ETHICS THEORY

BUSINESS PRACTICE

Mick Fryer

ETHICS THEORY

BUSINESS PRACTICE

Los Angeles | London | New Delhi
Singapore | Washington DC

Los Angeles | London | New Delhi
Singapore | Washington DC

SAGE Publications Ltd
1 Oliver's Yard
55 City Road
London EC1Y 1SP

SAGE Publications Inc.
2455 Teller Road
Thousand Oaks, California 91320

SAGE Publications India Pvt Ltd
B 1/I 1 Mohan Cooperative Industrial Area
Mathura Road
New Delhi 110 044

SAGE Publications Asia-Pacific Pte Ltd
3 Church Street
#10-04 Samsung Hub
Singapore 049483

Editor: Kirsty Smy
Assistant editor: Nina Smith
Production editor: Sarah Cooke
Marketing manager: Alison Borg
Cover design: Francis Kenney
Typeset by: C&M Digitals (P) Ltd, Chennai, India
Printed and bound by Great Britain by Ashford Colour Press Ltd

First published 2015

Library of Congress Control Number: 2014937904

British Library Cataloguing in Publication data

A catalogue record for this book is available from the British Library

ISBN 978-1-4462-7414-9
ISBN 978-1-4462-7415-6 (pbk)

Contents

List of Theory in Practice boxes vi
List of Video Activities viii
About this Book x
Companion Website xi
Acknowledgements xii

Introduction 1

1 Rights Theory: Considering Business Ethics in Terms of Stakeholder Rights 17

2 Utilitarianism: Maximizing the Good Consequences of Business 54

3 Kantian Theory: Reason-based Duty and Business 88

4 Social Contract Theory: Business Obligations, Corporate Wrongdoing and Just Distribution 126

5 Virtue Theory: Virtue, Purpose and Flourishing in Business 171

6 Ethical Relativism: Business Ethics and Personal Conviction 212

7 Discourse Ethics: Democratizing Business 249

8 Feminine Ethics: Offering a Different Ethical Perspective on Business 287

9 Environmental Ethics: Business, People and Nature 324

10 The Responsibilities of Business Executives: Just Looking after Shareholders' Interests or Taking all Stakeholders into Account? 363

11 Some Closing Thoughts 401

References 429
Index 450

List of Theory in Practice Boxes

A common ethical dilemma 9
Corporate impact: considering Coca-Cola 10
Union busting at bottling plants used by Coca-Cola 23
The Ilisu Dam, cultural rights and the general good 28
Glencore and stakeholder rights 37
A living wage for fast-food workers? 49
Will Ford's rationalization plan maximize the good? 59
Using Atlas Iron's profit to maximize the good 74
Oil spillages in the Niger Delta: is Shell neglecting its non-dependent stakeholders? 84
The formula of universal law and movie piracy 102
Suppliers: Simply a means to an end? Or an end in themselves? 105
Would UK water companies have wanted everyone to know what they were doing? 111
Rana Plaza: a disaster waiting to happen 121
The psychological contract: a tacit agreement between employers and employees 133
Starbucks wakes up and smells the coffee 138
Phone tapping at News International: bad businesspeople or bad business culture? 149
The contentious matter of senior-executive pay 166
The virtuous apprentice 180
Management buyouts: changing the purpose of business? 189
Bloodgate: Prioritizing external goods and the erosion of virtue 204
Ethical absolutist and ethical relativist approaches to Foxconn's employment practices 219
Bribery and corruption in the arms trade 242
Discourse and open door policies 265
Workplace democracy at Suma 274

BMW's sale of its 'English patient' 307
The Marine Stewardship Council: a case of enlightened anthropocentrism 330
Wind farms: an enlightened way of meeting human energy needs; or a blight on the landscape? 334
Is krill the only species endangered by the over fishing of krill? 338
Trafigura, Ivory Coast and environmental justice 348
The hamburger connection 359
Energy company executives: guilty of 'cold-blooded profiteering' or fulfilling responsibilities as shareholders' agents? 368
Making the world a better place while making money from selling healthcare products 376
Do banks have a responsibility to provide all customers with free access to their funds? 381
Offshoring: Good business sense or an abrogation of responsibility to stakeholders? 396
The Mondragon Corporation: another way of doing business 408
The banking crash: a trigger for legitimation crisis? 417
The tobacco industry: good guys or bad guys? 422

List of Video Activities

1.1 Corporate lobbying through expert groups 20
1.2 Suarez Gold: Afro-Colombian miners defending their heritage 25
1.3 30 words – the Universal Declaration of Human Rights 27
1.4 Australian banks sending jobs offshore despite healthy profits 40
1.5 The Power of Property Rights and Boundary Issues 45

2.1 *The Cruel Sea* 56
2.2 *Fortune*'s list of the 100 best companies to work for 65
2.3 Mitt Romney explains how profit can serve the common good 75

3.1 Pirate Nation 104
3.2 How Jhaqueil Reagan got a job at Papa Roox fast-food restaurant 114

4.1 What to expect when society breaks down after a crisis 129
4.2 Ben Affleck's *Boiler Room* Speech 143
4.3 Enron Scandal 146
4.4 We've been Fuld: Congress grills Lehman CEO on compensation 160
4.5 Types of Discrimination 164

5.1 Half the Man 174
5.2 *The Corporation* 183
5.3 What is the Purpose of Business? – John Mackey of Whole Foods Market 187
5.4 Tony Woods talks about his job as a garden designer 196

6.1 *Jurassic Park* 217
6.2 *Troy* 223
6.3 WSF 2013 – Social Movements against the power of corporations/ Brid Brennan 225
6.4 *Glengarry Glen Ross* 231
6.5 Britain's Barclays Investigated for Rigging Libor Rates 237
6.6 *Margin Call* 239

7.1 Deepwater Horizon disaster 259
7.2 Prof. Richard Wolff talks about workplace democracy 263
7.3 Google updates its privacy policy 284

8.1 Ben & Jerry's Join Our Core Roundtable 295
8.2 Niall Ferguson interviewing Christine Lagarde 300
8.3 Ethical Leadership 304
8.4 Dolce & Gabbana's 2013 Spring/ Summer fashion range 318
8.5 Volkswagen Force and Simon the Ogre for Thomson Holidays ads 319

9.1 *The Corporation* 326
9.2 Chumbawamba, 'You Can (Mass Trespass, 1932)' 332
9.3 Pumba Private Game Reserve, South Africa 344
9.4 Islands Going Under 345
9.5 Joseph DesJardins' three principles for sustainable business 354
9.6 Business Battle 357
9.7 Ancient forest destruction 358

10.1 Betting Britain: Social responsibility takes back seat as gambling flourishes 372
10.2 Brent Spar Greenpeace vs. Shell and The Case Against Shell: 'The Hanging of Ken Saro-Wiwa Showed the True Cost of Oil' 385

11.1 Milton Friedman lecturing to a group of students in 1977 406
11.2 Detox: A song about PeoplePower and Winning! 413
11.3 Alien Invasion 415
11.4 Anita Roddick discusses corporate social responsibility 421

About this Book

With a unique focus on ethics theory and how it relates to business practice, *Ethics Theory and Business Practice* will give you a grounded introduction to business ethics along with some tools to help you make ethical decisions in practical business contexts.

The book contains a number of features to help readers to engage with the ideas contained within it:

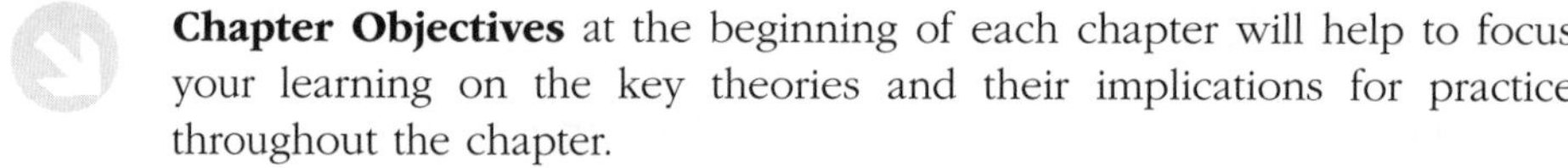

Chapter Objectives at the beginning of each chapter will help to focus your learning on the key theories and their implications for practice throughout the chapter.

Pause for Reflection boxes at regular intervals invite you to reflect critically on the theory and to think about how it relates to business or to you personally.

Video Activities, accompanied by QR codes, link to short videos on the Internet, which illustrate the ideas discussed in the book. If you find an inactive link to an external website, please try to locate that website by using a search engine or check the companion website where we will provide an alternative where possible.

Theory in Practice exercises give you the chance you to apply the theory introduced in the text to real-life business situations.

Discussion Questions towards the end of each chapter suggest ideas for group discussion and invite you to apply the theory to topical, ethically charged, business-related issues.

Each chapter concludes with some ideas for **Further Study**, including books, articles, and videos that explore in more detail the material introduced in that chapter.

Diagrams throughout will help you to understand how concepts explained in the text fit together and how they relate to business practice.

Companion Website

Visit the companion website for this book at **study.sagepub.com/fryer** to find a range of teaching and learning materials for both students and lecturers, including the following:

For students:

- Chapter Summaries will refresh your memory of the main topics covered in each chapter.
- Self-test Questions are designed to test your understanding of key ideas presented in the book, ideal for revision.
- Weblinks will direct you to some fascinating online resources to further enhance your learning and illustrate how theory translates into practice.

For lecturers:

- PowerPoint Slides.
- Additional Exercises.
- Notes on the Exercises and Video Activities in the book.
- Additional Videos.
- Assessment Activities.

Lecturers, for more detailed information on the above resources please visit **study.sagepub.com/fryer**

Acknowledgements

I am grateful to a number of people who have helped directly in preparing the contents of this book. Thank you to Nina Smith and Kirsty Smy at Sage for their encouragement since the book's inception. Thanks also to the following people whose feedback on draft chapters has been extremely helpful.

- Annette Cerne at Lund University;
- Chris Doran at the University of Salford;
- Steve Griffiths at University of Wales Trinity Saint David;
- Peter McGhee at Auckland University of Technology;
- Richard Warren at Manchester Metropolitan University; and
- Tracy Wilcox at the University of New South Wales.

Louise Fryer has also offered invaluable suggestions about content, as well as helping with copy reading and providing administrative support.

I am also grateful to many people who have contributed indirectly to the material presented here. They include, in chronological order: Tom Roberts and his colleagues in the philosophy department of UCW Aberystwyth during the 1970s, who nurtured my interest in moral philosophy; all those people whom I met during 25 years in business management, who gave me plenty of ethical quandaries upon which to reflect; George Chryssides and John Kaler, whose 1993 book *An Introduction to Business Ethics* exemplified for me the application of ethics theory to business practice; Peter Ackers and Laurie Cohen, who gave me the opportunity and the confidence to write about business ethics. Lastly, thank you to those students of Aberystwyth and Loughborough who have helped me to develop the ideas offered in the book.

Introduction

Chapter objectives

This chapter will:

- outline the aim of this book;
- explain how the words 'ethics', 'business' and some related terms are used in the book;
- outline the approach to the study of business ethics taken in this book and contrast it with some alternative approaches;
- offer some reasons for taking this approach;
- outline the content and structure of the book.

The aim of the book

The aim of this book is to encourage you to think about what ethical business practice and unethical business practice consist of and to apply this thinking to real-life business scenarios. This aim, and how the book hopes to achieve it, should become clearer as you read this introduction. First, though, I will say a little about ethics, business and some terms that are associated with each. I will then describe the approach to business ethics study that the book will take, and explain why I think this is a worthwhile approach.

What is ethics?

You are undoubtedly familiar with the words 'ethics' and 'ethical'. Both terms often appear in everyday conversations about all sorts of things. However, you will probably find this book easier to read if I give you some idea of how these words, along with a few related terms, will be used. Ethics is often associated with the words *right* and *good*, along with their opposites *wrong* and *bad*. For instance, we might speak of a particular action as being 'right' or 'wrong', meaning that it is an ethically correct or an ethically incorrect thing to do. Or we might refer to a particular state of affairs as 'good' or 'bad', meaning that it has some form of intrinsic ethical desirability or undesirability.

As well as referring to certain actions as being ethically right, we also use the word 'right' in a different sense when talking about ethics. That is, we talk of *a right* as being something that people have rather than as a quality of an action. To recognize someone's right to something is to acknowledge that they have an ethical claim to that thing. Furthermore, when we speak of people's rights in this way, we also sometimes speak of other people's *responsibility* to respect those rights. If somebody has an ethical claim to a certain thing, we tend to believe that others have an ethical responsibility to let them have that thing, or perhaps even to enable them to have it. And just as we speak of ethical responsibilities, we also assume that words like *obligations* and *duties* mean more or less the same thing. Responsibilities, obligations and duties, then, refer to things that we have some sort of ethical compulsion to do.

We also talk a lot about *fairness* when we discuss ethics. We tend to think that if a situation is 'fair' then it is ethical, and if it is 'unfair' then there is something unethical about it. Furthermore, ethics-related talk often includes references to *virtue*: we sometimes refer to a person who behaves ethically as 'a virtuous person', or we refer to an ethical act as 'a virtuous act'.

But perhaps the word that crops up most often in association with ethics is *morality*. Indeed, 'ethics' and 'morality' are often used interchangeably in everyday speech, as are the words 'ethical' and 'moral'. Philosophers frequently make a distinction between morality and ethics though. In philosophical texts, 'morality' often refers to a particular person's beliefs about what is right and wrong, good and bad, and so on; or perhaps it refers to what a particular community thinks about such matters. Meanwhile, 'ethics' is often taken by philosophers to refer to the study of morality. Ethics, then, might be understood as a subject that puts various moralities to the test; as the process of enquiring into the legitimacy of various notions of good, bad, right, wrong, fairness, unfairness, virtue and vice. And when philosophers say that something is 'ethical', they are usually implying that it has a value against which the 'morals' of a particular person or a particular community can be judged.

By and large, the book uses the words 'morality' and 'ethics' in this philosophical sense, especially when discussing specific theorists to whose work this distinction is particularly relevant. However, some of the quotations and discussions that appear in the text follow the everyday convention of using the words interchangeably. Moreover, the meaning of many of the statements you come across in the book would not be altered significantly if 'moral' were substituted for 'ethical' or vice versa. Therefore, although you may find it helpful to be aware of the philosophers' distinction between ethics and morality, it is not something that you should bother too much about.

Each of the above terms is likely to arise in general conversations about ethics. When this happens, they are mostly being used in a non-specific way to express or to explore ethical perspectives. Instead of describing something as ethical, we might call it right, good, fair, virtuous or moral. And instead of calling something unethical we might say it is wrong, bad, unfair or immoral. However, some of these terms also have particular relevance to specific ethics theories. Therefore, although they will be used in a general way throughout the book, you will also find them taking on more precise meanings in some chapters. For instance, Chapter 2 explores particular versions of what *good* consists of; Chapter 3 explores an ethics theory that revolves around a precise understanding of *duty*; the word *virtue* is used in a specific way in Chapter 5; and *morality* is used in a particular, philosophical sense during some parts of Chapters 3 and 6.

What is business?

One way of defining the subject matter of business ethics is to describe it as the study of how terms associated with ethics should be used in relation to business. Thus defined, business ethics invites us to think about what *right* and *wrong* consist of in relation to business activity; about the *goodness* and *badness* of specific business situations; about the *rights*, *responsibilities*, *obligations* and *duties* that ought to govern business relationships; about what a *fair* distribution of the benefits and burdens of business activity might involve; and about what constitutes a *virtuous* business or a virtuous businessperson.

However, in order to understand what business ethics, as defined in this way, involves, some familiarity with the word 'business' is needed. I expect you are even better acquainted with that word than you are with words like 'ethics' and 'ethical'. Nevertheless, it may help to say a little about how it, along with some related terms, will be used here.

A field of human activity

One way in which we use the word 'business' is to describe a particular type of human activity. When we use it in this way, we usually have in mind the production and supply of goods and services by organizations that are owned by private individuals or by groups of private individuals. This type of activity is usually contrasted to that which is organized by the state, or that which is carried out by charities, clubs and societies.

Of course, the dividing line between business and these other types of production and supply is not a precise one. This is partly because there is a lot of interaction between the state and business, with government policy and state funding having a big impact on what goes on in the business world. It is also because state-run organizations, charities, clubs and societies often use similar organizational methods and follow similar commercial imperatives to those that are common in business. Moreover, not all business is conducted in a conventional 'business-like' manner. Indeed, some types of business, such as that carried out by cooperatives and collectives, has a lot in common with what goes on in charities, clubs and societies.

It will help to keep the vagueness of the dividing line between business and other ways of providing goods and services in mind as you read this book. Given the extent to which business-like methods and priorities are found in state-run organizations, charities, clubs and societies, you may find that some of the insights that this book enables are as relevant to these other contexts as they are to business. But just as reflection about what happens in business can provide insights to what goes on in other types of organization, so might those other types of organization cast some interesting perspectives on business. It is tempting to limit our purview of business to conventional, hierarchically organized, profit-driven organizations. But, if we do this, we may deprive ourselves of the insights offered by the consideration of alternatives. It may be that some of the ethical concerns that are associated with contemporary business are specific to this conventional model and can be avoided, or at least reduced, if we move away from it and consider what different forms of organization might offer to business.

A type of institution

As well as using the word 'business' to describe a particular field of human activity, we also tend to use it to describe a particular type of institution; that is, an institution that carries out the activity we refer to as business. The word 'business' will be used in this book in both of these senses: to refer to a field of human activity and also to refer to institutions that carry out that activity. Of course, the precise nature of businesses varies greatly, from small, independent farmers, shopkeepers and plumbers to vast, global business institutions.

When we speak of businesses in the sense of a particular type of institution, we are also inclined to use other words such as 'firm', 'company', 'corporation' and 'enterprise'. Sometimes these words take on a precise meaning. For instance, when we speak of corporations we are usually referring to very big businesses that have a global scope. However, we are more likely to take these other words as meaning the same thing as the word 'business'. For the most part, then, that is how they will be used in this book; that is, interchangeably. The one exception is that 'corporation' will mostly be reserved for discussions of very big business organizations that operate internationally.

The subject matter of business ethics

The book aims to encourage you to think about ethics – as described above – in relation to business – as described above. Moreover, it will offer a range of theoretical perspectives that will help you do this. In taking this approach, the book will avoid some other approaches that are quite common in business ethics textbooks. One alternative approach is to focus on the relationship between ethics and corporate performance. This approach usually involves advising readers how to identify the ethical expectations of those people who are in a position to influence corporate success; people who are sometimes referred to as a company's *stakeholders*. Books that take this approach also tend to offer guidance on how to identify key stakeholders and on what businesses need to do in order to respond to their expectations concerning ethics. This may include advice about how to structure corporate activity so that it meets stakeholders' ethical expectations. It may also include advice on how corporations should communicate their ethical credentials to those key stakeholders so as to appear as ethical as they can be.

Another approach that is sometimes taken in business ethics textbooks is to tell readers what needs to be done in order to run a company in an ethical manner. This approach tends to involve applying taken-for-granted standards of ethical rightness to particular business disciplines such as marketing, accounting and human resource management so as to show how these disciplines can be carried out ethically. Sometimes the taken-for-granted standards of ethical rightness to which these books appeal are those which the book's writers assume we all share. Sometimes they are derived from a particular ethics theory that is favoured by the writers. Quite often this approach is combined with the one mentioned above, insofar as it aims to show that, by conforming to taken-for-granted ethical standards, businesses can become more profitable. In other words, these books are keen to convince their readers that being (ethically) good is (financially) good for business.

These alternative approaches have a lot to recommend them. However, they do not offer much assistance to readers who want to develop their own ideas about what ethical business consists of. The first approach helps us to think about business practice in relation to the ethical expectations of key stakeholders, but it does not help us to reflect on the legitimacy of those expectations. Nor does it have much to say about the expectations of people who are not critical to business success but who may nevertheless be affected by business activity. Meanwhile, the second approach helps us to think about how we can structure business practice in accordance with ethical standards that are presupposed by certain business ethicists, but it does not do much to encourage or assist reflection on the legitimacy of those standards. This book takes things back a stage. Rather than advising you how to respond to the expectations of influential stakeholders or to standards that particular business ethicists take for granted, it addresses the question: what *is* ethical in relation to business practice? And rather than answering this question for you, the book endeavours to help you to develop your own response.

The word 'develop' is very important in the last sentence. I am assuming that you have already given the topic of business ethics some thought and that you already have some ideas about what is ethical and what is unethical in relation to business practice. And you may already have some well thought-out rationales to back up those views. In that case, the book might serve to reinforce your convictions and provide you with even more solid grounds for holding them. Alternatively, the book may provide you with some solid justifications for opinions that, until now, have been based on nothing more than vague intuition. On the other hand, reading this book may encourage you to change your mind about certain things. Perhaps you will end up thinking that some things that you used to disapprove of are not so bad after all. Or maybe the theories discussed in the book will draw your attention to ethically problematic features of business practice that you had not previously considered. Whichever of these outcomes the book achieves in your case – perhaps it will be a bit of each – it will have performed a worthwhile purpose. I will explain why I think this purpose is worthwhile after I have said a little about the scope and nature of business ethics enquiry.

The scope of business ethics enquiry

A number of theorists have highlighted the merits of considering the relationship between ethics and business at more than one level (for example, De George, 1993/1978; Solomon, 1991). For a start, we might consider business ethics at a *micro* level; that is, we might explore ethicality in relation to the day-to-day activities and decisions of individual businesspeople. The sorts of question that arise at this micro level might include the following: Is it ethically acceptable for a business manager to withhold information from her colleagues about their impending redundancy in order to retain their commitment to the company and thus to avoid a downturn in corporate performance? In a supply-contract negotiation, is it OK for a company buyer to give preferential treatment to a supplier with whom he has developed a long-standing business relationship or should supplier arrangements be governed purely by financial considerations? And is it all right for a supplier to offer a gift to the buyer of a company with which she does business in order to thank that person for their custom? Moreover, is it ethically permissible for a company buyer to accept such gifts from a supplier?

Moving up a level, we can also consider business ethics at a *meso* level. That is, we might think about things like right, wrong, good and bad in relation to the activities of particular companies or specific industry sectors. For example, we might ask whether it is ethically acceptable for a firm to structure its accounts in such a way that it avoids paying taxes in the country within which its operations take place, paying them instead in another country that offers more favourable arrangements. Or we might question whether a global commodity-supply corporation is justified in disposing of waste products at low cost in developing nations. And we might ask if it is OK for financial-service firms to establish highly complex derivative trading structures, which offer the possibility of high returns but in which systemic risk is hard to predict or control.

Stepping up again to a *macro* level, we might consider the wider role that business plays, or should play, within society. At this macro level, business ethics touches on considerations of national and international economic policy. It also crosses into the realm of political ideology. The types of question that occur at a macro level might include whether economic markets alone should be allowed to govern business activity, or whether governments should exercise control over market activity in order to bring about specific social and environmental objectives. Macro-level enquiry might also ask whether corporations have an obligation to consider the impact of their activities on society and the natural environment, or whether they should just do all they can to maximize shareholder returns. And macro-level enquiry might consider whether the benefits and burdens of economic activity are fairly distributed between various communities.

The practical scenarios discussed in the book will encourage exploration of business ethics at micro, meso and macro levels. It is important, however, to emphasize the interconnections between these different levels. Micro, meso and macro levels should not be viewed as distinct, separate spheres that are unconnected to one another. Rather, we should be alert to the possibility that what goes on at each level may affect what goes on at others. Thus, dominant attitudes concerning the relationship between business and society may help to shape the activities and the decisions made within specific corporations and industry sectors, which can, in turn, influence the conduct of individual businesspeople. Similarly, the decisions made by specific people and groups within corporations can have a significant effect on meso-level corporate activity, while certain individuals and corporations may also exert a powerful influence over macro-level policy.

Business ethics in practice: about dilemmas

An important point about the study of business ethics, at all levels, is that it often involves consideration of *dilemmas*. Ethically charged business scenarios rarely involve a straightforward choice between what is self-evidently ethical and what is self-evidently unethical. Rather, they usually involve choices between conflicting courses of action, each of which has ethical attractions as well as ethical shortcomings. The task confronting businesspeople who have to make choices in such scenarios, as well as that confronting those of us who wish to evaluate their choices, is to work out which of these conflicting courses of action has the greater claim to ethical legitimacy.

This is not the image that is sometimes presented by media discussions of business ethics. When newspapers, TV, radio and internet news sites get hold of ethics-related stories about business, they often present them in quite a simplistic manner. For instance, few mainstream media sources did much to evoke sympathy for the banking chiefs and traders whom they held responsible for the banking crash of 2008. Similarly, while oil poured into the Gulf of Mexico following the Deepwater Horizon explosion in 2010, there were few attempts to deflect international condemnation from BP's CEO, Tony Hayward. And as revelations about bribery and corruption in the arms trade have seeped out in recent years, few media commentators have questioned the apparently self-evident immorality of the BAE Systems executives towards whom the finger of censure has been pointed.

Such media coverage tends to encourage a certain way of thinking about business ethics: a belief that we all know what is ethical and what is unethical; that some corporations and some businesspeople knowingly do unethical things; and that the task of business ethicists is to alert us so that these self-evidently unethical activities can be condemned and so that their repetition can be prevented. Unfortunately, things are rarely so simple. Even in the high-profile cases just mentioned, to paint the culprits as unethical chancers who knew they were doing wrong but who did it nevertheless is to misunderstand the extent to which their actions may have been driven, at least partly, by what they considered to be ethically sound intentions.

For instance, even if bankers were a little too enthusiastic in seizing the opportunity to feather their own nests offered by complex, derivative trading, many of them also believed that their high-risk and high-return investment practices would fulfil their ethical obligation to build the share value of their companies. Furthermore, BP's senior executives may have authorized drilling activities that, with hindsight, carried a level of environmental risk that many would find unacceptable. Nevertheless those executives may also have been driven by a desire to provide the affordable fuel that contemporary lifestyles demand, whilst meeting their obligations to BP's shareholders. And if BAE Systems executives had not made payments to Saudi princes and fixers, weighty defence contracts may have been lost, along with major sources of national revenue and the jobs of hundreds of BAE Systems employees. Those BAE Systems executives, then, may have had to wrestle with the conflicting claims of, on the one hand, their innate disapproval of corruption and, on the other hand, the welfare of their workers and the economic prosperity of their nation.

Now, to highlight ethical considerations in mitigation of actions such as these is not to say that the actions taken and choices made by bankers, Tony Hayward and BAE Systems executives were ethically sound after all. Even after taking their ethical agendas into account, we might still conclude that they acted wrongly. Moreover, with the benefit of hindsight, it could be suggested that their decisions did not even do much to further their ethical agendas. Such cases do, however, draw attention to the possibility that even what appear to be clear cases of corporate unethicality are not, as many critics suggest, necessarily motivated purely by egotistic self-interest. Those responsible for such actions may have had to weigh up conflicting ethical claims. And they may have done things that seem ethically problematic in order to avoid outcomes that they considered, at the time, to be even worse. Moreover, when we shift our attention from cases such as those mentioned above to the type of ethically charged scenarios that arise more commonly in business, the rights and wrongs may be even less obvious.

Theory in Practice

A common ethical dilemma

An ethical dilemma that often confronts senior business executives concerns workforce restructuring. Often, if a company is not performing as well as it could, there is a perception that it needs to trim its workforce in order to increase efficiency. To illustrate the ethical heart-searching that such situations can cause, I include below a short extract from a conversation with a former company finance director, in which she tells of making some of her employees redundant:

> That was the first time that I'd ever gone through a redundancy programme at all in my career and I found that horrifically difficult ... I think there were about 30-odd engineers in that instance. I talk about it easily now, but at the time I was in pieces. I found it personally extremely difficult. We had guys in their mid-50s in tears and it's incredibly difficult. And then [on another occasion I had to lay off] my own finance team. I felt an even stronger personal connection to those people because I'd helped train and develop them and bring them in and build a team ... But I have to look at the wider group. So at [one company] ... there were 200 other employees, and customers, and the shareholders ... you've come to do a role, there is an element of: try and detach myself, think of myself in my professional capacity, and think I'm doing this because the organization needs it.

In each of the situations that this executive describes, she has had to weigh her sense of ethical responsibility for those people she made redundant against her perceived responsibilities towards her company's other employees, its customers and its shareholders, all of whom depended on the continued survival of the business. She ended up putting in place redundancy programmes, which caused her a great deal of angst, in order to avoid the possibility that the companies might have gone bust, which, for her, would have had even more serious ethical implications.

Why study business ethics?

When I tell people that I am writing a book about business ethics they often smile and say things like 'I didn't think there was any such thing!', or 'that shouldn't take too long, then!' Such remarks are usually offered in jest. Nevertheless, they reveal something about the way that people tend to perceive the relationship between business and ethics. I doubt whether I would get such comments, even jokingly, if I said I was writing about business economics, business marketing or business strategy. Nor would such remarks be so likely if the topic of my book was medical ethics or teaching ethics. Such reactions reveal a commonly held belief that business and ethics do not really have much to do with one another. Despite the impressive rhetoric that comes out of some corporate PR departments about ethics, and despite the earnestness with which some business ethics academics approach their subject, many people have a sneaking suspicion that this is all a bit of a waste of time; that business is about making money and that ethics do not really come into it.

I usually smile politely and shrug when people say things like this to me. The situations in which these comments tend to be made – usually during casual social encounters – do not lend themselves to solemn declarations of my scholarly convictions! However, I happen to disagree with the sentiment that lies behind such observations.

I outlined earlier several possible approaches to business ethics. There are some solid justifications for taking any of these approaches. However, there is a particularly compelling rationale for the approach taken by this book. This is that businesses have a significant impact on everybody's lives (Deetz, 1992). Many of us will spend a substantial part of our waking hours at work in businesses. Those businesses therefore have a big influence over our financial, physical and psychological well-being. Businesses also, to an increasing extent, provide the goods and services upon which we all depend. Their effectiveness in doing this and the manner in which they do it are therefore critical to everybody's quality of life and, in some cases, to the very possibility of life. Moreover, the marketing activities undertaken by businesses do a lot to shape our attitudes about what is personally desirable and socially acceptable. The extent to which the aspirations thus created are realized or, indeed, realizable, has an important bearing on individual self-esteem and social harmony. And lastly, the resource usage and the waste production entailed in the production of goods and services by businesses have an enduring impact on the natural environment and on communities.

To propose that business should exercise this awesome influence over us and over the world that we occupy without a thought of its ethical ramifications would seem odd. And to suggest that practices that carry so much consequence should be immune to ethical appraisal by people like you and me would also seem curious. That is why I believe that business and ethics should go together.

Theory in Practice

Corporate impact: considering Coca-Cola

Coca-Cola is the world's foremost producer of sweet, carbonated drinks. For better or for worse, over one billion cans or bottles of Cola-Cola are consumed every day, which amounts to 12,500 every second (War on Want, 2006).

According to Coca-Cola's corporate website (Coca-Cola, 2013e), the company provides employment for over 700,000 people in its worldwide operations. Coca-Cola is thus in a position to influence the well-being of all those people and their families. Those jobs also have a knock-on effect on local economies, since the wages paid to Coca-Cola's workers get recycled through local shops, bars, clubs, garages, hairdressers, recreation facilities and so on. Moreover, Coca-Cola's operations continue to expand. For instance, in 2013, the company opened a brand new, $20m bottling plant in rural Ethiopia, which promises to bring a welcome source of economic activity to the region.

Each year, Coca-Cola spends over $2.5b advertising its products (Coca-Cola, 2013a). It thus creates images of personal desirability and social normality which impact on consumers and would-be consumers all over the world.

Coca Cola also has a considerable environmental impact. For instance, the company uses vast quantities of water to make its drinks. It is estimated by War on Want (2006) that it takes almost three litres of water to produce one litre of Coca-Cola.

Coca-Cola invests a great deal of money on charitable projects. Between 2002 and 2010, for instance, it spent over $690m on water-stewardship projects, healthy and active lifestyle initiatives, community recycling projects, and educational programs and other deserving causes (Coca-Cola, 2013d).

Questions

1 What ethically praiseworthy things might result from Coca-Cola's activities?
2 What ethically questionable things might Coca Cola bring about?

Content and structure of the book

Having said a little about the approach to business ethics taken in this book and, I hope, having convinced you that you are not wasting your time reading it, I will explain the rationale behind the choice of content and the way that content is structured. I have already mentioned that the aim of the book is to help you develop your ideas about business ethics. Fortunately, there are abundant theory resources available to assist in this endeavour, because philosophers have been talking about ethics for over 2,000 years. During this time, a wide range of theories and perspectives have been offered, many of which provide useful frameworks for considering ethically charged business scenarios.

Ethics theory: merit in diversity

A notable feature of these various ethical theories is that they say many different things about ethics. In one sense this is a bit frustrating. The fact that philosophers have offered so many different perspectives on ethics means that we do not have a commonly agreed set of standards to tell us what is right and what is wrong. While we may lament this lack of unity in ethical theories, it is perhaps unsurprising. After all, lots of different people, in different places and at different times, have contributed to ethics theory. Therefore, we should not be too surprised that they have come up with lots of different viewpoints. Furthermore, as the Greek philosopher Aristotle suggested over two millennia ago (2009/circa 323BC), maybe ethics is just not the sort of subject that is suited to one set of clear, uniform prescriptions.

But not only might this lack of a common approach to ethical evaluation be inevitable; it might also be a good thing since it means that ethical evaluation has a broad range of perspectives upon which to draw. Instead of seeing contrasting ethics theories as offering frustratingly conflicting bases of ethical evaluation then, their very diversity might be seen as an aid to the development of a comprehensive understanding. To take this view is to regard ethics theories as a collection of different viewpoints, each of which may permit insights not offered by others. Ethical enquiry can thus be seen in the same light as those slow-motion TV replays that are becoming common in top-class sport, which help referees and umpires tell whether they should award a goal, try, wicket or whatever. Just as a variety of TV-camera angles enable match officials to look at a particular incident from a range of perspectives to gain a thorough understanding of that incident, so might ethics theories be regarded as a range of angles from which we might examine a particular business scenario in order to develop a comprehensive understanding of its ethical ramifications.

Chapter content

With these considerations in mind, each of the chapters in the book introduces a specific ethics theory and explains how it might assist ethical evaluation of business practice. In other words, each chapter provides one particular angle from which ethically charged business scenarios can be viewed.

The first four chapters explore the insights offered by some theoretical perspectives that have figured prominently in the Western philosophical tradition over the last few hundred years. Chapter 1 considers how *rights* might inform our understanding of business ethics. It explores some features of the way that we often think about rights, as well as some challenges to the primacy that is accorded to certain rights in business contexts. The idea of stakeholding is offered as a basis for considering business-related rights, and some implications of different types of stakeholder relationship are explored.

Chapter 2 discusses the *utilitarian* notion that the most ethical action is that which promotes the best consequences for the greatest number of people. The chapter considers some contrasting ways of defining good consequences and reflects on the implications that these might have for business. One particular utilitarian approach, which is usually referred to as rule utilitarianism, is outlined and some of the pros and cons of using it as a practical guide to ethical business management are considered.

The duty-based moral philosophy of one of Europe's most influential philosophers, Immanuel Kant, is discussed in Chapter 3. *Kantian theory* places a great deal of emphasis on intentions, human reason and freedom, and the chapter explores some implications that these themes have for business practice. Some ways in which Kantian theory might help us to identify our duty in business situations are also explored. The chapter ends by applying these insights specifically to ethical evaluation of labour standards in offshore production.

Chapter 4 discusses a theme that has had a profound impact on European and American political thought: the notion of the *social contract*. Social contract theory considers ethical responsibilities in relation to contractual agreements. It provides the basis for exploration of the contractual obligations that prevail in business contexts; exploration which goes beyond consideration of explicit, written agreements. Social contract theorists have also offered contrasting ways of thinking about the relationship between human nature and social organization. This chapter draws on these contrasting analyses to suggest different ways of explaining unethical business conduct. The chapter also explores some insights that the more recent contract theory of John Rawls offers to ethical evaluation of the benefits and burdens associated with business activity.

The next three chapters move away from what are sometimes called the moral philosophies of the Enlightenment to explore insights offered by some other perspectives. Chapter 5 looks at the notion of *virtue*. Although virtue theory derives from Ancient Greek thought, especially the teachings of Aristotle, it has become popular again during the last 40 years. The chapter draws on Aristotelian theory to ask what it is for businesses and businesspeople to flourish, and considers how the doctrine of the virtuous mean might apply to corporate behaviour. The emphasis that virtue theory places on purpose is explained, and this is offered as a basis for considering the purpose of business. The chapter ends by explaining some themes introduced by virtue theory's most influential modern proponent, Alasdair MacIntyre, and considering how these might help us identify virtuous businesses and virtuous business management.

The approach to ethics discussed in Chapter 6, *ethical relativism*, is quite different from those considered in previous chapters. Instead of exploring absolute standards of right and wrong, ethical relativism highlights differences between the ethical understanding of different people and different communities. The chapter starts by outlining some distinctive features of ethical relativism and highlighting their implications for business ethics. Friedrich Nietzsche's account of the evolution of conventional morality is then outlined, and some ways in which Nietzsche's ideas might help us to reflect on our own beliefs about business ethics are considered. The chapter ends by introducing the existentialist notion of authenticity and explaining how this might help us to think about ethical conviction and accountability in business contexts.

The *discourse ethics theory* discussed in Chapter 7 is based around the idea that an ethical outcome is one that is agreed to by all those who are affected by it. The chapter explains the relationship between discourse ethics and democracy and introduces the notion of stakeholder democracy as a basis for ethical legitimacy. Some specific criteria that discourse needs to conform to in order to provide ethical legitimacy are considered with specific reference to workplaces. The importance of the public sphere to discourse is highlighted, and attention is drawn to the possibility that the public sphere might be colonized by corporate agendas. The chapter ends with consideration of the activities of ICT corporations in relation to the public sphere.

Chapter 8 discusses *feminine ethics theory*. It considers whether there is such a thing as a specifically feminine way of thinking about ethics, as well as exploring some insights that such a perspective might offer to business. The chapter also outlines contrasting ways of thinking about gender, as well as highlighting some ways in which corporate activity might be culpable of contributing to unhelpful, stereotypical images of femininity and masculinity.

Chapter 9 introduces some ethical perspectives that have emerged within the field of *environmental ethics*. It begins by describing various ways of attributing value to the natural environment, highlighting how these might relate to corporate activity. Western environmentalists' preoccupation with wilderness and wildlife conservation is then considered, and some ways in which this may deflect attention from issues that are important to people in other parts of the world are discussed. The notion of environmental justice is then considered with specific reference to the benefits and burdens of corporate activity. The chapter ends by discussing the possibility that contemporary ways of doing business may be intrinsically detrimental to environmental preservation, as well as outlining some suggestions for a more environmentally supportive approach.

Chapter 10 addresses a question that is central to business ethics: *what are the ethical responsibilities of corporate executives*. Two contrasting responses to this question are discussed. First, the approach of shareholder theory, which proposes that executives are primarily responsible to their shareholders, is explored. Next, a contrasting perspective, normative stakeholder theory, is outlined, which proposes that executives have broader ethical responsibilities. Some compelling rationales in favour of each of these perspectives are explored.

The book will end by discussing some possible reactions that you may have after reading the preceding chapters. The first possible reaction is that you may be left with feelings of *perplexity* about what is right and what is wrong. That is, after looking at ethically charged business issues from a range of different perspectives you may find it even harder to say what is ethical and what is unethical than you did before you started the book. Secondly, you may find that the book leaves you feeling *ambivalent* about the ethicality of business practice. In other words, you might end up thinking that there are aspects of contemporary business that you find ethically appealing, but that there are also aspects that you find ethically unappealing. Therefore, you may not know quite what to think about the ethicality of business practice; whether contemporary business is generally a good thing or whether it is generally a bad thing. And lastly, you may end up feeling *powerless*. Whatever conclusions you may have drawn about right and wrong, and about the ethical desirability of what you see happening in today's business world, you may conclude that you can do absolutely nothing to affect anything.

In this concluding chapter I will suggest that these are understandable reactions to a philosophically based study of business ethics. Many people who explore the topic in any depth end up feeling the same way. However, I will also suggest that perplexity need not stop you from forming firm ethical opinions; on the contrary, it might serve to enhance the quality of those opinions. I will also suggest that ambivalence about the ethicality of business activity need not mean that you have to accept the bad with the good; rather, it offers a sound basis for exploring ways of doing business which minimize the bad whilst retaining the good. And I will also suggest that, when it comes to influencing business practice, you may not be as powerless as you think.

Reading the book

Each chapter in this book has been written in such a way that it can stand alone. Although the chapters include occasional cross-references to other chapters, each can be approached as a self-contained unit of study. Therefore, there is no need to read the book sequentially: you do not have to read the early chapters in order to understand the theories discussed later in the book.

One last point to bear in mind is that this book does not pretend to offer a definitive classification of ethics theories. A lot more has been written about ethics, by Western and non-Western philosophers, than is discussed between these covers. Moreover, those theories that are included in the book could have been organized and presented differently to the way they have been organized and presented here. This book, therefore, should not be seen as an all-inclusive encyclopaedia. Rather, it should be seen as a compendium; as a collection of information about ethics theory which can be used to assist your understanding. It does not aim to tell you everything there is to know about business ethics. Rather, it seeks to broaden your awareness of the ethical implications of business practice, to encourage you to reflect on those implications, and to provide you with some useful frameworks for doing so.

Discussion questions

1. Discuss the following statement: Business is all about making money and businesspeople have no need to concern themselves with ethics.
2. You undoubtedly have some views about ethical right and wrong. Where do you think these views have come from? Have you always had the same beliefs or have they evolved over time? What might encourage you to alter your ethical opinions?
3. What sort of things do you think we can do to ensure that our ideas about business ethics are as well developed as they can be?

Rights Theory: Considering Business Ethics in Terms of Stakeholder Rights

1

Chapter objectives

This chapter will:

- outline a range of political, social and cultural rights, and discuss some ways in which they relate to business ethics;
- discuss some features of the way that we tend to think about rights;
- explain how stakeholding offers a basis for considering rights in business contexts;
- highlight the need for businesses to consider the rights of affected stakeholders as well as those of influential stakeholders;
- explain the importance placed on property rights in contemporary business contexts;
- introduce contrasting perspectives on the relationship between property and labour.

Introduction

What do we mean when we use the word 'right'? We tend to use this word in two different ways when talking about ethics. On the one hand, we often say that something is the *right* thing to do, meaning that it is the ethically correct thing to do. In such instances, 'right' is being used as an alternative to 'ethical' or 'moral'. Although 'right' is often used in this way, this is not the meaning that this chapter will discuss.

Instead, this chapter will focus on a more specific use of the word. It will explore what we mean when we say that someone *has a right*. When we talk about right or rights in this way we are referring to specific ethical entitlements that individuals or groups have.

This usage of the word often crops up when people talk about ethics. For instance, we might speak of our 'right to know', our 'right to speak' or our 'right to be heard'. More generally, we often refer to 'human rights' in the belief that there are certain ethical entitlements that all people share, regardless of gender, ethnicity, age or nationality. These human rights might include things like the right to life, the right to work or the right to be respected.

A discourse of rights is also common in business contexts. Most large corporations have a lot to say about the emphasis they put on respecting the rights of people who come into contact with them. If you look at the social-responsibility pages of most firms' websites, you are likely to find declarations of the firm's commitment to respecting consumer rights, employee rights, shareholder rights and the rights of local communities. Meanwhile, critics of corporations also tend to talk about rights, often claiming that there is a discrepancy between what corporations *say* about respecting people's rights and what those corporations actually *do*.

This chapter will explore the way that we speak about rights in more detail, considering some of the implications of rights talk for business. The first part of the chapter will describe how rights have come to assume such a prominent place in Western society. It will also highlight some features of the way we usually think about rights. The second part of the chapter will introduce the notion of stakeholding as a way of thinking about rights and business. I will explore some ways in which stakeholder relationships may entail rights to consideration on the part of specific groups. I will also highlight the importance of companies taking the rights of all their stakeholders into account, not just the rights of their most-influential stakeholders. The chapter will end by considering a particular set of rights, which hold a prominent place in contemporary ethics debate, especially in business contexts: that is, property rights. I will introduce some contrasting ideas about property rights offered by John Locke and Karl Marx, outlining their relevance to business ethics.

About rights theory

This first section of the chapter will offer a brief overview of how contemporary, Western understanding of rights has evolved and how political, social and cultural rights might relate to business activity. I will say a little about the *Universal Declaration of Human Rights* and how it might offer a reference point for ethical business conduct. I will then describe some features of the way that we usually think about rights, drawing out some implications for business ethics.

The development of modern rights theory

It is commonplace to talk about ethics in terms of rights nowadays. However, this has not always been so. Although the roots of the Western preoccupation with rights can be traced back over 2,000 years (Herbert, 2002; Campbell, 2006), it was not until the seventeenth century that explicit talk of rights began to shape our ethical understanding. Some commentators identify three stages in the evolution of rights theory since then. They speak of three 'generations', each of which has introduced different aspects to the way that we think about rights today. As Tom Campbell (2006) points out, we should use this three-stage classification with care, for trying to capture the evolution of any complex phenomenon in such simple terms runs the risk of over generalization. Nevertheless, the three-generation typology offers a helpful starting point for exploring some rights that we consider to be important today and for thinking about their relevance to business. I will therefore say a little about some key themes that emerged during each so-called 'generation', as well as outlining some ways in which these ideas can be applied to contemporary business ethics theory and practice.

First generation: political rights

Political rights relate to people's ability to have a say in how the communities within which they live and work are run, but they also concern broader aspects of people's treatment by those in positions of power. Words such as participation, justice, fairness, equality and freedom often crop up in discussions of political rights.

Over the last few centuries, when people spoke of political rights they were usually talking about the relationship between the state and citizens. 'The state' in this context is a generic term used to refer to the individuals, groups and institutions that govern a nation. Political rights, thus understood, were a major inspiration for revolutionary events that took place in Europe and North America during the seventeenth and eighteenth centuries (Almond, 1993; Freeman, 2002; Campbell, 2006; Mahoney, 2007). These included the so-called 'Glorious Revolution' in England, the American War of Independence and the French Revolution, each of which sought to limit the power of the state and grant political rights and a certain amount of economic autonomy to some of the citizens of those countries.[1]

However, despite this early focus on controlling the power of the state, political rights are also relevant to business in a number of ways. For one thing, as Tom Campbell suggests, in a world that is increasingly shaped by corporate activity, 'the state is no longer seen as the only significant danger to the rights of the individual'

---

[1]Usually these rights were limited to wealthier, male citizens. Recognition of political rights for the poor and for female citizens has taken longer to establish.

(2006: 126). As corporations get bigger and as their global spread escalates, their power over citizens, and even over governments, grows. Nowadays, the financial turnovers of the world's major corporations exceed that of many states. Those corporations spend vast sums shaping public perceptions and lobbying politicians to encourage economic and legal frameworks that support their interests. Their activities and influence span the globe, and they are able to hop from one country to another in order to locate their operations in nations that offer favourable conditions. Meanwhile, the governments of host nations, tempted by the economic benefits associated with the presence of major corporations in their country, may hesitate to oppose corporate power, even when the perceived rights of their own citizens are under threat.

There are therefore good grounds to suppose that corporations nowadays have a more significant impact on our lives than do the state frameworks upon which earlier rights theorists focused their attention. Therefore, while not losing sight of the threat that excessive state power presents to the political rights of individuals, it is as important today, given the power of modern corporations, to also reflect on the challenge that those corporations may present.

The issue of political rights is also relevant to the way that authority is distributed within most modern corporations. It is customary for corporations to be run in a top-down manner, with senior executives making key decisions on behalf of everyone else in the business (see for example Parker, 2002). Although business theorists and practitioners often speak of the merits of democratic decision making (see Johnson, 2006 for an overview), opportunities for democratic participation in corporations are generally fairly superficial and rarely involve matters of major importance (see discussion in Fryer, 2012). As a result, despite our apparent commitment to democracy outside of work, people who are employed in large businesses spend a substantial part of their lives in autocratic systems that allow them very little say in how things are done.

Whereas the revolutionaries of the seventeenth and eighteenth centuries focused on the application of power by the state, then, recent attention has fallen on the uses and abuses of corporate power. In particular, talk of political rights today needs to consider the treatment of citizens by those who wield corporate power, along with the challenges that such power might present to the rights of people inside and outside of those corporations to have a say in how their lives are organized.

Video Activity 1.1

The following video from Corporate Europe Observatory, entitled 'Corporate lobbying through expert groups', discusses how corporations try to get their representatives included in European Union Expert Groups. These Expert Groups play a prominent role in the drafting of EU legislation, to which all member states are expected to conform.

www.youtube.com/watch?v=_WPd-ASU0yM

The practice described in this video is just one instance of *corporate lobbying*. Corporate lobbying involves corporations using various forms of influence to try to get politicians and bureaucrats to pass laws that are favourable to the commercial interests of those corporations. Some examples of the types of agenda that might occupy corporate lobbyists are: oil companies might try to influence government environmental policy; tobacco companies might try to shape laws on tobacco advertising and packaging; a car manufacturer might try to influence end-of-life vehicle regulations; or a confectionery firm might try to shape laws concerning the advertising of sweets and chocolate to children. Often, corporations use specialist organizations for this purpose, which usually go under the name of 'public relations', 'public affairs', 'political consultancy' firms.

Questions

1 Why would corporations want to get their representatives onto the Expert Groups described in this video?
2 How might this undermine the *political rights* of the citizens of democratic European nations?

Second generation: social rights

The focus of what is sometimes referred to as a 'second generation' of rights theory was on so-called *social rights*. Social rights are understood as those rights that are concerned with basic human needs. At their most rudimentary level, social rights are about people's right to food, water and shelter. On a more advanced level, they include entitlement to services such as education, health care and leisure.

Interest in social rights, which became prominent in Western society during the nineteenth century, has been described as a response to the social consequences of the Industrial Revolution (Campbell, 2006). The political revolutions of the seventeenth and eighteenth centuries may have shifted power away from hereditary monarchs and land-owning aristocrats, helping to create a new, privileged class of merchant traders and manufacturers, but they brought few benefits to the impoverished masses of most European nations. And although the Industrial Revolution, which followed these political upheavals, enabled substantial improvements in human productivity and helped to generate considerable wealth, it also had some less desirable features. Chief amongst these was the hardship that characterized the life and work of most of the people who were employed in the factories, foundries, mines and mills of newly industrialized society (Hobsbawm, 2003/1962; 1997/1975). While a small minority of owners and investors became very rich through the revolution in industrial processes, most of the workers upon whose labour their wealth was built worked extremely long hours, often in unhygienic and unsafe conditions, earning just enough money to get by.

Initiatives by politicians, social reformers and the occasional philanthropic business owner began to change all this during the nineteenth and twentieth centuries, leading eventually to improvements in the provision of health care, education and leisure facilities in many Western nations, along with some form of welfare assistance for those in economic difficulty. Furthermore, employment legislation has done a great deal to improve the lot of working women and men throughout the developed world. Measures such as health and safety laws, minimum wage levels, regulation of working hours, laws that give part-time and temporary workers similar entitlements to full-time employees, and legislation concerning matters such as maternity and paternity rights are now common.

However, despite this apparent escalation in legal protection, the topic of workers' social rights continues to be an important one for Western corporations. This is partly due to a movement back towards looser employment regulation in some developed nations (see for example Saad-Filho and Johnston, 2005; Lloyd et al., 2008; Kalleberg, 2011). But the topic of workers' social rights is also important for Western corporations for another reason. This is that many corporations carry out a substantial proportion of their activities in developing nations, where legal protection of workers' rights is less rigorous than in the corporations' home countries. Those corporations therefore confront decisions about whether to respect the conventions of their home country in relation to the social rights of their workers, or whether to apply the less-stringent regime of their host nation. Some have chosen the latter approach and have faced criticism for doing so (see, for example Klein, 2001). It has been suggested that, by transferring their production and processing operations to developing nations in order to reduce labour costs, some corporations run the risk of resurrecting many of the social-rights abuses that characterized European industry during the early days of the Industrial Revolution. In other words, some of today's Western corporations may be guilty of treating their workers in the developing world just as badly as Britain's nineteenth-century mill owners, factory bosses and mine owners treated theirs.

Trade unions, the expression of political rights and the protection of social rights

The development of *trade unions* (more commonly known in the USA as *labor unions*) has been important for the expression of political rights and for the protection of social rights in workplaces (see for example Francis and Smith, 1980; Davis, 2009). By giving employees the opportunity to represent their views, union organization offers a corrective to autocratic, top-down decision making by senior management. It therefore has the potential to facilitate workers' *political right* to have a say in decisions that affect them. Membership of a union also puts employees in a better position to negotiate with their employers than if they acted individually. They may thus be better placed to assert their perceived *social rights* in matters such as pay, working conditions and job security.

It is unsurprising, then, that the right to belong to a union, or the right of labour to 'organize', is considered by the United Nations to be a universal human right: Article 23.4 of the *Universal Declaration of Human Rights* states that 'Everyone has the right to form and to join trade unions for the protection of his (sic) interests' (United Nations, 2013b).

Theory in Practice

Union busting at bottling plants used by Coca-Cola

Coca-Cola places a great deal of emphasis on employment rights. As the company states on its corporate website: 'In recent years, we have more clearly defined what we stand for with respect to human and workplace rights. We have also begun the complex work of ensuring that our entire business system and supply chain align with our policies' (Coca-Cola, 2013c). The company tells of its commitment to 'fostering open and inclusive workplaces that are based on recognized workplace human rights, where all employees are valued and inspired to be the best they can be' (Coca-Cola, 2013f: 1). Included in Coca-Cola's workplace rights policy is recognition of the right of its employees to 'freedom of association and collective bargaining', which accords to them a 'right to join, form or not to join a labor union without fear of reprisal, intimidation or harassment' (2013f: 2).

The emphasis that Coca-Cola has recently placed on workplace rights may be partly a response to problems it encountered a few years ago. In 2003, trade unions around the world launched a boycott of Coca-Cola's products in response to perceived breaches of workers' right to join a union at locally owned Coca-Cola bottling plants in Columbia (Brodzinski, 2003). That boycott followed legal action launched two years previously by the Colombian food and drink union, Sinaltrainal, against Coca-Cola and its bottlers. Sinaltrainal had alleged that the bottling companies 'contracted with or otherwise directed paramilitary security forces that utilised extreme violence and murdered, tortured, unlawfully detained or otherwise silenced trade union leaders' (cited by Brodzinski, 2003). The union's claims included an allegation that nine union members had been killed during the previous 13 years by far-right militias acting on behalf of Coca-Cola's Columbian bottlers to discourage union activity. This action followed similar allegations of anti-union activities carried out at bottling plants used by Coca-Cola in Guatemala, Nicaragua, Pakistan, Turkey and Russia (War on Want, 2006).

(Continued)

(Continued)

Questions

1. How might the anti-union activities alleged by Coca-Cola's critics be construed as a denial of the *political* and *social rights* of workers who bottle Coca-Cola's products?
2. In recent years, Coca-Cola seems to have changed its policy concerning union membership and union activity at its sub-contracted bottling plants. Why do you think Coca-Cola might have allowed its bottlers to discourage union membership and union activity in the past?
3. Do you think the change in emphasis by Coca-Cola indicates acknowledgement on the company's part that it has moral responsibility to ensure that the rights of the workers who bottle its products are respected, or might other factors have motivated this transformation in company policy?
4. The breaches of workers' rights referred to above are alleged to have taken place not on Coca-Cola's own premises but at bottling plants belonging to companies that have been subcontracted to bottle Coca-Cola's products. Do you think Coca-Cola should be held ethically responsible for alleged breaches in workers' rights on its subcontractors' premises?

Third generation: cultural rights

The political and social rights that were the focus of the first and second generations of rights theory have been augmented recently by a third generation. Tom Campbell (2006) refers to the preoccupation of this third generation as 'recognition rights', since they mostly concern the right of groups of people to be recognized by other groups of people. A broader term, which is perhaps more descriptive of the focus of late-twentieth-century and twenty-first-century rights talk, is *cultural rights*. Cultural rights include the right to recognition, but they also include other entitlements such as the right to preserve traditional ways of life, the right to maintain certain patterns of behaviour and belief, and the right to enjoy particular styles of social and artistic expression (Gilbert, 2005). The need to uphold cultural rights tends to be most pressing in situations where minority groups, or groups that are in some way disadvantaged or vulnerable, are marginalized or suppressed by dominant majorities. Such groups include those that are defined by race, ethnicity, religion, gender, sexual orientation or disability.

Cultural rights are relevant to business in a number of ways. For a start, consideration for cultural rights encourages companies to be sensitive to any specific, cultural needs that people like their employees and customers might have. The phrase 'equal opportunities' is relevant in this respect. However, it is also a little misleading, because respecting people's cultural rights may involve more than simply treating them equally.

Indeed, equal treatment may be construed as no more than giving people the opportunity to join in with a dominant mainstream. The exercise of cultural rights may demand more than this: it might require that differences are acknowledged, respected and accommodated. For instance, people of non-Western religious faith who work in American and European firms may not necessarily wish to be treated the same as Christian, Judaic and secular colleagues who comprise the majority of their companies' workforces. They may ask that any distinctiveness of dress or rituals of prayer that distinguish them are respected and that, where necessary, measures are put in place to accommodate these. Rather than treating all people the same, then, respect for cultural rights is about creating spaces within which diverse cultures might flourish; within which all may participate on an equal footing; and within which the characteristics that mark certain groups as different can be cultivated and respected.

Cultural rights are also relevant to business ethics in situations where corporate activity threatens to erode traditional ways of life, or where it undermines the social and economic fabric upon which vulnerable cultures rely. The tourism industry is particularly susceptible to critique in this respect (see for example Iyer, 2000/1988; Greenwood, 1989; Guha, 1997/1989). The movement of large numbers of people from affluent, Western countries to remote, underdeveloped destinations, along with the construction of Western-style accommodation and recreation amenities, often initiates stark contrasts between the behaviours and expectations of tourists and the cultural sensitivities of local people (UNEP, 2013).

But tourism is not the only industry sector that may impact on indigenous cultures. The clearance of rainforest for logging, agriculture and rubber production (BBC, 2008), the establishment of large-scale mining operations (Garvin et al., 2009; Urkidi and Walter, 2011) and industrial-scale trawling (Allen and Todd, 2013) can all endanger the habitats upon which traditional ways of life depend. So although business activity has the potential to spread economic development to impoverished communities, thus facilitating many of the social rights listed above, corporations should be sensitive to the potential for their activities to undermine the cultural cohesiveness of those communities.

Video Activity 1.2

The following video by Hollman Morris, entitled 'Suarez Gold: Afro-Colombian miners defending their heritage', is a brief section from a longer documentary which, according to the Theprisma website, concerns:

> traditional mining in the Colombian region of Cauca, located in the country's southwest, which has been carried out by Afro-Colombians who settled in this area of the country around 1637. Since then the descendants of these

(Continued)

(Continued)

first miners have continued their traditional mining with no accountability to anyone, and they can use the gold they find in whatever way they want. This activity is not only a way of life for these people but it has also become linked with their culture and ethnicity. Nevertheless, this is now under threat from the avarice of appropriation of resources by the companies, both national and foreign, that gained one of the 7,500 permits for exploratory mining granted by the Colombian government between the years of 2002 and 2012. (Theprisma, 2012)

www.youtube.com/watch?v=hxsnfUMPqj8

Questions

1 If large mining corporations take over the operation of mining activities in Cauca from local people, how might this affect the lives and work of those people?
2 How might this affect the ability of Cauca people to exercise their cultural rights?
3 Do you think mining corporations should concern themselves with such matters, or does the fact that a corporation has purchased a mining permit from the Columbian government give it the right to do as it wishes with this land, regardless of the impact on local people?

Universal Declaration of Human Rights

An indication of the importance with which rights are treated in modern society is offered by the agreement, in 1948, by the General Assembly of the United Nations to a *Universal Declaration of Human Rights*. The *Universal Declaration of Human Rights* was an attempt to get the world's most powerful nations to agree to minimum standards of conduct in their treatment of their own citizens and the citizens of other nations. It lists over 30 rights that are accorded to 'all members of the human family' (United Nations, 2013b) and which all its signatories agreed to respect. These rights include some from each of the three generations mentioned above.

The effectiveness of the *Universal Declaration of Human Rights* has been questioned on the basis that it may be more of an expression of aspiration than enforceable legislation, and also that some of its signatories contravene it with impunity when it suits their purposes (Almond, 1993).[2] Nevertheless, the *Universal Declaration of Human Rights* offers the first globally ratified agreement that fundamental rights exist, that they apply to all humans, and that they should be respected by everybody.

As far as business is concerned, the *Universal Declaration of Human Rights* offers a globally accredited blueprint that corporations can use to guide their interactions with people inside and outside of the business. The seriousness with which corporations treat the *Universal Declaration of Human Rights*, at least in theory, is apparent from the way that a lot of corporate marketing rhetoric resonates with its terminology (MacLeod, 2005). At the same time, the *Universal Declaration of Human Rights* offers to those who seek to comment on the ethicality of corporate behaviour a basis upon which to conduct their critique.

Video Activity 1.3

The following video, called '30 words – the Universal Declaration of Human Rights', lists 30 words that feature prominently in the *Universal Declaration of Human Rights*. As you watch the video, make a list of the words that are spoken.

www.youtube.com/watch?v=RNwL2mjApRw&feature=fvwre

Questions

1 Try to place all the words you have listed under the headings of 'political rights', 'social rights' and 'cultural rights'. In categorizing these words you might find it helpful to refer to a more-detailed statement of the *Universal Declaration of Human Rights*, which is available at: www.un.org/en/documents/udhr/#atop
2 For each of the words that you have listed, can you think of one practical step that a company can take to ensure that it respects the right referred to by that word?

Some characteristics of rights

So far, this chapter has introduced rights theory by highlighting some rights that are often talked about in Western society nowadays. This discussion has been placed in

[2]Consider, for example, Article 5 of the *Universal Declaration of Human Rights*, which states that 'No one shall be subjected to torture or to cruel, inhuman or degrading treatment or punishment', in relation to reports of the US military's treatment of prisoners in its so-called 'war on terror'.

a loose, historical framework of three different generations of rights discourse, each of which has highlighted the importance of different rights. I have also outlined some ways in which rights highlighted during each generation relate to contemporary business ethics. I will now talk a little more generally about rights, highlighting some features of rights as we think of them nowadays.

Rights trump other considerations

When we speak of someone as having a right, we generally assume that that right carries some sort of compulsion that overrides other considerations. Notably, we often think it ethically correct to respect a right even if doing so does not serve the general good. For instance, suppose a rich person lends me a thousand pounds. For the rich person, a thousand pounds may not be a lot of money, although she would probably expect me to give it back nevertheless. However, for people who are less wealthy, a thousand pounds is a great deal of money, which could make a big difference to their lives. So it might seem preferable for me to give the money to a charity rather than repaying the loan; perhaps a charity that provides food and shelter for survivors of an earthquake in the developing world. This would probably do a lot more good than giving the money back to the rich person. However, most of us would agree that we should pay the money back. And our reason for doing so is not only that we may want to borrow money again one day. We tend to think that if someone lends money to us, this creates a right to repayment on their part. And this right to repayment carries a compulsion that goes beyond considerations of the general good that would be achieved by giving the money to those in greater need.

This does not necessarily mean that we would always respect a right over and above all other considerations. The good that will be done by disregarding a right may be so overwhelming that we choose to disregard that right. Also, it may be the case that one right is trumped by another, more compelling, right (more about this shortly). However, it does mean that we think of rights as being special in a way that gives them a certain ethical force.

Theory in Practice

The Ilisu Dam, cultural rights and the general good

The British construction company Balfour Beatty and the Swiss Bank UBS found themselves weighing cultural rights against other considerations when they became involved in the construction of the Ilisu Dam in Turkey during the early 2000s (Smith-Spark, 2006).

The Ilisu Dam was to be built on the upper Tigris River. Its construction would have provided a much-needed, non-carbon energy source as well as bringing many new jobs to the area. However, the construction of the dam would lead to the flooding of a vast upstream area, formerly home to over 50,000 Kurdish people. The flooded area would include the ancient city of Hasankeyf, widely considered as a key architectural site and of tremendous cultural significance to the Kurdish people. This, along with other considerations, eventually caused Balfour Beatty and UBS to pull out of the project, leading to its temporary suspension (Smith-Spark, 2006).

Questions

1 In what ways might the construction of the Ilisu Dam contribute to the general good?
2 In what ways might the dam's construction interfere with the cultural rights of Kurdish people?
3 What other factors, apart from consideration for the cultural rights of the Kurds, might have persuaded Balfour Beatty and UBS to pull out of the Ilisu Dam project?

Rights entail responsibilities

A second assumption that we generally make when speaking about rights is that rights entail responsibilities (although we often use the word 'obligation' or 'duty' instead of 'responsibility'). In other words, if I recognize that someone has a right to something, this entails that other people have a responsibility to act in a manner that takes that right into account. So to say that someone has a right is not just to make a disinterested, factual statement about that person's situation. It is also to say something about how others ought to act. For instance, if I believe that a person has a right to speak and be heard, then I am also committing myself to the notion that other people, including myself, have a responsibility to allow that person to speak and to listen to what they have to say. Rights, then, are not just things that people have; they also create responsibilities/obligations/duties for others to act in particular ways.

This is important in a business context because the responsibilities that are entailed by someone having a right may rest with a corporation. Of course, when we speak of a corporation having responsibilities, what we actually mean is that the people who run that corporation have responsibilities. In this sense, the term 'corporate responsibility' is convenient shorthand. Thus, if a corporation's customers, employees, shareholders and suppliers, as well as the local communities that come into contact with that corporation, have rights, then it is the responsibility of the corporation, or the people who run it, to act in ways that respect those rights.

Negative responsibilities and positive responsibilities

Not only do rights entail responsibilities; they may also entail both negative and positive responsibilities. A *negative responsibility* is usually understood as a responsibility to not prevent someone from exercising a right. So if a person has a right to a certain thing, others have a negative responsibility to not prevent them from doing that thing. For instance, if we accept that all people have a right to life, then clearly we have a responsibility not to take anyone's life away from them.

However, fulfilling negative responsibilities may not be enough to enable people to exercise certain rights. It may be necessary for us also to do something *positive* to enable the exercise of a right. For instance, if we believe that all children have a right to education then someone (usually the state) needs to provide schools so that all children can exercise that right. Meanwhile, someone else (usually taxpayers) needs to pay for those schools. Thus, the right to universal education creates a *positive responsibility* for the state to provide schools and for citizens to contribute to the cost of providing those schools. A positive responsibility, then, should be understood as a responsibility to do something positive to enable someone to exercise a right.

The distinction between negative and positive responsibilities is useful for drawing our attention to steps that we may be ethically obliged to take in order for someone to exercise their rights. Consider the following example. Suppose that a company wishes to recruit a new member of staff. The managers of the company believe that all people, including people with disabilities, have a right to equal consideration for positions within the business. Therefore, the company clearly has a *negative responsibility* to not preclude applications from people with disabilities. However, this may not be enough for some people with disabilities to exercise their right to apply and to be considered equally. It may be that certain features of the job as it is currently structured make it difficult for people with certain forms of disability to do the work. Perhaps the job is located in an office that is up two flights of stairs, so a person with impaired mobility would find it hard to get to their work station. Or maybe the job involves telephone selling, which may cause difficulties for a person with impaired hearing. But if we accept that all people have a right to equal consideration for the job purely on job-related criteria, then the company has a *positive responsibility* to do certain things to enable applications from people with disabilities, such as offering to relocate the work station to a more accessible location, or offering to provide special telephone equipment so that a person with impaired hearing would be able to undertake the work.

Pause for Reflection

Clause 1 of Article 23 of the *Universal Declaration of Human Rights* states that 'Everyone has the right to work, to free choice of employment, to just and favourable conditions of work and to protection against unemployment' (United Nations, 2013b). Moreover, many countries have introduced equal-opportunities employment legislation upholding people's right to be considered for work opportunities purely on job-related criteria. However, family commitments prevent a lot of people from finding work which fully utilizes their skills. This is a particular issue for single parents who have to balance work with childcare responsibilities.

If people with childcare commitments have a right to be considered for work purely on job-related criteria, what *negative responsibilities* might this create for companies who are recruiting staff?

What *positive responsibilities* might it entail for those companies? In other words, what positive things might companies have a responsibility to do in order to help people with childcare commitments to work for them?

Conflicting rights

One last, very important feature of rights is that the rights of different people or different groups of people often conflict with one another. For instance, my right to play my music in my own home late at night may conflict with my neighbours' right to enjoy a good night's sleep. My right to keep the money that I earn may conflict with other people's right to health care, since that health care needs to be paid for partly by taxes on my wages. Similarly, the right of a global mining corporation to extract metal from land that it owns might, if its mining activities pollute local rivers, conflict with local people's right to clean water supplies. And within corporations, the perceived rights of people such as customers, employees and shareholders may conflict with one another. This issue of conflicting rights will be discussed several times during the rest of this chapter.

Rights and stakeholders

So far this chapter has discussed some rights that are relevant to business contexts, placing them under the headings of political, social and cultural rights. It has introduced the *Universal Declaration of Human Rights* as a rights-based reference point for ethical business practice and it has outlined some features of the way that we usually think about rights. This discussion has taken for granted the assumption that people have rights in relation to business. However, the question of *why* people have those rights has not yet been considered. This second section of the chapter will discuss that question. It will introduce the notion of *stakeholding* and explain why stakeholder relationships might entail rights to consideration on the part of certain groups. I will also distinguish between different types of stakeholder relationship, drawing attention to the possibility that the rights of some stakeholders might get overlooked as a result of business's preoccupation with the rights of other stakeholders.

Stakeholding as a basis for the creation of rights

The term *stakeholder* was introduced to business theory by Edward Freeman, who described a stakeholder as 'any group or individual who can affect or is affected by [a business] organizations' objectives' (1984: 46). Freeman's concept of stakeholding has had a big impact on business theory, and the word 'stakeholder' is often used by business academics and business practitioners nowadays.

In order to draw out the ethical implications of stakeholding, it helps to elaborate on Freeman's original definition. Note that Freeman alludes to two separate kinds of relationship, each of which might offer the basis for stakeholder rights and for corresponding business responsibilities. On the one hand, he speaks of any group or individual who *can affect* a business's objectives. Another way of describing people who have this first type of relationship with a business is to say that they are able to contribute in some way to the success of the business, or to influence its success. I will therefore refer to these people as *influential stakeholders*.

On the other hand, Freeman also mentions groups and individuals who *are affected by* a business organization's objectives. In this second type of relationship he is referring to stakeholders who are in some way impacted by the activities of the business. I will refer to this category of stakeholders as *affected stakeholders*.

You will find both of these types of stakeholder represented in Figure 1.1 by a circle: the circle on the left represents influential stakeholders; that on the right represents affected stakeholders. Both categories of stakeholder are linked to a company by arrows which represent their relationships to it. I will say more about those arrows shortly, but first I will explain who might fall into these two separate types of stakeholder group and why the relationships that they have with a business might create rights on their part.

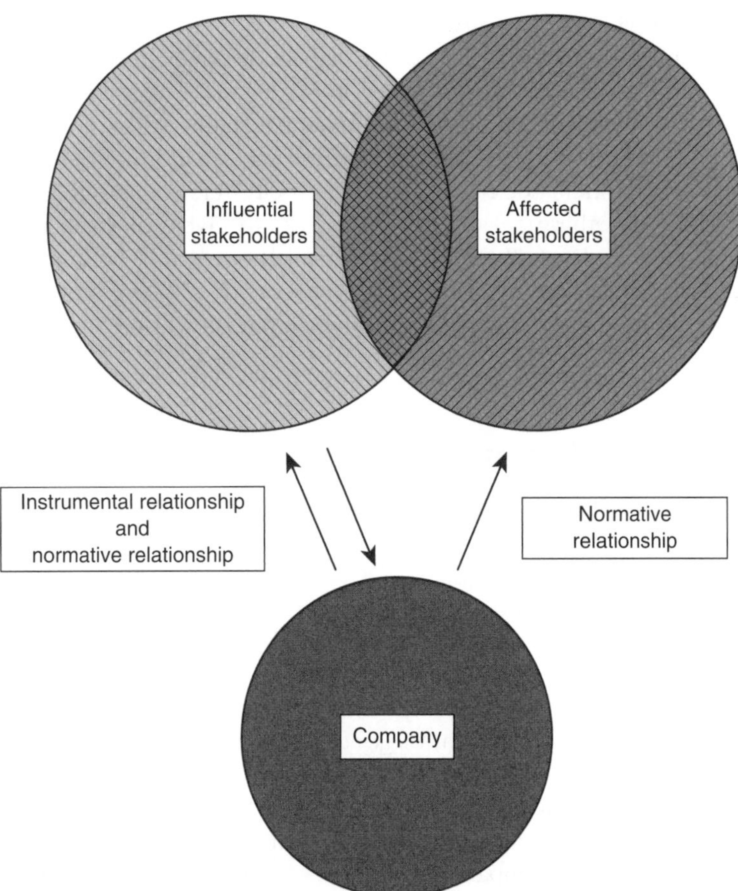

Figure 1.1 Relationships between influential stakeholders, affected stakeholders, and the company

Influential stakeholders: reciprocity rights

In the category of influential stakeholders – stakeholders who can influence a business's success – we might include its customers, for without the support of its customers a company is unlikely to succeed. After all, if nobody wants to buy the things that a company sells, that company will not be in business for long. Similarly, the people who work for a business can influence the achievement of its objectives. Without the efforts of its employees, some of whom might work for a company for many years, that company is unlikely to succeed. The same can be said of suppliers.

Those firms and individuals who sell goods and services to a company clearly influence its performance. Similarly, the banks that lend money to a business and the shareholders who invest in it by purchasing its shares make a vital contribution to its success. They too, then, can be classed as influential stakeholders.

The word *reciprocity* can be used to describe the creation of rights on the part of influential stakeholders such as these. Reciprocity refers to a situation in which one party gives something to another party and receives, or expects to receive, something in return. Applied to influential stakeholder relationships, reciprocity implies that, since stakeholders influence the success of a business by supporting it, they have, in return, a right to expect that their interests will be taken into account by that business.

Affected stakeholders: effect entails a right to consideration

So much for the first kind of relationship that Freeman mentions in his definition of stakeholders. What of the second kind: those relationships in which stakeholders *are affected by* the activities of the business? Of course, all of the influential stakeholders already referred to also fall into this second category. Customers support a business, so have influence over it, but they are also affected by its product, pricing and promotion strategies. Employees influence the success of a business, but they are also affected by the human resource management practices that it adopts. Similarly, suppliers will be affected by the amount of goods and services that a company chooses to buy from them and by the price that it is willing to pay. And the success or otherwise of a business will clearly have a significant effect on those people who invest in it. In the worst-case scenario, if the company goes bust they may lose their investment. On the other hand, if the company does well, investors may be able to share in its success through the interest payments it makes, through uplift in the value of their investment, or through the award of generous dividend payments.

So, customers, employees, suppliers and investors fall into both of the categories described by Freeman: they can affect business success *and* they are affected by it. In the terms used here, they can be considered as both influential stakeholders and as affected stakeholders. For this reason, you will notice that the two circles representing influential stakeholders and affected stakeholders in Figure 1.1 overlap. All of the groups mentioned above can be placed in the overlapping part at the centre of the diagram.

However, it is important to note that there may be other individuals or groups who only have the second kind of relationship with a business. In other words, they may be *affected by* its activities but they have no *influence over* its success. One group that may fall into this category is the community that lives close to a business. Local communities might be affected by noxious fumes that a business produces, by the noise that its operations make, perhaps by the light pollution it emits and by other forms of pollution that it might cause. People who live close to a company may also find their lifestyles affected in other ways. For instance, indigenous culture may be eroded by large numbers of people who come into an area to work for a company, or local roads may become congested by the traffic generated by business activity. Of course, some of those local people may work for the business themselves, so they will influence its success in their capacity as employees. Some may also buy its products, so they will have some influence over it. Some may supply it, or invest in it, so they could also be classed as influential stakeholders. In this case, even some of these local people can be placed in the overlap between the two circles in Figure 1.1. But there are likely to be many other local people who are not customers, employees, suppliers or investors and who therefore have no influence-relationship with the business whatsoever. They will, however, be affected by its activities. These, then, can be placed in the section on the right-hand side of the right-hand circle in Figure 1.1.

Given that such people make no contribution to the success of a business, so they have no reciprocity relationship with it, why should they have a right to be taken into account? One answer to this question lies in the assumption that *effect entails a right to consideration*. In other words, the rights of such people are based on the idea that the effect a business has over them creates, on their part, a right to be taken into account.

This idea chimes with commonsense ideas about ethics. Most of us would accept that, if our actions have an effect on other people, those people have a right to be taken into account by us. For instance, if I live in a flat with neighbours on all sides, then it seems reasonable to assume that those neighbours have a right to my consideration. And if I were to play my music very loud at three o'clock in the morning, then most people would agree that I am failing to respect that right. The same principle applies to companies. Corporations, particularly large corporations, have a considerable social and environmental effect. It therefore seems reasonable to suppose that the people who experience that effect have a right to consideration. In other words, they have a right to be taken into account by the people who make the key decisions in companies.

Pause for Reflection

This discussion of stakeholders has focused so far on *people* and *groups of people*. However, people are not the only ones affected by corporate activity. Corporations also have a significant effect on the natural environment. To what extent do you think that animals, insects, marine creatures, plants, and even the land and the oceans can be considered as stakeholders that have a right to consideration?

The normative and instrumental importance of stakeholders

This section has so far explained the difference between influential stakeholders and affected stakeholders. It has also described how each type of stakeholder relationship might provide a basis for the creation of stakeholder rights and corresponding business responsibilities. I will now highlight a further important distinction between different types of stakeholder relationship.

Normative relationships

Both influential stakeholders and affected stakeholders might be thought of as having an ethical relationship with a company: influential stakeholders on account of their *reciprocity rights*; affected stakeholders on the basis that *effect entails a right to consideration*. For this reason, Figure 1.1 shows arrows pointing from the company towards each type of stakeholder. These arrows represent the fact that the company has responsibilities towards the stakeholders that fall within each circle. Another way of putting this, to adopt Thomas Donaldson's and Lee Preston's (1995) terminology, is to say that both types of stakeholder are *normatively* important to the company. The word 'normative' is generally used to denote some form of ethical content. Therefore, because of the ethical rights and ethical responsibilities that characterize the relationship between the company and its stakeholders, it could be said that the company has a *normative* relationship with each category of stakeholder.

Instrumental relationships

Influential stakeholders, as well as being normatively important to – or having an ethical relationship with – a company, are also important in another way. Namely, their contribution is important to a company's commercial performance. This is why, in the case of influential stakeholders, Figure 1.1 shows an arrow going from influential stakeholders towards the company. This arrow denotes the influence that they have over it. In Donaldson and Preston's (1995) terminology, influential stakeholders are *instrumentally* important to a business insofar as their support is *instrumental* to corporate success. They could therefore be said to have an *instrumental* relationship with the company as well as having a normative relationship with it.

Concerning influential stakeholders: good ethics is (generally) good for business

Note that, as far as influential stakeholders are concerned, there is harmony between *normative* and *instrumental* considerations: if a company respects the rights of its influential stakeholders, this is likely to be good for business because, by respecting influential stakeholders' rights, a company is likely to retain their support. On the other hand, if a company does not respect the rights of its influential stakeholders those people may withdraw their support, which could have a damaging effect on the company. In the case of influential stakeholders, then, doing what is *normatively* important is consistent with doing what is *instrumentally* important; companies have compelling business reasons to respect the rights of influential stakeholders.

Concerning affected stakeholders: good ethics may not be good for business

As far as relationships with influential stakeholders are concerned, then, *good ethics* might be considered *good for business*. However, this is not necessarily the case with affected stakeholders. Consider the local communities already mentioned. Companies may have *normative* reasons to take these people into account on the basis that effect entails a right to consideration. However, they do not necessarily have any *instrumental* reason to do so, for the support of such people, from a purely instrumental point of view, may be irrelevant. Apart from those few local people who may buy its products, who may work for the company and so on, most local people are not in a position to influence a company's success. They are therefore of no direct instrumental importance to it. They have a normative relationship with the company but no instrumental relationship.

So, respecting the rights of non-influential, affected stakeholders is unlikely to have any direct impact on corporate success. As far as non-influential, affected stakeholders are concerned, good ethics is not necessarily good for business.

Theory in Practice

Glencore and stakeholder rights

Glencore is one of the world's largest commodity and mining corporations. Glencore was floated on the London stock exchange in 2011 at a value of £38bn (Wachman, 2011b). The flotation made five of the company's partners into billionaires, including chief executive, Ivan Glasenberg, whose ownership share was valued at £4 billion (Sweeney, 2012).

In a television interview the following year (BBC, 2012a), Ivan Glasenberg spoke of the seriousness with which Glencore treats its social and environmental responsibilities. The sustainability pages of the company's website reinforce this

(Continued)

(Continued)

commitment, stating: 'We recognise that our work can have an impact on society and the environment. We are committed to improving our performance in human rights, health and safety, environmental protection and compliance' (Glencore Xstrata, 2013).

However, a 2012 BBC Panorama documentary suggested that Glencore may not treat the rights of all its stakeholders with the same importance. One of several allegations made by the BBC relates to Glencore's copper-mining operation in the Democratic Republic of the Congo. Specifically, the programme claimed that Glencore had, for three years, pumped heavily polluted waste from its copper-refining plant in Katanga province into the Luilu River. The programme's presenter, Jonathan Sweeney, claimed that

> Glencore's acid waterfall stank of toxic fumes when I visited it a few weeks ago. Upstream, the river used by local people to wash and fish was clear; downstream of the Glencore pipe, there was brown sludge. One local complained: 'Fish can't survive the acid. Glencore lacks any respect for people. No one would do that to another human being. It's shocking'. A Swiss NGO tested the acidity of the wastewater and found a pH value of 1.9, where 1 is pure acid and 7 neutral. (Sweeney, 2012)

In Glencore's defence, Ivan Glasenberg said that toxic waste had been dumped into the river even before Glencore's arrival. On taking over the copper-refining operation, Glasenberg claimed that Glencore had undertaken to stop the pollution but admitted that this had taken three years so far and that, during that time, the pollution had continued unabated. When questioned on this, Glasenberg said: 'It was impossible to remedy faster ... What else could we do? We have 6,500 employees, the government insists we keep them employed' (cited by Sweeney, 2012).

Questions

1. Who would you classify as Glencore's *influential stakeholders*; that is, what groups does Glencore depend upon for its commercial success?
2. Why might the contribution these people make to Glencore's success give them a right to be taken into account by people such as Ivan Glasenberg?
3. From the above account, can you identify any people who are affected by Glencore's activities (that is, the company's *affected stakeholders*) who do not have an influence-based relationship with it?

4 What reasons might be given for the right of these people to be taken into account by people like Ivan Glasenberg?
5 In what way might Glencore be accused of not respecting the rights of some of its *non-influential, affected stakeholders*?
6 In this instance, Glencore's decision making seems to have favoured the rights of its *influential stakeholders* over those of some of its *non-influential, affected stakeholders*. Can you think of any reasons why Glencore's executives might have made that choice?
7 Glencore's decision to overlook the rights of some of its *non-influential, affected stakeholders* seems inconsistent with the claims of its web pages and its chief executive that it respects its social and environmental responsibilities. Can you think of any *instrumental* reasons why a company might want to project an image of social and environmental responsibility, even if it does not respect the *normative* responsibilities associated with this image?

Variations in stakeholder influence; variations in instrumental importance

Of course, the *instrumental* importance of taking the *reciprocity rights* of *influential stakeholders* into account will vary depending on just how influential those stakeholders are to corporate success. Not all influential stakeholders are equally influential, so while there are sound instrumental reasons to take the reciprocity rights of some into account, this may not be so with others. For instance, in the case of a company's employees, those workers who possess hard-to-find, specialist skills are likely to exercise more influence than unskilled workers who can easily be replaced. If the former decide to withdraw their support for a company by resigning, that company could be in trouble. This is not the case with the latter. Similarly, institutional investors such as pension and insurance firms, who may hold large shareholdings in a company, might wield more influence over it than private individuals who own just a few shares. Moreover, corporate customers, who buy large quantities of a company's product, will be more influential than occasional, private purchasers. And suppliers of scarce goods and services are likely to have more influence over a company than those who provide it with things that are easy to source elsewhere. Importantly, in each of these cases, it is of greater instrumental importance to keep the first group of influential stakeholders happy than it is to keep the second group happy. Companies therefore have sound instrumental reasons to respect their *normative* responsibilities to the first group but not necessarily the second group.

Now it may be that failing to take less-influential stakeholders into account will create bad publicity for a company, which might erode the support of its more-influential stakeholders. And this, in turn, may eventually undermine corporate success. In such cases, it is instrumentally important for a company to respect the rights of its less-influential, affected stakeholders. But this will only be the case insofar as such publicity reaches the company's more-influential stakeholders. Furthermore, it will only be the case insofar as those more-influential stakeholders care whether or not the rights of less-influential, affected stakeholders are respected. It is possible to envisage a situation in which corporate activity has a significant, adverse impact on the lives of many people, but in which none of its most-influential stakeholders know or care about this. In such a case, that firm would have no instrumental reason to take the rights of those affected stakeholders into account.

The implication of the distinction between, on the one hand, a firm's most-influential stakeholders and, on the other hand, its less-influential, affected stakeholders is that there are sound, instrumental reasons to take the former into account but there are not necessarily any sound, instrumental reasons to take the latter into account. In other words, taking the first into account is good for business; taking the second into account may not be. This is very important because there is a tendency in business communities and amongst some business ethics theorists to downplay tension between instrumental and normative considerations. In other words, many business practitioners and some business ethicists suggest that there is no conflict between doing what is best for business and acting ethically because if a company behaves unethically it will lose the support of its influential stakeholders, which, ultimately, will be bad for business. These commentators conclude that good ethics is therefore good for business and, conversely, what is good for business is ethically good. This may indeed be the case as far as a firm's most influential stakeholders are concerned. However, it is not always the case when it comes to its relationships with a firm's less-influential, affected stakeholders. As far as less-influential, affected stakeholders are concerned, a company may prosper – and, indeed, many have been accused of prospering – by treating them with absolute disregard.

Video Activity 1.4

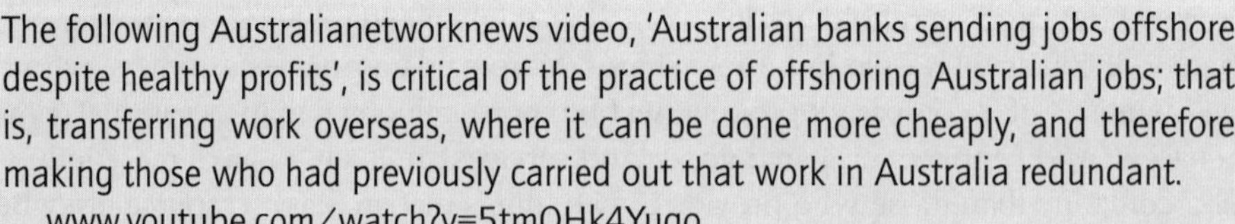

The following Australianetworknews video, 'Australian banks sending jobs offshore despite healthy profits', is critical of the practice of offshoring Australian jobs; that is, transferring work overseas, where it can be done more cheaply, and therefore making those who had previously carried out that work in Australia redundant.

www.youtube.com/watch?v=5tmOHk4Yugo

Questions

1 Can you identify any *influential stakeholders* whose *reciprocity rights* are served by the practice of offshoring jobs?

2 Can you identify any *less-influential stakeholders* whose *reciprocity rights* are not respected and who are adversely affected by offshoring?

3 The 'local labelling system' discussed in the video is designed to make one group of highly influential stakeholders aware of where corporate work actually takes place. Which *highly influential stakeholders* are these?
4 How do you feel about the ethics of offshoring as described in the video? Do you think such offshoring is ethically justified or not?
5 Do you think your views on the ethicality of offshoring would change if you owned a large number of shares in one of the corporations discussed in the video? What about if you were an Australian former-employee of one of these corporations who had lost their job as a result of offshoring?

Property rights

This chapter has so far explained how various sorts of right may be relevant in business contexts and how these rights might create responsibilities for companies and the people who run them. The notion of stakeholding has been offered as a framework for considering these rights and responsibilities. This last section of the chapter will consider one particular branch of rights that has received a lot of attention from philosophers over the last few hundred years, which continues to figure prominently in contemporary rights talk, and which has particular relevance to business ethics. These are *property rights*.

When people speak about the rights associated with property they are talking about more than the land and buildings that we often think of as property. To think purely in terms of land and buildings is to employ a narrow definition of property. A broader definition embraces everything that we own, including, for sure, our houses and our land but also including things like clothes, smartphones, cars, furniture, pets and the money in our wallets and our bank accounts. A broader definition also includes any investments we make. After all, by buying shares in a company, we become a part owner of that company. It, or at any rate a part of it, thus becomes our property. As I will explain shortly, some people also include our bodies and what we do with them under the heading of property. And, of course, it is customary to think of the products of our creative intellect as our property. Indeed, many nations today recognize intellectual property rights, which respect people's ownership of the ideas they have, the music and the literature they produce, and the things they invent.

Property is very important in business contexts. This is partly because the value of a corporation's property is usually taken as the key indicator of its prosperity. The buildings, fixtures and fittings, land, machinery, raw materials, products, cash reserves, investments, patented inventions, trademarks and copyrights that belong to a company therefore tell us a lot about whether that company is thriving or not. Moreover, the people who own a business – those people who have shares in it – are usually depicted as the indirect owners of all those things, and their ownership is widely considered to bestow on them certain important rights.

But property is also important to business in more fundamental ways. The capitalist system within which most contemporary business is conducted is generally understood as a set of economic arrangements that revolve around the exchange of property between stakeholders. In other words, the modern business model is usually depicted as a complex interplay of voluntary property exchange, in which corporations, consumers, investors, suppliers and employees exercise their right to exchange property with one another in the form of money, goods and services, labour and a range of derivative forms of ownership.

Given the significance of property to contemporary business, it is unsurprising that the right to accumulate, hold, transfer, and generally do as we wish with our property is taken very seriously in corporate environments. But where do property rights come from? Why do individuals and corporations have a right to own certain things and do with them as they choose? What justification can be given for this cornerstone of modern ethical understanding and contemporary business thinking?

This section will consider some responses to questions such as these. It will introduce an influential account of the origin of property rights: that offered by the seventeenth-century political philosopher John Locke. Although Locke wrote over 300 years ago, his ideas still resonate in the way we think about property today. Moreover, versions of Locke's ideas are often drawn on to justify the importance given to property rights in contemporary corporate environments. After outlining Locke's account, I will introduce an alternative perspective on property rights and business, which was offered by the nineteenth-century economist, philosopher and social theorist, Karl Marx. Marx's perspective offers reasons to be wary of placing too much emphasis on property rights in business ethics. In particular, it highlights tension that often occurs between the interests of two particular sets of stakeholders: shareholders and employees. It also draws attention to the possibility that employees will be exploited in the process of serving the property-related interests of shareholders.

John Locke's account of property rights

John Locke's justification of property rights is presented in his *Two Treatises of Government* (1988/1690). In this work, Locke put forward the view that the earth has been given by God to all humankind in common 'to make use of … to the best advantage of Life, and convenience' (Locke, 1988/1690: 286/II.26). In other words, as Locke saw it, the earth and all the resources it contains did not originally belong to anyone in particular; they belonged to us all. Nevertheless, Locke observed that we have moved from this state of common ownership to a state in which specific things are owned by specific people. He set out to explain how this transformation from common ownership to private ownership can be justified.

The merits of productive labour

Locke's explanation begins with the observation that if we are to make productive use of the things that have been given to humankind in common we must, as individuals, take control of them. In Locke's words, 'there must of necessity be a means *to appropriate* them some way or other before they can be of any use, or at all beneficial to any particular Man' (1988/1690: 286/II.26). Another way of putting this is to say that somebody must take hold of the things that nature has provided and work on them if they are to serve a useful, human purpose.

Self-ownership and the ownership of one's labour

To this, Locke added what he thought was a self-evident truth: that of self-ownership. It was obvious to him that each and every one of us owns our own self, and that it makes no sense to think of human beings in any other way. As he put it, it is clear that 'every Man has a *Property* in his own *Person*. This no Body has any Right to but himself' (Locke, 1988/1690: 287/II.27).

Since each one of us owns our own self, Locke believed that we must also own our own labour. In other words, since our bodies are ours, what we do with them must also be ours. For each person, then, 'The *Labour* of his Body, and the *Work* of his Hands, we may say, are properly his' (Locke, 1988/1690: 287–88/II.27). Therefore, as Locke described things, any effort that I choose to expend on tasks such as picking apples, digging metals out of the ground, drawing water from a well, hunting deer in the forest, or catching fish from the ocean belongs to me and to no one else: that labour is my property and I have a right to do with it whatever I wish.

Property as the outcome of application of one's own labour to common resources

Now, if we mix our labour, which is our own property, with the fruits of nature, which are our common inheritance, we can turn that common inheritance into something useful. As Locke saw it, we thus come to have a right of ownership of the outcome of this productive endeavour. In his terms, the apples that I gather, the metal that I dig, the water that I draw, the deer that I shoot and the fish that I catch transfer from being part of *everybody's* common inheritance to being *my* private property as a result of the application of *my* labour. And once these things become my property, nobody else has a claim to them. In Locke's words:

> Whatsoever then he removes out of the State that nature hath provided … he hath mixed his *Labour* with, and joyned to it something that is his own, and thereby makes it his *Property*. It being by him removed from the common state Nature placed it in, it hath by his *labour* something annexed to it, that excludes the common right of other Men. (1988/1690: 288/II.27)

Locke believed, therefore, that the common goods that we appropriate through the application of our labour are properly ours, since it is our labour that makes those things useful. As he put it, it is our labour that adds value to them: 'tis *Labour* indeed that *puts the difference of value* on everything' (Locke, 1988/1690: 296/II.40). And since we have acquired a right of ownership of these things through the application of our value-adding labour, Locke thought that no one else has a right to take them from us.

In this way, Locke suggested that the improvement of common resources, which is ultimately to the benefit of everybody, necessarily entails private property. If people were not able to own things, they would have no reason to appropriate them and make them more useful. And if this were the case, the things that have been given to us in common by God would remain forever in an unproductive state. Locke concluded that 'the Condition of Humane Life, which requires Labour and Materials to work on, necessarily introduces *private Possessions*' (Locke, 1988/1690: 292/II.35). Indeed, for these reasons, Locke considered the existence of private property and recognition of ownership rights to be essential features of a civilized and prosperous society.

Contemporary relevance of Locke's rationale

Aspects of Locke's justification characterize the way that we often think of property ownership today. We tend to believe that the things we acquire through our own endeavours are rightfully ours. We assume that we have a right to those things and that nobody should take them from us. For instance, if I study hard at school and university to gain the qualifications needed for a well-paid job, and if I then apply myself diligently to my career so that I get promoted and earn a good salary, I assume that I have a right to the money I earn and to the things that I buy with it. Furthermore, I assume that nobody should be allowed to take that money or those things from me.

This way of thinking also seems relevant to business ownership. We might characterize corporate activity as the productive application of a company's labour to pre-existing resources, which creates goods and services that people need and which thus become the property of the company. Companies then exchange that property for money (that is, for the property of their customers), which makes life better for everybody. A successful business might therefore be depicted, in a Lockean sense, as one which has productively applied its labour to humankind's common inheritance, and which has thus turned that inheritance into something useful; something that people need; something that makes everybody's life better. On this Lockean-style rationale, the benign consequences of this appropriation of common resources would justify a company's right to the property that it thus accumulates and its right to exchange that property as it chooses. Moreover, those people who facilitate this whole process by investing their money (their property) in a company, in the form of share ownership, and who therefore come to own the company, might be understood as having a right to the returns that they receive from their investment.

Video Activity 1.5

Watch the following two videos.

www.youtube.com/watch?v=jnjPFZV8Wqo

www.youtube.com/watch?v=lDMenqKCXdw&list=PLFA50FBC214A6CE87

The first video, entitled 'The Power of Property Rights', comes from Learn Liberty. In this video, Tom W. Bell offers a Lockean rationale, suggesting that property ownership is essential for the productive use of resources and that the acknowledgement of property rights is an essential feature of social and economic organization.

The second video, entitled 'Boundary Issues', which is taken from the film *The Corporation*, offers some different perspectives on property rights. In this video, several philosophers, economists, and public servants challenge the philosophical rationale for property rights and suggest that it is not good for everything to be privately owned. Rather, they suggest that it is better for everyone if certain things remain in common ownership.

This second video ends with economist Michael Walker offering a contrasting view. Walker suggests that it would be better for us all if absolutely everything, including the sea, the air, and all the earth, were privately owned. He suggests that only by becoming somebody's property will such resources be properly cared for.

Questions

1 From these videos, from the foregoing discussion of John Locke's account of property rights, and from your own reflections on this topic, how do you think society might benefit from the recognition of property rights?
2 What arguments might be offered for limiting private ownership of property?
3 Do you think that the provision of *all* goods and services should be in the hands of privately owned businesses, or should some goods and services be controlled by publicly owned and publicly run institutions?

John Locke was by no means an unreserved advocate of property rights. He believed that property rights should be subject to certain conditions. For instance, he suggested that each person's right to take common resources into private ownership should be conditional on that person only taking as much as they need. He also proposed that nobody should be allowed to take so much from the common store that others are deprived. Moreover, Locke suggested that property ownership places on owners an obligation to consider the needs of those who are less fortunate than themselves. Nevertheless, despite the conditions that he placed on the appropriation of common resources, Locke vigorously supported the notion of private property. In general, his theory of property offers an intuitively appealing justification for people's right to own those things that they acquire through the application of honest, human endeavour.

Karl Marx's critique of property rights

In contrast to Locke's generally supportive account, a less-supportive discussion of property rights was offered two centuries later by the influential German theorist, Karl Marx. Marx was critical of rights in general as a basis of ethical evaluation. He took the view that, by focusing our ethical attention on rights, we come to think about ethics purely in individualistic terms. That is, we are thus encouraged to think of people as separate, independent entities who need rules, based on individual rights, to govern interactions that come about as they pursue their separate, independent agendas. Like many philosophers, Marx saw this as a fundamentally misguided way of thinking about people. As he saw it, humans are essentially social creatures who depend on social interaction in all sorts of complex ways. He believed that the individualistic mindset that is associated with an ethic of rights diverts attention from that social interdependence. It encourages us to focus solely on personal entitlement instead of thinking about what we can do to contribute to social cohesion and to promote the common good. As Marx saw it, 'none of the so-called rights of man goes beyond egoistic man, … namely an individual withdrawn behind his private interests and whims and separated from the community' (2000/1843: 61).

Marx was particularly critical of property rights in this respect. In his view, to place too much emphasis on property rights is to create a society in which each person retreats within their separate domain, taking pleasure in their own possessions, and giving little thought to how this impacts on other people. In Marx's words, 'the right of man to property is the right to enjoy his possessions and dispose of the same arbitrarily, without regard for other men, independently from society, the right of selfishness' (2000/1843: 60).

Pause for Reflection

If Karl Marx were alive today, he might have described many of the conflicts that occur between neighbours as the outcome of the anti-social selfishness that is encouraged by our preoccupation with property rights. For instance, he might thus have explained the fact that some people feel entitled to grow trees on their land that block their neighbours' light; or that some choose to block roads and footpaths that cross their land, which provide access that others depend upon. He might have said that these problems occur because people believe that they have a right to do whatever they want on their own property, regardless of how this affects other people.

Can you think of any business practices that you are aware of for which Marx might have offered a similar account? That is, can you think of situations in which corporations use their property in a selfish manner which benefits them but which causes problems for others?

Marx also had a lot to say about the relationship between labour and property. You will recall that John Locke's account of property suggested that our right to enjoy our possessions was fair reward for the labour that we have invested in appropriating those possessions. Marx offered a contrasting perspective on the relationship between labour and property in capitalist business settings. Rather than seeing property as just reward for labour, he pointed out that capitalism tends to oppose labour to property. As Marx saw it, our preoccupation with property, along with the rights associated with it, has created a situation in which the owners of property and the providers of labour stand in opposition to one another. In order to appreciate how this opposition occurs, it helps to have some familiarity with Marx's explanation of how surplus value, or profit, is created, and how this entails the exploitation of workers.

The creation of profit, or surplus value

Marx saw business as a process of drawing together a range of resources – such as land, buildings, materials, machinery and labour – and using those resources to create products. He pointed out that each of those resources has a value, and a business has to pay a price which reflects that value. A business makes profit – or creates 'surplus value' (Marx 2000/1867) – when the value of the things it produces is greater than the combined value of all the resources used to make them. This enables the business to sell its products at that higher value and retain the difference.

Consider the generation of surplus value in relation to the activities of a clothing manufacturer. A clothing manufacturer gathers together all the resources that are needed to make and sell clothes. Those resources probably include: a factory in which to carry out production; some clothes-making machinery; some fabrics and other raw materials; electricity to power the machines and light the factory; perhaps some advertising space so that the manufacturer can tell people about its products and encourage them to buy them; and so on. The manufacturer also needs to hire people to work in its clothing factories. All these resources previously belonged to somebody else; that is, they were somebody else's property. Even the labour that the clothing manufacturer uses is the property of the factory workers, and it has to be purchased from them. The manufacturer pays for all these resources and combines them in order to make clothes, hoping to sell those clothes for more money than the combined cost of the factories, machinery, fabrics, electricity, advertising space, wages and so on. If it succeeds in doing this, it makes a profit or, in Marx's terms, it creates surplus value.

Exploitation of labour

Just as Locke believed that labour is the vital ingredient that turns God-given natural resources into something that will serve a useful purpose, Marx believed that labour is the most important component in the creation of surplus value. As he saw it, the labour provided by a clothing manufacturer's factory workers is the key element that enables all the other resources to be made into something of greater value. However, despite the contribution of labour to the creation of surplus value, Marx pointed out that the providers of labour (in this instance, the factory workers) usually receive very little for their efforts. Indeed, they are usually paid no more than a subsistence wage, which enables them to buy only the bare necessities of life. This ensures that they have to spend a substantial portion of their lives at work in order to earn a living. Meanwhile, most of the surplus value created by business activity, thanks to the input of workers, goes to those who own the business. The result of this is that business owners get richer and richer while their employees are locked in poverty.

To express Marx's account in contemporary terms, he would say that it is employees that enable businesses to make profit. However, despite the significance of their contribution, most employees in most businesses receive very little in return for their endeavours. In capitalist enterprise, the profits made by a business go mainly to those who own it; that is, to its shareholders (although senior managers usually get a substantial portion of surplus value nowadays). Meanwhile, most employees are paid as little as the business can get away with paying them, which is usually just enough for them to live on. This means that they have to work long hours to earn a living, which, in turn, ensures that all the necessary work gets done.

Marx believed this to be an exploitative system. Rather than being fairly rewarded for the application of their labour, workers are forced to sell it at a very low price so that the owners of businesses can build their own stash of property. Rather than being in harmony with labour, then, property ownership is in opposition to it. Marx thus noted that

> modern bourgeois private property is the final and most complete expression of the system of producing and appropriating products, that is based on class antagonisms, on the exploitation of the many by the few... But does wage-labour create any property for the labourer? Not a bit. It creates capital, i.e., that kind of property which exploits wage-labour, and which cannot increase except upon condition of begetting a new supply of wage-labour for fresh exploitation. Property, in its present form, is based on the antagonism of capital and wage labour. (Marx and Engels, 2000/1848: 256)

For reasons such as this, Marx considered the deference accorded to private property in modern society to be misguided. He pointed out that those who own property control businesses. Those owners tend to use their control purely as a means of further enriching themselves while keeping the working classes – those who have nothing to sell but their labour – in poverty. Thus, as a result of the primacy of property rights over most other ethical considerations, property owners are able to ratchet up their wealth and their power while the workers upon whose labour their affluence is built receive just enough to get by. This, as Marx saw it, leads to a situation of ever-increasing inequality and ever-increasing unfairness.

Theory in Practice

A living wage for fast-food workers?

Clause 3 of Article 23 of the *Universal Declaration of Human Rights* states that 'Everyone who works has the right to just and favourable remuneration ensuring for himself and his family an existence worthy of human dignity, and supplemented, if necessary, by other means of social protection' (United Nations, 2013b). This clause places a responsibility on employers and on national governments: it impels employers to pay their workers a living wage; and, where this is not possible, it obliges governments to augment wages to a level 'worthy of human dignity'.

Given the record-high levels reached repeatedly by the US stock market during 2013 (Rushe, 2013a, 2013b) it seems reasonable to suppose that the government would have little need to augment wages in the USA. Since the commercial performance of American corporations is generally strong, enabling substantial returns on investment for the owners of those corporations, one might expect employees to be well rewarded for their contribution. Given the vibrancy of American business, it seems reasonable to assume that corporate employees would have little trouble sustaining themselves and their families, and that they would have little need for state handouts.

It is surprising, therefore, to learn that employees of American fast-food corporations, including McDonald's, Wendy's, and KFC, participated in city-centre marches and strike action during 2013 to protest about low wages. Many of those workers receive no more than the minimum wage of $7.25 an hour, which they say is not enough for them and their families to survive on. Many claim that they need to apply for state aid to supplement their meagre earnings in order to live (Gabbatt, 2013; Helmore, 2013).

(Continued)

(Continued)

Fast-food employees are not alone in their belief that it is not possible to live on the current minimum wage in America. Indeed, American President Barack Obama is among those calling for an increase: Obama has suggested that the minimum wage needs to go up to at least $9 in order to return to the value that it had 30 years ago (Gabbatt, 2013).

The campaigning organization Fast Food Forward has been active in organizing protests about low pay. The Fast Food Forward website claims:

> In America, people who work hard should be able to afford basic necessities like groceries, rent, childcare and transportation. While fast food corporations reap the benefits of record profits, workers are barely getting by – many are forced to be on public assistance despite having a job. (Fast Food Forward, 2013)

Questions

1 Which group of stakeholders would you consider to be the owners of fast-food corporations such as McDonald's, Wendy's and KFC? In other words, whose property are these companies?

2 If the campaigning group Fast Food Forward is correct in its account of industry profits and employee wages, how might this support Karl Marx's contention that people who work in businesses are exploited so that those who own those businesses can get rich?

3 It could be suggested that if fast-food industry employees are unhappy with their wages, they should go and work somewhere else. Why do you think they do not do this?

Conclusion

Rights occupy an important place in contemporary ethics discourse: when we talk about ethics, we often do so in terms of rights. As such, the notion of stakeholder rights offers an intuitively appealing way of thinking about business ethics. It encourages us to consider the rights that stakeholders might have as a consequence of their relationship with a firm. It also highlights the responsibility of businesses and businesspeople to respect those rights.

However, thinking about business ethics in terms of stakeholder rights does not provide clear-cut prescriptions for practical decision making. This is because the rights of different stakeholders may entail conflicting business responsibilities. It may therefore be necessary to balance conflicting rights in order to identify ethical courses of action. Unfortunately, there are no simple formulas that we can use to help with this task of balancing stakeholders' rights; conflicting rights cannot be fed into some sort of ethical calculator that delivers precise answers. Consideration of rights is a qualitative matter rather than a quantitative matter and, in carrying out qualitative evaluation of conflicting, rights-based claims, different people may arrive at different conclusions. However, although it is hard to say, definitively, whose rights-based ethical evaluation is the correct one, it seems sensible to suppose that comprehensive consideration of rights is likely to deliver a more well-founded evaluation than limited consideration of rights. In other words, ethical evaluation that gives full consideration to all relevant rights is better than evaluation that only considers some rights.

This chapter has drawn attention to two particular points that should be kept in mind when trying to arrive at a comprehensive evaluation of rights in a business context. The first is that we should take into account the rights of *all* relevant stakeholders. In particular, we should be alert to the possibility that businesses may prioritize the rights of their most influential stakeholders while overlooking the rights of other people who have less influence over corporate performance but who are nevertheless affected by corporate activity. Although a company may have sound instrumental reasons to privilege the rights of its most influential stakeholders, normative – that is, ethical – considerations require that they also consider the rights of their less influential, affected stakeholders.

A second point that needs to be kept in mind when comparing rights is that we should not accord too much significance to any particular set of rights, for doing so might cause us to overlook other rights that are equally deserving of attention. In particular, we should remember that property rights are important, but they do not necessarily trump all other rights. Property rights are taken very seriously in contemporary society and in the contemporary business world. Moreover, there is a sound ethical rationale behind our preoccupation with property. Nevertheless, property is not everything. Property rights are only one set of rights; and property owners are only one set of business stakeholders. A comprehensive appraisal of the rights pertaining to any business situation may need to go beyond property rights, considering stakeholders other than shareholders. In particular, Marx's critique of capitalist enterprise highlights the possibility that privileging the rights of property owners may lead to exploitation of workers. In prioritizing the rights of property owners, then, we may fail to respect the rights of those people who, according to Marx, make the most significant contribution to corporate success; that is, its employees.

Discussion questions

1. Consider an ethically contentious business scenario that you are familiar with. Identify any political, social and cultural rights that are relevant to this scenario. What responsibilities might these rights entail for the company or companies in question? Do these responsibilities call for similar courses of action or are there conflicting responsibilities? Taking account of all relevant stakeholder rights and associated corporate responsibilities, what do you think would be the most ethical resolution to this scenario?
2. Discuss the following statement: Respecting the rights of stakeholders is good for business.
3. Watch the following video about the John Lewis group, entitled 'John Lewis Partnership Model Explained': www.youtube.com/watch?v=kDBbglknn9M. How might the partnership model outlined in this video address Karl Marx's concerns about the exploitation of labour by owners? In what ways might such a model also serve the political rights of employees?
4. In August 2013, demonstrators who were protesting against the establishment of hydraulic-fracturing oil-extraction ('fracking') operations by the company Cuadrilla in the UK blocked access to Cuadrilla's property in Sussex, preventing the company from carrying out its activities for a short while. Read the Guardian report and view the video of this incident, both of which can be found at: www.theguardian.com/environment/2013/aug/19/caroline-lucas-arrest-balcombe-anti-fracking. Drawing on the ideas introduced in this chapter, can you identify ethical arguments in support of and against the protesters' action?

Further study

Brenda Almond's (1993) chapter on rights offers a clear and concise discussion of some of the issues explored in this chapter as well as a few further aspects of rights theory.

A more detailed discussion of rights theory can be found in Tom Campbell's (2006) book, *Rights: A Critical Introduction*.

A discussion of stakeholder theory, and how it offers a basis for various ways of thinking about business's relationship with its stakeholders, can be found in Thomas Donaldson and Lee Preston's (1995) paper 'The stakeholder theory of the corporation: concepts, evidence and implications'.

John Locke's (1988/1690) account of property rights is laid out in Chapter V of the second treatise of his *Two Treatises of Government*. Copies of this work can be downloaded from the internet.

An exposition of Karl Marx's ideas about the relationship between labour and private property can be found on pages 273 to the end of page 284 under the heading of 'Wage labour and capital' in *Karl Marx Selected Writings* (2000/1849).

Jonathan Wolff's (2002) small book *Why Read Marx Today* offers a concise and accessible introduction to Marx's work, which draws out the contemporary relevance of Marx's writing and puts his ideas about property and labour into the broader context of his social and economic theory.

Utilitarianism: Maximizing the Good Consequences of Business 2

Chapter objectives

This chapter will:

- introduce consequentialism as a way of evaluating ethics;
- describe how utilitarians judge the ethicality of an action's consequences in relation to how much good it causes;
- explore some contrasting ideas about what is 'good' for people and how these might impact on utilitarian evaluation;
- outline some difficulties with using utilitarianism in practice;
- introduce rule utilitarianism as a response to these difficulties;
- explain how the principle of corporate maximization offers a rule-utilitarian guide to management decision making;
- outline some limitations of the principle of corporate maximization.

Introduction

Most people would agree that telling a lie is an ethically questionable thing to do. However, there are times when it seems ethically acceptable to tell a lie. Consider the following situation. Suppose you are soon to celebrate your twenty-first birthday. A few days before your birthday you visit your grandmother, who is a very keen cook. She has baked a birthday cake for you: a fruit cake, which she knows is your favourite. She has put a lot of effort into the cake, making it several months in advance so that its flavours will have matured and it will be in peak condition for your birthday. Your grandmother puts the cake in a tin and you take it with you when you leave, promising to share it with some friends on your birthday. However, you trip over in the railway station on your way home, dropping the cake tin down some steps. The tin falls open on hitting the concrete floor and the cake tumbles out. It rolls to the bottom of the steps, breaking into many fragments. You are very upset, partly because you were looking forward to eating the cake, and partly because you know how much effort your grandmother put into baking it and you realise how disappointed she would be if she knew what had become of it.

Next time you visit your grandmother, she asks if you enjoyed your birthday. You feel that you have to mention the cake. What should you say? Should you tell her the truth: that the cake ended up on the floor of the railway station, where it provided a feast for a flock of pigeons and a stray dog? Or should you tell a lie, saying that you and your friends ate the cake and that you all enjoyed it very much?

In such a situation, many people would opt for the latter course. And they would consider this the most ethical thing to do, even though it involves lying to their grandmother. If challenged about the ethical rightness of telling a lie to their grandmother, they would probably say something like this: 'What would happen if I told my grandmother what really happened to the cake? She would be upset. And what good would come of telling the truth? None whatsoever. On the other hand, what will happen if I tell her that my friends and I ate the cake and enjoyed it? My grandmother will be happy. And what harm will be caused by this lie? Absolutely none. Therefore, it is better that I lie to her'.

We often justify our actions in this way, saying that something is the right thing to do because it brings about more good than harm. Moral philosophers usually refer to this as a *consequentialist* approach to ethics. It is called consequentialist because it involves weighing up the consequences of various courses of action and choosing the course of action which brings about the best consequences. Consequentialism thus stands in contrast to *non-consequentialist* ethical approaches, which focus on the intrinsic right and wrong of doing particular things. For instance, a non-consequentialist might say that, regardless of the consequences, it is intrinsically wrong to tell lies; therefore, we should not do it. For a consequentialist, intrinsic properties of an act are not important. A consequentialist would say that we should promote the best consequences even if this means doing things which may *seem* unethical, like telling a lie.

This chapter will discuss *utilitarianism*, which is the most widely discussed consequentialist ethics theory. The first section of the chapter will explain some of the key features of utilitarianism, outlining a few different approaches that it might take. The second section will outline some practical difficulties associated with utilitarianism, before introducing an amended version, usually referred to as *rule utilitarianism*, which seeks to avoid these difficulties. The third and final section of the chapter will explain how the *principle of corporate maximization* is often used in business as a rule-utilitarian approach to management decision making. It will also highlight a potential problem with the principle of corporate maximization; a problem that risks seriously undermining its value as a credible approach to business ethics.

Utilitarianism: maximizing the good

One form of consequentialism that has gathered a lot of support over the last few hundred years is *utilitarianism*. The title 'utilitarianism' derives from the word 'utility'. *Utility* has come to take on a range of meanings in contemporary speech, but moral philosophers tend to use it in a particular way. Jeremy Bentham, an eighteenth-century theorist who is usually regarded as a founding father of utilitarianism, defined utility as 'that property in any object, whereby it tends to produce benefit, advantage, pleasure, good, or happiness … or … prevent the happening of mischief, pain, evil, or unhappiness to the party whose interest is considered' (2000/1789: 88). Utilitarianism, then, judges the ethicality of actions in relation to their propensity to promote desirable things like benefit, advantage, pleasure and happiness, and to avoid undesirable things like mischief, pain, evil and unhappiness.

The words 'good' and 'the good' often crop up in discussions about utilitarianism. These words refer to those things, or those states of affairs, that are regarded as desirable and which utilitarians seek to promote. As far as utilitarianism is concerned, an ethically right action is one which brings about the greatest amount of good for the greatest number of people or, as philosophers often put it, one which *maximizes the good*. Utilitarianism therefore proposes that, when confronting an ethically charged decision, we should consider the consequences of the various courses of action that are available to us and choose that which maximizes the good. Similarly, when we are evaluating the ethical legitimacy of someone else's actions, we should ask whether, from the various options open to them, that person chose the option that would cause the greatest amount of good for the greatest number of people.

Video Activity 2.1

The following video is taken from *The Cruel Sea*, a 1950s movie about the Second World War.

During the Second World War, Britain was heavily dependent on food brought across the Atlantic in shipping convoys from the United States. These convoys had to run the risk of being torpedoed by German submarines, which succeeded in sinking many ships and killing many people. In response, special anti-submarine vessels were deployed by the British navy to track down and destroy these submarines, thus protecting the convoys.

In this video clip, the captain of an anti-submarine vessel, played by Jack Hawkins, has to face a difficult choice when he believes that his boat has located an enemy submarine. The captain makes a utilitarian-style decision. Based on the information that is available to him at the time, he weighs up the good and bad things that are likely to result from two alternative courses of action: attacking or not attacking the submarine.

http://www.youtube.com/watch?v=XKQAflZrXpU

Questions

1 As the captain sees it, what are the consequences of attacking the submarine?
2 As he saw it at the time, what would have been the consequences of not attacking the submarine?
3 On a utilitarian analysis, given the information available to the captain at the time, do you think he made the right decision?
4 If so, why was he so upset at having made that decision?

Utilitarianism and business

Utilitarianism provides a useful framework for evaluating the ethicality of decisions that are made in business. Utilitarian-style rationales are often appealed to by managers to justify actions that are ethically contentious, particularly those which lead to bad consequences for some people. A rationale frequently offered for such actions is that, although some people are harmed, other people benefit from them. And since more people benefit than are harmed, the actions are thought to be justified.

Utilitarian rationales of this nature are sometimes offered when businesses undertake rationalization programmes. Rationalization usually involves restructuring a company's operations in an effort to make it more profitable. Such efficiency measures often involve some people losing their jobs. This may be because demand for a company's products is shrinking, so it does not need so many employees. It may be because the company has developed more efficient ways of working: perhaps through better use of technology; perhaps through concentrating its operations into fewer, larger units and thus achieving scale economies. Or it may even be because the company has decided to relocate some of its operations to another country, where wages and other production costs are lower. Whichever is the case, such rationalization programmes usually involve job losses somewhere in the company.

To apply utilitarian analysis to such scenarios we need to identify the various courses of action that are open to those senior executives who make the choice whether or not to rationalize. We then need to identify the good and bad consequences associated with these various courses of action. The ethically right thing to do, according to utilitarianism, is the thing that causes the greatest overall amount of good; or the thing that maximizes the good.

Such analysis of good and bad consequences might include some of the following considerations. By closing down part of its operation, a company will have to make some of its employees redundant. Clearly, this is not good for those people, because they will lose their jobs. But those employees will not be the only ones who lose out. For a start, their families are likely to suffer because of a reduction in family income. Such measures will probably also affect other local people, since the loss of jobs will cause a downturn in local economic activity; that is, there will be less money spent in local shops, bars, restaurants, recreation facilities, and so on. This is especially so when a large production plant, which has been an integral part of a region's economic framework, is closed. Consider, for example, the impact on a town when a large car manufacturer closes one of its factories, making thousands of people redundant. These, then, are some of the negative consequences of rationalization.

However, there are also positive consequences associated with rationalization. Work that had previously been carried out in a closed-down plant may be transferred to plants in other areas. This will benefit the people who work in those plants, who may have more work to do and may therefore be able to earn more money. And this will, of course, benefit their families and their local communities. Also, if a rationalization programme achieves its objective – that is, if it improves the company's profitability – this will increase the value of its shares, which is good for the company's shareholders. According to utilitarian analysis, then, these positive consequences of rationalization need to be balanced against its negative consequences.

These negative and positive consequences also need to be compared with the consequences that would flow from other possible courses of action. The most obvious alternative to rationalization would be to leave things precisely as they are. An obvious good consequence of this is that the immediate job losses associated with rationalization would be avoided. That would be beneficial for those employees whose livelihoods would thus be saved, their families, and those other businesses which depend on a vibrant local economy. These, then, would be some good consequences of leaving things as they are.

However, leaving things as they are might also lead to some very bad consequences. Rationalization is often carried out in an effort to arrest a downward spiral in a company's performance. In other words, managers often rationalize because they believe that, if they do not make changes, their company will become less competitive and may eventually go bust. Clearly, this would be bad for everybody associated with the company. This includes all its employees, who will probably lose their jobs; its shareholders, whose investment will be at risk; and those people who supply it, who will lose the custom of that company. A company going bust might even have bad consequences for its customers, who would lose any after-sale service provided by that company and who would have the inconvenience of searching out other places to buy the things they need.

A utilitarian, then, would weigh up all these considerations and support the course of action that they believe, on balance, will cause the greatest amount of good and the least amount of harm. Of course, it would be a mistake to expect utilitarian evaluation of this nature to always provide a definitive answer. Utilitarianism does not usually deliver neat, quantitative conclusions. The estimation of good and bad consequences tends to be a qualitative undertaking, which does not lend itself to precise calculation. Nevertheless, utilitarian analysis can serve a useful purpose. By encouraging us to think about good and bad consequences, it offers a seemingly impartial basis of evaluation. In particular, a thorough analysis of consequences may draw our attention to features of an ethically charged scenario that we might not otherwise have considered. Therefore, although utilitarianism does not deliver precision, it does help us to think systematically and comprehensively about a situation before reaching our own, qualitative conclusions.

Theory in Practice

Will Ford's rationalization plan maximize the good?

In October of 2012, Alan Mulally, Chief Executive Officer of the Ford Motor Company, announced major restructuring plans for Ford's European operation (Read, 2012). First, he revealed that Ford would close its car factory in Genk, Belgium, which employs 4,300 people. A few days later, he also announced the impending closure of Ford's UK Transit Van plant in Southampton, with the loss of 500 jobs, along with its stamping and tooling operation in Dagenham, which would lead to the loss of another 750 jobs. These moves were part of a rationalization strategy that would involve transferring production to Ford's plants in Spain and Turkey. This rationalization was a response to ongoing commercial performance issues with Ford's European business, which was expected to record a loss of 1.5m euros for the year.

Ford's announcements were met with mixed responses. On the one hand, some business analysts praised Mulally for taking decisive action to remedy poor commercial performance; action which resulted in an immediate two per cent increase in Ford's share price (Read, 2012). As far as these analysts were concerned, Ford's senior managers were doing the right thing. On the other hand, making 5,000

(Continued)

(Continued)

people redundant, many of whom had spent all their working lives with Ford, seems a harsh thing to do. Indeed, the Unite union, which represents many of Ford's UK workers, responded by accusing Ford of 'betrayal' and promising to fight the job cuts (Read, 2012). Clearly, then, this is an ethically contentious issue. So how might utilitarianism help us to evaluate Ford's plans?

Utilitarian evaluation would focus on the consequences of the courses of action that were open to Alan Mulally and his fellow senior managers. It would compare these contrasting sets of consequences and favour the course of action which brings about the greater amount of good for the greater number of people. Two options were open to Ford's managers: on the one hand, they could rationalize the business as planned; on the other hand, they could leave the operation as it was (other options might also have been considered by the management team; for the sake of this discussion, let us concentrate on these two).

Questions

1 What are the good and bad consequences of Ford's proposed rationalization?
2 What would be the good and bad consequences of leaving Ford's operations as they are?
3 Taking into account these good and bad consequences, do you think the proposed rationalization is ethically justified?
4 Do you think that consequentialist analysis offers an adequate account of the ethical dimensions of this issue, or are there other, non-consequential considerations that should also be taken into consideration?

Defining 'the good'

Utilitarianism, then, is concerned with maximizing the good. It proposes that ethical courses of action are those which bring about the greatest amount of good for the greatest number of people. Before applying utilitarian theory, however, we need to think about an important question: what do we mean by 'the good'? If we are to use utilitarianism as a practical guide to ethical evaluation, we must establish some criteria of goodness against which we can judge the consequences of our and other people's actions.

In the case discussed above, most of the 'goods' and 'bads' associated with Ford's proposed rationalization are self-evident. For instance, most people would agree that losing one's job is a bad thing; and most would agree that it is a good thing for shareholders that the value of their shares increases. However, the goodness and the badness of consequences are not always so obvious. Consider, for example, the pornography industry. On the one hand, it could be argued that pornography is an ethically uplifting product because some people take pleasure from viewing pornographic material, and surely pleasure is a good thing. So a utilitarian might argue that, as long as more people take pleasure from pornography than are harmed by it, pornography is ethically acceptable. On the other hand, it might be argued that utilitarian analysis of pornography should go beyond cost-benefit analysis of people's enjoyment. It could be suggested that some forms of enjoyment are good for people while other forms are bad. It might even be argued that more is at stake than pleasure when we weigh up the good and bad consequences of something like pornography.

Such controversy also arises in relation to utilitarian evaluation of other products, such as alcohol, tobacco and other recreational drugs. It even shapes utilitarian consideration of the respective desirability of various forms of entertainment and culture. For instance, should tabloid newspapers attract more ethical praise than broadsheets on the basis that more people get more enjoyment from the former than from the latter? And does the fact that most people take more pleasure from using social media than reading business ethics textbooks make Facebook ethically superior to the publisher of this book?

Different utilitarian theorists have offered different perspectives on the matter of defining the good. Here, I will briefly outline three common approaches: that which associates the good with pleasure; that which identifies it with some form of objective value other than pleasure; and that which differentiates between higher pleasures and lower pleasures. I will then explore some contrasting insights that these different conceptions of the good might offer to utilitarian evaluation of a specific business scenario.

Hedonistic utilitarianism

Jeremy Bentham's seminal account of utilitarian theory (2000/1789) defines good and bad in terms of pleasure and pain.[1] In other words, for Bentham, ethics consists of promoting pleasure and avoiding pain. As Bentham saw it, all other things that we might value, such as money, fame and fortune, friends and family are not valued in their own right. We only value them because we associate them with pleasure. That is, we value these things because we expect them to bring us pleasure. Take money as an example. Most of us value money. Indeed, a lot of people seem keen to accumulate as much money as they can. Some even appear to value money above anything else. But Bentham would ask: 'why do people want money?' For sure, the

[1]Bentham often uses the words 'happiness' and 'unhappiness' interchangeably with 'pleasure' and 'pain', as if they mean the same thing. For the sake of clarity, this chapter will stick with 'pleasure' and 'pain' when discussing Bentham's utilitarianism.

occasional eccentric may have an obsessive yearning to amass an enormous fortune just for the sake of possessing it. But most people only value money because they can use it to buy things; things for themselves, things for their family, and maybe things for their friends. And why do people want to buy things for themselves, their families, and their friends? According to Bentham's analysis, we buy things for ourselves because those things bring us pleasure. And we buy things for our family and friends because we expect this to bring them pleasure, and their pleasure gives us pleasure.

So, as far as Bentham was concerned, all human desires ultimately derive from a quest for pleasure. He believed that this is the way that human beings are: the only thing that we value *in its own right* is pleasure and the only thing that we seek to avoid *in its own right* is pain. As Bentham put it: 'Nature has placed mankind under the governance of two sovereign masters, *pain* and *pleasure*' (2000/1789: 87). And, since pleasure is the only thing that humans value in its own right, and since pain is the only thing that we seek to avoid in its own right, Bentham suggested that pleasure and pain should provide the basis for utilitarian evaluation: pleasure must be the ultimate good and pain must be the ultimate bad. Therefore, maximizing pleasure and minimizing pain must be the ethically correct thing to do.

Bentham's style of utilitarianism is sometimes referred to as *hedonistic utilitarianism*. Hedonism means the pursuit of pleasure, so hedonistic utilitarianism is utilitarianism which places the maximization of pleasure above all other things as a criterion of ethical rightness. Were we to use Bentham's hedonistic utilitarianism as a basis for evaluating business, then, we would approve or disapprove of business practice according to its tendency to maximize pleasure and minimize pain.

Objective-good utilitarianism

Not all utilitarians have agreed with Bentham's hedonistic equation of 'good' with pleasure. Some of his critics suggest that pleasure is not necessarily people's ultimate goal, suggesting that we tend to value many other things in their own right. Others point out that, even if people *do* value pleasure above all else, this does not necessarily mean that pleasure is what they *ought* to value above all else. Indeed, the idea that human beings should only be interested in the pursuit of pleasure might seem rather a demeaning depiction of humanity. As Robert Goodin puts it, it seems to present the human race as no more than 'a mad assembly of pleasure hogs constantly out for a buzz' (1993: 242).

Some utilitarians therefore propose that certain things are good for people, whether or not those things bring pleasure. Such things are sometimes referred to as *objective goods*. Used in this way, the word 'objective' refers to something that is the case independently of people's (subjective) opinion about it. In other words, objective goods are things which are good for people regardless of how they feel about those things. *Objective-good utilitarianism* (sometimes referred to as *ideal utilitarianism*) thus offers an alternative to Bentham's hedonistic version.

One theorist to propose the intrinsic merits of things other than pleasure was G.E. Moore (1993/1903; 2005/1912), who suggested that certain states of mind have merit regardless of their pleasantness or unpleasantness. Moore thought that the *appreciation of beauty* and the *acquisition of knowledge* fell into this category of intrinsically good states. *Personal freedom* is another thing that might be thought of as objectively good for a person: it might be suggested that it is good for people to make autonomous choices about how they live their lives, even though some find such choices difficult and would rather leave others to make them on their behalf. *Human dignity* might also be construed as an objective good: it might be thought good for people to preserve their dignity even if this means abstaining from things which, although undignified, are nevertheless pleasurable.

More generally, *self-actualization* might be thought of as an objective good. The term 'self-actualization' is used by some psychologists (Goldstein, 2000/1939; Maslow, 1943) to refer to people realizing their intellectual, cultural and physical potential. To include self-actualization as a criterion of the good would be to suggest that it is good for people to reach their full potential, whether or not this brings them pleasure. The intuitive appeal of self-actualization is apparent from the reaction that many of us feel when a gifted musician, artist or sportsperson becomes more interested in living the high-life of a celebrity than in developing and applying their exceptional talents. Stars who party instead of training and practising may be doing what brings them pleasure, but many of us would feel that such people are not doing themselves justice. By wasting their talents they are somehow harming themselves.

For an objective-good utilitarian, then, business practice should not be evaluated purely in terms of its capacity to promote pleasure and avoid pain. Other things might also be considered important, such as the creation and preservation of beautiful things, the furthering of knowledge and learning, promotion of freedom, preservation of people's dignity, and enabling those who are associated with the business to realize their full intellectual, cultural and physical potential. According to objective-good utilitarianism, all of these things are valuable in their own right.

Pause for Reflection

Which of the following statements offers the best description of your reasons for reading this book?

1 'I am reading this book because I am enjoying it (i.e. reading this book gives me *pleasure*).'
2 'Although I am not particularly enjoying this book, I believe that reading it will help me pass my degree, which will help me get a job, which will enable a way

(Continued)

(Continued)

of life that will, ultimately, bring me pleasure (i.e. reading the book is *a means to the end of pleasure*).'

3 'I believe that reading this book will help me to develop my intellect and I think that this is a good thing whether or not I get any enjoyment out of it (i.e. reading this book promotes something that is *objectively good*, regardless of the pleasure or displeasure that it gives me).'

Mill's utilitarianism: distinguishing higher pleasures from lower pleasures

Now, it might be suggested that so-called objective goods *do* bring people pleasure, but that this pleasure is a long-term accomplishment that is attained at the expense of a certain amount of short-term pain. Thus, although self-actualization may demand quite a lot of hard work and application, which is not always pleasant, the eventual pleasure that it brings justifies the hardships experienced along the way. John Stuart Mill, another classical utilitarian theorist, offered a compromise between hedonistic utilitarianism and objective-good utilitarianism which takes this into account. Like Bentham, Mill proposed that ethics consists of maximizing pleasure. However, he distinguished between different forms of pleasure, suggesting that some forms are innately superior to others. As Mill put it, 'It is quite compatible with the principle of utility to recognise the fact, that some *kinds* of pleasure are more desirable and more valuable than others' (1962/1861: 258). And in order to eventually experience the most exquisite pleasures, Mill suggested that we might need, in the short term, to resist some less appealing but nevertheless tempting pleasures.

Generally, Mill equated higher pleasures with intellectual and cultural refinement. He believed that the pleasures experienced by people who had developed their intellectual and cultural capacities are of a superior quality to those experienced by people of less refined taste. Mill also suggested that the most exquisite pleasures can only come as a reward for long-term endeavour, during which we cultivate our capacity to appreciate their superior attributes. Mill even suggested that people with the most refined minds may find life unsatisfying because they are consumed by a restless striving for intellectual and cultural enhancement. Nevertheless, as Mill put it, 'It is better to be a human being dissatisfied than a pig satisfied; better to be Socrates [a very clever Greek philosopher] dissatisfied than a fool satisfied' (1962/1861: 260).

Mill supported this idea with the observation that people who have taken the time and effort to cultivate their cultural tastes and intellectual capacity, and who have thus reached an advanced stage of refinement, tend to prefer more-refined pleasures. He pointed out that such people are best placed to compare the pleasures derived from more-refined and less-refined stages of personal advancement, having themselves once been at a less-advanced stage. Conversely, he did not feel that the judgement of people who have not reached higher stages of refinement could be relied upon, for they have only experienced the baser pleasures. They are therefore in no position to make informed comparisons.

Mill's reasoning can be illustrated if you imagine two friends who are comparing musical enjoyment. Jane only listens to popular boy bands and girl bands because she believes that this is the most enjoyable form of music. Meanwhile, Jane's friend Samir used to listen to boy bands and girl bands, and used to enjoy doing so. However, Samir has since cultivated a taste for classical choral music, which he now prefers. Mill would suggest that Samir is better placed to compare the enjoyment associated with pop music and classical music because, unlike Jane, he has experienced both.

As you can imagine, Mill was a great supporter of giving everybody access to educational opportunities and providing all with a broad range of cultural experience, since he thought that this would enhance their ability to appreciate higher pleasures. In this way, he believed that the overall amount of good in the world would be increased. Applied to the evaluation of business practice, Mill's ideas offer an ethical basis for promoting products and services which develop people's cultural and intellectual capacities. It also puts an ethical premium on workplace arrangements which enhance employees' intellectual and cultural development.

Video Activity 2.2

The following video is a CBS report on the US business magazine *Fortune*'s list of the 100 best companies to work for.

www.youtube.com/watch?v=li4HRGEjaZg

One of the reasons we go to work is to earn money. The wage we earn enables us to buy things for ourselves and our families, which, we hope, will bring us pleasure and which will avoid the pain of deprivation. Moreover, most of us find it more pleasurable to work in safe, comfortable environments than in unsafe, uncomfortable ones. It is also good if our work involves doing things that we find enjoyable. In these respects, companies that pay their staff a good wage, that care for their physical needs, and that give them enjoyable tasks to carry out would attract moral praise in *hedonistic utilitarian* terms. However, *objective-good utilitarianism* and J.S. Mill's emphasis on *higher pleasures* suggest that utilitarian evaluation of employment practices should go beyond such considerations.

(Continued)

(Continued)

Questions

1 In what ways would the companies discussed in this video attract praise from a hedonistic utilitarian?
2 In what ways might they attract praise from utilitarians who take objective goods into account or who accord added significance to higher pleasures?

Different ways of defining the good applied to utilitarian analysis of Spearmint Rhino

Spearmint Rhino is an American-owned company that runs a string of what it refers to as 'gentleman's clubs' – more commonly known as lap-dancing and strip clubs (Wachman, 2011a). Spearmint Rhino provides a setting within which its customers, who are mostly men, can buy food and drink while watching women strip and dance on a central stage. Customers can also hire female dancers to perform for them in private booths (further information about Spearmint Rhino can be accessed at the company's web site: http://www.spearmintrhino.com/).

Most of Spearmint Rhino's dancers work as freelancers. They pay a nightly fee of between £30 and £80 to Spearmint Rhino, which enables them to charge customers around £20 for each 3–4 minute, private dance (Doward, 2002; Wachman, 2011a). On a busy night, up to 200 dancers could be working the floor of a Spearmint Rhino club (Doward, 2002). According to Spearmint Rhino's senior management, the company expects its dancers and its customers to conform to strict standards of conduct. These include a 'no touch' policy, which forbids any physical contact other than holding hands and dancers placing their arm on a customer's shoulder. CCTV cameras survey the clubs and any customers who infringe the regulations are 'escorted from the premises by muscular bouncers' (Wachman, 2011a).

Spearmint Rhino seems to be a successful business. As well as the payment it receives from its dancers, the company makes money by selling drinks and food in its clubs. In addition, most of the fees paid to dancers by customers are paid in 'Rhino chips', which customers buy from the club and on which Spearmint Rhino takes a 20 per cent commission (Doward, 2002; Wachman, 2011a). The company has expanded considerably since it was founded in Las Vegas some 20 years ago. There are now over 20 Spearmint Rhino clubs in England, the USA and Australia, and the company also runs clubs under the Sixteen, Blue Zebra and Rouge brands.

So, what would a utilitarian make of a company like Spearmint Rhino? Would utilitarians consider this to be an ethical company? Is Spearmint Rhino a business that brings more good into the world than bad? Is it the type of company that a utilitarian would be happy to invest in, to patronize, to supply or to work for? How would a utilitarian feel if a Spearmint Rhino Club set up in his or her neighbourhood? The answers to such questions depend to a large extent on how 'the good' is defined. I will discuss how a hedonistic utilitarian might go about assessing the ethicality of Spearmint Rhino. I will then consider the approach that might be taken by an objective-good utilitarian. Lastly, I will consider some insights that John Stuart Mill's distinction between higher and lower pleasures might offer.

Hedonistic utilitarian analysis

A hedonistic utilitarian would want to know if Spearmint Rhino brings more pleasure into the world than pain. In Spearmint Rhino's favour, it could be argued that its customers freely choose to patronize it, which seems to suggest that doing so brings them pleasure. Indeed, it is not unusual for those customers to spend up to £10,000 during an evening at a Spearmint Rhino club (Wachman, 2011a), which indicates that they find the experience extremely pleasurable.

What of the dancers who work the floor at Spearmint Rhino? There is some debate about whether or not these women find their work pleasurable. According to John Gray, the company's founder and CEO, 'We make it nice for the girls, so they want to come and work at our clubs rather than anyone else's' (cited by Doward, 2002). Even those women who do not enjoy dancing at Spearmint Rhino, but who just do it for the money, may find their overall quality of life enhanced by their earnings. This, at least, is the view of John Specht, Spearmint Rhino's UK Vice President, who pointed out that 'We don't force anyone to come in. If the girls are looking do this type of entertainment and make good money in a safe, fun environment... then why not?... they could be doing a lot worse things'. Specht goes as far as to suggest that dancing in a Spearmint Rhino club offers an excellent way for university students to finance their studies: 'With the rising student fees the students know that they can come in and earn the money they need to survive' (cited in *The Telegraph*, 2012).

Hedonistic utilitarian analysis would also take into account the pleasure and pain experienced by those who work for Spearmint Rhino in other capacities, such as its bar staff, security guards, administrative staff, cleaners and managers. Presumably, some of these people enjoy their jobs, so working at Spearmint Rhino enhances their pleasure. Furthermore, it might be argued that even those who find the actual work unpleasant are compensated by being able to buy things that give them pleasure.

And what of Spearmint Rhino's shareholders? The company's success has probably bought a lot of pleasure to its investors. Its founder and CEO, John Gray, who has become very wealthy indeed, seemed particularly pleased about this success when he observed that:

> You could rip out 75 per cent of our turnover and we'd still be profitable… [the economic downturn following the terrorist attack on the New York World Trade Centre on] 11 September didn't happen to us. It had no effect at all. This business is phenomenally recession-proof. There's no logic to it. Nothing comes close to this… It's all about golden eggs. We're breeding geese. (cited by Doward, 2002)

This, then, is the hedonistic upside to Spearmint Rhino: the pleasure that it brings to its customers, its dancers, its employees, and its investors. But what of the downside; do these pleasures need to be weighed against any pain that the company might cause?

We might start by considering any longer-term displeasure that patronizing Spearmint Rhino brings to its customers. A visit to a Spearmint Rhino club is not a cheap undertaking, and we should be alert to any longer-term financial hardship that this expenditure might bring to the company's customers. However, since Spearmint Rhino's prime target market comprises bankers, lawyers and accountants, who are either spending substantial bonus payments or entertaining clients on expense accounts (Doward, 2002; Wachman, 2011a), it is unlikely that their expenditure at Spearmint Rhino will cause them too much long-term displeasure (although the customers of these bankers, lawyers and accountants may not be too pleased to learn that part of the substantial fees that they pay for financial and legal services goes towards funding excursions to lap-dancing clubs).

Hedonistic utilitarian evaluation might also need to look a little more closely at the pleasure and displeasure that working at Spearmint Rhino brings to its dancers. Notwithstanding the enjoyment and financial benefits to which the company's senior managers refer, the short-term and longer-term benefits for dancers may not be so apparent. The pressure group Object, which campaigns against the objectification of women, presents a rather different perspective on the pleasures associated with working in a lap-dancing club to that offered by the company's senior managers:

> High performer to punter ratios mean there is intense competition for the attention of male punters and it is in this context that the buying and selling of sex acts occurs in some clubs. Even in clubs where licensing conditions are adhered to many women report a heavy psychological toll linked to dealing with, in effect, normalised sexual harassment on a nightly basis. (Object, 2012a)

Hedonistic utilitarian analysis should also take account of any displeasure that the company's activities might cause for society at large. In this respect, Object also refers to the 'ever-accelerating pornification' of society represented by lads' mags, internet porn and establishments such as Spearmint Rhino clubs (cited by Wachman, 2011a). According to Object,

> Lap dancing clubs encourage their customers, and wider society, to see women as sex objects. They reinforce the idea that women are always sexually available, as long as you've got a bit of cash to spare. This has to be seen in the wider context of a society in which … violence against women is endemic … Those working with female victims of

> male violence believe that the mainstreaming of the sex industries legitimises the attitudes that ultimately lead to violence against women. (Object, 2012b)

These are important considerations that hedonistic utilitarian analysis would need to take into account. If a consequence of organizations such as Spearmint Rhino is escalation in objectification of women, which ultimately promotes domestic violence and other forms of female subordination, then the pain that this brings to its victims, their families, and, perhaps, even to its perpetrators needs to be balanced against the more evident hedonistic benefits that the company offers to its customers, its shareholders and its employees.

Objective-good utilitarian analysis

So if these are some of the considerations that hedonistic utilitarian analysis would take into account, how might objective-good utilitarian analysis regard Spearmint Rhino? All of the hedonistic considerations listed above would also be relevant to objective-good utilitarian evaluation, because most accounts of objective-good utilitarianism include pleasure as an objective good. However, for objective-good utilitarians, pleasure is not the whole story. Other factors would also need to be taken into account. For instance, objective-good utilitarianism would ask whether dancing in a Spearmint Rhino contributes to objective goods such as dancers' dignity, self-actualization and personal autonomy. The same question might be asked of Spearmint Rhino's customers: whether spending their money, and their customers' money, at Spearmint Rhino makes the most positive contribution to their self-actualization or whether there are more productive things that they could be doing with their spare time and money. On the one hand, John Gray, Spearmint Rhino's CEO, presents attending lap-dancing clubs in a positive light: 'We don't want people to feel embarrassed. … There's nothing seedy in it' (cited by Doward, 2002). On the other hand, the pressure group, Object, suggests that lap-dancing clubs may encourage in their customers a limited understanding of intimate, interpersonal relationships, which is not just socially harmful but also personally unfulfilling.

Analysis in terms of higher and lower pleasures

The pleasures and displeasures experienced by customers, shareholders and dancers would also be relevant to John Stuart Mill's version of utilitarianism. However, were Mill to enter a twenty-first century lap-dancing club, he might ponder whether the hedonism that he was observing fell into the category of 'higher pleasure' or 'lower pleasure'. As far as customers are concerned, he may consider that there are more 'refined' ways in which they could be taking their leisure; ways which would deliver, to those who had sufficiently developed their tastes, pleasure that is of a qualitatively higher order and which is thus more deserving of utilitarian esteem.

I would guess that Mill would not be overly impressed to see institutions such as Spearmint Rhino prospering in contemporary society. That such places attracted people of little education and limited refinement would not surprise him greatly, but he would probably be shocked to find them patronized by highly-educated professionals whom he would expect to take pleasure in more refined leisure pursuits.

Characteristics of contrasting basis of analysis

Generally speaking, hedonistic-utilitarian evaluation of a product or a service provided by a company such as Spearmint Rhino would take the following format: on the one hand, it would consider the immediate pleasures derived by consumers and providers; on the other hand, it would consider any longer-term pain caused to those customers as a consequence of their consumption, as well as any pleasure or pain caused to other members of society as a consequence of that business activity. In other words, for a hedonistic utilitarian, if people are enjoying themselves and causing little or no harm to anybody else, they should be left to get on with it.

Objective-good and Mill-style utilitarian analysis would take a broader view of 'the good'. These perspectives go beyond considerations of short-term and long-term pleasure; they also take account of the quality of pleasure as well as considering other things that might be considered 'good' for us. They thus offer the basis for a more comprehensive, and possibly a more critical analysis of products and services offered by companies such as Spearmint Rhino.

Utilitarianism in practice: some challenges and a response

Regardless of disagreements about precisely what the good consists of, the idea that the ethical thing to do is that which leads to the greatest amount of good for the greatest number of people seems, intuitively, to make a lot of sense. For this reason, utilitarianism occupies an important place in ethics theory and practice. However, utilitarianism presents challenges, especially in the form that has been described so far. This section will discuss some of these challenges before describing an amended version of utilitarianism, usually called 'rule-utilitarianism', which responds to them.

Two challenges to utilitarianism

Two particularly compelling challenges to utilitarianism are: firstly, that despite the intuitive appeal of its fundamental principle, utilitarianism's conclusions often conflict with commonly held ideas about what is ethical; and secondly, that it imposes upon decision makers a burden of information gathering and prediction that is both impractical and unreasonable. I will present these two challenges in a little more detail before considering how utilitarianism might mitigate them while remaining true to its basic principle of maximizing the good.

Utilitarian conclusions conflict with ethical intuition

The first problem with utilitarianism, as described so far, is that, despite the intuitive appeal of the fundamental principle of good maximization, its practical implications are often counter-intuitive. By this, I mean that, when applied to practice, utilitarianism frequently points in a different direction to that in which our ethical intuition would point. In other words, it tells us to do things that do not *feel* right. This is because, if we perform only those actions which maximize the good, we may have to set aside commitments and responsibilities that seem to hold a great deal of ethical significance. Richard Brandt, in his paper 'Toward a credible form of utilitarianism' gives some examples of utilitarianism's counter-intuitive implications:

> [Utilitarianism] has implications which it is difficult to accept. It implies that if you have employed a man to mow your lawn and he has finished the job and asks you for pay, you should pay him what you promised only if you cannot find a better use for your money. It implies that when you bring home your monthly pay-check you should use it to support your family and yourself only if it cannot be used more effectively to support the needs of others. It implies that if your father is ill and has no prospect of good in his life, and maintaining him is a drain on the energy and enjoyments of others, then, if you can end his life without provoking any public scandal or setting a bad example, it is your positive duty to take matters into your own hands and bring his life to a close. (Brandt, 1978/1963: 146–147)

In each of these cases, acting in a way that appears to maximize the good would involve doing something that does not seem right: breaking a prior agreement; putting the welfare of strangers over that of our own family; or ending the life of an elderly family member just because they have become a drain on society. All these things just *feel* wrong.

Now, the fact that an ethics theory points in directions that are counter-intuitive should not necessarily be taken as a reason to reject that theory. It may, rather, give us cause to question our ethical intuitions. After all, many members of the white community of South Africa in the 1980s felt that it would be counter-intuitive to treat black people the same as white people, despite ethics theories that challenged the fundamental principles of Apartheid. Most people in South Africa now look back on the ethical intuitions of their forbears, which were used to support appalling racial inequality, with dismay. They realise, in retrospect, that the ethical intuitions that were once so widely upheld in their society were faulty.

However, although an ethics theory should not necessarily be rejected in the face of countervailing ethical intuition, neither should we throw out all our intuitions just because a particular theory tells us to. It may be that those intuitions are alerting us to some significant limitations of that theory: ethical intuition may not always be right, but it sometimes rings important alarm bells. So if classical utilitarianism tells us too often to do things that feel wrong, then we should at least examine that theory a little more closely before adopting it as a practical guide.

Utilitarianism is an overly rigorous guide to action

A further difficulty presented by utilitarianism is that it imposes an extremely rigorous decision-making regime on people who wish to use it as a practical guide. It calls upon us to evaluate each of our actions in terms of their propensity to maximize the good. And in order to do this, we must make complex predictions about the likely consequences of the various courses of action that are open to us. This may not present too many difficulties for implementing utilitarianism in our private lives, since we may not confront too many ethically charged decisions in our day-to-day affairs and, when we do, the consequences of the available courses of action are usually fairly simple to predict. For businesspeople, however, the challenge is a lot greater. Decisions taken in business can affect large numbers of people, which magnifies their ethical significance. Moreover, predicting the consequences of business decisions is complicated by the fact that those consequences can be very far reaching indeed. This is particularly so for businesspeople who run global corporations, whose decisions can affect the lives of people all over the world. If we add to this the dynamic and unpredictable nature of the corporate environment, utilitarianism starts to look rather unworkable as a practical guide to action.

Utilitarianism, therefore, seems to place businesspeople under an excessive burden of prediction, calculation and comparison. Given the busy lives of most corporate decision-makers, utilitarianism, in this format, seems rather an impractical approach to business ethics. It is one thing for moral philosophers and business undergraduates to sit in their university libraries, reflecting at their leisure on decisions taken by people in business, undertaking complex analysis of various notions of the good, and arriving at eventual pronouncements concerning the rightness of those actions; but it is quite another thing for a hard-working, busy businessperson to do so.

Rule utilitarianism: a potential solution to these challenges

The classical approach to utilitarianism that has been discussed so far is usually called *act utilitarianism* (you may also find it referred to as *direct utilitarianism* or *extreme utilitarianism*). Act utilitarianism proposes that we should evaluate *specific* situations in terms of their good or bad consequences. Each time we confront an ethically charged choice, act utilitarianism would expect us to follow the course of action which, *on that particular occasion*, will maximize the good.

This act-specific feature of utilitarianism is largely responsible for both of the difficulties outlined above. As far as the first of these difficulties is concerned, act utilitarianism runs the risk of viewing specific acts in isolation of their broader context. The requirement that we consider each and every specific act on its utilitarian merits is also largely responsible for utilitarianism's heavy decision-making burden. There is, however, an alternative form of utilitarianism which goes a long way towards addressing these difficulties.

Bringing utilitarianism in line with ethical intuition

That act utilitarianism takes specific actions out of their broader context is exemplified by each of the Richard Brandt examples listed above. To refuse to pay someone what you promised for mowing your lawn on the basis that there are better ways of using the money is to overlook the broader ramifications of breaking contractual agreements. To neglect your own and your family's sustenance on the basis that others may be in greater need of your monthly pay cheque is to ignore the notion of personal and family responsibility that is fundamental to most societies. And to allow your father to die just because he has become a burden on society is to disregard not only family obligation but also the sanctity of human life.

Most importantly for a utilitarian, to disregard principles and obligations such as these is to disregard principles and obligations that can, themselves, be justified in utilitarian terms. It seems reasonable to suppose that more good than harm will come about if all people honour contractual obligations, take care of themselves and their family, and respect the sanctity of human life. Therefore, although there may be isolated instances in which contravening these principles will do more good than harm, if applied *as general rules*, they will maximize the good.

Considerations such as these have given rise to *rule utilitarianism* as an alternative, more practically feasible approach to ethical evaluation (Urmson, 1978/1953; Brandt, 1978/1963, 1971). Rule utilitarianism (sometimes referred to as *indirect utilitarianism*) does not expect us to consider specific decisions in isolation; rather it calls upon us to ask what general categories those decisions fall into. And once we have identified a general category, rule utilitarianism asks us to apply rules which are relevant to that general category; rules which, if applied consistently, will lead to the greatest amount of good for the greatest number of people.

So, to return to Brandt's examples, in deciding whether or not to pay the person who has mowed your lawn, you should ask what general category this decision falls into. And it seems to fall into the category of honouring contractual agreements (albeit, a contractual agreement that was probably not written down). In general, if all people honour contractual agreements, then it is reasonable to suppose that this will maximize the good. This is because honouring agreements seems to be a general rule that will help us to lead mutually supportive lives as members of a community, which must be good for us all. Therefore, in this instance, even though *act* utilitarianism says we should do something more worthwhile with our money, *rule* utilitarianism tells us we should pay the money as agreed.

Similarly, in Brandt's second example, the general rule of looking after oneself and one's family seems to be a rule which, if generally applied, will maximize the good. It seems reasonable to suppose that if each of us looks after our own welfare and that of our family, then everybody, ultimately, will be better off. Therefore, we should follow this rule instead of, as act utilitarianism would dictate, giving our wages to someone in greater need.

And even though act utilitarianism suggests that we should end the life of our father when he becomes a burden on society, this contravenes a rule concerning the sanctity of human life which, if generally applied, will lead to more good for more people. After all, imagine what the world would be like if we did not have respect for the sanctity of human life. For one thing, we would all live in a state of constant anxiety that we might be killed at any moment. And if we did manage to make it through to old age, we would have to endure the anticipation that we will be disposed of as soon as we are no longer able to make a positive contribution to society. These are not pleasant prospects.

Theory in Practice

Using Atlas Iron's profit to maximize the good

In its 2012 annual report, Atlas Iron Limited reported an underlying profit before tax of $98 million for the year (Atlas Iron, 2013). The company's board of directors announced that they would use some of this profit to pay a dividend of 3c in the dollar to shareholders, retaining the rest in the business.

Act utilitarianism would question whether Atlas Iron's directors should have used the money in this way. After all, there are probably many ways in which the money could have done more good than by giving a little cash to the company's shareholders and adding to Atlas Iron's cash reserves. For instance, the money could have been used to help relieve famine in West Africa. It could have been used to help the victims of earthquakes that had recently taken place in Iran and the Philippines. Or it could have helped to relieve the suffering of impoverished American citizens whose homes and livelihoods had been ravaged by extreme weather during the course of that year. All of these uses of Atlas Iron's profits would probably have brought about a greater amount of good for more people that paying shareholders a small dividend and topping up the company's cash reserves.

However, for Atlas Iron's directors to follow any of these courses of action would be highly controversial. For one thing, the company's shareholders would probably have had something to say if their expected dividend had been donated to a famine-relief fund. And many other stakeholders, such as employees, suppliers and customers, would also expect the company to bolster its own financial strength before looking after people who have nothing to do with the business.

Rule utilitarianism offers a way of addressing this tension between utilitarian conclusions and intuitive rightness. A rule utilitarian would ask us to consider what general, utility-maximizing rules might be relevant to this scenario. They would then expect us to apply those rules, even if doing so conflicts with the course of action which, in this specific instance, would bring about more good for more people.

Questions

1 What utility-maximizing rule do you think Atlas Iron directors applied when deciding how to spend the company's annual profits?
2 How might that rule, if applied consistently, maximize the good?
3 Can you think of any alternative, utility-maximizing rules that could be applied to the distribution of company profit?

Reducing utilitarianism's heavy decision-making burden

Rule utilitarianism, then, enables us to retain utilitarianism's intuitively appealing, good-maximizing, basic principle whilst avoiding some of the intuitively unappealing courses of action to which act utilitarianism points. But rule utilitarianism also has the benefit of reducing many of the practical difficulties associated with utilitarian decision making. If we adopt rule utilitarianism as a guide to action, rather than making complex predictions about consequences whenever we face an ethically contentious decision, we merely have to follow general rules which we believe will maximize the good. As well as making utilitarianism more intuitively appealing, then, rule utilitarianism makes it a lot simpler. This is particularly important in a business-management context, since anything that can be done to simplify an ethics theory will improve its chances of being used as a practical guide. The next section will therefore explain how rule utilitarianism is sometimes used by managers as a guide to ethical decision making.

Video Activity 2.3

In this CNBC video of a US Republican party presidential debate, Mitt Romney, the 2012 presidential candidate, explains briefly how he believes profit can serve the common good.

www.youtube.com/watch?v=-ElvJVKGfZ8

(Continued)

(Continued)

Question

How might Romney's point be represented in rule utilitarian terms? In other words, what utility-maximizing rule might it offer to people who run businesses?

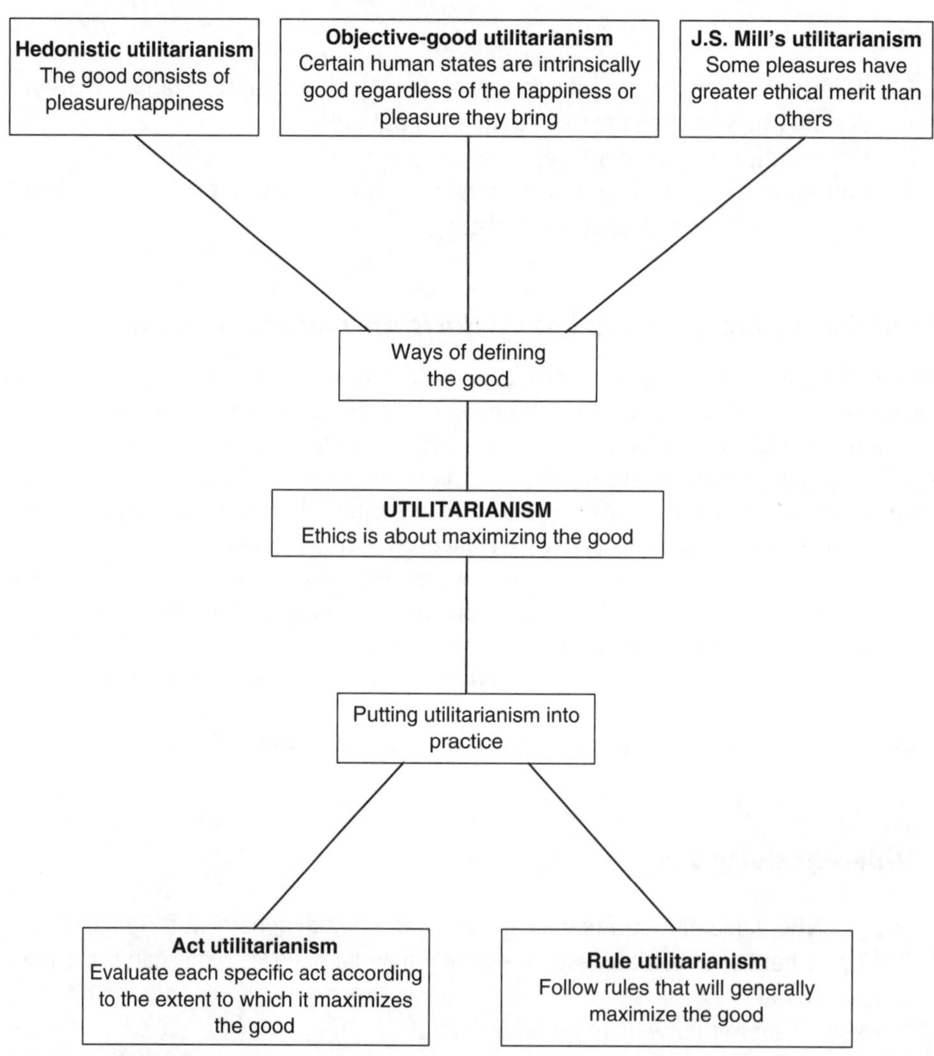

Figure 2.1 Utilitarianism: an overview

Utilitarianism and management

How do business managers go about making ethically contentious decisions? What rationales do they appeal to? How do they justify doing things which are troubling from an ethical perspective? A few years ago, as part of a research exercise into organizational leadership and ethics (fuller discussion is available in Fryer, 2011), I explored questions such as these with senior executives from a number of large corporations. The responses that I received indicated that utilitarian-style analysis forms an important part of the ethical toolkit of many managers.

This section will explain how utilitarianism featured in the ethical justifications offered by these managers. In particular, I will outline a *rule-utilitarian* rationale, which I refer to as the *principle of corporate maximization*, which figured prominently in their accounts. The principle of corporate maximization offers a handy guide to management decision making, avoiding a lot of the complexity that would be involved in an act-utilitarian approach. Nevertheless, it also presents a particular difficulty of its own; a difficulty which risks undermining its ethical credibility. The chapter will end by outlining this difficulty, illustrating it with reference to a particular scenario.

The principle of corporate maximization: a rule-utilitarian approach to management decision making

Part of my research into leadership and ethics involved trying to get an understanding of how senior executives think about ethics. In one-on-one interviews with chief executives and executive directors from various companies, I explored the approaches that they take to ethical decision making. I was particularly keen to find out how they justify doing things that they find troubling from an ethical perspective. The rationale that emerged most often in these discussions was a utilitarian-style one. Take the example offered by David, who was managing director of a global agribusiness. David told me that the thing that had caused him most moral anxiety during his management career was making people redundant. This was because he was well aware how devastating it can be for someone to lose their job. When I asked him how, given the ethical problems associated with making people redundant, he justified doing it, he replied: 'It sounds callous, but … you sacrifice a hundred to save the thousand. Sometimes you've got to make those decisions'. In other words, David felt that the redundancies that he had authorized were justified because more people benefited from them than were harmed by them.

A similar rationale was offered by many of the managers I met. They justified doing things that caused them a great deal of soul searching on the basis that more people benefitted from those things than were harmed by them. However, it would be wrong to describe these rationales as act-utilitarian. The managers that I met did not talk of weighing up each specific decision on its consequentialist merits before taking the course of action which promotes the greatest amount of good for the greatest number of people in that particular instance. And it would be surprising had they done so for, as discussed above, act utilitarianism does not offer a very practical ethical guide to running a business. Rather, the rationales that these senior executives offered would be better described as rule-utilitarian rationales. That is, they spoke of following a general rule which they believed would maximize the good.

Doing what is best for business in order to maximize the good

The utilitarian rule that managers tended to appeal to is that they should do whatever they could to promote the success of their corporation because they believed that this, ultimately, would maximize the good. So how does maximizing corporate performance bring about more good than harm? An insight into how this thinking works was offered by Susan, who was chief executive of a business-support organization. Susan had just described treating a former employee in a way that she felt was ethically questionable but which was nevertheless justified. I asked how she justified this action. Her reply was that:

> The health of the organization supports currently 128 families. You've only got to see the Christmas party, where suddenly your responsibilities are clear: when you see 400 people who depend on you getting it right. And, at the end of the day, the health of the many support the decisions you make about the few.

Susan was making the point that the well-being of her employees and their families depends on the success of her organization. And it is easy to see why: if the organization is not successful, these people could all lose their jobs, and that would not be good for them or their families. Therefore, by doing what is best for the organization she felt she was doing what is best for them. So, even when this means doing something which harmed one member of staff, or a few members of staff, she justified this with reference to the good that it causes for everyone else.

But employees and their families are not the only people whose well-being depends on the success of a company. There are many other people who prosper from corporate success and who may be harmed by corporate failure. Jane, who is managing director of a cider company, made this point when I asked her about her ethical responsibilities. She emphasized the responsibilities she feels to various groups:

> All our employees, all our local farmers – their main crop now is cider apples. We're not only looking after us as shareholders, as directors, but we've got the employees, we've got our suppliers. There's a huge knock-on effect … so I need to keep the company sound and that [ends up] looking after everybody that's involved with the business, whether it's a shareholder, whether it's an employee, whether it's a supplier or whether it's a customer.

As well as dwelling on her responsibility to look after her employees, then, Jane highlights the dependency that her shareholders have on her company: if her firm went bust, they would lose their investment. She also mentions the dependency of her customers. Presumably there are many cider drinkers who have acquired a taste for the cider that her firm makes, who take a pleasure from drinking it, and who would be sad if they had to switch to another brand. Jane was particularly conscious of the dependency relationship between her company and its local suppliers. Only certain types of apple are suited to cider production, and she knows that her suppliers have developed these strains in their orchards over many generations. If Jane's company went out of business, it would be hard for them to find alternative outlets for their specialized produce, and it would take a long time to turn their orchards to alternative uses. For Jane, then, promoting the success of her business serves the interests of not only its employees but also its shareholders, customers, and suppliers, all of whom depend on it.

The principle of corporate maximization: maximizing the good for dependent stakeholders

You may recall that the last chapter introduced the notion of stakeholders. A stakeholder was originally defined by Edward Freeman as 'any group or individual who can affect or is affected by the [business] organizations' objectives' (1984: 46). The last chapter made a distinction between influential stakeholder and affected stakeholders. *Influential stakeholders* were defined as those people who are in a position to influence a business's success. *Affected stakeholders* are those who are affected by the activities of the business. I pointed out that these are not mutually exclusive groups, since many people who have influence over a business are also affected by what it does. Rather, the influential-affected categorization offers a way of thinking about the kinds of relationship that might exist between stakeholders and business.

The views expressed by the executives that I referred to above draw attention to ways in which the *affect* relationship between a business and its stakeholders might work. That is, they highlight the *dependency* that some stakeholders have on a business. These executives were well aware that various stakeholders, such as employees, shareholders, and suppliers, depend on their companies. For example, employees depend on a company for their livelihood; shareholders depend on it for the security of their investments; suppliers depend on it as a source of income. Given that dependency relationship, if the company succeeds, those stakeholders stand to benefit; if the company fails, they are harmed.

People who have this dependency relationship with a business might be called 'dependent-affected stakeholders'. However, for the sake of simplicity, I will use the shorter term 'dependent stakeholders' when referring to those people. *Dependent stakeholders*, then, are all those people who, in one way or another, depend upon a company. The effect that that company has on them operates through that dependency relationship. These people can be placed in the top half of the right hand circle in Figure 2.2.

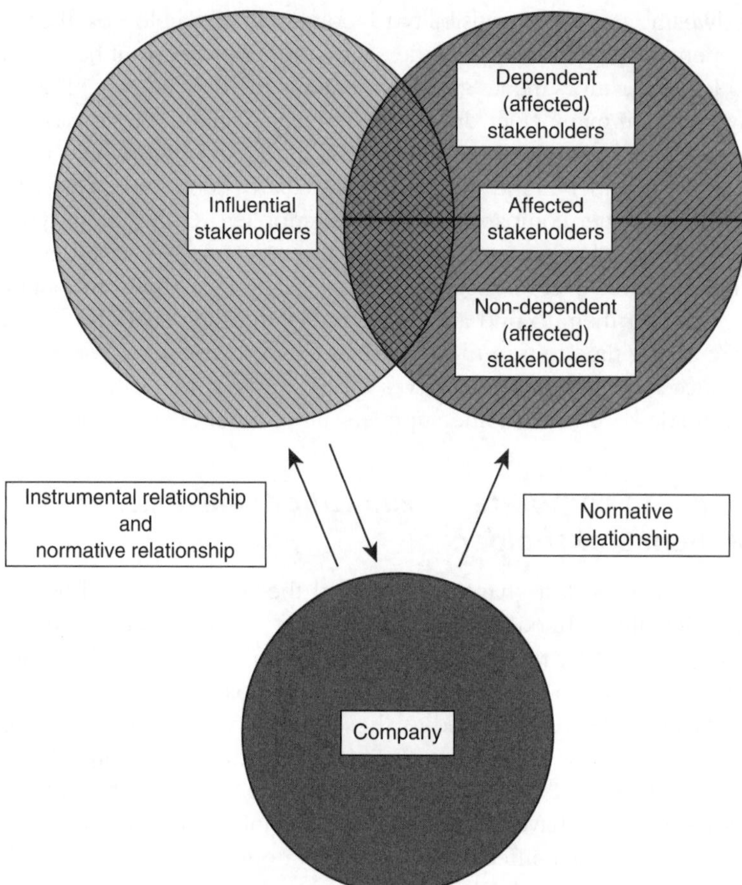

Figure 2.2 Dependent (affected) stakeholders and non-dependent (affected) stakeholders

The notion of dependent stakeholder helps us to pinpoint the rule-utilitarian nature of the executive views about ethics that were outlined above. These executives seemed to be saying that, since the interests of dependent stakeholders are tied up with the commercial success of their company, looking after the company looks after those interests. In other words, doing what is best for the company maximizes the good for dependent stakeholders. So, rather than weighing up each ethically charged decision on its utilitarian merits, as an act utilitarian would do, the executives believed they should do whatever they can to further the success of their company in the knowledge that they would thus maximize the good for all their dependent stakeholders. Importantly, even if the interests of some dependent stakeholders are harmed, for example by redundancies associated with a rationalization programme, this is justified because the interests of all other dependent stakeholders, who are far more numerous, will be promoted.

Another way of putting this is that these executives followed a simple rule-utilitarian principle, which I refer to as the *principle of corporate maximization*. The principle of corporate maximization might be expressed as follows:

> Business managers have a responsibility to do all they can to maximize the commercial performance of their corporation, because this, if applied as a consistent rule, will maximize the good for their dependent stakeholders.

The rationale behind the principle of corporate maximization was most clearly stated by another of the executives I met, the CEO of a travel company, who told me that

> if you compromise on [tough] decisions, the company doesn't perform so well... If you make the right decision, you are being more responsible to everybody else in the business because you are doing the best for the business, which is then doing the best for them. So you are doing the best for the majority in effect, but at the cost of some individual.

Pause for Reflection

Apart from the rule-utilitarian justification offered here, can you think of any other reasons why managers should be keen to maximize corporate performance?

Challenging the principle of corporate maximization

The principle of corporate maximization offers to managers a persuasive utilitarian rationale for doing what is best for business, even if this means doing things that are ethically contentious. Like rule utilitarian principles in general, it accords with ethical intuition. That is, the principle of corporate maximization conforms to executives' intuitive conviction that they should be looking after business, even if this harms a few individuals. It also takes a lot of the complexity out of utilitarian decision making: all managers need to do is put into practice a simple and straightforward principle; that is, as long as they do what is best for their company they will thereby maximize the good for all its dependent stakeholders, and they will thus be acting ethically.

However, despite its merits, as an ethical rationale, the principle of corporate maximization presents a serious difficulty. This difficulty concerns its preoccupation with dependent stakeholders. The principle of corporate maximization aims to maximize the good of all of those people who depend on a company. However, in focusing just on dependent stakeholders, it may overlook the interests of other stakeholders, who may not have a dependency relationship with a company but who are nevertheless affected by its activities. The people who may thus be overlooked could be referred to as 'non-dependent affected stakeholders', since they are affected by what a company does but they do not depend on it. However, I will use the simpler term of 'non-dependent stakeholder' to refer to these people. *Non-dependent stakeholders*, then, are people who do not have a dependency relationship with a company but who are nevertheless affected by its activities. These people could be placed in the bottom half of the right-hand circle in Figure 2.2.

What sort of people might fall into this category of non-dependent (affected) stakeholders? Take the example of a company that manufactures guns, tanks, fighter aircraft and other so-called 'defence' equipment. An armaments company's shareholders, employees, and suppliers, as well as other groups such as its customers, depend on the company in some way, so their 'good' will be linked with its commercial success. By following the principle of corporate maximization, executives will thus maximize the good for all these people. However, other groups are also affected by an armament company's activities even though they do not depend on it in any way. The most obvious category of non-dependent stakeholder is those people who are killed or maimed by its products, along with those communities whose lives and livelihoods are devastated by the destruction it enables.

Consider how this might relate to a concrete management decision. Suppose a manufacturer of armaments is deciding whether or not to produce anti-personnel landmines. Anti-personnel landmines are designed to explode when someone treads on them. They may kill their victim or they may blow off their victims' legs, feet, toes and hands, as well as firing shrapnel into their faces and bodies. If there is a ready market for landmines, and so long as it is legal to produce and sell them, it is in an armament company's commercial interest to do so. So, by producing landmines, an armament company's executives will help to maximize the good for their dependent stakeholders. The rule-utilitarian principle of corporate maximization would therefore suggest that it should begin production forthwith.

However, although this would benefit the company's dependent stakeholders, it will not benefit one group of non-dependent stakeholders: those non-combatants who are killed or maimed by stepping on landmines. And the number of people in this group is by no means insignificant. The United Nations estimates that landmines kill between 15,000 and 20,000 people every year, as well as severely maiming countless more (United Nations, 2013a). These victims include not only soldiers fighting in wars; they also include civilians, many of whom are children, who inadvertently tread on landmines that are left in the ground after a conflict. Indeed, the International Campaign to Ban Landmines estimates that between 70 and 85 per cent of landmine casualties are non-combatants (ICBL, 2013). But as well as the direct effect on their victims, landmines also have significant economic effects because an area that has been planted by landmines is useless for any form of agriculture or alternative use until it has been cleared. And clearing a minefield is an extremely hazardous and expensive process.

As well as highlighting the number of non-dependent stakeholders who are affected by a decision concerning landmine production, it is also instructive to compare the magnitude of effect on dependent and non-dependent stakeholders. First, consider the magnitude of the benefits that will flow to dependent stakeholders if a firm begins landmine production. Those benefits might include increments to share price for shareholders, slightly improved job security for employees, and an increase in custom for suppliers. Now consider the possible impact of landmine production on non-dependent stakeholders: perhaps the loss of a leg, the loss of a child, or the long-term loss of livelihood due to the fact that agricultural land has been rendered unusable. The benefits that might accrue to dependent stakeholders are undoubtable; however, they pale into insignificance compared to the associated burden borne by non-dependent stakeholders.

In the case of an armaments manufacturer, then, following the principle of corporate maximization may overlook the well-being of a lot of people. But the effects of corporate activity on non-dependent stakeholders may not always be so obvious as they are in the case of landmine production. Take the case of Spearmint Rhino's lap-dancing clubs, which was discussed earlier in this chapter. The campaign group, Object, suggests that entertainment venues such as lap-dancing and strip clubs are just one aspect of a 'pornification' of society, which encourages demeaning and harmful attitudes towards women. According to Object, the presentation of women as objects of sexual attention, which is associated with such venues, contributes, among other things, to sexual assault, harassment and domestic violence. So even if the commercial success of Spearmint Rhino maximizes the good for its dependent stakeholders, the negative consequences experienced by non-dependent stakeholders, which are far reaching and subtle, need to be included in any comprehensive utilitarian calculation.

Defending the principle of corporate maximization

In cases such as these, then, by focusing purely on maximizing the good for dependent stakeholders, the principle of corporate maximization risks ignoring the consequences of corporate activity for large numbers of non-dependent (affected) stakeholders. This need not necessarily negate the value of the principle of corporate maximization. For one thing, it could be argued that even if a lot of non-dependent stakeholders are harmed by corporate activity, the number of people who thus benefit is far greater. Therefore, the principle of corporate maximization still maximizes the good regardless of the problems it causes for non-dependent stakeholders.

Furthermore, it might be argued that even if, in isolated instances, more people are harmed by corporate activity than benefit from it, the overall impact of successful business is positive. In other words, flourishing businesses bring more good into the world than harm, so even if some businesses fail to match up to utilitarian evaluation, their executives should still follow the principle of corporate maximization because this is, in general, a utility-maximizing rule. A rationale of this nature has been offered by the American economist Milton Friedman (1970). Friedman's views will be discussed in more detail in Chapter 10.

However, while these arguments may offer some mitigation for the principle of corporate maximization, they do not completely absolve it from critique. It seems sensible to conclude that the principle of corporate maximization does indeed offer a handy guide to management decision making; a guide which may be supported by a persuasive utilitarian rationale. Nevertheless, its utilitarian credentials should be kept constantly under review to avoid it being used to justify actions which, on fuller utilitarian analysis, would be considered unethical. If managers are not careful they may find themselves doing things in the name of corporate maximization that bring incremental enhancements to corporate performance, and which thus bring small increases to the well-being of some dependent stakeholders, while causing a great deal of distress to a lot of non-dependent stakeholders who are affected by their activities.

Theory in Practice

Oil spillages in the Niger Delta: is Shell neglecting its non-dependent stakeholders?

Shell is one of the world's largest companies. In 2012, it was valued at over $200bn. In most years, Shell pays out millions of dollars in dividends to its shareholders. It provides transport fuel for 10 million customers every day at 44,000 service stations in 80 different countries. It also produces natural gas, oil and lubricants; fuels for aviation, industry and domestic heating; bitumen for making roads; and chemicals that help to make goods as varied as paints, detergents, mobile phones and waterproof clothing. Shell employs around 100,000 people worldwide. Every year, the company pays over $20bn in corporate tax and generates nearly $90bn in duty and sales taxes in the countries where it trades (Shell, 2012). Many people are therefore dependent upon Shell and many stakeholders benefit from its commercial success.

Fifty years ago, Shell began drilling for oil in the Niger Delta (Vidal, 2010, 2011b). A lot of the oil that the company drills is transported from the area though the Bodo-Bonny, trans-Niger pipeline (Vidal, 2011a). During 2008, the pipeline sprang two leaks in the swamps around Bodo, an area with a population of some 69,000. The first leak was noticed in August or October of that year (Shell's account differs from that of local people, Vidal, 2011b) and was repaired in November. A second leak sprang in December 2008, but Shell did not address the leak until February of 2009 (Vidal, 2011b). As a direct result of these leaks, as much as 311,000 barrels of oil have spilled from the pipeline into a 20 square kilometre network of creeks and inlets around Bodo (Vidal, 2011a; Amnesty International, 2012a).

The consequences of this spillage have been disastrous for local people and for the fragile Bodo ecosystem (Vidal, 2010; Naagbanton, 2011). The livelihoods of 80 per cent of local people depend on fishing in Bodo's creeks and inlets and, since the 2008 leaks, fish stocks have been devastated. Agriculture has also been affected, as pollution has seeped into the water table and has thus spread over farmland. Moreover, as John Vidal, who has visited the area, observes, 'the air stinks, the water stinks and even the fish and crabs caught in Bodo creek smell of pure ... crude oil' (Vidal, 2011b). Clearing up the mess is likely to take a great deal of time and money; indeed, international oil-spill assessment experts suggest that it could cost more than $100m to clean up the oil around Bodo and to restore the devastated mangrove forests that used to line the creeks and rivers but which have been killed by the oil (Vidal, 2011a).

The case of the Bodo leaks is not unusual. According to a United Nations Development Programme Report, more than 6,800 spills were recorded in the Niger Delta between 1976 and 2001, with many more going unreported (Naagbanton, 2011). Independent estimates put the total volume of oil spilled in the Delta over the last 50 years at between 9m and 13m barrels, which is twice the amount spilled during BP's Deepwater Horizon disaster (Naagbanton, 2011). Vidal (2010) reports that more than 1,000 lawsuits have been filed against Shell in Nigerian courts for pollution-related incidents, and that the company has been fined many times. However, local communities complain that they see little of the compensation money and the promised clean-ups do not happen (Vidal, 2011b). Patrick Naagbanton, Coordinator of the Centre for Environment, Human Rights and Development, has observed that 'the evidence of Shell's bad practice in the Niger Delta is mounting ... Shell seems more interested in conducting a PR operation than a clean-up operation. The problem is not going away; and sadly neither is the misery for the people of Bodo' (cited in Amnesty International, 2012a).

Questions

1 Can you list some of Shell's *dependent stakeholders* who are mentioned in the above report?

2 Can you identify some *non-dependent stakeholders* mentioned above; that is, people who are affected by Shell's activities who do not fall into the category of dependent stakeholders?

3 How would you compare the magnitude of the benefits that accrue to *dependent stakeholders* in this instance to the magnitude of the harm done to *non-dependent stakeholders*?

4 If Shell's executives were to follow the *principle of corporate maximization*, how would they respond to the spillages of oil in the Niger Delta that are referred to here?

5 Do you think this would be an adequate utilitarian response to the company's corporate responsibilities?

Conclusion

Utilitarianism focuses on the consequences of business actions and corporate decisions rather than on notions of intrinsic rightness. It encourages us to evaluate the amount of good and harm that those actions and decisions bring about. Utilitarianism thus offers an alternative way of thinking about business ethics to rights theory and other non-consequentialist theories. Moreover, although identifying precisely what is 'good' and 'bad' for people is no simple matter, it seems to make intuitive sense to think about business ethics in terms of maximizing the good.

Despite the intuitive reasonableness of utilitarianism's fundamental, good-maximizing principle, though, applying it in practice presents challenges. Some of the problems associated with classical, act utilitarianism can be relieved by adopting a rule-utilitarian approach. Not only does rule utilitarianism avoid some significant clashes with ethical intuition; it is also far easier and a lot more practical to apply broad principles which, in general, maximize the good than to carry out complex prediction and analysis of consequences every time we make an ethically charged decision. Rule utilitarianism may therefore offer a more feasible approach to business ethics than act utilitarianism.

This may explain the popularity of a rule-utilitarian-style approach to ethics amongst business managers. By maximizing corporate performance, many managers seem confident that they will maximize the good for those people who depend on their company. They therefore believe they should do what is best for business even though this may involve doing some ethically contentious things. However, although this is a compelling and pragmatically useful rationale, it may push corporations down avenues that present difficulties when subjected to a more comprehensive utilitarian analysis. Indeed, if managers get into the habit of just doing what is best for business without thinking more broadly about consequences, they may end up doing more harm than good. Therefore, despite the ethical and practical merits of the principle of corporate maximization, it needs to be applied with great care.

Discussion questions

1 What insights does utilitarianism offer that might help us to consider business from an ethical perspective? Can you identify any limitations of a utilitarian perspective as a basis for evaluating business practice?
2 How might a utilitarian approach to ethical evaluation of business differ from one that is based on rights theory?
3 Different utilitarian theorists have proposed different notions of what is 'good' for people. How might these various notions shape our ideas about regulation of the supply and promotion of products and services?

4 Most utilitarian theorists have focused on maximizing *human* good. However, humans are not the only creatures who experience the consequences of business activity. There is a case for including animals in utilitarian calculations. This issue is of direct importance for many businesses involved in the production of food, clothing, pharmaceuticals and cosmetics. However, it also relates to any type of business activity that impacts on the natural world. To what extent is it permissible to sacrifice the 'good' of animals in order to provide benefits to humans? Is it OK for animals to suffer to make human life better? For instance, in the testing of pharmaceuticals, how much animal suffering do you think is justified to provide cures for human disease?

5 This chapter has discussed a utilitarian rationale for the principle of corporate maximization. Can you think of any other, non-utilitarian justifications that might support the maximization of corporate success as a principle of ethical management? What challenges might be presented to these justifications?

Further study

A concise statement of some key aspects of Jeremy Bentham's seminal elaboration of utilitarian theory can be found in Chapter 1 of his *An Introduction to the Principles of Morals and Legislation* (2000/1789).

John Stuart Mill offers an interesting and clear discussion of the relative merits of different forms of pleasure in the first few pages of Chapter II of *Utilitarianism* (1962/1861).

J.J.C. Smart and Bernard Williams offer a clearly written and comprehensive account of utilitarian theory, its applications, its merits and its demerits in their book, *Utilitarianism: For and Against* (1973). Although published over 40 years ago, this remains a classic discussion of utilitarianism and its contemporary relevance.

Jones et al.'s (2005) book, *For Business Ethics*, includes a chapter on utilitarianism entitled 'Business Ethics I: Consequences'. This offers further discussion of some of the ideas introduced in this chapter as well as presenting some additional perspectives.

For an extended discussion of management, management ethics and some of the ethical challenges presented by management per se, which touches on utilitarianism and which also refers to several other theories introduced in this book, see Martin Parker's book, *Against Management* (2002). See, in particular, Chapter 1, 'Managerialism and its discontents', and Chapter 9, 'For organization'.

Kantian Theory: Reason-based Duty and Business

3

Chapter objectives

This chapter will:

- explain the emphasis that Kantian ethics theory places on intention, reason and freedom;
- explain why Kant believed actions that are motivated by a reason-based sense of duty to be most deserving of ethical esteem;
- explain three formulas that Kant suggested we might use to identify our duty;
- explain why Kant thought we have a duty to develop ethical sentiments;
- describe how Kantian theory can be applied to evaluate the ethicality of employment practices in an offshore production scenario.

Introduction

In matters of ethics, should the head rule the heart or should the heart be allowed to rule the head? When we make ethically charged decisions, should we use cool-headed reason or should we permit emotion to influence our choices? Immanuel Kant, one of the most distinguished figures in the history of European philosophy, was firmly of the view that the head should take precedence: reason, for Kant, should always come before sentiment. Accordingly, Kant based his moral philosophy on reason. He proposed that, by applying reason, we can work out what is ethical and what is unethical or, as Kant would put it, we can work out what is our duty. He also believed that, regardless of any countervailing emotions that we might feel, we should always do what we consider to be our duty.

The first section of this chapter will explain why Kant considered reason so important to ethics. It will also describe the importance he placed on good intentions and freedom. The second section will explain how Kant suggested we should identify our duty. Some implications of these ideas for business ethics will be explored as we go along. The chapter will conclude by applying Kant's ideas to a particular, ethically charged topic: the corporate practice of transferring manufacturing and assembly operations to developing nations in order to reduce costs.

First, a few words about Immanuel Kant. Kant was born in 1724 in Königsberg, which was then in East Prussia but is now the Russian exclave of Kaliningrad. Kant died 80 years later, having spent all his life in and around Königsberg. His writing had a profound impact during his lifetime and it continues to influence philosophical debate about ethics, politics, aesthetics and the nature of perception and reality. Even philosophers who take issue with some of Kant's ideas acknowledge the influence that engagement with those ideas has had on their own thought. Of course, Kant did not have much to say about business ethics as we understand it today: the ethical ramifications of twenty-first century capitalist enterprise were far from the mind of an eighteenth-century, Königsberg University philosophy professor. Nevertheless, although Kant's moral philosophy was developed in a very different context to that of present-day corporate activity, it offers some illuminating insights to contemporary business ethics.

Kant's moral philosophy

Kant's favoured approach to philosophical enquiry about any topic was to ask how a human mind must necessarily organize its understanding of that topic. As he put it in the *Critique of Pure Reason*, he was concerned with 'knowledge which is occupied not so much with objects as with the mode of our knowledge of objects' (2003/1787: 59/25). By taking this approach, Kant believed that he could identify certain features of the way that we will always think about a particular subject. He applied this approach to moral philosophy by asking how a human mind must begin if it wishes to think about ethics. In other words, he set out to identify things that anyone 'who takes morality to be something, and not merely a chimerical Idea without truth' (Kant, 1948/1785: 106/95–6) must take for granted.

By this method, Kant believed he could develop a detailed understanding of what ethical understanding must necessarily be like for humans; or at least, what it will always be like for humans who are prepared to spend a little time thinking about their ethical choices. This approach revealed to Kant the importance of three things: firstly, that ethical evaluation of a person's action must take that person's *intention* into account; secondly, that *reason-based choice* must be the basis of ethical conduct; and thirdly, that the notion of ethical responsibility presupposes *freedom*. Before considering the relevance of these ideas to business, I will explain them in a little more detail. I will also describe briefly why Kant considered intention, reason-based choice and freedom to be so central to ethics.

Taking intentions into account

Kant begins his *Groundwork of the Metaphysic of Morals* (1948/1785) by asking what commonsense opinion has to say about ethics. A contemporary scenario might help to illustrate some of his conclusions. Imagine that four friends have just finished the last of their university exams. Each of them is going home the following day and it may be some time before they see one another again. Since it is only just past five o'clock, and since none of the four plans to leave until late the next morning, the four friends embark on a night out to celebrate finishing their exams. However, it being late in the academic year, three of the students, Anna, Otis and Sofía, are broke. Fortunately, the fourth student, Harry, has just received some money from an investment fund that his great-aunt Maude had set up for him. Therefore, Harry offers to lend each of the others £20 on the condition that they pay him back when they can. The others agree and the four go on to enjoy a pleasant evening.

During the next few weeks, each of the students finds temporary work and starts to replenish their bank account. After a month or so, Anna, Otis and Sofía all return the £20 that Harry had lent them. However, each has different reasons for doing so. Anna considers not paying the money back. After all, she thinks to herself, she will not see Harry again for a long while and he may have forgotten all about the £20 by the next time they meet. However, on further reflection she decides that this is unlikely. He will probably remember that she owes him money and, although he may not mention it, he will think badly of her for not repaying the loan. He may even tell other people about the non-repayment. This, she thinks, will not be good for her popularity. She might even lose some friends as a result of not repaying Harry. Therefore, she decides to repay the money and sends Harry a cheque for £20.

Otis takes a very different approach to Anna. Otis often thinks about the money he owes Harry, reminding himself that he must pay the money back as soon as he has sufficient funds. This is because Otis is a kind and considerate young man. He cares about Harry and would not be able to forgive himself were he to take advantage of Harry's generosity. Therefore, on the day that he receives his first pay cheque, Otis immediately posts a cheque for £20 to Harry. He feels relieved at having repaid his debt.

Sofía, like Anna, wonders whether she should bother repaying the debt. On the one hand, she thinks, she may never see Harry again. Unlike Otis, Sofía is unlikely to lose much sleep if she fails to pay the money back. In fact, she is rather tempted to put the money towards a new smartphone that she wants to buy for herself. However, she asks herself: 'Would it be unethical to not repay the debt?' and she decides that it would. In borrowing the money from Harry, she reasons, she has incurred a duty to repay it. Therefore, she should repay it. So she overcomes her temptation to spend the money on a smartphone and posts a £20 cheque to Harry as soon as she has saved enough.

Were it possible to transport Kant from eighteenth-century Prussia to the world of twenty-first-century student finance, he would probably suggest that a few aspects of this scenario provide insights to the way that people necessarily think about ethics. Firstly, he would point out that, in each case, the consequences are the same: in all three cases, the debt has been repaid. Therefore, it could be said that an ethically desirable outcome has been reached in each of the three cases. Nevertheless, Kant would also suggest that the ethical esteem that most people would accord to Anna, Otis and Sofía would vary.

Consider, first, the case of Anna. Anna does not care too much about any so-called 'duty' she might have to repay Harry. She only repays her debt because she is concerned about her reputation and about the possibility of losing friends. Kant would suggest that this diminishes the ethical esteem to which she is entitled. Kant would also say that this tells us something very important about the way we attribute ethical esteem: this is that in attributing ethical esteem we do not just think about the nature of people's actions; we also think about what motivates them to perform those actions. In other words, it is not *what we do* that matters; it is *why we do it*. As Kant put it, 'if any action is to be morally good, it is not enough that it should *conform* to the moral law – it must also be done *for the sake of the moral law*' (1948/1785: 55–6/viii).

Using reason to make decisions

So, based on considerations such as these, Kant concluded that intentions matter more than consequences for apportioning ethical esteem and ethical culpability. And I expect most people would agree with him, at least in relation to Anna's intentions in repaying her debt. However, where Kant's views might differ from those of most people is in the way that he would attribute ethical esteem to Otis and Sofía. Many people would find Otis's innate kindness more appealing than Sofía's approach because, unlike Sofía, Otis is not tempted to dishonour his debt; indeed, he seems emotionally incapable of doing such a thing. However, Kant would suggest that Sofía is more deserving of ethical esteem that Otis. He would also suggest that, were we to think about Otis and Sofía's reasons for acting in a bit more detail, we would agree with him.

Kant's reasons for thinking this stem from his analysis of what makes humans do the things they do. He believed that human action is driven by two different factors. On the one hand, we are motivated by *sentiment*. Sentiment, for Kant, includes sensations such as hunger and thirst. It also includes emotional states such as affection and hatred, fear and bravery, charitableness and meanness. Our tendency to be motivated by sentiment – by sensations and emotions – is something that we share with animals, since they too act on sensations and emotions. However, Kant observed that human beings are also driven by *reason*. That is, we are able to think rationally about what we do and whether we should do it. This capacity for reason is something that, as Kant saw it, distinguishes humans from other creatures. Whereas non-human beings just act on sentiment – that is, on physical sensations and emotional stimuli – humans are able to think about those sentiments and reason about how they should respond to them.

It is because of this distinction between sentiment-driven action and reason-driven action that Kant would attribute greater ethical esteem to Sofía than to Otis. He would point out that Otis had acted purely on sentiment. Because Otis is a naturally kind and generous person, who likes to repay his debts, that is what he did: he did what he was naturally inclined to do. Importantly, Otis had made no reason-based choice to repay the debt: such a choice had not arisen because of the type of person that Otis is. Sofía, on the other hand, had made a conscious, reason-based decision to do what she considered to be her duty. And Sofía had done her duty even though she did not particularly want to. In other words, she had imposed reason over sentiment.

Kant would say that this element of reason-based choice makes Sofía's action more deserving of ethical esteem. Although most people would approve of Otis's sentiment, Kant would point out that Otis had not necessarily *chosen* to have those sentiments: he may just have been born a kind and generous person; or maybe kindness and generosity had been inculcated in him by his early life experiences. Therefore, Otis's sentiments are not necessarily something for which he can claim personal responsibility; they are just part of the way he happens to be. Sofía, on the other hand, had thought rationally about the ethical implications of repaying the debt and, although sentiment (an emotional urge to own a new smartphone) pushed her in the opposite direction, she had made a reason-based choice to do what she considered to be her duty. Thus, the act of repaying the debt is something for which she can claim personal responsibility: it is *her* choice.

Now, to say that Sofía is more deserving of ethical esteem than Otis is not to say that Otis's actions are devoid of ethical merit. Kant did not say that sentiments such as generosity and kindness have no ethical value whatsoever (I will explain a little later what Kant had to say about such sentiments). It is just that Kant believed that those actions that are *most* deserving of ethical esteem are those that result from a *conscious act of reason-based choice* on the part of the actor, where that actor *chooses* to do what they consider to be their *duty*.

Pause for Reflection

Do you agree with Kant that we do not choose to have the sentiments we have, so we cannot claim credit for them? Or do you think that we are able to make a reason-based choice to cultivate certain sentiments? Can we shape our own sentiments in this way? Can you think of any times when you have intentionally changed the emotional response that you have to a certain person or a certain issue; when you have taught yourself to like something you did not initially like, or to dislike something to which you previously felt attracted?

Freedom

Kant's approval of acts that are driven by reason-based choice is closely related to his belief in the necessity of human freedom. To understand the type of freedom that Kant had in mind here, it is helpful to contrast it to a particular way in which people might be thought not to make free choices. This is to think of human action as *causally determined*. To think of our actions as causally determined is to think of them as being caused by factors that are beyond our control.

A little historical perspective might help to explain why this opposition between freedom and causal determination was so important to Kant. Kant lived during a time often referred to as the European Enlightenment. This period had seen significant progress in many areas of human understanding, not least in the field of natural science. And many of the Enlightenment's advances in scientific understanding had been achieved through the study of cause-effect relationships. In other words, by studying how certain events caused certain other events, Enlightenment scientists had brought about huge improvements in the way that humans are able to understand and predict natural phenomena, and this knowledge enabled humans to control their world far more effectively than hitherto.

One particular development made by Enlightenment thinkers was to move beyond earlier worldviews that held supernatural and divine forces responsible for natural occurrences. Instead, they looked to sciences such as chemistry and physics to provide explanations for what goes on in the world. This had given rise to a particular way of thinking about the world: that those events that take place within it are causally determined. In other words, that every event is the necessary and inevitable outcome of a complex string of cause-effect sequences, which conform to the laws of nature. And because all events are the necessary consequence of cause-effect sequences, things cannot be other than as they are. Kant referred to this mode of enlightened scientific thought as one in which 'everything which takes place should be infallibly determined in accordance with the laws of nature; and this necessity of nature is… no concept of experience, precisely because it carries with it the concept of necessity' (1948/1785: 115/114).

Now, if we understand human beings as physical entities, it is possible to apply this same approach to human behaviour. That is, it is possible to view human actions as the outcome of complex sequences of cause and effect. And we do often talk about human behaviour in this way. For instance, we sometimes seek to explain a person's conduct by highlighting personal traits they have inherited from their parents (for instance, 'he's got his father's short temper'), or by enquiring into their early-life experiences (for instance, 'did her mother encourage her to behave like this when she was a child?'). This implies that their actions are in some way predetermined; that those actions are caused by psychological or social factors that are beyond that person's control. Thus, we look to disciplines such as psychology and sociology to provide similar scientific certainty with regard to human conduct that chemistry and physics offer in relation to non-human occurrences.

The problem is that if we account for human behaviour in this way, there seems to be no place for free will. If our actions are the outcome of complex sequences of causes and effects, which include our hereditary make-up and the things that have happened to us throughout their lives, then we cannot say that our actions are the outcome of free choices on our part. And if we cannot say that humans have free will – that they freely choose to act as they do – then it makes no sense to hold anyone ethically responsible for their actions. But we do tend to hold people ethically responsible, at least in part, for their actions. Indeed, the whole idea of ethics makes little sense unless we can hold people ethically responsible for their actions. We may acknowledge that social or psychological forces push people towards certain courses of action but we assume that, by an act of free will, they are able to overcome any such causal determination. Thus, the very notion of ethics presupposes free will.

This conundrum troubled philosophers of Kant's era, just as it exercises the minds of contemporary ethicists and social theorists: how can we reconcile causal determinism with free will? Kant's response was to say that different ways of thinking are suited to different areas of enquiry: that we must have one way of thinking about the physical world and another way of thinking about ethics. If we are thinking about the physical world, Kant believed that the notion of cause and effect is a fundamental precondition of such thought; that is, we cannot understand the world in a physical way unless we think of it in terms of cause-effect sequences. However, if we are thinking in terms of ethics we must think in terms of freedom: 'to every rational being possessed of a will we must also lend the Idea of freedom as the only one under which he can act' (Kant, 1948/1785: 109/100–1). This is because the very notion of ethics – along with that of ethical responsibility – presupposes free will. Unless we are able to think of people's actions as freely chosen by them, then it makes no sense whatsoever to hold them ethically responsible for those actions.

Combining this notion of free will with the notion of reason-based choice discussed earlier permits us to define a little more precisely what freedom means for Kant. To do this we must go back to Kant's distinction between sentiment and reason. Kant emphasised the physical nature of sentiment. He regarded the sensations and emotional drives that influence our choices as physical urges. As such, they are part of the physical world that should be understood in terms of cause-and-effect sequences. It could be said, therefore, that our sentiments *cause* us to act in particular ways. However, since humans are rational as well as physical creatures, it is up to us to decide whether we allow those sentiments to determine our action or whether we override them through the exercise of reason-based choice. And it is in this capacity to override the influences of sentiment that our freedom lies. Don Becker sums up Kant's views on this matter very well when he says that: 'Kant thinks of people in just this dual way, as sensible or physical beings, causally determined according to the laws of nature, and as intelligible or purely rational beings, independent of causal determinism and capable of acting in accord with the laws of freedom' (Becker, 1993: 70–1).

For Kant, then, our capacity to act out of a reason-based sense of duty is the essence of humanity; it is

> nothing less than what elevates a human being above himself (as a part of the sensible world), what connects him with an order of things that only the understanding can think and that at the same time has under it the whole sensible world ... that is, freedom and independence from the mechanism of the whole of nature, regarded nevertheless as also a capacity of a being subject to special laws – namely pure practical laws given by his own reason. (1997/1788: 74/86–7)

So, returning to our case of three students repaying their debt to their generous friend Harry, Sofía, by asserting reason over sentiment in order to do what she considered to be her duty, demonstrates her capacity for freedom. She exercises free will and thus, as Kant would see it, expresses her essential humanity. Otis, on the other hand, does not exercise free will in this instance; he does not take the opportunity to use his uniquely human capacity for making reason-based choices; he just does what his sentiment tells him to do. Although that was the right thing to do, insofar as it is what his reason-based sense of duty *would* have told him to do *had he* consulted it, he did not do this. Therefore, he cannot take responsibility, in a Kantian sense, for that act.

Four students – 20 years on

So far, this chapter has explained how Kant set out to identify aspects of the way that humans must always think about ethics. Kant concluded that the notion of ethics presupposes three things. Firstly, that we take account of *intentions* in attributing ethical esteem, which implies that people's reasons for acting are more important than the consequences of their actions. Secondly, he argued that *reason-based choice* is more important than sentiment for according ethical esteem; that is, as far as ethics is concerned, it is more important for people to do what they do because their reason tells them it is their duty than because they feel like doing it. And, thirdly, Kant supported this primacy of intention and reason-based choice by appealing to the notion of *free will*; he proposed that ethics makes no sense unless we assume that people are able to choose to do what they do.

In order to appreciate how these ideas might relate to ethical evaluation of business activity, it helps to imagine people like the students introduced earlier in corporate roles. Imagine, then, that all passed their exams and gained very good degrees. All went on to secure good jobs and, after 20 years or so, Anna, Otis and Sofía each found themselves working as Chief Executive of a large company. Harry, meanwhile, went into investment banking and now runs a private equity firm. He is still lending people money but, unlike with his loans to his university friends, he is now making a very good return on his investments. I will leave Harry to his investments, hope that he survived the banking crash of 2008, and write him out of the story because it is the other three friends that I want to focus on. Although Anna, Otis and Sofía are all twenty years older, none of them has changed all that much. In particular, each approaches ethics very much as they did in their student days.

Anna's story

I will begin with Anna's story. Anna, you will recall, considered not repaying her student debt to Harry but did so because she feared that other people would think badly of her otherwise. Anna is now running a company that is involved in the supply of construction materials. This company has mining, extraction and processing operations all over the world. Given the nature of its business, Anna's company has a significant environmental and social impact. Anna is not too concerned about this. She is more interested in meeting her commercial targets and boosting the value of the company's shares. After all, if she does these things she will be rewarded with handsome bonus payments. Moreover, since a large part of Anna's salary is paid in shares in her company, it is in her interest to maximize share value. These matters are therefore more pressing for Anna than the effect her company has on the natural environment and on society.

However, Anna is no fool. Although she does not care too much about the environment and the communities that are affected by her business, she realizes that many other people do. In particular, many of her customers and employees, and even some of her suppliers and shareholders, take an interest in such matters. In short, many of the stakeholders upon whose support Anna's company depends care about its environmental and social profile, so it is in Anna's interests to do likewise. Therefore, Anna makes sure that her company spends a lot of money hiring corporate social responsibility (CSR) consultants. These are very clever people who tell Anna what the ethical expectations of her company's key stakeholders are and, just as importantly, how these expectations are likely to change in coming years. These CSR consultants also advise Anna how her company might best respond to these shifting stakeholder expectations.

In response to the advice of their CSR consultants, Anna's managers take great care to minimize the company's environmental impact. They also give a lot of money to local community projects, because their CSR consultants have told them that this will be particularly well viewed by their customers. Anna also makes sure that all her suppliers are paid on time; after all, she does not want her company to get a bad reputation because it delays payment of its bills. Anna also realizes that a serious accident could be very bad for publicity, so she makes sure that the company implements high standards of health and safety in its mining and extraction operations. Moreover, Anna's company has a section on its corporate website entitled 'sustainability', which tells of all the good things it is doing for the environment, for local communities, for its suppliers and for its employees; after all, Anna thinks, there's no point doing all these nice things if you don't tell people you're doing them. As a result of all this CSR and public relations activity, Anna's company gets a reputation for being a very ethical business.

Pause for Reflection

How might Immanuel Kant assess the ethicality of Anna's company? Presumably, he, like most people, would approve of the outcomes of the company's CSR activities. But what do you think Kant would have to say about Anna's *intentions*? Would these attract his ethical esteem?

Otis's story

Otis is also running a large business: a company that sells designer clothing. Otis has not changed all that much. He is still a very kind, considerate and generous man. He has attracted many people who are very much like him to work in his company. As a result, his company is a very nice one with which to do business. It pays its bills on time, it treats its employees well, it markets its products in a respectful manner, it supports local charities, and it is very careful to recycle its waste. Otis and his fellow managers do not discuss such matters in much detail. They just do these things because that is the sort of people they are. Nor do they do these things in order to attract good publicity; they just do them because they want to.

Pause for Reflection

How do you think Kant would rate Otis's company in terms of its ethics? Presumably, he would think the company employs many nice people who do many good things. But why do they do these things? Are they motivated by sentiment or by reason? To what extent are their actions based on *reason-based* choices to do their *duty*? To what extent are they exercising *free will*, as Kant would understand it?

Sofía's story

Sofía went into the book trade when she left university and she now runs a publishing firm. She is still quite ambivalent about ethics. Her company works in a very competitive environment and she would rather focus all its efforts on commercial success than spend time worrying about environmental and social responsibilities. However, Sofía is still a very thoughtful person. She reasons that her company would not exist were it not for its customers, its employees, its suppliers and its shareholders. She also thinks about her company's broader relationship with society, reasoning that her company depends on society in all sorts of ways and that it must therefore have certain responsibilities towards society. Sofía believes that this relationship with her stakeholders and with society creates certain duties on the part of her company. She therefore encourages her employees to think about the social and environmental implications of what they do. She urges them to fulfil what they believe is their duty to the environment, to all their stakeholders and to society at large, even if this means making a little less profit than they would otherwise have made. Sofía thinks of this as a legitimate cost of doing business.

Pause for Reflection

What do you think Kant might have to say about the approach to ethics in Sofía's company? Would he approve of the resources that it devotes to *reason-based* discussion of *duty*? Would Kant approve of the extent to which people throughout the business are given the *freedom* to think rationally about their *duty* and follow their own ethical judgement?

Identifying duty: the categorical imperative

The previous section explained the emphasis that Immanuel Kant placed on good intention. It also pointed out that, for Kant, a well-intended act is one which aims to do what reason tells us is our duty, for only by obeying reason are we expressing the freedom that is a fundamental feature of being human. But if an ethically estimable act is one that is performed with the intention of doing one's duty, this begs an important question: how do we go about identifying our duty? For Kant, one way of answering this question is that we can do so by applying the *categorical imperative*. This section will explain what Kant meant by the categorical imperative. It will also outline three specific formulas of the categorical imperative, which Kant suggested we might use to identify precisely what our duty consists of in practical situations.

Distinguishing categorical imperatives from hypothetical imperatives

The term 'categorical imperative' is rather an imposing one that is apt to put people off Kantian ethics. However, it expresses a simple idea, which is best understood by explaining, firstly, what an 'imperative' is and, secondly, what 'categorical' means. The first bit is straightforward: an imperative is merely an authoritative command that tells us what we ought to do. The second bit is a little more complicated. Kant explains what categorical means, when applied to imperatives, by contrasting categorical imperatives to hypothetical imperatives. He explains that a *hypothetical* imperative tells us what we ought to do in order to achieve some objective that we desire. As he puts it, 'Hypothetical imperatives declare a possible action to be practically necessary as a means to the attainment of something else that one wills' (1948/1785: 78/39).

A hypothetical imperative thus takes the form 'do *x* in order to achieve *y*'. For instance, 'you ought to repay your debts if you want people to think well of you' is a hypothetical imperative. An important feature of a hypothetical imperative is that its force depends on the importance we place on a particular objective. In other words, whether or not we should do *x* depends on how much we wish to achieve *y*. In the example, 'you ought to repay your debts if you want people to think well of you', the importance of repaying our debts derives from the importance that we place on people thinking well of us.

A *categorical* imperative, on the other hand, does not relate to any further objective. It is an authoritative command that tells us what we ought to do *full stop*. In Kant's words, 'a categorical imperative would be one which represented an action as objectively necessary in itself apart from its relation to a further end' (1948/1785: 78/39). Its force does not depend upon something else that we may or may not value. It just tells us what we ought to do regardless of how we feel about anything. For instance, 'you ought to repay your debts' would be, for Kant, an example of a categorical imperative. It is something that we ought to do regardless of its consequences.

Kant's distinction between sentiment and reason is relevant to the distinction between hypothetical and categorical imperatives. Hypothetical imperatives relate to *sentiment* insofar as their force depends upon how we *feel* about a further objective. For example, the force of the imperative 'you ought to repay your debts if you want people to think well of you' depends on how we feel about being well thought of by other people. This sentimental dimension – this relationship with feeling – undermines the ethical force of a hypothetical imperative for Kant because, as already explained, Kant saw ethics as a reason-based undertaking. A categorical imperative, on the other hand, involves no sentiment-based attachment to any further objective. It is merely something that our reason tells us we ought to do. Since it is based on reason alone, it has ethical compulsion.

The way in which Kant believed that the categorical imperative relates to reason should become apparent when we consider some formulas of it. 'Formula' is the term that H.J. Paton uses in his translation of Kant's *Groundwork of the Metaphysic of Morals* (1948/1785) to refer to different expressions of the categorical imperative. It might be easier to think of formulas as practical tests that we can apply to specific situations to help us to identify our duty in those situations. I will outline three particular formulas. Paton calls the first two the 'formula of universal law' and the 'formula of the end in itself' and I will use his terminology here. I will call the third formula 'the formula of universal acceptability', since this reflects the way that it has been adapted by some business ethics writers. I will explain how Kant derives each of these formulas and illustrate how they might help us to think about duty in specific business contexts.

The formula of universal law

Kant expresses the first of these three formulas, *the formula of universal law*, as follows: '*Act only on that maxim through which you can at the same time will that it should become a universal law*' (1948/1785: 84/52 [italics in original]). It might help to translate some of Kant's eighteenth-century phrasing – particularly the words 'will' and 'maxim' – into terms with which you may be more familiar. When Kant uses the word 'will' – in the sense of willing something to happen – he means, quite simply, to want that thing to happen. And a maxim, for Kant, is a 'subjective principle of action' (1948/1785: 84/51*). In other words, it is a principle upon which a person acts. For example, suppose I decide to borrow some money from someone when I do not intend to pay it back. My maxim – my principle of acting – in this case could be expressed as follows: 'I will borrow money when I need it, even if I do not intend to pay it back'.

Kant's formula of universal law asks us to consider what would happen if our maxim became universal law. In other words, what would happen if everyone adopted that maxim? In the case of borrowing money without intending to pay it back, what would happen if everyone acted on the principle: 'I will borrow money when I need it, even if I do not intend to pay it back'? Well, one thing that would happen is that people would be far less willing to lend money to one another. After all, the custom of lending money depends on the expectation that borrowers will repay their debts. If non-repayment of debts became common practice, this expectation would diminish significantly. And, consequently, it would become very difficult to find anyone to lend money to me. Therefore, if I decide to borrow some money from someone without paying it back, the universal adoption of my maxim would lead to a situation in which I would not be able to borrow money. Thus, my maxim would be self-defeating.

Pause for Reflection

How might we apply the formula of universal law to assess the ethicality of telling a lie? What would happen if the telling of lies became universal custom (i.e. if everybody did it)? In such a situation, would telling a lie achieve its desired outcome?

It is important to stress the role that *reason* plays in the formula of universal law. Kant points out that it would be *irrational* to act on a maxim whose universal adoption would be self-defeating. And since ethics is based on reason and on reason alone, it would also be unethical. One way of applying Kant's formula of universal law to a particular action is to ask oneself the following succession of questions:

Question 1: what am I trying to achieve by my action?

Question 2: what is the maxim upon which I am acting?

Question 3: what would universal adoption of my maxim consist of?

Question 4: what would be the eventual result of universal adoption of my maxim?

Question 5: how would this result affect my success in achieving what I am trying to achieve?

Theory in Practice

The formula of universal law and movie piracy

In order to illustrate how the formula of universal law might help in a business ethics context, I will apply it to a particular scenario, which was related by Josh Halliday (2012) in *The Guardian* newspaper.

Halliday tells that in August of 2012, Anton Vickerman was sentenced to four years in prison by a British judge for conspiracy to facilitate copyright infringement. For several years, Vickerman had run a very successful internet-based business. That business consisted of a website, surfthechannel.com, which linked to pirated versions of films. Vickerman's business model was straightforward: users would log on to surfthechannel.com to select a film that they wanted to watch. The site would then direct them to other websites where they could watch their chosen film for nothing. Since, at its peak, surfthechannel.com was attracting 400,000 users a day, companies were keen to advertise on it. Consequently, Vickerman made a lot of money from selling advertising space on the site. For instance, according to Josh Halliday (2012), advertising revenue enabled Vickerman to make a profit of £250,000 in 2008.

The British court that tried Vickerman decided that he had broken the law. However, Vickerman's conviction was controversial, with one critic describing his four-year jail sentence as 'deeply concerning, inappropriate and disproportionate' (cited in Halliday, 2012) and others saying that the prosecution should never have been brought. It is therefore instructive to reflect on the ethics of what Vickerman did and, in particular, to consider the light that Kantian theory might shed on the matter.

Consider, then, how we might apply the *formula of universal law* to Vickerman's business model to evaluate the extent to which he was acting in accordance with reason-based duty. This would involve asking the five questions listed above, to which the following responses might be offered:

Question 1: what was Vickerman trying to achieve by his action?

It is fair to assume that Vickerman was hoping to make money from helping people access free films (he may also have had a philanthropic agenda to make artistic material available at minimal cost to impoverished consumers, but given the magnitude of his profit, making money seems to have been a major priority).

Question 2: what is the maxim upon which Vickerman was acting?

This could be expressed as follows: 'I will make money by helping people to access films for free'.

Question 3: what would universal adoption of Vickerman's maxim consist of?

If Vickerman's maxim were adopted universally, then many websites all over the world would try to find ways of making money by offering free access to films.

Question 4: what would be the eventual result of universal adoption of Vickerman's maxim?

In order to answer this question, we need to consider the likely impact of universal free-movie access on the economic viability of the film industry. If websites such as Vickerman's, which facilitate free access to films, became widespread, then anyone who wished to watch a film would be able to do so without paying. If this were the case, it is unlikely that many people would pay to rent or buy films. Therefore, revenues from the sale and rent of films would decline substantially. Of course, film-makers might still be able to raise revenue from advertising, but their overall income would probably fall considerably. Quite how this fall in revenue would affect the film industry is hard to say, but it is likely to have a serious impact on the quality and quantity of films. The commercial viability of big, high-budget, blockbuster movies, which are often the most popular, would be particularly hard hit. Indeed, the very survival of the film industry might be in jeopardy. If this happened, in a few years, websites such as surfthechannel.com would not have many new films to direct their users to. If this were to happen, it is unlikely that users would continue to use surfthechannel.com. And if this were to happen, advertisers would no longer be prepared to pay large sums of money to advertise on surfthechannel.com. Thus, Vickerman would lose his revenue stream.

Question 5: how would this affect Vickerman's success in achieving what he is trying to achieve?

If this were to happen, it is clear that surfthechannel.com would no longer enable Vickerman to make money by helping people to access free films.

It seems then, that the universal adoption of Vickerman's maxim would be self-defeating. If other companies were to adopt Vickerman's business model, the resources upon which that business model depends would dry up. Thus, as far as Kant's formula of universal law is concerned, Vickerman's business could be described as unethical. By making money from providing free access to movies, Vickerman was acting contrary to reason-based duty.

The notion of *freeloading* might help you to appreciate the ramifications of Kant's formula of universal law. Freeloading refers to the practice of taking something from a system without contributing to the sustenance of that system and, by doing so, undermining the system. If everyone who uses a system were to freeload, there would eventually be no system upon which to freeload. Therefore, to use Kant's terminology, it would be hard for a freeloader to 'will' that freeloading be universally adopted. In the case discussed above, it seems that Anton Vickerman's business was freeloading off the film industry: it was making money from that industry whilst undermining its ongoing viability.

Video Activity 3.1

The following video, entitled 'Pirate Nation', discusses the topic of music piracy. www.youtube.com/watch?v=rwQrq1dBHl0

Questions

1 How might the practice of music piracy be construed as freeloading; that is, of taking something from a system without contributing to the sustenance of that system?
2 How might the practice of music piracy stand up to Kant's formula of universal law? You can test this by applying the five questions listed above.
3 If the practice of music piracy is unethical, is it only the people who make pirated music available free of charge who are acting unethically? Or do you think their customers, who download music without paying, are also acting unethically?

The formula of the end in itself

Although Kant presents the formula of universal law as the most fundamental expression of the categorical imperative, the addition of several other formulas helps to make the demands of ethics more intuitively plausible (Schneewind, 1992; Becker, 1993). These other formulas also offer ways of identifying duty in business contexts that are a little more straightforward than that offered by the formula of universal law. The most commonly discussed of these additional formulas is *the formula of the end in itself*. Kant expresses this formula as follows: '*Act in such a way that you always treat humanity, whether in your own person or in the person of any other, never simply as a means, but always at the same time as an end*' (1948/1785: 91/66–7 [italics in original]).

To understand what Kant means by this, it is important to appreciate the difference between treating someone as a means to an end and treating them as an end. To treat someone *as a means to an end* is to value that person only insofar as they help you to achieve some further end that you happen to value. In other words, treating someone as a means to an end means *using* that person to achieve an objective that you wish to achieve. In such cases, the value that you place on that person may derive solely from the value that you place on the further objective. In other words, that person may only be important to you because they offer a convenient means of achieving what you want to achieve; you are according them no value in themself. To treat someone *as an end*, on the other hand, is to treat them as having value in their own right. In other words, it is to value that person regardless of their usefulness in helping you to achieve what you want to achieve. Thus, what Kant is saying in the formula of the end in itself is that people should not be used as a tool to achieve some further purpose; they should always be treated as if they are important in their own right.

This formula appeals to some of the ideas explored earlier, particularly those relating to the innate rationality and freedom of all human beings. These qualities, for Kant, give to human beings a certain dignity, and to use somebody purely as a means to an end would not be consistent with that dignity. In Kant's view, all people should be valued in their own right because of the dignity that they merit as rational, free beings.

At first glance, the formula of the end in itself may seem rather an impractical formula to use in a business context. If treating people as a means to an end is unethical, then it seems that business *per se* is unethical. After all, is it not the case that all businesses use all sorts of people in order to make profit? For instance, customers are 'used' to obtain the revenue that enables a company to be profitable; employees are 'used' to produce the goods and services that businesses sell; suppliers are 'used' to acquire the resources necessary to make those goods and services; and shareholders are 'used' to secure the capital that a business needs to survive and prosper. To prohibit treating people as a means to an end, then, seems to prohibit business as we know it.

However, it is important to distinguish between treating people as a means to an end and treating people *only* as a means to an end. Kant does not actually say that we should not treat people as a means to an end; he only says that we should not treat them *only* as a means to an end. In his words, we should treat people 'never *simply* as a means, but always at the same time as an end'. Treating people as a means to an end is acceptable, then, for Kant as long as we *also* treat them as an end in themselves. In other words, it is permissible to use someone to achieve a desired end as long as you also value them, at the same time, in their own right.

Theory in Practice

Suppliers: Simply a means to an end? Or an end in themselves?

The distinction between treating people simply as a means to an end and treating them also as an end in their own right can be illustrated with reference to contrasting ways that a company might treat its suppliers. Consider the following two

(Continued)

(Continued)

accounts. The first account, taken from Conor Woodman's (2012) book, *Unfair Trade*, describes how a business might treat its suppliers as a means to the end of making profit whilst also treating them as an end in their own right. The second account, from George Monbiot's (2001) *Captive State*, describes some companies that seem to regard their suppliers as no more than a means to an end. According to Kantian theory, the first company would be acting in accordance with reason-based duty; the companies described in the second account would not.

Treating suppliers as an end in themselves

Conor Woodman (2012) relates a discussion with Dave Keeper and Ian Meredith, who run the Ethical Addictions company. Ethical Addictions buys single-origin coffee from producers in Asia, Africa and Latin America and supplies it to restaurants, coffee shops, hotels and farm shops.

A short video from the Ethical Addictions website, in which the company explains its business model, can be viewed at:

www.eacoffee.co.uk/news_88065.html

One of the coffees on Ethical Addictions' list is from Orera, a small village on the slopes of Mount Kilimanjaro. Keeper and Meredith described to Woodman how they set up their supply arrangement with Orera. Until the arrival of Ethical Addictions, the farmers in Orera had received $1.38 per kilo for their coffee. This is less than half the price stipulated by the Fairtrade organization for the purchase of coffee in Tanzania. One reason why the price was so low is that the purchase of coffee was conducted through various intermediaries, each of which took a cut, which left little for the villagers of Orera. To avoid this unnecessary erosion in the villagers' income, Keeper and Meredith decided to buy direct from the farmers.

On the one hand, Keeper and Meredith note the importance of making a profit from their deal with the Orera farmers; after all, any business needs to make money in order to survive and Ethical Addictions is no different: 'We want to run a business and that means we have to make a profit' (Dave Keeper, cited in Woodman, 2012: 53). In Kantian terms, then, Ethical Addictions could be described as treating its suppliers as *a means to the end* of running a profitable business. However, Woodman's account of how Keeper and Meredith went about setting up the Orera deal suggests that they do not regard their suppliers purely as a means to an end; rather they also think of them as *an end in their own right*:

> Ian and Dave decided to make a direct offer to the Orera villagers ... [They] could have paid the lower price and made bumper profits but they didn't feel

> that fitted with their business model. The short-term profit-maximising approach would have been to screw the villagers and pocket the cash but Dave and Ian saw things differently. For them it was more important to encourage the village to become a long-term potential supplier of good coffee to fit their brand. (Woodman, 2012: 54)

The important thing about this account is that Keeper and Meredith could have persuaded the Orera farmers to sell their coffee direct to Ethical Addictions, instead of going through intermediaries, by paying a far lower price than they actually ended up paying. All they would have had to do was to offer more than the $1.38 that the villagers were currently getting. Had they wanted to treat their suppliers purely as a means to the end of profit maximization, this is what they would have done. And if the Orera villagers were eventually unable to supply coffee at these low prices, then Ethical Addictions could simply have taken its business elsewhere. However, this is not how Keeper and Meredith wanted to do business. They wanted to pay a price that would provide them with a profit whilst also enabling the villagers to carry on producing good quality coffee beans well into the future. Thus, in Kantian terms, they also treated the villagers as an end in their own right.

Now, it could be argued that, by paying a price that would ensure the long-term sustainability of coffee growing in Orera, Meredith and Keeper were just looking after their own, long-term, business interests. By ensuring ongoing supply from Orera, they were avoiding the need to seek out new suppliers every few years. And there is a sense in which valuing stakeholders in their own right is consistent with an enlightened, long-term, business strategy. Nevertheless, this long-term, mutually supportive approach is not one that all businesses are inclined to adopt, as is apparent from George Monbiot's account of some of the practices employed by supermarket chains.

Treating suppliers simply as a means to an end

Supermarket chains tend to buy in vast quantities from their suppliers. This gives them a great deal of negotiating power. George Monbiot relates the way that some use that power to persuade suppliers to do things that are not in their best interests and which may even undermine their commercial viability.

> In November 1999, Safeway sent the farmers it bought from a notice entitled 'Good News From Safeway'. Its 'new promotional strategy' would 'deliver a much improved level of availability for your product'. There was a

(Continued)

(Continued)

> catch, however. 'To take part in the programme we request a contribution from your product line of £20,000. ... We look forward to you joining us in this campaign, and anticipating a favourable response, we will take the liberty of sending you an invoice on Friday of this week. Thank you in advance for your support'. (Monbiot, 2001: 183)

The tacit understanding behind the message that Monbiot recounts was clear: if Safeway's suppliers refused to make the £20,000 donation asked of them, they risked losing the supermarket's custom. Monbiot goes on to allege that:

> At the end of the year, both bakers and fruit growers supplying the superstores may be forced to pay a 'rebate' to the chain they supply: if they refuse they will not be asked to sell their produce to the company again ...
>
> farmers often find themselves locked into selling food to the supermarket, simply because the collapsing wholesale market has left them with no choice. The supermarket can gradually reduce the price it pays until the farmer's business folds, whereupon it switches to a new supplier, who is less aware of the hidden costs of the relationship ...
>
> We hear little about practices like these because, as John Breach of the Fruit Growers' Association points out, 'farmers who dare to raise objections to terms and conditions run a very real risk of being delisted'. After a meeting of livestock farmers convened to protest against the demands that Tesco was making on the way in which they raised their animals, one of the organizers complained: 'The fear factor was immense. Few people felt brave enough to put their head up and speak publicly'. (Monbiot, 2001: 183–4)

The following Australian TV news report, entitled 'Australian farmers and growers squeezed by supermarket chains to breaking point', discusses similar conduct by large supermarkets in Australia:

www.youtube.com/watch?v=uxpaOs5np2A

Unlike the directors of Ethical Addictions, the managers of the supermarkets described here seem to have little regard for the long-term sustainability of their suppliers. They seem confident that, should one supply source fail, they can easily switch to an alternative source. According to Monbiot's account and the Australian news report, these managers do not seem to value their suppliers in their own right. Rather, suppliers are treated merely as a means to the end of acquiring meat, fruit and vegetables at the lowest possible price and thus maximizing profit. And if some of those suppliers go bust in the process, this seems to be of little concern to the supermarkets.

Questions

1 The distinction between treating people just as a means to an end and treating them as an end in their own right has been illustrated here in relation to suppliers. However, it can also be applied to other stakeholder groups. How might the formula of the end in itself be applied to identify an ethical approach to customer relations? What sort of things might a business do, and what sort of things should it avoid doing, if it wishes to treat its customers as an end in their own right?
2 How might measures such as those that you have identified impact on the short-term and long-term performance of a business?
3 So far, this discussion of Kant's second formula has talked about businesses' relationships with specific stakeholders; that is, with specific groups of people with whom a business has a formal relationship. However, can you think of ways in which it might help us to think about the ethicality of business relationships more generally? In other words, how might the notion of treating people as an end in themselves help us to identify corporate duties towards society in general?

The formula of universal acceptability

Some of Kant's commentators (for example Becker, 1993; Wood, 2000) also pick out a third formula from his discussion of the categorical imperative, which I will refer to here as the *formula of universal acceptability*. This third formula offers a basis from which some business ethicists have derived a useful test for assessing the ethicality of specific actions. I will briefly outline the formula and describe some implications that have been drawn from it. I will then outline the practical test of ethicality that it offers and illustrate how this might be used.

Kant's formula of universal law, which was discussed above, suggests that we should only perform an action if we would be happy for the maxim upon which that action is based to be universalized. Kant points out that this implies that we should think of ourselves as universal lawmakers. In other words, whenever we act we should imagine that we are creating a universal law that governs all other people, which says that the action we are performing is also appropriate for them. The ethical implication of this is described by Kant as follows:

> Thus morality consists in the relation of all action to the making of laws … This making of laws must be found in every rational being himself and must be able to spring from his will. The principle of his will is therefore never to perform an action except on a maxim such as can also be a universal law, and consequently such *that the will can regard itself as at the same time making universal law by means of its maxim*'. (1948/1785: 96/76)

To appreciate how we can derive the formula of universal acceptability from this, and how this formula, in turn, has been adapted by some business ethicists to provide a handy practical test, we need to consider it in relation to some of the other aspects of Kant's moral philosophy discussed earlier. Remember that Kant believed that the innate rationality and freedom of human beings gives them a certain dignity, and that this dignity should always be respected by other humans. You will recall that this fundamental dignity of human beings provides the basis for the second formula of the categorical imperative, the formula of the end in itself, which was discussed above. But human dignity also entails that we should not impose laws on other people that they would not be happy to accept. To expect others to follow laws that they do not agree with would be inconsistent with the dignity due to them as rational, free beings. Therefore, in considering the desirability of the imaginary law that we are creating by performing a particular action, we must ask ourselves whether everybody else would be happy to be subjected to that law. If we were to impose such a law against other people's will, we would not be treating them with the dignity that is their due. The *formula of universal acceptability* therefore suggests that we should only do things that we believe other people would find acceptable.

This, of course, begs the question: how do we know what laws other people would find acceptable? How can we be sure that everyone else would be happy to accept the law that we are tacitly establishing through our action? And the answer to this question is that we cannot be sure, because we cannot possibly go round asking everybody if they find the law that we are thus creating acceptable. Nevertheless, we can do the next best thing: we can imagine ourselves in a hypothetical position that helps us to reflect on whether we truly believe all others would be happy with that law. This involves asking ourselves how we would feel if news of what we are doing, along with our reasons for doing it, became public knowledge.

Pause for Reflection

Can you think of any way that you have treated another person that you would not want broadcast on Facebook, Twitter or any other social media sites that you use? Do you think this provides a reliable indication that you ought not to have treated that person in that way?

Andrew Crane and Dirk Matten (2010) have linked these ideas to Linda Trevino and Katherine Nelson's suggestion that 'in general, if you don't want to read about it in *The New York Times*, you shouldn't be doing it' (Trevino and Nelson, 2004: 99). Crane and Matten thus refer to 'the '*New York Times* test' (Crane and Matten, 2010: 106) as a practical application of the Kantian formula of universal acceptability. As they put it, 'if you would be uncomfortable if your actions were reported in the press, you can be fairly sure that they are of doubtful moral status' (2010: 106). This is because your unwillingness to see your actions reported in *The New York Times* probably indicates that you are well aware that other people would not be happy for the law that you are establishing through your actions to be universalized.

Theory in Practice

Would UK water companies have wanted everyone to know what they were doing?

In August of 2013, a report appeared in *The Observer* newspaper accusing the UK's biggest water companies of being 'the most persistent and frequent polluters of England's rivers and beaches' (Carrington and Barnes, 2013). The report, which draws on data obtained from the Environment Agency (England) under freedom of information rules, listed a number of ways in which the water companies, who are responsible for treating waste water and delivering clean water supplies, have been linked to pollution. These include overflowing of sewers, failure to clean up after spillages, and discharge of untreated sewage into rivers.

The report revealed that water companies are frequently fined for causing pollution and failing to clear it up. However, it suggests that the fines are so low that they have little deterrence effect. For instance, despite more than 1,000 pollution incidents in the past nine years, the companies had been fined a total of only £3.5m (Carrington and Barnes, 2013). Joan Walley MP, chair of the Environmental Audit Committee (EAC), summed up the situation as follows: 'In law, the "polluter pays" principle is supposed to deter companies from damaging the environment, but in this case the penalties appear to be so pitiful that water companies seem to be accepting them as the price of doing business' (cited in Carrington and Barnes, 2013).

Joan Walley's charge implies that water companies are making a cost-benefit comparison of the costs of delivering their business in a less-polluting way against the fines handed out for not doing so. They have concluded that it is cheaper to pay the fines than it would be to put measures in place to reduce pollution.

(Continued)

(Continued)

Therefore, they have not invested as much as they could have done in pollution-reduction measures; rather, they have gone for the cheaper option of allowing pollution and paying the fines when they get found out.

If this is so, water company executives could offer some firm ethical justifications for their actions. For instance, they could point to their responsibility to do what is best for business and their duty to maximize returns for their investors. But had they wished to undertake a more comprehensive ethical evaluation, they might have found the *formula of universal acceptability* useful. This would call on them to ask whether they believed the principle upon which they appeared to be acting would be universally accepted. And one way of conducting this thought experiment would be to ask themselves if they would be happy for their decisions, along with the reasons why they had taken those decisions, to appear in the national newspapers.

To some extent, this hypothetical thought experiment has become reality, since *The Observer*'s report has made the water companies' activities common knowledge. In this respect, the companies have been subjected to a real, rather than an imaginary, *New York Times* test. Of course, the reasons why the water companies did not reduce pollution are a matter of conjecture. However, many observers might agree with Joan Walley's suggestion that they were simply viewing pollution and the associated fines as a cost of doing business. Moreover, the public and political reaction to this issue (Carrington, 2013) suggests that many people agreed with the conclusion of Simon Hughes, deputy leader of the UK Liberal Democrat party, that 'the public is entitled to say that our monopoly water providers are neither good corporate citizens nor good stewards of our precious environmental assets' (cited in Carrington and Barnes, 2013).

Questions

1 Do you think that water company executives would put profit maximization before pollution reduction if they knew that this decision would be broadcast through the national press?
2 Can you think of any other cases of what you consider to be unethical corporate conduct to which the formula of universal acceptability might apply?

Rescuing ethical sentiment: perfect duties and imperfect duties

This second section of the chapter has outlined three ways of identifying reason-based duty, each of which draws on ideas introduced in the first section. It may have occurred to you throughout this discussion that Kant's approach to ethics is a particularly austere one, since it seems to allow no space for sentiment. This can be seen in the way that Kantian ethics would attribute ethical esteem to two of the students discussed earlier. Remember that Otis repaid his debt to Harry because he is a naturally kind and considerate person. He would not have been able to live with himself had he not paid the money back. Sofía, on the other hand, considered not repaying her debt but, after reason-based consideration of her duty, she decided that she ought to do so. I suggested that, of the two, Kant would consider Sofía more deserving of ethical esteem because she had used reason to identify her duty and had then acted accordingly, whereas Otis had acted purely on sentiment. I also asked you to think about how Kant would rate the companies that Otis and Sofía went on to run in terms of their ethical praiseworthiness. It is likely that Kant would find Sofía's company more praiseworthy because Sofía encouraged people to think rationally about their duty and to act on their own reason-based choices. Otis's company, on the other hand, just happened to be staffed by kind, generous people.

It may seem harsh to give so much ethical credit to reason compared to sentiment. As I have presented his philosophy so far, Kant does not have much to say about sentiments such as kindness, altruism and generosity, which is contrary to the way that we usually think about ethics. And Kant's moral philosophy has been criticized on that basis: that it is a stern, disciplinarian celebration of reason, which downplays the importance of ethical sentiment. However, Kant did not completely dismiss the caring sentiments. Although he considered reason-based sense of duty to be most deserving of ethical acclaim, he also approved of the type of sentiment that came so naturally to the young Otis and which characterized the company he went on to run.

In order to explain the role that Kant assigned to ethical sentiment, it is useful to distinguish between *perfect duty* and *imperfect duty*. Although Kant does not offer an explicit and unambiguous definition of these two types of duty, the distinction generally made (for example by Acton, 1970; Becker, 1993; O'Neill, 1993) is that a *perfect duty* is a duty to which, under any circumstances, one is bound. As Kant put it, a perfect duty 'allows no exception in the interest of inclination' (1948/1785: 85/53**). Those duties that we can work out by applying the categorical imperative fall into the category of perfect duty. For instance, we have a perfect duty to repay our debts come what may, because to do otherwise would offend the formula of universal law. Similarly, we have a perfect duty to never, under any circumstances, use people purely as a means to making money, because that would offend the formula of the end in itself. And the formula of universal acceptability suggests that we have a perfect duty to do nothing that we would not want to become public knowledge.

Imperfect duties, on the other hand, are not quite so compelling. They concern things that we should do wherever practically feasible, but not necessarily all the time. Developing our own predisposition to be kind, altruistic and generous would fall into this category. An imperfect duty such as this, for Kant, responds to the inevitability of relations of mutual dependency between people. For Kant, our duty to be kind, altruistic and generous can be worked out using reason: because of the mutual dependency between people, it would be irrational for us to will that sentiments such as kindness, altruism and generosity did not exist: each of us may, one day, need others to be kind, altruistic and generous to us. As Kant describes it:

> although it is possible that a universal law of nature could subsist in harmony with [ignoring the hardships of others], yet it is impossible to *will* that such a principle should hold everywhere as a law of nature. For a will which decided in this way would be in conflict with itself, since many a situation might arise in which the man needed love and sympathy from others, and in which, by such a law of nature sprung from his own will, he would rob himself of all hope of the help he wants for himself. (1948/1785: 86/56–7)

However, duties such as these are less complete than perfect duties (hence *imperfect*) because we cannot fulfil them absolutely: we cannot be completely kind, altruistic and generous to everyone.

Consideration of imperfect duty has certain implications for business. If we have a (albeit imperfect) duty to display sentiments such as kindness, altruism and generosity, then it seems reasonable to suppose that companies, which, like people, are embedded in relations of mutual dependency within society, have an imperfect duty to display such sentiments. And if companies have a duty to display sentiments such as these, then those who are in positions of responsibility in companies have a duty to encourage them in themselves and amongst their colleagues. Such considerations bring Kantian ethics close to some of the ideas of virtue ethics that are discussed in Chapter 5.

Video Activity 3.2

The following video shows a Wish TV news report about how Jhaqueil Reagan got a job at Papa Roox fast-food restaurant.

www.youtube.com/watch?v=Ydy1HiZ-Vio

Questions

1 Do you think Art Bouvier, the owner of Papa Roox, had a *perfect duty* to help Jhaqueil Reagan by giving him a lift to town and by offering him a job in his restaurant? In other words, had he not done these things, would he have breached Kant's *formula of universal law*, *formula of the end in itself* or *formula of universal acceptability*?

2 How might Art have been fulfilling what Kant would call an *imperfect duty* by doing these things?

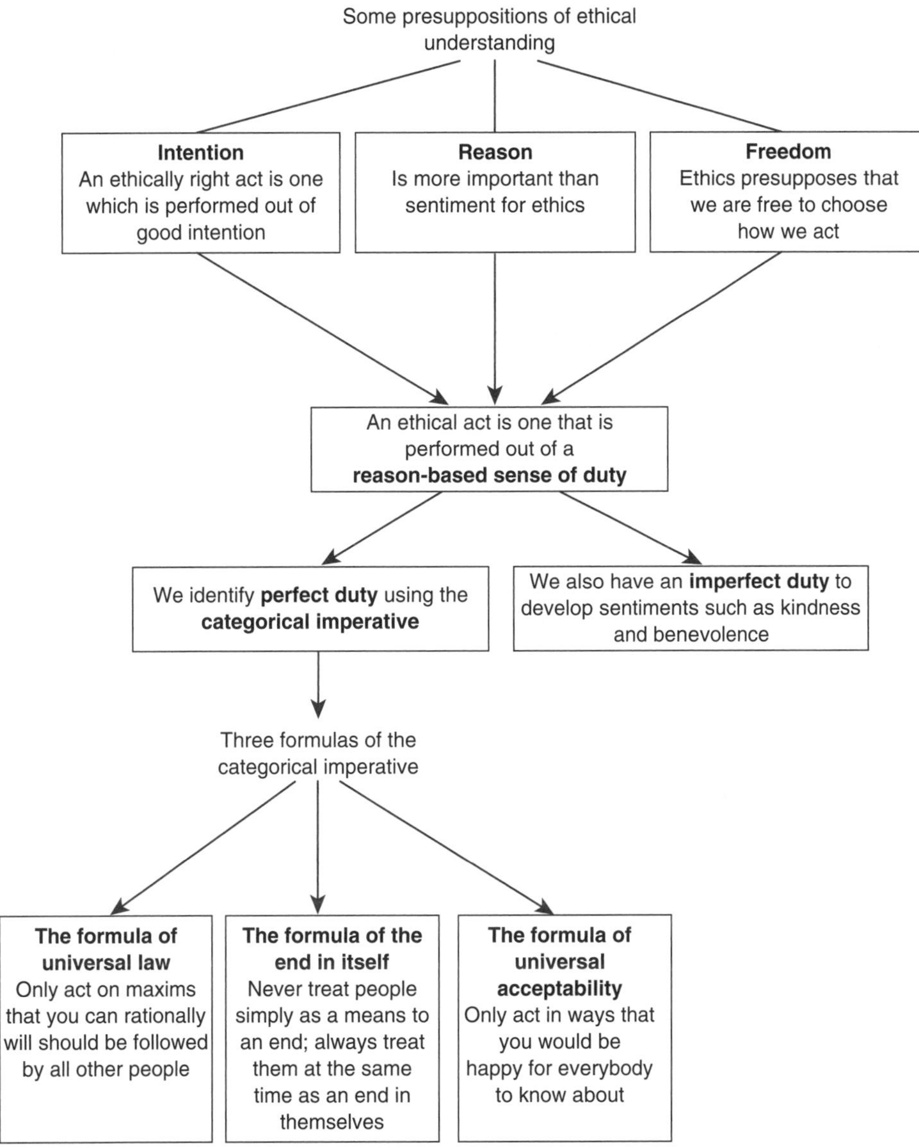

Figure 3.1 Kantian ethics theory: an overview

Kantian ethics theory applied to labour standards in offshore production

The first section of this chapter outlined some key features of a Kantian approach to ethics; that is, the importance it places on intention, reason and freedom. The second section described how Kant proposes we should identify our duty; that is, by using the categorical imperative. Three formulations of the categorical imperative have been introduced: the formula of universal law, the formula of the end in itself, and the formula of universal acceptability. The chapter will end by considering how some of these ideas might be used to assist reflection on the ethicality of an issue that has become very common in business: the practice of offshoring production. Offshoring raises a number of ethical questions. One of these relates to labour standards that are often implemented in offshore production operations.

Offshoring: a brief introduction

During the last 30 years, it has become common for Western businesses to transfer manufacturing and assembly operations to overseas locations, particularly to locations in the developing world. In some cases this practice, generally referred to as *offshoring*, is undertaken to locate manufacturing closer to supplies of raw material. Sometimes companies are keen to take advantage of tax breaks, which are offered by the governments of developing nations in order to attract overseas investment and thus stimulate their own economies. Most importantly, though, the cost of labour in the developing world tends to be much lower than it is in the West, so companies who offshore can usually achieve big reductions in their wage bills. Consequently, designer-label clothing and branded goods sold in Western shopping malls are more likely to have been made in the Philippines than in Western Europe or the USA, and most of the smartphones that have become a must-have item for many people in the West are assembled in vast manufacturing estates in China.

Western companies do not often run offshored operations themselves. More often, they outsource production to specialist factory operators. These operators might run units within extensive Export Processing Zones (EPZs); that is, in sealed-off manufacturing enclaves that offer tax benefits to the corporations that use them. Alternatively, they may operate huge factory estates that carry out production on behalf of global corporations.

Offshoring can deliver benefits to various stakeholders. The cost savings associated with cheaper production might be passed on to consumers, who thus pay less for the stuff they buy. Offshoring can also drive increased profitability, which means that shareholders get higher returns on their investment. Furthermore, the EPZs of Asia and Central America and the giant assembly factories in China provide work for local people that might not exist otherwise. Not only is this potentially advantageous for those workers; it can also benefit local communities as wages get recycled through the economy. Supporters of offshoring also point out that taxes associated with economic activity in the developing world can pay for improvements to public services. Moreover, offshoring might facilitate the transfer of technical skills and knowledge from rich, Western nations to struggling economies.

Nevertheless, the ethicality of offshoring has been challenged on a number of fronts. Some of the strongest criticism concerns the labour standards that are common in offshored production facilities. For instance, Naomi Klein's (2001) book *No Logo* provides a detailed account of manufacturing operations at the Cavite EPZ in Indonesia, which assembles products for many well-known, global brands. Klein describes the labour conditions that she found at Cavite. Migrant workers, who were mainly young women who had travelled to Cavite from other parts of Indonesia, were expected to work extremely long hours, with enforced overtime whenever particularly large orders needed to be processed. Klein found that management control was strict, authoritarian and sometimes abusive. She also reports that most of the work was tedious, and that health and safety provision fell well short of the standards expected in the West. Moreover, although wages were sufficient to pay for rudimentary accommodation and food, Klein notes that they would not be enough to allow the workers to save or to spend money on discretionary items. Cavite workers certainly could not have afforded to buy the products they were employed to assemble. Furthermore, Klein reports that there was little or no job security, and that any form of union activity, which might have improved the lot of workers, was actively discouraged.

A practical scenario

Imagine that you are senior executive of a large sports goods manufacturer, who has been asked to establish a new manufacturing base for making training shoes. You are considering subcontracting this work to a Taiwanese-owned company that operates assembly plants on EPZs throughout Asia and Central America. You are attracted to this particular company because it can make your goods far more cheaply than they could be made anywhere else. But you are also aware that it achieves its low-cost base by using many of the labour practices criticized by Naomi Klein. This company is able to do this because it usually sets up its manufacturing operations in areas where there are few other employment opportunities, so its workers are unlikely to leave for better-paid jobs elsewhere with better working conditions. Also, the company operates in countries whose governments are eager for the economic stimulus that EPZ operators provide, so local officials are disinclined to intervene on behalf of the workforce. Furthermore, if economic development, or the arrival of other employers, leads to an increase in the cost of labour in one of its operations, this production company simply moves to another, less-developed location where it can once again run its operation at minimum cost.

The employment practices of your potential supplier make you feel rather uncomfortable. On the one hand, you think about the ethical upside of doing business with this company, such as cheaper trainers for your customers and an increase in share value for your shareholders. And as far as the company's workers are concerned, surely any job is better than no job. However, you wonder if there is a way of getting your trainers made in a manner that causes you less ethical discomfort. You ask yourself what Immanuel Kant might say about this issue.

Applying the categorical imperative

Well, Kant would probably say that it is a good thing for you and your company to care about the welfare of the workers who make your products. Indeed, he would suggest that you have an *imperfect* duty to develop sentiments such as kindness and generosity in your business and to display these sentiments towards all people, especially those over whose lives you have so much influence. However, whilst imperfect duties such as this are important, it is *perfect* duty that is most important for Kant. And perfect duty can only be identified using reason. Ultimately, then, you should identify your ethical responsibilities using reason, not sentiment. And to do this, you need to apply the categorical imperative. So, what insights might the three formulas of the categorical imperative discussed earlier enable in this case?

Applying the formula of universal law

How would using this supplier stand up to the test of the formula of universal law? The formula of universal law would call upon you to act only on maxims that you could rationally wish to be universalized. One way of applying this formula to the present situation would be to apply the five questions listed earlier in this chapter to doing business with your proposed production company.

Question 1: what am I trying to achieve by my action?

One way of answering this question is that your ultimate objective in getting trainers made by this company would be to maximize profit for your company. And to do this, you need to sell as many trainers as you can. After all, that is what you are in business to do: to make profits by making and selling sports kit.

Question 2: what is the maxim upon which I am acting?

Perhaps the maxim upon which you would be acting, should you choose to work with this supplier, would be as follows: 'Use a manufacturing company that pays low wages and observes low labour standards in order to minimize costs and thus maximize profit'.

Question 3: what would universal adoption of my maxim consist of?

Perhaps universal adoption of this maxim would look something like this: 'All employers, all over the world, would use manufacturing companies that pay low wages and observe low labour standards in order to minimize costs and thus maximize profit'.

Question 4: what would be the eventual result of universal adoption of my maxim?

One consequence of universalization of your supplier's employment policy is that all companies would spend less on manufacturing so could, if they chose to do so, sell their products more cheaply. However, given the relatively high proportion of corporate costs taken up by things like marketing, product prices may not drop by very much. A more obvious consequence of companies all over the world treating their employees like your prospective supplier does, and particularly of paying such low wages, is that there would be very few people around with enough spare cash to buy expensive items such as the trainers that you sell.

Question 5: how would this affect my success in achieving what I am trying to achieve?

If there were not many people around with enough disposable income to buy expensive sports kit, then your company would not sell many trainers. Therefore, you would not achieve your objective of maximizing company profit. So it seems that universal adoption of your maxim in using this manufacturing company would be self-defeating.

It seems, therefore, that you could not rationally will the universal adoption of your maxim. It follows that, if we apply the formula of universal law in this manner, using this company would not sit well with Kantian theory.

Pause for Thought

Can you think of any other ways in which the formula of universal law might be applied to this case? Would these deliver the same conclusions or different ones?

Applying the formula of the end in itself

What of Kant's second formula: the formula of the end in itself? Remember that the formula of the end in itself asks us not to treat people purely as a means to an end without also treating them as an end in themselves. In other words, we must not simply use people to achieve some objective that we desire; we must also value them in their own right.

So, do the employment practices of your prospective supplier conform to this requirement? In getting this company's employees to make your trainers at very low cost, you would certainly seem to be treating them as a means to the end of maximizing profit. But would you also be treating them as an end in their own right? On the one hand, it might be argued that you would be providing them with work that they may not otherwise have, so this treats them as an end in their own right. But would this be enough to satisfy Kant? Is this all that it takes to value someone in their own right, or are other things also required? What else might you, as an executive charged with the manufacture of sports kit, expect your subcontractor to do that would convince you that it is fulfilling its duty to treat its workers as an end in their own right?

You might take a lead from some employment practices that are expected in most developed nations; practices which this company is not observing. You could begin by insisting on the payment of a wage that permits a comfortable standard of living, rather than one that just secures basic needs. You might also ask your subcontractor to observe similar health and safety standards in its factories to those expected in the West. You could also ask it to provide those who make your trainers with opportunities to develop their skills. You might insist on a degree of job security. Moreover, you might demand that workers are able to participate in company decision making. You might even insist that your prospective subcontractor permits its employees to join a union so that they can represent their interests more effectively. All of these things would seem to be more in keeping with treating people as an end in themselves than the production company's usual employment practices.

More generally, you might expect subcontractors who make your trainers to treat the communities within which they set up their factories with respect. Offshoring has been criticized for encouraging a short-term, exploitative approach, in which global corporations and their subcontractors regard the developing world as no more than a source of cheap labour. Instead, you could identify opportunities to establish longer-term, mutually beneficial relationships with the communities in which your products are assembled.

Pause for Thought

In order to demonstrate that it is treating the communities in which its products are assembled as an end in their own right, rather than merely using them as a source of cheap labour, a company might want to invest in local services and amenities. What sort of specific actions do you think it could take in this respect?

Applying the formula of universal acceptability

The third formula of the categorical imperative, the formula of universal acceptability, is probably the simplest to apply in this case. In order to estimate the universal acceptability of using this manufacturer to make trainers for your company, with its employment practices as they currently stand, you simply have to ask yourself if you would be happy for that information to appear in a national newspaper. If so, then, as far as this formula is concerned, you are justified in using the subcontractor with its present labour standards. However, if the thought of this becoming public knowledge concerns you, then you have a duty either to use another supplier that treats its workers better or to encourage your proposed subcontractor to amend its employment practices.

Theory in Practice

Rana Plaza: a disaster waiting to happen

On 24 April 2013, the eight-storey Rana Plaza building collapsed in Savar, a sub-district in the Greater Dhaka Area in Bangladesh, killing over 1,130 people and injuring thousands more. Rana Plaza housed several garment factories, which made clothing for many well-known Western brands and retailers (BBC, 2013d; Saul, 2013). Most of the victims of the disaster had been working in these factories when the building collapsed.

A Bangladesh government enquiry into the disaster found that the builders of Rana Plaza had failed to follow usual building codes and had used substandard construction materials (*The Telegraph*, 2013). Moreover, concerns had been raised about the building shortly before its collapse. According to Bangladeshi media reports, building inspectors had discovered cracks in the building the day before the collapse and had requested its evacuation and closure (War on Want, 2013). However, War on Want (2013) reports that garment workers were told to return to work the following day.

It has been suggested that the disaster was a result of Asian garment producers and Western corporations putting profit before workers' safety. For instance, one source sums up the disaster as follows:

> The reasons for this slaughter are depressingly predictable; in the cost equation between periodic loss of workers' lives and effective workplace health & safety measures the cheaper option always wins out ... All involved know that workplace deaths from factory fires and building collapses are inevitable under present conditions in Bangladesh – and that these conditions contribute greatly to the low costs of wages, price and profits. The country is the world's cheapest supplier of clothing. The details of the disaster show the operation of this logic at work. (libcom, 2013)

(Continued)

(Continued)

Following the disaster, various trade unions and labour rights organizations have tried to persuade corporations whose garments were produced in Rana Plaza to commit to compensation payments to the victims and their families. They have also tried to get corporations to agree to minimal standards of safety in garment factories in the developing world. These agreements include the Bangladesh Accord on Fire and Building Safety, which asks brands, retailers, trade unions and manufacturers to commit to a comprehensive program to address safety in garment factories in Bangladesh (Industriall, 2013; War on Want, 2013).

These efforts have met with varying degrees of success. Some companies, such as Primark and the owners of the Zara chain, were proactive in providing relief in the aftermath of the disaster and have also committed to compensation payments (Butler and Hammadi, 2013; Saul, 2013). Moreover, over 100 companies had signed up to the Bangladesh Accord on Fire and Building Safety by October 2013 (Industriall, 2013).

However, some other companies have been less willing to commit to such measures. For instance, War on Want (2013) reports that several users of Rana Plaza have so far refused to offer any form of financial assistance or compensation, while some corporations have declined to sign up to the Bangladesh Accord on Fire and Building Safety. Amongst these are the American corporation, Walmart, which, according to War on Want, is the single largest buyer from Bangladesh, and Gap. Rather than commit to a binding agreement, these companies have preferred to put their own measures in place, which involve no consultation with trade unions and contain no binding commitments (War on Want, 2013).

Questions

1 What questions would you want to ask the companies whose garments were manufactured in Rana Plaza factories to find out if they had carried out their duty prior to the accident according to Immanuel Kant's formula of universal law?

2 How would you go about establishing if those companies had acted in accordance with the formula of the end in itself?

3 How might the formula of universal acceptability be used to assess whether the companies were acting in accordance with reason-based duty?

4 What *imperfect duties* might the companies have had in relation to working conditions in Rana Plaza?

5 How might Kant's emphasis on *good intention* and on *free, reason-based choice* relate to the decision about whether or not to sign up to agreements such as the Bangladesh Accord on Fire and Building Safety?
6 Do you think the corporations that bought garments produced in Rana Plaza had a duty to ensure the safety of the building within which those goods were made, or was this entirely the responsibility of the garment producers?

Conclusion

Immanuel Kant's moral philosophy offers an alternative way of thinking about business ethics to the consequentialist approach that was outlined in the last chapter and which characterizes a lot of business ethics discussion. In other words, Kantian ethics highlights the importance of not only taking account of the consequences of our actions but of also considering the reasons why we carry out those actions. It suggests that, as far as ethical evaluation is concerned, outcomes are not everything; intentions also matter. The emphasis that Kantian theory places on reason has been challenged by some philosophers, who suggest that intuition plays an important role in ethical evaluation. Nevertheless, Kant's categorical imperative offers ways of applying reason which correspond to intuitive notions of right and wrong and which therefore offers a degree of rational justification for some of our ethical intuitions. These formulas might best be thought of as useful rules, which are relatively simple to apply to ethical dilemmas to help us think about the rights and wrongs of those dilemmas.

Kant's emphasis on freedom is particularly important for business ethics. Freedom is a key feature of the human dignity that Kant considered so important, and which is upheld by treating every person as an end in themself rather than just as a means to an end. But freedom is also crucial in another sense: for Kant, each of us should be free to apply our own reason in order to identify right and wrong. The importance that Kant places on freedom of ethical thought calls into question the desirability of ethical prescription. People should not be told what is right and what is wrong; they should be encouraged to work it out for themselves. In other words, duties should not be handed down from on high. As J.B. Schneewind describes it, for Kant

> There is no place for others to tell us what morality requires, nor has anyone the authority to do so … Because we are autonomous, each of us must be allowed a social space within which we may freely determine our own action. This freedom cannot be limited to members of some privileged class. (1992: 310)

Such considerations call into question the top-down management style that characterizes some corporate approaches to ethics. Kant's celebration of ethical freedom does not sit easily with formalized ethical codes, designed by senior executives, communicated by ethical training programmes, and administered via performance-management systems. However, it does sit easily with employees being encouraged to reflect, rationally, about right and wrong; to use this reason-based reflection to identify their duty; and to act in accordance with it.

Discussion questions

1. Global corporations have been accused of treating the developing world as no more than a source of cheap labour (for example, Global Exchange, 2011). Critics have suggested that many corporations show little interest in building long-term, mutually beneficial relationships with the communities within which their products are assembled. Conversely, a glance at the corporate websites of many corporations tells us of their commitment to doing good wherever they operate. If those corporations really are committed to establishing and sustaining supportive relationships with the communities where their goods are produced, what might they do to put this commitment into practice? Can you list five specific measures that a corporation could adopt that would constitute treating those communities as an end (rather than just as a means to the end of making profit)?
2. Kantian theory is not the only lens through which to consider labour standards in offshore production. Other ethical perspectives also provide useful insights, some of which contrast with those discussed in this chapter. You might like to consider, for instance, how *rights theory* and *utilitarianism* might apply to some of the issues raised here. Would they point in different directions to Kantian theory or would they support similar conclusions?
3. Kant placed a great deal of emphasis on human reason. In this respect, he was an important representative of the European Enlightenment. Do you agree with Kant that reason is all-important to ethical evaluation, or do sentiments also give important messages about right and wrong?
4. Kant believed that human rationality is universal. In other words, he thought that all people reason in the same way and, as long as they think long and hard enough about things, they will come to similar conclusions. Do you agree? Or do you think that different regions, different cultures, different types of people, maybe even different genders, have their own notions of what is rational?

Further study

Kant's *Groundwork to the Metaphysic of Morals*, which was first published in 1785, is a relatively accessible and concise account of his moral philosophy. Many copies of this work are available in published form or online.

H.B. Acton's (1970) book, *Kant's Moral Philosophy* offers, in a very readable format, further discussion of the theory explained in this chapter.

If you would like to read more about offshored production, you might like to look at Naomi Klein's (2001) account of 'The Discarded Factory' in Chapter 9 of her book, *No Logo*.

If you wish to read some alternative discussions of Kant's moral philosophy, you could look at Norman Bowie's (2002) 'A Kantian approach to business ethics', in Robert Frederick's *A Companion to Business Ethics*. The ideas presented in that chapter are developed more fully in Bowie's (1999) book, *Business Ethics: A Kantian Perspective*. You should also read a critique of Bowie's interpretation and application of Kant, which can be found in Chapter 4 of Jones et al.'s (2005) *For Business Ethics*.

4 Social Contract Theory: Business Obligations, Corporate Wrongdoing and Just Distribution

Chapter objectives

This chapter will:

- outline social contract theory in its classical format;
- explain the importance of voluntarism, tacit agreements and hypothetical constructions in a business context;
- discuss two contrasting perspectives on the relationship between human nature and social organization;
- explain how these offer the basis for person-focused and culture-focused approaches to explaining and preventing unethical business conduct;
- introduce John Rawls's theory of justice;
- explain how Rawls's ideas can be applied to ethical evaluation of the distribution of benefits and burdens associated with business activity.

Introduction

Social contract theory is generally associated with political philosophy. This is because, as it is usually presented, social contract theory provides a basis for justifying state authority. It therefore helps us to think about the rights and obligations of queens, kings, presidents and prime ministers as well as those of their citizens. However, despite its politics-based heritage, the insights offered by social contract theory can be applied in other contexts. This chapter will explore, in particular, what social contract theory has to say to business relationships; that is, it will discuss ways in which social contract theory helps us to identify rights and obligations that are associated with relationships between corporations and their stakeholders, and how it helps us to think about the broader relationship between business and society.

The chapter will begin with a brief explanation of social contract theory, particularly as it appears in the writing of three of its most celebrated classical exponents, Thomas Hobbes, John Locke and Jean-Jacques Rousseau. I will highlight some key aspects of these accounts, explaining how they might help us think about business ethics today. The second part of the chapter will focus specifically on the work of Hobbes and Rousseau, showing how their ideas about human nature and social organization might help us to reflect on why unethical business conduct happens, how it might be avoided, and how it can be remedied. The chapter will end by considering the work of a more recent social contract theorist, John Rawls. I will outline Rawls's ideas about just distribution, indicating how these ideas can be used to evaluate distribution of the benefits and burdens of business activity.

Social contract theory: some key themes

This first section will draw attention to some key features of social contract theory and explain how these help us to consider some of the obligations that corporations take on just by doing business within a particular society. In order to do this, it is necessary to offer a brief account of social contract theory in its original political context. Once we understand social contract theory's political significance, it will be easier for us to appreciate the insights it offers to business ethics.

Classical social contract theory

It is hard to offer a simple definition of social contract theory because it is such a broad and diverse field of political philosophy (Boucher and Kelly, 1994). Nevertheless, there are common threads in the accounts offered by three philosophers who are often regarded as its 'classical' proponents: Thomas Hobbes, John Locke and Jean-Jacques Rousseau (Morris, 1999). I will begin therefore by offering a brief overview of social contract theory as it appears in the political writing of these theorists, before dwelling in a little more detail on some of its key features and explaining how these might help us to think about the ethicality of business practice.

Society and the state of nature

Most people nowadays live in some form of society. This means that they develop ties of mutual dependency and work together on all sorts of joint projects. It also means that they use common resources and facilities like roads, communication networks, schools and hospitals. In addition, society usually offers some form of political structure, with a recognized government supported by government agencies. Society also tends to have laws and ethical conventions, to which most people conform. If people in society disobey its laws and ethical conventions, they are usually constrained or punished in some way.

Classical social contract theorists ask us to imagine what life would be like without society; a situation they refer to as the *state of nature*. In the state of nature, people would live in a solitary and self-contained manner. There would be little or no cooperation; people would just satisfy their own needs as best they could and pay little attention to others. There would be no social organization, no hierarchies, no government, and no state authorities telling people what to do. In this situation, people would mostly do as they pleased.

The state of nature is quite difficult for us to imagine because few of us have experienced it. For sure, we may have encountered situations that resemble a state of nature in some respects. However, in such situations there is usually some form of organization and hierarchical control lurking in the background. The state of nature, then, is a very rare thing. A key question that social contract theorists set out to address is: how has this come about? Why is it that we all live in society rather than in a state of nature? Furthermore, how can this situation, in which our natural freedom to act as we please is sacrificed to the hierarchical control of government and its agencies, be justified? Or as Jean-Jacques Rousseau famously put it, how is it that 'Man is born free, and [yet] everywhere he is in chains' (Rousseau, 1993/1762: 181)?

The advantages of society

Social contract theory's response to these questions goes something like this. It begins with the observation that there are certain advantages to living as part of society. In describing these advantages, different theorists offer slightly different accounts. According to Thomas Hobbes, the main benefit of living within society is that it allows us to escape the physical hazards associated with the state of nature. And in talking about the physical hazards of the state of nature, Hobbes was not referring to things like extreme weather and wild animals; he was talking about the threat presented by other people. Hobbes believed that, without clearly defined political structures, human relationships would be highly antagonistic and everybody would be in a constant state of war against everybody else. As he saw it, people therefore come together in society out of 'the foresight of their own preservation, and of a more contented life thereby' (Hobbes, 1994/1651: 106/xvii, 1).

John Locke's explanation of society placed rather more emphasis on the preservation of property than on physical safety. Locke believed that people who lived without some form of social organization would have little respect for one another's possessions. Consequently, there would be no incentive for people to invest time and effort building a home, cultivating land, and accumulating useful items because others would just take these things from them. He therefore suggested that the main advantage of living in organized, governed groups is that it permits systems of control, which ensure the respect for property that would be lacking in a state of nature. As Locke described it, 'The great and *chief end* therefore, of Mens uniting into Commonwealths, and putting themselves under Government, *is the Preservation of their Property*' (Locke, 1988/1690: 350–1/124).

Video Activity 4.1

The following video by Pistak Paisder, entitled 'What to expect when society breaks down after a crisis', comprises a collection of amateur and media footage of riots in Los Angeles in 1992 and of looting that followed Hurricane Katrina in 2005. This video gives some idea of what, according to some social contract theorists, a contemporary state of nature might look like.

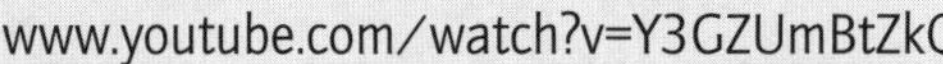
www.youtube.com/watch?v=Y3GZUmBtZkQ

Questions

1. How do the scenes shown in this video evoke the state of nature envisaged by Thomas Hobbes?
2. How do these scenes manifest the main disadvantage that John Locke associated with the state of nature?

Jean-Jacques Rousseau offered yet another perspective on the benefits of living in society. Rousseau believed that the chief merit of society is that it enables information to be shared and knowledge to be captured; things which are essential for the development of the human race. As he saw it, in a state of nature, 'Every art would necessarily perish with its inventor … and generations [would succeed] generations without the least advance' (Rousseau, 1993/1755: 79–80). Deprived of technological or cultural progress, humankind would remain locked forever in a condition of simplistic ignorance. In social groups, on the other hand, people are able to communicate, which enables them to pool expertise and build on one another's achievements. And since everybody is able to benefit from human progress, Rousseau believed that society has the potential to deliver significant advantages to all.

Pause for Reflection

You may be reading this book as part of a university course. How might universities such as yours be understood as social groupings that enable the achievement of the main benefit that Jean-Jacques Rousseau associates with society?

According to social contract theory, then, the reason why people live in society is that it serves their interests to do so. People realise that social living secures their personal safety, guarantees respect for their property, and facilitates human progress. They also realise that these things would be hard to achieve if people lived in a state of nature, outside of society. People therefore make an agreement – a *social contract* – to participate in society instead of living in a state of nature.

The disadvantage of society

Despite the advantages presented by society, however, social contract theorists pointed out that it also demands sacrifices on the part of those who inhabit it. And although Hobbes, Locke and Rousseau offered rather different accounts of the benefits of society, they were united in their assessment of its biggest sacrifice. This is that, in entering society, we give up our freedom to do whatever we want to do. We have to agree, instead, to do what is needed to ensure the smooth running of society. Moreover, this is no small sacrifice, for the classical theorists regarded freedom as a fundamental human right. Nevertheless, they believed that, in agreeing to the social contract, we agree to give up our right to freedom in order to enjoy the benefits of society.

Agreeing to take the rough with the smooth

That we have agreed to make the sacrifices demanded of society is an important feature of the social contract. Social contract theorists took the view that, by enjoying the benefits of society, we agree to surrender our natural freedom. And having made that agreement we can have no just cause for complaint when we are called upon to do what society requires of us, even if this means doing things we do not want to do. Once we have agreed to the social contract, we must be willing to put up with its downsides as well as its upsides.

For the classical theorists, this justifies government authority. They suggested that the main role of government was to ensure that society was organized so as to promote the common good. And since citizens have agreed to surrender their natural freedom in the interests of the general good of society, they have an obligation to do what government tells them to do. In other words, citizens enjoy the benefit of other people being controlled by government; therefore, they must be prepared to surrender their own freedom to government control.

Three features of social contract theory

These, then, are some fundamentals of social contract theory in its classical, political format. But what does this all have to do with business? In order to draw out the relevance of social contract theory for business, it helps to emphasize three of its key features: firstly, the notion of *voluntarism*, which underpins social contract theory's ethical appeal; secondly the *tacit* character of the agreement to which it usually refers; and thirdly, the idea that the social contract is a *hypothetical construction*.

Voluntarism

The ethical appeal of social contract theory lies in the notion of *voluntarism*. In a political context, voluntarism has been defined by Patrick Riley as 'emphasis on the assent of individuals as the standard of political legitimacy' (Riley, 1999/1970). Another way of putting this is that social contract theory bases the ethical legitimacy of government authority on the fact that people have *voluntarily* agreed to obey government as a condition of membership of society. And since citizens have voluntarily assented to government authority, that authority is legitimate.

To take voluntarism out of its political context and apply it to relationships more generally is to suggest that the ethical legitimacy of social arrangements derives from the fact that those who are involved in those arrangements have voluntarily agreed to their involvement. Furthermore, they have agreed to be involved whilst fully aware of the advantages and disadvantages that this presents. In other words, we enter into relationships voluntarily and with our eyes open; therefore we must be prepared to accept the negative consequences of those relationships as well as the positive.

Consider voluntarism in relation to a business-supplier relationship. Suppose a farmer agrees to supply milk to a supermarket at a given price over a period of, say, six months. Both the farmer and the supermarket buyer weigh up the advantages and disadvantages of entering into the supply relationship for a fixed period of time. The main advantage, for both parties, is security: the supermarket has an assured supply of milk at a set price for the six-month period; the farmer has a guaranteed outlet for her milk. The disadvantage is that both parties surrender certain freedoms by entering into the supply relationship. One important freedom that they give up is the freedom to enter into more profitable relationships with other people should the opportunity arise. So, for the duration of the six-month period of the relationship, the farmer surrenders her freedom to switch to any alternative retailer who may pay a higher price for her milk. Similarly, the supermarket is committed to buying its milk from the farmer, even if another farmer offers milk at a lower price. Neither the farmer nor the supermarket would be justified in complaining about this loss of freedom because it is something that they *voluntarily* agreed to when they entered into the supply relationship.

Tacit agreements

So far this all seems fairly straightforward, in politics, in life and in business. We all make voluntary agreements with friends, family and even with strangers. We thus feel ethically obliged to stick to those agreements, even if they call upon us to do things we would rather not do. Similarly, corporations make voluntary agreements with their suppliers, employees, customers and other stakeholders, which confer rights and obligations on all sides. However, where social contract theory offers something a little special to this topic of voluntarism is in the idea that the voluntary agreements we make may be *tacit* ones.

The word 'tacit' is generally used in contrast to the term 'explicit'. According to the *Oxford English Dictionary*, 'explicit' means 'stated clearly and precisely'. So an explicit agreement would be an agreement that has been clearly and precisely stated. Clearly, the voluntary agreement that social contract theory refers to is not of this type; it is not clearly and precisely stated. When people agree to participate in society in order to enjoy the benefits of citizenship and to put up with the associated drawbacks, they do not usually do so explicitly. It is more accurate to describe citizenship agreements as *tacit*, which means that they are, as defined by the *Oxford English Dictionary*, 'understood or implied without being stated'. According to social contract theory, by participating in society we make a tacit agreement to conform to the laws and conventions of that society. As John Locke describes this state of affairs, 'every Man, that hath any Possession, or Enjoyment, of any part of the Dominions of any Government, doth thereby give his *tacit Consent*, and is as far forth obliged to Obedience to the Laws of that Government, during such Enjoyment' (Locke, 1988/1690: 348/119).

Explicit and tacit agreements are both likely to feature in business relationships. Consider, again, the supply agreement that our farmer makes with a supermarket. A number of aspects of that agreement are likely to be explicit. For instance, the price of the milk, the terms of payment and the delivery schedule will, in all probability, be clearly and precisely stated. These explicit conditions may even be written down in a legally binding contract. It is worth noting, however, that an agreement does not have to be part of a legally binding contract in order to be explicit, nor must it necessarily be written down: it is quite feasible for the terms of an agreement to be verbally stated in a clear and precise manner without them being written down on a piece of paper.

In addition to these explicit agreements, though, there may also be aspects of a supply agreement that are tacit. For instance, both the farmer and the supermarket buyer, in entering into the supply relationship, will probably expect the other to treat them with a certain amount of courtesy and respect. And, conversely, they will be aware that the other expects courtesy and respect from them. In entering into the relationship they therefore voluntarily agree to treat one another with courtesy and respect, even if this commitment is not clearly and precisely stated. In other words, their agreement to be courteous and respectful to one another is a tacit agreement.

Theory in Practice

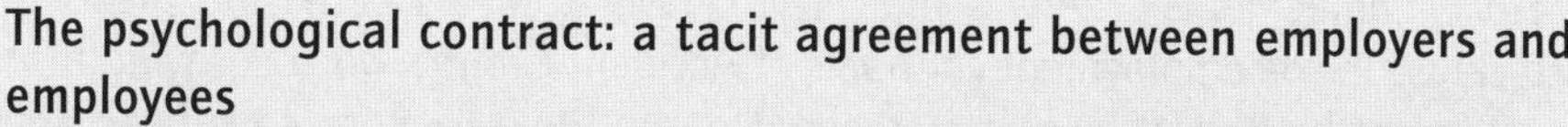

The psychological contract: a tacit agreement between employers and employees

In many countries, employees are legally entitled to a contract of employment. The contract of employment usually provides a statement of a range of obligations and rights on the part of the employer and the employee. For instance, it will probably say how much the employee is to be paid, what hours they are expected to work, and what duties are required of them. It may also say something about standards of conduct and dress. And it will probably contain some information about disciplinary procedures and notice period. All these things will be clearly and precisely stated. In other words, they will be *explicit*.

In addition to these explicit terms, though, employers and employees tend to have expectations of one another that are not stated clearly and precisely. Within contemporary human resource management theory, the term *psychological contract* has been adopted to describe such expectations (Guest and Conway, 2002; Conway and Briner, 2005). The psychological contract is likely to shape employees' and employers' understanding of what is fair in matters such as task allocation, consideration for promotion, and the provision of development opportunities. It may include expectations of job security on the part of employees as well as expectations of employee loyalty on the part of employers. It will probably include, more generally, a mutual understanding of what is an appropriate way for employees and employers to behave towards one another. It may be that none of these things appear in the contract of employment. Furthermore, they may not even be stated verbally at any time. They are therefore *tacit* rather than explicit. Despite their tacit nature, though, they have an important bearing on people's notions of what is ethical and what is unethical as far as the treatment of employees is concerned.

(Continued)

(Continued)

In 2003, 2,400 employees of the UK's largest personal injury claims firm, Accident Group, lost their jobs when the company was put into liquidation by its parent company, Amulet Group. Employees were understandably disappointed to lose their jobs. However, the feature of this episode that surprised many of them the most was that they were informed of their redundancy by text message. According to a BBC report (BBC, 2003), staff with company mobile phones first received a message telling them to 'check your e-mail for salary news', before being told later by text that 'unfortunately salary is not paid'.

Informing employees by text that they are to lose their jobs did not contravene any *explicit* agreements. There is unlikely to have been a clearly and precisely stated clause in the employment contracts of Accident Group's workers saying that they could not be sacked by text message. Nor are there likely to have been any explicit verbal commitments to that effect. Nevertheless, many employees considered this an inappropriate way of telling people they are to lose their jobs. Their feelings were summed up by one former Accident Group employee, who observed: 'I am absolutely disgusted by the whole thing ... I have worked so hard for this company and all they could manage to do was send me an impersonal text message to say I no longer had a job and "unfortunately my wage had not been paid"!' (cited in BBC, 2003).

In this instance, Accident Group seems to have contravened a *tacit* expectation on the part of its employees that the company will treat them in a respectful and considerate manner. This expectation seems to have formed part of their *psychological contract*. And sacking them by text does not seem consistent with this tacitly agreed respect and consideration.

Questions

1 If the company that you worked for had to make you redundant, how would you expect them to inform you?

2 Most employees have a tacit expectation that their employer treats them in a respectful and considerate manner. Apart from the issue discussed here, can you think of other concrete forms that respectful and considerate treatment might take?

3 Can you think of any tacit obligations that employees might have towards their employer and their work colleagues, which may not be stated clearly and precisely?

A hypothetical construction

So, social contract theory draws attention to the voluntary, tacit nature of many of the agreements that we make in business. But it also highlights a further important feature of such agreements. This is that they need not necessarily be thought of as *actual* events. Although the notion of a social contract conjures up images of people getting together at some historical moment, many centuries ago, and making a formal agreement to pass from the state of nature into society, it is unlikely that theorists such as Hobbes, Locke and Rousseau had such a meeting in mind. Indeed, even if such an event had taken place in the dim and distant past, there is no reason why members of today's society should feel ethically bound by its terms: contemporary citizens may have an obligation to respect the terms of voluntary agreements that they have made, but there is no reason why they should honour contracts made by their distant forebears.

Rather than an actual, historical event, then, the social contract is best thought of, in the words of Jeremy Waldron, as a *hypothetical construction*; that is, as a device

> that generates the basis of a normative standard for testing laws and social arrangements. We do not ask whether the arrangements were in fact agreed to; we ask instead whether they *could have been agreed* by people working out the basis of a life together under conditions of initial freedom and equality. (Waldron, 1994: 51)

According to social contract theory, then, citizenship relationships and the ethical obligations associated with them should not be thought of as deriving from an actual, historical agreement. Instead, they should be thought of *as if* some form of voluntary agreement had been made, even though such an agreement has never actually been made. Social contract theorists take the view that by remaining in society, and by enjoying its benefits, we act *as if* we have agreed to a social contract.

If we take social contract theory out of its political context and apply it to a business relationship, the notion of a hypothetical construction can still be applied. It suggests that the legitimacy of the rights and obligations associated with a business relationship derives from people's participation in that relationship. By participating in, and by enjoying the benefits of a particular business relationship, we signal assent to a hypothetical agreement to make the associated sacrifices. That is, we act *as if* we have made an *actual* agreement to do so, even though no such agreement has ever actually been made.

Social contract theory: some insights for business ethics

To sum up the discussion so far, social contract theory offers several useful insights to business ethics. For one thing, it highlights the ethical significance of voluntary agreements that are made in business contexts. The notion of *voluntarism* draws attention to the ethical force that our voluntary agreement to participate in a business relationship gives to the obligations and rights associated with that relationship. In particular, it emphasizes our obligation to do things that we may not want to do: if we voluntarily enter into a relationship that has benefits and burdens, then we are ethically obliged to accept the burdens as well as the benefits.

Social contract theory also highlights the possibility that aspects of the voluntary business agreements that we make may be *tacit*. Nevertheless, tacit agreements do not necessarily carry less ethical rigour than explicit ones. So, in identifying ethical rights and obligations that shape business relationships, we should look beyond agreements that are stated clearly and precisely; we should also consider agreements that are understood or implied without being stated.

Furthermore, social contract theory encourages us to think about *hypothetical* agreements as well as actual ones. In order for us to be ethically bound by certain conventions we need not necessarily have made an actual agreement to respect those conventions; hypothetical agreement may suffice. By participating in a relationship, even one that did not originate in a specific, actual agreement, we could be thought of as having given our voluntary assent to respect its conventions.

Social contract theory and the relationship between business and society

In drawing attention to the importance of *voluntary*, *tacit*, *hypothetical* agreements, social contract theory has some important things to say about corporate relationships with specific stakeholders such as employees, suppliers, managers, customers, shareholders and suchlike. In other words, the insights that it provides can be applied in a *micro* context, helping us to evaluate the conduct of individuals within business environments. However, social contract theory also helps us to think about business ethics on a *macro* scale. That is, it helps us to consider the broader relationship between business and society.

The benefits that society offers to business

In order to elaborate these insights, it helps to reflect on the advantages and disadvantages that society offers to business. Rather than comparing the respective merits of the state of nature and society for individuals, consider instead what a state of nature might mean for business. In this respect, it is instructive to refer to Thomas Hobbes for, in highlighting some benefits that society offers to individual citizens, Hobbes made allusions that are also relevant to business. Hobbes describes the state of nature as follows:

> In such condition there is no place for industry, because the fruit thereof is uncertain, and consequently, no culture of the earth, no navigation, nor use of commodities that may be imported by sea, no commodious building, no instruments of moving and removing such things as require much force, no knowledge of the face of the earth, no account of time, no arts, no letters, no society, and which is worst of all, continual fear and danger of violent death. (Hobbes, 1994/1651: 76/x111, 9)

One point that Hobbes is making here is that it would be very hard to conduct business without the security, resources and facilities that society provides. Consider a few examples. Business uses society's transport and communication infrastructure to move its products around and to sell them. Businesses employ qualified, skilled people, whose education, for the most part, has been provided by society. Businesses draw on accumulated technical and scientific knowledge that has been developed over many generations by society. Business also relies on law-enforcement agencies to ensure security of its property and to make sure people honour the contracts that are essential to its investments. All this is provided by society, at public cost.

Pause for Reflection

Hobbes, Locke and Rousseau each emphasized different benefits that society offers to its citizens. Hobbes focused on personal security, Locke highlighted the protection of property, and Rousseau stressed the accumulation and development of knowledge. Can you think of specific ways in which society provides each of these benefits to businesses?

The sacrifice that business makes in order to enjoy those benefits

Of course, all these benefits provided by society have to be paid for somehow. The usual way of paying for these resources, services and facilities is via taxation. Individual citizens pay tax, usually on their wages (income tax) and very often on the purchases they make (value added tax). But, importantly, businesses are also expected to make a contribution. This contribution usually takes the form of corporation tax. The rationale behind corporation tax is that businesses use the facilities and resources provided by society to make a profit; therefore businesses should make a contribution to the cost of those resources and facilities. The usual way of arranging those contributions is for companies to pay a fixed proportion of their yearly profit in tax.

A voluntary, tacit, hypothetical agreement between business and society

The relationship between business and society might be conceptualized, then, in terms of a social contract. Business makes a *voluntary* agreement to accept the benefits offered by society; that is, to make use of resources and facilities such as those referred to above, without which it would not be able to exist. And it does so on the *tacit* understanding that it makes the associated sacrifices, of which the most obvious is regular payment of corporation tax to help cover the costs of these resources and facilities. Corporations may not make an actual, historical agreement to do this. Therefore, the agreement between business and society is best described as a *hypothetical construction*. To put this in more practical terms, by trading within a particular country, a corporation *voluntarily* gives its *tacit* consent to a *hypothetical* agreement to use the services provided by that country on the condition that it pays something towards the cost of those services.

Theory in Practice

Starbucks wakes up and smells the coffee

In 2012 and 2013, the British media carried a number of articles about large, global corporations such as Google, Amazon, Vodafone and Starbucks, which trade extensively in the UK but which pay relatively little corporation tax (for example, BBC, 2012d; Murphy, 2012; Street-Porter, 2012; *The Economist*, 2012). These articles did not suggest that companies were breaking the law, for they seemed to be paying taxes in line with their reported UK profits. However, the media articles suggested that the companies may have been presenting their accounts in a way that minimizes their tax liability in the UK.

This is not an uncommon practice. Indeed, many large, complex businesses use clever accounting methods to ensure that their accounts show very low profits in the UK, despite the magnitude of their UK operations. For an explanation of how companies are able to do this, view the *Money Week* video by Tim Bennett, entitled 'Why does Starbucks pay so little tax?', at: www.moneyweek.com/investment-advice/how-to-invest/video-tutorials/why-does-starbucks-pay-so-litle-tax-61302.

These revelations about corporate tax avoidance evoked a great deal of public anger. Even the British Prime Minister, David Cameron, who is not noted for criticizing corporations, attacked this practice when speaking to the World Economic

Forum in Davos. In what might be interpreted as a direct criticism of Starbucks, Cameron suggested that multinational corporations who dodge their tax liabilities in this way needed to 'wake up and smell the coffee' (cited by Chu, 2013). But Cameron was not only criticizing tax avoidance in the UK. He was also speaking of the way that multinational corporations avoid tax liabilities in developing nations, thus minimizing their contribution to the development of much-needed infrastructures in these countries.

Questions

1 Drawing on the notions of *voluntarism*, *tacit agreements* and *hypothetical constructions*, can you explain why it might be unethical for corporations to use complex accounting practices to minimize tax liabilities, even though these accounting practices are legal?
2 In most countries, the law provides an explicit statement of corporate responsibilities in that particular country. However, in some developing nations, corporate responsibilities may not be so explicitly enshrined in law. Do you think corporations should only honour responsibilities that are enshrined in law, or should it also consider tacit responsibilities that relate to the countries they are trading in?

Do bad people make businesses bad, or do bad businesses make people bad?

This section will draw on social contract theory to explore the relationship between businesspeople, business culture and business ethics. In particular, it will consider whether the prime responsibility for unethical business conduct lies with 'bad' people, or whether we should also look for explanations in the culture that prevails within a particular company. This discussion will proceed in three stages. It will begin by outlining two contrasting ways of thinking about the state of nature and society: those offered by Thomas Hobbes and Jean-Jacques Rousseau. Then, in the second stage, these contrasting perspectives will be used to develop contrasting ways of thinking about the relationship between human nature and social organization. The third and final stage will use these contrasting perspectives on human nature and social organization to outline two rather different ways of thinking about unethical business conduct: a *person-focused* approach and a *culture-focused* approach. An overview of these three stages is offered in Figure 4.1.

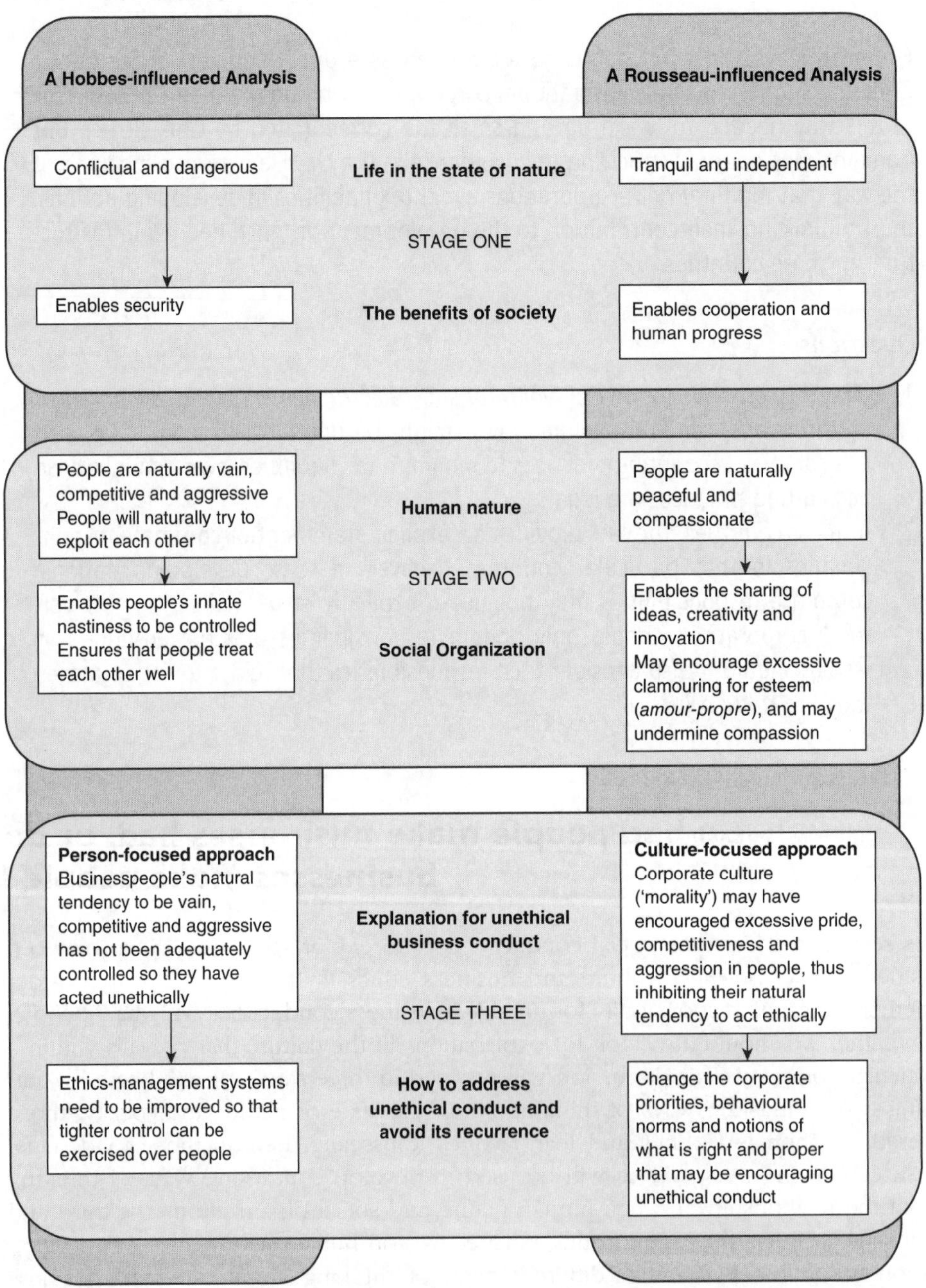

Figure 4.1 Contrasting analyses of unethical business conduct, why it happens, and how to avoid it

Stage One: Hobbes and Rousseau: contrasting perspectives on the state of nature and society

As pointed out earlier in this chapter, Thomas Hobbes and Jean-Jacques Rousseau had very different ideas about the benefits of society. They also had different views concerning the role that government should play in relation to society. These contrasting ideas were based on very different understandings about what life would be like in a state of nature.

Hobbes's account of the state of nature and society

As far as Thomas Hobbes was concerned, the state of nature would necessarily be a highly quarrelsome environment. In the absence of regulatory organizational structures, Hobbes did not envisage people getting on quietly with their own lives. Rather, he believed that a state of perpetual war of 'every man against every man' (Hobbes, 1994/1651: 76/xiii, 8) would prevail. People would be driven by unwholesome sentiments such as pride, partiality, acquisitiveness, revenge, competitiveness and a quest for glory. Even those who were not predisposed to aggression would find it necessary to engage in what has been referred to as 'anticipatory violence' (Kavka, 1999/1983: 18). That is, they would assume that all other people bore aggressive intent towards them, so they would be compelled to attack others in order to avoid being, themselves, the victims of predatory attack. All people would thus be drawn into an endless spiral of hostility as each sought to 'master the persons of all men he can, so long till he see no other power great enough to endanger him' (Hobbes, 1994/1651: 75/xiii, 4). The result, as Hobbes saw it, is that life would be 'solitary, poor, nasty, brutish and short' (1994/1651: 76/xiii, 9).

For Hobbes, then, the decision to opt for society over the state of nature is not a hard one to make. The state of nature that he had in mind was so awful that any form of society would be preferable to it. Furthermore, given people's innate predisposition to self-serving, acquisitive aggression, Hobbes suggested that society needs to be run along very strict lines. He believed that absolute authority should be placed in the hands of an all-powerful sovereign, since this was the only way to avoid chaotic, mutually destructive anarchy. As he described it:

> The only way to erect such a common power as may be able to defend [citizens] from the invasion of foreigners and the injuries of one another … is to confer all their power and strength upon one man, or upon one assembly or men, that may reduce all their wills, by plurality of voices, unto one will … as if every man should say to every man *I authorise and give up my right of governing myself to this man, or to this assembly or men, on this condition, that thou give up thy right to him, and authorise all his actions in like manner.* (Hobbes, 1994/1651: 109/xvii, 13)

Rousseau's account of the state of nature and society

Summarizing Jean-Jacques Rousseau's ideas about the state of nature and society is not quite as straightforward as summarizing those of Hobbes. This is partly because Rousseau's account was not as unequivocal as Hobbes's; partly because Rousseau did not always present his ideas in a systematic fashion; and partly because he offered rather different views at different times (Bertram, 2004). Nevertheless, it is clear that the state of nature Rousseau had in mind was very different to that envisioned by Hobbes. Whereas Hobbes thought that all the worst aspects of humanity would come to the fore in the state of nature, Rousseau believed them to be product of society.

For sure, Rousseau's state of nature would have its drawbacks. As mentioned earlier, Rousseau thought that its major shortcoming would be lack of any innovation, creativity, knowledge accumulation, or human progress. This is mainly because, in the state of nature, people would only be interested in meeting their own, immediate needs. Since their projects would 'hardly extend to the close of day' (1993/1755: 62), Rousseau thought it unlikely that they would share ideas or engage in the forward planning necessary for technical innovation and intellectual development.

Nevertheless, Rousseau did not envisage life in the state of nature being disrupted by the anti-social passions described by Hobbes. Indeed, outside of society, Rousseau believed humans to be peaceable creatures, who are 'strangers to vanity, deference, esteem, and contempt'; who do not have 'the least idea of "mine" and "thine"'; and who would look 'upon every violence to which they were subjected, rather as an injury that might easily be repaired than as a crime that ought to be punished' (Rousseau, 1993/1755: 76). Although the inhabitants of Rousseau's state of nature would live solitary, independent lives, he believed that their existence would be tranquil and secure. It would be an environment 'in which all things proceed in a uniform manner, and the face of the earth is not subject to those sudden and continual changes which arise from the passions and caprices of bodies of men living together' (1993/1755: 54).

In contrast to the state of nature, Rousseau believed that society has the potential to facilitate innovation, creativity, the accumulation of knowledge, and human progress. However, he also believed that society has the potential to bring out the darker side in people. Indeed, whereas Hobbes believed that the regulatory structures of society were necessary to control people's innate vices and to ensure a peaceable existence, Rousseau thought that society could actually disrupt the peace that would be found in the state of nature. For Rousseau it is not human nature that makes people competitive, vain, aggressive, and acquisitive; it is society. Three particular aspects of Rousseau's account set his ideas apart from those of Hobbes and give some indication why he thought certain types of social structure liable to corrupt people's innate placidity: the first aspect is Rousseau's discussion of the notion of *amour-propre*; the second relates to the way that he speaks about *compassion*; and the third involves his usage of the term *morality*.

Amour-propre

Thomas Hobbes observed that 'men are continually in competition for honour and dignity' (1994/1651: 108/xvii, 7). He considered this to be an unavoidable aspect of the human condition, since pride and vanity are elemental features of human nature. Even in the state of nature, Hobbes believed that people would clamour for the esteem of others. Rousseau, on the other hand, believed such traits to be a product of society. Rousseau's account of *amour-propre* is important in this context. There is not an English word that expresses exactly what Rousseau meant by *amour-propre,* but he used the term generally to describe people's desire to be well thought of by other people.

In the solitary, autonomous existence that would prevail in the state of nature, Rousseau suggested that people would not be motivated by *amour-propre*, for they would have little need for the regard of others:

> in the true state of nature, *amour-propre* did not exist; for as each man regarded himself as the only observer of his actions, the only being in the universe who took any interest in him, and the sole judge of his deserts, no feeling arising from comparisons he could not be led to make could take root in his soul. (Rousseau, 1993/1755: 73fn)

For Rousseau, *amour-propre* only emerges as a human characteristic because of the interdependency that develops in society. Since, in society, the fulfilment of our own aspirations often demands the support of other people, we come to value the esteem of others: people would not lend their support to our agendas if they did not think well of us; therefore, we want to be well thought of. But although a certain amount of *amour-propre* is an inevitable feature of society, Rousseau observed that it can get out of hand. That is, in certain circumstances, society may descend into a highly competitive jostling for status in which every person tries to elevate themselves above others in the public esteem. As Rousseau saw it, then, far from being an essential feature of human nature, *amour-propre* is 'a purely relative and factious feeling, which arises in the state of society, leads each individual to make more of himself than of any other, [and] causes all the mutual damage men inflict one on another' (1993/1755: 73fn).

Video Activity 4.2

The following video, 'Ben Affleck's "Boiler Room" Speech', shows a scene from the film *Boiler Room.*

www.youtube.com/watch?v=w4Pu_JuPILw

(Continued)

(Continued)

Questions

1 In this scene, the main character speaks of the wealth that he has already accrued, which his audience can also achieve if they join his firm. However, his speech seems to appeal to more than a simple desire for money. How might his speech be interpreted as an appeal to the *amour-propre* of the prospective traders in the room?

2 In what ways does the main character seek to establish his own *amour-propre* in this scene; in other words, what does he do to make sure that the others in the room think well of him? Why do you think he does this?

3 If people in business behave like this character, do you think this is because they are naturally inclined to do so? Or is this type of behaviour encouraged by specific circumstances such as the people we mix with and the types of company we work for?

Compassion

Rousseau also expressed concern that certain features of society might discourage people from behaving compassionately towards one another. He thought that compassion comes naturally to humans, believing it to be a 'pure emotion of nature, prior to all kinds of reflection' (Rousseau, 1993/1755: 74). He regarded it as an automatic response that is evoked when we see someone in distress; 'an innate repugnance at seeing a fellow-creature suffer' (1993/1755: 73). As such, compassion is something that would be present in the state of nature, for even in their solitary, independent lives, people who lived in the state of nature would sometimes come across others in difficulty.

Rousseau also believed compassion to be a very important human sentiment. For one thing, he saw it as the basis for many intuitively ethical human traits: 'what is generosity, clemency, or humanity but compassion applied to the weak, to the guilty, or to mankind in general? Even benevolence and friendship are, if we judge rightly, only the effects of compassion' (Rousseau, 1993/1755: 75). Moreover, Rousseau considered compassion to be important for the preservation of the human race, since it restrains us from pursuing our own self-interest at the expense of others. Thus, 'by moderating the activity of love of self in each individual, [compassion] contributes to the preservation of the whole species' (1993/1755: 75–6).

However, despite the prevalence of compassion as a natural human response, despite its importance as a prompt to intuitively ethical action, and despite its importance to the preservation of the human race, Rousseau believed that compassion can get suppressed by society. In short, certain types of social structures and conventions can inhibit people's innate predisposition to treat one another compassionately.

'Morality'

In his 'Discourse on the origin of equality', Rousseau makes a seemingly contradictory statement when he refers to 'the force of natural compassion, which the greatest depravity of morals has as yet hardly been able to destroy!' (1993/1755: 74). Here, Rousseau seems to be saying that compassion, which he describes elsewhere as the root of intuitively ethical action, can be destroyed by morality. How can this be? How could it be that morals can destroy the basis of ethics?

In order to unravel this apparent paradox, it helps to understand just what Rousseau meant by 'morals' in this context, for when he spoke of morals and morality he was using these words rather differently from the way that we often use them today. It is common nowadays to use the word morality in the same way as we use the word ethics. That is, when we talk of somebody being moral, we mean that they are ethical; when we speak of morality and morals, we speak of ethics. However, this is not the way that Rousseau used the term. When Rousseau spoke about morality, he was speaking of the values that prevailed within a particular society. And when the term is used in this way, it may be that a set of morals, or a morality, is considered by people outside that society to be ethical. However, it is also possible for a particular morality to be seen as unethical by people outside the society within which it prevails.

Consider the example of the 'morals' (in Rousseau's sense) of Nazi Germany. During the 1930s and 1940s, the Nazi leaders of Germany were committed to a certain set of values. This included a belief in the innate superiority of certain racial characteristics, which they used to justify the extermination of people who did not conform to their racial ideal. Now, few people outside of extreme fascist groups would consider Nazi values to be ethical, so we would find it curious to refer to them as a morality. Nevertheless, this is how Rousseau would have referred to them. He would undoubtedly have been as appalled as we are by the nature of Nazi values, but he would nevertheless have referred to them as a set of 'morals'; albeit an unethical set.

What Rousseau is claiming in his seemingly paradoxical suggestion that 'morals' destroy compassion, then, is that the particular types of values that prevail in particular types of society may inhibit compassion. It is easy to see how this was so in Nazi Germany: the 'morals' of Hitler and his cronies certainly seemed to have undermined their compassion. Rousseau believed that aspects of the morals that prevailed in eighteenth-century Europe also undermined compassion. And since compassion provides a basis for ethical conduct, 'morals', when the term is used in this way, can undermine ethics. In short, Rousseau is drawing attention to the fact that the values that prevail in a specific social context may inhibit people from acting ethically and may, instead, encourage them to act unethically.

Video Activity 4.3

When Enron went bust in 2001, it left billions of dollars of unpaid debts, its shareholders lost their investment, its 21,000 employees lost their jobs and many also lost their pensions. The following video discusses the activities and eventual collapse of Enron.

www.youtube.com/watch?v=Mi2O1bH8pvw

Questions

1 If Jean-Jacques Rousseau watched this video, how might he remark on the 'morality' that prevailed at Enron? What would you say is the overriding principle of that 'morality'?
2 Geoffrey Skilling, the former CEO of Enron, resigned shortly before its collapse, reassuring shareholders that all was well with the company whilst selling millions of dollars' worth of his own shares. Skilling seems to have shown little compassion for those who lost their investments, jobs and pensions as a consequence of his duplicity. How might Enron's 'morality' have inhibited compassion amongst Skilling and his colleagues?
3 Would you describe the 'morality' that prevailed at Enron as an ethical one?

Stage Two: Contrasting ways of thinking about human nature and social organization

In Hobbes's and Rousseau's accounts, then, we have two very different views about human nature and the role that social organization can play in relation to it. On the one hand, Hobbes's pessimistic outlook on human nature depicts humans as inherently competitive, aggressive, vengeful and proud. It proposes that they are naturally inclined to put themselves first, to seek status and glory, and to thrive on the misfortunes of others. According to Hobbes's analysis, if people find themselves in a position of power over other people, they will probably try to exploit that situation to their own advantage. On this understanding of human nature, the role of social organization is to control the innate viciousness in people. If people are to come together in social groups to enjoy the benefits of social living, they need to be strictly controlled. If such controls are lacking, people will inevitably try to get one over on everybody else.

On the other hand, Rousseau's account offers a more optimistic view of human nature. It suggests that, when people are left to their own devices, they will not necessarily try to injure or dominate one another. Indeed, by highlighting people's innate compassion, Rousseau points to the possibility of peaceful co-existence. As far as social organization is concerned, Rousseau draws attention to its potential to enable communication, to facilitate the sharing of knowledge, and to encourage creativity. The benefit of social organization, according to Rousseau's analysis, is not that it enables people's innate viciousness to be controlled but that it can accelerate human progress.

Nevertheless, Rousseau also highlights potential challenges presented by social organization. In particular, his analysis suggests that certain types of social organization may have a corrupting influence on people. For a start, social organization may encourage too much *amour-propre*; that is, it has the potential to engender excessive pride, extreme competitiveness, and an overwhelming yearning for honour and status. Moreover, he suggests that the values that prevail within certain forms of social organization may suppress our innate compassion and thus inhibit our capacity for generosity, clemency, humanity, benevolence and friendship. In particular, he draws attention to the way that particular types of 'morality' may challenge universally respected notions of right and wrong, rather than supporting them.

Stage Three: Contrasting explanations of unethical business conduct and how to address it

So far, this section has drawn attention to some differences between Hobbes's and Rousseau's accounts of the state of nature and society. It has also highlighted the contrasting understandings of human nature and social organization that flow from these contrasting accounts of the state of nature and society. I will now move on to a third stage. This involves outlining two distinctive ways of thinking about business ethics, which flow from these contrasting ways of thinking about human nature and social organization. These offer contrasting insights into why unethical business conduct takes place, how it might be avoided, and how it should be addressed when it does occur.

A person-focused approach

A Hobbes-inspired approach might be referred to as a *person-focused* approach. It is person-focused because, when apportioning blame for unethical business conduct, it encourages us to reflect on the part played by unethical individuals and to ask whether those individuals have been adequately controlled. It begins with the presupposition that, if not appropriately controlled, people are likely to behave badly. It suggests that competitiveness, pride, aggression and acquisitiveness are likely to prevail amongst humans unless they are tightly regulated.

This entails that, in order to avoid unethical conduct, businesses need to exercise firm supervision of their people. Companies would therefore be well advised to define strict codes of ethics, which clearly state what type of conduct is acceptable and what is unacceptable. They should also ensure that these codes of ethics are communicated to all employees through briefings and ethics training, so that people know precisely what is expected of them. And if people within a business still behave unethically, this is probably because ethics management procedures have not been sufficiently rigorous. Therefore, to avoid a repeat of unethical conduct, a company needs to step up its ethics management systems.

A culture-focused approach

A contrasting perspective on business ethics, which is indicated by Rousseau's account, is a *culture-focused* approach. This approach is culture focused because it looks for explanations for unethical business conduct not in individuals but in culture. That is, it considers the priorities, the behavioural norms, and the notions of what is right and proper within a company, and it asks whether these may have encouraged people to behave unethically. It suggests that blame for unethical conduct should not be directed entirely at specific individuals. Rather, it proposes that explanations may also be found in the culture within which those people work.

According to a culture-focused approach, in order to address unethical conduct we may need to look beyond tighter regulation of individuals. Specifically, Rousseau's approach would highlight the need to ask how a firm's culture may have encouraged *amour-propre* in its employees. That is, it would enjoin us to consider whether the firm's prevailing *morality* might have fostered excessive pride, extreme competitiveness, and an overwhelming quest for status. And it would ask whether corporate culture, and the morality it encourages, may have inhibited peoples' innate *compassion*.

Of course, to consider the role that culture plays in fostering unethical conduct is not to deflect attention entirely from individual actors. Indeed, it is possible that some individuals will behave improperly no matter what cultural influences they are exposed to. A culture-focused approach does, however, encourage us to look beyond specific individuals who carry out unethical acts. It invites us to look also at the culture within which those individuals work and, insofar as we consider the culpability of individuals, it encourages us to look at those who play a significant role in creating and sustaining that culture. In other words, a culture-focused enquiry into unethical conduct would look beyond those relatively junior employees who are often held responsible for corporate misconduct and focus, instead, on senior employees who set the priorities, the behavioural norms, and the notions of what is right and proper that might have encouraged those acts.

The following *Theory in Practice* section offers the opportunity to apply these contrasting person-focused and culture-focused approaches to a specific instance of unethical conduct, and to consider some specific insights that each permits.

Theory in Practice

Phone tapping at News International: bad businesspeople or bad business culture?

The *News of the World* was closed down by its owners in July of 2011, thus ending 168 years of uninterrupted publication during which it had become one of the UK's most popular Sunday newspapers.

The story leading to the *News of the World's* closure began several years earlier. In 2007, the paper's royal affairs editor, Clive Goodman, and a private investigator called Glenn Mulcaire were sent to prison for plotting to intercept mobile phone messages. The charges against them related mainly to Mulcaire hacking into the voicemail box of a royal aide in order to provide information for Goodman, which was subsequently used for a story about the British royal family. Mulcaire also pleaded guilty to hacking into the voicemail boxes of various other public figures (BBC, 2007).

On the face of it, justice had been done. It seemed that, in order to get a story, one rogue journalist had conspired with an unscrupulous private investigator; both had broken the law; and both had been suitably punished. However, the matter did not end there. Two years later, a report in *The Guardian* newspaper (Davies, 2009) claimed that News International, the company that owned *News of the World*, had made confidential settlements totalling £1m to other people whose phones had been hacked. The report suggested that

> payments secured secrecy over out-of-court settlements in three cases that threatened to expose evidence of [News International] journalists using private investigators who illegally hacked into the mobile phone messages of numerous public figures as well as gaining unlawful access to confidential personal data, including tax records, social security files, bank statements and itemised phone bills. (Davies, 2009)

During 2009 and 2010 several other well-known people, who suspected that their voicemail had been tapped by investigators working for the *News of the World*, began legal action against News International. Meanwhile, the Metropolitan Police, suspecting that the paper's phone-hacking activities may have been far more widespread than had first appeared, reopened their enquiry. Eventually, more

(Continued)

(Continued)

than 4,000 people, including politicians, actors and sports personalities, were identified as possible victims of the *News of the World's* phone hacking. Furthermore, the investigation has subsequently broadened to include allegations of improper payments by the newspaper to public officials as well as claims of computer hacking (BBC, 2012c).

Despite the magnitude of the phone-hacking affair, it occupied a fairly low profile in the public consciousness before July 2011. Up to then, its alleged targets had been political figures and wealthy celebrities. Although the possibility that the privacy of high-profile, public figures had been invaded by phone hacking, story-hungry journalists caused a great deal of consternation amongst those alleged victims, it aroused no more than mild interest amongst the general public.

However, on 5 July 2011, the phone-hacking scandal took on a very different meaning in the hearts and minds of the British public. On that day, a report in *The Guardian* (Davies and Hill, 2011) alleged that private detectives working for the *News of the World* may have accessed and tampered with messages in the voicemail box of Milly Dowler, a 13-year-old girl who had been murdered in 2002. *The Guardian*'s report alleged that, during the period between Milly Dowler's disappearance and the discovery of her body, her voicemail had been hacked by Glenn Mulcaire on behalf of the *News of the World*. The report claimed that 'As her friends and parents called and left messages imploring Milly to get in touch with them, the *News of the World* was listening and recording their every private word'. *The Guardian*'s report also claimed that, as Milly's voicemail box filled up, messages were deleted to make room for more: 'Apparently thirsty for more information from more voicemails, the paper intervened – and deleted the messages that had been left in the first few days after [Milly's] disappearance'. As a result of this tampering, friends and relatives of the missing girl were led to believe that she might still be alive. Moreover, *The Guardian*'s article claimed that the police search for Milly may have been hampered by this illegal activity and that the deletion of her voicemail messages may have destroyed vital evidence.

Two days later, public anger with the *News of the World* was further inflamed when *The Telegraph* reported (Hughes et al., 2011) that Mulcaire may also have hacked into the voicemail boxes of families of British soldiers who had died in Iraq and Afghanistan, and those belonging to victims of the 7 July 2005 terrorist bombing in London. Moreover, it has subsequently been claimed that the voicemail box of a spokesperson for the family of Madeleine McCann, a British girl who disappeared whilst on holiday in Portugal in 2007, had been accessed illegally (Chandrasekhar et al., 2012).

These accusations were hugely damaging for the *News of the World*. As far as the public was concerned, it was one thing for journalists to invade the privacy of publicity-seeking celebrities in order to get a good story; it was quite another thing to do this to the victims of tragedy. As public anger against the *News of the World* mounted, one company after another cancelled their advertising campaigns with the paper. It seemed that nobody wished to be associated with an organization that was allegedly responsible for such heinous activity. News International's executives believed they had to take drastic action and, on 7 July 2011, James Murdoch, News International's Chairman, announced the paper's closure. The last edition of the *News of the World* appeared on Sunday, 10 July.

Figures at the top of News International and its parent company, News Corporation, were quick to condemn the actions of those *News of the World* journalists and private investigators whom they considered responsible for this illegal phone hacking. Announcing the closure of the paper, James Murdoch, observed that 'The good things the *News of the World* does ... have been sullied by behaviour that was wrong ... if recent allegations are true, it was inhuman and has no place in our Company ... Wrongdoers turned a good newsroom bad' (Politics Home, 2011). Rebekah Brooks, who was then News International's Chief Executive and had been editor of the *News of the World* at the time of the alleged Milly Dowler hacking, was quoted as being 'sickened' by the affair (*The Sun*, 2011). And Rupert Murdoch, father of James and Chairman of News Corporation, later observed that 'we felt ashamed at what had happened and thought we ought to bring it to a close ... We had broken our trust with our readers' (Commons Select Committee, 2011).

There seems little doubt that unethical conduct had occurred at the *News of the World*. But how are we to explain why this unethical conduct took place, and how might the company have avoided it? Moreover, how should News International prevent such unethical behaviour from happening again?

Applying a person-focused approach

A Hobbes-inspired, *person-focused* explanation of the phone-hacking episode would focus on bad behaviour by specific individuals. It would assume that those individuals had been ineffectively controlled by the company's ethics management systems. Moreover, it would seek a solution to such problems in enhanced ethics management. This seemed to be the approach taken by James Murdoch, News International's Chairman. When he appeared before a Parliamentary inquiry into

(Continued)

(Continued)

the affair, Murdoch spoke proudly of News Corporation's code of ethics, which every employee in all of its businesses is expected to follow, and of the ethics training that the company carries out to that end:

> Every employee, every colleague around the world of News Corporation receives the code of conduct. It is a pamphlet that has some detail in it – not too much, so that people read it. With respect to what ethical conduct is required ... It is about ethical conduct, the law, breaking the rules and so on. Everyone who becomes an employee is required to do that. Our legal counsel also internally conducts workshops around the world with staff, from Mumbai to Manchester, around those rules and code of conduct. That is something we try hard to communicate as crisply as we can to everyone in the business. (Commons Select Committee, 2011)

However, these control measures had clearly been insufficient to regulate the activities of certain people. James Murdoch explicitly put the blame for the phone-hacking affair on specific individuals: 'the actions of some reporters and people some years ago have fundamentally tarnished the trust that the *News of the World* had with its readers', and his father Rupert Murdoch added 'I feel that people I trusted ... have let me down. I think that they behaved disgracefully and betrayed the company and me' (Commons Select Committee, 2011).

Furthermore, as far as James Murdoch is concerned, the solution to such errant behaviour by isolated individuals lies in tighter control of ethics:

> These actions do not live up to the standards that our company aspires to everywhere around the world, and it is our determination to put things right, to make sure that these things do not happen again and to be the company that I know we have always aspired to be ... At the end of the day, we have to have a set of standards that we believe in, and we have to have titles and journalists who operate to the highest possible standard. We have to make sure that, when they don't live up to that, they are held to account. That is the focus for us. (Commons Select Committee, 2011)

For James Murdoch, then, it is his company's task to ensure that the people who work within it are aware of the high ethical standards that are expected of them and to make sure that they conform to those standards. When unethical conduct occurs, it is because errant individuals have not been adequately controlled. So, the solution is to step up control procedures to avoid any repetition of such unethical conduct.

Applying culture-focused approach

A Rousseau-influenced, *culture-focused* approach would offer rather different insights to the phone-hacking scandal. This approach would look at ways in which the particular priorities and norms that prevailed at the *News of the World*, and possibly more widely throughout News Corporation, may have encouraged unethical conduct. In this respect it is interesting to consider a description published on the BBC website by Dan Arnold, who had worked as a journalist at the *News of the World* several years prior to the phone hacking scandal. Arnold observed that:

> Those working at the *News of the World* knew they had 'made it' – it was the biggest selling paper in the English-speaking world. Moral qualms? Rarely ... Who would care about the ethics if you exposed a dodgy politician or a paedophile? Certainly not me. You could put the fear of God into an MP just by phoning and saying: 'Hi, I'm a reporter from the *News of the World*'. Kind of 'ignore me at your peril'. Definitely a thrill ... It was absolutely dog-eat-dog in the office ... Suspicion and paranoia were how you survived. And it was so competitive ... There simply wasn't room for all the stories produced to appear in the paper, so only the best ones made it. ... It was a bubble too. Most [journalists] were so focused on their stories and not getting fired that the 'real' world did not exist. We were on call 24 hours a day with our pagers, and often worked evenings and weekends ... The stress was visible on colleagues' faces and often led to huge drinking binges and troubles at home. (Arnold, 2011)

It should be emphasized that the above account is one report by one individual who worked at the *News of the World* some time before the phone-hacking scandal. As such, it does not necessarily offer a valid and reliable overview of the prevailing ethos at the newspaper in its latter years. Nevertheless, Arnold's account does give some idea of the pressures and expectations that those who work in certain journalistic contexts might be subjected to. It also says something about the competitive and aggressive nature of the work environment within which some journalists operate.

It is also instructive to consider the evidence given by Rupert Murdoch, father of James, when he attended a Parliamentary inquiry into the scandal. As Chairman of News Corporation, Rupert Murdoch carries overall responsibility for corporate governance throughout the organization and its constituent businesses, including the *News of the World*. As such, he would be expected to take a keen interest in

(Continued)

(Continued)

any allegations of illegality or unethicality within the business, since ultimate responsibility for such misdemeanours lies with him. Nevertheless, to the astonishment of Members of Parliament who interviewed Murdoch at that Parliamentary inquiry, he seemed remarkably ill-informed about such matters. For instance, Murdoch claimed to have been unaware of the £1m settlement that had been made to buy secrecy from some of the early plaintiffs in the hacking affair. He was also unaware of alleged serious wrongdoing in a related context, as indicated in the following exchange with Tom Watson, one of his interviewers:

Mr Watson:	In 2008, another two years, why did you not dismiss *News of the World* chief reporter Neville Thurlbeck, following the Mosley case?
Rupert Murdoch:	I had never heard of him.
Mr Watson:	Okay. Despite a judge making clear that Thurlbeck set out to blame two of the women involved?
Rupert Murdoch:	I didn't hear that.
Mr Watson:	A judge made it clear Thurlbeck set out to blackmail two of the women involved in the case.
Rupert Murdoch:	That is the first I have heard of that.
Mr Watson:	So none of your UK staff drew your attention to this serious wrongdoing, even though the case received widespread media attention? ... Despite the fact that blackmail can result in a 14-year prison sentence, nobody in your UK company brought this fact to your attention?
Rupert Murdoch:	The blackmail charge, no.
Mr Watson:	Do you think that might be because they knew you would think nothing of it?
Rupert Murdoch:	No. I can't answer. I don't know. (Commons Select Committee, 2011)

Murdoch excused his ignorance of such matters by pointing out that the *News of the World* is one small part of a very large and complex business empire, and that he could not possibly be expected to know about everything that happened in his many subsidiaries. Nevertheless, one matter on which Rupert Murdoch did seem to be extremely well-informed was the commercial performance of his newspapers all over the world. When the topic of each newspaper's sales-and-advertising income and week-by-week profitability was raised with James Murdoch at the inquiry, Rupert Murdoch quickly interjected to point out that: 'I certainly get that [information] from all over the world, every week' (Commons Select Committee, 2011).

Questions

1 To what extent do you think responsibility for the problems at the *News of the World* can be laid at the feet of specific individuals who were inadequately controlled by the paper's ethics management systems?
2 According to Dan Arnold's account of his time at the News of the World, how might *amour-propre* have been taken to unacceptable extremes at the paper? How might this have contributed to the events described here?
3 In what ways might the prevailing '*morals*' (as Rousseau used the word) at the paper have undermined journalists' innate capacity for *compassion*?
4 James Murdoch has blamed unethical conduct at the *News of the World* on relatively junior figures within his company, whom he considers have let down him and the organization. To what extent do you feel that responsibility can also be laid at the feet of more senior people within News Corporation for setting priorities and establishing norms that were inconsistent with the company's explicit code of ethics?

John Rawls's theory of justice

So far this chapter has drawn on classical social contract theory to facilitate reflection on obligations that might prevail in business contexts and to outline contrasting ways of accounting for and responding to unethical business conduct. This third and last section will discuss a more up-to-date contribution to social contract theory, that of the twentieth-century philosopher, John Rawls. Specifically, I will explain some frameworks proposed by Rawls for identifying just distribution of the benefits and burdens associated with social relationships, and how these might be applied in business contexts.

Social contract theory and justice

As the title of his book *A Theory of Justice* suggests, John Rawls (1999/1971) approaches social contract theory from the point of view of justice. When he speaks of *justice* Rawls is not referring to the criminal justice system, which prosecutes people who do not obey the law and which decides how they should be punished. Rather, justice for

Rawls relates more broadly to 'distributive principles for the basic structure of society' and to the 'role of its principles in assigning rights and duties and in defining the appropriate division of social advantages' (1999/1971: 9). Justice, then, as Rawls understands it, is concerned with distribution of the benefits and burdens of society, along with the ethical rights and obligations that are associated with that distribution.

Like the classical social contract theorists already discussed, Rawls's preoccupation was with political, social and economic structures in society at large. Nevertheless, his treatment of distributive justice on a societal scale offers useful insights for considering the ethical legitimacy of distribution in smaller forms of organization, such as businesses. It also offers some interesting ways of considering the relationship between business and society. I will therefore begin this discussion of Rawls's work by sketching in broad outline how he goes about identifying general principles of social and economic justice. I will then offer some suggestions as to how this approach might be applied to evaluate the distribution of benefits and burdens associated with business activity.

Identifying general principles of justice

In common with earlier social contract theorists, Rawls thought that life in society offers benefits but that it also creates burdens. He suggested that society therefore needs *principles of distributive justice* to determine how these benefits and burdens should be shared. Such principles could determine, for instance, how wealth and status should be allocated, along with the amount that each person should contribute to the costs of providing services that everybody uses. Working out such principles of justice is a core focus of Rawls's work. In other words, he sets out to identify a just decision procedure for saying who gets what and who gives what.

In defining principles of justice, Rawls places a lot of importance on three ideals: *freedom*, *rationality* and *equality*. I will describe how he embraces the first two ideals, freedom and rationality, in the concept of the *original position*. I will then outline how he uses the idea of a *veil of ignorance* to address the third ideal, equality. I will go on to explain how the original position and the veil of ignorance are used by Rawls to identify fair principles of justice.

An overview of the relationship between the ideals of freedom, rationality and equality; the notions of the original position and the veil of ignorance; and the principles of justice derived by Rawls from these notions is depicted in Figure 4.2.

The original position: embracing the ideals of freedom and rationality

As far as *freedom* is concerned, Rawls proposes that, ideally, people should be free to choose the principles of justice to which they are subjected. In other words, people

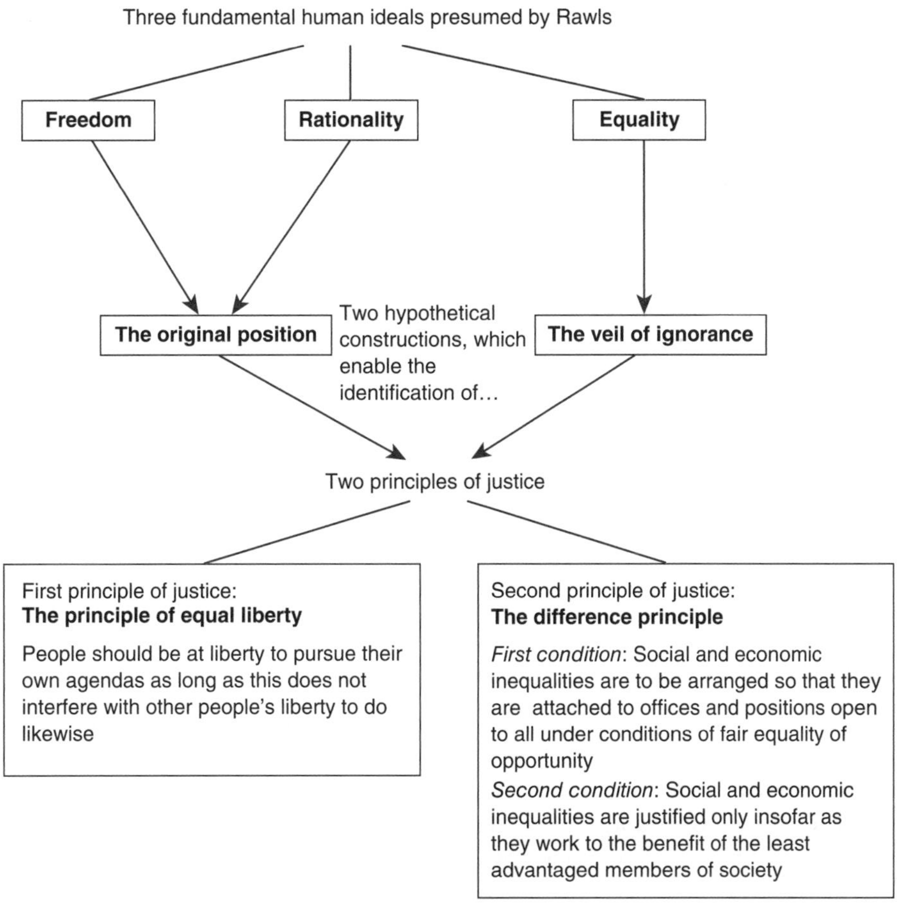

Figure 4.2 John Rawls's theory of justice: working out principles of justice

should have a say in who gets what and who gives what. His recipe for justice thus satisfies the expectation of *voluntarism* to which classical social contract theory appealed. That is, it bases the legitimacy of social arrangements on the free choice of those who are subjected to those arrangements. Of course, people are not able to actually choose the principles of justice to which they are subjected. It is too late for that; society is already up and running so we cannot start anew. Therefore, Rawls settles for the next best thing. Like the earlier contract theorists, he appeals to the notion of *hypothetical construction*; that is, he proposes that since we cannot *actually* choose our principles of justice, we should be subjected to those principles that we *would* choose were we in a position to do so.

Rawls also bases his theory of justice on *rationality*. According to Rawls's notion of rationality, it is rational for people to want to further our own interests. Therefore, rational decision makers, if given the opportunity to choose, will select those principles of justice which promote their own interests. Therefore, he believes that principles of justice should reflect the choices that would be made by rational decision makers who are primarily motivated to further their own interests.

In order to identify principles of justice that we, acting as rational decision makers, would freely choose, Rawls invites us to occupy an imaginary *original position*. Rawls's use of the original position is, in some ways, similar to earlier theorists' usage of the state of nature. That is, he proposes that we should imagine ourselves in some pre-social situation, prior to the establishment of the society of which we are part, in which we are choosing the principles of justice that should govern the distribution of benefits and burdens in that society. By imagining ourselves in this original position, we are able to identify those principles of justice that we would choose were we free to do so. Since the choices that we would make in the original position would, according to Rawls, reflect rational consideration of our best interests, they would also conform to his criterion of rationality. The principles of justice that we would choose in this imaginary original position are thus those that 'free and rational persons concerned to further their own interests would accept' (Rawls, 1999/1971: 10).

Introducing equality: a veil of ignorance

However, there is a major problem with this recipe for identifying principles of justice; a problem of which Rawls was well aware. This is that the principles of justice that would be chosen by 'free and rational persons concerned to further their own interests' would vary considerably. The reason for this inevitable variation is that all people are different. Their socio-economic statuses differ: some are rich; some are poor. They have different capabilities: some are intellectually capable, some less so; some are physically strong, others are less strong; some are talented in certain ways; some in other ways. And their aspirations are also likely to vary considerably: different people enjoy different things; different people have different ideas about what a good life consists of.

As a result of such variations, each of the 'free and rational persons' that Rawls invites to occupy his original position is likely to opt for principles of justice that favour people like them. For instance, rich people of elevated rank would probably opt for principles which favour the better off, whereas less-affluent people would choose a more egalitarian set of principles. Moreover, each person is likely to choose principles which reward those who possess capabilities, skills and talents that they possess. For instance, people whose skills enable them to excel at a particular type of work are likely to propose that such work is rewarded more generously than jobs that demand other sets of skills, which they do not happen to possess. And every person is likely to select principles that help them to achieve things that they want to achieve. In other words, the fact that society is characterized by inequality means that every free and rational person, when placed in an imaginary original position, is likely to choose different principles of justice.

To overcome this problem, Rawls appeals to a third notion, the notion of *equality*. He suggests that the principles of justice that should prevail are those that would be chosen by people who found themselves in an original position of 'equality as defining the fundamental terms of their association' (Rawls, 1999/1971: 10). By this, he means that just principles are those that would be chosen by members of a society if inequality of status, capability and aspiration did not exist. Of course, we cannot eradicate those inequalities that do actually exist in our society. However, Rawls believed that, by pretending we know nothing of those actual inequalities, we can prevent them from influencing our choice of principles of justice. To achieve this he suggests that, when we step into an imaginary original position to choose principles of justice, we leave our status, our capabilities, and our aspirations at the door. We can thus place ourselves in an original position in which:

> no one knows his place in society, his class position or social status, nor does anyone know his fortune in the distribution of natural assets and abilities, his intelligence, strength, and the like. I shall even assume that the parties do not know their conceptions of the good or their special psychological propensities. (Rawls, 1999/1971: 11)

In order to incorporate the condition of equality into the original position, then, Rawls asks us to assume that we are choosing principles of justice from behind a *veil of ignorance*, which shields us from any knowledge about our actual situation. By donning this veil of ignorance, we nullify the inequalities that would otherwise shape our choice. We thus contrive a position of equality.

The original position, the veil of ignorance and business ethics

To sum up Rawls's approach, the principles that he believes should govern the distribution of benefits and burdens in a particular society are those that would be chosen by members of that society if they were in a position to choose and if they made that choice without knowledge of their actual status, capabilities and aspirations. In order to identify such principles, we should place ourselves in an imaginary *original position* in which we wear a *veil of ignorance* concerning our actual place in society, our actual interests and our actual aspirations. According to Rawls, the principles that we choose from this imaginary position will be just ones.

I will discuss the general principles of justice that Rawls thinks would be chosen by 'free and rational persons concerned to further their own interests' shortly. Before doing so, however, I will dwell for a moment on a general way in which the original position and the veil of ignorance might be used to help us think about ethics in relation to business. Quite simply, in order to identify an ethically acceptable outcome – in Rawls's terminology, a 'just' outcome – to an ethically contentious situation, we should imagine ourselves in an original position in which we consider that issue from the perspective of someone who is involved in it. But we should also imagine that we are doing so from behind a veil of ignorance that conceals the precise nature of our involvement. To put this another way, if you wish to evaluate an ethically contentious issue, you should ask yourself the question: how would I wish that issue to be addressed if I were somehow affected by it but if I did not know precisely how I was affected?

Video Activity 4.4

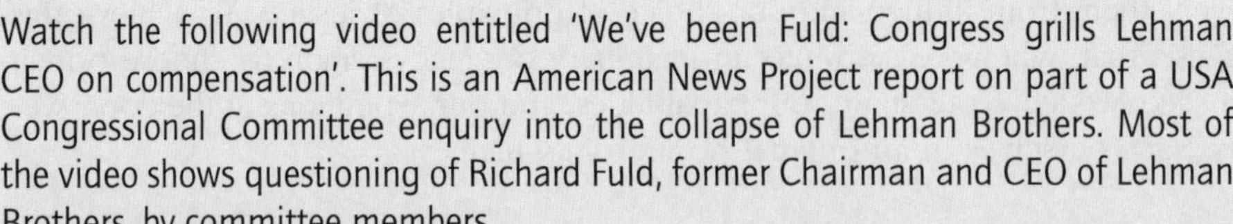

Watch the following video entitled 'We've been Fuld: Congress grills Lehman CEO on compensation'. This is an American News Project report on part of a USA Congressional Committee enquiry into the collapse of Lehman Brothers. Most of the video shows questioning of Richard Fuld, former Chairman and CEO of Lehman Brothers, by committee members.

http://www.youtube.com/watch?v=0GGV3GGHD2Q

During his questioning of Richard Fuld, the committee chairman, Henry Waxman, asks Fuld several times if he thinks the eventual outcome of the Lehman collapse, in which investors and creditors lost everything while Fuld took home over $400 million, was 'fair'. Fuld seems to have difficulty answering this question.

If Fuld had wanted to apply John Rawls's ideas to evaluate the fairness (or the justice) of this distribution of benefits and burdens, he could have placed himself in an *original position* concerning these arrangements and put on a *veil of ignorance* concerning his actual status, capabilities and aspirations. That is, Fuld could have asked himself how he would respond to Waxman's question if he knew that he was to be somehow involved in the collapse of Lehman Brothers but if he did not know if his involvement was to be that of a shareholder (who was to lose his investment), an employee (who was to lose his job), or CEO (who was to walk away from the collapse with over $400 million). He would then ask himself whether he would have chosen this distribution of benefits and burdens.

Question

If Richard Fuld had applied Rawls's theory to evaluate the distribution of benefits and burdens associated with the collapse of Lehman Brothers, do you think he would have answered 'yes' or 'no' to Waxman's question?

Rawls's two principles of justice

An alternative way of applying Rawls's theory of justice to the evaluation of business ethics scenarios is to apply specific principles of justice that he believed people would choose were they placed in a hypothetical original position. Rawls suggested that, if placed behind a veil of ignorance in an imaginary original position, people would be inclined to choose two principles. He referred to the first of these as the *principle of equal liberty*, and he called the second the *difference principle*.

The principle of equal liberty

Rawls thought that any person who reflects, from a hypothetical original position, on the conditions of their involvement in society would wish, first and foremost, for a certain amount of individual liberty. He suggested that we would all want to be able to pursue our own aspirations and develop our own capabilities, so we would accept liberty as a general principle. However, we would also realise that, in certain cases, if other people did the things they wanted to do this could impact negatively on us, preventing us from doing what we wanted to do. Rawls proposes, therefore, that people who choose from their hypothetical original position would place a condition on liberty. This condition is that people should only be able to pursue their own agendas insofar as this does not interfere with other people doing likewise.

Consider this principle in relation to a simple example. I may want to be able to drive my car into the middle of town, park in the most convenient spot, which is on the main road in the town centre, and do my shopping. I would like to be free to do this. However, if I park my car on the main road, this will make it hard for other people to exercise their freedom to get into town to do their shopping. Therefore, I accept a limitation to my freedom. That is, instead of parking on the main road I agree to park in a car park, pay the necessary fee, and walk the short distance to the town centre. By accepting this slight restraint on my freedom to do what I want to do, I ensure that everybody else can do what they want to do. Similarly, all those other people accept a slight limitation to their freedom: they also use the car park rather than leaving their cars by the side of the road in the town centre. In this way we are all at liberty to achieve what we want to achieve, which is to get into town to do our shopping, with a very slight restriction placed on how we do this.

Based on these considerations, Rawls derived his first principle of justice, the *principle of equal liberty*, which he expressed as follows: 'Each person is to have an equal right to the most extensive total system of equal basic liberties compatible with a similar system of liberty for all' (Rawls, 1999/1971: 266). This principle of equal liberty is widely proclaimed in contemporary, Western society – at least in theory – so it clearly has a great deal of intuitive appeal. However, I will not elaborate further on it here because it is Rawls's second principle, which flows from the first one, which offers more fruitful, practical insights as far as business ethics is concerned.

The difference principle

Rawls's second principle relates to inequalities that are likely to emerge in any society that allows people the liberty advocated by his first principle. Such inequalities are inevitable because, as long as people are free to apply their respective capabilities and pursue their aspirations, different members of society will end up in different situations: some will accumulate wealth and possessions, some will not; some will be well respected by their fellows and accorded superior status, some will not; some will be motivated to seek fame and fortune, others will not.

To disallow such differences would be to interfere with the principle of equal liberty. The principle of equal liberty calls for people to be free to follow their separate aspirations and apply their distinctive capabilities as they choose, as long as this does not prevent others from doing likewise. If this leads to differences in status and wealth, so be it. Furthermore, Rawls observed that society in general can benefit from people developing and applying their specific talents to the fulfilment of their respective agendas. It is only by each person using their respective skills to achieve what they want to achieve that communities are able to progress. Therefore, although certain inequalities may result from application of the principle of equal liberty, such application will, in the long term, be to everyone's benefit. However, Rawls also proposed that, were we to find ourselves in an original position and were we choosing from behind a veil of ignorance, we would want to place two conditions on those inequalities. He referred to these two conditions together as the *difference principle.*

The first condition of Rawls's difference principle is that we would only approve of differences insofar as everybody has the opportunity to strive for those positions that are more advantageous. As Rawls put it, 'Social and economic inequalities are to be arranged so that they are … attached to offices and positions open to all under conditions of fair equality of opportunity' (1999/1971: 266).

Of course, in proposing this principle of fair equality of opportunity, Rawls was not suggesting that everyone should be able to take up whatever position in society they like. Not only would this be rather impractical; it is also likely to be in everybody's interest that certain people do certain things. For instance, there may be many students who would like to become President of their Student Union when they have finished their studies. However, not only is it impossible for everyone who wants to do that job to do it; it is also in the interest of all students that the post is open only to those who are well suited to it. Therefore, selection procedures for such roles are justified. But the important point is that such selection procedures should focus on what is best for everybody concerned. That is, our criteria for selecting the President of the Student Union should be designed so that the person who ends up doing the job is the person who will best serve the interests of all those students who are members of the union.

The second condition of Rawls's difference principle supposes that, if placed in a hypothetical original position, we would only consent to differences in people's individual circumstances insofar as those differences serve the interests of the least well-off. In other words, we would not mind some people doing better than others, as long as the situation of those others was also improved as a result of such inequality. As Rawls put it:

> the higher expectations of those better situated are just if and only if they work as part of a scheme which improves the expectations of the least advantaged members of society. The intuitive idea is that the social order is not to establish and secure the more attractive prospects of those better off unless doing so is to the advantage of those less fortunate. (Rawls, 1999/1971: 65)

Consider this condition in relation to our example of the President of the Student Union. That person, on taking up their job, will probably be paid a salary. A situation of inequality between the President and most other students is thus created, in which the President is better off than most of the students she represents. She may therefore be able to own a car, live in a nicer flat, and afford a better smartphone than most. She will also be accorded a certain status, which few other members of the student community can attain. All these advantages would only be considered justified, according to Rawls's difference principle, if the lot of even the least well-off students were enhanced as a consequence.

So, how might the situation of ordinary, impoverished students be improved as a consequence of the President of the Student Union enjoying benefits such as these? One answer to this question is that it is in the interests of all students that the job of President is filled by somebody who is well suited to the role and who is able to represent students' interests in the best possible manner. Now, if the post were not salaried, it is likely that only people who have some form of private financial support would run for election. Similarly, were the person who filled the role of President regularly subjected to ridicule and abuse, some well-qualified people may be disinclined to apply. This would rule out a lot of very good candidates, and the Student Union would not end up with the best possible President. For these reasons, it is sensible to pay a salary to the President and to accord them a certain amount of respect. In this way, people who are well suited to the role, and who can further the interests of even the most impoverished student, are likely to put themselves forward for election.

According to the second condition of Rawls's difference principle then, inequalities in affluence and status between the president and other students are justified on the basis that these inequalities work in the interests of the least well-placed student. However, inequalities which went beyond this would not be considered just.

The difference principle and business

This discussion of Rawls's theory of justice can be summarized as follows: Rawls suggests that *just principles* for sharing the benefits and burdens of society are those principles that we would choose were we ignorant of our actual place in that society. He believed that, if placed in this hypothetical original position, we would permit inequalities insofar as these were subjected to the following conditions: firstly, that selection for more advantageous positions should be subject to fair equality of opportunity; and secondly, that only those inequalities that work to the benefit of the least advantaged would be permitted.

Applying the first condition: fair equality of opportunity

The relevance of the first condition of Rawls's difference principle to business is straightforward. Rawls's proposal that 'social and economic inequalities are to be arranged so that they are … attached to offices and positions open to all under conditions of fair equality of opportunity' offers a resounding endorsement to equal opportunity in corporate contexts. It suggests that participation in business activity, along with distribution of the associated benefits, should be subject to fair and equal selection criteria, which reflect individuals' suitability for such participation. Opportunities to participate should not be hindered by personal characteristics such as socio-economic background, gender, disability, race, ethnicity, religious conviction or sexual orientation.

Video Activity 4.5

The following SkillBoostersTV video, 'Types of Discrimination', highlights various ways in which discrimination might occur in workplaces.
www.youtube.com/watch?v=_TbvuqRMUO4

Questions

1. To what extent do you think each of the scenes shown in the video breaches the *first condition of John Rawls's difference principle* concerning fair equality of opportunity?
2. When a breach of fair equality of opportunity occurs in a workplace, do you think is it always those in charge who should be held responsible, or might junior employees also contribute sometimes to unfair inequality?
3. Do you think those responsible for undermining fair equality of opportunity always do so intentionally, or can unfairness also be a result of unintentional ignorance on the part of those responsible?

Applying the second condition: benefitting least-advantaged groups

The second condition of Rawls's difference principle offers more varied insights to business. While it permits unequal distribution of the benefits and burdens of business activity, this second condition proposes that those inequalities should only be permitted insofar as least-advantaged stakeholders benefit from them. In other words, it is OK for some people to do better than others out of business activity, so long as the situation of those others is also improved as a consequence. Clearly, this would preclude business activity which serves the interests of privileged groups while undermining the interests of less-privileged groups.

This condition can be applied to evaluate business activity on a macro level and on a micro level. *Macro-level* consideration is concerned with distributions between communities on a regional or an international scale. The issue of *environmental justice* is relevant in this respect. Environmental justice is concerned with distribution between communities of the benefits and burdens of economic activity. It is particularly concerned to highlight situations 'in which wealthy communities enjoy benefits of industrialization without shouldering costs, and poor communities shoulder costs without enjoying benefits' (Keller, 2010: 418). Environmental justice commentators draw attention to a growing tendency for transnational corporations to undertake large-scale industrial activity in less-developed nations. Their concern is that communities within those less-developed nations bear heavy environmental and social costs associated with such operations, while the benefits flow primarily to customers, shareholders and senior managers who live far away in wealthy nations. In other words, the Third World is picking up the social and environmental tab so that people in the First World can enjoy a better lifestyle.[1]

But even within nations, distribution of the benefits and burdens of industrial activity often fails to meet the second condition of Rawls's difference principle. In this context, researchers have drawn attention to a tendency for corporations to locate industrial plants and waste-disposal facilities close to less-affluent communities, while their affluent consumers, shareholders and senior managers live in relatively unpolluted, semi-rural tranquillity in leafy suburbs and pleasant, provincial towns (Bullard, 2010/1994; Wenz, 2010/1995). Clearly, international and inter-regional instances of environmental injustice contravene the second condition of Rawls's difference principle, since they increase national and regional inequalities by benefiting affluent communities at the cost of less-affluent communities. Rather than those inequalities being justified on the basis that they uplift the circumstances of the least well-off, then, they only serve to increase socio-economic polarization to the benefit of the wealthiest.

As well as being applied at a macro level of regional and global distribution, Rawls's difference principle can be applied at a *micro level*. That is, it can be used to help us think about the ethicality of distribution in relation to specific business communities or specific individuals within those communities. At this level, a key question we should ask when we witness disproportionate distributions of the benefits and burdens of corporate activity between various stakeholders is the following one: is the lot of the least well-off person being improved as a result of these inequalities?

[1]The topic of environmental justice is discussed in more detail in Chapter 9 of this book.

Theory in Practice

The contentious matter of senior-executive pay

The topic of executive pay has aroused considerable interest in recent years. This is partly because of the vast amounts paid to senior managers and directors in large corporations. For example, the average pay earned by the chief executives of the 100 most valuable companies traded on the London Stock Exchange – that is, FTSE100 companies – in 2012 was £4.2m (Garside, 2012).

But not only do senior executives in big companies earn a lot; their pay rates seem to be going up. Between 2004 and 2008, the total amount awarded to the 10 most highly paid FTSE executives rose from £70m to £170m (Finch and Bowers, 2009) while, between 2000 and 2010, the total amounts paid to the top executives at FTSE100 and FTSE250 companies rose by more than 160 per cent and 118 per cent respectively (Goodley and Wearden, 2010). In 2010 alone, total FTSE100 chief-executive pay rose by 55 per cent (Goodley and Wearden, 2010).

Senior executive pay seems particularly high when compared to other people's wages. For instance, the average earnings of a FTSE100 boss in 2010 were nearly 200 times the average UK wage (Goodley and Weardon, 2010). Moreover, the gap between the wages of senior and junior workers in the biggest companies seems to be getting bigger. Average FTSE100 chief executives' pay was 47 times their employees' average wage in 1998, but that figure had risen to 120 times by 2010. (Groom, 2011). Over a longer timescale, Brian Groom (2011) of the *Financial Times* observes a 30-year global trend towards inequality. For example, Groom points out that pre-tax income of the top one per cent of earners in the USA rose from eight per cent of total national earnings in 1974 to 18 per cent in 2008.

There has been considerable debate about the fairness of senior executives being paid so much. On the one hand, it is argued that a good boss can make a big difference to a firm's commercial performance, so, if a firm needs to pay a lot of money to attract the right person, this is what it must do. Furthermore, since a large part of senior executive pay tends to be made up of bonus payments and share awards, it is often suggested that this is a good way of motivating bosses to do what is best for their shareholders.

On the other hand, it could be argued that paying such huge performance-related bonuses and share awards may motivate bosses to do what is best for their shareholders but it does not necessarily serve the interests of other people. For instance, a Chartered Management Institute survey found that during 2012–13, despite a difficult year in which many junior employees lost their jobs, UK chief executives' earnings rose by nearly 16 per cent (Groom, 2013). Indeed, in some cases top executives are awarded handsome bonuses for hitting performance targets, while the jobs of junior employees are sacrificed in the interests of achieving those targets.

But critics also point out that the link between high senior executive pay and the interests of shareholders may not be as clear as is often claimed. For instance, 2008 saw the onset of the worst global recession in decades, in which FTSE companies lost almost a third of their share value, yet senior executive salaries rose overall by ten per cent (Finch and Bowers, 2009). And in 2010, chief executives at FTSE 100 companies saw their median earnings rise 32 per cent, which was three times as much as the rise in share prices (Groom, 2011).

So, how might we go about assessing the fairness of senior executive remuneration, the huge differentials between senior and junior employees' pay, and comparisons between the rewards of company bosses and other stakeholders?

Applying Rawls's theory of justice to the issue of senior executive pay

John Rawls's theory of justice might assist with ethical evaluation of senior executive pay levels in at least two ways.

One way of applying Rawls's theory is via direct application of the concepts of the *original position* and the *veil of ignorance*. To do this, you might find it helpful to do the following three things:

- Firstly, imagine yourself in an *original position*. That is, imagine that you are to be involved in some way with a particular company. Your impending involvement may be, for example, as a customer, a shareholder, a junior employee, a senior executive, or somebody who lives locally and who therefore experiences the environmental and economic impact of the company's operations.
- Secondly, put on your *veil of ignorance*. That is, although you know you are to be involved with the company, pretend that you do not know the precise nature of your impending involvement. In other words, you do not know if you are to be a customer, a shareholder, a junior employee, a senior executive, or a local resident.
- Now, from this *original position*, shrouded in your *veil of ignorance*, ask yourself whether you would choose for senior executives to be paid so much.

A second way of applying Rawls's insights to this issue would be to apply the *difference principle*. Let us assume, for argument's sake, that the appointment of senior executives meets Rawls's fair equality of opportunity condition (although

(Continued)

(Continued)

many commentators would question this assumption). What you need to do now, then, is apply the second condition: the condition that differences in people's individual circumstances are only deemed fair insofar as those differences serve the interests of the least well-off. This would involve asking whether paying senior executives such high wages serves the interests of a corporation's least-advantaged stakeholders. This is a complex question, the response to which requires you to do the following:

- Firstly, you should identify those least-advantaged stakeholders. They might include junior employees, some suppliers, and members of the local communities who are affected by the operation of a business.
- Secondly, you should ask whether paying senior executives so much money is improving the lot of these stakeholders.

Questions

1 In what ways might paying very high salaries to senior executives further the interests of least-advantaged stakeholders?
2 In what ways might paying very high salaries to senior executives undermine the interests of least-advantaged stakeholders?
3 What do you think could be done to bring senior executive pay more into line with the interests of less-advantaged stakeholders?

Conclusion

Although social contract theory is a branch of political philosophy, it offers some useful insights to business ethics. By emphasizing the ethical significance of *voluntary choice*, social contract theory encourages us to think about ethical rights and obligations that are created when business stakeholders voluntarily enter into relationships with one another. Furthermore, social contract theory highlights the possibility that *tacit agreements* associated with those relationships may carry just as much ethical force as agreements that are clearly and precisely stated. Moreover, the concept of a *hypothetical construction* encourages us to think about ethical rights and obligations that we may take on just by participating in a particular relationship. In order to assess the duties and obligations that prevail in business environments, then, we may need to look beyond explicit, actual agreements that are legally enshrined or which are clearly stated in some other way.

The contrasting accounts of the state of nature and society offered by Thomas Hobbes and Jean-Jacques Rousseau suggest different ways of thinking about the causes and remedies of unethical business conduct. In particular, Rousseau's account, along with the *culture-focused perspective* to which it points, suggests that we may need to look beyond the conduct of individual businesspeople if we are to find an adequate explanation for unethical business conduct. We should also consider the possibility that the culture that prevails within a particular business environment may encourage people to behave as they do. And when we are considering the personal culpability of specific individuals we would do well to look not only at relatively junior workers who actually carry out unethical acts; we should also look to those individuals who are responsible for setting the cultural priorities and norms towards which those people strive.

And finally, John Rawls's theory of justice proposes a model for thinking about business ethics in terms of just distribution of the benefits and burdens associated with corporate activity. In particular, the notions of an *original position*, a *veil of ignorance*, and the *difference principle* provide a framework of egalitarian impartiality for thinking about what just distribution might consist of.

Discussion questions

1. Voluntarism is an important feature of social contract theory. It proposes that, since people have voluntarily agreed to be involved in a relationship, they should respect the rights and obligations associated with it. How relevant do you think voluntarism is to specific business relationships? To suggest that people have voluntarily agreed to something implies that they had a choice. Do all stakeholders who are involved in a relationship with a corporation have a choice whether or not to be thus involved? For instance, do employees always have other employment options open to them? Do suppliers always have alternative outlets for their produce? Do customers always have other sources of supply? If not, can they really be said to have voluntarily agreed to the rights and obligations associated with that relationship?
2. How might Hobbes's and Rousseau's contrasting versions of the relationship between the state of nature and society, along with the person-focused and culture-focused perspectives to which they point, help us to think about the causes of the 2008 banking crisis?
3. How might John Rawls's difference principle assist ethical evaluation of the *Trafigura, Ivory Coast, and Environmental Justice* controversy that is discussed in Chapter 9?

Further study

Nigel Warburton's (2001) book, *Philosophy: The Classics* includes brief, clearly written summaries of the accounts of social contract theory offered in Hobbes's *Leviathan*, Locke's *Two Treatises of Government*, and Rousseau's *The Social Contract*.

You might like to engage directly with the work of Hobbes, Locke and Rousseau. There are many hard and electronic copies of these classical texts available. The following sections are particularly relevant to the theory discussed in this chapter.

Some key aspects of each theorist's account of the social contract are presented in:

- Chapter XVII, entitled 'Of the Causes, Generation, and Definition of a Common-Wealth', of Thomas Hobbes's (1994/1651) *Leviathan*.
- Chapter VIII, 'Of the Beginning of Political Societies' and Chapter IX, 'Of the Ends of Political Society and Government' in the *Second Treatise* of John Locke's (1988/1690) *Two Treatises of Government*.
- Chapter 6, entitled 'The Social Compact', of Jean-Jacques Rousseau's (1993/1755) *The Social Contract*.

Hobbes's and Rousseau's contrasting accounts of life in the state of nature can be found in:

- Part II, Chapter XIII, entitled 'Of the Natural Condition of Mankind, as concerning their Felicity, and Misery', of Hobbes's (1994/1651) *Leviathan*.
- 'The First Part' of Rousseau's (1993/1755) *A Discourse of the Origins of Inequality*.

To read the outline of John Rawls's (1999/1971) description of the original position and the veil of ignorance, see *A Theory of Justice*, Chapter I, sections 3 and 4 on pages 10–19. The difference principle is discussed in Chapter II, sections 13 and 14, on pages 265–78.

Virtue Theory: Virtue, Purpose and Flourishing in Business

5

Chapter objectives

This chapter will:

- explain how being virtuous might help businesspeople and businesses to flourish;
- introduce the doctrine of the virtuous mean and discuss its relevance to business;
- outline the relationship between virtue, human flourishing and community;
- explain how virtue can be linked to purpose;
- explore some conceptions of business purpose and some associated virtues;
- consider how the achievement of excellence in practices delivers internal and external goods, which help people to flourish;
- explain how the prioritization of external goods in business might inhibit the cultivation of virtue, the attainment of excellence, and the achievement of internal goods;
- outline some practical steps that managers can take to encourage virtue in business.

Introduction

When philosophers speak of *virtue theory* they are referring to ideas that are over 2,000 years old. In particular, Western virtue theory is usually associated with the

Ancient Greek philosopher Aristotle and his *Nicomachean Ethics*. Despite its ancient heritage, though, virtue theory is alive and kicking today. A number of contemporary philosophers have revived the work of Aristotle, proposing that virtue theory offers useful insights into many of the ethical conundrums that we face in contemporary life.

Virtue theory differs from the approaches that have been explored so far in this book in that its prime focus is on *character* rather than on actions. The theories introduced in the preceding chapters have offered a range of principles that we can use to evaluate the actions of businesses and businesspeople in terms of their ethicality. Virtue theory, on the other hand, encourages us to think about the type of person we need to be in order to be ethical. It focuses on personal qualities, or *virtues*, that an ethical person needs to have. In the context of business ethics, then, virtue theory helps us to think about what it is for a business or a businessperson to *be* ethical.

Some of the insights offered by virtue theory will be elaborated in this chapter. The chapter will begin by introducing Aristotle's ideas about the relationship between virtue and *human flourishing*. I will explain how flourishing, for Aristotle, involves an appropriate amount of virtue – not too much, not too little – and I will draw out some implications that this has for business. The second part of the chapter will discuss the relationship between virtue and *purpose*. In particular, I will outline contrasting ways of thinking about the purpose of business, exploring how these contrasting approaches might help us to think about business virtue. The chapter will end by discussing the relationship between virtue and *excellence*, along with those goods that the achievement of excellence enables. These ideas will then be used to develop some ideas about what virtuous business management might consist of.

Although the chapter will discuss flourishing, purpose and excellence in different sections, it will become clear as the chapter progresses that there is a great deal of crossover between these themes. Moreover, the unifying theme of *community*, which is central to virtue theory and which has important ramifications for business, will crop up throughout the chapter. So although each of these ideas is presented separately, you will find it helpful to keep their interconnection in mind as you read the chapter.

Human flourishing and the virtuous mean

This first part of the chapter will explore the relationship between virtue and *human flourishing*. It will consider the Ancient Greek view, expressed by Aristotle, that it is not possible to flourish or to be truly fulfilled as a human being without being virtuous. Having considered what this might mean for business, I will introduce Aristotle's doctrine of the *virtuous mean* as a way of thinking about just how virtuous businesspeople and businesses should be in order to flourish in an Aristotelian sense.

Virtue and human flourishing

Aristotle took the view that virtue is a vital ingredient of human flourishing.[1] In other words, he thought that nobody is able to be truly fulfilled as a human being unless they are virtuous. To explain Aristotle's understanding of the relationship between virtue and human flourishing, I will outline two different ways of thinking about relationships; that is, I will explain how the *internal* relationship that he had in mind differs from *external* relationships. I will offer an example of how the relationship between virtue and fulfilment might work in relation to a businessperson and a business. I will also explain how the notion of community provides, for Aristotle, an essential link between virtue and flourishing.

Internal relationships and external relationships

There is an obvious way in which being virtuous might help us to flourish. This is that, if we are virtuous, people are likely to think well of us. And if people think well of us we will, for instance, make friends more easily, get invited to lots of parties, and find it easier to borrow money when we need it. And since all these things seem to be associated with leading a fulfilled life, or flourishing as a human being, there seems to be an obvious relationship between virtue and human flourishing.

We might think of the relationship between being a virtuous business and being a flourishing business in the same way. If a company gets a reputation for being virtuous, customers may be more likely to buy its products, investors may be more likely to buy shares in it, and potential employees may be more willing to work for it. Since all these things help to make businesses profitable, there is a clear link between being an ethical company – or a virtuous company – and being a profitable company. And, as we all know, being profitable will help a business to flourish.

However, this is not quite what Aristotle had in mind when he said that virtue helps us to flourish. To think of virtue and flourishing in this way is to present them as two separate things. Alasdair MacIntyre (1985/1981) describes this as envisaging an 'external' relationship between them. That is, virtue and flourishing are regarded as *external* to one another; they are seen as different things that can be kept apart and thought of

[1]Here, I am following Richard Kraut (2010) and Gerard Hughes (2001) respectively in referring to the Aristotelian term *eudemonia* as 'flourishing' or 'fulfilment'. Aristotle defines *eudemonia* as 'a sort of living and faring well' (2009/circa 323BC: 13/1098b). It has also been described in such terms as 'well-being' (Taylor, 2005: 271); 'doing well' (Irwin, 1999: 333); 'blessedness', 'prosperity', or 'the state of being well and doing well in being well' (MacIntyre, 1985/1981: 148). If you read Aristotle's work, you will probably find *eudemonia* translated as 'happiness'. However, this translation can be misleading because we often associate happiness with pleasure and we often think of it as a short-lived, emotional state. *Eudemonia* meant a lot more to Aristotle than fleeting moments of pleasure.

in isolation from each other. Notably, in this external type of relationship, there may be other ways of achieving those things that are associated with flourishing. For example, there are various ways, other than being virtuous, of getting people to think well of us: being a good guitar player, being good at sport, or buying drinks for all our friends in the pub are just as likely to achieve that end. And in the case of a company, virtue is not the only route to profitability: lying, cheating and swindling might also bring profitability, at least in the short term.

The type of relationship that Aristotle envisaged between virtue and human flourishing was not like this. Rather, he thought of it as an 'internal' relationship (MacIntyre, 1985/1981). For Aristotle, virtue and flourishing are not separate things that can be considered in isolation from one another. As he saw it, virtue is not just one way of achieving human flourishing, which could conceivably be replaced by other ways. Flourishing, for Aristotle, is not something that we achieve *as a result* of being virtuous; rather, it is achieved *through* being virtuous. MacIntyre describes Aristotle's position as follows:

> the exercise of the virtues is not in this sense *a* means to the end of the good for man. For what constitutes the good for man is a complete human life lived at its best, and the exercise of the virtues is a necessary and central part of such a life, not a mere preparatory exercise to secure such a life. We thus cannot characterize the good for man adequately without already having made reference to the virtues. (MacIntyre, 1985/1981: 149)

Another way of putting this is to say that virtue is its own reward. As Aristotle saw it, virtue brings significant benefits to virtuous people, but those benefits are not separate goods that are realized at some point in the future as a result of virtue; they are integral to being virtuous. Being virtuous and the good things that flow from it to a virtuous person cannot be separated. Each is integral to the other.

Video Activity 5.1

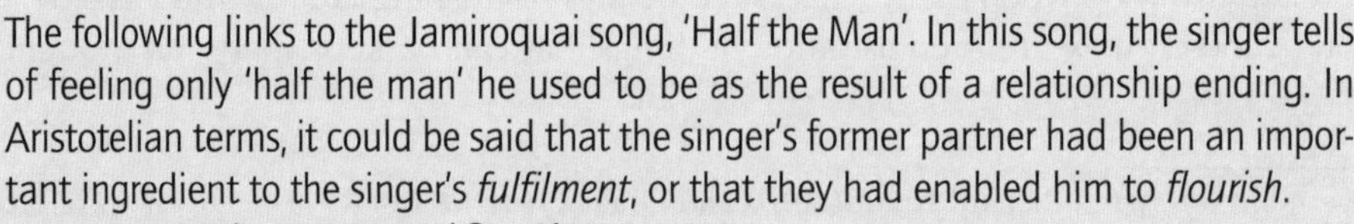

The following links to the Jamiroquai song, 'Half the Man'. In this song, the singer tells of feeling only 'half the man' he used to be as the result of a relationship ending. In Aristotelian terms, it could be said that the singer's former partner had been an important ingredient to the singer's *fulfilment*, or that they had enabled him to *flourish*.

www.youtube.com/watch?v=GkL7cVqIZHU

Questions

1 Do you think that the relationship between the singer's former partner and the singer's own fulfilment is best described as an *external* one or an *internal* one? In other words, does the singer seem to regard the former partner as a

means to the end of his own fulfilment; a means that could easily be replaced by other means? Or does the relationship seem to have been one in which, like the relationship between virtue and fulfilment, the partner was an integral, irreplaceable feature of the singer's fulfilment?

2 Think of a person that you hold dear. This might be a partner, a family member, or a very close friend. Do you consider the relationship between that person and your own flourishing as an external or an internal one? In other words, do you regard that person as a means to your own personal fulfilment, who could be replaced by somebody else? Or is that particular person so integral to your fulfilment that you cannot think of being truly fulfilled without them?

Virtue and a flourishing businessperson

The way in which Aristotle believed virtue to be linked to human flourishing, or human fulfilment, may become clearer if we consider two analogies. For the first analogy, imagine two elderly people, Sarah and Bob, who are approaching the end of their lives and who are well aware that they do not have much longer to live. Suppose that both Sarah and Bob are wealthy. Each has spent most of their life running successful businesses. And each is able to leave a comfortable inheritance to their family. However, the methods that Sarah and Bob have used to achieve business success have been very different. In Sarah's case, she has always been fair and honest in her business dealings. She has treated her employees with respect, she has paid her suppliers on time, and she has never misled her customers. Moreover, she has been considerate towards local residents, and she has always been truthful with her investors. It seems reasonable to describe Sarah as a virtuous businesswoman.

Bob, on the other hand, has chosen a very different route to business success. He has lied and cheated whenever he could get away with it. He has let down his customers when it was in his interests to do so. He has tried to avoid paying his suppliers whenever possible, caring little about how this might affect them. And he has treated his employees as a disposable resource, hiring and firing people with little thought for their personal circumstances. Furthermore, Bob has treated people who live close to his business with disdain. Therefore, although Bob has managed to run a profitable business, not many people would call him a virtuous businessman.

Although it would be inappropriate to call either Sarah or Bob happy, given their impending demise, it might not seem so out of place to refer to them in terms of 'fulfilment', or 'flourishing'. Moreover, it would seem more reasonable to apply such terms to Sarah than to Bob. Of course, it may be that Bob also *feels* fulfilled because of all the money he has made in his life. However, I suspect that most people would find Bob's state of fulfilment harder to identify with than Sarah's. Aristotle, were he acquainted with Sarah and Bob, would certainly reach that conclusion. He would probably say that Sarah had achieved fulfilment, or that her life had flourished, and that her achievement of this state is intimately connected to her virtuous character. But I doubt if he would have said the same of Bob. According to an Aristotelian analysis, then, Sarah's virtue has enabled her to flourish in a way that Bob, with his lack of virtue, has failed to achieve.

Virtue and a flourishing business

For a second analogy, consider the two companies that Sarah and Bob are leaving behind. Of the two, Sarah's seems to be the more virtuous business. It is a company which treats people fairly and which has a mutually supportive and respectful relationship with its stakeholders. Bob's company, on the other hand, treats people in an inconsiderate and disrespectful manner, worrying only about the bottom line. Both Sarah's and Bob's companies have flourished financially. However, were we to take a more comprehensive view of flourishing, we might say that Sarah's company is a more flourishing one than Bob's. Had Aristotle been a twenty-first-century business consultant, advising both Sarah and Bob's management teams, we can be sure that he would have considered the former to be a more flourishing organization.

Virtue, flourishing business and community

One reason why Aristotle would consider Sarah to be more fulfilled than Bob, and why he would consider her company to be a more flourishing company, relates to the connection he made between human flourishing and *community*. Aristotle tended to talk of human fulfilment as a condition that is achieved through social interaction. It is not something that can be attained apart from membership of some form of community. As he put it, 'it is strange … to make the supremely [fulfilled] man a solitary; for no one would choose the whole world on condition of being alone, since man is a … creature … whose nature is to live with others' (2009/circa 323BC: 176/1169b). And by focusing on the connection between community and human fulfilment, Aristotle also drew attention to the need for human virtue to be developed within, and exercised in relation to, a community.

It is important to appreciate, though, the nature of the relationship that Aristotle envisaged between community and human flourishing. We might think of community as important to human flourishing insofar as being part of a community ensures people's safety and helps them to satisfy their physical needs.[2] However, this is not the understanding that comes across in Aristotle's teachings. According to his understanding, it is not *as a result of* being part of a community that we achieve fulfilment; it is *through* being part of community.

[2]This is the way that some classical social contract theorists such as Thomas Hobbes thought of community, as explained in Chapter 4.

Like the relationship between virtue and human flourishing, then, Aristotle understood the relationship between community and flourishing as an *internal* one rather than an *external* one. He would have found the very notion of human flourishing hard to conceive in isolation from the notion of community. According to his understanding, being part of a community does not serve as a means to the end of a fulfilled life; it is the context through and within which a fulfilled life is lived.

Consider Sarah's and Bob's companies in terms of community. It could be said of Sarah's company that it is part of an extended community; a community which embraces groups such as its employees, customers, suppliers, investors and local residents. It identifies itself in relation to that community of stakeholders and it behaves towards its members in a respectful, truthful and considerate manner. You could even say that Sarah defines her company in relation to its community: that is, she would have trouble conceiving of her company without referring to its community of stakeholders. However, it would be hard to say such things of Bob's company. Unlike Sarah, Bob has tried to set his company apart from its community of stakeholders, taking from them what it needs to get by with little thought for communal interaction. Instead of regarding customers, employees, shareholders and suppliers as members of a mutually supportive community, he has treated them as a means to an end; he has used them as tools to bring about the commercial success of his business.

On an Aristotelian analysis, then, Sarah and her company could be said to have behaved virtuously as part of a mutually supportive community of stakeholders, while Bob has viewed his own interests as distinct from those of his stakeholders. For this reason, Sarah would be regarded as a more fulfilled person and her company as a more flourishing company. Her very being, and the being of her company, is embedded in notions of community. Bob, on the other hand, by separating himself from his wider community and by treating stakeholders purely as resources to be exploited, has undermined both his and his company's virtue. And in so doing, he has limited both his and his company's ability to flourish in a comprehensive, Aristotelian sense.

Pause for Reflection

Think of a business which you believe has conducted itself in an unethical manner. Does the importance Aristotle placed on community help to explain your view that that company has been unethical? That is, has the company treated some of its community of stakeholders in a manner that is inconsiderate or lacking in respect?

Do you feel that that company is somehow less fulfilled or less flourishing as a result of its unethical conduct? Imagine that you were an employee of that company. Do you feel that your own virtue and your own fulfilment as a human being would be impaired in some way by your association with the company?

How virtuous should we be in order to flourish?

So far, I have drawn attention to the connection that Aristotle made between being virtuous and human flourishing. I have also explained the emphasis that he placed on community in relation to virtue and human fulfilment. To apply these ideas to a business context would be to suggest that a business cannot truly flourish unless it is a virtuous business. And the way for a business to be virtuous is to understand itself as being embedded in a community that comprises all its stakeholders, and to act in a respectful and considerate manner towards that community.

Now, to suggest that we need to be virtuous in order to be truly fulfilled is not to say that we must live a life of ascetic self-denial. Even Aristotle did not take the possibility of humans displaying 'heroic excellence' too seriously (Urmson, 1980/1973: 158). Equally, businesspeople and businesses do not need to renounce things like profitability, competitiveness and corporate interests in order to flourish in an Aristotelian sense. For one thing, neither people nor companies can flourish in *any* sense unless they attend to the practicalities of self-preservation. In most societies, as well as being virtuous, people must achieve a certain amount of financial security in order to flourish. Equally, a company that wishes to flourish in an Aristotelian way must secure its commercial viability. So how virtuous do we actually need to be in order to be fulfilled? And how virtuous must a business be in order to flourish?

The virtuous mean

The Aristotelian notion of the *virtuous mean* is important to questions about how virtuous we should be. Aristotle thought of virtue as the avoidance of extremes: 'virtue is a kind of mean, since … it aims at what is intermediate' (2009/circa 323BC: 30/1106b), while 'the extremes [are] neither praiseworthy nor right, but worthy of blame' (2009/circa 323BC: 33/1108a).

In this respect Aristotle thought rather differently to the way that we often think today about desirable and undesirable human characteristics. We tend to think of such matters in terms of pairs: that is, we contrast a desirable human trait – a virtue – with its opposite, which we often call a vice. For instance, we might consider generosity to be a virtue and its opposite, stinginess, to be a vice. But this is not the way that Aristotle saw human virtue. He thought of virtues and vices in terms of triads rather than pairs. He would have regarded generosity as a virtue and stinginess as a vice, but he would also have considered profligacy – that is, an excess of generosity – be a vice. For Aristotle, you can be *too* generous.

To think about virtue, then, we have to think not only about the vice of *deficiency* but also the vice of *excess*. And to be virtuous we need to avoid excess as well as deficiency in relation to various character traits. Aristotle offers many examples of how a virtuous mean avoids both extremes. For instance, he considered it virtuous for a person to have an appropriate amount of pride but, as well as contrasting 'proper pride' with its excess, 'empty vanity', he also contrasted it to its deficiency, 'undue humility' (2009/circa 323BC: 32/1107b). Similarly, he contrasted courage with its excessive extreme, 'rashness', as well as its deficient extreme, 'cowardice' (2009/circa 323BC: 32/1107b). Moreover, the virtue of 'ready wit' is contrasted with both 'buffoonery' and 'boorishness' (2009/circa 323BC: 33/1108a), while somebody who wishes to be friendly in a virtuous way needs to avoid not only being a 'quarrelsome and surly sort of person' but also being an 'obsequious' person (2009/circa 323BC: 33-34/1108a).

To be fulfilled, then, a person does not need to be a saint. Rather they need to possess certain desirable traits in good measure, but not to excess. And a company that seeks to flourish need not get involved in such extravagant philanthropy that it overlooks its own commercial prosperity. Rather, that company should display the right amount of virtue; it needs to hit the virtuous mean.

Identifying the virtuous mean

The question of what constitutes the right amount of virtue is not an easy one to answer. Aristotle was well aware that it is not possible to calculate a virtuous amount of pride, courage, wit, or whatever else with precision, so it is not always easy to tell where each virtuous mean sits in relation to excess and deficiency. This is partly because ethics is not the sort of subject that lends itself to precise calculation. But it is also because what constitutes a virtuous response to a particular set of circumstances will depend very much on those circumstances. For example, Aristotle would not have expected a person who possessed the virtue of good temper to get angry if subjected to some small insult. However, if somebody inflicted extreme cruelty on that person's friends or their family, he would have expected them to get very angry indeed. For Aristotle, then, virtue is all about responding in an appropriate manner. As he put it, to feel emotions 'at the right times, with reference to the right objects, towards the right people, with the right motive, and in the right way, is what is both intermediate and best, and this is characteristic of virtue' (2009/circa 323BC: 30/1106b).

Knowing precisely what the virtuous mean consists of, then, is not easy. Indeed, Aristotle believed that a sound grasp of virtue is only available to somebody who has developed sufficient practical wisdom to be able to judge what is appropriate to each given set of circumstances. Moreover, he thought that such practical wisdom only came with experience. Aristotle did, however, offer some tips on how we might go about identifying the virtuous mean in relation to specific characteristics. His first piece of advice is that we should steer away from the extreme to which virtue is more often contrasted, since this is the extreme to which we are more likely to succumb. Take the example of courage. Since courage is more often contrasted to its deficiency, cowardice, than to its excess, rashness, Aristotle suggested that we should err on the side of rashness. In other words, we should try harder to avoid cowardice than rashness. In so doing, he suggested, we are most likely to exhibit a virtuous amount of courage.

Aristotle's second tip is that we should steer away from those extremes to which we are habitually inclined, and we should avoid those that we find most pleasurable. For instance, someone who finds herself inclined towards conceit and who takes pleasure in talking about her own achievements is more likely to display the virtuous mean of 'proper pride' if she makes a point of reigning in her vanity. On the other hand, a person who is habitually inclined to humility would be well advised to err on the side of vanity, since she would thus be more likely to exhibit the virtuous mean of proper pride.

Theory in Practice

The virtuous apprentice

During recent years, a reality television programme called *The Apprentice* has become very popular in the UK and the USA. The basic formula of the programme is that a group of ambitious young businesspeople undertake a range of tasks to compete for the approval of a well-known, wealthy businessman. The presiding business magnate in the UK edition of the programme is Alan Sugar, while Donald Trump plays the lead role in the USA version. Each contest lasts for several weeks, during which time contestants are gradually eliminated – or 'fired' – until an eventual winner is declared. The prizes for winning the contest have varied as the programme has evolved, but victory usually brings either an extremely well-paid job in one of Sugar's or Trump's companies, or some form of investment partnership with them. It is clear from the enthusiasm with which contestants approach the competition that they are very keen to win, and that they value these prizes very highly.

To give you an idea of how the programme works, you can find some excerpts from the UK version at:

www.youtube.com/watch?v=35yGOWXodt4

Some excerpts from the USA version can be found at:

www.youtube.com/watch?v=dq1Vpf3ddml

In order to succeed in *The Apprentice*, contestants must display characteristics that will help them to be successful businesspeople. Presumably, Alan Sugar and Donald Trump are very knowledgeable about what these characteristics are. I assume that they are also well versed in identifying such characteristics in their aspirant employees and investment partners. Therefore, they are capable of choosing a winning apprentice without any help from you or me.

However, it may be that neither Alan Sugar nor Donald Trump has paid quite so much attention to the qualities needed to be a *virtuous* businessperson. So perhaps you could help them here. Imagine that you have been appointed as an advisor for a special series of the programme. This series will be called *The Virtuous Apprentice*. Instead of identifying the candidate who has the potential to make the greatest amount of money for Sugar and Trump, this series will try to identify the most virtuous candidate.

In order to carry out this consultancy task, you will need to do four things:

1 Firstly, you will need to envisage what it means to be a flourishing business in an Aristotelian sense, rather than in a purely financial sense. It might help you to think about some businesses with which you are familiar. These may flourish insofar as they are big and successful companies, but ask yourself whether they are also flourishing in a broader, Aristotelian sense. You might also like to think of these companies in relation to their communities of stakeholders. Do they treat these communities with respect and consideration, or do they just treat people like customers, employees and suppliers as a means to the end of making profit?
2 Once you have thought about what it is for a company to flourish, you can think about the qualities its employees will need to have in order to enable this. You might like to take some ideas from business ethicists who have written about virtue theory in relation to business. For example, Ron Beadle and Geoff Moore (2006) suggest that virtues like *courage*, *truthfulness* and *constancy* will help a business to flourish. Robert Solomon (1992) says that *trust* is important, since a virtuous businessperson must be prepared to trust others and must also be deserving of trust themselves. Try to choose a list of five business virtues that you think Alan Sugar and Donald Trump should look out for.
3 Having drawn up a list of five virtues, you are ready to complete the third part of your task. This is to identify extremes of excess and deficiency with respect to each virtue. These are the extremes that contestants in this special edition of programme will need to avoid if they are to persuade Sugar and Trump that they are demonstrating the virtuous mean. In identifying these extremes, you may struggle to find single words to express them. This does not matter; indeed, Aristotle was unable to find single words to describe the extremes of most of the virtues that he discussed. Instead, as Aristotle did, you can use

(Continued)

(Continued)

sentences or phrases, which describe what deficiency or excess would consist of in relation to each virtue.

4 You are now ready for the fourth and final part of the task. Since it will be difficult for Sugar and Trump to identify precisely where the virtuous mean lies in relation to each virtue, you can offer them some assistance. As Aristotle suggests, it is helpful to steer clear of those extremes to which the virtuous mean is usually contrasted. It is also useful to steer away from the extreme to which a specific individual is more prone. So, for each of the business virtues you have identified, to which of its two extremes do you think *The Apprentice's* contestants are most likely to be predisposed? Equipped with this information, Alan Sugar and Donald Trump can look out for candidates who are able to avoid those particular extremes.

You might also like to carry out one additional task. From what you see of Alan Sugar and Donald Trump in the above videos and in any other versions of *The Apprentice* that you may have watched, and from what you have heard about them elsewhere, how would you rate them in terms of each of the virtues you have identified? Do they display a virtuous mean, or does their behaviour suggest that they tend towards one extreme or the other?

The virtuous mean: knowing how much is enough

In his documentary film *The Big One* (Moore, 1998), Michael Moore asks Nike's Chairman Phil Knight the following question: 'How much is enough? If you are a billionaire, would it be OK to be just a half a billionaire? Would it be OK for your company to make just a little less money if it meant providing some jobs here in this country?'

The Aristotelian notion of the virtuous mean is relevant to Moore's question. The virtuous mean offers a commercially realistic ethical template for business insofar as it acknowledges that businesses need to ensure their financial prosperity. However, although applying the virtuous mean in a corporate context leaves space for corporate executives to look after the bottom line and compete energetically in their resource markets, it also cautions financial restraint. Corporations often exercise a great deal of power in relation to their suppliers, employees and customers. They may also exercise a great deal of influence over the lives of those who live close to their operations. Observing a virtuous mean would involve resisting the opportunities for exploitation that such power may present. It involves doing what is necessary for the company to survive whilst, at the same time, treating those who are affected by corporate activity with consideration.

Video Activity 5.2

The following link will take you to some excerpts from the Achbar, Abbott and Bakan film, *The Corporation* (2005). Watch the first excerpt. In this clip, the speakers suggest that business corporations are designed to maximize profitability and growth whilst externalizing as many of the associated costs as they can. In other words, people who work in corporations have no choice but to do whatever they can to maximize corporate growth and profitability whilst getting other people to deal with the social and environmental consequences.

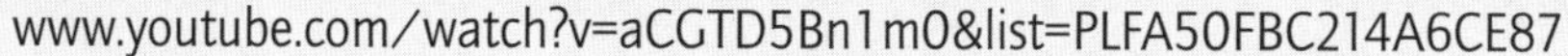
www.youtube.com/watch?v=aCGTD5Bn1m0&list=PLFA50FBC214A6CE87

Questions

1 If these speakers are correct in their assessment of corporations, what implications might this have for those businesspeople who want to follow a *virtuous mean* in their business dealings? You might like to think about this question in relation to the five virtues that you identified in the last Theory in Practice exercise.
2 Do you agree that corporations are inherently predisposed to maximize growth and profitability at all costs, or do you think it is possible for a businessperson to balance the interests of the corporation with the interests of those who are affected by its activities, and to thus follow a virtuous mean? Can you think of any specific companies that you think observe a *virtuous mean*?

Defining virtue in relation to purpose

So far, this chapter has described the connection Aristotle makes between human flourishing, virtue and community. It has also introduced his doctrine of the virtuous mean. It has explored some of the implications that these ideas have for business: namely, that a company that seeks to flourish in an Aristotelian sense should embrace virtue, should acknowledge the role that it plays within a community of stakeholders, and should seek to avoid excess. This second section of the chapter will explore a further theme in Aristotle's moral philosophy: that is, the connection he makes between virtue and purpose. In particular, I will consider how thinking about the purpose of business might help us to understand what business virtue consists of.

Purpose, flourishing and virtue

Aristotle (2009/circa 323BC) speaks of human flourishing in relation to achieving one's *purpose* as a human being, or carrying out one's human *function*. In other words, he suggests that a flourishing person is one who achieves their human purpose. It therefore follows that, if we can establish the purpose – or the function – of human beings, we can get some idea of what human flourishing consists of. Gerard Hughes describes Aristotle's position thus: 'We might discover what fulfilment consists in if we can grasp what is the function of a human being. To inquire about the function of something … is to inquire about what it is supposed to do, what its purpose is' (2001: 36). Furthermore, according to Aristotle, since virtues are qualities that enable humans to flourish, they are also those qualities that help us to achieve our purpose. So as well as helping to establish what human flourishing consists of, identifying the purpose of humans may help us to think about what human virtue consists of.

One way of illustrating the connection between purpose, flourishing and virtue is to consider it in relation to a simple, everyday implement that has a fairly obvious purpose. Take the example of a kitchen knife. It may seem curious nowadays to talk about a 'flourishing' kitchen knife, or about a kitchen knife being 'virtuous', but such statements would not have been so odd to Aristotle. Were he asked to describe a flourishing kitchen knife, he would probably have said that it is one which fulfils the purpose of a kitchen knife. Moreover, he might have suggested that virtues in relation to a kitchen knife are those qualities that enable it to fulfil that purpose.

So what is the purpose of a kitchen knife? Although kitchen knives are sometimes used for other things, most people would agree that their fundamental purpose is to cut and chop food. Therefore, a flourishing kitchen knife could be described as one which serves that purpose well. And virtues in relation to a kitchen knife would be those qualities that enable it to cut and chop food effectively. Since qualities such as sharpness, balance and rigidity will help a kitchen knife to fulfil this fundamental purpose, it could be said that, from an Aristotelian perspective, a virtuous kitchen knife is one that is sharp, well-balanced and rigid.

Aristotle's teaching encourages us to think about human virtue in a similar way: if we can agree about the purpose of humans, we might be able to define human virtues as those qualities that enable the achievement of that purpose. Now, defining the purpose of human beings is no simple matter. A great deal has been said and written on this topic and this is not the place to contribute to this vexing philosophical and theological discussion. Even Aristotle seemed a little unclear about what he considered the purpose of humans to be, and his ideas on the topic have aroused quite a lot of debate in their own right. So neither will it help us to dwell on Aristotle's notion of human purpose here.

However, while it does not serve our current needs to enquire into the content of Aristotle's or anyone else's views about the purpose of human beings, this does not stop us from adopting his general method of defining virtue in relation to purpose. Nor does it prevent us from exploring the insights that this approach might offer to business ethics. This section will therefore do just that. It will explore some ideas about the purpose of business, using these ideas as a basis for considering business virtue.

The purpose of business

The question 'what is the purpose of business?' has aroused quite a lot of interest amongst business ethicists. Unsurprisingly, a range of responses has been offered to it. I will outline here two contrasting views. The first view is offered by Elaine Sternberg, who focuses on the role that companies play in generating wealth for their shareholders. A second perspective draws on the work of Robert Solomon and provides the basis for a somewhat broader understanding of business purpose.

Business purpose and the maximization of shareholder value

In her book *Just Business* (2000) Elaine Sternberg uses a broadly Aristotelian method to identify business virtue. That is, she offers a definition of the purpose of business and uses this to get some idea of what business virtues consist of. As far as Sternberg is concerned, the 'defining purpose' of business is the thing that characterizes it and distinguishes it from other types of institution such as clubs, charities and public-sector organizations. This defining purpose, according to Sternberg, is *'maximising owner value over the long term by selling goods or services'* (Sternberg, 2000: 32). Moreover, Sternberg proposes that 'this simple statement is the key to understanding business, and consequently one of the foundations of understanding business ethics' (2000: 32).

Sternberg goes on to outline a range of virtues that she believes will help businesses to achieve this purpose. Among them, she includes 'ordinary decency' (2000: 83), which embraces qualities such as *courage*, *responsibility* and *integrity*. She also speaks of the importance of *fairness*, which involves treating people 'without favour or capricious exception' (2000: 84) and honouring agreements. Furthermore, Sternberg emphasises the importance of *honesty* to maximizing long-term shareholder value.

Now, some of the virtues that Sternberg identifies might seem curious given her focus on maximizing share value. After all, share value is largely determined by profitability, and it may sometimes be possible to achieve higher profit by *not* behaving with integrity, by *not* treating people fairly, and by *not* being honest. It is important to note, however, that Sternberg stipulates that the purpose of business is to maximize owner value *over the long term*. It is possible that a business might be more profitable *in the short term*, and that it might maximize shareholder value *in the short term,* if it fails to show the virtues that Sternberg lists. However, Sternberg believes that this would erode the respect and trust upon which longer-term business success depends. Therefore, although non-virtuous behaviour may offer certain short-term benefits, it will not help a company to achieve its purpose over the long term.

Distinguishing purpose from goals

Other business ethicists have drawn on Aristotelian-style rationales to derive a rather different understanding of purpose to that proposed by Sternberg. Robert Solomon offers a basis for this alternative understanding when he distinguishes between the purpose of business and the goals of business. As Solomon points out, goals and purpose, 'though necessarily connected, are not the same' (1992: 119).

For Solomon, the *goals* of an activity relate to the way that activity happens to be structured. Goals can be identified simply by observing the activity: if we look at an activity closely enough we will be able to identify the goals that happen to prevail within it. Now, if we observe the way that business is usually conducted, and if we examine the priorities of many businesspeople, we might conclude that maximizing shareholder wealth is an important business goal. As Elaine Sternberg points out, the creation of shareholder wealth certainly seems to be accorded a great deal of importance in many corporate environments. However, according to Solomon's analysis, the apparent fact that maximizing shareholder wealth happens to be an important goal of business does not necessarily make it the *purpose* of business. Solomon believes that in order to identify the purpose of business we have to do more than just look at the way it happens to be structured; we need to look at the role that it plays in society.

Before considering the role that business plays in society, it might help to illustrate Solomon's distinction between goals and purpose in relation to another form of human activity. Take the game of tennis as an example. Tennis is usually structured in such a way that those who play it try to score more points than their opponent by hitting a ball over a net with a racquet while preventing their opponent from doing the same thing. That is the *goal* of tennis: to score more points than one's opponent by doing these things. That is the way tennis happens to be structured. It could be structured differently. Indeed, as with any game, the way in which tennis is structured has evolved over the years; its goals have not always been identical to those which now shape the laws of the game. But that is the way that tennis is usually structured nowadays; that is its goal as things currently stand.

In order to ascertain the purpose of tennis, on the other hand, we need to do more than just observe the way that it happens to be structured. We need also to look outside of the activity to see how it interrelates with its social context. This will enable us to identify the purpose that it serves in relation to that broader context. Looked at in this way, tennis does many things. It helps people to keep fit and healthy. It provides opportunities for social interaction. It offers entertainment for spectators. It sometimes provides a focal point for community identity and national consciousness. It supplies role models from whom young people can learn socially desirable behaviour. It instils valued personal qualities such as endurance, tenacity and respect for one's opponent. And it offers to its players and spectators a welcome release from the stresses of their working lives. These are just some of the things that tennis does. Such things, in totality, comprise the purpose of tennis according to Solomon's definition.

Business goals and business purpose

If we apply this goal-purpose distinction to business, the 'defining purpose' of business as identified by Elaine Sternberg (2000) might be better termed its goal. Business may be structured around maximizing shareholder value in the long term, at least in some corporate environments, but that does not tell us much about the purpose that business serves in its wider social context. In order to appreciate that broader purpose we need to look at ways in which business interacts with the society that surrounds it. We also need to look at the many good things that accrue, or can accrue, from that interaction.

When we do this, we will certainly see that *part* of business's purpose is to create wealth for its owners. In this respect, business's goal also forms part of its purpose. Business also provides people with goods and services that they require, so this is another way in which its goal coincides with its purpose. However, business also does many other things. For instance, it provides opportunities for people to earn a living, to make and sustain interpersonal relationships, to acquire a broad range of skills and capabilities, to develop their careers, and to participate in something that they consider to be a worthwhile, common endeavour. Business also sustains communities by providing forums within which people can interact and by supporting local economic infrastructures via the payments it makes to suppliers, employees and shareholders. Moreover, the taxes that business pays help to support public services upon which it depends and which also serve other members of the communities within which it trades.

Solomon proposes that, in order to truly appreciate the purpose of business in an Aristotelian sense, we need to take this broader view. It is this wider understanding of business purpose that captures the reasons why business is usually considered to be a socially beneficial phenomenon. After all, national and regional governments, with the approval of their electorates, often invest considerable resources to attract and develop business activity within their territories. They do not do this just to create wealth for the shareholders of those businesses. This may be part of the reason why they do it, but it is not the whole reason. To appreciate the whole reason we have to look at the many different ways that business can contribute to the well-being of the communities that those governments represent. And to do that we have to consider not only how business can serve the interests of its shareholders but how it can improve the lives of all the stakeholders that it affects.

Video Activity 5.3

In the following video, 'What is the Purpose of Business? – John Mackey of Whole Foods Market', Professor R. Edward Freeman and John Mackey discuss various conceptions of the purpose of business.

www.youtube.com/watch?v=6ncsJGxkZdQ

(Continued)

(Continued)

Questions

1 What are John Mackey's views about the idea that the *purpose* of business is to maximize shareholder wealth?
2 What other ways of thinking about business purpose does Mackey attribute to the entrepreneurs he has met?
3 What do you think is the purpose of business?

Business purpose and community

One way of comparing these contrasting ways of defining the purpose of business is to do so in relation to the *communities* to which they refer. The emphasis that Aristotle placed on community has already been highlighted in the first part of this chapter. Community is also important for the definitions of business purpose that are offered by Elaine Sternberg and Robert Solomon. However, Sternberg and Solomon's contrasting definitions entail rather different understandings of community. For Sternberg, the community that business serves comprises its shareholders. Of course, businesspeople need to interact with a broader community of stakeholders, such as customers, suppliers and employees, in order to serve their shareholders. But those other stakeholders are only important on Sternberg's account insofar as they enable companies to maximize the wealth of their shareholders.

Solomon's definition of purpose, on the other hand, embraces a broader understanding of community. It identifies purpose in terms of what business can do for the wider community within which it trades, not just what it can do for its shareholders. Solomon's definition of business purpose thus entails a notion of community which includes all those people who are potentially implicated in or affected by the activities of a business.

Pause for Reflection

Elaine Sternberg's definition of business purpose offers a basis for identifying a number of business virtues. Some of these virtues are outlined above. They include qualities such as honesty, integrity, responsibility and courage. For Sternberg, the ethical desirability of these virtues derives from their usefulness in helping businesses to maximize owner value over the long term by producing goods and services.

Consider the alternative definition of purpose offered by Robert Solomon. Can you identify other virtues, which are not included in Sternberg's list, which would help to fulfil Solomon's broader notion of business purpose? You might like to think in particular about the importance that Solomon places on a wider community of stakeholders. What personal qualities might help businesspeople to interact with and serve the needs of this wider community?

Theory in Practice

Management buyouts: changing the purpose of business?

During the last 35 years, management buyouts (MBOs) have become a prominent feature of the UK business landscape (Wright et al., 2005; Amess and Wright, 2007; Wright et al., 2009). MBOs involve a company being bought from its previous owners by a group of managers. Those previous owners might be shareholders, in the case of a publicly quoted company, or private owners such as the company's founders and their families (Wood and Wright, 2010). Sometimes an MBO involves managers buying part of a larger company and running it as a separate entity (Wood and Wright, 2010).

At first glance, the notion of an MBO seems benign from an ethical point of view. It conjures up images of a team of managers, who are well acquainted with a company and its people, taking control of the company and running it on behalf of those people. To those who work for a company, managers are usually seen in a different light from distant groups of shareholders and wealthy private owners, with whom employees have little or no acquaintance. Many employees would regard their manager as 'one of us': someone they greet when they pass them in the corridor; someone who regularly communicates with them and who seems to want to support them; someone who asks about their family; maybe even someone they have worked alongside in the past. Employees tend to identify with their managers and they usually assume that their managers identify with them. So what employee would not want their company to be owned by its managers?

(Continued)

(Continued)

This impression may be misleading, however (Jones and Hunt, 1991; ITUC, 2007; PSE, 2007). For one thing, the managers who buy a company are not always its incumbent team. Sometimes they are 'bought-in' managers who have not previously worked for the company, but who find themselves in a position to take control of it (Amess and Wright, 2007; Bacon et al., 2010; Wood and Wright, 2010) and who believe that doing so may bring them substantial financial gain (MORI, 2001). But also, in order to appreciate the ethical ramifications of an MBO, even one that involves incumbent managers, we need to understand just what it involves.

To buy a company costs a lot of money. For instance, the average value of UK MBO deals in 2007 was £68 million (Jelic and Wright, 2011), and very few managers have that sort of money sitting in their bank account. Therefore, they need to acquire the necessary funding from somewhere. Fortunately for those managers, many financial organizations are willing to support an MBO. What usually happens is that a private equity (PE) firm oversees the purchase (Wright et al., 2005; ITUC, 2007; PSE, 2007). That PE firm will use some of its own money (that is, the money of its own investors) to partially fund the purchase, which allows it to become a co-owner of the company along with its managers.

Of course, purchasing managers also tend to put in some of their own money. Indeed, PE firms like managers to invest a significant amount (Amess and Wright, 2007) of their own money; maybe something in the region of a few hundred thousand pounds. They reason that, although this management stake represents only a small portion of the total purchase price, it is a lot of money to those managers; money which they can ill afford to lose. Therefore, by contributing even such a small proportion of the purchase price, managers have a strong financial incentive to look after the company they have bought into (Wright et al., 2005; Amess and Wright, 2007).

So, in this way a PE firm and a management team, which usually comprises the company chief executive and several senior executives, get together to buy a company. However, even with the contribution of a PE firm and several managers, the combined ownership funds usually only amount to a small proportion of the total purchase price of the target company. Therefore, there is still a lot of money to find. This remaining amount is usually provided as debt. That is, the PE firm and the managers go to another financial institution, such as a bank, and ask it to lend them the necessary additional money to buy the company. This additional amount is usually between $\frac{2}{3}$ and $\frac{7}{8}$ of the total purchase price (Wright et al., 2005).

Now, it is important to note that the bank that lends this extra money to fund the purchase does not thus become a part owner of the purchased company. It is the PE firm and the managers who own the company. All the bank does is lend them the money to buy it, rather like a bank might lend you or me the money to buy a new car. Of course, if the PE firm and managers fail to repay their debt to the bank, that bank may then seize the company – just as a bank that lends me the money to buy a car may take possession of it if I fail to pay back my loan. In this case, the bank would become the owner of the company. However, this is an eventuality that managers, PE firms and banks usually try to avoid.

This sort of deal, where the new owners (the PE firm and the managers) borrow such a large proportion of the funds needed to buy a company is called a 'highly leveraged' deal. Highly leveraged deals can be very advantageous to PE firms and managers. To understand why, consider the following analogy. Suppose you see an antique table for sale in a shop for £500. It is clear to you that the shop owner does not realise the true value of that table. You, on the other hand, are an antiques enthusiast and you are well aware that the table is worth at least £700. So you decide to buy the table for £500 with the intention of reselling it for £700. However, you only have £20 in spare cash so you cannot afford to pay for the table as things stand. Therefore, you go to a bank, explain what you intend to do, and ask the bank to lend you the remaining £480 that you need to buy the table. The bank happily agrees to lend you the money because you say you will pay interest on your loan. Moreover, the bank knows that if your plan to resell the table does not succeed it can take the table from you so, whatever happens, it will not be left empty handed.

So, you buy the table with your £20 and the bank's £480. You take it to another shop, whose owner is more tuned-in to the value of antique tables. The owner of this shop agrees to buy the table from you for £700. You repay your bank loan of £480 and you are left with £220, thus making a profit of £200. The important point about this is that, by borrowing such a large proportion of the purchase price of the table, you are able to turn your investment of £20 into £220. Another way of putting this is that, even though the value of the table has only risen by 40 per cent, the value of your investment has risen by 1,000 per cent!

This is why managers and PE companies are keen to get involved in highly leveraged MBOs. By borrowing so much of the purchase price of the target company from a bank, they have a chance to make a huge return on their investment. They believe that, as long as the company is managed in a particular way, its value can be increased. This belief is usually based on the supposition that, rather like the first owner of the antique table described above, the company's present owners are not extracting maximum value from it (Jones and Hunt, 1991). Moreover, buyers

(Continued)

(Continued)

usually proceed on the assumption that they have the necessary skills, knowledge and commitment to extract maximum value. Their intention is therefore to buy the company, manage it in such a way that its value increases over a period of perhaps three or four years (PSE, 2007), and then sell it. By borrowing most of the money needed to buy the company in the first place, they can achieve a very high return on their investment even if they only increase its value by a relatively small amount. For example, a manager who contributes, say, £100,000 to the purchase price of a company, and who succeeds in increasing its value by 10 or 20 per cent, may walk away with millions of pounds. This is a very good way for managers, who are prepared to risk some of their own money and who are prepared to do what is necessary to increase the commercial value of their company, to become very rich indeed.

In the following Corporate Finance Television video, 'What is a Management Buy Out', Neil Ackroyd offers a brief overview of how MBOs work. The video also offers some links to further information about MBOs:

www.youtube.com/watch?v=_HRJE-d-IRY

Questions

1 Imagine you are a manager involved in an MBO. During the period of your ownership of the purchased company, what do you think you would consider its key *purpose* to be?
2 What *virtues* do you think that perceived purpose might encourage in you?
3 How might the *management virtues* encouraged by an MBO scenario differ from those associated with Sternberg's and Solomon's definitions of *business purpose*?
4 Can you think of other ways in which a company could be bought from its present owners, which might involve other parties as well as managers in the deal and which might thus embrace a wider *community* of stakeholders?

Virtue, work practices and human flourishing

Although virtue theory is rooted in Ancient Greek thought, and particularly in the philosophy of Aristotle, the last 35 years have seen renewed interest in it. A lot of this interest has been inspired by the work of Alasdair MacIntyre. MacIntyre (1985/1981) puts forward the view that the moral philosophies of the last few hundred years have failed to provide a satisfactory account of ethics because they have overlooked key insights that were fundamental to virtue theory. He therefore suggests that we need to go back to the work of Aristotle and the virtue theorists who succeeded him if we are to construct an adequate understanding of ethics.

The first section of this chapter discussed Aristotle's view that virtue helps people to lead a fulfilled and flourishing life. MacIntyre (1985/1981, 1994) develops this theme, drawing attention to the contribution that different types of 'good' can make to human flourishing. He explains how these goods can be realized through the achievement of *excellence* in *practices*, and how *virtues* can enable the achievement of excellence. In so doing, he highlights the importance of work practices to human flourishing, as well as the need for the businesses within which those work practices take place to focus on excellence, to cultivate virtue and to ensure the right balance of various types of good.

This last section will elaborate on some of MacIntyre's ideas and highlight their relevance to business ethics. It will then outline some further suggestions offered by Geoff Moore and Ron Beadle, who have drawn on MacIntyre's work to identify some practical steps that business managers might take to encourage the achievement of excellence, an appropriate balance of goods, and the cultivation of virtue in the companies that they run.

How external goods and internal goods help us to flourish

In his book *After Virtue* (1985/1981), Alasdair MacIntyre draws attention to the contribution that various types of 'good' can make to human flourishing. He places these goods into two categories: on the one hand, there are *external goods* such as money and status. It is easy to see how these goods can help people to flourish. Money enables us to buy things that ensure a comfortable life for us and for those who depend upon us. Status is also important because we like to be well thought of by other people. However, MacIntyre points out that these are not the only goods that contribute to a fulfilled life. As well as these external goods, he highlights the importance of *internal goods* to human flourishing. Internal goods include things like the enjoyment, sense of achievement, exhilaration and pride that we get from the things we do in life. Internal goods also include the knowledge, skills and capabilities that we acquire whilst doing these things. MacIntyre suggests that without these internal goods it would be hard for someone to flourish as a human being: money and status, along with the benefits that they enable, will not suffice for those who seek to lead a fulfilled life.

Excellence in practices, goods and virtue

MacIntyre also draws attention to the fact that we tend to derive both internal goods and external goods from participation in *practices*. Moreover, he highlights the relationship between the achievement of *excellence* in practices and each type of goods. I will outline what he means by a practice before explaining how the achievement of excellence in practices can relate to internal goods and external goods, and how the virtues help us to achieve excellence.

Practices

MacIntyre defines a practice as 'any coherent and complex form of socially established, cooperative human activity' (1985/1981: 187). Most people take part in the type of practices MacIntyre has in mind. For example, we participate in a practice if we play sport, if we act in a play, or if we play a musical instrument. All of these activities are socially established, and they usually involve some form of cooperation with other human beings. Pastimes like bird watching and train spotting are practices as well. They are socially established activities and, although people often do them alone, those people tend to share their findings with other bird watchers and train spotters and, in so doing, they contribute to the development of those practices.

Part of the relevance of MacIntyre's ideas for business ethics lies in the fact that, for many people, their job involves participation in a practice. For instance, building a house is usually a socially established, cooperative human activity; so are coalmining, farming, designing IT systems, making clothes, working in a bar, providing financial services and many other types of work.

Practices, excellence and internal goods

An important feature of practices is that participation in them enables us to derive both the internal goods and external goods that are essential for human flourishing. Consider, first, the internal goods that we might derive from participation in a practice. These might include the pleasure a footballer gets from playing a game well, the satisfaction a musician gets from participating in a good concert, the exhilaration a surfer enjoys while catching a wave, the sense of achievement that an IT-system designer derives from creating an efficient and user-friendly IT system, and the pride that a bank employee might take in providing financial services that people appreciate. Each of these situations is also likely to involve a certain amount of skill enhancement. By participating in the things we do, whether these are leisure activities or work activities, we develop our capability in those activities.

MacIntyre points out that internal goods such as these tend to be associated with the achievement of *excellence*. The pleasure, satisfaction, sense of achievement, exhilaration, pride and personal development that practices enable usually come when we carry out those practices well. When we fail to do them well, we are more likely to be left with feelings of dissatisfaction, exasperation and discontentment. Furthermore, if something prevents us from carrying out a practice as well as we can, this may leave us with nothing but a sense of frustration. Achieving excellence therefore helps us to derive the internal goods associated with practices.

To fully appreciate the relationship between excellence and internal goods, though, it is important to understand precisely how MacIntyre uses the word 'excellence'. To say that internal goods can only come through the achievement of excellence could be interpreted as saying that one needs to be an outstanding exponent of a particular practice in order to derive any internal goods from participating in it. However, this is not what MacIntyre means. As far as he is concerned, in order to derive internal goods from a practice, you do not need to be an expert; you just need to be able to apply yourself with some success to the achievement of standards of expertise that are widely accepted within that practice. For example, to derive internal goods from the practice of surfing, you do not have to ride a 30-foot wave with the control of a champion. Someone who has just taken up surfing can derive internal goods just by staying upright on a surf board for a few seconds on a very small wave. The important thing is that they are progressing in accordance with standards of excellence that are widely accepted within the surfing community. In other words, there is a socially established understanding of what surfing excellence involves, and the surfing debutant derives internal goods by making some progress against those standards. Even the tiniest achievements can be considered 'excellent' if they comprise a step in the right direction. As MacIntyre puts it,

> A practice involves standards of excellence and obedience to rules as well as the achievement of goods. To enter into a practice is to accept the authority of those standards and the inadequacy of my own performance as judged by them. It is to subject my own attitudes, choices, preferences and tastes to the standards which currently and partially define the practice. (MacIntyre, 1985/1981: 190)

Pause for Reflection

Think of a *practice* that you take part in regularly. When was the last time you experienced some degree of *excellence* in that practice? What did that excellence consist of? What *internal goods* did you derive from your success?

Practices, excellence and external goods

Participation in practices also enables us to derive external goods. For instance, a person who plays football well, who is a good musician, who is a good surfer, who designs efficient and user-friendly IT systems, or who provides financial services that people appreciate is likely to be well thought of, so they will derive a certain status from their participation. Moreover, if they carry out that practice as part of their work, they are also likely to get paid for it.

Note that external goods can also be associated with the achievement of excellence in practices. We do not usually derive money and status just from participating in practices; we only derive these external goods when other people believe that we have participated in those practices successfully. Neither a footballer nor an IT-system designer is likely to be well paid and highly thought of unless they are generally considered to be good at what they do.

Practices, excellence and community

MacIntyre also draws attention to the relationship between practices, excellence and community. He points out that practices and the standards of excellence that prevail within them are created, developed and sustained by communities of practitioners. In other words, all those people who have participated in a practice in the past have contributed to its development. They have also helped to establish our ideas about what excellence consists of. Moreover, it is the people who participate in a practice today and into the future who will shape its ongoing development and determine how those notions of excellence evolve. MacIntyre points out that anybody who participates in a practice should respect that community of fellow practitioners, for without them the practice could not exist. Moreover, every practitioner should do their bit to perpetuate the practitioner community and to contribute to the development of future notions of excellence.

Video Activity 5.4

In the following Royal Horticultural Society video, Tony Woods talks about his job as a garden designer and mentions some of the rewards that he derives from achieving excellence in his work.

www.youtube.com/watch?v=a7p2TCW4zVo

Questions

1 Do you get the impression that Tony's job helps him to *flourish* as a human being?
2 Which of the good things that Tony associates with his work might fall into Alasdair MacIntyre's category of *internal goods*?

3 What other rewards do you think the job of a garden designer might offer, which would fit into MacIntyre's category of *external goods*?
4 How do you think the standards of *excellence* in garden design, which Tony aspires to achieve, have come about?
5 In what way might Tony be able to contribute to the ongoing development of those standards of *excellence*?

Practices and virtue

MacIntyre points out that *virtue* plays an important role in relation to practices and the achievement of excellence in them. As he sees it, virtues are those personal qualities that enable people to achieve excellence in practices. And since virtues enable the achievement of excellence, they also help us to derive the goods that are associated with it. In his words, *'A virtue is an acquired human quality the possession and exercise of which tends to enable us to achieve those goods which are internal to practices and the lack of which effectively prevents us from achieving any such goods'* (1985/1981: 191).

Clearly, the precise nature of virtue will vary from practice to practice, since different human qualities enable the achievement of excellence in different practices. For instance, balance and poise will help someone to achieve excellence at surfing; an excellent actor needs to have a clear voice; and an excellent provider of financial services needs to be able to empathize with the needs of her customers. These, then, are just a few of the virtues that are specific to those practices. However, in addition to these practice-specific virtues, MacIntyre suggests that certain virtues support the achievement of excellence in any practice. Chief amongst these are *courage*, *justice* and *honesty*. The importance of these particular virtues derives from the importance that MacIntyre places on community. Since, like Aristotle, MacIntyre proposes that courage, justice and honesty are essential to the survival of any community, he suggests that they are also critical to the perpetuation of any practice and to the achievement of excellence in it.

To summarize these ideas then, practices are leisure or work activities from which people derive internal and external goods through the achievement of excellence. And virtue is important because it is virtue which enables the achievement of excellence. Virtue therefore enables the achievement of those goods which are essential to human fulfilment.

Contrasting external goods to internal goods

Despite this productive relationship between, on the one hand, virtue and the achievement of excellence in practices and, on the other hand, those internal and external goods that help people to flourish, there are some important differences between internal goods and external goods. It is important to understand these differences if we are to appreciate the implications of MacIntyre's work for business ethics.

The extent to which internal goods and external goods are dispersed throughout communities

The first distinction between internal goods and external goods is that the supply of internal goods is not limited, nor is there a limit on the number of people who can benefit from them. Indeed, it is often the case that the achievement of excellence by a practitioner brings internal goods not only to that person but to many other people who are associated with their practice. This is most evident when we consider practices such as entertainment and sport. For example, when a musician plays a great concert, it is not only she who derives the associated internal goods; all those who attend the concert share her enjoyment, satisfaction and exhilaration, as do her fans who listen to recordings and watch videos of the concert. Moreover, the musical techniques that she pioneers in her live performances may inspire other musicians to develop their own skills accordingly. Her performance therefore pushes back the boundaries of excellence in her practice, an achievement from which all members of the practitioner community can benefit.

This is also the case with work practices. Consider, for instance, tour operation; that is, the job carried out by someone who works for a travel agent or for some other business that arranges holidays and travel. Tour operation is a practice in MacIntyre's terms. It is socially established and, in order to participate in it, one needs to coordinate with other people in various ways. For instance, a tour operator needs to coordinate with her colleagues and her customers. She also needs to coordinate with hoteliers, airlines, ferry companies, restaurateurs and a range of other service providers. She may also need to coordinate with public officials in holiday destinations, with regulatory bodies, and maybe even with academic institutions. Note that the principles and protocols of tour operation, along with standards of tour-operating excellence, have been established over many years within the tour-operating community, particularly during the second half of the twentieth century when overseas travel became an established part of many people's lives.

When a tour operator does her job well, she is likely to derive the job satisfaction, pleasure, sense of achievement, pride and personal development that come from providing high-quality customer service, maintaining productive relationships with her colleagues and partners, and generally by doing her work well. All these internal goods will help her to lead a fulfilled life, or to flourish as a human being. However, she is not the only person who will benefit from her achievement of excellence in tour operating. Those who enjoy the holidays that she arranges will also derive some of these goods. It is even possible that, by arranging excellent holidays, she is able to push forward the standards of customer service in the travel industry so that all people who take part in organized holidays and travel in the future, either as providers or consumers, are able to benefit from her excellence.

The internal goods that accrue from achieving excellence in practices are therefore often widely distributed: there are plenty for everybody involved. It is not only the excellent practitioner who flourishes through the achievement of excellence then; her efforts also help others who are involved in the practitioner community to flourish. As MacIntyre points out 'it is characteristic of [internal goods] that their achievement is good for the whole community who participate in a practice' (MacIntyre, 1985/1981: 190–1). However, this is not the case with external goods. This is because external goods are usually limited in supply, so if one person gets them somebody else is deprived of them. External goods, then, tend to be things for which people compete: 'External goods are therefore characteristically objects of competition in which there must be losers as well as winners' (MacIntyre, 1985/1981: 190).

Consider, for instance the external goods that our tour operator derives from her work. For a start, she will expect to receive a wage. She may also get a handsome bonus on top of her wage if she meets performance standards associated with excellence in the practice of tour operation. The achievement of excellence may also enable a certain social standing amongst her peers. Moreover, as she develops her skills as a tour operator, she is likely to get promoted, which will mean that she gets paid even more money and that her social and professional status are further enhanced. Of course, just like the internal goods outlined above, external goods such as these help a tour operator to lead a fulfilled life. Unlike with internal goods, though, other people are unlikely to share in them. We tend to think of the money and status that a tour operator gets from doing her job well as 'her' money and 'her' status. The more of these external goods she comes to 'possess', the less there are for other people. Of course she may share her money with her friends and family but, in so doing, she will have less for herself. The human flourishing that comes from the acquisition of external goods, then, is limited. There is only so much money and status to go round, so if one person gets them others do not.

Relationship with the achievement of excellence

A second important distinction between internal goods and external goods is that internal goods can only be achieved through the achievement of excellence, whereas external goods can be achieved by other means.

MacIntyre points out that it is in the nature of internal goods that they are necessarily linked to excellence in practices. Indeed, this is why he calls them 'internal'. By this, he means that they can only be specified in terms of the particular practice through which they are derived. However, this is not necessarily the case with external goods. MacIntyre points out that things like money and status are external to the achievement of excellence. That is, they can be specified without reference to excellence and practices: the achievement of excellence in a practice is one thing; the external goods that are derived from it are separate things that just happen to follow from it. As MacIntyre puts it, external goods are 'externally and contingently attached to ... practices by the accidents of social circumstances' (1985/1981: 188).

MacIntyre highlights an important implication of this external relationship. This is that there are always other ways of achieving external goods. Their achievement is not necessarily linked to the achievement of excellence in practices. For instance, we may cheat in a practice so that we derive external goods not through the *actual achievement* of excellence but through the *appearance* of excellence. Consider, for instance, what might happen if our tour operator decides to seek money and status other than by the achievement of excellence. Suppose she takes credit for the work of her colleagues, she bribes travel correspondents to write good reviews of the holidays that she organizes, she fails to reveal hidden extras in order to misrepresent the price of the holidays that she sells, or she treats resort-based suppliers shoddily in order to minimize costs. All of these things may help her to become wealthy and to achieve the status of a successful tour operator. However, they will not bring her those internal goods that can only come from arranging holidays that meet standards of excellence that have been developed in the tour operating community over many years.

MacIntyre suggests that this sort of problem is especially likely to occur when external goods get prioritized over internal goods. When people come to value things like money and status more than things like job satisfaction, pleasure, a sense of achievement, pride, exhilaration and personal development, there is a danger that the former will undermine the achievement of the latter.

Relationship with virtue

The contrasting relationships that internal goods and external goods have with the achievement of excellence entail a further distinction between them. This is that the relationship between virtue and internal goods is rather different from that between virtue and external goods.

Consider, first, the relationship between internal goods and virtue. Internal goods cannot be achieved other than by the achievement of excellence in practices. And since virtues are those human qualities that enable the achievement of excellence in a particular practice, virtues are essential to the achievement of internal goods. However, this is not so with external goods. This is because, as pointed out above, external goods such as money and status can be derived other than by the achievement of excellence. And since these external goods do not necessarily demand the achievement of excellence, they do not necessarily require virtue for their attainment.

Indeed, MacIntyre suggests that in some situations 'the possession of the virtues may perfectly well hinder us in achieving external goods' (MacIntyre, 1985/1981: 196). He has in mind situations in which it has become customary to acquire external goods by means other than through the achievement of excellence; situations in which, for instance, cheating has become commonplace. In such situations, those who focus on the achievement of excellence, and who act virtuously, may be at a positive disadvantage to those who use any means at their disposal to get external goods. MacIntyre warns, therefore, that 'if in a particular society the pursuit of external goods were to become dominant, the concept of the virtues might suffer first attrition and then perhaps something near total effacement' (1985/1981: 196).

The importance of keeping external goods in their proper place

To summarize so far, MacIntyre highlights the contribution that internal goods and external goods can make to human fulfilment, their relationship with the achievement of excellence in practices, and the link between virtue and excellence. He also highlights some differences between internal goods and external goods, which suggest that the latter may, in some cases, be problematic. The first difference is that external goods do not tend to get dispersed throughout practitioner communities. This means that the human fulfilment that comes from external goods is less likely to be shared than that accruing from internal goods. The second is that external goods can be attained other than through the achievement of excellence. Consequently, if somebody becomes overly focused on external goods, they may forget all about the achievement of excellence and just do what they have to do to acquire those external goods. And the third difference is that external goods are not necessarily linked to virtue. Therefore, to strive too hard for external goods is to run the risk of undermining virtue.

In general, then, if the quest for external goods gets out of hand, it is likely to erode virtue, to detract from the achievement of excellence, and to hinder the attainment of internal goods. To place too much emphasis on external goods such as money and status therefore runs the risk of preventing everybody from flourishing in a comprehensive way.

Now, it is important to note that, in alerting us to the hazards presented by external goods, MacIntyre is not saying we should not desire them: external goods are 'goods' after all; they are not 'bads'. As he describes them, 'external goods genuinely are goods. Not only are they characteristic objects of human desire ... but no one can despise them altogether without a certain hypocrisy' (1985/1981: 196). All he is saying is that they should be kept in their place. In the case of the tour operator discussed earlier, there is nothing wrong with her wanting to be wealthy and well-respected. Such things will help her to lead a fulfilled life. However, MacIntyre highlights the danger that, if she becomes overly focused on these external goods, she may lose sight of the importance of excellence, the need for virtue, and the internal goods associated with her work. She will thus undermine the capacity of the practice of tour operation to contribute to human fulfilment.

The link made by MacIntyre between virtue and human flourishing, which includes their relationship with the achievement of excellence in practices and the associated internal and external goods, is summarized in Figure 5.1.

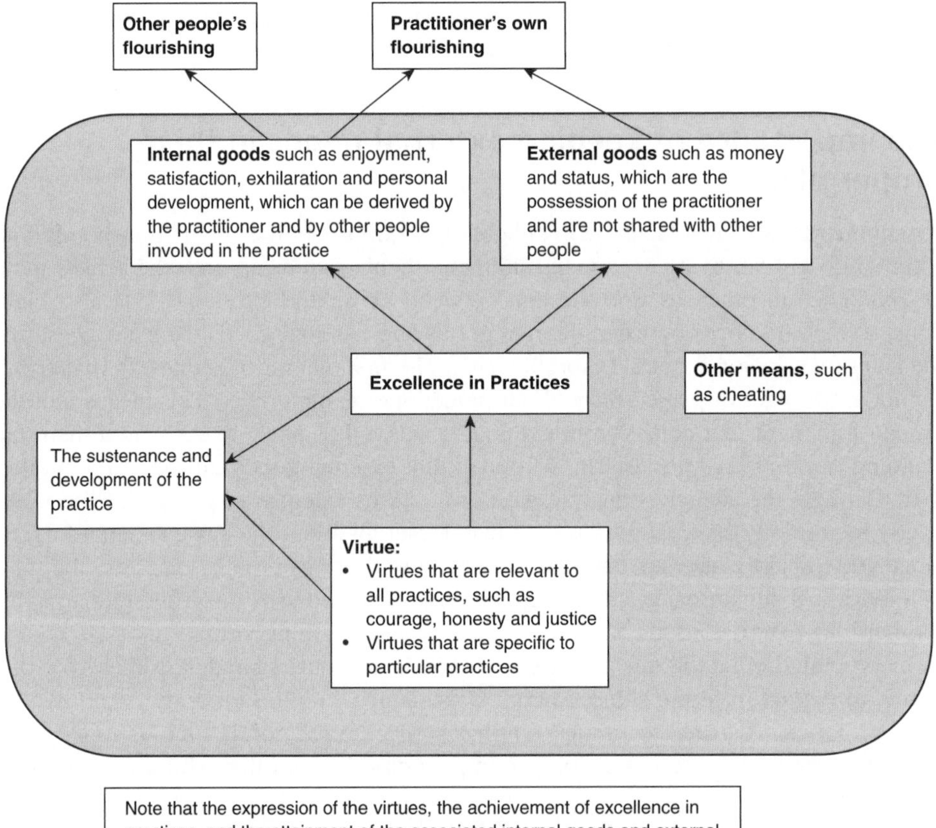

Figure 5.1 Alasdair MacIntyre: The link between virtue and human flourishing

The role of institutions

For MacIntyre, then, it is important to avoid external goods becoming too important. A key role in helping to keep external goods in their proper place is played by what MacIntyre refers to as *institutions*. Institutions provide the frameworks within which practices take place. As MacIntyre describes it, if 'Chess, physics and medicine are practices; chess clubs, laboratories, universities and hospitals are institutions' (MacIntyre, 1985/1981: 194).

Clearly, business corporations can be regarded as institutions, since they provide the organizational frameworks within which certain work practices take place. And the bodies that are charged with regulating companies within a particular industry can also be thought of as institutions, since these regulatory bodies also provide organizational frameworks for work practices. In the example of tour operation, then, the travel company that provides the organizational framework within which the practice of tour operation takes place can be regarded as an institution. Moreover, regulatory organizations such as the Association of British Travel Agents, which supervises tour operators in the UK, might also be classed as institutions in MacIntyre's terms.

Taking care of external goods

In MacIntyre's view, the primary role of institutions is to take care of external goods. As such, institutions fulfil an essential role in relation to practices: it is institutions that ensure the availability of the external goods that a practice needs in order to take place; and it is institutions that arrange the distribution of those external goods amongst practitioners. As MacIntyre puts it,

> Institutions are characteristically and necessarily concerned with what I have called external goods. They are involved in acquiring money and other material goods; they are structured in terms of power and status, and they distribute money, power and status as rewards ... no practices can survive for any length of time unsustained by institutions. (MacIntyre, 1985/1981: 194)

To appreciate how institutions relate to the external goods associated with a particular practice, consider again the practice of tour operation. Travel companies – within which the practice of tour operation takes place – provide the resources and facilities that tour operators need to carry out their work. The buildings, communications systems, financial resources, and all the other paraphernalia that is needed by tour operators if they are to do their job well must be made available, and it is the role of travel companies to provide these things. As the institutions within which tour operation takes place, travel companies must also arrange the allocation of external goods amongst the tour operators who work within them. That is, it is their role to ensure appropriate distribution of wages and status amongst tour operation practitioners.

Keeping external goods in their proper place

MacIntyre suggests that it is also the role of institutions to ensure an appropriate relationship between, on the one hand, external goods and, on the other hand, internal goods, excellence and virtue. Although institutions have to look after external goods, they also have to make sure that external goods do not get out of kilter with these other important things. Rather, external goods should be distributed in accordance with excellence and virtue. And if external goods are distributed in accordance with excellence and virtue, their achievement will correspond to the achievement of internal goods. It would be the responsibility of a travel company, then, to ensure that wealth and status are distributed amongst its employees in accordance with the amount of excellence they achieve. In other words, tour operators should be paid and promoted in accordance with the extent to which they meet relevant standards of tour operating excellence.

However, MacIntyre warns that this may not always happen. Institutions may get things wrong; they may place more importance on external goods than on excellence, virtue and internal goods. And in so doing, they may undermine the very things that they are there to preserve. Thus, as MacIntyre sees it, 'Practices are often distorted by their modes of institutionalization, when irrelevant considerations relating to money, power and status are allowed to invade the practice' (1994: 289).

To envisage how this might happen, consider once more the practice of tour operating and the institution of a travel company. Instead of concentrating on delivering excellent holidays, a particular travel company might prioritize short-term profitability. In order to achieve this, it might promote a highly competitive, sales-driven culture, which focuses on revenue maximization and cost minimization. It might celebrate short-term financial performance, paying bonuses and promoting sales staff according to sales figures, regardless of the implications for service quality and relationships with in-resort providers. It might also skimp on staff, training, IT-system development and office facilities to further cut costs. All of these measures would maximize revenue and reduce expenditure in the short term whilst impairing the company's ability to deliver excellence into the future.

The challenge facing institutions such as business corporations and the bodies that regulate them, then, is to ensure an appropriate balance between internal goods and external goods. It is to encourage virtues that are consistent with the achievement of excellence in the work practices that they house. And it is to prevent the allure of external goods from eroding virtue and excellence. In short, a virtuous business institution is one that prevents money and status from becoming overwhelming corporate imperatives.

Theory in Practice

Bloodgate: Prioritizing external goods and the erosion of virtue

Sports corporations occupy an increasingly significant place in global economic activity, with the likes of soccer clubs, cricket clubs and American football clubs being run as multi-million pound enterprises. These businesses provide the *institutional* frameworks within which work *practices* such as playing soccer, cricket and

American football take place. Within this professional context, sports people such as soccer players, cricketers and American footballers are not just players practising their sport in their spare time; they are full-time company employees, whose practices are managed by the sports corporations for which they work.

Since 1997, the game of rugby union has embraced professionalism, with the consequence that the world's biggest rugby clubs are run as corporations nowadays. As well as being a business activity for many people, rugby is also a *practice* in MacIntyre's terms. It is a socially established, cooperative form of human activity. Like any practice, rugby has its own, characteristic standards of *excellence*. People who achieve those standards of excellence are thus able to derive a range of *internal goods* and *external goods*.

Harlequins is one of the oldest and most famous rugby clubs in England. As a professional rugby club, Harlequins is now part of a corporation known as Harlequin FC. The Harlequins team plays in the English Premiership, which organizes England's top-end, professional competition. Harlequins is also a member of the Rugby Football Union, which oversees all rugby in England. And because it plays in European competitions, Harlequins is subject to the control of European Rugby Cup, which has organized cross-border competitions in Europe in recent years.

Harlequins has a long and distinguished history. Many fine players from all over the world have been proud to represent the club, drawn by its reputation for hospitality and fair play as well as by its competitive achievements. For over a century, Harlequins has epitomized characteristic *virtues* of rugby such as honesty, camaraderie, good sportsmanship and respect for opponents. On 12 April 2009, however, Harlequins became embroiled in a scandal whose reverberations shook the rugby world and which was to have a profound impact on the club's status as a business and as an iconic sporting institution.

On that day, Harlequins were playing the Irish side, Leinster, in the semi-final of rugby's European Cup, which is the most prestigious club competition in the Northern Hemisphere. The match was tightly poised as it entered its dying minutes. Leinster were leading by six points to five. Harlequins were pressing hard on the Leinster line but could not breach the Irish team's defence. Unable to score a winning try, it seemed that Harlequins' only opportunity to snatch victory would be to kick a drop goal or a penalty goal. However, the player who was most likely to kick a goal for them had been substituted earlier in the game. Harlequins badly needed him on the field now but, according to the substitution rules of rugby, the only circumstance under which they could bring back their star goal kicker would be if another player had to be replaced because of injury.

(Continued)

(Continued)

The Harlequins coaching team then put in motion a cunning ruse to get their goal kicker back into play. A blood capsule was smuggled onto the field (Rees, 2010). One of the Harlequins players bit into the capsule and feigned a cut to his mouth. There seemed to be no alternative but to replace him, and the star kicker returned to the field.

Ultimately, Harlequins' ruse was unsuccessful. Their kicker did not get the opportunity to kick a goal, and they lost the match. However, as events unfolded, this was the least of their worries. The Leinster coaches and match officials became suspicious of the substitution and a delegation was sent to the Harlequins changing room to investigate the 'injury'. As the officials approached, the 'injured' player implored the Harlequins team doctor to cut his lip to try to convince them that he had been legitimately substituted. Although she was initially unwilling to do this, the doctor eventually made a small incision to the inside of the player's mouth with a scalpel (Rees, 2009a).

But this attempt to cover up Harlequins' deception did not work. An official enquiry into the incident was launched, the findings of which had severe repercussions for the club. Dean Richards, who was Harlequins' Director of Rugby, and who was a hugely respected figure in the history of English rugby, took responsibility for the deception and resigned his post (BBC, 2009a). Richards was later banned from taking any part in European competitive rugby for three years (BBC, 2009b). The chairman of Harlequin FC, Charles Jillings, also resigned, saying that 'As a result of the board's failure to exercise control, the club cheated ... Ultimately this happened under my watch and the failure to control must fall at my door' (cited in Rees, 2009b). Meanwhile, the team physiotherapist, who admitted issuing the blood capsule, was suspended from practising by the Health Professions Council for two years (Rees, 2010), although his suspension was subsequently rescinded (Averis, 2011). The player who had feigned injury was banned from playing for four months and the doctor who cut his lip in an effort to cover up the deception was cautioned by a General Medical Council disciplinary hearing (*The Guardian*, 2010). Moreover, European Rugby Cup, the organizing body of the competition, imposed on Harlequins a fine of 300,000 euros (*The Telegraph*, 2009).

Despite these heavy sanctions, though, the most significant effect of the scandal was the damage it caused to Harlequins' reputation. The company's Chief Executive, Mark Evans, observed that it was unlikely that the stigma surrounding what came to be called 'bloodgate' would ever completely disappear (BBC, 2010a). Key figures in one of the world's most respected rugby clubs, which had for over a century been regarded as a bastion of the game's traditional virtues, had been exposed as cheats.

Questions

1 A number of *institutions* associated with the *practice* of rugby are referred to in the above account. Can you identify them?
2 What *internal goods* might be derived by Harlequins' players through achieving some measure of excellence at rugby?
3 What sort of *external goods* would have been maximized by those associated with Harlequins if they had succeeded in winning against Leinster?
4 In what way might Harlequins' efforts to achieve those *external goods* have undermined *virtues* that are traditionally associated with rugby?
5 Can you identify actions taken by the *institutions* named in this account to preserve those *virtues* and to ensure that the *external goods* associated with playing rugby did not get out of kilter with *excellence* and *internal goods* in future?
6 Do you think any of the *institutions* named here might have contributed to the prioritization of external goods which led to these events?
7 This account has focused on tensions between *external goods* and the *virtues* associated with the *practice* of rugby. Can you identify ways in which virtues associated with other practices were also put under pressure by the prioritization of external goods in this particular business?

Creating and sustaining a virtuous business

The implications of MacIntyre's ideas for business ethics have been explored at length by Geoff Moore (2002, 2005, 2008, 2012) and Ron Beadle (Beadle and Moore, 2006; Moore and Beadle, 2006). By thinking of corporations as institutions and by thinking of the activities that take place within those corporations as practices, Moore and Beadle suggest that we can develop an understanding of what it is to be a virtuous corporation. Their proposals also provide a template for virtuous business management.[3] That is, they offer a number of recommendations that might help business managers to create and sustain virtuous corporations.

For a start, Moore and Beadle propose that managers should do what they can to encourage the pursuit of excellence in their corporations. Whichever practices may be housed within a corporation – whether they include tour operating, financial services provision, coalmining, clothing manufacture, music, sport or any other coherent and

[3]This topic is addressed explicitly by Moore in his (2008) paper, 'Re-imagining the morality of management: a modern virtue ethics approach', but this discussion will also draw on other papers by these writers.

complex form of socially established, cooperative human activity – it is essential that the people who carry out those practices are encouraged to do so to the best of their ability. Most importantly, the quest for external goods should not be permitted to overshadow the pursuit of excellence in practices. Any corporation that permits this may 'in effect, kill itself from the inside' (Moore, 2002: 28) by failing to sustain the basis upon which its long-term viability depends.

A second recommendation is that external goods should be regarded as a means to achieving the end of excellence, rather than as an end in themselves. For sure, external goods such as money and reputation are critical to corporate prosperity. Their care and cultivation is therefore 'both a necessary and worthwhile function of the organization' (Moore, 2012: 366). And responsibility for caring for and cultivating these essential external goods falls to business managers, since they are the stewards of the institutions (the corporations) for which they work. However, external goods should not be allowed to become an overwhelming priority. The achievement of excellence in practices should always be the ultimate objective within a corporation; and external goods such as money and reputation should be valued only insofar as they support this. As Moore puts it, companies need money and status, but they should be prized '*only to the extent necessary to the sustenance and development of the practice*' (2008: 499).

Geoff Moore also emphasizes the importance of celebrating internal goods over external goods. In his words: 'individuals would need to concentrate on the *intrinsic* value of work in business organizations rather than its *instrumental* value' (2005: 249). Moore thus draws attention to the connection between internal goods, as defined by MacIntyre, and what human resource management theorists often refer to as 'intrinsic rewards'; that is, things like job satisfaction, collegiality, self-esteem and personal development. These are often contrasted to 'extrinsic rewards' such as money and status, which equate to MacIntyre's external goods. Moore thus highlights the value of human resource management processes that celebrate the intrinsic rewards associated with excellence, as opposed to those that focus primarily on individually based, financial incentives.

And a fourth point made by Moore and Beadle is that managers may need to resist pressure from outside the business to maximize short-term financial performance. As they put it, a virtuous corporation needs 'to be able to resist the corrupting power of institutions in its environment with which it, in turn, relates, such as competitors, suppliers or those that represent the financial market, where these encourage single minded concentration on external goods' (Moore and Beadle, 2006: 375). If managers wish to manage their corporations in a virtuous manner, then, they may have to challenge values and priorities that prevail in the corporate world. In particular, those who run publicly owned companies may need to manage the expectations of shareholders and market analysts, for whom short-term, financial measures are often taken to be the most important indicators of corporate flourishing.

Conclusion

This chapter has outlined a number of insights that virtue theory offers to business ethics. Aristotle's teaching encourages us to think of corporate flourishing in terms that go beyond financial prosperity. In particular, it alerts us to the possibility that for a business and the people within it to flourish, they need to develop and sustain an appropriate amount of virtue, and they need to express that virtue within the context of a community. Virtue theory's focus on community also encourages us to challenge a business ethos that focuses only on the interests of shareholders. It points to a more comprehensive understanding of business purpose; one which entails respectful and considerate relationships with the wider community of stakeholders with which business interacts.

The importance of keeping financial considerations in their proper place is also suggested by MacIntyre's discussion of internal goods, external goods and excellence. MacIntyre's account suggests that, although things like money and status need to be cultivated by corporations, if managers get too carried away with these external goods, they may lose track of more comprehensive and long-term benefits that business can deliver. By applying MacIntyre's ideas to business management, it is possible to identify practical measures that will help managers foster virtue, excellence and internal goods in the businesses they run, and which may also help them to build sustainable, flourishing companies.

Discussion questions

1. How might virtue theory help us to think about the banking crisis of 2008? Could the near collapse of the financial services industry be explained by the decline in virtues that have traditionally been associated with banking? Could it be accounted for in terms of an overly limited conception of purpose, in which the achievement of short-term financial return became an overarching personal and organizational imperative? And to what extent could this be seen as a case of excellence, internal goods and virtue being subsumed under an overwhelming quest for external goods? Drawing on virtue theory, what advice could you give to financial service regulators and directors of banks that might help them to re-orientate priorities within the institutions that they manage and reinvigorate some traditional banking virtues?
2. Alejo José Sison (2003) suggests that virtue theory might help to explain the fall of Enron in 2001. As well as Sison's book, there is plenty of information on

(Continued)

(Continued)

the internet about Enron. A video called *Enron: The Smartest Guys in the Room* has also been made about the company. If you are not already familiar with the Enron story, you might like to look at some of this material before discussing the following questions: In what ways did the actions of senior managers and traders at Enron prevent the company from flourishing in an Aristotelian sense? How did Enron's senior managers and traders perceive the purpose of the business? In what ways did the prioritization of external goods erode virtue, undermine the achievement of excellence and inhibit internal goods within the company?

3. The account of the 'bloodgate' scandal towards the end of this chapter illustrates how virtue and excellence might be undermined if a sports business places too much emphasis on external goods. The professionalization of sport is an increasingly common phenomenon today, with many sports organizations run by business managers who pay as much attention to the bottom line as they do to sporting excellence. Do you believe that the professionalization of sport inevitably erodes the traditional virtues of sport? Can you identify some things that managers of sports corporations can do to ensure that external goods are kept in their proper place and that the achievement of excellence and internal goods, and the preservation of virtue, remain key objectives?
4. The notion of community is very important to virtue theory. Can you identify ways in which this community orientation contrasts with the individualism that characterizes some of the ethics theories discussed in previous chapters?

Further study

If you would like to read Aristotle's ideas at first hand, you might like to begin with Book I, Chapters 1–8 of his *Nicomachean Ethics*. In reading Aristotle's work, however, it helps to remember that *eudemonia* appears in English translations simply as 'happiness', whereas the words 'flourishing' and 'fulfilment' have been used in this chapter. A better understanding of Aristotle's work will be achieved if you bear in mind that, for him, *eudemonia* meant far more than 'happiness' as we usually understand it.

Robert Solomon's ideas about virtue and business are developed in his (1992) book *Ethics and Excellence: Cooperation and Integrity in Business*. See, in particular, Chapter 11 'The Aristotelian approach to business ethics' and Chapter 13 'Business as a practice'.

Alasdair MacIntyre's book *After Virtue* (1985/1981) is the most important recent work on virtue theory. Two chapters that are of particular relevance to the ideas discussed here are Chapter 12, 'Aristotle's account of the virtues', which discusses Aristotle's theory, and Chapter 14, 'The nature of the virtues', in which MacIntyre builds on Aristotelian theory to develop his own ideas on the relationship between virtue and the achievement of excellence in practices.

Stephen Darwall's *Virtue Ethics* (2003) offers a diverse collection of ancient and modern writings on virtue theory, including some of the above.

Geoff Moore's (2008) paper, 'Re-imagining the morality of management: a modern virtue ethics approach' proposes that MacIntyre's ideas can be adapted to provide a model of virtuous management whose objective is to ensure an appropriate relationship between excellence, external and internal goods within organizations.

All of the Geoff Moore and Ron Beadle papers cited in the bibliography of this book discuss MacIntyre's work and explore how his ideas can be applied in business contexts. See, in particular, Moore's (2002) paper 'On the implications of the practice-institution distinction: MacIntyre and the application of modern virtue ethics to business' and Beadle and Moore's (2006) paper 'MacIntyre on virtue and organization'.

6 Ethical Relativism: Business Ethics and Personal Conviction

Chapter objectives

This chapter will:

- outline some ways in which an ethical relativist approach to business ethics differs from an ethical absolutist approach;
- explore Friedrich Nietzsche's ideas about the relationship between power and morality;
- introduce the idea that personal interests and power agendas might influence the way we think about business ethics;
- explain why ethical relativism does not necessarily entail ethical indifference;
- explain how the existentialist notions of bad faith and authenticity relate to business ethics;
- consider how authenticity might be encouraged in business settings.

Introduction

The first few chapters in this book have outlined some principles that can be used to help us think about the ethical rights and wrongs of business practice. Principles such as 'promoting the greatest good for the greatest number', 'treating people as ends rather than just as a means to an end' and 'respecting universal human rights' were offered as criteria of ethicality that can be applied to business scenarios. The implicit presupposition underlying this approach is that there are absolute notions of ethicality against which business practice can be evaluated. According to this understanding, the task of business ethicists is to identify those absolute notions of ethicality and evaluate the actions and decisions of businesses and businesspeople in accordance with them.

The theory that will be discussed in this chapter, *ethical relativism*, takes a rather different approach and, in so doing, it offers some different insights to business ethics. Instead of trying to identify absolute notions of ethical rightness that hold good in all places at all times, ethical relativism is more concerned with exploring variations in people's attitudes towards ethics and considering why these variations might exist. Ethical relativists also tend to put a lot of emphasis on ethical autonomy. That is, instead of advising people how to apply absolute principles that are provided by some external source, such as moral philosophy, ethical relativism encourages people to give expression to their own, deepest ethical convictions.

The second and third parts of this chapter will discuss each of these ethical relativist themes in turn. The second section of the chapter will consider some aspects of Friedrich Nietzsche's contribution to ethics theory. Nietzsche is one of the most influential philosophers of modern times. He is also one of the most controversial. Some of the detailed content of his writing is quite contentious, particularly if it is read literally. Nevertheless, it is worthwhile engaging with Nietzsche's ideas, partly because they have been so influential and partly because, when considered in a less-literal way, they offer some useful insights into why different people might hold contrasting views about what constitutes ethical business practice.

As well as encouraging us to reflect on why particular people hold particular sets of ethical convictions, Nietzsche had some interesting things to say about the desirability of people expressing those convictions. In this respect, he made a significant contribution to what is often referred to as *existentialist* philosophy. However, other existentialist theorists have presented similar ideas more explicitly than Nietzsche. I will therefore, in the third part of this chapter, draw primarily on the work of one of the most renowned existentialist thinkers, Jean-Paul Sartre, to develop this particular aspect of ethical relativism and to explain how it might help us to think about ethical autonomy in business.

Before addressing these two themes, though, it is worthwhile spending some time describing in more detail how ethical relativism differs from some of the approaches explored in earlier chapters. The first section of this chapter will therefore contrast ethical relativism to *ethical absolutism*, drawing out some of the implications that the former holds for business ethics.

Some features of ethical relativism

This first section of the chapter will outline some characteristics of ethical-relativist theory. I will begin by listing some ways in which ethical relativism differs from some approaches with which you may be more familiar. I will then introduce two attitudes that ethical relativism engenders, each of which will be explored more fully in the remaining sections of the chapter.

Contrasting ethical relativism to ethical absolutism

The theories discussed in the first four chapters of this book are sometimes referred to as *ethical absolutist* theories.[1] Ethical absolutism encourages us to think about ethics in terms of *universal* principles that have *objective* validity. It also tends to put a lot of faith in *human reason* for working out what is right and what is wrong. Ethical relativist theories differ from ethical absolutism across each of these dimensions. In drawing attention to variations in views about ethics, ethical relativism challenges the feasibility of applying the same ethical standards everywhere, suggesting that ethics is, to some extent, *relative* to time and place. Ethical relativism also questions the objective validity of ethical statements, proposing that ethics is largely a matter of *subjective* judgement. Moreover, rather than using human reason to tell right from wrong, ethical relativists highlight the role played by *emotion* in the formation of our ethical convictions and in the making of ethical judgements. I will begin this section by spelling out these distinctions in a little more detail. In the process, I will describe what terms such as 'universal', 'relativist', 'objective' and 'subjective' mean when used in discussions about ethics.

The relevance of place: contrasting relativism to universalism

One important dimension across which ethical relativism and ethical absolutism differs concerns the relevance of place. Ethical absolutists tend to think about ethics in terms of *universal* standards that can be applied everywhere. In other words, ethical absolutism encourages us to think that if something is the right thing for me to do where I live it is also the right thing for somebody else to do wherever they happen to live. To apply this universal presupposition to business ethics is to assume that the same standards of ethical conduct should apply to businesses wherever they operate. It implies, for instance, that transnational corporations should follow the same ethical standards in their overseas operations as they do in their home country.

[1]Ethical absolutism is sometimes referred to as 'ethical universalism', but I will stick with the former title in this chapter.

As its name suggests, ethical relativism takes a *relativist* approach to the significance of place. Relativism challenges the notion that the same ethical principles ought to be applied everywhere. It draws attention, instead, to variations in ideas about right and wrong, suggesting that what is right in one place may not be right in another. To apply a relativist approach to business ethics, then, is to suggest that business ethics is relative to place; that what constitutes ethically acceptable business practice in one place may not do so in others. According to an ethical relativist perspective, then, it may be appropriate for a corporation to apply one set of ethical standards in its operations in one part of the world while applying a different set of standards elsewhere.

The nature of ethical statements: contrasting subjectivism to objectivism

Ethical relativists also tend to think differently to ethical absolutists about the nature of ethical statements. Ethical absolutist theories encourage us to think of ethics in terms of *objective* truths. That is, when we say that something is right or wrong, ethical absolutists assume that we are making a factual statement, which can be evaluated in terms of its factual accuracy. According to this objectivist way of seeing things, certain things *are* ethically right and other things *are* ethically wrong, regardless of anybody's opinions on the matter. This implies that if somebody fails to perceive the ethical rightness of a particular situation, that person is simply incorrect in their ethical appraisal. Either they have failed to perceive relevant ethical criteria or they have failed to apply those criteria correctly. In a business context, ethical absolutism encourages us to think of certain business situations as being ethically desirable and others as being ethically undesirable no matter what anybody may think about them. Certain things in business simply *are* right, while other things simply *are* wrong. The statements that we make about the ethicality of business practice can therefore be evaluated against those objective criteria of right and wrong.

Ethical relativists challenge the idea that ethical statements can be objectively true, drawing attention instead to their *subjective* quality. In other words, when we say that something is ethically right or wrong, ethical relativists assume that we are expressing an opinion, rather than stating a fact. According to this understanding, notions of right and wrong are no more than constructions of the human mind; they have no external validity. This implies that if a person or a community believes something to be right, then it is right *for them*; if they believe that thing to be wrong, then it is wrong *for them*. For an ethical relativist, then, business conduct is ethical insofar as people think of it as ethical. And if people consider business conduct to be unethical, then that is what it is. Views about business ethics are just opinions and, just as different people can have contrasting opinions, so certain business practices may be ethical for some people, while being unethical for others.

Working out what is right and wrong: relying on emotion rather than reason

Ethical absolutists and ethical relativists also tend to think differently about how we should work out what is right and what is wrong. Many (although not all) ethical absolutist theories emphasize the role that *reason* can play in ethical judgement. Immanuel Kant, for instance, was a notable rationalist (see Chapter 3). He believed that we can work out our duty purely by using reason. Indeed, Kant placed so much faith in human reason that he thought people who just do the right thing because they feel like it are less deserving of ethical esteem than those who do it because reason tells them to. For Kant, the head should rule the heart when it comes to ethics.

The reason-based character of ethical absolutist theories encourages us to think about business ethics in terms of abstract, theoretically derived principles, which we should apply to specific business contexts in a detached, dispassionate manner. In order to apply ethical absolutist theory to business ethics, then, one need not get too close to the situation being evaluated. For sure, it is important to have a comprehensive understanding of the relevant principles and the relevant facts, but there is no reason why such an understanding cannot be gathered from afar. We do not necessarily need to have direct, personal exposure to a situation in order to evaluate it ethically. Indeed, such exposure might even evoke emotional responses that would undermine detached, reason-based consideration. Ethical absolutist theory, then, may be best applied to business at a distance.

Ethical relativism, on the other hand, does not rely so heavily on reason. Instead, it emphasizes the role that *emotion* plays in ethical evaluation. It encourages us to think of ethical judgements as emotional responses to specific situations rather than in terms of emotionally detached applications of abstract principles. Ethical relativism

Ethical Absolutism		**Ethical Relativism**
Ethics is *universal*: right is right and wrong is wrong no matter where you are.	**The relevance of place**	Ethical right and wrong are *relative*: what is right for one person in one place may be wrong for another person in another place.
Ethical statements are statements of *objective* fact.	**The nature of ethical statements**	Ethics is *subjective*: ethical statements are statements of opinion.
We can work out what is right and wrong using human *reason*. We can do this from a distance.	**Working out what is ethical**	Ethical judgements are *emotional* responses to specific situations. Therefore, to tell right from wrong, we need to get up close.

Figure 6.1 Contrasting ethical absolutism to ethical relativism: a summary

therefore implies that, when we make ethical judgements, we should allow ourselves to be informed as much, and perhaps more, by the heart as by the head.

The emphasis that ethical relativists place on emotion leads them to challenge the idea that we can stand back from a business scenario and pass ethical judgement in a neutral, dispassionate manner. Ethical relativist theories tend to emphasize proximity rather than distance. That is, they suggest that those who are best placed to pass ethical judgement on a business-related situation are those who are closest to it and who therefore experience the most acute emotional responses to it. Indeed, it has been suggested (for example, by Bauman, 1993) that large business organizations are intrinsically corrosive of ethics because they deprive people of the close contact upon which ethical sensitivity depends.

Video Activity 6.1

In the 1993 film Jurassic Park, a company run by John Hammond creates a theme park on a tropical island, which contains prehistoric creatures that have been scientifically produced by bioengineers working for Hammond. The following URL links to a scene from the film. The scene features a discussion about the ethics of Hammond's enterprise. In this discussion, Donald Gennaro, a lawyer working for Hammond, outlines some entry-pricing strategies designed to maximize revenue from the park. Hammond takes issue with Gennaro's profit-maximizing approach, arguing that everybody should be able to visit the park and suggesting that the strategies Gennaro has in mind might preclude all but the richest people from doing so. Meanwhile, Dr Ian Malcolm challenges the ethicality of the whole idea of using science to recreate prehistoric creatures, proposing that this involves interfering with the natural course of evolutionary development. The other scientists present also express reservations about the project.

www.youtube.com/watch?v=0Nz8YrCC9X8

Questions

1 Would an ethical relativist be more likely to regard the disagreement between Ian Malcolm and John Hammond about the ethics of bioengineering as: (a) a disagreement about ethical fact; or (b) a difference of ethical opinion?
2 In observing Donald Gennaro's and John Hammond's disagreement about pricing strategies, would an ethical relativist be more likely to: (a) explore possible reasons why each of these men held their respective views about the ethics of admission pricing; or (b) try to apply abstract, universal principles to identify which of the two has the best grasp of ethical truth?

(Continued)

(Continued)

3 In order to develop our understanding of the ethicality of bioengineering in Jurassic Park, would an ethical relativist be more likely to propose: (a) that we keep our distance from the park and carry out a detached, rational appraisal of the ethical rights and wrongs of the matter using abstract ethical principles; or (b) that we visit the park, see the animals and meet the people who work there in order to develop a well-informed emotional response to its ethical ramifications?
4 Can you think of any reasons why the scientists in the film might have ethical reservations about bioengineering, while characters such as John Hammond and Donald Gennaro have so few reservations?
5 Can you think of any reasons why Gennaro and Hammond might have such different views about entry-pricing strategies?

Ethical relativism: no reason for ethical indifference, but good reason for ethical reflection

It is important to point out that ethical relativism does not provide a justification for dismissing the importance of ethics. To apply ethical relativism to business is not to say that businesspeople should not bother about ethics. Just because there are no absolute standards that we can use to evaluate the ethicality of business practice does not mean that business is an ethics-free zone. The absence of universal, objective standards of right and wrong does not mean that we should no longer worry if a company pollutes the environment, if it misleads its customers, or if it expects its employees to work in unhealthy, unsafe or demeaning conditions. It just means that we cannot look to universal, objective, rationally accessible principles to support our ethical convictions about such issues. But removing the handrails that guide our personal ethical convictions does not mean that those convictions no longer matter. Indeed, as I will explain in the third section of this chapter, some ethical relativists believe that the force of ethical opinion actually derives from its subjective nature. Those theorists therefore place a great deal of importance on people being able to develop and express their deepest and most heartfelt ethical beliefs.

Although ethical relativism need not undermine the worth of ethical conviction, though, it does encourage reflection on it. In particular, it encourages us to think about why we may have come to hold those ethical convictions that seem so self-evident to us. Ethical relativism invites us to question our taken-for-granted assumptions about right and wrong; to ask whether they really are as certain as we think, or whether they are, at least to some extent, shaped by our life experiences, the social influences to which we have been exposed, and the things that matter to us. It is to this aspect of ethical relativism that I will turn in the next section of this chapter.

Theory in Practice

Ethical absolutist and ethical relativist approaches to Foxconn's employment practices

The differences between ethical relativist and ethical absolutist approaches can be illustrated by considering the contrasting insights that they might offer on a specific, ethically charged, business-related issue. In recent years, a number of media reports have thrown the spotlight on employment practices in Chinese factories in which iPads, iPods and iPhones are assembled (for example Chamberlain, 2011; Dihigg and Barboza, 2012). These reports suggest that Foxconn Technology, which undertakes assembly on Apple's behalf in China, allows working conditions that would be considered unethical in Western nations. For instance, reports tell of employees being forced to work excessive overtime in order to meet demand for Apple's products; of draconian supervisory practices, which include public humiliation of workers whose performance is considered substandard; and of workers being accommodated in overcrowded dormitories and being expected to follow strict rules. The pressure group China Labor Watch (2014) has even linked a spate of suicides amongst Foxconn workers to the intense pressure that they are under to produce Apple goods. Charles Dihigg and David Barboza (2012) also refer to reports of unsafe and unhealthy working conditions. For instance, they suggest that inadequate extraction in Foxconn's Chengdu plant allowed a build-up of aluminium dust from the polishing of iPad cases, which may have been responsible for a fatal explosion in 2011.

If these reports are correct, the labour standards that are permitted in China, at least in Foxconn's factories, are very different from those that would be expected by the people who buy Apple's products in the West. So how should we interpret, understand and evaluate this issue from an ethical perspective? Ethical absolutists and ethical relativists are likely to approach this task in contrasting ways, and each would enable different insights.

An ethical absolutist approach

Ethical absolutism would help us to establish *universal* ethical standards that should be applied by corporations in their assembly plants, wherever they happen to be. If ethical absolutist evaluation reveals that Foxconn has failed to observe those universal standards, then it would be considered ethically culpable. In this case, critique might also be levelled at Apple for allowing its subcontractors to get

(Continued)

(Continued)

away with unethical labour practices. On the other hand, if ethical absolutist critique reveals that the standards being applied in the manufacture of Apple's products conform to universal rightness, then both Apple and Foxconn can be absolved of ethical wrongdoing.

These labour standards would also be considered by ethical absolutists to have *objective* validity. That is, they would be thought to exist regardless of whether Apple's and Foxconn's managers realise it. If it is decided that objectively valid labour standards have been breached in Foxconn's Chinese factories, there are two possible explanations. The first is that Foxconn and Apple's managers did not realise that they were doing anything unethical. The second is that they knew that these practices were unethical but they chose to continue with them anyway. Conversely, if Foxconn's working practices are found to conform to the objective standards that ethical absolutism helps us to identify, then Foxconn and Apple would be considered to have done nothing wrong. In this case, it is those who criticize these companies that would be regarded as having made an incorrect ethical assessment.

Ethical absolutism would also provide a basis upon which companies like Apple can establish a global code of practice that can be used to ensure that their operations all over the world conform to universal, objective standards of employment ethics. Indeed, following criticism of working conditions in Foxconn factories this is precisely what Apple has started to do, although critics suggest that these standards may not have been applied as rigorously as Apple claim (Dihigg and Barboza, 2012).

Ethical absolutism would also assume that enquiry into the ethicality of this issue can be carried out at a distance. For sure, it is important to get the facts straight before we pass ethical judgement, but this does not necessarily require first-hand exposure to Chinese factory conditions. Ethical absolutism places a lot of faith in *reason* to help us identify universally, objectively valid labour standards. It also looks to reason to help us establish whether these standards are being applied in this instance. These tasks do not require that we go and visit Foxconn's factories in Shenzhen and Chengdu, and they do not demand that we meet Foxconn's employees face-to-face to get their views. They just require that we gather accurate, factual information. Indeed, according to some ethical absolutist theories, intimate contact with the practicalities of this issue might hinder our capacity to make a dispassionate, reason-based evaluation of its ethical ramifications.

An ethical relativist approach

Ethical relativists would probably approach this issue differently, and their enquiry might offer different insights. Rather than trying to identify universal labour standards that can be applied in the West and in China, ethical relativists might seek to understand why the practices that Foxconn encourages in China are so different from those that would be accepted in the West. Such enquiry might look at cultural, economic and social factors that shape employment practices in China and which have resulted in ethical expectations that differ so much from those that prevail in the West.

Ethical relativists would also take the view that the ethicality of Foxconn's employment practices is a matter of *subjective* judgement. In other words, it is a matter of opinion, not a matter of factual truth. However, ethical relativist theory may also offer insights into why different people have come to hold contrasting opinions on this topic. Furthermore, it might offer some insights into why managers at Foxconn and Apple had chosen to adhere to ethical standards which differ so much from those that prevail in the West.

Whereas ethical absolutism would suggest that ethical evaluation of Foxconn's employment practices could be carried out at a distance, some ethical relativist theorists would advocate intimate engagement with the issue. For such theorists, those who are best placed to pass ethical judgement on Foxconn's employment practices are those who are able to get up close to them: those who are able to speak with Foxconn employees; to observe their working conditions at first hand; and to experience the disciplinary regime to which they are exposed. Direct exposure of this nature would be expected to enable the emotional responses upon which ethical-relativist theory places so much importance.

Questions

1 Do you think that Chinese attitudes towards employment ethics are really so different to Western attitudes, or is Foxconn just doing things that even Chinese people would consider unethical?
2 Can you think of any other reasons why Foxconn implements employment practices in its Chinese factories that would be unacceptable in most Western countries?
3 Can you think of any reasons why Apple has allowed its iPhones, iPads and iPods to be produced in accordance with employment standards that would not be approved of in most of the countries in which they are sold?

Friedrich Nietzsche: morality and power

The German philosopher Friedrich Nietzsche, who lived through the second half of the nineteenth century, has had a major influence on ethical relativist theory. Nietzsche had little time for the religion-influenced morality that pervaded European society during his time and which continues to exert a powerful hold over Western ethical thought today. His concerns with this system of morality, which he referred to as 'slave morality' (2003/1887), were twofold. Firstly, he objected to its universalist and objectivist pretensions. Nietzsche was a severe critic of ethical absolutism; he did not believe that any set of moral principles could have universal, objective validity. Rather, he was keen to show that morality is no more than a set of social conventions that hold sway within a particular community at a particular time. But Nietzsche's concerns with prevailing morality went beyond its claim to a universal, objective validity to which it is not entitled. He also proposed that the predominance of the particular values and beliefs that comprise 'slave morality' are preventing the human race from achieving its full potential. For Nietzsche, then, our attachment to the prevailing, religion-influenced morality of the Western world is not only misguided; it also undermines human progress.

This section of the chapter will introduce some of Nietzsche's ideas. It will begin by explaining how Nietzsche went about refuting ethical absolutism. This involves outlining some of the things Nietzsche wrote about power, and about the desirability of strong people exercising power over weak people. These ideas are quite controversial, offering a justification for a highly elitist, meritocratic and competitive business environment, which many people find unattractive. Nevertheless, given the influence that Nietzsche's work has had, particularly when implemented by less-scrupulous wielders of power, it is worth spending a little time spent getting to grips with it. Moreover, although Nietzsche may seem quite explicit about celebrating power and advocating competitive meritocracy, other themes can also be found in his discussion of the relationship between morality and power. I will therefore end this section by outlining what is arguably a more important feature of his discussion of power. This is that it alerts us to the extent that people's beliefs concerning business ethics are shaped by their personal interests and, in particular, by their desire to exert power over other people.

Nietzsche's refutation of ethical absolutism

Nietzsche based his refutation of ethical absolutism on an enquiry into the origins of Western morality. He was particularly interested in the writings of Greek philosophers of the fifth and sixth centuries BC and in what they told us about attitudes to ethics in the ancient world (Leiter, 2002). This genealogical enquiry, Nietzsche claimed, demonstrated that any system of morality is nothing more than a human construction; a set of beliefs and values that prevail amongst a certain group of people in a particular place at a particular time. Moreover, he suggested that the reason why the beliefs and values that comprise a particular system of morality hold sway within a particular community is that they help influential groups within that community to realise their interests and achieve their agendas. In other words, morality for Nietzsche is no more than a set of principles which help a certain group of people do what they want to do and get what they want to get.

Masters and slaves

To appreciate how Nietzsche came to this conclusion, it helps to be aware of several ideas that figure prominently in his writing. The first of these is that Nietzsche often spoke of people in explicitly hierarchical terms. Words such as 'master' and 'slave' appear frequently and, although these terms are sometimes intended literally, they are also used to refer to contrasting 'types' of people. On the one hand, 'master' refers to members of physically or intellectually superior elites, who tend to occupy dominant roles within society. Traditionally, these are 'the "aristocrats," the "mighty," the "masters," the "holders of power"' (Nietzsche, 2003/1887: 16/I.7). Nietzsche observes that, in order to attain and hold onto their elevated status, these gifted elites must be willing to endure considerable hardship and to take great risks. Indeed, in the ancient world where notions of morality first evolved, master types regularly had to put their own lives on the line, since maintaining their position in society demanded continual success in bloody, physical conflict.

When Nietzsche spoke of 'slaves' on the other hand, he was referring to people at the other end of the social hierarchy: 'the slaves, or the populace, or the herd, or whatever name you care to give them' (Nietzsche, 2003/1887: 18/I.9). Slaves, for Nietzsche, were not necessarily captive workers. They were, rather, the less-capable and less-privileged multitudes that make up the majority in most societies. Unlike their masters, slaves had not been willing to risk their lives and endure hardship in order to attain privileged status. Instead, they had contented themselves with subordinate, less-challenging roles, allowing their masters to fight their battles on their behalf.

Video Activity 6.2

The film *Troy* gives some idea of the Ancient world that Nietzsche had in mind when he spoke of 'slave types' and 'master types' in their early historical context. The film is loosely based on the Homeric legend that relates events surrounding the fall of Troy.

The following URL links to a scene from this film, in which the greatest of the Greek fighters, Achilles, takes on and kills Boagrius, who is presented in the film as the champion of Thessaly's army. The scene is interesting for the fact that it is Achilles who represents the Greeks in this battle rather than Agamemnon, who is overall leader of the Greek armies. In Nietzschean terms, Achilles, as Prince of the Myrmidons, is a 'master type' in his own right. However, as supreme leader of the Greek armies, Agamemnon would be counted as the master of all masters. As such, he might have been expected to fight against the king of Thessaly instead of Achilles being called upon to fight Boagrius. Achilles alludes to this when he mutters to Agamemnon as he

(Continued)

(Continued)

passes: 'Imagine a king who fights his own battles. Wouldn't that be a sight?' Indeed, so indignant is Achilles about being called upon to stand in for his commander that he only agrees to do so when urged by the wise counsellor, Nestor.

www.youtube.com/watch?v=Sq-uMIZGETs&list=PLFC0EB75314EE3AE4

Questions

1 On a Nietzschean analysis, how might Agamemnon's unwillingness to risk his own life in mortal combat undermine his legitimacy as supreme *master* of the Greeks?
2 In this scene, the fictitious character Boagrius demonstrates many of the qualities that Nietzsche associates with *master types*. He is physically strong, and he is clearly willing to undergo hardship and risk his life in order to achieve his objectives. But can you think of one particular Nietzschean *master* quality that Boagrius seems to lack?

Will to power

A second idea that figures prominently in Nietzsche's account of morality is his suggestion that all living things are fundamentally motivated by a desire to assert themselves over everything and everyone around them. He often uses the term *will to power* in this context. Thus, he writes in 'Beyond good and evil' of 'a world whose essence is the will to power' (2006/1886: 340/186), and in the *Genealogy of Morals* he refers to the 'real essence of life, its will to power' (2003/1887: 52/II.12). Contrary to accounts of human nature which emphasize the motivational primacy of survival needs, such as the quest for food, drink and shelter, Nietzsche believed that the struggle for supremacy is what really drives the world. As he saw it, 'a living being wants above all else to *release* its strength; life itself is the will to power, and self-preservation is only one of its indirect and most frequent *consequences*' (Nietzsche, 2006/1886: 318/13).

Nietzsche believed that, since the will to power is a fundamental motivating force in all living things, it is a prime mover of human activity. According to his psychological analysis, all other human urges must therefore be understood as secondary to our desire to impose ourselves over others. As he described it, 'The great and small struggle always revolves around superiority, around growth and expansion, around power – in accordance with the will to power which is the will of life' (2006/1887: 366/349).

Nietzsche's preoccupation with power struggles offers one way of thinking about the jostling for status that often occurs in contemporary workplaces. Although we often explain these struggles by highlighting the financial rewards that accrue to those who achieve the highest rank, Nietzsche would suggest that the desire to assert power over other people is what really spurs professional ambition. Similarly, were Nietzsche to observe the competitive skirmishes that pervade relationships between large corporations today, he would not put these down to financial ambition on the part of 'corporate masters'. Rather, he would suggest that such acquisitive behaviour is fundamentally driven by the desire of corporate masters to grow their power base.

The inevitability of will to power

Given the all-encompassing and pervasive character of the will to power, Nietzsche suggested that it would be foolish to deny its significance and it would also be futile to try to prevent its expression:

> to require of strength that it should *not* express itself as strength, that it should not be a wish to overpower, a wish to overthrow, a wish to become master, a thirst for enemies and antagonisms and triumphs, is just as absurd as to require of weakness that it should express itself as strength. (2003/1887: 25/I.13)

In these respects, Nietzsche's view of power is quite different from contemporary attitudes. Nowadays, we tend to regard people who overtly strive for power with a certain amount of suspicion. For instance, we tend to express disapproval of politicians who we suspect of hankering after office just to satisfy their lust for power. Instead, we hope for public figures who will be motivated by a public-service ethic. Similarly, senior executives in large corporations are disinclined to speak openly of the pleasure they take from holding power. Rather, they tend to dwell on their commitment to their company, their customers and their shareholders; or on their dedication to producing high-quality goods and services; or on their wish to do things that benefit society. Nietzsche would have thought of all this as rather foolish. For a start, he would have suggested that it is pointless to expect politicians, businesspeople or anyone else to be motivated by anything other than will to power. Moreover, he suggested that we should not try to conceal this fundamental human drive; rather we should admit to it and feel justified in flaunting whatever power we may have.

Video Activity 6.3

The following URL links to a video entitled 'WSF 2013 – Social Movements against the power of corporations/Brid Brennan'.

www.youtube.com/watch?v=D7DAt-TKcQo

In this video Brid Brennan, who coordinates the Transnational Institute's economic justice programme, talks about social movements that seek to counter the power of large corporations and place power, instead, in the hands of ordinary people.

(Continued)

(Continued)

Questions

1 Brid Brennan is critical of the extent to which the lives of people around the world are increasingly dominated by powerful corporations. How might Nietzsche have responded to this criticism?
2 In contrast to her criticism of corporate power, Brennan speaks approvingly of international campaigns to put power back into the hands of ordinary people. This implies that power is legitimate when it is in the hands of ordinary people but not when it is in the hands of corporations. How do you think Nietzsche would have felt about this distinction between 'legitimate' people power and 'illegitimate' corporate power?

Morality as an expression of the interests of dominant groups

Friedrich Nietzsche believed that the denial of our will to power is a relatively recent phenomenon. He suggested that, if we go back to antiquity, we find that those who held power were not only happy to flaunt it; also they were not constrained from doing so by misguided egalitarian ideals. The warrior kings of early Greek society, for instance, were blatant in the exercise of their power. As far as they were concerned, they had endured the hardship and taken the personal risks that the acquisition of power demanded; therefore, they saw no reason to be modest about exercising it. Conversely, the 'slave types' over whom these Greek 'masters' ruled accepted their subordinate status as a consequence of their own disinclination to endure similar hardship and take similar risks. The value systems that prevailed in that ancient society were therefore consistent with the imposition of power by those elite 'master types'. Nietzsche drew attention to the manner in which early notions of 'good' thus referred to qualities associated with 'master types'. Those human qualities that were consistent with their imposition of power, such as courage, strength, endurance, arrogance, pride, competitiveness and ruthlessness, were thus considered to be 'good'.

As a consequence, not only did early 'master types' exercise social, economic and military power; the value systems of ancient society also provided ethical justification for their doing so. Thus, in earlier epochs,

> has it been the good themselves, that is, the aristocratic, the powerful, the high stationed, the high minded, who have felt that they themselves were good, and that their actions were good, that is to say of the first order, in contradistinction to all the low, the low-minded, the vulgar, and the plebeian. (Nietzsche, 2003/1887: 11/I.2)

However, Nietzsche observed that things are very different in the modern era. An alternative system of morality prevails in Western society, in Nietzsche's time and in our own, which contrasts with the harsh, elitist values of the warrior king. This contemporary 'slave morality' (2003/1887) disapproves of the imposition of power by the brave, the intelligent and the strong. Instead, it privileges the interests of the masses. So how has this transformation of morality come about?

The triumph of slave morality

Nietzsche's account of the triumph of 'slave morality' over earlier value systems goes something like this. Clearly, the 'master morality' of former times had served the interests of warrior kings. In particular, it had provided a justification for the imposition of their will to power over the masses. Since everything that was associated with the warrior kings was considered 'good', it seemed reasonable that they should dominate social, economic and military affairs. However, in privileging the interests of the warrior elite, 'master morality' had helped to keep the masses in subordinate roles. In particular, it had inhibited the expression of *their* will to power. According to Nietzsche, in order to break out of this repressive situation, and to enable themselves to impose their own will to power, the masses set about redefining morality. Instead of relating goodness to qualities associated with their masters, and thus justifying their own subjugation, the masses reshaped notions of good in a way that would serve their own agendas. They were thus able to facilitate the expression of what Linda Williams (2001) calls their own 'reactive' will to power as an alternative to the 'active' will to power of the 'master types'.

Pause for Reflection

If you were one of the Nietzschean *master types* – that is a member of the physically strong, intellectually capable elite, willing to take risks and endure hardship to achieve your agendas – your interests, and particularly your *will to power*, would be well served by a system of morality which rewarded your exceptional capabilities and which justified you in imposing your power over the masses. A moral system which rewards intellectual accomplishment, cultural achievement and physical prowess, and which legitimizes inequality, meritocracy, selfishness and arrogance would therefore be to your advantage.

However, if you were a member of the less-fortunate masses, your interests might be better served by a different system of morality. What sort of qualities and social arrangements do you think would be approved of by this alternative, *slave morality*?

According to Nietzsche, religious leaders of various denominations played an important role in this triumph of 'slave morality' over 'master morality', since it offered them the opportunity to build their own power base. What Nietzsche called a 'priestly mode of valuation' (2003/1887: 16/I.7) therefore evolved, in contrast to the earlier 'knightly, aristocratic mode' (ibid). This inversion of morality saw the master morality replaced by a

> contrary equation … [in which] … the wretched are alone the good; the poor, the weak, the lowly, are alone the good; the suffering, the needy, the sick, the loathsome, are the only ones who are pious, the only ones who are blessed, for them alone is salvation … [while] … on the other hand, you aristocrats, you men of power, you are to all eternity the evil, the horrible, the covetous, the insatiate, the godless; eternally also shall you be the unblessed, the cursed, the damned! (ibid: 17/I.7)

In order to grasp the significance of Nietzsche's account for business ethics, it is important to appreciate the link that he makes between systems of morality and the imposition of power by particular groups. In Greek antiquity, the warrior kings had been able to establish a basis of moral evaluation that was consistent with the imposition of their power. However, as the masses realized the potential offered by their numerical superiority, and as they became organized by the scheming 'priests of antiquity', they managed to reshape morality so that it served their interests. The egalitarian, altruistic, cooperative values of 'slave morality' have thus come to dominate public notions of ethicality, taking the place that was previously held by the selfish, egotistical, competitive values of 'master morality'. The key point is that, in either case, morality is no more than a human construction that promotes the objectives of a specific set of people. And, as Nietzsche saw it, any person's ultimate objective is to acquire and hold on to power.

Pause for Reflection

If Nietzsche were alive today, and were he acquainted with the world of large corporations, who do you think he would identify as *master types* in the corporate world? Who would he think of as the *slave types*?

The interests of these contrasting sets of people – today's corporate *masters* and today's corporate *slaves* – would be supported by contrasting systems of morality. How do you think a contemporary corporate *master morality* would evaluate the ethicality of paying senior executives salaries and bonuses that exceed those of junior employees by multiples of several hundred? What contrasting perspectives would a contemporary corporate *slave morality* offer on this topic?

The *will to power* of Nietzschean corporate *masters* and corporate *slaves* would be served by contrasting approaches to corporate decision making. What type of decision-making structures would promote the will to power of corporate masters? What form of decision making would serve the will to power of corporate slaves?

Nietzsche's call for a return to master morality

I pointed out earlier that Nietzsche's concerns with prevailing morality were twofold. On the one hand, he wanted to make his readers aware that the 'slave morality' that has come to dominate Western thought is nothing but a vehicle for the expression of the interests of certain groups, particularly their will to power, and that it therefore has no universal, objective validity. However, he also wanted to alert his readers to the hazards associated with the prevailing 'slave morality'. Nietzsche took a dim view of the specific values and beliefs that characterize modern, Western, ethical thought. He believed that these have had a damaging effect on the human race and that, if they continue to prevail, they will further constrain human progress.

Nietzsche's disquiet with 'slave morality' relates particularly to the ways in which it holds back human elites from achieving their full potential and thus contributing to the advancement of the human species. For one thing, he was concerned that the emphasis that modern society places on happiness, peace and tranquillity inhibits our capacity to endure suffering, risk and danger. And he believed that, in order to push forward the boundaries of human progress, we must be prepared to suffer, we must be willing to take risks, and we must court danger. He also disapproved of the way in which 'slave morality' values altruism above egotism, so that people feel they have to look after others rather than making the most of themselves. As far as he was concerned, the strong must be prepared to forge ahead on the path towards human progress, unhindered by misplaced concern for those they leave behind. Most of all, Nietzsche objected to the pernicious cult of egalitarianism; that is, the advocacy of equality, which he considered to be 'no more than a naïve humanitarian concoction, a contortion of meaning that allows you to succeed in accommodating the democratic instincts of the modern soul!' (2006/1886: 323/22).

Nietzsche's concern with slave morality, then, is that by discouraging risk taking, endurance, ruthlessness and competition, and by championing misplaced notions of equality, altruism and benevolence, it prevents the most capable people from doing what they can to further human excellence. Precisely what this human excellence consists of is not particularly clear from Nietzsche's discussion. It seems to correspond to some vague notion of the self-actualization of the human species. Despite his equivocation in defining excellence, though, Nietzsche seems fairly clear about the conditions necessary for its attainment. Most importantly, it requires prioritisation of the interests of 'master types' over the masses; it is inherently unequal. The crux of Nietzsche's concern is that the values of 'slave morality', having become embedded in modern culture, are constraining the most gifted elites from cultivating and manifesting those traits whose expression is essential to the realization of their potential and thus to the advancement of humankind. As he saw it, the quest for excellence has been smothered under a blanket of flaccid mediocrity: 'the morality of the vulgar man has triumphed' (2003/1887: 18/I.9) and in the consequent 'dwarfing and levelling of the European man lurks *our* greatest peril' (ibid: 25/I.12).

Applying Nietzsche to business

There are various ways in which Friedrich Nietzsche's philosophy might be applied to business. The variety of applications that his writing permits is partly due to the fact that it is open to different interpretations. Nietzsche was by no means a methodical writer. He tended to use a flamboyant, impassioned and enigmatic writing style, which makes it hard to work out precisely what was on his mind. Even when he does seem to offer straightforward accounts, it may be misleading to take his words at face value. Indeed, some commentators suggest that, rather than offering concrete prescriptions of his own, Nietzsche's main objective was to shake his readers out of their comfort zone in an effort to encourage them to question attitudes and presuppositions with which they have become accustomed (see, for example, Danto, 1994/1986; White, 1994/1988; Williams, 2001).

Justifying competitive, meritocratic elitism

Given the complexities associated with establishing quite what Nietzsche meant and what he expected to achieve through his writing, it is not surprising that his ideas have been used to support a broad and varied range of actions and ideologies. Most alarmingly, Nietzsche's philosophy has been co-opted by extreme right-wing political and social movements. For instance, Adolf Hitler and the National Socialists of 1930s Germany found justification for their cruel agenda in Nietzsche's celebration of meritocracy and his repudiation of any humanistic values that might have tempered their savage excesses. Many of Nietzsche's commentators (e.g. Kaufman, 1956; Langiulli, 1971; Williams, 2001; Leiter, 2002) suggest that to paint Nietzsche with the brush of Nazism is unfair, since he was neither a German nationalist nor anti-Semitic, and since he would probably have been appalled by the selective appropriation of his philosophy by right-wing extremists. Nevertheless, considering his apparent celebration of hierarchy, his unashamed elitism, his criticism of 'slave morality', and his repudiation of values such as kindness, altruism and equality, it is easy to understand why fascists should have found his philosophy so attractive.

Nietzsche's criticism of 'slave morality', his advocacy of those values which promote the will to power of 'master types', and his call for 'master morality' to be put back in its rightful place of cultural pre-eminence might also be used to support meritocratic business arrangements. On this interpretation, Nietzsche seems to say that those people who are the most capable should be encouraged to flourish; that those who are prepared to take risks, to endure hardship, and to observe harsh self-discipline should be rewarded; and that domination by business elites should not be constrained by misguided values such as equality, kindness and concern for others. In short, the business world should be dominated by gifted high-flyers.

Video Activity 6.4

The following video clip shows a scene from the 1992 film *Glengarry Glen Ross*. The scene is set in the office of a property sales company. The salesmen who usually work in the office are exhorted by their new sales manager, Blake, to be more aggressive in their sales activities.

www.youtube.com/watch?v=eIrnAl6ygeM

Questions

1 In what ways does the character Blake express the values of *master morality*, which are celebrated in Nietzsche's writing?
2 Do you believe that this approach to business is common?

Reflecting on our ethical convictions

Nietzsche's ideas seem to justify a highly competitive corporate world, in which the strongest and the most resolute are allowed to flourish while the weakest are left to fall by the wayside. Moreover, in establishing power in the corporate world, businesspeople need not spare any thought for the social consequences of their actions: if the playing out of corporate power games eventually makes the world a better place, then we need not worry too much if a few people get hurt along the way. According to this interpretation of Nietzsche, businesses and businesspeople should be tough, and if their toughness is undermined by a misplaced social conscience this will ultimately curtail human progress.

However, these are not the only insights that Nietzsche's philosophy offers to business ethics. Nietzsche's celebration of 'master morality' may be amongst the most striking aspects of his work, but it is by no means the only message that we can take from it. Arguably, his most important contribution to ethics theory is not his legitimation of competitive elitism but the fact that he encourages us to think about the role that self-interest, and particularly power agendas, play in the formation of people's ethical judgement. We are accustomed to thinking of our ethical views as impartial, detached responses to the situations that we encounter. We thus downplay the possibility that our beliefs about right and wrong might be influenced, consciously or subconsciously, by our own interests and our own aspirations. By highlighting the role that power agendas play in the formation of morality, Nietzsche encourages us to think otherwise. He thus offers us good reason to be suspicious of the apparent purity of ethical conviction.

When we evaluate the ethical beliefs expressed by particular business communities, then, Nietzsche would urge us to reflect on the extent to which those beliefs may be shaped by interests and power agendas that prevail within those communities. Consider, for instance, how attitudes to the matter of senior-executive pay may vary between corporate bosses and their junior employees. Senior managers may consider themselves ethically entitled to their generous salaries by virtue of all the hard work they put in, the considerable responsibility they take on, and the magnitude of their contribution to corporate success. And they may struggle to come to terms with contrasting viewpoints that call into question what appears to them to be a self-evident entitlement to their just rewards. Junior employees, on the other hand, may see things otherwise. They may contest the fairness of paying their corporate masters hundreds of times more than they receive in their own salaries. In this instance, Nietzsche would advise both sides to consider whether their respective ideas about ethical entitlement are quite as objectively based as they seem. Nietzschean analysis would suggest that the ethical perspective of senior executives on such a matter is partly influenced by financial self-interest, and particularly by a yearning for the power that wealth enables. On the other hand, the ethical resentment that less-privileged employees feel towards their senior colleagues may be partly shaped by their realization that they are unlikely to ever be able to share the latter's good fortune, so their own capacity to wield power will be forever constrained.

Consider, also, the insights that Nietzsche's ideas might offer to the ethicality of contrasting corporate decision-making processes. Senior managers may consider that their experience, knowledge and superior judgement give them the ethical prerogative to make key decisions affecting the firm and its stakeholders. On the other hand, stakeholders such as employees, suppliers, local communities, shareholders and customers, whose lives may be deeply affected by those decisions, are likely to think that they are ethically entitled to participate in them. Nietzschean theory encourages us to ask whether these conflicting moral perspectives are at least partly shaped by considerations of the contrasting distributions of power that would be enabled by contrasting decision-making regimes.

Existentialism: endorsing personal, ethical conviction

The first section of this chapter contrasted ethical relativism to ethical absolutism. It explained that ethical relativism questions the existence of objective standards of right and wrong that can be applied universally and that can be worked out using human reason. Ethical relativism draws attention, instead, to variations in people's understanding of right and wrong. It suggests that ethics is a matter of opinion, and it encourages us to consider why different people might have contrasting ethical opinions. The chapter's second section outlined Nietzsche's refutation of ethical absolutism. I explained how Nietzsche's philosophy might be used to justify elitist business arrangements, but that it might also encourage us to reflect on the extent to which agendas that we hold dear might influence our views about the ethicality of business practice.

To apply this Nietzschean-style ethical relativism to business is potentially a troubling prospect since it seems to undermine the worth of ethical conviction. If, as Nietzsche suggests, there is no such thing as objective, universal, ethical legitimacy, and if any system of morality is no more than a set of conventions that secure the interests of a particular group, then there seems to be no point to ethics. We appear to be left with nothing but moral emptiness; an ethics vacuum in which there is nowhere to turn for guidance. This is the spectre of *nihilism*; a rejection of the very notion of ethical right and wrong, which leads some to the view that life has no meaning. Applied to business, this approach seems to justify an attitude of ethical indifference; a view that, since there are no irrefutable ethical standards to regulate business activity, there is no point in bothering about ethics. And if there is no reason to bother about ethics in business, anything goes.

However, ethical relativism need not lead to an attitude of ethical indifference. Despite Nietzsche's apparent demolition of ethical certainty, a more positive theme can also be drawn from his work; a theme which points towards a more productive relationship between ethical relativism and business ethics. In order to identify that theme, it helps to interpret Nietzsche's writing about ethics metaphorically instead of taking his words at face value. One Nietzsche commentator who has taken this approach is Richard White. White suggests that, when Nietzsche seems to advocate a return to master morality by speaking hopefully of the 'return of the master' (White, 1994/1988), he is doing nothing more than urging every 'sovereign individual' (Nietzsche, cited by White, 1994/1988: 72) to come to terms with the potency of their own, autonomous, ethical conviction. As White sees it, Nietzsche is railing against the human tendency to follow the herd rather than make our own minds up about right and wrong. According to this interpretation, Nietzsche is not telling us to abandon ethics. On the contrary, he is telling us to embrace it wholeheartedly. But he is also telling us that, ultimately, we have to make up our own minds about what is right and what is wrong; that when it comes to ethical judgement, each of us has to grasp the power of our own sovereign will. See Figure 6.2 for an illustration of how these contrasting interpretations might apply to business. This representation differentiates the *nihilistic* response referred to above with the *authentic* response that will be elaborated in this last section.

Fortunately, we do not have to depend on contestable, metaphorical interpretations of Nietzsche's *Genealogy of Morals* to find this type of advocacy of ethical self-empowerment. This is because other writers have provided us with far more explicit articulations of this theme. In this last section of the chapter, I will introduce some ideas that other so-called *existential* thinkers have used to highlight the importance of personal ethical conviction. I will focus particularly on the work of Jean-Paul Sartre, a French, existentialist philosopher, author and playwright who had a big influence in Parisian intellectual circles during the 1960s. I will then explain how these ideas help us think about ethical accountability and authenticity in business.

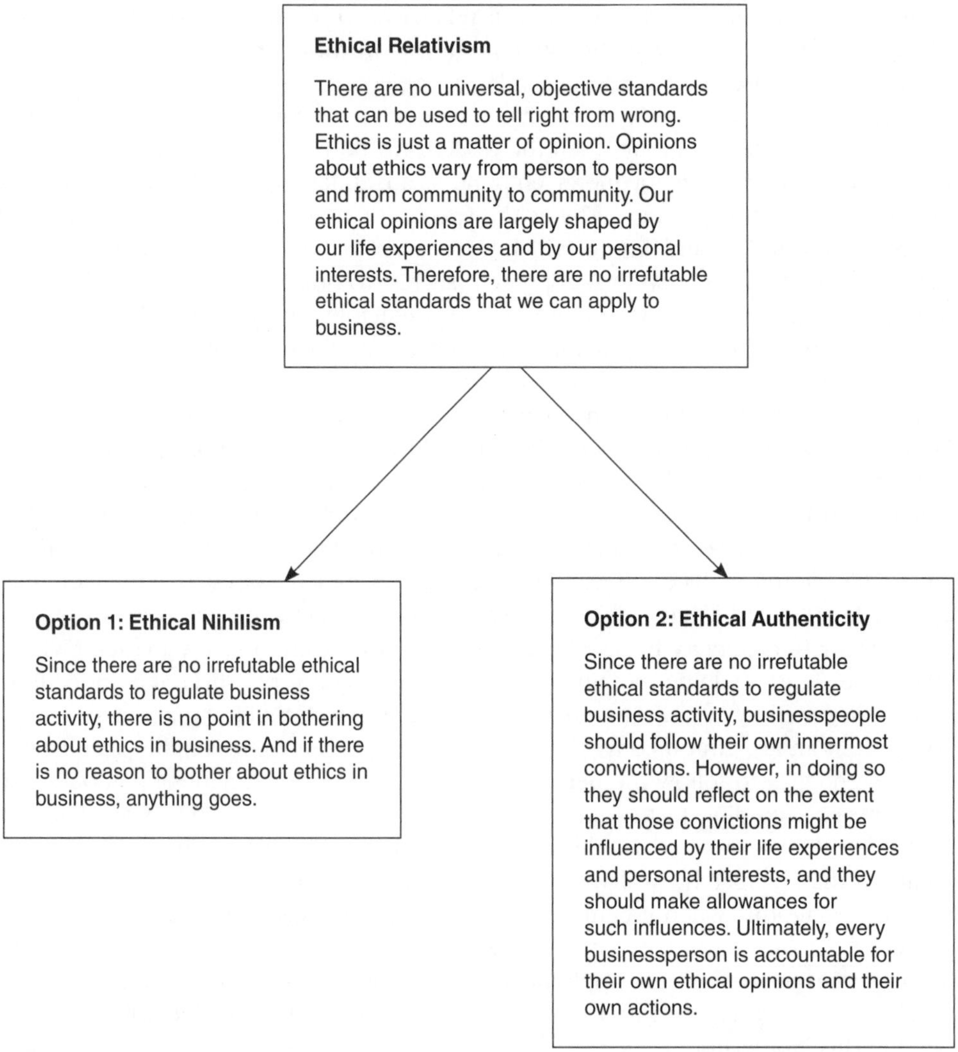

Figure 6.2 Some contrasting ways of applying ethical relativism to business

Our unavoidable freedom to make committed ethical choices and to act in accordance with them

Freedom is very important for existentialism. In particular, existentialists emphasize our freedom to make what we will of the world around us and to respond to that world as we choose. When existentialists speak of freedom, though, they are not usually concerned so much with freedom from coercion by other people. Rather, their focus is on freedom from the constraints that we place upon ourselves. According to an existentialist understanding, we are all a lot freer than we are usually willing to acknowledge. Life may not quite be a blank canvas, but it is certainly a canvas upon which we have far more freedom than we think to construct our own meanings and choose our own directions. As Jean-Paul Sartre put it, 'Man is nothing else but that which he makes of himself. That is the first principle of existentialism' (1973/1946: 28).

Freedom and ethical conviction

Our freedom to make our own meanings and to act in accordance with them has important implications for ethics. For one thing, it entails that we should not lean too heavily on other people's guidance to justify our own ethical choices. For sure, other people may be able to offer us advice about ethics, and listening to their advice may enhance our ability to make well-informed ethical choices rather than poorly informed ones. Nevertheless, the ultimate decision about how to respond to that advice is ours to make. This attitude is summed up by Sartre's statement to somebody who approaches him for advice about an ethical dilemma: 'You are free, therefore choose – that is to say, invent' (Sartre, 1973/1946: 38). The point Sartre is making is that we should not pass off responsibility for ethical decision making to anybody else. To do so would be a cop out of our responsibility as makers of our own ethical choices; it would be to shirk a freedom that is a fundamental feature of the human condition.

This emphasis on individual freedom also implies that we should not feel ourselves bound by particular sets of ethical principles. Existentialists are suspicious of philosophical and religious authorities that tell people what to think about ethics, because they believe this discourages us from making our own free choices concerning right and wrong. Søren Kierkegaard, a Danish philosopher whose writing is often regarded as the inspiration for existentialism, proposed that the energy and commitment that we invest in ethical choices is what actually gives those choices their worth. As Kierkegaard saw it, by making ethical decisions in accordance with the dictates of external authorities or pre-defined principles, we adopt a passive relationship with those decisions. We thus stand back from them and treat them as something that is not really part of us. For him, this passivity is inherently limiting because our decisions are thus deprived of emotional commitment. Decisions that derive from personal conviction, on the other hand, are characterised by the vibrancy of emotional resolve. For Kierkegaard, 'what is important in choosing is not so much to choose the right thing as the energy, the earnestness, and the pathos with which one chooses' (1997/1843: 73–4). Kierkegaard even goes as far as to suggest that emotional engagement with the decisions we make helps us to become better people. He believed that it is by making emotionally engaged choices that the human spirit flourishes; deprived of such choices, it 'withers away in atrophy' (ibid: 72).

In order to draw out some of the implications for business ethics of existentialism's emphasis on ethical conviction, it helps to be aware of two concepts that figure prominently in the work of Jean-Paul Sartre. That is, the contrasting notions of *bad faith* and *authenticity*. I will therefore describe what Sartre means by bad faith and authenticity before drawing out some implications that these ideas have for business ethics.

Bad faith

Bad faith, for Sartre, is a form of self-deceit. He describes it in the following terms: 'one who practices bad faith is hiding a displeasing truth or presenting as truth a pleasing untruth. Bad faith then has in appearance the structure of lying. Only what changes everything is the fact that in bad faith it is from myself that I am hiding the truth' (Sartre, 2003/1943: 72).

To be guilty of bad faith, then, is to be guilty of concealing something from oneself. Sartre has particular forms of self-deceit in mind, though, when he speaks of bad faith. He uses the term in two specific senses, for he is especially concerned about two things that we might conceal from ourselves. The first is that we may hide from ourselves the extent to which our lives are shaped by our circumstances. Sartre, like Nietzsche, felt that it is important to acknowledge the broad range of factors that influence our perceptions, our beliefs and our actions. Whereas Nietzsche focused primarily on the influence that power agendas have over us, Sartre also spoke of the way in which our personal interests, our physical and psychological make-up, our life experiences, and the social pressures that are brought to bear on us influence the way that we see the world and the choices that we make in life. Sartre used the term *facticity* to describe such influences. Facticity refers to the factors that constitute our situation in life. To deny facticity – to deny the influence that such factors have on the choices that we make – would, for Sartre, be one form of bad faith.

However, this is not the only form of bad faith with which Sartre was concerned. Although we are sometimes inclined to overlook the significance of facticity, Sartre believed we are even more prone to a second type of bad faith. This second form consists of pretending that we are unable to choose how to respond to facticity. As far as Sartre was concerned, all of the features that comprise facticity may point us in certain directions, but we are nevertheless free to choose whether or not to go in those directions. Our personal interests, our life history and the pressure that influential others exert over us may encourage us to see the world in a particular light or to act in a certain way, but it is up to us to decide whether we succumb to those influences or assert our capacity to do otherwise. For Sartre, it is bad faith to believe differently. The second form of bad faith, then, which Sartre takes even more seriously than the first, is to conceal from ourselves our freedom of choice; to pretend that we must give in to the various influences to which we are subjected.

Bad faith and business ethics

Consider how bad faith might relate to businesspeople's freedom to make ethical choices and their freedom to respond to those choices. As far as the making of ethical choices is concerned, it would be bad faith for a businessperson to fail to acknowledge the range of influences that may influence her ethical views; influences such as her upbringing, her life experiences, and the values that prevail in the communities within which she lives and works. These influences comprise part of the facticity of her situation. As such, they shape her attitudes about right and wrong in relation to business practice. However, it would also be bad faith for businesspeople to fail to acknowledge their capacity to transcend those influences and assert their own independent ethical judgement. A businessperson's ethical attitudes may be shaped by the influences that comprise facticity, but she is always free to withstand those influences and develop her own, sovereign, ethical convictions.

Bad faith is also relevant to businesspeople's freedom to respond to their ethical convictions. A range of factors may encourage them to act against those convictions. For instance, a businessperson's personal interests may be better served by doing something she believes to be wrong; work colleagues might encourage her to take action which contravenes her ethical beliefs; or maybe the managers to whom she reports might urge her to do something that she finds ethically troubling. It may even be that the ethical conventions that prevail within her work environment push her in a direction that, to her, just does not seem right. For Sartre, it would be bad faith for a businessperson to deny the existence of influences such as these, since they all form part of her facticity. They are powerful motivators for her to act against her inner convictions. Nevertheless, it would also be bad faith for her to deny her freedom to respond to those influences as she chooses. It is up to her whether she acts in accordance with her ethical convictions or against them. If we act in a way that we consider to be unethical, it is because we have chosen to do so. We never *have* to act unethically.

Video Activity 6.5

The following video clip is a report from PBS News Hour entitled 'Britain's Barclays Investigated for Rigging Libor Rates'. It discusses the scandal concerning the manipulation of LIBOR, which initially involved Barclays Bank in London but in which a number of other banks subsequently became involved.

www.youtube.com/watch?v=yjWUwGbyf7w

(Continued)

(Continued)

Questions

1 Those bank employees who provided inaccurate and misleading data to the LIBOR panel may have believed that they were acting ethically. Alternatively, they may have believed that they were acting unethically but chose to do what they did nevertheless. In either case, they were probably influenced by what Sartre would call the *facticity* of their situation. In other words, the way that they thought and acted was probably influenced by a range of situational factors. Some of these factors are alluded to in the video; you may be able to think of some others yourself. What aspects of these bank employees' *facticity* might have encouraged them to provide false data?

2 Some of the employees who supplied false data may have believed they were acting unethically, but that they had no choice but to do what they did. How might this, in Sartre's terms, be construed as a form of *bad faith*?

Authenticity

Whereas bad faith consists of either denying the influence of facticity or denying our capacity to transcend it, Sartre uses the term *authenticity* to refer to coming to terms with the freedom of choice that is an unavoidable feature of the human condition. An authentic person, for Sartre, is one who acknowledges the influences that facticity exerts over the choices that they make but who nevertheless asserts their capacity to transcend facticity.

An important feature of authenticity is that we should not feel constrained by previous choices we have made. Each choice we confront should be seen as a fresh beginning, and as we confront each new beginning we should not feel that we have to carry any baggage from the past into it. The fact that we have believed certain things and acted in certain ways in the past does not commit us to doing the same in the future. To be authentic is to acknowledge the inescapable truth that we are always free to be the person we choose to be, to believe the things we choose to believe, and to follow the courses of action we choose to follow. As Sartre put it, it is to come to terms with the truth that 'my future is virgin; everything is allowed to me' (2003/1943: 88).

Authenticity and business ethics

As far as ethics is concerned, an authentic person is one who acknowledges the factors that influence her ethical beliefs, but who also asserts her ethical autonomy. This includes coming to terms with the fact that we have to make our own ethical choices;

that nobody else can make them for us. This, Sartre acknowledges, can be an unnerving realization. In a business context, not only does it mean that a businessperson cannot depend on others to provide ethical justifications for the things that she does; it may also entail questioning value systems that she has grown accustomed to relying upon. Authenticity is all about letting go of any handrails that have guided our ethical choices in the past and giving free rein to our own ethical inventiveness.

Authenticity also entails asserting our capacity to transcend the various influences that may have a bearing on our actions and grasp the implications of our own sovereign choice. In other words, authenticity involves following our ethical convictions regardless of factors that push us in other directions. An authentic businessperson, then, is one who acknowledges any factors that may encourage her to do something that she considers to be unethical, but who nevertheless transcends those influences and acts in accordance with her deepest ethical convictions.

Video Activity 6.6

The following two videos show scenes from the film *Margin Call*. The action takes place in the head office of a Wall Street investment bank at the beginning of the banking crash of 2008. Both scenes feature the bank's Chief Executive, John Tuld (played by Jeremy Irons), and senior trader, Sam Rogers (played by Kevin Spacey). In the first scene, the bankers discuss a plan to offload the bank's toxic assets before the market has the opportunity to learn of their worthlessness. Sam Rogers objects strongly to this, but eventually agrees to go along with it. In the second scene, which takes place after the toxic assets have been sold, Rogers tries to hand in his resignation but John Tuld persuades him to stay. Rogers clearly does not want to stay, but he agrees to because, as he puts it, he needs the money. In each scene, Rogers displays ethical discomfort with what the bank is doing and with what is expected of him, but he goes along with it nevertheless.

http://movieclips.com/QJzRq-margin-call-movie-be-first-be-smarter-or-cheat/
http://movieclips.com/EAwXc-margin-call-movie-its-just-money/

Questions

1 To what extent would you say that Sam Rogers forms his ethical opinion in an *authentic* way? That is, to what extent does he exercise his freedom to develop his own ethical views about offloading toxic assets, instead of just conforming to the ethical views of his colleagues?

(Continued)

(Continued)

2 Do you think Rogers behaves authentically? In other words, does he exercise his freedom to act in accordance with his ethical convictions, or does he give in to the *facticity* of his situation and act in ways that go against his convictions?
3 In the second video, John Tuld reminds Sam Rogers that he has been doing deals that benefit himself and his company, but which have put other people out of business, 'every day for almost 40 years'. Tuld seems to imply that, since this is what Rogers has always done, he is in no place to criticise its ethicality and he has no choice but to carry on doing it. Later, Tuld tells Rogers 'we can't help ourselves. You and I can't control it or stop it or even slow it down or even ever so slightly alter it. We just react'. How might these be interpreted as expressions of *bad faith* on Tuld's part?

Accountability and authenticity in business

For existentialists, then, freedom is an inescapable feature of the human condition. We cannot be human without being free. In Sartre's words:

> Human freedom precedes essence in man and makes it possible; the essence of the human being is suspended in his freedom. What we call freedom is impossible to distinguish from the *being* of 'human reality'. Man does not exist first in order to be free *subsequently*; there is no difference between the being of man and his *being-free*. (2003/1943: 49)

For Sartre, freedom of choice is particularly important in the field of ethics. The inescapable freedom that defines the human condition entails that our ethical choices are our own; that they cannot be passed off to anybody else or to any external authority. It also entails our freedom to act in accordance with our ethical convictions. Remember that the freedom with which Sartre is concerned is not freedom from coercion by others; it is freedom from the constraints that we place on ourselves. If somebody uses extreme force to compel us physically to do something, then, of course, we may have little choice but to do as that person says. However, for most people, such situations are pretty rare, in life in general and in business. Far more common are situations in which we confront a range of pressures to think or act in particular ways, but in which we can nevertheless choose how we respond to those pressures. This is the freedom that Sartre highlights; the unavoidable freedom that we have, at such times, to transcend facticity. To be authentic is to acknowledge that freedom. To fail to acknowledge it is bad faith.

Ethical accountability

These ideas have two particular implications for business ethics. The first implication is that businesspeople can always be held accountable for the ethical choices that they make and the things that they do. Except in those very rare instances where we are physically constrained to do something that we would not otherwise do, there is no sense in which we could be described as having 'no choice' but to act as we do. Businesspeople may confront a range of pressures to think and act in certain ways. However, as Sartre points out, no matter how constrained a businessperson may feel by these pressures, she is nevertheless free to decide how much attention she pays them. Whether she goes with the facticity of those pressures or stands against it is, ultimately, her choice and her choice alone. Therefore, it is she who must accept responsibility for what she believes and what she does.

Encouraging authenticity

A second implication concerns the ethical desirability of business structures and organizational processes that facilitate authenticity. It is important to note in this respect that authenticity is not an easy route to take. Sartre spoke of the *anguish* that people feel when confronted with the enormity of their own freedom. It is far easier to pass off responsibility for our ethical choices to others, to lean on seemingly authoritative principles to guide our decision making, and to assume that we have no choice but to go where facticity leads, than it is to take personal responsibility for our beliefs and our actions. Sartre likens the anguish of authenticity to the feeling of vertigo that many of us experience if we stand next to a high precipice. For Sartre, the fear that grips us in such situations is not that we may fall or that somebody may push us; it is the fear that we may jump. Anguish, then, comes from acknowledging the awful potency of our own capacity to choose. My anguish flows from my realization that it is *I* who must choose, and from my awareness of the awesome responsibility that this places on me.

We might imagine, then, that people who work in businesses will be more inclined to take shelter in bad faith than to confront what Sartre calls 'the reflective apprehension of freedom by itself' (2003/1943: 63). Given the desirability of authenticity, though, measures which encourage it, and which discourage bad faith, must be seen as a good thing. In this respect, just as existentialists are critical of philosophical and religious authorities that encourage people to follow prescribed ethical principles rather than listening to their own inner convictions, they would be equally suspicious of the tendency for large firms to define ethical standards on behalf of their employees. It is customary nowadays for corporations to establish codes of ethics, which prescribe values and behaviours for their employees; to use ethics training programmes to disseminate these standards amongst their workforces; and to apply ethics management systems to encourage people to obey them. According to an existentialist analysis, to prescribe ethics in this manner, rather than permitting employees to develop and follow their own ethical convictions, runs the risk of discouraging authenticity. Ethics management systems of this type thus constitute one of the 'veritable breeding grounds for bad faith' that Kevin Jackson (2005: 320) associates with today's corporate world.

Far better, then, for those who design business structures and organizational processes to consider ways in which they might encourage employees to develop their own ethical understanding and to act in accordance with their own ethical convictions. Ian Ashman and Diane Winstanley make this point in their discussion of existentialism and business. As they put it, 'The concern [for corporations] is to recognize that ethical decisions stem from an individual's freely chosen values, which results in commitment towards certain actions. They do not arise from obligations or duties drawn from abstract doctrines or codes that negate a sense of ownership or responsibility' (2006: 227).

From an existentialist perspective, then, rather than focusing on prescriptive ethics management procedures, corporations should do what they can to encourage employees to develop their own capacity to make informed ethical judgements, to act on those judgements, and to assume personal responsibility for their actions.

Theory in Practice

Bribery and corruption in the arms trade

This case study offers you the opportunity to apply some of the ideas that have been outlined in the second and third sections of this chapter to a specific, business-related scenario.

Within Western nations, it is usually considered unethical for corporations to use bribery as a method of getting business. Indeed, it is not uncommon for Western businesspeople to pride themselves on the ethical purity of their own business environment in this respect, whilst reproaching developing nations for their corrupt practices.

It therefore came as a surprise to many when, in 2003, a report appeared in *The Guardian* newspaper (Leigh and Evans, 2003) alleging that one of Britain's biggest companies had been involved in bribery on a massive scale. BAE Systems is the UK's largest manufacturer of weapons, military aircraft and security equipment. According to *The Guardian*'s report, the company had paid bribes over many years to officials in Saudi Arabia in order to win contracts worth tens of billions of pounds to supply defence equipment to the Saudi Government.

Although subsequent reports by David Leigh and Rob Evans allege a litany of corruption going back to 1970s payments to the Shah of Iran (Leigh and Evans, 2011a), the biggest deal seems to have been BAE's lucrative al-Yamamah contract, which was agreed in 1985 and which has continued into the 2000s. Of this contract, Leigh and Evans allege that

> Over the past 20 years, the warplane programme has brought £43bn in revenue for BAE ... Police later calculated that more than £6bn may have been distributed in corrupt commissions, via an array of agents and middlemen ... A relatively minor, although colourful, aspect of this torrent of cash was a £60m 'slush fund' maintained by BAE to keep Prince Turki bin Nasser sweet on his visits to the west. The arms firm provided him with extravagant holidays, fleets of classic cars, planeloads of shopping and blond girlfriends. (Leigh and Evans, 2011b)

The aspect of this affair that surprised many observers the most, though, was not that corporate executives and unscrupulous autocratic leaders of client nations had colluded in this manner, but that they appear to have done so with the approval and support of the UK government. Attracted by the boost that such deals brought to the UK economy, and by the influence in Middle-East affairs that they enabled, successive British governments seem to have done whatever was needed to facilitate bribery in the arms trade and to subsequently keep it quiet. Indeed, it has even been claimed that British fixers and middlemen, who smoothed the way for the payment of bribes, have been rewarded with knighthoods and other state honours (Leigh and Evans, 2011a).

Leigh and Evans allege that official support for BAE's corrupt payments continued even after the UK government had signed up to a 1999 international convention agreeing to prevent such practices: 'Instead of fulfilling their international promises, officials merely tried to put more distance between themselves and the companies doing the bribery' (Leigh and Evans, 2011c). Moreover, it has been reported that when, under pressure from the media and the British police, the British Serious Fraud Office commenced enquiries into BAE's affairs in Saudi Arabia, British Prime Minister Tony Blair stepped in to get the investigation halted in the interests of 'national security'. Leigh and Evans (2011d) suggest that Blair was concerned that ongoing investigations might embarrass the Saudi royal family and stop them sharing with the UK security information that would help the UK's fight against terrorism.

(Continued)

(Continued)

Ethical concerns about this affair relate partly to the perception that bribery and corruption in business dealings is intrinsically unethical. However, concerns also relate to the additional costs that bribes may have entailed for client countries; costs which were ultimately borne by their citizens. In relation to the initial round of payments associated with the al-Yamamah deal, Leigh and Evans suggest that 'The cash for all these payoffs came, simply enough, from overcharging. Accidentally released UK documents reveal that the basic price of the planes was inflated by 32%, to allow for an initial £600m in commissions' (2011b). Referring to an earlier deal with Iran, which is alleged to have involved payment of massive bribes to the Shah, Leigh and Evans observe that 'Such duplicity was a fraud on the Iranian people. They were ultimately the ones who had to pay for the Shah's thieving' (2011a).

The main cause for concern about these practices, then, is that a Western company was able to boost its commercial performance by paying well-placed officials in the Middle East enormous sums of money, and that the bill for all this was picked up by ordinary people in Saudi Arabia and Iran who could least afford to pay it.

Nevertheless, a number of British politicians have defended their and their government's role in the affair. Dennis Healey, a former Labour Defence Secretary, observed that bribery was endemic in the arms trade, implying that corporate executives and government ministers had little choice but to go with the flow: 'Bribery has always played a role in the sale of weapons ... in the Middle East people couldn't buy weapons unless you bribed them to do so, and that was particularly true in Saudi Arabia' (cited by Leigh and Evans, 2011e). Ian Gilmour, Secretary for Defence in the Conservative government of 1974, has also expressed this view, pointing out that 'You either got the business and bribed, or you didn't bribe and didn't get the business' (cited by Leigh and Evans, 2011f). Furthermore, Harold Hubert, a former director of army sales for the UK government's Defence and Security Organisation, has suggested that the benefits that accrue from sales of weapons should take precedence over any ethical scruples concerning the way in which those sales are carried out: 'I am not keen to educate the Persians in virtuous ways. My task is to sell British equipment.' (cited in Leigh and Evans, 2011g).

Some recipients of bribes have also mounted a spirited defence of their part in the affair. For instance, Prince Bandar of Saudi Arabia, who is alleged to have collected more than £100 million a year in bribes on behalf of Saudi officials (Leigh and Evans, 2011d), has suggested that the good things that he and his colleagues have done for their country more than justify the payments they have received as a consequence of defence contracts: 'If you tell me that building this whole country ... out of $400bn, that we misused, or got, $50bn, I'll tell you, "Yes. So what?"' (cited in Leigh and Evans, 2011b). And anyway, as Bandar pointed out, he was just doing what anyone in his position would have done: 'We did not invent corruption ... This has happened since Adam and Eve. It's human nature' (ibid).

Questions

1 Some BAE Systems executives, UK politicians and overseas officials who have been interviewed recently say that they see nothing wrong with giving and accepting bribes in this instance. How might self-interest, and particularly considerations of personal *power*, explain these people's attitudes towards the ethicality of bribery?
2 Some of the British politicians who were implicated in this affair have claimed that they had no choice but to facilitate bribes; that they would not have secured valuable contracts otherwise; and that this was just part and parcel of doing business in some parts of the world. How might the two types of *bad faith* described above relate to this justification?
3 Do you think that the executives, politicians and overseas officials involved in this issue have acted in an *authentic* manner?
4 What sort of measures would an existentialist advise BAE Systems to put in place to avoid things like bribery and corruption becoming institutionally embedded in the company and to thus avoid a recurrence of the corporate embarrassment and long-term commercial problems that this episode has caused?

Conclusion

Ethical relativism draws attention to variations in ethical attitudes in different places and at different times. It thus encourages us to question whether any one set of ideas about ethical business can be applied everywhere. It also invites us to explore reasons for variations in people's views about business ethics. The contributions made by certain philosophers to ethical relativist theory offer specific insights for business. This chapter has drawn out the implications of three particular themes.

Firstly, Friedrich Nietzsche encourages us to consider the relationship between power and morality. Nietzsche's own discussion of this relationship offers the basis for some contentious ideas about the application of power and the desirability of competitive meritocracy in business. However, while these ideas may seem to be the most explicitly stated in Nietzsche's writing, they should not divert attention from a second important theme. This concerns the extent to which our ideas about ethics may be shaped by our own interests. Nietzsche's writing encourages us to reflect specifically on the influence that power agendas might have on our ethical beliefs. However, in applying this insight to business, we need not be constrained by Nietzsche's power-oriented analysis of human psychology. We might also ask whether broader, self-interested agendas might play a subtle role in shaping the way we think about business ethics. Although we like to think of ethical evaluation of business practice as an unbiased, rational process, Nietzsche encourages us to consider whether our judgements are shaped partly by our own personal interests or by the interests of the communities of which we are part.

Considerations such as these might drive us towards feelings of ethical indifference or even to nihilistic despair. If ethics is just a matter of opinion, shaped largely by people's personal agendas, there seems little point in having ethical convictions or standing up for them. If this is the case, we might be tempted to conclude that businesses and businesspeople need take no notice of ethics. However, existentialism suggests otherwise. Philosophers such as Sartre propose that, rather than undermining the worth of ethical conviction, the absence of any basis for external verification might serve to reinforce it. If there are no absolute standards against which we can validate personal ethical conviction, personal ethical conviction assumes a position of pre-eminence. The very fact that our ideas about the ethicality of business practice have nothing to prop them up except the emotional fervour that we invest in them actually boosts their vitality. Considerations such as these highlight the importance of ethical autonomy in business. As well as drawing attention to businesspeople's ethical accountability, they underpin the importance of those businesspeople being able to act according to their own ethical convictions.

It should be stressed, however, that to champion ethical conviction is not to preclude ethical debate. Just because ethics is a matter of opinion does not mean that there cannot be well-informed and poorly informed opinion; and it does not entail that our ethical convictions cannot be improved by exposure to other people's views. Indeed, engaging with other people's ethical convictions may permit the development of a more rounded and comprehensive overview than if we try to form them in a discursive vacuum. The desirability of interchanges of ethical opinions will be explored in more detail in the next chapter.

Discussion questions

1. Discuss the following statement: 'Ethical relativists suggest that there are no objective, universal standards that can be used to evaluate business practice. Therefore, it follows that businesspeople can do whatever they choose, without thinking about ethics.'
2. If we agree with ethical relativists that there are no objectively valid, universal ethical principles that can be used to evaluate business practice, does this mean that theories such as rights theory, utilitarianism and Kantian theory serve no useful purpose? Or do you think there might be ways in which these theories can still be used to help us develop our ethical convictions?

3. *Whistle-blowing* is relevant to the issue of facilitating existentialist *authenticity*. In a business ethics context, whistle-blowers are employees who see something that they consider to be unethical going on in their company and who report it to people inside or outside the company who are in a position to address it. Many countries have introduced laws protecting whistle-blowers and a lot of companies have established procedures which encourage whistle-blowers to report wrongdoing (see Near and Miceli, 1985; Miceli et al., 2008). Indeed, in some situations financial rewards are even offered to encourage whistle-blowing (see Perlis and Chais, 2010). On a Sartrean analysis, how might whistle-blowing procedures help to encourage people who work in businesses to be *authentic*? Do you think paying people to whistle-blow might inhibit the *authenticity* of their actions?
4. The topic of bribery in corporations was discussed in this chapter. It was pointed out that bribery is usually disapproved of in Western nations. However, the practice of *corporate hospitality* is increasingly prominent in the West. Corporate hospitality involves firms taking valued clients and business partners to expensive restaurants, exclusive clubs, popular cultural events and high-profile sporting occasions, where they lavish generous hospitality upon them. Do you believe that a distinction can be drawn between corporate hospitality and bribery so that the former can be considered ethical and the latter unethical? Or, if bribery is considered unethical, should corporate hospitality also be considered unethical?
5. In many developed and developing nations, recent decades have seen a significant concentration of capital and economic polarization (Unger, 2009/2005; Callinicos, 2010; Therborn, 2011). In other words, small groups of people have become increasingly wealthy as a consequence of economic activity, and the gap between rich and poor has grown wider. Meanwhile, as the power of organized labour has diminished with declining membership of trade unions (ibid), senior executives of large corporations are increasingly able to dictate what goes on in the business world. To a large extent, as far as business activity is concerned, it could be said that Nietzsche's explicit call for 'return of the master' has been answered: *master morality* seems to be gaining ground in economic affairs. Nietzsche seems to suggest that this state of affairs will help the human race to achieve its full potential. Do you agree that this is happening? Is the world becoming a better place as a consequence of increasing concentration of capital, growing economic polarization, and the domination of global economic affairs by powerful elites? Or would human progress be better served if economic affairs were more strongly influenced by the values that Nietzsche refers to as *slave morality*?

Further study

Charles Dihigg and David Barboza's (2012) *New York Times* article, which discusses the production of iPads in China, offers an interesting account of some of the cross-cultural, ethical tensions associated with international business.

Zygmunt Bauman's (1993) book *Postmodern Ethics* offers a detailed discussion of the implication of ethical relativism for contemporary life. Bauman has some interesting things to say about how organizational structures can inhibit ethical sensitivity in businesses. René ten Bos's (1997) paper, 'Business ethics and Bauman ethics', contains an excellent overview of Bauman's ideas, drawing out their specific implications for business ethics.

If you would like to engage directly with Friedrich Nietzsche's ideas about ethics, the Preface and Essay I of his (2003/1887) *Genealogy of Morals* are good places to start.

Richard White's (1994/1988) 'The return of the master: an interpretation of Nietzsche's genealogy of morals' is also worth reading as a corrective to an overly literal interpretation of Nietzsche's work.

Jean-Paul Sartre's major philosophical work, in which he elaborates his version of existentialism at great length, is *Being and Nothingness* (2003/1943). Reading *Being and Nothingness* is, however, an imposing undertaking, which I would not recommend as an entry point to his work. Fortunately, his (1973/1946) book *Existentialism and Humanism* offers a short, relatively clear and engaging introduction of some of the ideas contained in his longer work.

Kevin Jackson's (2005) paper, 'Towards authenticity: a Sartrean perspective on business ethics', develops some of the ideas introduced here at greater length, as well as drawing on other aspects of Sartre's philosophy.

7 Discourse Ethics: Democratizing Business

Chapter objectives

This chapter will:

- specify the democratic nature of discourse ethics;
- explain how discourse ethics theory appeals to ethical consensus as a basis for evaluating right and wrong;
- explain how discourse ethics envisages the achievement of ethical consensus through dialectical opposition;
- consider the ethically legitimating potential of workplace discourse;
- outline some criteria that workplace discourse needs to meet if it is to conform to the expectations of discourse ethics;
- describe some structural features of communication that might help these criteria to be met;
- explain why the public sphere is important to discourse;
- consider the internet's potential to contribute to a vigorous public sphere;
- explore one way in which corporate colonization might inhibit that potential.

Introduction

There are various ways in which we might think about the nature of ethical right and wrong. Firstly, we might imagine that certain things just *are* right and other things just *are* wrong; that ethical rightness and wrongness are enduring truths that exist independently of any particular person's awareness of them. This way of thinking about ethics implies that, even if nobody realized that particular acts were wrong, they would still be wrong. This is the stance of ethical absolutism, which, as pointed out at the beginning of Chapter 6, tends to be associated with some of the theories introduced in the earlier chapters of this book.

A second way of thinking about the nature of ethical right and wrong was described in Chapter 6. This is the position of ethical relativism; the idea that there are no absolute standards of right and wrong that exist 'out there' beyond our awareness. According to this view, right and wrong are a matter of subjective, human judgement, so what is right for one person may not be right for others.

The discourse ethics theory that will be discussed in this chapter takes neither of these positions. As Richard Bernstein (1983) observes, it draws on philosophical ideas that go 'Beyond Objectivism and Relativism'. Discourse ethics theory challenges the ethical absolutist notion that right and wrong exist independently of people's awareness of them. However, it also challenges ethical relativism's view that right and wrong are matters of personal opinion. Instead, it takes the view that a particular state of affairs is ethically right if those who are affected by it agree that it is right. Conversely, it proposes that a state of affairs is ethically wrong if those who are affected by it think it is wrong. According to this perspective, then, an ethical course of action is not the course of action advocated by the person who has the clearest understanding of objective right and wrong. Nor is it the course of action that a particular individual considers to be ethical. It is the course of action that all who are affected by it agree is ethical.

Discourse ethics places a premium on *discourse*, since it is through discourse that agreement about ethics can be reached. The word 'discourse' can be used as a noun or a verb. Used as a noun, it is defined in the *Oxford English Dictionary* as 'written or spoken communication or debate'. Used as a verb, it refers to the act of engaging in such communication or debate.[1] Discourse ethics can therefore be described as an approach which relies on written or spoken communication and debate to define ethical right and wrong.

This chapter will explain discourse ethics in more detail and explore some of its implications for business. The first section of the chapter will outline some features of discourse ethics theory. It will explain the democratic nature of discourse ethics, discussing its dependency on the achievement of ethical consensus amongst affected stakeholders, and explaining how such consensus might be achieved through dialectical opposition. The second section of the chapter will outline some criteria that discourse in work contexts needs to meet if it is to confer ethical legitimacy on business practice,

[1]The word 'discourse' is sometimes used by philosophers and social theorists in other senses. However, when discourse ethics theorists use the word, it is usually the *Oxford English Dictionary* sense as defined here that they have in mind.

applying these specifically to employment relationships. These criteria relate to the stakeholders who are included in discourse and the manner of their inclusion, along with the structure of discourse. The third and last section of the chapter will introduce two further concepts that are important to discourse ethics – the public sphere and colonization – in order to explore some features of modern information and communication technology (ICT) through the lens of discourse ethics theory. The importance of the public sphere for discourse, along with the potential of ICT to facilitate it, will be highlighted. The chapter will end by drawing attention to one way in which the realization of that discursive potential might be undermined by corporate colonization of ICT-related media platforms.

In discussing discourse ethics, I will rely primarily on the work of Jürgen Habermas, one of discourse ethics theory's best-known proponents. In presenting Habermas's ideas, I will draw not only on his explicit discussion of discourse ethics (1990/1983, 1994/1991) but also on some of his earlier writing about communication in which his observations about discourse ethics are implicit (for example, 1984/1981, 1987/1981). In doing so, I will try to simplify some of the complexities of Habermas's theory and present its implications in terms of discourse ethics.

Some features of discourse ethics

The fundamental principle of discourse ethics has been described by Jürgen Habermas as follows: 'only those norms can claim to be valid that meet (or could meet) with the approval of all affected in their capacity as participants in a practical discourse' (1990/1983: 93). What Habermas means by this is that, if we wish to find out what the ethical resolution to a particular situation consists of, we need to involve all of the people who are affected by that situation in discourse about it. Whichever resolution all of those people agree to is ethical. Similarly, if we want to evaluate the ethicality of a decision, we should examine the extent to which those who are affected by that decision have been able to participate in it and the extent to which they reached agreement.

For Habermas, then, it is the processes by which situations and decisions come about that define their ethicality or unethicality. Ethical rightness is the outcome of processes of frank, open discourse involving members of the community of stakeholders who are affected by an issue, which permits that community of stakeholders to reach shared ethical understanding about it. Insofar as a situation has come about as a result of such processes, it is ethical. Insofar as a decision has been made without embracing such processes, it lacks ethical legitimacy.

This section will outline some ideas that underpin discourse ethics theory. It will explain how discourse ethics theorists believe that a group of people who are affected by a particular situation can reach consensus about its ethical legitimacy through processes of dialectical discourse, which involves the exchange of contrasting points of view. First, though, I will say a little about the explicitly democratic character of discourse ethics theory, differentiating the type of democracy that is associated with it from a rather different democratic approach.

Discourse ethics: a particular kind of democracy

Discourse ethics theory offers a distinctly democratic approach to business ethics, since it highlights the desirability of people being able to participate in decision making. According to discourse ethics, business activity is ethical insofar as those who are affected by it agree that it is ethical. It is therefore important that those affected stakeholders (that is, those people who are affected by business activity) are able to engage in discourse (that is, in written or verbal communication or debate) about the ethicality of business activity. It is important to emphasise, however, that although discourse ethics offers a democratic approach to corporate decision making, this approach is a little different to the democracy with which you may be more familiar.[2]

Conventional democracy

Quite often, when we speak of democracy, we refer to people being able to choose from a list of options. Depending on the context, those options may include political parties who seek election to government, a list of candidates who are vying for a position of authority, or a range of prospective courses of action. Whichever is the case, people vote for their preferred option and the option that receives the most votes gets adopted. Importantly, this type of democracy does not necessarily involve any exchange of views; it merely acknowledges the right of individuals to hold their respective views about matters of general importance and to register their preference through a ballot. Nor does it entail the development of alternatives to the options that are on offer. Voters are able to choose between some fixed alternatives but this type of democratic process may do nothing to broaden their choice.

Discourse-ethics style democracy

The approach associated with discourse ethics goes beyond this understanding of democracy in two respects. Firstly, discourse is integral to it. That is, discourse-ethics style democracy necessarily includes communication and debate in which all parties are able to express their views whilst having the opportunity to listen to the views of

---

[2]This more conventional style of democracy is sometimes referred to as 'liberal democracy', while the discourse-ethics style of democracy that contrasts with it is sometimes called 'discursive democracy'.

others. According to discourse ethics, then, the ethical legitimacy of a course of action is not determined by the number of votes that it receives; it is determined by the quality of communication and debate from which it proceeds and by the extent to which that communication and debate ends in consensus.

And the second way in which discourse ethics goes beyond the more usual democratic approach is that it entails openness to options that have not yet been considered. Instead of allowing people to choose only from a set menu of alternatives, discourse ethics envisages the exploration of new possibilities. Whereas the more usual style of democracy gives us a set list of political parties, candidates or courses of action to choose from, the democracy associated with discourse ethics expects that, during the process of discourse, new possibilities may emerge.

Discourse-ethics style democracy applied to a practical business scenario

Consider these contrasting types of democracy in relation to a specific example involving a small business. Imagine a local bar or pub that has been the social hub of the community for many years. There has never been a TV set in the bar because people have mostly gone there to meet friends and talk, and the landlady and her predecessors have always thought that TV would interfere with this. However, not all the bar's customers agree with this and some regulars ask the landlady if she will install a TV set in the main room so that they can watch popular programmes and top-level sports events while they are having a drink. They point out that most bars and pubs have TV sets nowadays. They also suggest that installing a TV would be good for business, since it would encourage them to come to the bar more often and because other people who usually watch big games elsewhere may also want to come in on match days. However, some other regular customers are strongly opposed to this suggestion. This is partly because they are not interested in watching the soaps, reality shows and male sport that dominate TV programming and it is partly because they fear that a TV set will inhibit conversation, thus radically altering the bar's atmosphere and interfering with the role it plays in forming and sustaining community bonds.

The landlady is in a quandary. She wants to do what is good for her business; she feels a sense of responsibility to give her customers what they want; and she also feels a sense of responsibility to ensure that the bar continues to be at the hub of local life. She wants to do the right thing by everybody concerned but she is not sure what that is. She wonders how to proceed.

On the one hand, she considers organizing a ballot. This would give all her customers the chance to vote for or against the installation of a TV. She could then do whatever the majority chooses. However, although she finds a democratic solution of this nature appealing, she fears that she may just end up upsetting some of her customers in order to keep the others happy. She is therefore very interested when she hears one of her customers, who is studying business ethics at a nearby university, talking about discourse ethics to his friends. This starts her thinking about a different sort of democratic resolution to her dilemma.

The landlady decides to arrange a meeting in the bar one evening to discuss the matter of the TV. Those who are for it will be able to present their case, and those who are against it can explain their objections. She reasons that not only will this give all her customers the opportunity to express their views, it will also give everybody the chance to hear what the others say so that they can take these views on board and amend their own perspectives accordingly. It may even be that some compromise solutions that have not yet been considered will get suggested, which avoid a straightforward TV-or-no-TV choice. Whatever happens, she believes that this is the surest route to achieving a consensus that will keep everybody happy.

Pause for Reflection

In the case just described, as far as discourse ethics is concerned, it is not possible for you or me to say what would be the ethical thing for the landlady to do regarding the TV. Discourse ethics would suggest that the ethical resolution will be that which is agreed to by all the bar's customers at their forthcoming meeting, and we are not able to predict that outcome. However, you may be able to think of some further options that might be suggested at that meeting, which would avoid a straight choice between having a TV and not having a TV in the main room and which might therefore keep everybody happy.

The landlady proposes to offer all her customers the chance to take part in the forthcoming meeting. Can you think of other people (other stakeholders), who may also be affected by this issue, who could also be included in discourse about it?

Discourse ethics and ethical consensus

Discourse ethics proposes that an ethical course of action is one that all affected parties can agree on. The practical feasibility of discourse ethics therefore depends on the likelihood that those who are affected by an issue will achieve consensus about it. And this may seem like a big hurdle to overcome. After all, people are likely to have widely disparate views on a topic so the possibility of consensus may seem like a distant one. In the bar-TV example discussed above, for instance, some people will want to watch TV in the bar and some will not. It seems unlikely that those preferences will change.

However, it is important to bear in mind that agreement about interests and preferences is not the sort of consensus that discourse ethicists aspire to. Rather, discourse-ethics theory envisages consensus about what is ethical.[3] And a person's opinion about what is ethical may be different from their view of what is in their interests, or what they prefer. For instance, I currently live in a remote house in the Cambrian Mountains and I would *prefer* it if large, articulated lorries did not drive past my house on the small, one-track mountain road throughout the day. However, I realize that these lorries are collecting wood from local forests and that this forestry activity is a key contributor to the local economy, providing jobs for local people and tax revenue that helps fund local services. I therefore believe that it is ethically acceptable for these lorries to use my road, even though I would prefer it if they did not.

While it may not be possible to reach consensus about personal preferences or personal interests, then, achieving a shared understanding about what is ethical may not be so challenging. Of course, ethics is not a separate realm that is completely cut off from the realm of interests and preferences. Indeed, a lot of ethical discourse involves debate about the legitimacy of various interests and preferences. By focusing on ethical discourse, then, discourse ethics does not dismiss the relevance of preferences and interests: we all have interests and preferences, and they matter. The important point, though, is that debate about the respective legitimacy of conflicting preferences and interests appeals to standards which operate at a deeper level. To return to the example of logging lorries discussed above, although I would prefer it if those lorries did not drive past my house, I go deeper into my inner convictions in order to evaluate the ethical legitimacy of my preference. And in doing so, I realize that my superficial preference is not backed up by feelings of ethical legitimacy. It is to this deeper level of conviction that discourse ethics appeals, and it presumes that consensus at this level is an achievable goal.

The merits of dialectical opposition

Discourse ethics theorists take the view, then, that although people may have widely diverging interests and preferences, this need not prevent them from reaching *ethical* consensus. It proposes that although conflicting preferences and interests may be hard to resolve, conflicting views about what is ethical can be overcome. But discourse ethics goes even further than this. Not only does it envisage that ethical disagreement might eventually result in ethical consensus; it also proposes that the quality of ethical

[3]To say that discourse ethics seeks ethical consensus is perhaps an overly simplified representation of Habermas's aspiration that communicative action will result in normative agreement reached at the level of lifeworld. However, this simplification seems justified in the interests of offering an approachable introduction to this topic.

consensus can be enhanced through the expression of opposition. There are several reasons for this. For a start, there is the pragmatic reason that people are more likely to commit themselves to a consensus that takes their views into account. Discourse-ethics theorists also propose that the expression of divergent opinions through processes of dialectical discourse will actually enrich the agreement that is eventually reached. This is partly because every person may have something important to add to discourse; but it is also based on a philosophical belief in the intrinsically uplifting value of dialectical opposition. I will say a little more about each of these three justifications for the expression of opposition.

The pragmatic benefit of the expression of opposition

Consider, first, a simple, practical benefit of expressing opposition. This is that any accord which arises from the expression of conflicting views is likely to be more committing and therefore more lasting than one in which dissent is silenced. The suppression of opposition may seem superficially beneficial. It may seem that if people are to achieve ethical consensus, it would be better if dissenters fell in line with the dominant perspective rather than expressing their opposition to it. However, any agreement that is reached in this manner is unlikely to represent true consensus. Instead, it will comprise nothing more than a fake accord, in which some people end up committing themselves to things they do not really believe in. In such cases, it is probable that dominant perspectives will hold sway while dissenting viewpoints just become marginalized. Although it may be quicker to reach an artificial agreement of this nature, such an agreement is unlikely to be a robust one. A more lasting consensus, and one to which all will be more likely to commit themselves, is a consensus which expresses a shared understanding that reflects the views of all people. And this will not happen unless those people are able to express disagreement.

Every ethical perspective may have something important to add

But not only are people more likely to commit themselves to an accord that has taken their views into account; discourse ethics also proposes that that accord is likely to be of a higher quality than one which has not embraced everybody's perspectives. This is partly based on the ideas that, if someone holds a particular ethical viewpoint, that viewpoint is likely to have some merit. After all, a person is unlikely to have firm ethical views on an issue unless they have good reasons for holding those views. Of course, this does not mean that that person has a comprehensive understanding of the issue, or that their ethical perspective cannot be improved in any way. There may, for instance, be factual aspects of the issue that they have not taken into account; or there may be ethical insights that they have not considered. It does mean, however, that they probably have something worthwhile to say.

Given that people who hold firm ethical views on a topic usually have something important to say about it, it is likely that if we listen with an open mind to what people who hold contrasting ethical viewpoints to our own have to say, our own understanding of the ethical implications of that topic will be enhanced. This does not mean that we will end up agreeing with everything the other person says. It just means that, when we listen to one another with open minds, we are likely to take something positive from what we hear.

We can therefore imagine a situation in which people exchange ethical viewpoints and thus gradually move towards convergence. Discourse ethics theory envisages that, if ethics-related discourse is allowed to run its course, and if participants approach it in an appropriate frame of mind (more about this later), each person will progressively amend their own perspective in response to the points made by others until they eventually achieve consensus. In this manner a resolution will ultimately be achieved in which the ethical convictions of each individual are in tune with the perspective that is held in common by the whole group.

How dialectical opposition might enhance the quality of consensus

The philosophical concept of *dialectic* builds upon these ideas, adding further to the desirability of expressions of opposition.[4] Dialectic, when used in this context, refers to the exchange of opposing perspectives and the consequent movement to a further perspective which is an improvement on either of the earlier perspectives. It involves using each perspective as a basis for exposing the limitations of, and contradictions contained in the other, thus allowing the contribution that each can make to an enhanced perspective to be drawn out. Dialectical enquiry can thus be contrasted to enquiry that moves in a straight line without diverging to explore oppositional possibilities. Of course, a non-dialectical, linear form of enquiry, by moving in a straight line, generally gets where it is going faster than dialectical enquiry. The problem is that the conclusions it reaches may be of limited value. Dialectical enquiry, on the other hand, vacillates from side to side in order to move forward. As a consequence of these side-to-side vacillations, it usually proceeds more slowly than linear, non-dialectical enquiry. Nevertheless, the conclusions that it eventually reaches are likely to be of a far higher quality than those which non-dialectical movement permits.

[4]The notion of *dialectic* is a complex and multi-faceted one which appears in many guises in philosophical writing. An explicit, systematic application of dialectical method can be found in the work of G.W.F Hegel (1977/1807; 1975/1830, 1969/1831). I will not delve too far into those complexities. Instead, I will just build on the idea that dialectic involves moving beyond a particular perspective by exploring the opposition that is implicit in it but which may need to be made explicit.

To illustrate how dialectical enquiry might work, and how it differs from non-dialectical enquiry, consider the following example. Suppose we are enquiring into the social desirability of an armaments factory. A non-dialectical approach to such enquiry might begin with the premise 'economic growth is socially beneficial', which seems to have a great deal of intuitive merit. From this, we could move promptly, in a non-dialectical fashion, to a second proposition: 'increased production is good for economic growth; therefore increased production is also socially beneficial'. And from this proposition, we might move briskly on to a further one: 'the construction of a large armaments factory will increase production, thus contributing to economic growth; therefore the construction of a large armaments factory is socially beneficial'.

Conversely, consider the approach that dialectical enquiry might take to the same issue. Again, it could begin with the same intuitively appealing premise: 'economic growth is socially beneficial'. However, instead of moving quickly on to a further proposition without challenging this initial premise, dialectical enquiry would oppose it with its opposite: 'economic growth is not always socially beneficial'. This might encourage us to think about which types of economic growth are socially beneficial and which forms are not so beneficial. It would thus permit us to move on to a third position, which is an improvement on either of these two previous positions. We might thus, in a dialectical fashion, reach the conclusion that the type of economic growth represented by the construction of a shoe factory is socially beneficial, but that an armaments factory offers a far more dubious social benefit. Not only have we thus achieved a richer understanding of the social desirability of an armaments factory; we have also reached a more comprehensive appreciation of the benefits of economic growth than we would have done if we had relied only on non-dialectical reasoning. However, it has taken us a bit longer to get there.

For discourse ethics, then, disagreement is not only a characteristic feature of discourse; it is to be positively encouraged. By encouraging dialectical exchanges of opposing perspectives, not only do we allow views to be expressed that would otherwise simmer under the surface; we also expose dominant perspectives to challenges that may enhance the quality of the ethical consensus that is ultimately achieved.

Discourse ethics in practice: Deepwater Horizon

The ideas that have been introduced so far in this chapter can be illustrated in relation to a practical business scenario. On 20 April 2010, BP's Deepwater Horizon oil rig exploded in the Gulf of Mexico killing 11 workers and beginning the worst environmental disaster in US history (BBC, 2010b). For 84 days, over 200 million gallons of oil flowed into the waters of the Gulf, devastating the marine environment and causing massive problems for local communities.

Video Activity 7.1

To remind you of the events surrounding the Deepwater Horizon disaster, you might like to view this video:

www.youtube.com/watch?v=gExZYxtdzrU

Question

List as many affected stakeholders as you can in relation to the explosion on Deepwater Horizon and subsequent events. In other words, list those stakeholders that were in some way affected by this episode.

This episode raised a lot of ethical questions for BP. For a start, BP's executives had to decide how they should respond to the disaster. For instance, they had to consider questions such as: what were BP's ethical responsibilities concerning the clear up? Should they compensate local communities for the economic damage inflicted by the spill? Did their responsibilities go beyond their duty to compensate for the economic cost? Did they also have obligations towards the environment? They also had to think about their responsibilities towards their shareholders: should they pay the dividend that corporate performance up to this point had merited, or should they withhold dividend payments and use the money instead to cover compensation and clean-up costs? And what about BP's obligations towards its employees and their families: did executives have a duty to reassess safety procedures in relation to deep-water drilling of this nature? Furthermore, this episode posed some important questions about deep-water oil extraction in general. It may have encouraged BP's executives to have a radical rethink about the economic benefits and environmental risks associated with drilling for oil in deep water.

A community of stakeholders

To appreciate how discourse-ethics theory would approach such questions, it helps to think of a corporation like BP as the nexus for an extended community; a community which involves all those stakeholders who are affected, or who are likely to be affected, by BP's activities. Those stakeholders include the most obvious groups, such as the families of employees who were killed in the explosion, along with other employees whose lives may be put at risk by future drilling and exploration. They also include the fishing and tourism communities of the Gulf of Mexico, whose livelihoods were affected by the spill, along with other communities who might bear the consequences of similar incidents in the future. This affair also had a significant impact on the natural world, so the birds and sea creatures killed or otherwise affected by oil spills, along with the marine environment in general, could also be regarded as stakeholders. And stakeholders might also include other groups who we usually associate with business activity, such as customers, suppliers and shareholders, all of whom are ultimately affected by BP's response and by its impact on the company. We might even include BP's competitors, since the actions taken by BP in this instance may also have an indirect effect on them.

Ethical consensus

Discourse-ethics theory would propose that this extended community of stakeholders has the potential to reach ethical consensus about what BP's executives ought to do. Moreover, it would suggest that this consensus can be reached through a process of dialectical discourse during which stakeholders exchange contrasting opinions. The first action that discourse ethics would recommend for BP's executives, then, would be that they make the necessary arrangements for such discourse to take place.

Discourse involving stakeholders' representatives

Of course, arranging discourse amongst stakeholders in this particular instance would be complicated by the sheer number of stakeholders involved, their geographical spread, and the fact that some of them – notably birds and sea creatures – are not able to participate in verbal communication and debate. Given the impossibility of getting all these hundreds of thousands of people and creatures together for a discussion about BP's ethical responsibilities, some form of representative discourse would need to be substituted for direct discourse. That is, representatives of all these different groups of stakeholders – including environmental and wildlife groups representing non-human stakeholders – would need to get together to discuss the issue.

This forum of representatives would itself need to be part of wider discursive processes, in which groups of stakeholders debate relevant questions amongst themselves. This would give their representatives some ideas to take forward to general, inter-stakeholder forums. After those general forums have taken place, representatives would need to report back to their constituencies, thus enhancing the ethical understanding of individual stakeholders. This process would need to be ongoing, enabling the views of each individual stakeholder to be exchanged with those of the broader community of stakeholders, thus allowing each to shape the other. The aspiration of discourse ethics theory would be that all stakeholders – including BP's customers, employees, shareholders and suppliers; the tourism providers and fishing people of the Gulf; other oil companies; wildlife and environmental pressure groups; and political representatives – take part in such discourse and eventually reach consensus about what is the ethical thing for BP to do.

Of course, the many stakeholders who would take part in such discourse are likely to have widely divergent views about what BP should do, so consensus may be hard to achieve. Several points need to be borne in mind though. The first is that discourse is about what is the ethically right thing for BP to do; it is not about what is in each stakeholder's own interests. The second point is that each person's ethical perspective is likely to have something positive to add to the debate. Therefore, every person should be receptive to what others have to say and should be prepared to modify their own viewpoint in response to what they hear. And the third point is that such divergence of perspectives should not be seen as a bad thing. Rather it should be welcomed as a productive resource that will ultimately enhance the quality of BP's response to the disaster.

Some criteria for the practical application of discourse ethics to employment relations

This second section of the chapter will consider the application of discourse ethics with particular reference to the workplace; that is, it will discuss how discourse might provide ethical legitimation for what goes on between companies and their employees. The term *workplace democracy* is sometimes used to describe a situation where employees engage in such discourse. After highlighting some instrumental merits that have been claimed for workplace democracy, I will outline some conditions that Jürgen Habermas has suggested discourse needs to meet if it is to provide ethical legitimation. These conditions will be explained with specific reference to workplace democracy.

The practical feasibility and commercial benefits of workplace democracy

One area of business activity that seems well suited to the application of discourse ethics is employee relations. Although stakeholder discourse may present practical challenges when applied to other groups of stakeholders, these challenges are less pronounced when it comes to the workplace. It is a lot easier to involve employees in discussions about corporate activity than it would be to involve the likes of customers, affected communities and the natural environment, who are often widely dispersed and sometimes hard to identify. Employees comprise an easily identifiable, readily accessible constituency, amongst whom arranging discourse should present few practical difficulties.

The desirability of workplace discourse is also supported by some management theorists, who have drawn attention to the instrumental merits of democratic management practices. Contrary to the idea that bosses should make decisions while junior employees just follow orders, it has been suggested that giving people at all levels a say in how firms are run helps to make those firms more successful (see discussions in Johnson, 2006; Knudsen et al., 2011). This advocacy of workplace democracy is partly based on the observation that all employees, including those at junior levels, may possess valuable knowledge, which it would be unwise for senior managers to ignore. It is also based on the motivational benefits of democratic participation. It has been suggested that workers will be happier and more productive if they believe that their input is valued and if they are able to have a say in what goes on in the company they work for.

Not only is it relatively easy to involve employees in discourse, then; contemporary management theory also indicates that there are sound instrumental reasons for doing so. However, as already suggested, not all forms of democratic engagement meet the

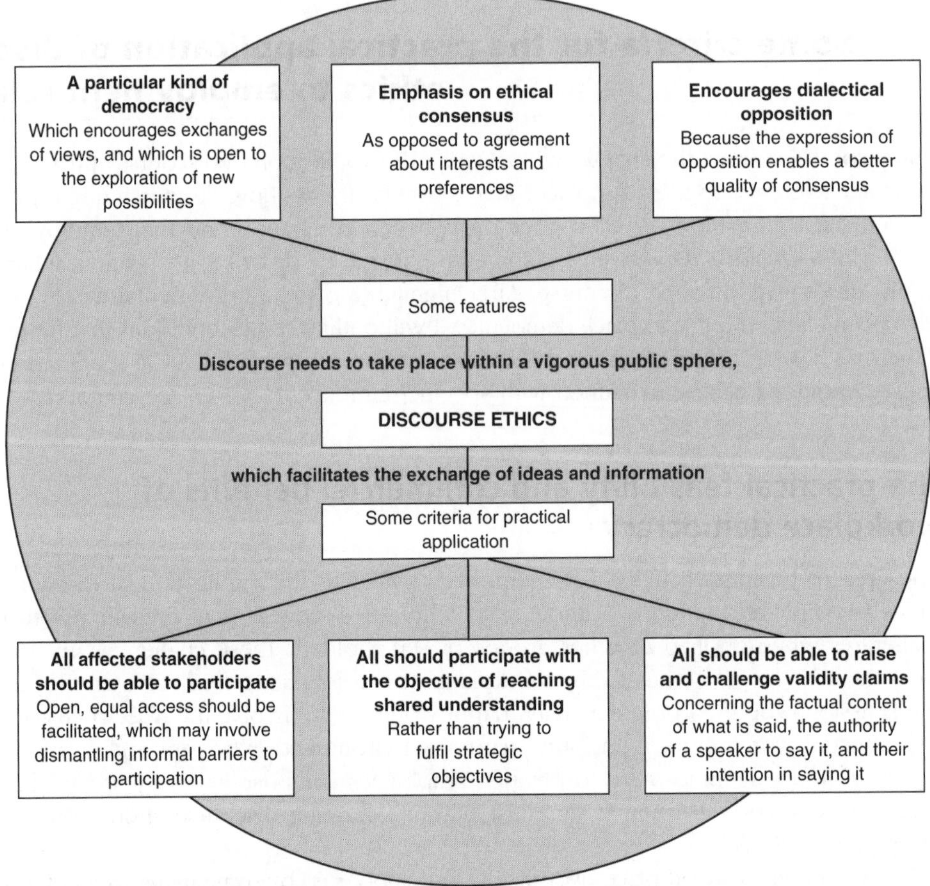

Figure 7.1 Discourse ethics: some features, some criteria for practical application and the role of the public sphere

ethically legitimating criteria of discourse ethics. So what form should workplace democracy take if, as well as providing the instrumental benefits that have been associated with it, it is to also meet the requirements of discourse ethics?

Jürgen Habermas and other discourse ethics theorists have suggested a number of criteria that discourse needs to meet if it is to provide ethical legitimation. These include the need for discourse to be arranged in a manner which encourages full and equal participation, and the need for those who take part in discourse to do so with the aim of achieving shared understanding. This section will begin by discussing each of these criteria, indicating how they might relate to discourse in the workplace. It will then explore some structural features that, according to Habermas, will help discourse to meet these criteria in practice.

Figure 7.1 graphically represents the criteria for practical application that were outlined in this section along with the key features of discourse ethics discussed in the first section of this chapter. These are shown within the framework of the public sphere, which is discussed in the next section.

Video Activity 7.2

Watch the following video, in which Prof. Richard Wolff talks for a few minutes about workplace democracy:

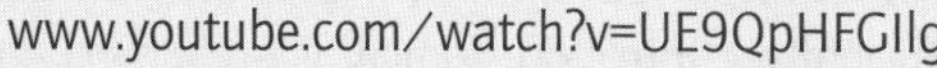

www.youtube.com/watch?v=UE9QpHFGIlg

Questions

1. Do you think everybody wants to be involved in discourse about what their companies do, or are some people happy to just do as they are told and take home their pay at the end of the week?
2. Why do you think some people might be more willing to participate in workplace democracy than others?
3. What might an employer do to encourage employees to want to take part in discourse?

Involvement of all employees

The importance that discourse ethics theory places on all who are affected by an issue being able to participate in discourse about it has already been stressed. According to discourse ethics theory, if discourse in the workplace is to provide ethical legitimation, it needs to be open to *all* affected parties. Moreover, all should be able to participate on an equal footing.

Open, equal access

Therefore, if democratic processes in the workplace are to offer a source of ethical legitimation, *all* employees should be able to take part in them on an equal footing. Forums need to be in place, then, that will allow everyone to share their views, no matter what their job is and no matter where they work. It is not enough, for instance, to allow only head-office staff to take part; and it is not sufficient if only employees above a certain hierarchical level are able to contribute. All employees, even the most junior and even those who work in a company's most remote operations, should be consulted and all need to be treated equally during discourse. Furthermore, part-time and temporary employees, as well as full-time staff, should be given equal opportunities to take part. This means that, in large corporations, a broad range of forums may need to be put in place so that everybody, or at least everybody's representative, can participate.

Informal barriers to participation

However, even when everybody has a formal right to take part in discourse, subtle, informal factors may interfere with the open exchange of views. For instance, some people may feel more comfortable expressing their opinions in public than others, or status differentials may mean that some perspectives are accorded more weight than others, irrespective of their quality. As a result, the status of a speaker, or their confidence in speaking, may have a bigger impact on outcomes than the content of what they say. It has even been suggested (for example Young, 1996) that the way that we habitually think of discourse – as emotionally controlled, logically presented, verbal, face-to-face debate – may disadvantage people who have something important to say but who are not at ease with this style of communication.

To address such issues it may help to expand the available modes of discourse to include forms with which otherwise marginalized groups might feel more comfortable (Young, 1996; Sanders, 1997). In particular, some writers (for example Fraser, 1992; Honig, 1996; Mansbridge, 1996) have advocated the creation of sheltered spaces where people who are less confident about sharing their views in large, open forums can debate their ideas and develop their confidence to express them.

The potential of ICT

ICT may also offer interesting possibilities in this respect. There is, of course, a danger that ICT will be used in firms to enable centralized control and surveillance of workers (Agger, 1987; Luke and White, 1987; Zuboff, 1988). However, if used sympathetically, ICT might also facilitate participation in workplace democracy. Not only might it help to overcome challenges presented by employees' geographic remoteness; it could also shift channels of discourse away from conventional forms of debate. As a result, those whose discursive preferences may otherwise preclude whole-hearted participation might feel more comfortable putting forward their perspectives and challenging those offered by more self-assured colleagues.

Theory in Practice

Discourse and open door policies

The following dialogue is taken from an interview with the managing director of a medium-sized company, who I will refer to here as Alex. Alex tells the interviewer how keen he is to encourage his employees to engage with him in discourse about business matters. He describes some measures that he takes to encourage this:

Alex: I am the sort of manager that has an open-door policy ... I like to be involved with the employees ... we have this sort of open policy which I find has worked very well. ... I think that's quite important in management that you are as open as you can be ...

Interviewer: Yes, ok. What you refer to as an open-door policy; can you give me an idea of how that actually operates in terms of employees?

Alex: In terms of employees, I have structured meetings during the day but I [also] have periods in my day where the door is left open for people to come in and interact with me ... Also, rather than them just having to come in here, I walk around the building at least three times a day and go to every department and just make sure that they can see me. I also try to meet with the whole company and present to them, at least when there is something significant to say... they can come at any time of the day but I encourage it [at particular times]... I think it's better to try and encourage them to have some dialogue with you and not be intimidated, and for them to think you're part of the team as well as they are, and that everybody's necessary.

Interviewer: But perhaps it's a tough thing for a junior employee to do; to walk in here and feel comfortable.

Alex: Well, they don't tend to walk in here ... But the open-door bit at least it gives people the opportunity to talk to you...

(Continued)

(Continued)

Interviewer: So does it tend to be more managers that come in and talk to you?

Alex: Yes it would tend to be more the middle managers and senior managers that would come in here and talk to me.

Questions

1 Despite Alex's desire to engage with employees from all levels in the company, he notes, with some regret, that junior employees do not often come into his office and offer their views. Why do you think that might be?
2 What other measures do you think Alex could put in place to supplement his 'open-door policy' and to encourage junior employees to offer their ideas, raise their concerns, and share their perspectives with him?

Participating in discourse with the right motivation

Some difficulties associated with achieving consensus through discourse have already been mentioned earlier in this chapter. I suggested that ethical consensus is a more realizable goal than consensus about what is in people's interests. It is important, therefore, that people do not try to conceal their self-interested agendas beneath the façade of an ethical rationale. Moreover, even discourse about the ethics of a situation may be undermined if people do not enter it with the intention of reaching shared understanding. Discourse should not be about getting one's own way, and it should not be aimed at winning the ethical debate. Rather, participants need to be committed to listening to other people's views, amending their own perspectives accordingly, and thus reaching a common agreement about the ethical rights and wrongs of an issue. Dogmatic assertion of one's own views and a refusal to engage with other people's perspectives will not do.

Contrasting communicative action to strategic action

Habermas makes an important distinction in this respect between acting *communicatively* and acting *strategically*. When we act strategically, we act with the intention of imposing some agenda that we value and we use discourse as a means of gaining other people's support for that agenda. When we act communicatively, on the other hand, we act with the intention of reaching shared understanding. As Habermas puts it,

> I call interactions *communicative* when the participants coordinate their plans of action consensually, with the agreement reached at any point being evaluated in terms of the

> intersubjective recognition of validity claims ... Whereas in strategic action one actor seeks to *influence* the behaviour of another by means of the threat of sanctions or the prospect of gratification in order to *cause* the interaction to continue as the first actor desires. (1990/1983: 58)

Ethically legitimating discourse, then, is a form of what Habermas calls 'communicative action' (1984/1981, 1987/1981, 1990/1983). And in order for it to work, participants must enter with a communicative intent – that is, with a desire to reach shared understanding – rather than with a strategic intent.

Of course, to expect people to drop their strategic agendas when they enter into discourse may seem unrealistic. However much we may commit ourselves to a cooperative search for ethical consensus, it is not easy for us to leave aside our personal agendas and group interests. Habermas acknowledges this when he notes that 'Pure types of action oriented to mutual understanding are merely limit cases. In fact, communicative utterances are always embedded in various world relations at the same time' (1987/1981: 120).

It is partly in response to such problems that Habermas offers some suggestions about how discourse should be structured. If these suggestions are followed, any strategic agendas are likely to become apparent and can be allowed for. It is to these structural criteria that I will turn next, particularly Habermas's call for people to be able to raise and challenge what he calls 'validity claims'.

The structure of ethically legitimating discourse

In his book, *Moral Consciousness and Communicative Action*, Habermas suggests some rules that should govern discourse if it is to provide ethical legitimation. These include the requirements that 'Everyone is allowed to introduce any assertion whatever into the discourse' and that 'Everyone is allowed to question any assertion whatever' (Habermas, 1990/1983: 89). To appreciate how Habermas arrives at these principles of ethically legitimating discourse, it helps to understand how Habermas justifies them in terms of *validity claims*. It also helps to be aware of how they relate to the achievement of shared understanding through discourse.

Communication and shared understanding

Discourse is a form of human communication. And Habermas (1984/1981, 1987/1981, 1990/1983) takes the view that the fundamental purpose of all human communication is to reach shared understanding. Another way of saying this is that the main reason we communicate with one another is to achieve common understanding about our world and our relationships within it. Of course, we also communicate for other reasons, such as to get people to do things that we want them to do. As pointed out above, this involves acting strategically rather than communicatively. However,

Habermas points out that we would not achieve these strategic objectives unless we first achieved shared understanding. This leads him to observe that 'Reaching understanding is the inherent telos of human speech … The concepts of speech and understanding reciprocally interpret one another' (1984/1981: 287).

From this starting point, Habermas works out some conditions that must be presupposed if communication is to achieve its objective of enabling shared understanding. In his words, these are 'The general symmetry conditions that every competent speaker must presuppose are sufficiently satisfied insofar as he intends to enter into argumentation at all' (1984/1981: 25). In particular, Habermas points out that, if people are to achieve shared understanding, they must be of the same mind across several different dimensions. Briefly, they need to be of one mind concerning the *factual* content of things that are said, the *authority* of speakers to say what they say, and the *reasons why* speakers say the things that they say.

Habermas proposes that, in order for this to happen, participants need to be able to raise and challenge *validity claims* across each of these dimensions. I will say a little about these three dimensions before explaining what Habermas means by raising and challenging validity claims. I will then explain how Habermas applies these general observations about communication to the specific matter of ethically legitimating discourse. This section will end by applying these ideas to a hypothetical workplace scenario, illustrating how they might help us to analyse the ethical quality of discourse about that scenario.

Shared understanding about the factual content of a statement

The first dimension of communication across which Habermas proposes that shared understanding needs to be achieved concerns the *factual* content of what is said. He observes that, when a speaker makes a statement, he or she makes a claim about the factual truth of that statement and, for speaker and listeners to reach shared understanding, all need to accept that factual truth. As Habermas describes it, all must accept 'That the statement made is true (or that the existential presuppositions of the propositional content mentioned are in fact satisfied)' (1984/1981: 99).

But in order for this to happen, clarification may be required. Of course, speaker and listeners must understand the words that are being used. However, Habermas points out that factual understanding demands more than linguistic familiarity because, even within one language, a word can have various meanings. Consider a simple example. Suppose Irene is Curtly's line manager. Irene tells Curtly that a project he is currently working on is so *important* that he ought to focus all his efforts on it. Curtly may understand the words Irene is using without fully grasping the factual content of her statement. For instance, Irene may be thinking of 'importance' in terms of the company's commercial performance, or in terms of the needs of the customer for whom the project is being undertaken. Curtly, on the other hand, may have different criteria of importance in mind; perhaps the project's contribution to the company's social responsibility profile, or maybe its significance in terms of his career progression. Therefore, in order to clarify the factual content of Irene's statement he may need to ask her for more information. Only after he has done this can Curtly and Irene be said to have reached shared understanding on the factual dimension of her statement.

Shared understanding about a speaker's authority to make a statement

However, Habermas points out that achieving shared understanding requires more than just clarifying the factual content of a statement. Shared understanding also needs to be reached on the dimension of a speaker's *authority* to say what they are saying. As Habermas puts it, participants in communication must accept 'That the speech act is right with respect to the existing normative context (or that the normative context that it is supposed to satisfy is itself legitimate)' (1984/1981: 99). In other words, speaker and listeners must agree that a speaker is well placed to make the statement that he or she makes. And in order to accept a speaker's authority to make a statement, listeners must know precisely what authority the speaker is claiming for themself.

Consider, again, Irene's statement to Curtly. Once both have agreed on criteria of importance, they must also agree on Irene's authority to rate the project, and thus the importance of Curtly's commitment to it, against those particular criteria. Irene and Curtly will not achieve shared understanding on the dimension of authority until they have done this. For example, suppose they establish that the urgent need of a customer is the criterion of importance to which Irene is appealing. It may be that Irene is basing her statement on nothing more than a hunch; that she has not actually spoken to the customer about the urgency of their need but that she is making an inspired guess. But Curtly might have different expectations of authority. He might expect Irene to have been explicitly told by the customer that they wanted the project completed as soon as possible before she made such a statement.

It is important, then, that Curtly is able to question Irene's authority to make her statement. He needs to be able to ask her how she knows that the customer needs the project completed urgently. Only by doing this can they reach shared understanding of not only the factual content of Irene's statement but also of how well qualified she is to make it.

Shared understanding about why a speaker is making a statement

But even this, in Habermas's view, may not be enough for shared understanding to be achieved. As well as reaching shared understanding about the factual content of a statement and a speaker's authority to make that statement, participants in communication must also achieve shared understanding about *why* statements are made; that is, they must be of the same mind concerning a speaker's *intention* in making a statement. As Habermas puts it, listeners must accept 'That the manifest intention of the speaker is meant as it is expressed' (Habermas, 1984/1981: 99), and in order to do this they may need to clarify that intention.

In the example of Curtly's project, he is likely to assume that Irene's intention in telling him that the project is important is that she wants him to complete it as soon as possible. But Irene may have some other reason for persuading Curtly to focus his efforts on this particular project. Perhaps she wants to distract his attention from other projects, which she wants to hold back for personal reasons. So, if he has any doubts about her intention, he needs to be able to ask what she hopes to achieve by asking him to prioritize this project. Only after Irene and Curtly have identified and resolved discrepancies between their respective understandings can they be of one mind about the meaning of Irene's statement.

Raising and challenging validity claims

Habermas uses some rather complex terminology to make these points. He uses the term 'speech act' to refer to the statements that are made by people when they engage in communication. He says that when we perform a speech act – that is, when we make a statement – we 'raise validity claims' in relation to the factual content of our speech act, our authority to perform that speech act, and what we hope to achieve by performing it.[5] That is, we ask our listeners to accept our version of the factual content of our statement, we ask them to accept our authority to make that statement, and we ask them to accept our intent in making the statement.

The ability of participants in communication to raise and challenge validity claims across the various dimensions of a speech act is very important to Habermas. As he puts it, 'The speech act of one person succeeds only if the other accepts the offer contained in it by taking (however implicitly) a "yes" or "no" position on a validity claim that is in principle criticizable' (1984/1981: 287). This means that speakers must be able to raise whatever validity claims they see fit, and also that listeners must be able to challenge those validity claims whenever they wish. Only by doing this will they be able to reach shared understanding.

Applying these insights to discourse

Habermas uses these general observations about human communication to derive some fundamental principles of ethically legitimating discourse. Discourse, as conceived by

---

[5]Habermas actually uses the terms 'locutionary', 'illocutionary', and 'perlocutionary' to refer to dimensions of a speech act. However, for the sake of simplicity, I will stick with 'factual content', 'authority', and 'intention'.

discourse ethics theory, is a form of communication that involves the frank and open exchange of ethical perspectives, undertaken with the express aim of achieving ethical consensus about a particular matter. For this aim to be achieved, it is essential that participants in discourse reach shared understanding of what one another says. Applying the insights outlined above, shared understanding needs to be achieved across the dimensions of fact, authority and intention concerning the statements that are made by those who take part in discourse.

Habermas thus derives the two principles of ethically legitimating discourse referred to earlier. The first principle, that 'Everyone is allowed to introduce any assertion whatever into the discourse' (1990/1983: 89), is another way of saying that all participants in discourse should be able to raise whatever validity claims they choose to raise. And the second principle, that 'Everyone is allowed to question any assertion whatever' (1990/1983: 89), expresses the requirement that all participants in discourse must be able to challenge the validity claims raised by other participants.

In summary, then, ethically legitimating discourse requires that all participants are able to make whatever statements they like, thus raising whatever validity claims they choose. Equally, everybody must be at liberty to challenge the validity claims made by everybody else across the dimensions of fact, authority and intention. All must therefore be able to ask questions like 'what do you mean?' or 'are you sure about that?' in order to achieve shared understanding of the factual content of a statement. All must be able to ask questions like 'how do you know?', or 'what gives you the right to say that?' in order to ensure shared understanding of a speaker's authority to make a statement. And all participants in discourse must be able to say things like 'why are you telling me this?' or 'what do you hope to achieve by saying that?' in order to ensure common understanding about a speaker's intentions. Only after questions such as these have been asked, answered and, if necessary, only after the responses have been debated and clarified, can participants in discourse be said to have reached shared understanding.

Importantly, during this process of raising, challenging and negotiating validity claims, any strategic agendas that may suffuse discourse are likely to be identified. Those agendas can then be allowed for and perhaps even set aside so that the fundamental purpose of achieving shared understanding can proceed.

Raising and challenging validity claims in workplace discourse

To illustrate how the raising and challenging of validity claims might happen in a more complex and more ethically charged workplace-discourse context, consider the following scenario. Suppose that, during a period of economic recession, a company is facing difficult trading conditions and its executives are thinking about how to respond. They believe that they must trim production capacity in order to bring it in line with falling demand for the company's products. However, they want to do this in the most ethical way. They are considering several options. One possibility is to close one of their production plants, making all its employees redundant. A second option is to make ten per cent of employees redundant in each production plant, thus reducing capacity throughout the business. A third option is to reduce all employees' hours of work and to lower their wages accordingly. And a fourth option is to leave their workforce at its present level but to ask all employees to take a wage cut.

This situation is ethically contentious because all of the options under consideration involve hardship for some people. Discourse ethics would propose that the most ethical course of action is that which is agreed after discussions involving all of those people who are likely to be affected by it. Since those who will be most profoundly affected are the company's employees, discourse ethics would propose that executives arrange for all employees, or at least the representatives of all employees, to participate in discourse in an effort to agree on the most ethical way forward.

The criteria that have already been discussed require that all workers should be represented in discourse. That is, representatives of full-time, part-time and temporary employees of all levels of seniority from all the company's locations should be able to participate. Moreover, consideration should be given to the nature of discourse: a range of different types of discourse may be needed if everyone is to be able to share their views in a manner with which they feel comfortable.

In addition to these conditions, Habermas's structural criteria would entail that all participants should be at liberty to raise whatever validity claims they wish. Furthermore, all should be free to challenge the validity claims raised by other speakers on the dimensions of factual content, authority and intention. What practical implications might this have in this instance?

Suppose the discursive forums put in place to debate this matter include a meeting, at which the company's chief executive discusses the issue with employee representatives. She begins the meeting by reminding everybody of the difficult economic situation, by observing that the company needs to take drastic steps, and by outlining the various options that have been proposed by senior executives to trim the company's production capacity. In making this statement – or, as Habermas would say, in *performing this speech act* – the chief executive is raising a number of *validity claims* about its *factual content*, which all other participants should feel able to challenge. For instance, they might want to question whether the economic situation is as bad as she says, or whether the company really needs to trim production capacity as she proposes. They might want to ask if other options could be considered to cut costs or to enhance commercial performance. They might even seek factual clarification of whether the company actually needs to do anything at all, or whether it could just ride out the recession and maintain its production capacity in anticipation of a subsequent boost in demand. Only once such matters have been clarified can all participants be said to have reached shared understanding about the factual content of the chief executive's statement.

Participants also need to be able to challenge the chief executive's *authority* to make her statement. For instance, they should feel free to ask her how she knows that the economic situation is so bad. Where has she got her data from? How can she be so sure that these conditions will continue? How can she be certain that any of the options under consideration will work? How does she know that these are the only feasible options? How much effort has she invested in considering other alternatives? The representatives taking part in the discourse need to be able to ask questions such as these to ensure that they are all of one mind concerning the chief executive's authority to say what she says.

Lastly, participants in discourse need to be able to challenge the validity claims that the chief executive raises on the dimension of *intention*. They must be able to ensure that her intention really is to propose a way of surviving the economic recession and that she has no ulterior motive. For instance, they need to be sure that she is not proposing redundancies just in order to bring marginal enhancements to commercial performance, which will enable a slight increase in the value of the company and which may also enhance her own remuneration. They may want to be assured that she is not using this situation as an opportunity to improve her own career prospects by demonstrating her willingness to make tough decisions. Or they may seek reassurance that she is not using economic recession as an excuse to put in place non-essential efficiencies that intensify the workload of junior employees and reduce their wages.

All those who take part in the meeting organized by the chief executive should also be at liberty to make whatever statements they wish, thus raising validity claims of their own. For instance, other employees may wish to suggest that substantial savings could be made if the chief executive were to reduce her own remuneration and that of her senior colleagues. Ethically legitimating discourse would require that participants feel that they are able to make such suggestions in the knowledge that they will be considered purely on their ethical merits and that they will be subjected to full and open debate.

Of course, the action that is agreed after discourse has run its course may be none of those that were initially proposed by senior executives. A different way of reducing capacity might be suggested during the meeting and it could be that this option is the one that everyone eventually agrees to. Indeed, given the value that discourse ethics places on the expression of opposing perspectives, alternatives which present radical challenges to the options suggested by senior management should be welcomed. It may even be that, following the presentation of alternatives, the plan to trim production capacity is abandoned altogether and the company decides to adopt an entirely different response to economic recession. Whichever is the case, the key point is that, as far as discourse ethics is concerned, the ethical course of action is the one that is agreed to after full and open discourse involving all affected parties and in which all feel that they are able to raise and challenge validity claims as they see fit.

Theory in Practice

Workplace democracy at Suma

Suma is the UK's largest independent wholesaler and distributor of wholefood (Co-operative News, 2011). In 2011, despite recessionary economic conditions, Suma's annual turnover grew by eight per cent to £30 million (Kingsley, 2012b). It is not just Suma's ability to prosper during adverse trading conditions that is unusual though; the company also has unconventional ownership and management structures. Not only is Suma a cooperative that is entirely owned by its employees; it also has no managers in the usual sense of the word. Instead, it has a 'management committee' comprising six members, who serve for a maximum of two years and who are otherwise treated no differently from the company's other 150 employees. Decisions taken by the management committee are based on consultation with the rest of Suma's workforce and any contentious matters are discussed at bimonthly general meetings (Suma, 2013). All of Suma's employees are therefore actively involved in the running of their business. As one employee, who has worked for Suma for over 30 years, remarked: 'Everyone's talking about the business, all of the time' (cited in Kingsley, 2012b).

Suma's website describes the company's approach to management as follows:

> Suma operates a truly democratic system of management that isn't bound by the conventional notions of hierarchy that often hinder progress and stand in the way of fairness. While we do use an elected Management Committee to implement decisions and business plans, the decisions themselves are made at regular General Meetings with the consent of every cooperative member – there's no chief executive, no managing director and no company chairman. In practice, this means that our day-to-day work is carried out by self-managing teams of employees who are all paid the same wage, and who all enjoy an equal voice and an equal stake in the success of the business. (Suma, 2013)

Suma has been in business for over 35 years. During that time it has won many industry awards for excellence including the 2011 Phillip Baxendale Award for People and Culture, whose judges remarked on Suma's 'ethos of employee-ownership, transparency and meaningful engagement with employees and driving notable activity to strengthen a culture of productive partnership' (cited in Co-operative News, 2011).

Questions

1 In what ways does the decision-making structure at Suma seem to conform to the ideals of discourse ethics?
2 What further information would you need in order to say that Suma's employee-engagement practices conform fully to the criteria that have been mentioned in this chapter?
3 What difficulties might the Suma cooperative model present for larger organizations that are more geographically dispersed?
4 How might such difficulties be overcome?

Discourse and the public sphere: the role of media and marketing corporations

So far this chapter has outlined some characteristics of discourse ethics. It has described how discourse ethics theory accords ethical legitimacy to decisions that result from discourse involving those who are affected by those agreements. Some specific conditions that discourse needs to meet if its outcomes are to have ethical legitimacy have also been outlined. This last section of the chapter will discuss some ways in which discourse that meets such criteria can be facilitated or inhibited by a particular type of corporate activity.

To begin with, the notion of the *public sphere* will be introduced and its relevance to discourse will be explained. The importance of a vigorous public sphere to stakeholder discourse will be highlighted and attention will be drawn to the role played by media corporations in facilitating the public sphere. The possibility that the effectiveness of the public sphere in facilitating discourse might be inhibited as a consequence of *colonization* by commercial and/or political considerations will then be highlighted. One particular form of colonization of the public sphere will be considered. This is the possibility that, although ICT corporations are able to promote a diverse and vigorous online public sphere, they may, in pursuing their commercial agendas, also undermine the effectiveness of that public sphere.

The public sphere and its importance to discourse

Imagine that you have been given the opportunity to take part in stakeholder discourse about a particular topic. Suppose, for instance, that a company is proposing to build some electricity-generating wind turbines near your house and, as a local resident, you have been invited to participate in a meeting with representatives of the company and with other interested parties. You feel quite strongly about this topic but you do not consider yourself very well informed about it. You have not been able to read much about the ethical pros and cons of wind turbines in the media or on the internet, and there has not been much discussion of it on the TV or radio. Moreover, you are not used to debating things like this in public. You have your own opinions on the subject, but you have never expressed them in front of other people. Nor have you spent much time listening to the views of others who may think differently from you about wind energy. In this case, you might find the prospect of taking part in the forthcoming meeting quite daunting.

Now consider a different scenario. Again, you have been asked to attend a meeting to discuss wind turbines but, in this case, you are quite well informed about the subject. You have read a number of articles about wind turbines in the newspaper, you have seen a couple of programmes about them on the TV, and you have listened to some discussions on the radio. And by putting 'wind turbines' into an internet search engine, you have been able to access a vast array of web pages which discuss the topic from various points of view. You also feel comfortable with the idea of taking part in a public discussion about ethics. You have seen other people doing this on the TV and you often read articles in newspapers and on the internet that discuss topics from contrasting points of view. Furthermore, you are used to expressing your views and debating about the ethicality of a wide range of issues on internet discussion forums and social media sites. In this case, you will probably feel far better equipped to take part in the forthcoming meeting.

This example illustrates an important feature of discourse ethics: that it would be hard to apply it in a vacuum. If people are to take part in discourse in a productive manner, it helps if they have access to information, if they are accustomed to exposing their own views to critique, and if they are used to engaging with other people's opinions, particularly those which challenge their own. It also helps if they have some experience of trying to reach a consensus that takes all people's points of view into account. Individual instances of discourse, then, need to take place within a broader framework that facilitates dialectical communication and which equips people to take part in it. Discourse is unlikely to work if it only consists of occasional discussions. It must be supported by ongoing provision of information, by exposure to diverse ideas, and by dialectical processes that accustom people to critical engagement with a range of perspectives.

It is for reasons such as these that discourse-ethics theorists speak of the importance of a vigorous public sphere. *Public sphere* is a term that is often used to denote a collection of physical, literary, media (press, radio and TV) and virtual spaces where people can access information, exchange ideas and debate matters of general interest. In Habermas's words, a public sphere is

> a realm of our social life in which something approaching public opinion can be formed. Access is guaranteed to all citizens … Citizens behave as a public body when they confer in an unrestricted fashion – that is, with the guarantee of freedom of assembly and association and the freedom to express and publish their opinions – about matters of general interest. (Habermas, 1974/1964: 49)

Corporations and the public sphere

The relationship between corporations, discourse and the public sphere is important in a number of ways. For one thing, if discourse involving stakeholders is to fulfil its role of providing ethical legitimization to corporate activity, corporations need to do more than arrange occasional meetings to discuss important topics. They should also do what they can to make relevant information available to stakeholders and to ensure that a range of perspectives are represented. They might also arrange for people such as employees to familiarize themselves with participation in discussions about ethically contentious matters and thus to develop their competence and confidence to play a productive role in stakeholder discourse.

But corporations are also important to discourse and the public sphere insofar as particular types of corporation play a key role in making information and ideas publicly available. For a long time, citizens of many countries have gathered information about topics of general interest by reading newspapers produced by news corporations, by listening to commercially produced radio programmes, and by watching TV stations run by private companies. Even in nations where state-run media institutions exist, these are usually supplemented by privately owned firms. Moreover, as well as disseminating information and ideas, these traditional media sources often encourage readers, watchers and listeners to send in letters, emails and texts and to take part in live phone-ins. They thus provide platforms upon which people can express and exchange their own viewpoints.

In brief, newspapers produced by large corporations, commercially produced radio stations, and programmes offered by privately owned TV companies have given people the opportunity to access information and develop their views about public affairs. For sure, a reader may not get access to a broad range of views if they read just one newspaper and a viewer may not be exposed to conflicting perspectives if they watch a single TV station, because papers and stations sometimes favour particular perspectives. Nevertheless, most of us are aware of the editorial slant of the papers we read, the radio programmes we listen to, or the TV shows we watch, so we can take this into account when we read or hear what they say. Furthermore, if we want to get a different perspective, we usually know which paper or station we can get it from. It seems reasonable to say, then, that media-related businesses have traditionally played a very important role in providing a vigorous and diverse public sphere.

A reinvigorated public sphere: the discursive potential of ICT

To some extent, however, the role played by newspaper, radio and TV corporations in relation to the public sphere is changing. With the development of the internet towards the end of the twentieth century and at the beginning of the twenty-first, we increasingly look to it, rather than traditional media, as an information source and as a platform upon which to exchange ideas. It has been suggested that this is a very good thing for discourse because, in principle, the internet offers a far more democratic forum for exchanging ideas and information than do corporate-run media institutions. Not only does it enable access to a vast range of perspectives; this access is also more-or-less instantaneous. Furthermore, our consumption of ideas is not filtered by the intermediation of press owners and editors, whose political ideologies may shape content. Instead, every citizen can directly download whatever they want to download. Having accessed one point of view on a topic, we can immediately switch to contrasting perspectives in order to gain a broad-based, comprehensive understanding. Potentially, then, the internet is a fertile source of dialectical consciousness formation. It thus presents interesting possibilities for reinvigorating a public sphere that observers such as Habermas suggest may have become somewhat moribund in recent times.

A number of writers have explicitly reflected on the discursive promise of the internet. Nick Harkaway, for instance, remembers the aspirations that suffused the internet-pioneering years of the 1990s:

> The promise and rhetoric of the Internet as given in the 1990s … was of open systems, free speech, individual privacy and governmental transparency. The electronic realm would be the crucible in which the physical one was remade. An untouchable refuge for revolution and experiment, the Net was the venue where anything that was suppressed could be given voice. (2012: 26)

Similarly, Jonathan Crary recalls ruefully that 'The interactive possibilities of these new tools were touted as empowering, and as intrinsically democratic and anti-hierarchical' (2013: 83), while Eli Pariser remembers that 'For a time, it seemed that the Internet was going to entirely redemocratize society. Bloggers and citizen journalists would single-handedly rebuild the public media' (2011: 5). A particularly optimistic prophet of the democratizing potential of the internet was Thomas Friedman (2005), who predicted that ICT would flatten hierarchies and transform information exchange, as well as spreading the affluence enjoyed by many in the West to other parts of the globe.

Just as corporations were central to the provision of traditional media platforms, they are also playing a central role in promoting this new, virtual, public sphere. For instance, the firms that run social-networking sites have put us in touch with contributors all over the world, who are able to share their opinions and exchange ideas with us. Meanwhile, corporations that provide internet search engines help us to access a staggering array of information about any topic we choose to research. It is unsurprising, then, that one of these corporations proclaims proudly that, of the 'Ten things we know to be true', one is that 'Democracy on the web works' (Google, 2013).

Corporate colonization of the public sphere

As well as contributing to the availability of a vigorous and diverse public sphere, however, corporations may also be culpable of closing it down. The manner in which this happens can be described in terms of a phenomenon that Habermas calls colonization.

The term *colonization*, when used in this context, refers to something entering a territory that it ought not to enter and taking control of processes that it ought not to control. The result of colonization, thus understood, is that, instead of processes being structured in a manner that allows them to fulfil their fundamental purpose, they become structured in ways that inhibit the achievement of that purpose.

In relation to discourse, colonization describes a situation whereby, instead of being structured in ways that permit the achievement of shared understanding, discourse gets sidetracked by other agendas and thus becomes orientated towards other purposes. Habermas is particularly concerned about ways in which considerations of power and money enter into discursive forums so that, instead of those forums enabling people to achieve shared understanding, they become dominated by financial and political considerations. Instead of discourse achieving its fundamental purpose, then, it becomes focused on the generation of wealth and the capture of power for the benefit of particular people.

Habermas believes that this is something to which modern society is especially prone. He warns of 'the fact that the capitalist economy and modern administration expand at the expense of other domains of life that are structurally disposed to moral-practical and expressive forms of rationality and squeeze them into forms of economic or administrative rationality' (1984/1981: 183). Habermas has identified ways in which the public sphere has become impoverished as a consequence of commercial and political colonization, as well as ways in which it might rejuvenate itself (see Calhoun, 1992 for discussion and critique of Habermas's ideas).

Undermining the internet's democratizing potential

As an example of how colonization of the public sphere, particularly by financial considerations, might take place, it is instructive to consider in more detail the internet's potential to promote a vigorous public sphere, and to reflect on some ways in which this potential may be undermined by commercial considerations.

The need for discourse to embrace diverse perspectives has been emphasized throughout this chapter. According to discourse ethics, it is through the dialectical interplay of contrasting points of view that we are able to move towards enhanced understanding. And only through this dialectical interplay can the ethical quality of agreements that eventually emerge be guaranteed. Part of the importance of the public sphere, then, lies in its capacity to enable the expression of a broad range of perspectives and to put people in touch with viewpoints that challenge their own. If the internet is to realize its potential to contribute to the public sphere and thus to facilitate discourse, then, it needs to do just this. It is not enough for it to link users to information and opinions that support their own convictions; it is important that it also exposes them to ideas that challenge those convictions.

Of course, one way in which the internet's capacity to present a diverse range of ideas and information to its users may be undermined is through meddling by government authorities. Such activity could be described as an instance of the power-oriented dimension of colonization to which Habermas refers. For instance, Evgeny Morozov (2011), in challenging 'cyber-utopian' claims for the essentially democratizing quality of the internet, points out that it might equally well be used as a mode of political surveillance and repression and for the manipulation of information and ideas. Of more relevance to business ethics, however, is the money-oriented dimension of colonization. That is, the way in which commercially driven corporate activity, instead of opening up internet users' exposure to diverse perspectives and thus facilitating dialectical discourse, may actually inhibit such exposure. In so doing, those corporations may be undermining the capacity of ICT to provide the vigorous and diverse public sphere upon which the practical implementation of discourse ethics relies.

Harvesting personal data

Eli Pariser explains how this happens in his book *The Filter Bubble* (2011), which describes corporations' increasingly sophisticated personalization of internet use. When we use the internet we often gain apparently free access to information and services. However, Pariser points out that that access is not as 'free' as it seems. Although we do not pay in cash for the information and services that are made available to us online, we pay in a different way: that is, we supply data about ourselves. And this data is used by corporations to construct a detailed picture of who we are, what we like, and what type of things we might be interested in buying.

The sort of data that we make available to the providers of internet services may seem harmless enough. For one thing we access most websites anonymously, so surfing the internet seems, on the face of it, no more revealing of our personal details than browsing the window displays in a shopping mall. And even if we do need to sign in in order to use the occasional website, we often do so with a pseudonym: we rarely provide details like our real name, address, or phone number that would enable someone to identify who we really are.

However, even if we do not share personal details with a website, we may still identify ourselves as a specific user. When we log on to a particular site we provide data which enables that site to recognize us and, more importantly, it allows it to construct a detailed profile of our interests and buying habits. And even when we access sites without logging in, those sites may still gather such data, as well as transferring cookies onto the PC, tablet, smartphone, or whatever internet-connection device we are using, which enable them to identify us as the user of that particular device and to start building a personal profile based on that mode of identification.

How the data we provide shapes what we see

The important point about this recognition process is that sites use the personal data we provide to shape the information they subsequently show us. For instance, if you go to an online clothing retailer's site and download some pages about beach shorts, a special offer on beach shorts may be the first thing you see the next time you log on to that site. The site has worked out that you might be interested in buying some beach shorts, so it will provide you with as much information as it can about beach shorts to try to persuade you to actually make a purchase.

A similar thing may happen if you put 'beach shorts' into a search engine to find that retailer's site in the first place. In this case, though, that data may get shared with other sites so that when you download those sites you see advertisements for beach shorts. For example, when you log on to the BigSalty site to get a wind and surf forecast for your kite-surfing trip on Saturday, you will see some adverts for beach shorts displayed prominently on the page that you view. You may also find an advert for that kite-surfing book that you searched for on Amazon yesterday, but which you decided not to buy. And, if you have looked on the internet for credit facilities lately, you may also see an advert for payday loans. In other words the user of your internet connection device – that is, you – has been identified as a kite-surfing enthusiast who is interested in buying some new beach shorts and who may need to borrow some money. That information has been shared with a number of corporations. And those corporations are using it to encourage you to buy their products and use their services.

Eli Pariser (2011) explains how the personal data that we hand over when we use the internet gets passed through the 'data market' and how it subsequently shapes what we see. One example is that, when we use a search engine, we tell the company that runs it some things about the type of issues that interest us and the type of products we might want to buy. That search engine provider then sells that information to data-handling companies, who use it in various ways. For one thing, they may use it to compile generic market-segmentation information, which will tell marketing professionals about the profiles and aspirations of the people who are interested in their products; information which will help them to market those products more effectively.

Of greater concern for Pariser, however, is that data-handling companies are able to build an increasingly detailed picture of each of the users listed on their databases. For example, according to Pariser, Acxiom, which is currently the largest data-handling corporation, has accumulated on average 1,500 pieces of data on each person on its database, which includes 96 per cent of all Americans.[6] Data handlers sell this information on to retailers that wish to advertise their products to those users. Those retailers are thus able to target their advertisements specifically at people who they think are most likely to buy. Moreover, the websites upon which those retailers advertise their products are able to charge a premium for enabling highly targeted advertising, which shows to each individual user only those specific advertisements that are deemed most relevant to them. Pariser sums up this activity thus: 'In the view of the "behaviour market" vendors, every "click signal" you create is a commodity, and every move of your mouse can be auctioned off within microseconds to the highest commercial bidder' (2011: 7).

---

[6]Pariser does not mention users outside the USA, but we can assume that data-handling companies are gathering similar data globally.

Special news bulletins, tailored just for you

Of course, if we do not want sites to trade information about us and use that information to sell us things, there are a number of things we can do to prevent cookies from accumulating on our internet connection device, or to opt-out of interest-based advertising. However, few people bother with such things because they usually involve complex processes and they tend to have a negative impact on user convenience. Therefore, most of us, even if we are aware of the capture and manipulation of information that is going on in the background, do little to prevent it.

And maybe we are right to not bother too much about all this. Perhaps it is not a bad thing that we only see adverts for stuff that we might want to buy rather than being exposed to loads of irrelevant pitches about things that are of no interest to us. Anyway, if sharing a bit of information about our purchasing aspirations means that we can access things like wind and surf forecasts for free, then why worry?

However, this process of personalization becomes worrying from a discourse ethics perspective when we consider some other ways in which we use the internet. Pariser highlights, in particular, the means by which we access information about public affairs nowadays. He offers two particular examples: firstly, the way that we increasingly depend on social-networking sites to gather information and opinions about matters of public interest; and secondly the way in which internet-based news sites are replacing traditional media sources as providers of information and forums for debate about current affairs. He suggests that, in each of these cases, data-driven personalization means that we are increasingly exposed only to news that service providers think we will want to hear.

Personalization by social-networking sites

Consider, first, the case of social-networking sites, which, according to Pariser (2011), 36 per cent of Americans aged under 30 depend on as their primary news source. We do not pay money to use social-networking sites. Instead, the sites receive most of their funding from the corporations who place adverts on them. Social-networking site providers clearly want to maximize revenue from those adverts. They do this by ensuring that advertisers are able to place their ads in front of users who are most likely to buy their products and by ensuring that those users log on as often as possible. Social-networking sites therefore gather a broad range of data about their users from the registration details that they provide, the things that they 'like', and the posts that they read. This enables those sites to build a detailed picture of each user and to predict the sort of things that he or she might want to buy. It also allows them to predict the sort of posts that need to be put at the top of a user's home page if that user is to be encouraged to use the site regularly.

In short, some social-networking sites create a detailed picture of each user so that they can show that user the posts that they predict will be of most interest to her or him. Pariser is concerned that the news that we read thus becomes increasingly narrowed down: we read a post from someone whose ideas we find interesting; the social-networking site registers our interest in that person's views, so places their next post at the top of our news feed next time we log on. So, again, we read what they have to say on a new topic. And because we have clicked again on one of their posts, their subsequent posts are even more likely to appear at the top of our news feed in future. Furthermore, the social-networking site may draw our attention to groups that that person belongs to or to people whose posts they follow, suggesting that we may also want to look at those groups or read what those people have to say. So we follow the site's advice and take a quick peek at these groups and people, which further reinforces the site's conviction that this is the sort of stuff that we want to be exposed to, so it shows us even more of the same. The eventual consequence is that we become locked into what Pariser calls a 'filter bubble': we become stereotypical versions of ourselves. 'You can get stuck in a static, ever-narrowing version of yourself – an endless you-loop' (Pariser, 2011: 16).

As far as discourse is concerned, the problem with all this is that, instead of getting exposed to a range of perspectives, which will allow us to proceed in a dialectical manner to a comprehensive understanding of an issue, our ideas just get narrowed down. We only see one side of the argument: that which is offered by those people our social-networking site thinks will interest us the most. Our favourite social-networking site never seems to say to us: 'take a look at what this person has to say on the topic; it might give you a different point of view'!

Pause for Reflection

If you are a Facebook user, look at any ads or suggested apps that appear on your home page. How do you think Facebook has worked out that you might be interested in these particular links? Look at the posts that appear at the top of your feed. Why might Facebook have prioritized these? What might you do to access some opinions on a particular topic that differ from those expressed in those posts? What might you be able to do to prevent Facebook from placing you within a highly personalized 'filter bubble'?

Personalization of internet-based news

Eli Pariser also highlights the challenges presented to the public sphere by the personalization of internet-based news. He observes that sites such as Yahoo News are becoming important sources of information about public affairs. The corporations that run those sites are as keen as those that run social-networking sites to maximize advertising revenue. And Pariser suggests that they are also looking at ways of building detailed profiles of their users so that they can show each user adverts and specific news features that they consider most relevant to them. The end result, Pariser fears, is that each user will be offered personalized news pages that fuel their own interests and opinions and which do nothing to challenge them. Our ideas about specific topics that interest us will thus be continually reinforced. Our awareness of significant events that do not fall within what is deemed to be our personalized sphere of interest will diminish. And we will become increasingly less likely to be troubled by perspectives that challenge our own.

Pariser concludes that processes such as these will not be helpful to discourse. Nor are they supportive of the discursive form of democracy that is usually associated with it.

> Ultimately, democracy works only if we citizens are capable of thinking beyond our narrow self-interest. But to do so, we need a shared view of the world we cohabit. We need to come into contact with other peoples' lives and needs and desires. The filter bubble pushes us in the opposite direction – it creates the impression that our narrow self-interest is all that exists. And while this is great for getting people to shop online, it's not great for getting people to make better decisions together. (Pariser, 2011: 164)

In Habermas's terms, this might be described as a process of colonization of the public sphere by financial interests. Instead of the internet-based public sphere being an open network, which exposes users to a diverse range of perspectives about a broad selection of topics, key players like internet marketing companies, search engine providers, social-networking site providers, and news providers are taking hold of that platform and using it merely as a tool to further their own commercial agendas.

Video Activity 7.3

In 2009 Google stated on its website that it was updating its 'privacy policy'. In essence, Google would, from that moment, collate the data that it gathered on users of its various services, including Chrome, Gmail and YouTube, and use this data to personalize the search results that it showed to those users. This meant that, instead of every user who searches on a particular word or phrase being shown the same list of links, each user would be shown a personalized list. That personalized list would be ordered according to what Google's algorithms had calculated was most relevant to that particular user (Pariser, 2011).

The following link shows a BBC report on this issue: www.youtube.com/watch?v=uEWmNwRHY2U.

This report focuses on the privacy implications of Google storing so much data about its users. However, this change in Google's privacy policy also has implications for the internet's usefulness as a platform for accessing diverse information and ideas.

Questions

1 How might personalization of search results benefit Google's users?
2 How might it serve Google's commercial purposes and those of its partner organizations?
3 In what way might personalized search results inhibit the usefulness of the internet as a public sphere; in other words how might personalization make it harder for users to access a diverse range of opinions on a particular topic?
4 What steps could you take to reduce the extent to which you are shown highly personalized information by Google?

Conclusion

Discourse ethics theory places a premium on people being able to have a say about matters that affect them. It therefore resonates with democratic principles that occupy a prominent place in most contemporary value systems. It encourages us to reflect on ways in which those democratic principles might be embraced by corporate decision-making processes, thus providing one form of ethical legitimacy for business activity. It also draws attention to some ways in which apparently democratic processes, particularly in business contexts, might not be as democratic as they could be.

Although the template for ethical legitimacy offered by discourse-ethics theory holds a great deal of intuitive appeal, its application also presents a number of practical challenges. These include problems associated with reaching consensus, the likelihood that ethical discourse will be influenced by strategic agendas, and the difficulty of arranging discourse in a corporate environment that, to an increasing extent, is geographically dispersed. However, these challenges need not undermine the relevance of discourse to business ethics. Rather, they can serve to highlight issues that need to be addressed if business is to conform to democratic ideals that most of us hold dear.

Discussion questions

1. List some practical difficulties associated with arranging discourse about matters of ethical significance in corporate settings. How might such challenges be overcome?
2. Can you identify any trends in contemporary corporate settings that make it particularly hard to apply discourse ethics theory to workplace relations? Do you

(Continued)

(Continued)

think these difficulties should be taken as a reason to abandon aspirations to make workplace practices more democratic? Or do they offer grounds for resisting those trends and striving for alternative corporate forms that are less erosive of discourse?

3. We tend to expect business managers to show leadership to their subordinates and to other business stakeholders. And we often think about leadership in impositional terms. That is, we expect our leaders to *lead*. There is a sense, then, that our expectations of business management are incompatible with the practical application of discourse in corporations. If we expect visionary leader-managers to show us where we should go and tell us how to get there, there seems little need for discourse in corporations. But does this have to be the case? Can you think of things that people in business-leadership positions might do to facilitate discourse and to ensure that all their stakeholders have the opportunity to participate in setting the direction of corporate activity?

Further study

Richard Bernstein's 'Introduction' to his (1985) edited collection, *Habermas and Modernity*, offers an excellent overview of Habermas's work, which relates his ideas about communication to other aspects of his social philosophy as well as contextualizing it in relation to the broader tradition of critical theory and twentieth-century European history.

Stanley Deetz's (1992) book, *Democracy in an Age of Corporate Colonization*, draws on Habermas's ideas and those of other critical theorists to explore in detail the relationship between democracy and corporate activity.

Mick Fryer's (2012) paper, 'Facilitative leadership: drawing on Jürgen Habermas' model of ideal speech to propose a less impositional way to lead', discusses ways in which Habermas's ideas might be applied to develop a facilitative style of business leadership that is consistent with the expectations of discourse-ethics theory.

Watch a short video at http://www.youtube.com/watch?v=dP3fsXAADAo, in which Eli Pariser outlines some ways in which the internet's capacity to contribute to a diverse public sphere may be closed down as a consequence of the commercial agenda of large ICT corporations that mediate public access to information and ideas.

8 Feminine Ethics: Offering a Different Ethical Perspective on Business

Chapter objectives

This chapter will:

- introduce the idea that there may be a characteristically feminine way of thinking about ethics;
- explore some insights that a feminine ethical perspective might offer to business;
- outline some challenges to the idea that there is a characteristically feminine way of thinking about ethics;
- propose that, notwithstanding these challenges, feminine ethics theory foregrounds some important themes that might otherwise be overlooked;
- consider how essentialist and constructionist perspectives on the nature of femininity might relate to business ethics;
- consider how consumer marketing might be responsible for sustaining stereotypical images of gender that contribute to the subordination of women.

Introduction

This chapter will explore some perspectives that are sometimes placed under the heading of 'feminine ethics'. In some respects, the title is misleading since it might seem to imply that this chapter will address issues that are only of interest to women. This is not the case. Indeed, as I will argue later, the ideas introduced under the general rubric of feminine ethics have as much to say to men as they do to women. The title is also potentially misleading in that it might be taken as a suggestion that the book's other chapters are more suited to men than they are to women. Again this is not the case. The reason for including this chapter is, rather, to introduce some important ideas that have been offered by theorists who have explored the relationship between gender and ethics. Some of these ideas provide unique insights to business ethics; others highlight the significance of themes that are present in other ethics theories but which may not receive the prominence they merit.

The first section of the chapter will draw on the work of Carol Gilligan and Nel Noddings to introduce the idea that there may be a characteristically feminine way of thinking about ethics and that, by focusing purely on masculine perspectives, business ethics may miss out on some important insights that this feminine approach enables. The second section will outline some challenges to the notion of a characteristically feminine ethical perspective. Some of these challenges take issue with this notion on factual grounds, proposing that it portrays a misleading simplification of how women and men think about ethics. Other critics warn that depictions of a characteristically feminine ethical perspective may not only be factually misleading, but that they may also encourage some unhelpful ways of thinking about gender and hierarchy. The second section will conclude by suggesting that, regardless of whether or not women think differently to men about ethics, the perspective that some consider to be uniquely feminine foregrounds important themes that might otherwise get overlooked.

The chapter's third section will explore a question that is implicit in the first two sections: to what extent are femininity and masculinity predetermined characteristics and to what extent are established ways of thinking about gender conditioned by social factors? Consideration of this question prompts reflection on whether certain types of business activity might be culpable of contributing to harmful gender stereotypes. The third and last section of this chapter will therefore outline some responses to such questions, along with some implications for business practice. These ideas will be explored with specific reference to consumer marketing.

Feminine ethics: an alternative to the masculine mainstream

During the last 35 years, a number of commentators have explored the possibility of a specifically feminine ethical perspective. In other words, researchers have begun to ask whether women are inclined to talk about ethics 'in a different voice' (Gilligan, 1993/1982) to that used by men. If there is indeed a characteristically feminine moral voice, then it may highlight some themes that are either overlooked or downplayed in the mainstream – or what Alison Jaggar (1991) calls the 'malestream' – ethics tradition.[1] This first section of the chapter will therefore consider some contributions to the idea that women are inclined to think differently to men about ethics. I will also consider how these ideas might help us to think about business ethics.

Two writers who have been particularly influential in this respect are Carol Gilligan and Nel Noddings. Here, I will outline some of the ideas offered by Gilligan and Noddings in elaborating a feminine *ethic of care*.

Carol Gilligan: identifying a different moral voice

Carol Gilligan's book, *In a Different Voice* (1993/1982), has made a significant contribution to the idea that women think differently from men about ethics. In her book, Gilligan discusses ways in which children and young adults develop and express their ideas about ethics. In the process, she identifies a distinctively feminine 'moral voice', which she distinguishes from the masculine approach that had informed earlier discussions of moral development. In particular, Gilligan challenges the work of Laurence Kohlberg, who had proposed that, because girls and young women discuss ethics in a different way to boys and young men, females do not tend to progress as far as males in their moral development. Gilligan suggests that Kohlberg's work was carried out from within a specifically masculine point of view. She points out that, since Kohlberg was applying uniquely masculine standards to his study of moral development, it is no surprise that he should find that males reach a higher stage of development than females. In contrast to Kohlberg's findings, Gilligan sets out to demonstrate that, rather than reaching a less-advanced stage of moral development, women are inclined to follow a different developmental path to that taken by most men.

Gilligan observes that males and females think differently about ethics in a number of ways. In particular, she identifies contrasting ways of perceiving human relationships, contrasting ways of thinking about ethical dilemmas, and contrasting expectations of ethics. Gilligan sums up these differences by referring to a female *ethic of care* and a masculine *justice perspective*. I will say a little about each of these differences before drawing out some of their implications for business.

---

[1]You may have noticed that most of the ethics theorists that have been discussed in this book so far are male. This is mainly because, until the second half of the twentieth century, very few women had written much about ethics. This, in itself, is an ethically charged state of affairs, since it begs the question of why women have been shut out from a very important arena of intellectual activity for so long. However, the intrinsic undesirability of exclusion and the disrespect that it entails are not issues that will be addressed here directly, although some of the ideas introduced in the chapter may offer some insights to these issues.

Contrasting ways of viewing human relations

Gilligan proposes that divergent masculine and feminine ethical perspectives are rooted in contrasting ways of understanding the human situation. According to Gilligan, boys tend to think about human relations in an individualistic way. That is, they see the world as comprising autonomous entities who navigate their way through life, following their own, separate agendas and only coming into contact with one another in the process of achieving those agendas. This way of thinking is an essentially atomistic one: it focuses on separation rather than interdependence. Moreover, those encounters with other autonomous entities that do occur as part of the human predicament are seen by males as offering the potential for 'dangerous confrontation and explosive connection' (Gilligan, 1993/1982: 38), so they need to be regulated by rules of engagement that are clearly understood by all.

In contrast to this individualistic, masculine perspective, Gilligan finds that girls tend to think of social arrangements in terms of connection. They are inclined to focus on relationships, seeing the human condition as one of interdependency between people rather than as one of autonomy. So, while boys emphasize the separations that exist between people, girls see 'a world comprised of relationships … a world that coheres through human connection' (Gilligan, 1993/1982: 29).

Contrasting ways of thinking about ethical dilemmas and resolving them

Partly as a result of these contrasting ways of thinking about the human condition, Gilligan finds that males and females think differently about ethical dilemmas and how they might be addressed. She observes that boys tend to see ethical dilemmas in terms of encounters between separate, discrete individuals, each of whom has claims that may conflict with the claims of others. Resolving such conflicting claims involves seeking definitive verdicts, which clearly apportion right and wrong to specific individuals.

Ethical evaluation, according to this masculine perspective, is a matter of detached, impersonal judgement; of standing back from the issue at hand and applying abstract principles in a dispassionate manner to achieve a just outcome. As one of Gilligan's research participants put it, an ethical dilemma is thus viewed as 'sort of like a math problem with humans' (Gilligan, 1993/1982: 26).

Conversely, Gilligan finds that girls are inclined to see those implicated in an ethical dilemma 'arrayed not as opponents in a contest of rights but as members of a network of relationships on whose continuation they all depend' (Gilligan, 1993/1982: 30). According to this characteristically feminine point of view, an ethical dilemma is a 'problem of care and responsibility in relationships rather than … one of rights and rules' (1993/1982: 73). Its resolution does not consist of applying abstract principles in order to reach a definitive judgement of right and wrong, from which separate individuals emerge either as ethically culpable or ethically vindicated.

Rather, resolution consists of preserving the communal bonds that an ethical dilemma threatens to rupture. Therefore, instead of applying ethical principles to arrive at a just verdict, girls are inclined to ask how enhanced understanding amongst participants in a conflict might lead to an outcome that serves the interests of all. According to Gilligan, then, girls are more inclined to emphasize everyone's responsibility to do what they can to make the whole thing work than they are to get tied up in analysis of the competing claims of specific antagonists.

Importantly, on this feminine understanding, the resolution of ethical conflict is not achieved through the dispassionate application of abstract principles. Rather, it requires familiarity with the complex situational factors that prevail within a specific context. It requires that everyone gets up close so that they can understand other people's perspectives. Feminine ethical evaluation, then, is not something that can be done at a distance. It demands intimate familiarity with the contextual intricacies of the situation under consideration.

Contrasting expectations of ethics

According to Gilligan's findings, these divergent perspectives lead to contrasting expectations of ethical enquiry and what it can achieve. Gilligan finds that males tend to look to ethics to protect the legitimate claims of individuals, which are often conceived in terms of rights. Females, on the other hand, expect ethical enquiry to point the way towards solutions that ultimately serve the interests of all. They see it as 'a way of solving conflicts so that no one will be hurt' (Gilligan, 1993/1982: 65). Ethics, on this feminine view, is not a 'contest of rights but a problem of relationships, centering on a question of responsibility which in the end must be faced' (1993/1982: 59).

Associated with these contrasting expectations of ethics are distinctive understandings of what it is to be an ethical person. According to the masculine perspective that Gilligan describes, an ethical person is one who respects people's rights; who steers a course through life without disobeying categorical, ethical rules of the road; and who, in the event of a collision, appeals to those rules to decide on culpability and reparation. The feminine view, on the other hand, understands ethicality in terms of concern for other people. Gilligan thus describes the feminine ethical agent as 'defining the self and proclaiming its worth on the basis of the ability to care for and protect others' (Gilligan, 1993/1982: 79).

Contrasting an 'ethic of care' to a 'justice perspective'

Gilligan adopts the terms an *ethic of care* (Gilligan, 1993/1982) or a *care perspective* (Gilligan, 1987) to refer to the characteristically feminine moral voice that she thus identifies. This she contrasts to a male *justice perspective*. She proposes that, for males, ethics is equated to justice because it involves applying ethical rules in the disinterested and impartial manner of a criminal court with the expectation of arriving at just outcomes. A feminine ethic of care, on the other hand, is rooted in a vision of communities of interdependence, in which all are seen as having responsibility for one another. Figure 8.1 offers a summary of these contrasting perspectives and of some of their respective implications.

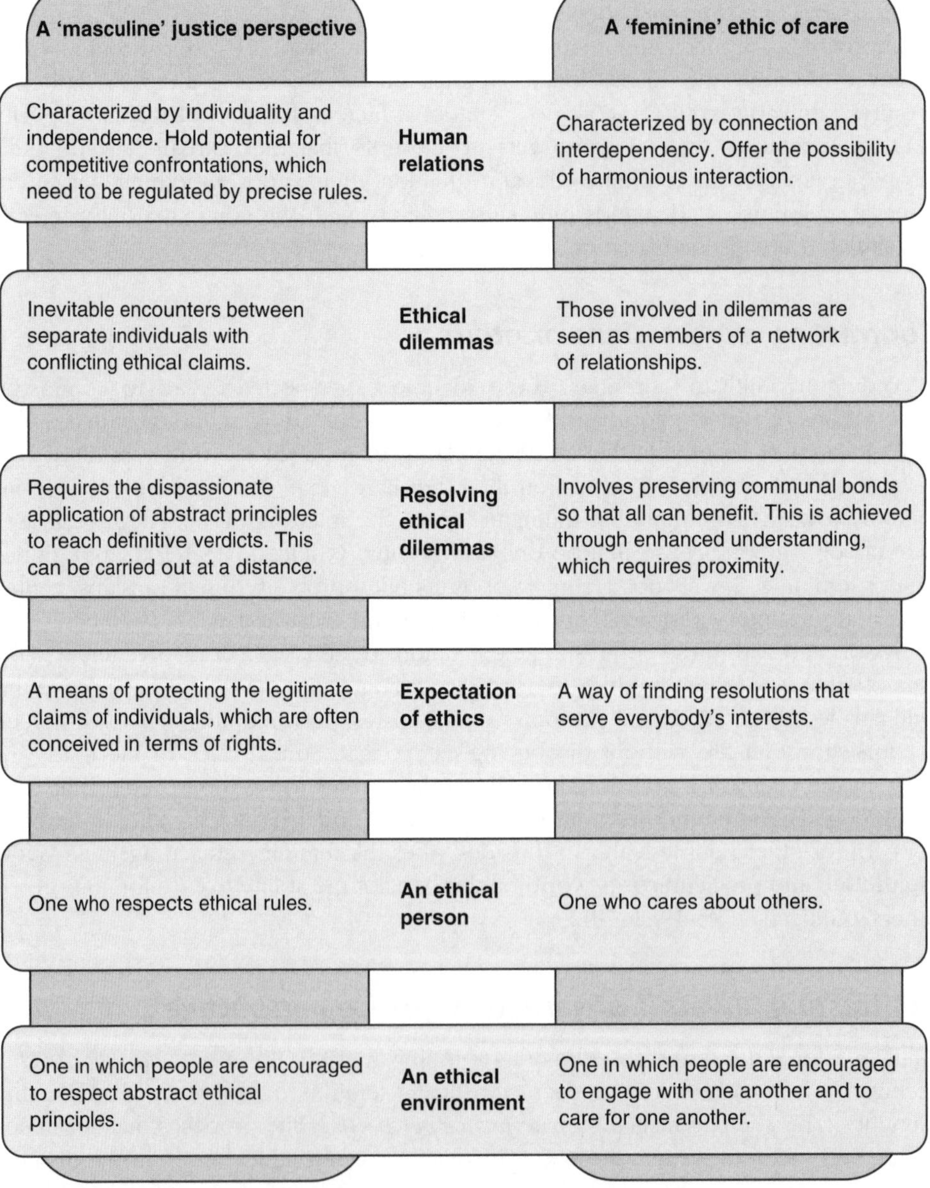

Figure 8.1 Contrasting a 'masculine' justice perspective to a 'feminine' ethic of care

Pause for Reflection

Do you find that women's attitudes to ethics are characterized by *care* and that men tend to think predominantly in terms of *justice*? How well do Gilligan's descriptions of distinctively masculine and feminine approaches to ethics apply to the way that you, yourself think? What about members of your family and your close friends: does Gilligan's analysis match the way they tend to talk about ethics?

Talking about stakeholders in a different moral voice

Relationships between businesses and their stakeholders have already been discussed several times in this book. Stakeholders are usually thought of as people who have some form of influence over a company, or perhaps as people who are affected in some way by a company's activities (Freeman, 1984). As already pointed out, it has become quite common to think about the ethical responsibilities of businesses in terms of responsibilities towards various stakeholders.

Andrew Wicks, Daniel Gilbert and Edward Freeman (1994) observe that theorizing about stakeholder relationships has traditionally been conducted in terms that Gilligan would describe as characteristically masculine. Moreover, Wicks et al. suggest that this limited, masculine perspective has restricted the usefulness of the stakeholder concept to business ethics theory. They propose that the alternative, feminine perspective identified by Gilligan provides a basis for a richer and more comprehensive understanding of the interconnections between businesses and their stakeholders. They therefore propose that 'The stakeholder concept can be enriched by replacing some of the masculine metaphors with feminine alternatives and, in so doing, [that we may] more fully express its latent possibilities' (Wicks et al., 1994: 477).

In order to achieve this objective, Wicks et al. identify several 'masculine metaphors' which, they suggest, prevail in business theory and practice. They point to ways in which each of these masculine metaphors might be augmented by alternative feminine metaphors, thus offering a 'feminist re-interpretation of the stakeholder concept [which] helps us better express the meaning and purposes of corporations' (Wicks et al., 1994: 477). Their findings also have important ethical implications for stakeholder relationships.

Some prevailing masculine metaphors concerning stakeholder relationships

The first masculine metaphor identified by Wicks et al. (1994) concerns a tendency for corporations and their stakeholders to be depicted in atomistic terms. That is, corporations are often portrayed as autonomous entities that are fundamentally separate from stakeholders such as their customers, their shareholders, their suppliers and the local communities within which they operate. Of course, stakeholders such as these may be able to influence the achievement of corporate objectives, and they may be affected by corporate activity. Corporations and stakeholders are therefore connected in that minimal respect. Nevertheless, according to the traditional depiction identified by Wicks et al., stakeholders are not regarded as being integral to a corporation's identity. Seen from this atomistic point of view, a corporation stands apart from its stakeholders and it can be thought of in isolation from them.

Wicks et al. (1994) also observe that traditional business theory tends to analyse the corporate environment in terms of competition. In other words, the business world is typically viewed as a context in which corporations and various groups of stakeholders contest their competing claims, their conflicting agendas and their contrasting objectives. According to this characteristically masculine analysis, corporations need to establish control if they are to operate successfully. That is, they need to ensure that their environment is structured in a manner which privileges their claims, their agendas and their objectives over those of their stakeholders. Importantly, in order to achieve this degree of control, corporations must exercise mastery over any stakeholders whose interests may conflict with their own.

The traditional, masculine perspective on stakeholder relationships identified by Wicks et al. also tends to present corporate decision making as a rational, dispassionate undertaking, which responds to hard, factual data and which can be carried out at a distance from the views of stakeholders. A certain amount of communication with stakeholders whose support is essential to corporate success may be advocated by this approach, but other, less-significant stakeholders are unlikely to be consulted. Thus, a situation is envisaged in which the opinions of many people who are affected by corporate activity go unacknowledged 'as we move toward a form of thinking which detaches us from the identities, emotions, needs, and perceptions of particular individuals' (Wicks et al., 1994: 481).

In accordance with this expectation of detached, rational decision making, the dominant, masculine approach to stakeholder relationships tends to structure power and authority in strict, hierarchical terms. As Wicks et al. put it,

> This conception of power and authority in the organization establishes a clear chain of command all the way from people on the assembly line up to the CEO and specifies the tasks that are appropriate to each role. In this type of system, people are primarily responsible for carrying out assigned duties rather than acting as a creative agent set free to make decisions and exercise judgement over important matters. (1994: 482)

An important feature of this strict, hierarchical-control metaphor is that participation in decision making tends to be limited to those at the top of the company. Voices and perspectives of external stakeholders such as suppliers and local communities tend to be excluded, as are those of less senior employees. A privileged decision-making role is thus reserved for those who occupy senior management positions within corporations, while any wider stakeholder engagement is generally precluded.

Some alternative, feminine metaphors concerning stakeholder relationships

In contrast to this prevailing, masculine approach to stakeholder relationships, Wicks et al. (1994) suggest that a feminine approach would not conceive of corporations in terms of autonomous entities but as webs of relationships, in which they are inextricably tied to their stakeholders. Thus, 'the us/them and internal/external distinctions [would] fade into a sense of communal solidarity in which one sees the corporate identity as manifest within an entire network of stakeholders and a broader social context' (Wicks et al., 1994: 483). Such an approach would focus management attention on responsibilities that the corporation has towards sustaining that environment for the benefit of all its members, rather than using it as a resource pool upon which to nourish itself.

Instead of corporate decision making being viewed as a detached, rational activity, the feminine reinterpretation envisaged by Wicks et al. (1994) would conceive of it as a matter of communication and collective action. This would involve proactive engagement with all stakeholders who are affected by corporate activity, not just those who are most important to the achievement of corporate objectives. It would also involve moving away from hierarchical, centralized decision-making procedures, since the involvement of stakeholders is best achieved through intimate engagement at a local level.

Most of all, a feminine reinterpretation of the stakeholder concept would emphasize a corporation's responsibility of care for those who are affected by its activities. Indeed, adding to Wicks et al.'s observations, Brian Burton and Craig Dunn (1996) propose that the primary feature of a feminine approach to stakeholder relationships would be an attitude of care for those stakeholders whose interests are most vulnerable to corporate activity, particularly where those groups are in some way disadvantaged or otherwise unable to represent their points of view.

Video Activity 8.1

In the following video clip, entitled 'Ben & Jerry's Join Our Core Roundtable', Rob Michelak of Ben and Jerry's Ice Cream discusses the approach his company takes to stakeholder relationships.

www.youtube.com/watch?v=HbWN9lSsdOM

(Continued)

(Continued)

Question

Can you identify ways in which Rob Michelak's description of Ben and Jerry's approach towards stakeholder relationships expresses what Andrew Wicks, Daniel Gilbert and Edward Freeman (1984) would call *feminine metaphors*?

Nel Noddings: favouring a feminine ethic of care over a masculine justice perspective

Nel Noddings (2003) book *Caring* supports and builds on some of the themes introduced by Carol Gilligan. However, whereas Gilligan (1993/1982; 1987) presents a feminine ethical perspective as an alternative to the dominant masculine view, Noddings goes further in proposing that a feminine ethic of care provides the basis for a response to human situations that is more profoundly ethical than that permitted by a masculine approach.

Getting up close to ethically charged situations

The basis for Noddings' preference for feminine over masculine ethics lies in her belief that women tend to base their responses to ethically charged situations on intimate contact with those situations. In this respect, Noddings reinforces Gilligan's observation that women are more likely than men to try to get close to ethical dilemmas. As she puts it,

> Faced with a hypothetical moral dilemma, women often ask for more information. … Ideally, we need to talk to the participants, to see their eyes and facial expressions, to receive what they are feeling. Moral decisions are, after all, made in real situations; they are qualitatively different from the solution of geometry problems. (Noddings, 2003: 2–3)

To understand why Noddings believes an intimate, feminine approach to be more profoundly ethical than a detached, masculine approach, it helps to be acquainted with three concepts that are central to her work: the ethical ideal; natural caring; and ethical caring. It also helps to appreciate how those concepts relate to one another.

The ethical ideal, natural caring and ethical caring

The *ethical ideal*, for Noddings, is the impulse that makes us want to act ethically rather than unethically. It is the basis of our ethical motivation, or 'the source of ethical behaviour' (Noddings, 2003: 80). As Noddings describes it, 'when we commit ourselves to obey the "I must" even at its weakest and most fleeting, we are under the guidance of [the ethical] ideal' (2003: 80).

Noddings suggests that the ethical ideal, this motivation to be ethical, comes partly from a natural sympathy that human beings feel for one another. More significantly, though, the ethical ideal is developed in instances of what Noddings calls *natural care*. Natural care describes situations in which we care for another person because it comes naturally to us to do so. For Noddings, the most obvious and most influential expression of natural care is maternal care; that is, a mother's care for her child. Noddings points out that it comes naturally to a mother to provide maternal care. In other words, a mother does not care for her child because she feels that she ought to; because she feels under some moral compulsion to do so. Rather, she cares because she wants to: she is emotionally compelled to care.

Of course, not all caring situations are instances of natural care. We sometimes care for others not because we feel emotionally compelled to but because we feel that we ought to. Noddings refers to such instances of care as *ethical care*. Ethical care is the care that we give when natural care may be absent. Ethical caring situations are situations in which we care because we feel we have a responsibility to care rather than those in which care comes naturally to us.

In such situations, where natural care is absent, why are we motivated to provide care? As Noddings sees it, this is where the ethical ideal comes in. The ethical ideal is formed during our experiences of natural care – most notably in those moments of intimacy between mother and child – and it returns to us when we come across somebody in need of care but when we have no natural compulsion to give that care. At such times, according to Noddings, the ethical ideal touches our emotions in the manner of a nostalgic recollection of previous moments of naturally caring intimacy; it springs from 'the longing to maintain, recapture, or enhance our most caring and tender moments' (Noddings, 2003: 104). Ethical care, then, derives from natural care in the sense that our experiences of natural care strengthen our ethical ideal, which in turn motivates us to provide ethical care when natural care is absent. Thus, the ethical ideal acts as a 'memory of our own best moments of caring and being cared for [which] sweeps over us as a feeling – as an "I must" – in response to the plight of the other' (2003: 79–80).

Overcoming inclinations to disregard ethics

The ethical ideal, then, is a compelling motivating force, which encourages us to act ethically. However, Noddings points out that there may be times when the ethical ideal conflicts with other motivations that are even more compelling. We have all experienced such situations. For instance, we may feel disinclined to give care to a person who is in need of it because we dislike that person. Or it may be that our own interests are better served by ignoring a person's need of our care. At such times, what determines the capacity of the ethical ideal to override these competing compulsions?

Noddings highlights two factors in particular, which encourage us to respond to the ethical ideal even when it is opposed by other compelling motivations. The first factor is the amount of natural care and ethical care that we have previously experienced. As Noddings sees it, care – whether natural or ethical – breeds care. This is partly because the more natural care we have experienced, both as givers of care and as receivers of it, the greater the reservoir of naturally caring moments we have to fuel our ethical ideal. But it is also because previous experiences of ethical care also strengthen the ethical ideal. Although the ethical ideal is initially formed in moments of natural care, each instance of ethical care adds to that store of caring moments upon which the ethical ideal draws.

But Noddings also proposes that, just as care is self-reinforcing, so is the absence of care. She suggests that a person who has had little experience of natural care may have little capacity for ethical care. This is because they lack exposure to what Noddings considers to be the most fertile incubators of the ethical ideal. Similarly, Noddings suggests that if we have little experience of giving care – whether natural or ethical – our reservoir of caring moments is similarly diminished. It follows, then, that the more care we experience, as carers and as cared-for, the stronger will be our ethical ideal, and the more likely we are to give care in those moments when we confront conflicting emotions.

A second factor that determines the likelihood of the ethical ideal overcoming conflicting motives and evoking an ethical response is proximity to an ethically charged situation. Noddings takes the view that the closer we are to a person in need of care, the more likely we are to give that care. This is because the ethical ideal is essentially an emotional response, which is aroused by emotional engagement with an ethically charged situation. Although the ethical ideal works as a recollection of our own previous caring moments, the closer we get to a situation in which somebody needs care, the more powerfully that recollection is aroused.

And this is the reason why, for Noddings, the feminine ethical perspective, which seeks close contextual proximity to ethically charged situations, permits a more profound ethical response. According to her account of the ethical ideal, it is evoked more powerfully when we get close to a situation. When we have intimate experience of a person or people in need of care, then, we are more inclined to act ethically and less inclined to follow other, conflicting impulses. And, as Noddings sees it, since women are more inclined to get close, women are more inclined to act ethically.

Applying Noddings's care ethics to stakeholder relationships

If we apply Nel Noddings's philosophy of care to the ideas already discussed concerning stakeholder relationships, several further implications emerge. For one thing, according to Noddings's appraisal, a feminine ethic of care does not only offer a different take on stakeholder relationships to a masculine approach; it also offers an outlook that is more profoundly ethical. Thus the 'feminine metaphors' identified by Wicks et al. (1994) would provide a basis for viewing stakeholder relationships which have greater ethical legitimacy than those metaphors described by Wicks et al. as masculine.

Noddings's ideas also have a number of further implications for business. Here, I will highlight three in particular: the propensity for corporate care to create more corporate care; the ethical desirability of small, intimate corporate contexts; and the ethical merits of women being employed in senior-management roles.

The self-reinforcing quality of care

One implication of Noddings's account of care is that, given the self-perpetuating nature of care, it is reasonable to suppose that people who work within a caring business environment will become more caring. Thus, an ethic of care is likely to flourish within companies where employees are encouraged to adopt a caring attitude towards their stakeholders. Moreover, not only will those employees be more likely to exhibit care; experiences of caring encounters with a company will also encourage other stakeholders such as customers, suppliers and local communities to care for that company. A self-reinforcing cycle of ethicality can thus be created within a caring company; a cycle in which the company cares for its stakeholders and stakeholders care for the company, with each being spurred on to ever greater expressions of their respective ethical ideal.

Conversely, just as experience of a caring context might enhance people's propensity to care, experience of a corporate environment within which care is not a common feature may have the opposite effect: people who operate within cut-throat, competitive environments are likely to become less-caring individuals. Therefore, if employees work within a non-caring company they will be disinclined to care for their customers, suppliers, local communities and so on. And those stakeholders, in turn, will be less inclined to care for the company. Just as care has the potential to initiate a self-reinforcing cycle of ethicality, then, its absence may initiate a self-perpetuating spiral of unethicality.

Care, proximity and company size

A further implication of Noddings's account follows from the ethical desirability of proximity. By drawing attention to the way that close, first-hand contact with ethically charged situations arouses the ethical ideal, and thus stimulates people to act ethically, Noddings highlights the ethical merits of small, intimate, locally responsive businesses. In such companies, stakeholders are likely to be in closer contact with one another than in a large, dispersed corporation. In particular, on Nodding's analysis, the hierarchical and geographical distances which large, global corporations create between decision makers and those who are affected by their decisions are likely to have an ethically corrosive effect. Noddings's philosophy of care thus provides some support for the contention that, as far as business ethics is concerned, 'small is beautiful' (Schumacher, 1993/1973).

Pause for Reflection

Nel Noddings suggests that care is the essence of ethics and that, in order for ethical care for people to be evoked, we need to have close contact with ethically charged situations. Can you identify trends in contemporary business which serve to distance decision makers from the consequences of their decisions, and which might thus supress their *ethical care* for those who are affected by those decisions?

Women in management

One last implication of Noddings's assertion of the ethical superiority of feminine ethics is that companies that appoint women to senior roles, and which permit those women to give full expression to their feminine, ethical convictions, are likely to be more ethically sustainable places than those which are run by justice-oriented men. This perhaps provides some support for the measures that are currently underway to increase female representation in senior management and on the boards of directors of major corporations. According to Noddings's analysis, not only will this result in a business environment that is less discriminatory towards women; it may also enhance the ethical responsiveness of that environment.

Video Activity 8.2

This video clip shows Niall Ferguson interviewing Christine Lagarde, who is Managing Director of the International Monetary Fund, during the Women and Crisis in Women in the World 2012 Forum.

www.youtube.com/watch?v=Xtl_BpqoZ30

During this conversation, Lagarde reflects on the influence that gender might have had on the financial crash of 2008, suggesting that 'If Lehman Brothers had been a bit more Lehman Sisters we would not have had the degree of tragedy that we had as a result of what happened'. Lagarde refers to the effect that levels of testosterone can have in a trading environment. She is implying, here, that the ultra-competitive, masculine environment that prevailed in the financial services industry may have had a significant impact on the crash and the resulting social and economic problems.

Questions

1 How might the masculine competitiveness to which Lagarde refers have supressed the *ethical ideal* in people who worked in trading environments?
2 How, according to Nel Noddings's theory, might the absence of *natural care* and *ethical care* in financial service institutions have created a self-reinforcing spiral of unethicality within the industry?
3 How might the presence of more women in senior roles in the financial services industry encourage greater ethical responsiveness in that industry?

Challenging the idea that there is a characteristically feminine moral voice

The work of Carol Gilligan and Nel Noddings has encouraged the idea that there is a typically feminine way of thinking about ethics, which is characterized by care, and that ethical evaluation may be the worse for excluding the insights it affords. However, Gilligan's and Noddings's work has not been without its critics. This section of the chapter will therefore discuss some challenges to care ethics theory.

Challenges to the feminine ethic of care perspective

Challenges to care ethics theory can be placed into several categories. Some critics have highlighted empirical shortcomings of care ethics research, suggesting that these shortcomings cast doubt on the accuracy of Gilligan's and Noddings's findings. Others critics suggest that care ethics theory offers misleading, simplified representations, which mask the variety and complexity of feminine and masculine ethical perspectives. It has also been suggested that the stereotypical depictions encouraged by care ethics theorists may serve to perpetuate women's subordination and their marginalization in public affairs. It has even been suggested that care ethics theory may be responsible for supporting authoritarian social arrangements in which people are denied a say in how they are treated by those in authority. I will say a little about each of these challenges to care ethics theory in turn. I end this section by suggesting that, even if we accept these challenges to care ethics theory as valid, the work of writers like Gilligan and Noddings may still offer unique and valuable insights to business ethics.

Care ethics theory may present a misleading, over-simplified depiction of women's ethical perspective

One criticism of care ethics theory is that the research on which it draws is not sufficiently comprehensive to justify its conclusions. Critics of Gilligan's work, in particular, have observed that her earlier research focused on the attitudes of white, middle-class, American females and that her findings may not apply to women who do not match this profile. In this respect, Claudia Card notes that Gilligan 'described several themes distinguishing the ethical thinking of many women from that of most men in her experience of many years' listening to mostly white, middle-class speakers reflect upon themselves and upon certain moral problems' (1991: 17). Meanwhile, Alison Jaggar draws attention not only to the ethnic and social exclusiveness of Gilligan's research; she also questions the assumption that the caring ethics that Gilligan identifies are necessarily shared by lesbians, or by women who have not experienced or who do not aspire to childrearing:

> certain groups of women, such as women of color, lesbians, or nonmothers, have complained that the claims made by feminists about 'women's' moral experience have excluded them. Gilligan's early work was criticized for making claims about women on the basis of a study of female students at Harvard, clearly an elite and extremely nonrepresentative sample. And women without children, especially those opposed to having children, have complained that the emphasis on mothering in current feminist ethics does not resonate with their own moral experience. (Jaggar, 1991: 91)

It has also been suggested that Gilligan's findings may have been limited by the nature of the ethically charged issues that she chose to discuss with her research subjects. For instance, Michele Moody-Adams suggests that Gilligan places too much emphasis on one particular study, in which research subjects discussed the topic of abortion whilst avoiding 'sustained discussion of many other concerns about which many women have become increasingly vocal' (Moody-Adams, 1991: 202). Moody-Adams asks, for instance, whether discussions about rape, physical abuse, sexual harassment and sexual discrimination might have evoked a very different moral voice in these women. Specifically, she questions whether, in discussing such issues, the females that Gilligan interviewed might have spoken in a more 'masculine' voice, appealing to categorical, universal principles such as the right to non-interference, the right to equal treatment, and respect for the integrity of individuals. Moody-Adams suggests that 'surely most women would simply pronounce all these actions, from rape to sexual discrimination in employment, categorically unacceptable' (1991: 204) rather than contextualizing them in terms of care.

Perhaps as a consequence of the focus of Gilligan's and Noddings's research programmes, it has been suggested that they have arrived at overly simplistic categorizations of masculine and feminine ethical perspectives, which mask the diversity that is likely to be found in the way that both men and women think about ethics. Accordingly, Alison Jaggar suggests that 'It may well be that women's moral sensibilities vary so much, not only from culture to culture but even within cultures, that it is impossible to identify a single distinctively feminine approach to ethics, even within a given culture' (1991: 91–92). Meanwhile, Michelle Moody-Adams suggests that, contrary to the simple care-justice dualism proposed by care ethics theorists, 'there is a very good case for thinking that both women and men structure the moral domain in a variety of ways' (1991: 210).

As far as attitudes towards business ethics are concerned, then, it may indeed be that white, middle-class, heterosexual businesswomen, who are mothers or who aspire to motherhood, are inclined towards an ethic of care when confronting particular types of ethically charged issue. Nevertheless, it may also be that businesswomen who do not fit this profile would judge ethicality in accordance with different criteria. Moreover, in considering issues in which perceived fundamental rights are at stake, such as matters of employment discrimination and sexual harassment at work, even white, middle-class, maternal businesswomen might be more predisposed to the judging approach that Gilligan associates with masculinity than they would be to a 'feminine' ethic of care.

Care ethics theory may encourage unhelpful gender stereotypes

As well as suggesting that care ethics theory offers an inaccurate, over-simplified depiction of feminine ethical perspectives, some commentators highlight difficulties that such a depiction might present to the status of women. One concern is that to make such a simplistic, two-fold categorization of masculine and feminine ethical perspectives runs the risk of perpetuating a 'troublesome and damaging sexist dualism' (Borgerson, 2007: 491) which has, for centuries, been deeply implicated in the disempowerment and subordination of women. In particular, it has been suggested that the characterization of women's ethical perspective in terms of care runs the risk of legitimizing traditional, hierarchical gender roles in which the man is the dominant partner, while women are expected to fulfil a subordinate, caring role (Tong, 1997/1989; Bartky, 1990).

Such hierarchical depictions could be troublesome in business contexts, where they might support the notion that men are uniquely fit for senior roles, which are conventionally presented as demanding detached, rational, decisive judgement, while women are hived off to administrative-support roles or, insofar as they are allowed to occupy a seat at the management top table, only do so in the traditionally caring, feminine enclave of Human Resource Management (Marshall, 1995).

Care ethics theory may foster paternalistic authority relationships

A further concern with care ethics theory is that the emphasis it places on maternal care may, instead of fostering mutually respectful interpersonal relationships, encourage maternalistic or paternalistic authoritarianism. That is, by supporting notions of ethicality that are based around stronger parties taking care of weaker parties, care ethics theory might be used to justify the subordination of the weak 'for their own good'.

Sarah Hoagland (1991) is particularly critical of Nel Noddings's discussion of caring in this respect. Hoagland applauds Noddings's agenda in offering an ethic of care which provides an alternative to characteristically masculine ethics of principle and duty. However, she is concerned that, by rooting her ethic of care in the relationship between mothers and their children, and also those between teachers and pupils and between therapists and patients, Noddings privileges a form of care that is fundamentally unequal and unidirectional. This, according to Hoagland, has several undesirable implications, the most disturbing of which is that caring relationships that are constructed around this template inevitably become relationships involving asymmetrical distributions of power. In other words, power lies with the carer and the cared-for has little say in what goes on.

Applied to a business context, instead of promoting mutually respectful interaction between managers and non-managers, or between corporations and their stakeholders, such an attitude of care may just reinforce the power of senior business executives by asking them to provide unidirectional and maternalistic care for their stakeholders without involving the views of those stakeholders in the suitability of that care or their desire to receive it. In other words, the proliferation of an ethic of care in business relationships might encourage senior managers to consider themselves ethically entitled to do what they think is best for their customers, suppliers, employees, and so on, without feeling the need to ask those stakeholders their opinion on the matter. Thus, care ethics theory might provide ethical legitimation for the power of corporations to do whatever their senior executives decide is best for everybody else.

Thus, according to Hoagland, instead of offering an alternative to asymmetrical power relationships, care ethics theory may offer to them a supportive complement. Applied to business environments, care ethics theory that is built upon such a maternalistic understanding of care may do little to challenge the unequal power distributions which characterize contemporary business and which result in the views of ethnically, socio-economically and gendered groups being pushed aside. Indeed, it may even serve to justify such distributions of power. Hoagland appeals instead for an ethics that calls upon us to confront other people as independent decision makers, competent and empowered to make choices about their own interests and agendas.

Video Activity 8.3

The following video, entitled 'Ethical Leadership', is made by James Michael Haley, H.J. Heinz Chair of Management at Point Park University. The all-male speakers in this video draw attention to the merits of ethical leadership. They highlight the need for businesses to get people into leadership roles who know the difference between right and wrong and who are committed to doing right. They also highlight the need for universities to provide ethical education for their students so as to produce ethical leaders. And they speak of the need for ethics training in corporations to ensure that everybody acts in accordance with the ethical standards set by ethically perspicacious leaders.

www.youtube.com/watch?v=B9K9pNxljjg

Questions

1 This video places a lot of emphasis on business leaders using the influence of their roles to raise the profile of ethics in their companies. How might this sort of ethical leadership encourage expressions of what Nel Noddings would call the *ethical ideal*?
2 Care ethics theory might be criticized for encouraging senior business executives to overemphasize their responsibility to care for their stakeholders, without consulting those stakeholders on the matter. Can you think of any ways in which the style of ethical leadership and ethics training described by John L. Krauss in this video might encourage in business leaders a unidirectional approach to ethics, in which employees are called upon to conform to the ethical expectations of senior executives, with little opportunity to develop and express their own ethical perspectives?
3 Do you think it is the role of business leaders (who have been trained in business ethics) to tell their employees what is ethical and what is unethical?

The potential contribution of feminine ethics to business ethics

This section of the chapter has outlined some challenges to the idea that there is a typically feminine ethical perspective, and that this perspective is characterized by care. These challenges highlight the importance of avoiding overly simplified depictions of male and female ethical perspectives, suggesting that both men and women may speak with a variety of moral voices. However, these challenges need not negate the value of Carol Gilligan's and Nel Noddings's work in identifying an alternative way of thinking about ethics. Neither should they preclude the usefulness of care ethics as a lens through which to consider ethically charged issues in business. For it is possible to appreciate the merits of care ethics without presenting it as an exclusive preserve of women or as definitive of women's ethical thought. Whether or not the moral voice described by the likes of Gilligan and Noddings is characteristically feminine, it seems to offer a way of thinking about ethics that, insofar as it differs from a justice perspective, may go relatively unheard in business contexts. As such, it may open the door to points of view that, as Alison Jaggar puts it, 'seek to broaden the Enlightenment tradition's perceived focus on individuality, impartiality, and reason so as to include an appreciation of the moral significance of community, particularity, and emotion' (1991: 83).

A 'masculine' justice perspective		A 'feminine' ethic of care
A competitive environment in which corporations stand apart from their stakeholders, and in which they need to establish control.	**The business environment**	Requires communication and cooperation if potential for mutual benefit is to be realized.
Unavoidable conflicts between the ethical claims of separate, autonomous stakeholders.	**Business ethics dilemmas**	A threat to harmonious relationships between stakeholders.
A rational undertaking, which requires the dispassionate application of principles, and which can be carried out at a distance from the views of stakeholders.	**Resolving business ethics dilemmas**	Requires the facilitation of communication between stakeholders, so that all can reach agreement on mutually beneficial outcomes.
Establishing which stakeholders' ethical entitlements should take precedence.	**Expectation of business ethics**	Generating understanding and helping all involved in business to perceive mutual interests and to act in ways which promote them.
One who is able to recognize which ethical entitlements should take precedence, and who acts accordingly.	**An ethical business-person**	One who conducts business in a manner which shows respect for the needs and expectations of stakeholders.
One in which people are encouraged to respect abstract principles and ethical codes.	**An ethical business**	One in which people are encouraged to communicate with stakeholders, to understand their needs, and to care.

Figure 8.2 A 'masculine' justice perspective and a 'feminine' ethic of care applied to business

It may also be the case that many people – women and men alike -- are predisposed to thinking about ethics in terms of care, but that their point of view goes unheard for not being expressed in a moral language that usually holds currency in corporate environments. By elevating the profile of care ethics, writers such as Gilligan and Noddings may thus offer to those women and men a voice that they would otherwise be denied. The insights offered by so-called 'feminine ethics' may have a lot to offer to business ethics, irrespective of whether they truly are expressive of the moral voice of women or whether they articulate ethical perspectives to which many men, as well as many women, feel predisposed.

Figure 8.2 reproduces the earlier Figure 8.1, drawing on the ideas that have been introduced in this chapter to offer a depiction of how the 'feminine' and 'masculine' ways of thinking about ethics summarized in this earlier diagram might be applied to business contexts.

Theory in Practice

BMW's sale of its 'English patient'

In 1994, the German manufacturer of luxury cars BMW bought the British company Rover from its previous owner British Aerospace for £800m. Precisely why BMW wanted to buy the Rover group is a matter of some debate, but commentators have suggested several reasons for the purchase. The first is that the acquisition of Rover permitted BMW to expand and diversify its own product range by moving into the mass-car market whilst, in the process, eliminating a possible rival in that market (Brady and Lorenz, 2005). Furthermore, the Rover group's prestigious Land Rover division would have been particularly attractive to BMW, since its acquisition allowed BMW to compete strongly in the growing 4-wheel drive market (Bailey and de Ruyter, 2012). It has also been suggested that BMW was keen to develop its transnational production facilities in order to give it bargaining power over workers in each country and to compete more effectively for funding from national governments (Bailey and de Ruyter, 2012). Moreover, some commentators have suggested that BMW was particularly keen to establish production facilities in the UK where, at that time, labour costs were lower than in Germany and where there was a relatively stable industrial-relations environment (Owen, 1999).

However, six years later, BMW put most of the Rover group up for sale. Again, the reasons why BMW decided to dispose of a company that it had been so keen to acquire just a few years earlier are a matter of debate (see Bailey and de Ruyter, 2012 for an overview). Whatever the reasons, widespread references to Rover as

(Continued)

(Continued)

BMW's 'English Patient' indicate that arrangements were not working well either for the Rover group (which was thus cast as a 'patient' in need of treatment) or for BMW (which had the unenviable task of providing, and funding, that treatment).

Despite these problems, BMW did manage to salvage some positives from its involvement with Rover. Although keen to sell the rest of the business in 2000, BMW retained the Rover group's Oxford-Cowley plant, now called Plant Oxford. This allowed BMW to continue production of the new Mini, which had become a great success. Another positive was that BMW managed to sell the attractive Land Rover, 4-wheel drive division to the Ford motor company for £1.8b – considerably more than it had paid for the whole company six years earlier (Bailey and de Ruyter, 2012). BMW's hardest task, however, was disposing of the MG and Rover brands, which were made at the Longbridge plant in Birmingham. MG-Rover was a far less attractive proposition for potential purchasers, partly because, after decades of under-investment, the Longbridge plant was not well attuned to the needs of twenty-first century car production.

Eventually, BMW did manage to sell MG-Rover, along with the Longbridge plant, for a token sum of £10. The buyers were a group of local businessmen, who called themselves the Phoenix consortium. The inducements offered by BMW to encourage Phoenix to take MG-Rover off its hands included giving the consortium £75m in cash, a £427m interest-free loan, and thousands of unsold cars. The Phoenix consortium planned to rejuvenate the MG and Rover brands, building the value of the business, before selling it on to a Chinese car manufacturer (O'Connell, 2009).

Unfortunately for the Longbridge workers, and also for the community that lived around the MG-Rover factory, the Phoenix consortium did not make a success of the business. Five years after the purchase, the company went bankrupt owing £1.3b to its creditors and putting its 6,300 employees out of work. Therefore, a car production plant that had been at the heart of the local economy for nearly a century faced closure. Although the Chinese NAC company eventually took over part of the Longbridge plant, subsequent employment was at fraction of its earlier levels.

The BMW-Rover episode is laden with ethical issues. Some of the most stringent criticism relates to the activities of the Phoenix consortium, whose directors accumulated considerable personal wealth through their brief ownership of MG-Rover whilst running it into the ground and saddling it with enormous debt (see Brady and Lorenz, 2005; O'Connell, 2009). Questions have also been raised about the UK government's involvement in the whole affair, with critics suggesting that politicians could have guided Rover towards a more suitable purchaser in 1994 than

BMW and that the disastrous re-sale of MG-Rover to Phoenix may have been averted had the government taken a firmer lead (Bailey and de Ruyter, 2012).

Here, though, I will focus specifically on BMW's involvement, which has also been subjected to ethical scrutiny on several fronts. Firstly, commentators have questioned BMW's motives for buying the business in 1994, suggesting that the company may have only ever been interested in the Rover group's 'healthy' brands, notably Mini and Land Rover, and that it never had any real interest in the rest of the company (Brady, 2005). If true, this might have evoked a rather cavalier attitude on BMW management's part towards those less-attractive parts of the business and towards the thousands of people whose livelihoods depended upon them.

Questions have also been asked about BMW's strategy in relation to its workers and the British government during the time of its ownership. Bailey and de Ruyter refer to a strategy of 'divide and rule' (2012: 11), suggesting that one of BMW's reasons for developing a transnational manufacturing operation was that it allowed top management to play off employees in one country against those in another, using threats of plant closure and redundancy to encourage workers to accept less-attractive employment terms. Furthermore, these same authors suggest that BMW may have used similar tactics to attract investment funding from national governments, proposing that they would develop manufacturing operations only in the countries whose government offered them the most generous financial inducements.

BMW's eventual sale of MG-Rover and the Longbridge plant to Phoenix has also been criticized on the basis that BMW showed little concern for what eventually became of the division and its workforce. Indeed, it has been noted that BMW became so desperate to find a purchaser for this part of the business that they 'didn't care who bought it as long as they could get rid of it' (Brady, 2005).

How then, might the *justice ethical perspective*, which Carol Gilligan suggests is characteristically masculine, perceive these issues? And what alternative insights into the ethicality of BMW's actions might be offered by the *care perspective* that, rightly or wrongly, has been associated with femininity?

Here, I will offer some fairly extreme suggestions so as to highlight differences between the insights offered by a justice perspective and those offered by a care perspective.

Considering BMW's activities from a justice perspective

A justice perspective would view BMW, the Rover group, and their respective stakeholders as independent entities, standing apart from one another, and pursuing

(Continued)

(Continued)

their separate agendas. Although each of these independent entities is likely to come into contact with others, such contacts would be regarded by each as a necessary means to the end of fulfilling its own, separate objectives. The business environment would be regarded as an essentially competitive one, in which BMW, Rover and their stakeholders are only likely to fulfil their own objectives if they can establish dominance over the others.

Viewed in this way, BMW's attempt to establish transnational production facilities, and thus to pursue a divide-and-rule policy in relation to its employees and national governments, would be regarded as a legitimate and necessary tactic to establish dominance in this competitive business environment. Similarly, if buying Rover gave BMW competitive advantage in the mass-car market, whilst also taking out a major rival, this too would be seen as justified. BMW's subsequent break-up of Rover and its separation of profitable divisions from non-profitable ones would also be considered legitimate competitive activity. Of course, BMW would be expected to respect abstract ethical principles in carrying out activities such as these. For instance, the company would be expected to conduct all of its transactions in a fair and open manner, without breaching anybody's explicit rights. But as long as this had happened, then BMW would not be held ethically culpable for the hardship experienced by any stakeholders as a consequence of its acquisition, break-up and sale of Rover. Such hardship would be seen as an unavoidable corollary of doing business in a competitive corporate world.

Viewed from a justice perspective, BMW's eventual sale of MG-Rover and the Longbridge plant to the Phoenix Consortium might also be regarded as a legitimate tactic on its part. As long as the sale was not influenced by any form of deception, and as long as the rights of all parties were respected, BMW was ethically entitled to dispense with these assets as it saw fit. A justice perspective might suggest that any hardship this may have entailed for those who worked at Longbridge was of no concern of BMW: by buying the division, Phoenix took on responsibility for such matters. By getting shot of the division, BMW offloaded any ethical obligations in relation to it.

A justice perspective might also consider that an ethically acceptable acquisition of Rover and eventual disposal of its constituent parts could be arranged from afar. The senior executives that masterminded the Rover episode would have had no need to visit Rover's British plants in order to assess the ethicality of their proposed actions. Evaluation of the ethicality of their acquisition and disposal strategy could be carried out quite adequately from BMW's head office in Munich.

Considering BMW's activities from a care perspective

Instead of viewing BMW, Rover and their respective stakeholders as separate entities, in which each tries to achieve its own, separate, commercial objectives within a competitive trading environment, a care perspective would emphasize the connections and interdependencies between them. According to this way of thinking, instead of seeking to dominate other entities that occupy their trading environment, BMW would be expected to establish mutually beneficial communication with them in order to seek outcomes that would benefit all. On this understanding, BMW's emphasis during this episode should have been on securing arrangements that would also enable Rover and its stakeholders to prosper, rather than securing its own interests at the expense of those of all other players.

A care perspective would expect BMW to care for those who were affected by its activities. Therefore, BMW would be expected to take into account the interests of those stakeholders – such as employees and local communities – who were affected by its acquisition, break-up and sale of Rover. An ethical acquisition and disposal strategy would therefore have taken the welfare of all those stakeholders into account. Viewing the acquisition of Rover purely as an opportunity to secure its own dominance would be considered ethically inadmissible from a care perspective.

A care perspective might also propose that BMW's duty of care would have continued beyond the eventual sale of Rover. Rather than viewing the sale of the unprofitable parts of Rover purely as an opportunity to dispose of unwanted liabilities, BMW would have been expected to do what it could to ensure that MG-Rover, the Longbridge plant, and all those employees and local communities who depended on them were taken good care of.

Furthermore, a care perspective would have called upon those who made the key decisions throughout the acquisition, break up and sale of Rover to get close to Rover's operations in order to assess the ethicality of their actions. Rather than making rational, dispassionate decisions from an office block in Munich, they would have been expected to visit the communities that would be affected by their acquisition-and-disposal strategy so as to engage on an emotional level with the plight of those stakeholders.

Questions

1. From the above account of the acquisition, break up and sale of Rover, do you think BMW's decision makers adopted a *justice perspective* or a *care perspective* to the ethicality of their actions?
2. According to your own, personal assessment of ethicality, do you think a *justice approach* or a *care approach* would have ensured the more ethically sustainable outcomes?

Business activity and notions of femininity

This chapter has so far discussed the suggestion that there is a characteristically feminine way of thinking about ethics. I have introduced some theory that supports the notion of a specifically feminine moral voice, and I have also outlined some challenges to that theory. I have also suggested that, regardless of whether or not the care perspective that some theorists associate with women is a specifically feminine approach, it may well offer some important insights to business ethics. I have also suggested that those insights may be precluded if we only consider business ethics from the justice perspective that may traditionally have been accorded greater prominence in academic and corporate discussions.

The question of whether there is a specifically feminine way of thinking about ethics might be viewed as part of a broader question concerning the nature of gender. That question concerns the extent to which femininity and masculinity are predetermined characteristics, which shape the way women and men think and behave, and the extent to which they are the outcome of social conventions. However we respond to this question – whether we consider gender to be innate or whether we regard it as a learned response to social conditioning – we might ask whether certain depictions of gender are harmful to the experiences of women and possibly also to the experiences of men. Given the prominent role that consumer marketing plays in establishing and sustaining images of what are normal and desirable personal identities, it is clear that corporate marketers can play a significant role in this respect.

This last section will consider these questions. It will begin by explaining the difference between *essentialist* and *social constructionist* perspectives on gender, drawing out some implications that each might have for business. I will then end the chapter by highlighting some ways in which corporate marketers might be culpable of sustaining images of gender that make it harder for women to play a full and active role in public affairs.

The nature of gender

The discussions that have occupied this chapter so far raise important questions about gender or, more specifically, about what it means to be feminine. That is, they encourage us to ask whether femininity is something that women are born with, which is an essential part of their being, and which confers on them certain ways of thinking and acting, or whether femininity is a role that women learn to play in response to social conditioning. To adopt the former view, which is sometimes referred to as an *essentialist* view, is not to say that all women conform to the same template. It is just to say that certain characteristics, which are definitive of femininity, are somehow 'hard wired' into women and that these characteristics, in general, distinguish them from men. And to adopt the latter view, which is sometimes referred to as a *social constructionist* position, is not to deny biological differences between men and women; it is just to suggest that these differences do not necessarily offer such a crucial basis for differentiating between people as is conventionally assumed.

How we think about these matters will shape, to a large extent, the way that we respond to the topics considered in the last two sections. For instance, Carol Gilligan's (1993/1982) depiction of a characteristically feminine moral voice can be interpreted either in an essentialist or in a social constructionist way. An essentialist stance would suggest that there are essential aspects of being a woman which evoke a certain way of thinking about ethics. Alternatively, a social constructionist might interpret Gilligan's findings as indicating that women are culturally and socially conditioned to play a different role from men and that this accounts for the distinctive moral voice that Gilligan identifies.

I will offer here a brief outline of some ideas that have been offered on this topic by two notable philosophers, Luce Irigaray and Judith Butler. I will then reflect on how these contrasting views about the nature of femininity can usefully be applied to illuminate issues associated with business.

Luce Irigaray: an essentialist perspective on gender

The French philosopher Luce Irigaray (2004/1984) offers an essentialist perspective on gender, building upon this foundation to propose that a major priority for humanity should be to improve understanding between the sexes. Irigaray suggests that there are fundamental differences between men and women, and that the unique contributions of the feminine and the masculine need to be embraced if the human species is to realise its full potential. As Irigaray puts it, 'To remember that we must go on living and creating worlds is our task. But it can be accomplished only through the combined efforts of the two halves of the world: the masculine and the feminine' (2004/1984: 108).

For this to happen, Irigaray proposes that both men and women need to understand and respect the contributions that the other can make. However, she suggests that we are far from achieving such a state of harmony and mutual respect between the sexes. The main reason for this, as Irigaray sees it, is a self-perpetuating cycle of male dominance and female subordination. As a result of centuries in which men have dominated political, economic and social life, qualities associated with masculinity have come to shape public notions of personal worth. And since men tend to manifest these prized, masculine qualities more emphatically than women, men are regarded as better suited than women to participation in public life. Thus, Irigaray highlights an unending process: men occupy prominent roles in public affairs, so masculinity is held in greater esteem than femininity. Consequently, the ongoing dominion of men over women seems to be justified, so it continues. And so on.

Irigaray's analysis offers a useful lens for thinking about business management and the role that is traditionally accorded to women in management. Just as men have dominated public life in general, they have also been pre-eminent in business leadership roles. As a result, characteristics that are traditionally considered to be masculine have become associated with successful business leadership. Thus, qualities such as assertiveness, decisiveness, rationality, competitiveness and dominance, which are usually associated with men, have come to be prized in business leaders. Consequently, in appointing senior business managers, we have become accustomed to appointing people who demonstrate these qualities, who, unsurprisingly, tend to be men. Meanwhile, women, whose essential characteristics are not seen as being so well-suited to such roles, are more likely to be found in administrative support positions, where a similarly self-reinforcing cycle prevails.

Just as Irigaray has suggested that characteristically masculine and feminine contributions must come to be appreciated if the self-perpetuating cycle of male domination and female subordination is to be broken, so a number of researchers have suggested that the unique contributions that men and women can make to business management should also be acknowledged. Thus, writers such as Paula Johnson (1976), Sally Hegelsen (1990) and Katie Rosener (1990) have highlighted distinctive qualities that women bring to leadership roles. These researchers have found that female leaders demonstrate, to a greater extent than their male counterparts, qualities such as nurturing, empathy, a willingness to share power and information, listening skills and a readiness to involve other people in decision making. But most significantly, these researchers also find that the feminine qualities that they identify are just as important in helping businesses to flourish as those qualities traditionally associated with men. An implication of this research is that if greater worth is attached to traditionally feminine qualities, not only are we likely to see more women in senior management roles, but also the businesses in which those women manage are more likely to thrive.

Whether we apply Irigaray's essentialist perspective to life in general or specifically to the business arena, then, the conclusions are similar: a call for enhanced understanding and respect for the distinctive contributions that men and women can make. The route to such an enhanced understanding, for Irigaray (2004/1984), lies in adopting an attitude of *wonder* toward difference. That is, Irigaray proposes that we should not conceive of the difference between men and women in hierarchical terms, so that one has to be 'better' and the other has to be 'worse'. Rather, we should adopt an attitude in which each respects the other for its integrity and its uniqueness, whilst embracing the insights and contributions that the other affords and by thus finding better ways of doing things.

Judith Butler: a social constructionist perspective on gender

If Luce Irigaray's essentialist perspective calls for enhanced understanding between men and women, Judith Butler offers a social constructionist view that challenges dualistic depictions of masculinity and femininity but which, like Irigaray, calls for respect for difference. Butler rejects the notion that gender is a stable, universal essence that necessarily confers upon people fixed behavioural, intellectual, emotional and ethical characteristics. Gender, for Butler, is not an essential feature of what we are. Rather, it is a human construction; a way of categorizing people that we have become accustomed to using, but which has no real existence beyond that. As far as Butler is concerned, 'gender identity rests on the unstable bedrock of human invention' (Butler, 2004/1987: 27).

To say that gender is a social construction is not to deny the existence of physiological differences between people. Nor is it to deny that those physiological differences can, if we so choose, provide a basis for categorizing people. However, Butler (2004/1987) argues that there is no reason why we should accord those physiological characteristics such a key role in identifying self and others. We do so because that is what we are accustomed to doing. But the fact that we are accustomed to thinking about people in a particular way does not mean that we must always think about them in that way. According to Butler, we are used to differentiating between people on the basis of particular physiological characteristics, but we could equally well do so according to a range of other physical, emotional or intellectual criteria. According to her perspective, the shape and function of people's genitalia offers no more compelling a basis for dividing the human race into two than the shape of their ear lobes, their mathematical ability or their musical preferences. That we have accorded it such significance is a purely arbitrary choice on our part.

Despite its arbitrary nature, though, Butler points out that gender has become fundamental to the way that we think of ourselves and others. Indeed, it is so crucial to our notions of identity that, if people do not conform to some predefined gender category, they struggle to achieve any sort of identity at all: 'If human existence is always gendered existence, then to stray outside of established gender is in some sense to put one's very existence into question' (Butler, 2004/1987: 27). For Butler, the emphasis that we place on predefined notions of gender creates difficulties for many people. This is because we do not only accord to gender an essential quality to which it has no legitimate claim; we also create ideal depictions of gendered identity upon which to base criteria of desirability and normality. And this can impact negatively on the self-esteem and self-identity for people who do not conform to those stereotypical depictions.

While Irigaray's essentialist perspective might call upon recognition of unique contributions that women can bring to business management, Butler's social-constructionist point of view encourages respect for the unique contribution that each and every person can make. According to Butler's way of thinking, we should not celebrate a particular set of business aptitudes because they are associated with a particular gender. Rather, we should welcome the specific talents that each individual brings to the table, without feeling the need to categorize them in terms of masculinity and femininity. If we are able to do this, not only will each person be able to contribute their unique capabilities in the most effective manner; they will also be released from stereotypical expectations concerning what is appropriate to their gender or to any other gender.

Avoiding stereotypical depictions of gender

In summary, Irigaray's essentialist perspective towards gender calls for a more respectful relationship between masculinity and femininity, which she believes can help to unravel traditional, hierarchical relationships of male dominance and female subordination. Meanwhile Judith Butler's social constructionist perspective highlights the problems that traditional depictions of femininity and masculinity may cause for those women and men who do not readily conform to them. Whereas Irigaray's writing calls for the unique contributions of men and women to be recognized, in life and in business, Butler's writing calls for the uniqueness of each individual to be respected. A common feature of both is that they alert us to the harm that might be caused when stereotypical depictions of gender are used to justify people's allocation to certain arenas and their preclusion from others.

Whether we feel inclined towards an essentialist or a social constructionist stance on gender, then, we have good reason to be suspicious of stereotypical depictions of femininity and masculinity. Furthermore, some commentators have suggested that we should also be wary of a tendency for certain forms of corporate activity to perpetuate such stereotypes. In this respect, the influential role that consumer marketing images play in creating and sustaining gender roles has received a lot of attention. I will therefore turn to this matter next, outlining some research which suggests that consumer marketing may be guilty of sustaining images of gender, which, in particular, inhibit women's participation in public life.

Consumer marketing and gender stereotyping

A number of researchers have explored the role played by marketing images in creating and sustaining notions of femininity and masculinity. Here, I will outline some seminal work carried out by Erving Goffman over 40 years ago, before introducing some more recent contributions to the themes explored by Goffman.

Erving Goffman: gender displays

Erving Goffman was interested in the way that people habitually position themselves in relation to one another. He believed that these 'displays' tell us a lot about how people perceive their respective status roles. As Goffman put it, displays 'tentatively establish the terms of the contact, the mode or style or formula for the dealings that are to ensue between the persons providing the display and the persons perceiving it' (Goffman, 1979/1974: 1).

Goffman was particularly interested in *gender displays*; that is, in the stances that men and women tend to adopt in relation to one another. He suggested that, by observing gender displays, we can gain important insights into conventional attitudes concerning the respective roles of, and status differentials between, men and women. Goffman focused especially on the way that gender displays are presented in consumer advertising. He was well aware of the power of advertising images to shape the attitudes of those who view them; after all, companies expend considerable resources and a great deal of ingenuity to achieve precisely that aim. And although the primary objective of advertisers is to shape peoples' attitudes towards their products, the images that they use to achieve that objective also have a significant corollary affect: this is that they *normalize* the roles and status differentials that they depict. In other words, by showing certain relationships between men and women in advertisements, corporate marketers encourage their audience to regard those relationships as normal.

Therefore, by presenting gender displays in such an influential manner, Goffman believed that marketers play a very important role in shaping social attitudes towards masculinity, femininity and the relationship between men and women. To identify and demonstrate some key features of these conventional understandings, Goffman gathered together several hundred advertising photographs. This enabled him to highlight some prominent features of the gender displays depicted in those photographs. For instance, he noted that women in adverts usually use hands and fingers to cradle or caress the article that is being promoted, rather than grasping it firmly or manipulating it. This depiction of 'the feminine touch' (Goffman, 1979/1974: 29) echoes the caring role identified by writers such as Gilligan and Noddings, which some of their critics associate with women's confinement to a supporting role.

Goffman also identified two further features of gender displays; features which, arguably, are of more direct significance to the perpetuation of masculine dominance and feminine subordination. The first, *function ranking*, refers to the way that, when a man and a woman are pictured interacting in face-to-face situations, the man is most likely to be depicted playing the 'executive role' (Goffman, 1979/1974: 32). The executive role usually involves issuing instructions and structuring activity. Women, on the other hand, are more likely to be depicted in the role of follower, showing deference to their dominant, male leaders. This is particularly apparent in advertising images showing occupational situations, such as male doctors attended by female nurses, but it is also evident in pictures which depict a range of social, recreational and family settings.

The second feature, *ritualization of subordination*, refers to the way that women are often presented occupying a passive position, such as sitting or lying down on beds or on the floor. Goffman associates such a stance with the adoption of a role of deference. Men, on the other hand, are more likely to be presented in upright positions, standing erect and holding their heads high, which Goffman considers to be a stereotypical mark of superiority and disdain. Goffman also notes that the tendency to depict women lying on the floor or on a bed might be associated with a 'conventionalized expression of sexual availability' (Goffman, 1979/1974: 41).

In summary, Goffman draws attention to the tendency of product advertisements to conform to a certain understanding of the feminine role; one which has women offering deferential support and care to their dominant, male partners. In other words, while men take the lead and make the big decisions, women provide supportive and caring back-up. Most importantly, though, Goffman suggests that, in presenting these gender displays so evocatively in product advertising, marketers perpetuate the understandings and assumptions that they depict. Thus, by depicting a relationship of feminine subordination to the masculine, advertising images perpetuate that subordination. So, for Goffman, the alignment between men and women that features in advertisements 'does not merely express subordination but in part constitutes it' (1979/1974: 8).

Video Activity 8.4

The following video from Dolce & Gabbana promotes the company's 2013 Spring/Summer fashion range.

www.youtube.com/watch?v=GkhIle2nl1U

Questions

1. Can you identify in this video any examples of what Erving Goffman would call displays of the *feminine touch*?
2. Can you identify any features of the facial expressions of the males and females in this video that might be described as *function ranking*?
3. Write a list of the actions that the males in the video are performing, and a list of the actions that the females are performing. How might these contrasting depictions support what Goffman refers to as the *ritualization of subordination*?
4. Do you think the video just shows *essential* differences between males and females, or do videos like this play a part in *socially constructing* our ideas about gender? In other words, does the video just show males and females as they naturally are, or do you think its portrayal of females and males might perpetuate stereotypical understandings of gender?

Some recent research

More recently, other researchers have explored similar themes to those highlighted by Erving Goffman. For instance, Adrian Furnham and Twiggy Mak (1999) have reviewed a range of studies of gender representation in television adverts around the world, noting a number of common features.

Amongst Furnham and Mak's findings is that men are more likely than women to be shown in professional and autonomous roles, whereas women are more often portrayed in dependent roles. Moreover, men are more often shown away from the home, most notably in the workplace, whereas women are more likely to be pictured at home or indoors. Adverts also tend to depict women as more compliant than men. Women may be shown offering opinions but they do not necessarily offer factual arguments to support those opinions. Men, on the other hand, are more likely to be shown offering reasoned, factual arguments in support of their statements. Furthermore, Furnham and Mak's overview finds that men are far more likely than women to give an 'end comment' in adverts, thus having the last word. Lastly, research shows marked differences in the types of product that are associated with men and women. Furnham and Mak find that women tend to be shown displaying domestic goods and body products, whereas men are more likely to feature in adverts promoting automotive products, sports equipment and business-related goods.

Video Activity 8.5

Here are two recent advertisements: the first advertises a car, the Volkswagen Force; the second, featuring Simon the Ogre, promotes Thomson Holidays.

www.youtube.com/watch?v=R55e-uHQna0
www.youtube.com/watch?v=JXNJA1yGn-8

Questions

1 Can you identify ways in which the images in these videos might perpetuate stereotypical ideas of men's and women's roles?
2 Can you think of ways in which these stereotypical depictions might hinder opportunities for women to progress their careers?

Jonathan Schroeder and Janet Borgerson (2005) have also highlighted a number of features of visual representation which, they suggest, contribute to the normalization of certain social structures. Building on earlier work by Archer et al. (1983), Schroeder and Borgerson, draw attention to *face-ism* in advertisements. Face-ism refers to the extent that an advertising image presents a person's face and head, rather than showing their neck, shoulders and lower parts of their body.

Schroeder and Borgerson point out that the face and the head are usually regarded as the centre of a person's intellect, personality, identity and character. Therefore, by focusing on someone's face and head, a photograph emphasizes the intellect, personality, identity and character of that person. Furthermore, Schroeder and Borgerson cite research which indicates that when people look at photographs, they rate those with more prominent faces as more intelligent, more ambitious and more attractive than those given less facial prominence. They go on to observe that, in advertising images, men's faces tend to be given more prominence than those of women. Thus, qualities such as intellect, ambition, personality and character are emphasized in men to a greater extent than in women. Meanwhile, by giving less facial prominence to women, those photographs place greater emphasis on women's bodies.

> **Practical Activity**
>
> Next time you watch commercial TV, or next time you read a glossy magazine, make a note of the depictions of males and females in the advertisements that you see. Do you find evidence to support the *face-ism* highlighted by Schroeder and Borgerson? In other words, do you find that the adverts focus more on men's faces and heads, whilst showing the shoulders and upper bodies of women to a greater extent?

Responding to concerns about stereotypical depictions of gender

Now, it might be argued that in depicting relationships between men and women, by showing the roles that are usually adopted by men and women in these relationships, and by portraying conventional status differentials between men and women, advertisers are just showing the way things are. The role of advertising, according to this line of argument, is not to challenge conventional cultural and social norms; it is to sell products and services. And, if showing photographs of people behaving the way people usually behave helps to achieve this end, then so be it. Advertisers are expected to sell things, not to judge the ethicality of gender roles that society has established over many centuries.

This is an argument that Schroeder and Borgerson challenge. For a start they suggest that, given the influence wielded by product marketers, it is not acceptable for them to remain 'morally myopic' (2005: 579). Advertisers have a significant capacity to shape public attitudes; that, after all, is why corporations spend such huge sums on advertising. Schroeder and Borgerson suggest this capacity to shape public attitudes comes with a responsibility to remain alert to its ethical implications. Furthermore, Schroeder and Borgerson propose that exploration of marketing ethics needs to move beyond traditional avenues of ethical critique. They observe that discussions of marketing ethics have tended to focus on the presentation of incomplete or misleading product information by marketers, or on the role played by marketing in encouraging socially and environmentally harmful consumerism. Although these issues are important, Schroeder and Borgerson suggest that attention should also be paid to the *pedagogical* role played by marketing. That is, to the role consumer marketing plays in educating people, particularly young people, and in creating and sustaining conventional images of normality and desirability.

Schroeder and Borgerson suggest that, in order to respond to this challenge, marketers should give more consideration to the broader impact of the images they portray, rather than just thinking about how effectively those images will sell their products. In this way, the sophistication of marketers' manipulation of images to sell goods might be matched by a more sensitive appreciation of how those images, if used irresponsibly, might create difficulties for their target market and for others who are exposed to them. In particular, Schroeder and Borgerson refer to the need to avoid *epistemic closure*. Epistemic closure refers to:

> the danger of typified representations of identity that increase the probability of human subjects interpreting what they experience or have represented to them as (stereo) typical [and which] may undermine a group's dignity and historical integrity and cast a demeaning light upon their physical and intellectual habits and ontological status as human beings. (Borgerson and Schroeder, 2005: 583–84, drawing on Gordon, 1997 and Miller, 1994)

To put this another way, epistemic closure consists of presenting a narrow, stereotypical depiction of a particular group, which in some way undermines the interests and dignity of that group. Avoiding epistemic closure, on the other hand, involves exploring the many, diverse ways in which that group might otherwise be depicted; particularly ways which challenge long-standing, entrenched forms of disadvantage and repression. Applied to the issue of gender, epistemic closure might include the presentation of stereotypical images of men and women which depict, either overtly or subtly, men in positions of dominance and women in roles of subservience. Conversely, challenging epistemic closure would involve exploring alternative ways of presenting gender which challenge that domination-subordination template.

Conclusion

Feminine, care ethics theory offers insights to contemporary life and contemporary business practice that may be overlooked by the mainstream ethics tradition. This chapter has drawn attention to some of those insights. Whether or not care ethics is a characteristically female phenomenon is open to question. But disagreement on this matter need not detract from the novel perspectives that care ethics offers. The so-called 'feminine' ethical approach identified by writers such as Carol Gilligan and Nel Noddings might come just as naturally to many men as it does to some women. The important thing is that, by drawing attention to care ethics, these theorists highlight approaches to ethics and to business which challenge dominant, so-called 'masculine' ways of thinking and which may therefore offer some valuable alternative insights.

However we think of gender, whether as a predetermined condition that accounts for certain attitudes and behaviours, including characteristic ways of thinking about ethics; or whether we regard it as a set of traits that we learn as a consequence of social conditioning, it is clear that certain forms of communication play a significant role in emphasizing particular features of masculinity and femininity and in sustaining our understanding of what it is to be male and female. Moreover, given the lavish resources invested in consumer marketing and the sophisticated techniques employed by consumer marketers to shape public perceptions, it is clear that they wield considerable influence in this respect. Given the magnitude of this influence, it seems reasonable to suppose that consumer marketers should think carefully about the responsibility it entails. In particular, they should remain alert to the possibility that the images of femininity and masculinity they portray may perpetuate stereotypical gender stereotypes that inhibit the self-actualization of women and perhaps also of men.

Discussion questions

1. Critically discuss the suggestion that women think differently to men about ethics.
2. What specific insights might an ethic of care offer to business ethics and how might these insights differ from those offered by a justice perspective?
3. Look at a woman's magazine. Take some specific adverts and articles and consider: to what extent do these represent women 'as they are'; and to what extent do they portray a stereotypical image of femininity? How might these images of femininity impact, either negatively or positively, on women's career development and on their life experiences in general?
4. Carry out this same exercise in relation to adverts and articles in a 'lad mag'. What constructions of masculinity and femininity, and what relationships between men and women, might be normalized by these images? How might these images impact on women's career development and on their life experiences in general?
5. Should consumer marketers just present images of men and women in advertisements in a way that is most likely to sell their products, or do marketers also have a responsibility to think about the images of normality and desirability that they thus depict?

Further study

Carol Gilligan's seminal work concerning feminine ethics of care is discussed in this chapter. A more recent treatment of the topic by Gilligan can be found in her (1995) *Hypatia* paper, 'Hearing the difference: theorizing connection'.

Sarah Hoagland's (1991) chapter entitled 'Some thoughts about "caring"', which appears in Claudia Card's *Feminist Ethics*, offers a critical discussion of care ethics, with particular reference to Nel Noddings's work.

Andrew Wicks, Daniel Gilbert and Edward Freeman's (1994) paper in *Business Ethics Quarterly* entitled 'A feminist reinterpretation of the stakeholder concept' offers an interesting discussion of feminine ethics and business stakeholders.

If you would like to read in more depth about the role played by marketing in creating and sustaining social understanding, Jonathan Schroeder and Janet Borgerson's (2005) paper, 'An ethics of representation for international marketing communication', which appeared in *International Marketing Review*, is a good place to start.

9 Environmental Ethics: Business, People and Nature

Chapter objectives

This chapter will:

- explain the difference between anthropocentric and biocentric approaches to environmental ethics;
- explore some implications of anthropocentrism and biocentrism for business;
- discuss some issues associated with environmentalists' preoccupation with wilderness and wildlife conservation;
- explore some ways in which the environmental benefits and burdens of business activity might get distributed unfairly;
- introduce the notion that developing a more sustainable relationship with the environment may demand a rethink of prevailing social and economic structures.

Introduction

During the last 30 years, environmentalism has become an important topic for business. There are a number of reasons for this. For a start, environmental concerns now occupy a high profile in the public consciousness. Most people pay attention to issues such as climate change, the depletion of natural resources, and the pollution of land, air and water. Therefore, any business that wishes to meet the expectations of influential stakeholders – that is, those people, such as its shareholders, customers and employees, upon whose support it depends – must take environmentalism seriously.

But there is another reason why business should take environmentalism seriously. This is that corporations are in a position to make a huge impact, negative or positive, on the environment. If you or I change the way we lead our lives so as to minimize our resource consumption or the amount of pollution we produce, this will have some effect on the natural environment. However, that effect will be small. On the other hand, the choices made by large corporations with regard to resource usage and waste disposal have an enormous environmental impact. This is most evidently the case with corporations that interact directly with the natural world, such as mining firms, oil companies and providers of agricultural commodities. But it is also the case for businesses that do not have such an obvious environmental link. Consider, for instance, the case of a large accountancy firm. Such a firm does not have much direct interaction with the natural world. Nevertheless, it is likely to run large office complexes, organize a lot of business travel, and large quantities of waste will be removed from its premises. Therefore its policies concerning energy usage, communication, waste disposal and recycling can have a big environmental impact.

For reasons such as these, many companies pay a lot of attention to the development and communication of environmental policies. But this is no simple matter, for even if we accept the importance of treating the environment in a responsible way, it is by no means clear precisely what that means in practice. The complexity of environmental ethics is partly a result of the many ways in which we might think about the relationship between humans and the natural world. For instance, is environmental responsibility just about safeguarding the natural world so that humans can continue to use the resources it provides, or should we also value it in its own right? Further complexity is added by the possibility that acting in accordance with one person's environmental priorities may challenge those of another person. Moreover, there are issues of distribution to consider: environmental and economic benefits that accrue to people in one part of the world may cause problems for people who live in other parts. Then there is the relationship between environmental sustainability and society: should environmentalism be treated as a separate matter from social and economic theory, or are these topics closely interlinked?

This chapter will explore some of these complexities. The purpose of this exploration is not to provide definitive answers concerning what is ethical in relation to the natural world. Rather, in keeping with the overall agenda of this book, it is to offer some conceptual frameworks that might help you to develop your own views on such matters.

This exploration will begin by outlining various ways of valuing the natural world. This discussion will contrast two different approaches. The first is that the natural world is valuable insofar as it serves the interests of humans; the second is that the natural world has intrinsic value, so we should treat it with respect irrespective of the consequences for humans. I will then discuss the environmental conservation agenda, which occupies a high profile in developed nations, and outline some reservations with this agenda; reservations that are usually expressive of the perspective of less-developed countries. The issue of environmental justice will then be considered; that is, the extent to which the benefits and burdens of environmentally harmful business activity are fairly distributed. The chapter will end by asking whether, in order to develop more sustainable ways of living with the natural environment, we may need to challenge social and economic structures that we usually take for granted. Each of these themes has important ramifications for business, and I will highlight these as the discussion evolves.

Video Activity 9.1

The following video clip is from the film *The Corporation*. It shows Ray Anderson, founder and former chairman of Interlink Inc., which is one of the world's largest manufacturers of modular carpet. In this clip, Anderson describes how he came to appreciate the environmental significance of his business and how he resolved to respond to the responsibility which that entailed.

www.youtube.com/watch?v=D9hetZuPzS4

Questions

1 How might the expectations of influential stakeholders have initiated Anderson's change in perspective towards the environment?
2 In what ways does a large carpet producer like Interface Inc. impact on the environment?

Some contrasting ways of valuing the natural world

Why do trees, plants, animals, mountains, rivers and oceans matter? Why should we care about them? Responses to questions such as these are often placed into two different categories: anthropocentrism and biocentrism. The meaning of the noun *anthropocentrism* and the associated adjective *anthropocentric* derive from the stem 'anthropo', which means 'relating to human beings'. Anthropocentrism, then, is a 'human-centric' approach; it is an approach that accords value to the natural world insofar as it makes things better or worse for human beings.

Biocentrism, on the other hand, proposes that the natural world has intrinsic value. That is, even if trees, plants, animals, mountains, rivers and oceans were of no use whatsoever to human beings, biocentrism suggests that they still matter so we still have a reason to care for and preserve them. According to a biocentric perspective, the natural world is not just there to make life better for humans; it has value in itself.

The complexities of attributing value to natural phenomena go beyond a simple anthropocentric-biocentric distinction, however. This is partly because there are various ways in which the natural environment might be thought to serve human purposes, so different anthropocentric stances, when applied to business practice, might point toward contrasting courses of action. Similarly, a range of different rationales can be put forward in support of biocentrism. This first section of the chapter will outline some of these different perspectives.

Some anthropocentric rationales

Anthropocentrism is based on the idea that the natural environment is there to serve human interests. Therefore, any value that may be attributed to nature derives from ways in which it improves human life. However, there is more than one way in which the natural world might be thought to serve human purposes.

Resource anthropocentrism: nature as a resource to be controlled and exploited

Traditional accounts of anthropocentrism focused on how the natural environment can be used to meet the physical needs of humans. These accounts take for granted the superior status of human beings, proposing that everything else that exists can legitimately be put to human use. The thirteenth-century philosopher and theologian Thomas Aquinas expressed this perspective. Aquinas thought about the universe in terms of a hierarchy, with God at the top, humans on the next tier and animals and plants occupying lower levels. This hierarchy, for Aquinas, is quite rightly ruled in a top-down fashion. Therefore, just as humans are ruled by God, those entities that occupy lower levels in the hierarchy can legitimately be ruled by humans.

One reason why Aquinas placed humans near the top of the universal hierarchy, next to God, relates to qualities that we, alone, share with God: 'of all the parts of the universe, intellectual creatures hold the highest place, because they approach nearest to the divine likeness' (Aquinas, 2010/1264–73: 63). Chief amongst these qualities is our ability to use reason. As Aquinas saw it, this capacity for reason differentiates humans from plants, which only act in order to seek nourishment. It also distinguishes us from animals, which, according to Aquinas, are only able to act instinctively. Human reason, on the other hand, enables us to deliberate, to make free choices, and to think about our place in the grand scheme of things. This, Aquinas believed, makes us qualitatively different from non-human entities.

For Aquinas, this privileged, hierarchical position gives humans the right to use lower beings to serve their purposes. Just as humans exist to serve the ends of God, so lower beings are put on earth to serve the ends of humans: 'intellectual substances are governed for their own sake, as it were; and others for the sake of intellectual substances' (Aquinas, 2010/1264–73: 64). And since nature is there to serve us, we cannot be criticized for using it as we please:

> Hereby is refuted the error of those who said it is sinful for a man to kill dumb animals: for by divine providence they are intended for man's use in the natural order. Hence it is no wrong for man to make use of them, either by killing or in any other way whatever. (Aquinas, 2010/1264–73: 64)

Four hundred years later, John Locke, an influential political philosopher, also emphasized nature's subservience to humans. Whereas some religious sources had emphasized the stewardship responsibilities entailed by humans' elevated hierarchical rank – that is, our responsibility to care for the non-human world – Locke followed Aquinas in expressing the view that God has given nature to humans to use for their own purposes: 'God, who hath given the World to Men in common, hath also given them reason to make use of it to the best advantage of Life, and convenience. The Earth, and all that is therein, is given to Men for the Support and Comfort of their being' (Locke, 1988/1690: 286).

Locke also stressed the need for humans to improve what nature has provided in order to enhance its usefulness. As he saw it, land that has been transformed from its natural state and brought under human control is considerably more productive than pristine wilderness. To illustrate this point, Locke contrasted the hunter-gatherer lifestyle of the Native American, prior to the settlement of North America by Europeans, with the advanced husbandry of rural England. He reflected on the unlikelihood that 'in the wild woods and uncultivated [waste] of America left to Nature, without any improvement, tillage or husbandry, a thousand acres will yield the needy and wretched inhabitants as many conveniences of life as ten acres of equally fertile land [do] in Devonshire where they are well cultivated' (Locke, 1988/1690: 294). For Locke, then, the correct approach to the natural world is not that of the hunter-gatherer; it is that of the cultivator.

Two hundred years after Locke wrote about the importance of cultivating the natural environment in order to make it more productive, the social theorist and moral philosopher John Stuart Mill highlighted the darker side of nature. For Mill, the natural world does not only present opportunities for meeting human needs; it also presents dangers. This creates an even more pressing need to control and shackle nature: not only must we put it to productive human use; we must also defuse the threat that it presents. As Mill put it, we must acknowledge that: 'the ways of Nature are to be conquered, not obeyed: that her powers are often towards man in the position of enemies, from whom he must wrest, by force and ingenuity, what little he can for his own use' (Mill, 2010/1874: 76).

Pause for Reflection

Throughout the twentieth century, a great deal of 'land improvement' was carried out in parts of South America, Asia and Africa. This involved the clearance of large areas of tropical rainforest, partly to provide timber for human needs and partly so that the cleared land could be used to supply global demand for commodities such as rubber, palm oil and beef. This activity conformed to the prescriptions of the philosophers mentioned above, who believed that natural resources should be controlled, cultivated and put to productive human use. But can you identify any anthropocentric problems with such an approach to the environment in this particular context?

Enlightened anthropocentrism: emphasizing the need to conserve scarce resources

The idea that the natural world is there to serve humankind does not necessarily imply that we can go and take what we want from it without a thought for the consequences. In the days of Aquinas, Locke and Mill, the greatest challenges confronting the human race revolved around cultivating and controlling nature in order to meet human needs. In a sparsely populated, largely agrarian world, there appeared to be abundant natural resources; all humans had to do was transform those resources as effectively as possible so they could be put to productive human use. Although some writers of the time expressed concern about the consequences of the industrialization of production and agriculture, the belief that we should control nature and take from it what we need was a pervasive one, particularly in Europe.

Nowadays, we tend to think differently. For a start, the world is a lot more crowded than it once was. There is no longer a vast wilderness awaiting human cultivation, and some of our biggest contemporary challenges concern dwindling natural resources and the accumulation of waste. We are therefore inclined to take a longer-term view of the way that we use the natural world. We are well aware that what we do now may have severe consequences for the future. Therefore, expressions of resource anthropocentrism nowadays are more likely to take the form of *enlightened anthropocentrism*. Enlightened anthropocentrism is the view that the natural world derives its value from its usefulness to humans, but that we need to be careful how we use nature because, if we are not, future generations will suffer the consequences.

Enlightened anthropocentrism, then, tends to focus more on long-term preservation of natural resources than on short-term exploitation of them. Nevertheless, the value system upon which its preoccupation with preservation is based is still an anthropocentric one. Enlightened anthropocentrism does not seek to preserve the environment for its own sake; it does so because we and our descendants will depend upon it in the future. Although enlightened anthropocentrism talks of sustainability, its emphasis remains on what the natural world can offer to human beings.

Theory in Practice

The Marine Stewardship Council: a case of enlightened anthropocentrism

An example of an enlightened anthropocentric initiative, involving cooperation between an environmental-protection organization and one of the world's largest corporations, is the Marine Stewardship Council (MSC). The MSC is an independent, non-profit organization, whose aim is to ensure that 'seafood supplies [are] safeguarded for this and future generations' (Marine Stewardship Council, 2013). It was set up in the late 1990s by the World Wildlife Fund and Unilever. At that time Unilever was one of the world's largest buyers of frozen fish, which it retailed under brand names such as Birds Eye and Findus. Unilever's interest in setting up the MSC was to ensure the availability of fish into the future and thus 'to safeguard its frozen fish business in the long-term' (United Nations Global Compact, 2006).

Nowadays, the MSC plays a prominent role in the fisheries industry. It advises where and how much fish may be caught by trawlers without endangering the future sustainability of fisheries. It also raises awareness amongst retailers and consumers of the dangers of over fishing. It certifies sustainably caught fish so that, when you or I buy fish from a retailer, we can be assured that it has been caught in a way that does not damage the viability of fish stocks into the future.

Questions

1. Nowadays a lot of fishing is carried out by huge trawlers, which are equipped with high level technology to locate shoals of fish, and which drag vast nets fitted with heavy weights across the seafloor, scooping up everything in their path. How might such industrial-scale fishing help to meet the short-term, *resource-anthropocentric* needs of humans?
2. How might it present a challenge to *enlightened-anthropocentric* considerations?

Aesthetic anthropocentrism: nature as a source of artistic pleasure

Despite the emphasis traditionally placed on the environment as a resource for meeting people's physical needs, its anthropocentric value does not end there. A great deal of contemporary environmental concern highlights the *aesthetic* value of nature. In other words, it stresses nature's artistic merits. According to this perspective, artistic value is not only located in human-made artefacts; it can also be found in nature (Hepburn, 1966). Those who emphasize the aesthetic appeal of nature propose that we should not just conserve the environment so that it will continue to feed us into the future; we should also do so because it provides other forms of valuable human experience.

There are several ways in which nature has been considered to have aesthetic value. Perhaps the most obvious is the opportunity it affords to gaze over picturesque scenes of rural tranquillity, peaceful sunsets across serene bays, or colourful flora and fauna. However, aesthetic value has also been identified in more intimidating settings. According to this view, it is not just the picturesque that has aesthetic merit; it is also the *sublime*. The eighteenth-century philosopher Immanuel Kant explained the appeal of the sublime by contrasting it to *beauty* (Schaper, 1992; Gardiner, 1993). For Kant, beauty can be appreciated on a small scale. The sublime, on the other hand, is made of sterner stuff. Its aesthetic appeal comes from apprehending vastness; of looking at something that threatens to overwhelm us. Whereas beauty might be found in neatly manicured, city gardens or in cultivated rural landscapes, the sublime needs to be encountered in its raw and natural state. As Kant put it, sublimity is found in:

> Bold, overhanging, and, as it were, threatening rocks, thunderclouds piled up the vault of heaven, borne along with flashes and peals, volcanoes in all their violence of destruction, hurricanes leaving desolation in their track, the boundless ocean rising with rebellious force, the high waterfall of some mighty river, and the like, [which] make our power of resistance of trifling moment in comparison with their might. (*Critique of Judgement*, cited in Schaper, 1992: 383)

More recently, aesthetic merit has been found in even less obvious, natural sources. For instance, contemporary environmentalists (Saito, 1998; Rolston, 2000; Callicott, 2003) highlight the aesthetic appeal of natural environments such as swamps, bogs and other wetland landscapes, which do not conform either to conventional notions of beauty or awe-inspiring, sublime grandeur. Aesthetic merit has even been identified in creatures hitherto considered ugly, such as snakes and other reptiles. According to such views, the aesthetic value of the natural world comes in many forms. Therefore, environmental conservation campaigns should do more than preserve the most overtly picturesque landscapes and the cutest creatures; they should embrace everything that is 'natural', for everything in nature has its own, idiosyncratic, aesthetic appeal.

Emotional anthropocentrism: emphasizing the importance of nature experience to being human

Preserving the aesthetic qualities of nature is not the only anthropocentric reason that has been put forward for protecting natural resources from human exploitation.

A slightly different rationale holds that direct exposure to nature is an important ingredient of a fulfilled human life. Whereas writers such as John Stuart Mill (2010/1874) emphasized the opposition between the forces of nature and humanity, suggesting that the latter should be controlled and shackled, more recent environmental perspectives emphasize the human benefits of experiencing nature in the raw. I refer to this approach to environmentalism as *emotional anthropocentrism* because it implies that intimate connection with the natural world is essential to the emotional well-being of humans.

The term *wilderness* is often used in environmentalist circles in the context of preserving pristine landscapes. Early champions of the emotional-anthropocentric importance of wilderness (Thoreau, 2010/1883; Muir, 2010/1901) proposed that city life and the trappings of civilization tend to deprive humans of connection with nature, and that human life is consequently impoverished. For these writers, the way to address this rupture from our primeval roots is to reconnect with nature on a regular basis. And they were not talking here about quiet strolls in cultivated urban parks; they were advocating encounters with wild, uncultivated spaces.

In order to facilitate wilderness experience for the citizens of the USA, John Muir became an influential advocate for the creation of National Parks. For Muir, National Parks would provide protected wilderness habitats in which people could commune with nature and thus rediscover their true selves. As he put it:

> Thousands of tired, nerve-shaken, over-civilized people are beginning to find out that going to the mountains is going home; that wildness is a necessity; and that mountain parks and reservations are useful not only as fountains of timber and irrigating rivers, but as fountains of life. Awakening from the stupefying effects of the vice of over-industry and the deadly apathy of luxury, they are trying as best they can to mix and enrich their own little ongoings with those of Nature, and to get rid of rust and disease. (Muir, 2010/1901: 96)

Video Activity 9.2

The following link is to a song by Chumbawamba called 'You Can (Mass Trespass, 1932)', along with accompanying photographs. The song's title refers to the Kinder Scout Mass Trespass of 1932, when hundreds of people joined an organized trespass on Kinder Scout mountain to protest their right to walk on the moors. Many of the trespassers spent their working week in the factories and mills of North-West England. Walking the moors at the weekend gave them their only opportunity to get away from the noisy, dirty, crowded environment where they spent most of their lives and to experience nature at first hand. Their right to do so was opposed by landowners, who wanted to preserve the moors for the lucrative business of grouse shooting.

The Mass Trespass was an important event in the restoration of ancient rights of way over Britain's mountains. Amongst other things, it led to the eventual recognition of a right to roam on mountain, moor, heath, down and common land throughout England and Wales.

www.youtube.com/watch?v=knzUMCZX8-w

Questions

1 How did preserving the moors for grouse shooting serve the *resource-anthropocentric* needs of certain people?
2 How did the trespass campaign aim to serve the *emotional-anthropocentric* needs of many more people?

Many people nowadays reap the benefits of wilderness experience that were advocated by pioneers such as Thoreau and Muir. However, the term *wilderness and wildlife* is a more apt description of the focus of contemporary interest in nature than simply calling it *wilderness*. Whereas the explicit focus of early campaigners was on experiencing pristine landscapes, contemporary wilderness advocates also emphasize the merits of exposure to the creatures that are indigenous to those landscapes. A wide variety of nature sanctuaries and wildlife reserves have therefore augmented the National Parks created by early North American campaigners.

Moreover, a vibrant industry sector has emerged to facilitate access to those wilderness and wildlife environments. There is no single term that adequately describes this industry, although 'adventure tourism', 'nature tourism', 'responsible tourism', and 'ecotourism' all cover some of its territory. In the absence of a better term, I will use here the expression *wilderness and wildlife tourism*. Given its vague parameters, it is hard to quantify the size and development of the wilderness and wildlife tourism industry. Nevertheless, it is clear that this is a tourism sector that has developed considerably in recent decades and that will continue to grow into the foreseeable future (Guha and Martinez-Alier, 1997; The International Ecotourism Society, 2000; Center for Emerging Issues, 2001; Zebich-Knos, 2008; Center for Responsible Travel, 2013).

Wilderness and wildlife tourism helps people to realize the emotional-anthropocentric benefits of nature, insofar as these benefits relate to wilderness and wildlife experience. On this particular understanding of the value of nature, businesses that provide transport, accommodation, information, tour guidance and other necessary amenities in and around wilderness and wildlife environments are performing a beneficial role. Nevertheless, concerns have been raised about the contemporary preoccupation with exposing people to wilderness and wildlife. These concerns will be discussed later in this chapter.

Theory in Practice

Wind farms: an enlightened way of meeting human energy needs; or a blight on the landscape?

The last 20 years have seen a big increase in the number of wind farms in the United Kingdom as the country tries to reduce environmentally harmful emissions in line with European and global policy commitments. A wind farm is a collection of turbines, whose purpose is to provide renewable, wind-driven energy. There are currently around 4,400 turbines in operation in the UK, providing 10 per cent of the country's energy needs. Considerable further investment in wind power is envisaged, involving UK and overseas companies supported by generous government subsidies. Approval is already in place for 7,850 more turbines, and it is envisaged that, by 2020, 15 per cent of UK energy will be wind powered (Gray, 2013; Macalister, 2013a; Mendick, 2013).

The creation of wind farms is a contentious topic. On the one hand wind farms provide a renewable energy source, which reduces dependency on environmentally harmful fossil fuels. On the other hand, they can have a significant impact on the landscape. Wind farms are usually built in prominent, upland locations, on islands, or at sea. Turbines currently stand up to 150 metres tall. They are usually mounted on concrete bases, and onshore turbines are linked by networks of tarmacked roads.

Wind farms in heavily populated areas tend to be fairly small in scale, usually comprising just one or a handful of turbines. However, those in rural areas can be far larger. For instance, a 36-turbine farm is planned for the remote Scottish island of Lewis (Stornoway Wind Farm, 2013). An even bigger development is envisaged for the Cambrian Mountains in Mid-Wales, a wild, sparsely populated area that is sometimes referred to as the 'Welsh Wilderness'. Here, there are plans to construct a total of 840 turbines (Mid Wales Wind Farm Planning, 2013).

Questions

1. In what ways does the creation of wind farms conform to an *enlightened-anthropocentric* agenda?
2. How might wind farms undermine the *aesthetic-anthropocentric* or *emotional-anthropocentric* value of the natural environments in which they are created?
3. Can you think of ways in which the construction of a wind farm might serve or undermine the economic interests of local communities in remote locations?

Some biocentric perspectives

Many environmental writers have taken issue with the notion that the natural environment should only be valued insofar as it serves the interests of humans. They argue that other sentient creatures, non-sentient organisms, and maybe even rocks, rivers, oceans and ecosystems are valuable in themselves, regardless of any purpose they might serve for human beings. This is the view of *biocentrism*: that the natural environment has intrinsic value and that we should treat it with respect because of that intrinsic value, not just because doing so benefits humans.

To apply biocentrism to ethical evaluation of corporate activity is to question the entitlement of corporations to treat the natural world as a resource pool to meet human needs, even if they do so in an enlightened manner that takes the needs of future generations into account. It is to suggest that those corporations should also think about the impact that resource extraction might have on the creatures and organisms that occupy that world. Biocentrism also entails that, in capitalizing on the aesthetic and emotional benefits that nature offers to humans, businesses should think of the impact that human encounters with the natural world might have on that world.

To follow are a few arguments that have been put forward in support of biocentrism.

Last-person argument

Richard Sylvan (2003/1973) offers what is often referred to as the *last-person argument* to show that the natural world has intrinsic value. Sylvan asks us to undertake a thought experiment, which goes something like this: suppose that some catastrophic human illness has ravaged the world and that you are the last person left on earth. Suppose, moreover, that you are in a position to inflict widespread environmental devastation after your death, perhaps by the delayed detonation of a series of massive nuclear explosions that would lay waste to the whole planet. According to anthropocentrism, there would be no reason not to inflict this devastation because, after the last person has died, it does not matter what happens to the planet.

Sylvan points out that most people would think this an unethical thing to do. Most of us would agree that, even after the last people have ceased to exist, it is better that the environment is not irreparably damaged. Sylvan takes this to indicate that, despite the apparent pervasiveness of anthropocentrism in our culture, when we think about things a little more deeply we find that anthropocentrism is actually contrary to most people's fundamental ethical intuitions. According to those fundamental ethical intuitions, the natural environment does have intrinsic value and we should therefore treat it accordingly.

Redefining the moral community

A further argument in favour of biocentrism revolves around Andrew Brennan's (1995) observation that the very notion of ethics presupposes the idea of a moral community.

That is, when we speak of ethics, we cannot avoid the idea that there is a community of beings who matter, ethically, who we should therefore take into consideration when we act. Ethics theory, according to Brennan, starts from this presupposition of a moral community, and it then seeks to define precisely who belongs to that community and precisely what their responsibilities are towards one another.

Brennan points out that traditional Western ethics theory has tended to define this moral community purely in terms of human beings. But he questions whether there is any legitimate justification for this. For instance, Thomas Aquinas's rationale for anthropocentrism, which was outlined earlier, proposed that humans are closer to God in a hierarchical chain of being, so they matter in a way that animals and plants do not. This argument is based upon a belief in an all-powerful God, who has accorded this hierarchically elevated role to humans and who has told them they may use it to serve their own interests. But this is a presupposition that many people do not share. Even some religious perspectives put more emphasis on the responsibility that our proximity to God confers on us to care for the rest of creation than on the right it gives us to use the world for our own purposes.

Another popular justification for elevating humans above the rest of the natural world is that, unlike all other entities, humans are capable of rational thought. This idea was embraced by some of the anthropocentric rationales presented above and has underpinned a great deal of Western philosophy. But why should human reason be such an important criterion for the attribution of value? Even if we accept that humans are able to reason in a way that other creatures cannot, why should this justify special privileges? Animals and insects may not reason as humans do, but they can do a great many things that we cannot do. After all, I may have been born with a greater faculty for human-style, rational thought than my dog but my dog's sense of hearing, sight and smell are many times better than mine. She also remembers routes through the mountains many years after they have escaped my memory, and she knows precisely who or what is outside my house long before I even know that anyone or anything is there. Furthermore, my dog is not given to bearing grudges, and the need to build a weapon of mass destruction has occurred neither to her nor her forebears. So what is so special about human rationality?

Richard Sylvan refers to our unfounded hierarchical elevation of humans as 'human chauvinism'; that is, an unsubstantiated presupposition that 'humans, or people, come first and everything else a bad last' (Sylvan, 2003/1973: 49). Similarly, Richard Ryder (2011) talks of 'speciesism'. Ryder points out that, like other 'isms' such as sexism and racism, speciesism involves a group of beings specifying a criterion of value that only they meet, and then asserting their superiority on the basis that nothing except them meets that criterion of value. Speciesism is thus based on a fallacious, circular argument. Andrew Brennan proposes that, instead, we should embrace a wider moral community, thus taking seriously 'the idea that trees, flowers, rocks, rivers and even ecosystems deserve moral consideration from us' (Brennan, 1995: 800).

A number of writers have pointed out that we can broaden the moral community, as Brennan proposes, without rejecting insights that have been afforded by a rich heritage of moral philosophy. All we have to do is apply those insights to a wider moral community than we have done hitherto. For instance, Tom Regan (1983) has offered persuasive arguments for the *rights* of animals to be acknowledged in addition to those of humans; Peter Singer (1995) has proposed that *utilitarianism* be extended to embrace the happiness of animals as well as humans; William Wright (1993) has suggested ways in which the *Kantian principle* of treating-people-as-ends might be extended to include animals; and Ronald Sandler (2010/2005) broadens the scope of *virtue theory* by applying its insights to the natural environment.

Pause for Reflection

One branch of environmental activism campaigns against what its supporters consider to be the unethical treatment of animals by businesses. Industries that attract particular attention in this respect include: pharmaceuticals and cosmetics, which test products on live animals; the fashion industry, which uses animal products to make clothing for humans; and agriculture, which may involve various forms of animal cruelty. *Resource anthropocentrism* might justify such treatment on the basis that humans can legitimately use other creatures to serve their own purposes. How might the *biocentric* arguments outlined above be used to challenge this resource-anthropocentric approach?

Challenging anthropocentrism's atomistic presupposition

A third critique of anthropocentrism suggests that it is premised upon a misguided *atomistic* understanding of the world and of the relationship between the human and non-human entities that inhabit it. Atomism sees the world in terms of distinct, autonomous entities, which exist separately from one another and which only come into contact insofar as this is necessary to achieve specific purposes. Applied to environmental thinking, atomism assumes that human beings can stand apart from nature, taking from it what they need when they need it, but otherwise leading their lives in isolation from it. This way of thinking is perhaps encouraged by the urbanized character of many people's lives nowadays: many of us spend most of our time in human-made environments, interacting only with other humans, using human-made technology, and rarely encountering the environment in its natural, unrefined state. We thus come to think of nature as no more than a resource pool, as a dumping ground for the stuff that we no longer need in our human domain, or maybe as something nice to look at when we are in need of a bit of aesthetic or emotional inspiration. Otherwise, we have little interest in it.

Critics of this atomistic perspective suggest that it misunderstands the unavoidable interconnections that pervade our world; interconnections which mean that humans and so-called 'nature' are so deeply implicated in mutual dependency that neither can be considered apart from the other. Several metaphors have been put forward to capture this interdependency and to illustrate the folly of trying to consider humans and the natural world in isolation from one another.

Aldo Leopold's *biotic pyramid* (2003/1949: 42) is one such metaphor. Leopold suggested that we should think of the natural environment as a pyramid, in which lower layers absorb energy from the sun and the atmosphere, transmitting that energy upwards via food chains involving, on successively higher layers, plants, insects, birds and small mammals, and humans and larger mammals. As Leopold describes it, 'The pyramid is a tangle of chains so complex as to seem disorderly, yet the stability of the system proves it to be a highly organized structure. Its functioning depends on the co-operation and competition of its diverse parts' (Leopold, 2003/1949: 43). Importantly, human beings form an integral part of the biotic pyramid. As such, we cannot stand apart from it and use it merely to serve our ends. Whatever we do to it, we do to ourselves.

An important feature of biotic pyramids, for Leopold, is that they are held in delicate tension. The integrity of the whole pyramid is dependent upon the presence of each of its constituent parts, their respective proportions, and the fragile connections that hold them together. And this integrity can be disrupted by sudden interference.

This does not mean that change should not occur in a biotic pyramid. Indeed, Leopold regarded gradual, evolutionary change as an inevitable feature, which facilitates the developing complexity of the pyramid and the flow circuits that sustain it. However, evolutionary change is a slow, gradual process, which allows for adaptation within the pyramid. Therefore, disruptions that result from slow, evolutionary change are unlikely to damage the harmonious interconnections that hold biotic pyramids together. However, changes to biotic pyramids brought about by human intervention may not be slow, evolutionary ones. Human-inspired changes can be both substantial and abrupt. Indeed, humans have the capacity to lop off an entire layer within a biotic pyramid by, for instance, polluting waters and land, or by hunting to extinction the creatures that comprise a key part of one of its layers. Such major interventions can have disastrous consequences for the sustainability of the pyramid as a whole and therefore for the beings that comprise it – including the humans who brought about the disruption in the first place.

Theory in Practice

Is krill the only species endangered by the over fishing of krill?

One of the most high-profile environmentalist movements of the 1970s was Greenpeace's campaign to 'Save the Whale'. Largely as a result of Greenpeace's efforts, an international moratorium on the hunting of whales is observed today by every nation in the world except Japan, Iceland and Norway (Greenpeace, 2014).

More recently, the concern of environmentalists has focused on a far less obvious ocean dweller. Whereas whales are the largest creatures in the sea, the Antarctic krill is one of its smallest. It is a shrimp-like creature, about 6cm long, which populates the Antarctic Ocean in vast quantities. Up to 30,000 of these minute crustaceans can occupy one cubic metre of water and it is estimated that the total weight of Antarctic krill is somewhere between 100 and 500 million metric tonnes – more than the weight of the entire human population (Greenpeace, 2009; Jowit, 2008).

Krill forms the principal food source for many creatures in the Southern Ocean, including seals, penguins, albatross, various fish species and baleen whales (Greenpeace, 2009). It therefore constitutes the base layer in a *biotic pyramid* that includes all these creatures as well as any other beings whose ecological equilibrium depends on them. But krill also perform a further important function. The regular movement of huge shoals of krill between the ocean surface and deeper levels serves the purpose of removing vast quantities of carbon from the atmosphere. Indeed, Dr Geraint Tarling from the British Antarctic Survey estimates the annual sequestration of carbon by Antarctic krill may be equivalent to the annual emissions of 35 million cars (Greenpeace, 2009).

But why should environmentalists be worried about krill, given that they exist in such vast quantities? The problem is that the krill population is believed to have declined by around 80 per cent since the 1970s (Jowit, 2008). Global warming is thought to be partly responsible for this decline. However, the harvesting of krill by humans is also to blame. Krill are increasingly in demand by humans for two reasons. Firstly, they provide a source of Omega 3 oil, which constitutes a key ingredient in fish-oil supplements and other health products that comprise a growing industry sector. Secondly, although some types of krill do not have a high enough oil content for human-health uses, they provide an abundant source of cheap animal and fish feed so are greatly in demand in the pet food industry and for fish farms.

As a result of this demand, krill are being fished in growing numbers. Of particular concern to environmentalists are the increasingly technological methods used for tracking shoals of krill and for harvesting them – a single state-of-the-art trawler can vacuum up as much as 45,000 tonnes of krill in a single fishing season (Greenpeace, 2009).

Questions

1 *Resource anthropocentrism* might be used as a rationale to support the increasingly efficient methods used to harvest krill for health products, pet food and fish-farm feed. How might an *enlightened-anthropocentric* perspective propose a more cautious approach to krill fishing?

(Continued)

(Continued)

2 In what ways might krill fishing indirectly undermine the *aesthetic-anthropocentric* and/or *emotional-anthropocentric* value of the Antarctic environment?
3 Do you think humans have *biocentric* responsibility to preserve the ecological balance of the Antarctic?
4 How might the over fishing of krill impact on a *biotic pyramid* that includes humans?

Some Anthropocentric Rationales	Some Implications for Business Ethics
Resource anthropocentrism: viewing nature as a resource to be controlled and exploited.	Businesses should harness the natural world and put it to productive human use.
Enlightened anthropocentrism: emphasizing the need to conserve scarce resources.	Businesses should put the natural world to productive human use, but should also be careful to preserve scare resources for future use.
Aesthetic anthropocentrism: regarding nature as a source of artistic pleasure.	Businesses which offer customers the opportunity to experience beauty in nature are performing a valuable role. Other businesses should ensure that their activities do not diminish people's opportunity to experience the beauty of the natural landscape.
Emotional anthropocentrism: emphasizing the importance of nature experience to being human.	Businesses which give people the opportunity to experience nature in the raw are playing a worthwhile role. Other businesses should avoid either contaminating the wild spaces that humans might want to visit or preventing human access to them.

Some Biocentric Rationales	Some Implications for Business Ethics
Last-person argument: even if there were no humans to experience it, nature would still matter.	Businesses should not view the natural world as a resource to be exploited for human use; they should respect its intrinsic value and avoid doing anything that might impair that value.
Redefining the moral community: people are not the only creatures deserving of ethical consideration.	Animals and other non-human creatures are deserving of ethical consideration, so businesses which impact on non-human creatures should treat them with respect. Animals are not just there for human use; they matter in themselves.
Challenging anthropocentrism's atomistic presupposition: humans and the natural world are linked in fragile, complex, interdependent eco-systems.	Businesses should consider the impact of their activities on nature. They should be aware that in altering nature they may damage the balance within complex eco-systems upon which everything and everybody depends.

Figure 9.1 A summary of anthropocentric and biocentric ways of thinking about the environment and some implications for business

Wilderness and wildlife preservation: rich person's crusade; poor person's burden?

So far, this chapter has outlined some ways in which value might be attributed to the natural environment, organizing these under the headings of *anthropocentrism* and *biocentrism*. The remainder of the chapter will explore some contentious topics that often crop up in environmentalist debate, each of which has particular relevance for business. Some of these topics touch on the approaches that have already been considered, and in some cases they can be contextualized in terms of a conflict between different approaches to valuing the natural environment.

One topic that raises a certain amount of controversy in global environmentalist debate concerns the importance that is attached to wilderness and wildlife conservation, particularly by people who live in more affluent nations. On the one hand, this particular environmentalist preoccupation can be justified in several ways. An *aesthetic-anthropocentric* justification might highlight the aesthetic pleasure that humans take from experiencing wilderness and wildlife. Alternatively, an *emotional-anthropocentric* rationale could point to the importance of conserving pristine wilderness spaces where humans can reconnect with nature. Furthermore, given recent growth in wilderness and wildlife tourism as an economic activity, an *enlightened-anthropocentric* rationale might point out that conserving the natural environment today may deliver significant economic benefits in the future through the development of tourism destinations. But wilderness and wildlife conservation can also be championed on *biocentric* grounds on the basis that animals, insects, plants, landscapes and ecosystems are part of the moral community and are thus deserving of respect. Therefore, pristine wilderness areas should be set aside within which these non-human entities can thrive, free from contamination by human activity.

However, despite the compelling rationales put forward to justify wilderness and wildlife conservation, the priority often accorded to it has been criticized. Critics of the conservation agenda do not necessarily disagree with its intrinsic merits; they do not challenge the desirability of preserving wilderness and wildlife *per se*. Their concern, rather, relates to the difficulties that conservation activities may cause for people whose lives and livelihoods are affected by it.

In this debate, the terms *North* and *South* are often used to refer to a distinction that is made elsewhere between the 'West' and the 'non-West', between the 'first world' and the 'third world', or between 'developed nations' and 'developing nations'. The distinction is thus drawn between, on the one hand, regions such as Western Europe, the USA, and (rather illogically) Australia, which have been more affluent for some time and, on the other hand, those regions which remain less developed, such as large parts of Africa, Asia, and South America, and nations whose economies have only recently expanded, such as the so-called BRIC group (Brazil, Russia, India and China).

Criticism of the wilderness and wildlife agenda is based on the observation that it privileges the values and interests of wealthy people from the North over the values and interests of less-wealthy communities in the South, where it is often put into practice. As Ramachandra Guha and Juan Martinez-Alier describe it, the high profile accorded to wilderness and wildlife conservation therefore represents the primacy of the 'full-stomach' environmentalism of the North over the 'empty-belly' environmentalism of the South (1997: xxi).

This section of the chapter will offer two contrasting accounts of the implementation of wilderness and wildlife conservation. The first describes some projects that have been set up in India and Africa, highlighting their negative implications for local people. The second account describes some similar projects established in Latin America. Whilst mindful of the potential of such projects to subordinate the interests of local people to the agendas of outsiders, this second account also illustrates some ways in which this might be avoided.

Wilderness and wildlife reserves in India and Africa

A particularly trenchant critique of wilderness and wildlife conservation is offered by Ramachandra Guha (1997/1989). Guha is especially concerned about the proliferation of wildlife reserves in the South, which have become popular tourism destinations for wealthy visitors from the North but whose creation often has serious repercussions for less-wealthy, indigenous people. Guha cites Project Tiger in India as an example. Launched over 40 years ago, Project Tiger seeks to preserve Indian tigers by creating wildlife habitats within which they can thrive and in which they can be observed by visitors. It currently runs 27 reserves across India, which cover just over one per cent of the country's total land area. The project's stated aim is 'to ensure a viable population of tiger in India for scientific, economic, aesthetic, cultural and ecological values and to preserve for all time, areas of biological importance as a natural heritage for the benefit, education and enjoyment of the people' (Project Tiger, 2013).

Guha points out that, as a result of this and similar initiatives to conserve the natural habitats of other iconic indigenous mammals, tens of thousands of local inhabitants, who had previously lived within newly created reserves, have lost their homes. Furthermore, those who live close by and who have, for generations, farmed and hunted the land upon which reserves have been established, now find themselves unable to do so. As Guha puts it:

> All over India, the management of parks has sharply posited the interests of poor tribals who have traditionally lived there against those of wilderness lovers and urban pleasure seekers who wish to keep parks 'free of human interference' … Everywhere, Indian wildlifers have ganged up behind the forest department to evict the tribals and rehabilitate them far outside the forests. In this they have drawn sustenance from American biologists and conservation organisations, who have thrown the prestige of science and the power of the dollar behind the crusade to kick the original owners of the forest out of their home. (Guha, 1997/1989: 106)

Guha also cites the work of Raymond Bonner (1993) who speaks of similar instances in Africa, where indigenous Africans have been disadvantaged so that reserves and wildlife parks can be created for the benefit of rich, northern tourists. As Bonner describes it:

> Above all, Africans [have been] ignored, overwhelmed, manipulated and outmanoeuvred – by a conservation crusade led, orchestrated and dominated by white Westerners …
>
> As many Africans see it, white people are making rules to protect animals that white people want to see in parks that white people visit …
>
> Africans do not use the parks and they do not receive any significant benefits from them. Yet they are paying the costs. There are indirect economic costs – government revenues that go to parks instead of schools. And there are direct personal costs [i.e., of the ban on hunting and fuel collecting, or of displacement]. (Bonner, 1993, cited by Guha, 1997/1989: 105; wording in parentheses is added by Guha)

Now, in these instances, the conflict between the conservation agenda and the interests of local communities might be conceptualized in terms of a conflict between different ways of valuing the natural world. In this respect, Guha observes that the values and interests of the affluent North have triumphed over those of the less wealthy South. As he sees it, the creation of Indian wildlife parks is the outcome of the combined efforts of local economic elites and North-based international campaigning organizations, which have privileged wildlife preservation over the resource needs of local people. Construed as a clash of values, it is clearly the values of the wealthy that have won out, whether these values are stated in (anthropocentric) terms of the aesthetic and emotional needs of humans, or whether they are presented under the (biocentric) heading of the rights of animals, plants and ecosystems to exist.

But Guha (1997/1989) also offers another way of conceptualizing this conflict. This is that the creation of parks involves a simple clash of economic interests. On the one hand, there are groups who stand to benefit financially from the creation and operation of wildlife reserves: hoteliers, airlines, souvenir sellers, tour operators and the like. On the other hand, there are the local communities whose livelihoods are thus undermined. And since most of the financial benefits associated with the reserves are reaped by large corporations, such as airlines and hotel groups, or by local, economic elites, it is the wealthy that win out over the poor. Considered in this way, the wilderness crusade might be seen as a convenient, 'soft' rationale, which has been co-opted by economically powerful groups to further their own financial interests while undermining the interests of poor, indigenous communities. Thus, as Guha puts it, a 'direct transfer of resources from the poor to the rich' (1997/1989: 95) is effected.

Wilderness and wildlife reserves in Latin America

A more nuanced discussion of this topic is offered by Michele Zebich-Knos (2008). Zebich-Knos describes some wilderness and wildlife conservation initiatives in Latin

America, which present similar threats to the interests of indigenous people to those discussed by Guha. However, Zebich-Knos distinguishes between projects that are driven by national government and NGOs, in which the opinions of local people are not represented, and those in which community dialogue and involvement is actively sought. Furthermore, she observes that in the former type of projects, economic benefits tend to flow primarily to international corporations, with little money trickling down to locals. In projects which encourage community involvement, on the other hand, a range of measures tend to be in place to ensure that local people are able to share in the economic fruits of wilderness and wildlife tourism.

Zebich-Knos (2008) also identifies concrete measures that have been adopted in some of these initiatives to avoid the worst of the problems that might otherwise be associated with them. These measures include the provision of ongoing job training for local people, which avoids situations in which locals are only employed in menial roles while highly paid, skilled roles are filled by incomers. Zebich-Knos also stresses the importance of integrating newly created reserves with traditional economic activities, thus augmenting, rather than replacing, those traditional activities. Moreover, she observes that the least-contentious projects are those that encourage respect for local cultural traditions through tourist education programmes and even by enforcing behavioural guidelines on tourists. Lastly, she suggests that a harmonious relationship between local and national/international players can be established as long as control for conservation projects remains with local people, while national and international agencies offer the business expertise and resources that those locals may lack.

Contrary to Guha's vehement critique of what he refers to as 'Radical American Environmentalism' (1997/1989), then, Zebich-Knos's enquiry indicates that wilderness and wildlife conservation can be pursued in a manner that respects its anthropocentric and biocentric ideals without necessarily undermining the resource needs or cultural traditions of local communities. However, for such a reconciliation to occur, attention needs to be paid to integrating conservation, and the tourist activity associated with it, with local economic practices and customary lifestyles. According to Zebich-Knos, this is best achieved by allowing local people to be actively involved in the planning, creation and operation of reserves. And, perhaps most importantly, it demands fair distribution of the economic benefits that accrue from the creation of wilderness parks and wildlife reserves. This last issue of distribution of economic benefits is part of a broader discussion which will be considered in the next section of this chapter under the heading of environmental justice.

Video Activity 9.3

The following link will take you to a promotional video for the Pumba Private Game Reserve in South Africa:

www.youtube.com/watch?v=i3S_nraulkQ

Questions

1 In what ways might the creation of reserves like the Pumba Private Game Reserve serve *anthropocentric* and/or *biocentric* agendas?
2 Do you think the Pumba Private Game Reserve draws most of its customers from what is referred to above as the *North* or from the countries of the *South*?
3 How might the creation of reserves like the Pumba Private Game Reserve serve the interests of local people?
4 How might the creation of such reserves harm the interests of local people?
5 What questions would you want to ask the people who run the Pumba Private Game Reserve to find out if it respects the economic and cultural needs of local people?

Environmental justice and environmental injustice

This section will consider a second environmentally related topic that has evoked a lot of debate. This topic is *anthropocentrically* focused insofar as it concerns the relationship between humans and the natural environment. Specifically, it concerns the questions: who benefits from human activity that impacts negatively on the environment? And who bears the associated burden? The name that is usually given to this topic is *environmental justice*. Questions of environmental justice draw attention, in particular, to instances in which the benefits of environmentally damaging economic activity accrue to certain groups while the burden is borne by others.

Video Activity 9.4

The following video, 'Islands Going Under', describes the impact of rising sea levels on Pacific island communities.

www.greenpeace.org/international/en/multimedia/videos/Islands-Going-Under-/

Most climatologists agree that the world is becoming progressively warmer. It is anticipated that melting ice will cause sea levels to rise, which will flood islands and other low-lying land. This is not the only impact of climate change though. It is likely to result in increased drought in hotter areas, causing famine and resource

(Continued)

(Continued)

scarcity. Furthermore, extreme weather events such as flash flooding and high winds have been linked to global warming.

Some scientists deny a link between human activity and climate change. However, most authoritative sources agree that increased industrial activity, growing consumption of fossil fuels, and depletion of certain forms of vegetation and marine life over the last 200 years have caused significant changes in the earth's atmospheric make-up which, in turn, are largely responsible for global warming.

Questions

1 Which areas of the world do you think have benefited most, in material and economic terms, from increases in industrial activity, the consumption of fossil fuels and depletion of resources over the last 200 years?
2 Which communities in what parts of the world do you think are most likely to suffer the consequences of global warming?

A form of economic activity that has an especially significant environmental impact, and which thus creates particularly weighty environmental burdens, is large-scale industrial activity. It is therefore unsurprising that such activity has attracted a lot of attention from those who concern themselves with environmental justice. In this respect, a number of researchers have highlighted the extent to which the fruits of large-scale industrial projects that take place in the South flow mainly to North-based, global corporations, to their North-based shareholders, and to their North-based customers. Meanwhile, the associated burdens are experienced by indigenous communities in the South (Bunker, 1985; Jorgenson, 2003 and 2006; Rice, 2007; Jorgenson et al., 2009; Shandra et al., 2009).

Environmental justice and the mining industry

One sector that has attracted a great deal of attention in this respect is the mining industry. In recent years, North-based mining corporations have looked increasingly to the South, particularly to Latin America, South-East Asia and Africa, to feed escalating global demand for metals such as copper and gold (Bridge, 2004). There are a number of reasons why the South has become so popular for mining projects. Environmental regulation in traditional mining areas in the North has become increasingly restrictive, so companies are attracted by looser standards in developing nations (Urkidi, 2010). Moreover, several decades of economic liberalization, encouraged by organizations such as the World Bank and the International Monetary Fund, have facilitated investment by transnational corporations in southern nations. This trend has been further helped by a political climate that is generally supportive of inward investment by overseas firms (Bridge, 2004; Garvin et al., 2009; Urkidi, 2010). As a consequence, the 1990s and 2000s saw considerable growth in mining activity in the South. For instance, gold production in Latin America nearly doubled during the ten years up to 2006 (Urkidi, 2010).

Investment in large mining projects by transnational corporations has the potential to make a significant contribution to a developing country's national economy. Mining companies also claim that their operations deliver many other benefits at a local level (see for example Barrick, 2013; BHP Billiton, 2013; Goldcorp, 2013; Newmont, 2013; and Rio Tinto, 2013). For a start, there are the employment opportunities created by mining projects. Moreover, mining companies claim that they make substantial contributions to local services, which helps to improve health, housing, education and transportation facilities. Corporations also highlight the efforts they make to take account of local concerns while planning and implementing their projects. They speak of the generous compensation and resettlement programmes they put in place, and they tell of the lengths to which they go to minimize disruption of traditional cultures and lifestyles.

However, despite all this, mining projects in the South have met with considerable opposition, particularly at a local level (Martinez-Alier, 2001; Acselrad, 2008; Urkidi, 2010). Much of this opposition relates to the environmental impact of large-scale mining activity and its implications for local economic and social arrangements. Mining can be a messy business. For example, the 'ecological rucksack' (Martinez-Alier, 2001: 158) of mining for copper and gold includes the release of sulphur dioxide into the air, which can be detrimental to human health and agricultural production. Mining can also cause acid drainage and the release of toxic deposits into rivers upon which human consumption and agriculture depend. Emissions from cyanide leaching, which is often used to extract gold, present a particularly potent environmental threat (Garvin et al., 2009; Urkidi, 2010; BBC, 2012a). In remote parts of the Andes Mountains, which have become a focal point for gold mining, there is also concern about the impact of industrial activity on glaciers, which has repercussions for water systems at lower altitudes (Urkidi, 2010). These environmental issues become even more pronounced as more efficient, but more risky, technologies make the exploitation of low-grade ore deposits technically feasible and profitable (Urkidi and Walter, 2011).

Many of the regions in which mining operations have been established in recent years have long traditions of subsistence farming and other small-scale agricultural practices. Not only are critics worried about the economic impact of mining operations on agricultural communities through air and water pollution, the destruction of arable land, and the private takeover of land to which there had previously been common access (Garvin et al., 2009; Urkidi, 2010; Urkidi and Walter, 2011); they also express concern about the cultural and social impact of large-scale mining activity. For instance, Leire Urkidi and Mariana Walter (2011) speak of local people's anxiety that the close, communal relationships that characterize traditional farming communities will be disrupted by vast, industrial operations in the Chilean Andes. Similarly, research by Theresa Garvin and her colleagues (2009) finds that local people who have experienced large, gold-mining projects in Ghana associate them with disruption of social norms, decreasing sense of community, the erosion of family ties, and a rise in criminal behaviour.

Critics also suggest that the economic benefits of mining activity rarely flow to local communities. Garvin et al. (2009) suggest that, although inward investment in mining operations may register at the level of the national economy, little of this is likely to filter down to a local, community level. Furthermore, the new jobs that are created by large-scale mining projects often demand specific skills, which are not found in agriculturally based communities. Most of these jobs are therefore taken up by suitably skilled incomers. Moreover it is claimed that, where money is promised by mining corporations to compensate for disruption to traditional economic activity, this is often inadequate, delayed, or not forthcoming at all. Juan Martinez-Alier (2001) points out that, even if communities do receive financial compensation and improvements to local services, this does little to atone for the loss of social cohesion and environmental degradation that tends to accompany large-scale mining projects.

In summary, as with many cases of perceived environmental injustice, large-scale mining projects are often viewed in the South as an unwelcome burden for which local communities receive few compensatory benefits. They are undertaken by global corporations to feed growing demand in the North for certain commodities. By extracting and refining these commodities in the South, corporations are able to do so at reduced cost. This delivers benefits for their customers, who live mostly in the North. It also benefits their shareholders, who live mostly in the North. Yet the environmental devastation that is an unavoidable corollary of large-scale industrial projects, along with its ramifications for traditional economic activity and cultural practices, is experienced by less-affluent communities in the South. For this reason, such developments are often seen as instances of transference of the environmental costs of consumption from wealthier nations, where most of that consumption takes place, to the less-wealthy countries, in which primary production takes place.

Theory in Practice

Trafigura, Ivory Coast and environmental justice

This section has described a growing tendency for large-scale, primary-extraction operations to be located in developing countries. As a result, the demand for certain products in wealthy, developed nations may be met to the detriment of less-affluent communities in less-developed countries. But there are other ways in which industrial detritus is conveniently taken out of sight of those who benefit most from it. Developed nations are increasingly shipping the waste products of industrial production to developing nations, where disposal can be carried out at lower cost (Clapp, 1994; Kokou, 2006; Milmo, 2009). The following case considers one particular instance of this.

Trafigura is one of the world's largest companies. It sources and trades crude oil, petroleum products, renewable energies, metals, metal ores, coal and concentrates around the globe (Trafigura, 2014a). The company has 167 offices in 58 countries on six continents (Trafigura, 2014b). In 2006, Trafigura's turnover was $45 billion (Amnesty International and Greenpeace Netherlands, 2012). Trafigura takes its corporate responsibilities seriously. A section on its website is dedicated to 'Responsibility' and the subtitle to this section, displayed in large type, is: 'We make it our responsibility to contribute positively to the lives of those affected by our operations' (Trafigura, 2014c).

Ivory Coast is small nation on the west coast of Africa. Its gross national product in 2006 was $18 billion – less than half of Trafigura's annual turnover (Amnesty International and Greenpeace Netherlands, 2012). Abidjan is the economic centre of Ivory Coast and one of the largest cities in West Africa (BBC, 2013c). Abidjan's citizens have borne more than their fair share of the environmental burden of modern industrial production. The city is heavily industrialized, and many of its inhabitants eke out a meagre living by sorting through lorry loads of waste that are delivered daily to Abidjan's many rubbish tips (BBC, 2009c). However, in August of 2006, Abidjan was subjected to still further hardship when it received a consignment of industrial waste that even its beleaguered, rubbish-tip scavengers did not want to touch (Amnesty International and Greenpeace Netherlands, 2012).

The tale of how this waste made its way to Abidjan, and the part played by Trafigura in its voyage, has been the subject of a report by Amnesty International and Greenpeace Netherlands (2012). According to the report the story began towards the end of 2005, when Trafigura bought large quantities of unrefined petroleum, called coker naphtha, from a Mexican oil company. As petroleum products go, coker naphtha is very cheap to buy because it has an extremely high sulphur content, which needs to be significantly reduced before it can be used legally as fuel. However, a relatively simple refining process, referred to as caustic washing, can be used to reduce coker naptha's sulphur content. Therefore, by buying coker naphtha at a low price, refining it, and selling it on, Trafigura stood to make a very good profit.

The problem is that caustic washing of coker naphtha produces a residue that is so toxic that the process is banned in many counties. So, according to the

(Continued)

(Continued)

Amnesty International and Greenpeace Netherlands report, after trying unsuccessfully to arrange caustic washing of its coker naphtha shipment in Africa and the Middle East, Trafigura decided to carry out the refining process at sea. The company commissioned the vessel Probo Koala and conducted caustic washing whilst afloat in the Mediterranean. With the refining process completed, Trafigura now had its cheap, refined oil ready for onward sale at a handsome profit.

However, the Amnesty International and Greenpeace Netherlands report points out that Trafigura now faced a further problem: what should it do with the toxic residue left over from the refining process, which remained on board the Probo Koala? Initially, the waste was taken to the Netherlands for treatment. However, according to the report, when Trafigura was made aware of the cost of the extensive treatment that would be required to neutralize its toxicity, the company decided to look for a cheaper means of disposal elsewhere.

Accordingly, the Probo Koala set sail for West Africa in the hope of finding a suitable location to unload its unwanted cargo at lower cost. Amnesty International and Greenpeace Netherlands (2012) say that several attempts to dispose of the waste in Nigeria were unsuccessful. However, the report says that the company eventually struck lucky in Ivory Coast when the Ivorian firm Compagnie Tommy agreed to take the waste off Trafigura's hands for the knock-down price of $20,000.

According to the report from Amnesty International and Greenpeace Netherlands (2012), reservations have been expressed about Compagnie Tommy's capability to undertake the task for which it was contracted by Trafigura. The report suggests that, when offered the job by Trafigura, Compagnie Tommy had only just received its licence to operate and had limited experience of such work. Furthermore, the report alleges that the Akouédo open-air dumpsite at which Compagnie Tommy proposed to unload the waste did not have the facilities needed to treat it properly. Nevertheless, on 19 August 2006, the Probo Koala arrived in Abidjan and unloaded its cargo. According to the report, some of the waste was dumped at the Akouédo site. The rest was distributed around a range of locations, including local drainage ditches and tips, by a fleet of truck drivers hired by Compagnie Tommy.

The Amnesty International and Greenpeace Netherlands (2012) report says that, the following day, many of the residents of Abidjan woke to an appalling smell. In the following weeks, tens of thousands fell ill with headaches, vomiting, diarrhoea, skin irritations, breathing difficulties and bleeding noses.

Trafigura has denied responsibility for the health problems experienced by the people of Abidjan. It has argued that no definitive link has been established between the dumping of its waste and the illnesses experienced by local people.

Moreover, it claims that the Amnesty International and Greenpeace Netherlands report on the episode 'does not set out a fair or balanced account of the Probo Koala incident, but is rather a report that has been designed to support the stated position of Greenpeace' (cited by Amnesty International, 2012b). Meanwhile, Bell Pottinger, a public relations firm that represents Trafigura, has claimed to be 'appalled' by the report, saying it was 'premature', 'inaccurate', 'potentially damaging', 'poorly researched' and 'deeply flawed' (cited by Leigh, 2009). Lawyers representing Trafigura have also threatened libel action against media companies, including the BBC, *The Times*, *The Guardian*, *Volkskrant* and Norwegian TV, who have reported on the incident (Leigh, 2009).

Nevertheless, the Amnesty International and Greenpeace Netherlands (2012) account of the aftermath of the incident reports the following developments. In return for immunity from prosecution in Ivory Coast in relation to this incident, Trafigura has agreed to pay nearly $200 million to the Ivory Coast government. Trafigura also paid a further $45 million in 2009 to settle a legal case for additional compensation that had been brought by Abidjan residents in a UK court. Moreover, on 23 July 2010, a Dutch court handed down a guilty verdict on a number of counts against Trafigura Beheer BV, a London-based executive of Trafigura Ltd, and the captain of the Probo Koala for illegally exporting waste from the Netherlands. Meanwhile, the owner of Compagnie Tommy has been jailed for 20 years in Ivory Coast for poisoning local people by illegally dumping untreated toxic waste.

Questions

1 It is alleged by the Amnesty International and Greenpeace Netherlands report that, by refining coker naphtha cheaply and disposing of the waste at low cost in Ivory Coast, Trafigura hoped to produce low-cost oil. If this is the case, who stood to benefit from this operation?
2 If the Amnesty International and Greenpeace Netherlands report is accurate, who bore the burden of this cut-price oil production?
3 According to the Amnesty International and Greenpeace Netherlands report, Trafigura appointed the Ivory Coast firm, Compagnie Tommy, to dispose of large quantities of toxic waste on its behalf; a task for which Compagnie Tommy seems to have been ill equipped. If this allegation is correct, do you think Trafigura should be held responsible for the consequences of the subsequent illegal dumping? Or, by contracting Compagnie Tommy to do the job, would Trafigura have absolved itself of ethical responsibility for what happened to the waste thereafter?

Some comprehensive approaches to environmental sustainability

This chapter began by considering various *anthropocentric* and *biocentric* ways of attributing value to the natural world. The last two sections have explored the possibility that a characteristically northern preoccupation with wilderness and wildlife preservation, along with the growth of industrial activity in southern nations, may uphold the values and interests of wealthy people in the North whilst undermining those of less affluent communities in the South. The chapter will end by introducing the idea that a sustainable solution to the environmental challenges that confront us may demand a radical rethink of the way that we live our lives and the way that we do business.

The work of Arne Næss has been particularly influential in this respect. Næss contrasts 'shallow ecology' with 'deep ecology' (1973, 2010/2008), proposing that the former offers an inadequate basis for developing a sustainable relationship with the environment. As Næss sees it, *shallow ecology* takes as its prime concern 'the health and affluence of people in developed countries' (1973: 95) and it identifies pollution and resource depletion as the greatest barriers to achieving this objective. The environmental policies of shallow ecology tend, therefore, to focus on issues such as recycling and developing alternative energy sources. The aim of these policies is to maintain the lifestyles to which those in the developed world have become accustomed whilst minimizing environmental harm.

Deep ecology, on the other hand, proposes a more comprehensive response to environmental challenges. It shares shallow ecology's concern about pollution and resource depletion, but proposes that these issues cannot be addressed without altering the lifestyles that shallow ecology seeks to preserve. Deep ecology finds attitudes that pervade contemporary society to be inherently unsupportive of a sustainable relationship with nature. And, of particular importance for business ethics, it finds some of those attitudes manifested most obviously in prevailing economic structures. Addressing environmental challenges, for Næss, thus requires changes to those structures. Rather than carrying on with business as usual, it demands 'reforms that will have consequences for all aspects of human life' (Næss, 2010/2008: 231).

The rest of this chapter will outline some issues that have been identified by Næss and others, along with some responses that they propose for developing a more sustainable relationship with the natural world. Specifically, the environmental implications of *consumer culture*, *logic of domination* and *denial of proximity* will be considered, and some ramifications for business will be identified.

Consumer society and environmental degradation

An obvious way in which business activity might conflict with environmental sustainability is through its contribution to resource depletion and waste production. In this respect, the developed nations of the North are considerably more profligate than the less-developed nations of the South. Bill McKibbin (2010/1998) uses the metaphor of a balloon to illustrate this issue. He invites us to imagine that a balloon floats above each person's head, carrying the natural resources that are consumed in order to provide for that person's daily needs. As McKibbin points out, the size of balloon that each of us would require would depend a lot on how we lead our lives. For instance, he notes that an average citizen of the USA would need to carry a balloon that is 20 times bigger than that of a Costa Rican, 50 times bigger than a Malagasi's, and 70 times the size of a Bangladeshi's.

McKibbin's balloon metaphor encourages us to reflect on what those of us who carry the biggest balloons could do to reduce their size. In other words, he invites us to think about how we could lead our lives in ways that are less consumptive of natural resources. He also highlights the need for people in developing nations to think about how economic development is likely to increase the size of their ecological balloons. He thus encourages reflection on how developing nations might improve their people's lifestyles without emulating the environmental recklessness that has so far characterized the developed world.

In this respect, the culture of consumerism has received a lot of attention, with a number of commentators highlighting the link between our fascination with buying and selling things and what McKibbin might refer to as our ecological balloon (see for example Galbraith, 1999/1958; Marcuse, 2002/1964; Baudrillard, 1997/1970; Bookchin, 2010/1993; Hamilton, 2003). Consumer culture has a pervasive hold in contemporary society. For most of us, our ability to buy new things and to display our purchases conspicuously says a lot about who we are and what we are. Similarly, at a national level, most countries evaluate their prosperity in terms of economic growth, which mainly reflects the amount of stuff that is being made, bought and sold within them. Consumption is therefore an important component of each person's individual identity and social status, while the ability to consume is taken as a key indicator of national well-being.

The self-evident problem with all of this is that the more we consume, the more resources we use up, and the more waste we produce in making stuff and disposing of the stuff that we no longer want. Of course, shallow ecology encourages us to enhance the efficiency of production and to dispose of waste in less-polluting ways. However, as Næss points out, any benefits that accrue from such measures are likely to be minimal as long as we remain so committed to consumption. In order to lead more environmentally sustainable lives, therefore, changing the way that we do things may not be enough; we may also need to have a radical rethink about the individual, social and political priorities that define contemporary society.

This creates a particular challenge for business, which plays a key role in sustaining consumer culture. In a competitive, free-market economy, it is part of the raison d'être of any business to sell its produce. Corporations therefore seem to be unavoidably programmed to do whatever they can to encourage sales. Consequently, the wheels of production and consumption are continually oiled by well-resourced corporate marketing departments, which bombard potential customers with sophisticated advertising messages encouraging them to buy new stuff that they may not really need, and to throw away the old stuff that is thus rendered obsolete. For this reason, critics of consumer culture urge us to evolve less environmentally damaging ways of organizing economic activity. In particular, they highlight the need to consider alternative ways of doing things that do not place so much emphasis on maximizing consumption.

Video Activity 9.5

In the following video, Joseph DesJardins proposes three principles for sustainable business. He calls these principles *eco-efficiency*, *bio-mimicry* and a *shift from products to services*.

www.youtube.com/watch?v=FrTElMJGXTE

Question

This section has highlighted Arne Næss's distinction between *shallow ecology* and *deep ecology*. A *shallow-ecology* approach might encourage businesses to change *how* they do things, by using resources and disposing of waste in a more environmentally responsive fashion. *Deep ecology*, on the other hand, demands a rethink of the individual, social and political priorities that define contemporary society; it calls upon us to change *what* we do. Consider each of the sustainable-business principles suggested by DesJardins. To what extent do you think each principle proposes changes to *how* businesses do things and to what extent does it suggest more fundamental changes to *what* businesses do?

Unravelling the logic of domination

Many environmentalists propose that if we are to develop a more sustainable relationship with nature, we need to live in harmony with it. That is, we should not set out to dominate nature; rather, we should acknowledge our interdependency with the natural environment and establish respectful coexistence with it. However, environmental writers have also suggested that establishing a mutually respectful, harmonious relationship with the natural world is hard to do when we do not even live in mutually respectful harmony with other humans. They suggest that attitudes towards other humans and those towards nature are two aspects of the same mindset, and if we are to change one aspect we must also address the other. Therefore, in order to establish a more-sustainable relationship with nature, we need to develop more-sustainable relationships with one another.

In particular, a number of commentators have highlighted ways in which human relationships are shaped by a *logic of domination* (Marcuse, 2002/1964; Warren, 2010/1990; Bookchin, 2010/1993). Moreover, some observe that that same logic of domination gets carried over to our attitudes towards the environment. As Murray Bookchin describes it:

> With the rise of hierarchy and human domination … the seeds are planted for a belief that nature not only exists as a world apart, but that it is hierarchically organized and can be dominated … the *idea* of dominating nature has its primary source in the domination of human by human and the structuring of the natural world into a hierarchical Chain of Being. (2010/1993: 272)

The roots of this logic of domination have been located in the *hierarchical* approach that we often take towards *difference* (Warren, 2010/1990; Bookchin, 2010/1993; Næss, 2010/2008). In other words, when we identify things as being different from one another, we try to categorize them and, in doing so, we tend to do it in hierarchical terms. We are not content to view categories as being merely different from one another; we also feel the need to establish a value hierarchy so that we can judge some categories as better than others. And once we have judged some categories as better and others as worse, we are inclined to use this hierarchical classification to justify the domination of the 'worse' by the 'better'.

Pause for Reflection

Think back to the *resource anthropocentrism* that was discussed at the beginning of this chapter. Can you see any relationship between this and the hierarchy-based *logic of domination* referred to here?

The workings of a hierarchy-based logic of domination have been identified in various aspects of human relations. For instance, *ecological feminists* (see Warren, 1994) highlight its effect on relationships between men and women. They perceive a link between the long-standing domination of women by men and humans' domination of nature, suggesting that both forms of domination need to be viewed as examples of the same, wider phenomenon. Ecological feminists propose that, if we are to develop a more sustainable relationship with nature, we must also unravel the relationships of domination which prevail between the sexes.

The pervasive influence of the logic of domination has also been identified in relationships between *socio-economic classes*. Writers such as Bookchin (2010/1993) and Næss (2010/2008) observe that the perceived superiority of certain human characteristics has been used to justify the hierarchical elevation of certain groups of people over others. This hierarchical elevation is then used to justify the domination of the latter by the former. Hierarchy and domination have also been highlighted in *international relations*. In particular, they have been found to suffuse relationships between the developing world and the developed world, finding expression in the historical colonization of large parts of Africa, Asia and South America by wealthy, European nations and, more recently, in the economic domination of the South by the North (Guha and Martinez-Alier, 1997; Næss, 2010/2008).

A common theme of these critiques is that they highlight a link between the domination of some humans by other humans and the domination of nature by humans. Both are regarded as outcomes of a common feature of human thought: our desire to order things hierarchically and to use this hierarchical classification as a justification for domination. Therefore, if we are to establish a more sustainable relationship with nature, we must challenge our desire to arrange things in hierarchical terms. We must get used to a new way of thinking about difference; of things as just being *different*, rather than as better or worse. We may then be able to establish relationships amongst humans in which domination is not so pervasive. And we might also develop a less-dominating attitude towards nature.

These considerations highlight the environmental benefits of establishing less-dominating relationships between sexes, classes and regions. They also hold specific implications for business insofar as they focus attention on the link between a firm's environmental policies and its broader cultural and structural arrangements. If a hierarchy-based logic of domination prevails in relationships within a company and in its relationship with various stakeholders, that logic of domination is also likely to shape its relationship with the environment. Conversely, a business that encourages supportive, mutually respectful cooperation in its internal and external affairs may also find it easier to engender a sustainable approach towards nature.

In this respect, Robert Solomon reflects ruefully on the 'macho myths and metaphors' (1992: 22) that pervade contemporary business thinking, which encourage businesspeople to conceive the business environment as a competitive battle for survival in which each feels he or she must dominate in order to avoid being dominated. Similarly, Gareth Morgan (1998) has highlighted the shortcomings of metaphors that portray organizations in purely political terms and which encourage employees to jostle for supremacy in hierarchical systems of control. The competitive, domination-oriented approach to business highlighted by Solomon and Morgan seem inappropriate to the establishment of a business culture that is consistent with environmental sustainability.

Video Activity 9.6

The following WKUK video, 'Business Battle', offers a light-hearted caricature of the 'macho myths and metaphors' that Robert Solomon identifies in some corporate contexts.

www.youtube.com/watch?v=e52dOCxWXiw

The business world is sometimes presented as a highly competitive environment, in which success demands domination of colleagues, customers, suppliers and other firms. Some environmental theorists would see this as an example of the *logic of domination* that shapes human relationships, which spills over into our relationship with the natural world.

Questions

1 The culture that prevails in any business is shaped partly by the management priorities that are set and the attitudes that are encouraged within that business. Can you identify any priorities and attitudes that might promote hierarchy and competition within companies, and which might therefore encourage *logic of domination*?

2 Can you identify alternative attitudes and priorities that might discourage *logic of domination* and which might thus engender a more-sustainable corporate relationship with the natural world?

The importance of proximity

So far, this section has drawn attention to some ways in which *consumer culture* and *logic of domination*, both of which are prevalent features of the corporate environment, might inhibit environmental sustainability. I will end by highlighting a third feature of contemporary business arrangements that may be unsupportive of sustainable relationships with the environment; that is, the increasing geographic dispersal of businesses. Of particular importance in this respect is what Zygmunt Bauman (1993), in a slightly different context, refers to as the *denial of proximity*.

A number of ethics theorists have highlighted the importance of proximity, or closeness, to ethical sensitivity (Levinas, 1969/1961; Bauman, 1993; Noddings, 2003). They suggest that we are more likely to act in an ethically responsive fashion towards other people if we have direct experience of the impact of our actions on those people, because this direct experience will arouse ethical sensitivity to their predicament. In other words, we are more inclined to care about what we do to people if we actually see it with our own eyes. And that first-hand experience is more likely if we are close to those people. Therefore, according to these theorists, the closer we get to people, the more likely we are to treat them ethically.

Arne Næss has applied these ideas about the ethically sensitizing force of proximity specifically to the context of environmental sustainability. He draws attention to the fragile nature of ecosystems and their vulnerability to ill-informed or irresponsible action by humans. He suggests that humans will show greater sensitivity to that fragility if they have direct exposure to the environmental consequences of their actions. For one thing, those who have direct exposure are likely to have the best understanding of how their actions impact on nature. But also, we are more likely to care about that impact if we experience it directly. For instance, I am more likely to care about the degeneration caused to a marine ecosystem by an oil spill if I witness that degeneration with my own eyes. The upshot of this is that the natural environment is likely to be treated with greater consideration by actors who are close to the consequences of their actions.

Just as Bauman (1993) highlights trends in contemporary business that deny decision makers proximity to the social implications of their decisions, Næss (2010/2008) identifies corporate trends that disconnect decision makers from the environmental consequences of business activity. In particular, he focuses on the increasing scale and geographic scope of corporations. He suggests that decision makers in large, centralized, global corporations are inevitably distanced from the environments that are impacted by their decisions. Decisions made in corporate head offices, in big cities, in developed nations, may have devastating impacts on distant ecosystems but, given their remoteness from those consequences, those who make those decisions may know or care little about their environmental impact. Conversely, Næss highlights the environmental merits of small, locally based firms, which supply local customers, which are supplied by local suppliers, which employ local people, and which impact mostly on their local environment. A localized business context is therefore, in Næss's view, inherently more supportive of environmental sustainability than a business context that is dominated by vast, global corporations.

Video Activity 9.7

Watch the following Greenpeace video, 'Ancient forest destruction':
www.greenpeace.org.uk/blog/forests/ancient-forest-destruction-video

Question

When you watched the opening scenes of this video, did it make you more sensitive to the plight of rainforest-dwelling animals that lose their home as a consequence of deforestation? If so, why do you think this is?

Some implications for business

The ideas introduced above highlight three features of prevailing social and economic structures that may hinder environmental sustainability: our fascination with consumerism; the logic of domination; and the distancing of decision makers from the environmental consequences of their decisions. Each of these features has significant implications for business, and in each respect the news does not seem to be particularly good for Næss's prescription for deep ecology. For a start, businesses are deeply implicated in the reproduction of consumer culture and this seems unlikely to change. Moreover, hierarchical structures and the logic of domination seem to be firmly entrenched in contemporary business. And lastly, the business environment is increasingly dominated by vast, global corporations, with whom local businesses compete at a significant disadvantage. Therefore, firms are getting bigger and their geographic scope is spreading, rather than becoming more locally and environmentally responsive.

These considerations indicate a fundamental tension between the tenets of deep ecology and contemporary business practice. However, they also draw attention to the need to think about alternative ways of doing business. Namely, they call into question the merits of consumer capitalism, underlining the desirability of exploring different ways of arranging the provision of goods and services. These considerations also highlight the merits of business structures and business cultures that are not based around hierarchy and domination, and in which business stakeholders can interact in a spirit of mutual cooperation. And finally, they draw attention to the advantages of political and economic measures which might help local businesses to resist the predatory avarice of global corporations.

Theory in Practice

The hamburger connection

Over 30 years ago, Norman Myers (1981) used the term 'hamburger connection' in relation to large-scale deforestation in Latin America. Myers's theory was that American rainforest is being cleared to provide grazing for cattle which, in turn, is being used to supply the USA fast-food industry's growing demand for cheap beef. Myers pointed out that the average beef consumption of a USA citizen had almost doubled in little over 15 years, largely due to the growing popularity of hamburgers. Conversely, beef consumption in some Latin American countries had actually gone down. Meanwhile, the extent of American rainforest had reduced by 40 per cent over a similar period.

(Continued)

(Continued)

Environmentalists are anxious about the clearance of rainforest for a number of reasons. As well as concern about the destruction of a vibrant ecosystem and the many species that depend upon it, there are also worries about losing the rainforest's capacity to absorb carbon and thus to counteract global warming.

Recent research indicates that the hamburger connection is still strong (Austin, 2010; Kaimowitz et al., 2013). Since Myers wrote his paper, global demand for beef has continued to escalate as fast-food culture – especially our passion for eating hamburgers – has spread around the world. Kelly Austin concludes that 'the vertical flow of beef up the world system is positively associated with deforestation in less-developed countries ... Thus, the hamburger connection can be conceptualized as a form of ecologically unequal exchange that increases deforestation in less-developed nations, and particularly so in Latin American nations' (2010: 295).

Questions

1 What *enlightened-anthropocentric* concerns might be raised about clearing rainforest to produce hamburgers?
2 What *biocentric* criticisms might be levelled at the clearance of rainforest to provide grazing for cattle?
3 Who do you think benefits most from the clearance of rainforest to provide cheap beef?
4 Why do you think people have become so keen to eat hamburgers in the last 50 years?
5 How might our treatment of rainforest be conceptualized as an instance of the *logic of domination*?
6 Do you think people in the developed world would be so ready to eat hamburgers if they witnessed, with their own eyes, some of the things that happen to animals and the natural world in order to make hamburger beef readily available?

Conclusion

Many people are concerned about environmentalism nowadays. It therefore seems sensible for businesses to think about how their activities might impact on the natural world. However, environmentalism is a complex topic, for there are many ways of valuing nature and many different agendas can be placed under the heading of 'environmentalism'. Exploration of the significance of the natural world for business ethics needs to take account of this complexity.

It is particularly important to recognize that our own environmental preoccupations may not be universally shared. In this respect, less-affluent parts of the world may have very different priorities to those which occupy people in more-developed nations. Moreover, we should be alert to the possibility that economic activity may offer benefits to some groups only by imposing considerable environmental burdens on other groups. Again, the contrast between affluent, developed nations and less-affluent, less-developed nations is important to such matters of environmental justice.

It is also important to consider the implications of prevailing economic arrangements for environmental sustainability. It may not be possible, in the longer term, to achieve the harmonious relationship with nature to which many aspire without changing the way we do business. Global corporations may proclaim their environmental credentials, telling their stakeholders of their sustainable sourcing policies, their responsible attitudes to waste disposal, and the lengths to which they go to mitigate their carbon footprint. However, all this may be of little consequence if their commercial imperatives, cultural priorities, and structural arrangements are fundamentally at odds with environmental sustainability.

Discussion questions

1. Drawing on the ideas introduced in this chapter, debate the ethical rights and wrongs of taking a job slaughtering cattle in an abattoir.
2. A lot of contemporary environmentalist debate revolves around the issue of climate change. Can you identify *anthropocentric* reasons why we should be worried about climate change? Can you identify *biocentric* reasons to be worried about it? Do you think concerns about global warming nowadays tend to be expressed in anthropocentric terms or in biocentric terms?
3. Can an adequate response to the problem of climate change be achieved without altering prevailing economic and social practices, or does it require fundamental changes to the way that we lead our lives and do business? If the latter, what sort of changes might be required?
4. Globalization is usually thought of as the increasing movement of goods, people, finance and ideas around the world. Identify ways in which globalization might help or hinder environmental justice and environmental sustainability.

Further study

David Keller's (2010) edited book, *Environmental Ethics: The Big Questions*, is an excellent collection of original writings on the topic. Some of the perspectives that are discussed in this chapter are explored more fully by Keller's contributors, as are some issues that have not been considered here. You might find the following of particular interest:

- A recent version of Arne Næss' seminal 1970s paper, 'The shallow and the deep ecology movement' is on pp. 230–34.
- A paper by Murray Bookchin, 'What is social ecology?' is on pp. 268–75. In this paper, Bookchin highlights some inherent tensions between capitalist economic structures and environmental sustainability.
- The topic of *environmental justice* is closely related to discussions of *environmental racism*. Two papers that address this issue are 'Environmental justice for all' by Robert Bullard (pp. 491–501) and 'Just garbage' by Peter Wenz (pp. 501–08).

Ramachandra Guha and Juan Martinez-Alier's (1997) book *Varieties of Environmentalism: Essays North and South* offers a critical challenge to the Northern environmentalist perspectives that are common in Europe and the USA. Guha's chapter on 'Radical American environmentalism and wilderness preservation: a Third World critique' is particularly thought provoking.

The topic of environmental justice is discussed in some detail in Leire Urkidi's (2010) paper, 'A glocal environmental movement against gold mining: Pascua–Lama in Chile'. As its title suggests, this paper considers environmental justice specifically in relation to a particularly contentious mining project in Chile. A rather different account of this particular project can be found on the website of Barrick Gold, the company that has undertaken it: www.barrick.com/operations/projects/pascua-lama/faq/default.aspx.

10 The Responsibilities of Business Executives: Just Looking after Shareholders' Interests or Taking all Stakeholders into Account?

Chapter objectives

This chapter will:

- explain how shareholder theory and normative stakeholder theory offer contrasting approaches to executive responsibilities;
- outline Milton Friedman's agency, free-market and usurpation arguments in support of shareholder theory;
- describe how normative stakeholder theory differs from instrumental stakeholder theory and enlightened shareholder theory;
- outline a stakeholder-investments argument, a respect-for-persons argument, and a reciprocity argument in support of normative stakeholder theory;
- highlight some characteristics of shareholder theory and normative stakeholder theory rationales.

Introduction

Most companies are run in a hierarchical manner. In other words, people at the top make the key decisions concerning those companies.[1] Those people are usually

[1]Whether this is an ethically desirable way of doing things, and whether it is the only way of doing things, are important questions in their own right. However, these are not questions that I will explore here – see Martin Parker's (2002) *Against Management* for an interesting discussion of such issues.

referred to as executives, or sometimes as managers. Executives/managers may also be directors, which means they have additional legal obligations in relation to their company. In this chapter, I will use the general term 'executives' to refer to these people. *Executives* should therefore be understood as people who hold senior positions in companies and who are their primary decision makers.

Executives sometimes own the company that they run. This may be the case where a company has been founded by an individual or a family and where that individual or family continues to manage it. It may also be the case when a team of executives buys a business from its previous owners. In large companies, though, it is more common to find executives running the business on behalf of somebody else. And even in those cases where executives do own the business that they manage, their ownership is likely to be shared with other people who do not have a role in running it. Generally speaking, then, there tends to be a *separation of ownership and control* in large companies: one set of people – usually referred to as shareholders – owns the company and another group – referred to here as executives – is employed to run the company on their behalf.

Clearly, executives perform an important role as far as business ethics is concerned. Although we often speak about companies being ethical or unethical, what we usually mean is that the people who control those companies are running them in an ethical or an unethical manner. Those people, those executives, therefore carry an onerous responsibility on behalf of the company that they manage. This raises a question that is fundamental to business ethics: what are the responsibilities of a business executive? In other words: who are business executives there to serve, and in whose interests should they run their company?

Questions such as these are often conceptualized in terms of a conflict between two contrasting perspectives. On the one hand there is the view, usually referred to as *shareholder theory*, which proposes that business executives' prime responsibility is to the shareholders – that is, to the owners – of the company that they run. According to this view, the goal of any business executive ought to be to make their company as profitable as possible since this is likely to enhance the company's value and will therefore serve the interests of those shareholders.

An alternative perspective has been referred to as *normative stakeholder theory* (Donaldson and Preston, 1995). This view holds that business executives have responsibilities to all the stakeholders who are associated with their company. This includes shareholders, of course, but it also includes groups such as employees, customers, suppliers, and people who live close to a business. It might even include society at large and the natural environment, since society and nature are usually affected by corporate activity. According to normative stakeholder theory, then, executives should not focus all their efforts on serving their shareholders by building share value; they should also take into account the needs and expectations of all those other stakeholders.

This chapter will explore both of these perspectives. It will begin by outlining some ethical rationales that have been offered in favour of shareholder theory. In particular, three arguments that have been put forward by Milton Friedman, one of shareholder theory's most outspoken proponents, will be discussed. The second half of the chapter will consider the other side of the argument. It will begin by describing some ways in which normative stakeholder theory differs from other approaches with which it might get confused. Three supporting rationales for normative stakeholder theory will then be outlined. The chapter will also draw attention to some characteristics of shareholder theory and normative stakeholder theory rationales. In particular, I will highlight some contrasting presuppositions made by either camp concerning the relative importance of various ethical considerations and the nature of business-stakeholder relationships.

The primacy of shareholders

When we speak of *shareholders* we may be referring to individual entrepreneurs, who founded and continue to own a company. Alternatively we might have in mind families or groups of private investors, who jointly own a business. More often, though, when we speak of shareholders, we are talking about people and institutions who hold shares in publicly quoted companies and who are able to buy and sell those shares on stock markets such as the New York Stock Exchange, the Tokyo Stock Exchange, Deutsche Börse, the London Stock Exchange, BM&F Bovespa, and the Australian Securities Exchange. You might find it helpful to bear in mind that, in the USA, people who own shares in publicly quoted companies tend to be referred to as *stockholders* rather than as shareholders.

The images that spring to mind when we think of shareholders, or stockholders, are not always flattering. Traditionally, shareholders have been depicted in the public imagination as wealthy speculators who make fortunes by trading on stock markets. However, to think of all shareholders in this way would be misleading. Indeed, some of the largest shareholdings in publicly quoted companies are held nowadays by so-called *institutional investors*. Institutional investors are large organizations, such as pension companies, insurance firms and banks, who invest money on behalf of their customers. By looking after shareholders, then, company executives are not just serving the interests of opportunistic, wheeler-dealing fat-cats, who gamble on the stock market; they are ensuring the financial viability of the pension funds, the insurance payouts, and the savings upon which many ordinary people depend.

The idea that a business executive's primary responsibility is to her or his shareholders is a pervasive one in the corporate world. Marc Goergen (2012) notes that this has long been the case in the USA and the UK, where there is a traditional expectation in firms that shareholder-value maximization will be pursued above all else. The rest of Europe and Japan have taken a broader view of corporate governance in the past; one which gives greater consideration to the interests of multiple stakeholders. Nevertheless, Goergen notes international convergence towards the Anglo-American model during the last 20 years. In general, then, there is an expectation that companies will be run in the interests of their shareholders and that 'while directors are expected to take into account the interests of other stakeholders, they should only do so if this is in the long term interests of the company, and ultimately its shareholders, i.e. its owners' (Goergen, 2012: 6). Moreover, the primacy of shareholders is supported by law in many nations. Although there is a certain amount of international variation in legal protection, shareholders' rights are enshrined in law in many countries whereas those of other stakeholders are not (Mallin, 2007).

Perhaps the most influential and frequently quoted statement of the ethical primacy of shareholders was offered by Milton Friedman in his 1970, *New York Times Magazine* article entitled 'The social responsibility of business is to increase its profits'. In this article, Friedman responded to what he considered to be a worrying development in American business discourse: that is, the importance that was increasingly being placed on so-called 'corporate social responsibility'. Friedman depicted corporate social responsibility as the idea 'that business is not concerned "merely" with profit but also with promoting desirable "social" ends; that business has a "social conscience" and takes seriously its responsibilities for providing employment, eliminating discrimination, avoiding pollution and whatever else may be the catchwords of the contemporary crop of reformers' (Friedman, 1970).

Friedman thought corporate social responsibility was a preposterous notion. As far as he was concerned, company executives should worry about one thing and one thing only: making as much money as they can for their shareholders. In his view, no other matter is the proper concern of an executive.

Some supporting rationales for shareholder theory

In his 1970 article, Friedman offered a number of reasons why executives should focus their efforts on generating shareholder value. I will outline here three of Friedman's arguments, which I will refer to as his *agency argument*, his *free-market argument*, and his *usurpation argument*. I focus on these particular arguments because they are arguably the most compelling of the rationales presented in Friedman's paper, and because they often crop up when people offer ethical justifications of shareholder theory.

Agency argument

The first of Friedman's arguments, the *agency argument*, proposes that since executives act as the agents of shareholders they should put shareholders' wishes above all other considerations. And since, according to Friedman, shareholders only wish is to make as much money as possible from their association with a company, this is what executives should seek to promote.

Separation of ownership and control

In order to understand Friedman's agency argument, it is important to appreciate the separation of ownership and control that exists in most large companies nowadays. As mentioned above, separation of ownership and control refers to the fact that one group of people (shareholders or, as Friedman calls them, stockholders) owns a company, while another group (executives) controls it. Of course, even where there is separation of ownership and control, there may be a certain amount of overlap because executives may own some shares in the company that they run. This is particularly so in large corporations, where shares and share options often form a substantial part of senior executives' reward packages. Nevertheless, in most cases, executives will only own a small proportion of a company's shares so, by and large, we can think of those who own a company and those who run it on their behalf as two separate groups of people.

Acting as a principal and acting as an agent

Friedman's agency argument hinges on this distinction between ownership and control. It also draws upon a further distinction that he makes between *acting as a principal* and *acting as an agent.* According to Friedman's definition, when I make decisions about my own life and my own possessions I am acting *as a principal.* At such times, I am controlling things that belong to me – *my* life and *my* property. It is therefore up to me what I do with them. When I act as a principal, then, I am at liberty to act however I choose: since the things that I am making decisions about are mine, I can use them as I wish.

When I *act as an agent*, on the other hand, I am not controlling my own property. Rather, I am looking after someone else's property on their behalf. And if I am looking after somebody else's possessions, Friedman suggests that I have a moral responsibility to do whatever that person asks me to do with them. Therefore, when acting as an agent I am not at liberty to do whatever I choose with the things under my control. I must, instead, do what the owner of those things wants me to do with them.

Business executives act as the agents of shareholders

Friedman points out that in most companies, in which separation of ownership and control exists, shareholders own a company and they appoint executives to run that company on their behalf. Executives therefore act as the agents of shareholders: 'The whole justification for permitting the corporate executive to be selected by the stockholders [shareholders] is that the executive is an agent serving the interests of his principal' (Friedman, 1970). And since executives act as the agents of shareholders, Friedman believes that executives have a moral responsibility to do with the company whatever those shareholders want them to do with it.

Business executives therefore have an ethical responsibility to maximize share value

Friedman also assumes that shareholders want to make as much money as possible out of the company that they own – that, after all, is usually why people buy shares in a company. Therefore, executives, as shareholders' agents, have a responsibility to make as much money for those shareholders as they can: they must do whatever they can to maximize share value. As Friedman describes it:

> In a free-enterprise, private-property system, a corporate executive is an employee of the owners of the business. He has direct responsibility to his employers. That responsibility is to conduct the business in accordance with their desires, which generally will be to make as much money as possible while conforming to the basic rules of the society … , in his capacity as a corporate executive, the manager is the agent of the individuals who own the corporation … and his primary responsibility is to them. (Friedman, 1970)

Friedman allows that when executives act outside of their corporate role, spending their own money, using their own possessions, and making use of their own time, they are acting as principals. Therefore, at such times they can do whatever they like. If they want to devote *their own* money to charity, or if they want to spend *their own* time working for environmental or social causes, that is up to them:

> As a person, [an executive] may have many other responsibilities that he recognizes or assumes voluntarily – to his family, his conscience, his feelings of charity, his church, his clubs, his city, his country … If we wish, we may refer to some of these responsibilities as 'social responsibilities.' But in these respects he is acting as a principal, not an agent; he is spending his own money or time or energy, not the money of his employers or the time or energy he has contracted to devote to their purposes. (Friedman, 1970)

However, when executives act on company business they are not acting as principals. At such times, they are acting as the agents of shareholders. At such times, then, Friedman demands that executives must do what shareholders want them to do with their property: that is, they must use it to make as much money as possible for those shareholders. They therefore have a responsibility to maximize share value, which they will usually do by making the company as profitable as they can.

Theory in Practice

Energy company executives: guilty of 'cold-blooded profiteering' or fulfilling responsibilities as shareholders' agents?

During 2013, Britain's largest energy companies were accused of making excessive profit to the detriment of their customers. A report in *The Guardian* newspaper

(Macalister, 2013b) revealed that the country's biggest gas and electricity suppliers had more than doubled their retail profit margins over the previous 18 months and were now earning an average of £95 annual profit per household on dual-fuel bills.

These profit levels were particularly contentious given that the UK had been hit by economic recession during this period, and many of the utility companies' customers had experienced financial hardship. Sam Robertson, a campaigner with the pressure group Fuel Poverty Action, referred to the companies' approach as 'cold-blooded profiteering' (cited by Macalister, 2013b), while Caroline Flint, the UK's shadow energy and climate-change secretary, suggested that 'What these figures show once and for all is that energy companies have increased their profits on the back of spiralling bills for hard-pressed consumers' (ibid).

On behalf of the energy companies, a spokesman for Centrica said his company's post-tax profit margin on the retail market had averaged 5% for the previous five years and was currently the equivalent of £50 per customer. However, he said that prices needed to go up because his company's costs and investment commitments had increased. In his view, the projected price rises represented 'a fair margin' (ibid).

Questions

1. Who would you consider to be the owners of the UK's big energy companies?
2. Why do you think those people have bought shares in the energy companies?
3. Who acts as the *agents* of these owners, looking after the energy companies on their behalf?
4. According to Friedman's agency argument, what is the responsibility of those agents?
5. Critics of the energy companies accuse them of sacrificing the interests of one particular stakeholder group to profit maximization. Which stakeholder group is this?
6. How would Friedman's agency argument respond to this criticism?

Agency argument and property rights

Milton Friedman's agency argument places a great deal of ethical importance on *property rights*. It proposes that, as the owners of a company, shareholders have a right to do whatever they wish with that company as long as this conforms to 'the basic rules of society' (Friedman, 1970). Since Friedman assumes that shareholders want to make as much money as possible from their company, they are entitled to do this: it is their property, so they can do with it as they wish. Friedman's agency argument also proposes that, when an owner asks an executive to look after their property (the company) for them, they have a right to expect that executive to do whatever they ask. And since shareholders want to make as much money as possible from their company, executives are ethically obliged to do this.

According to Friedman's analysis of rights, then, property rights take precedence over any other ethical considerations. Interestingly, when he speaks of the need for property owners to conform to 'the basic rules of society' Friedman does briefly mention 'those embodied in ethical custom'. However, he does not develop this point and, in general, property rights seem, for Friedman, to come first in ethical evaluation.

It seems that, for Friedman, if I own something I have a right to do whatever I want with that thing, as long as I do not break the law. This implies that any ethical obligations on my part to show consideration for my neighbours, for the environment, or for society at large take second place to my right to use my property as I choose. Moreover, if I give my property to someone else to look after, that person has an overriding obligation to do with it as I ask. Since that person is acting as my agent, they should not feel constrained by any other ethical obligations; they should put my property rights first and do with my property as I ask of them.

Pause for Reflection

Friedman's agency argument rests on the assumption that if I own property, then I am ethically entitled to do whatever I wish with that property so long as I do not break the law. Do you agree that property ownership gives a person a right to do whatever they want with their property, within legal limits? Or do you think we have an ethical obligation to use our property in a considerate manner?

A free-market argument

I will refer to a second argument Friedman offers in support of shareholder theory as his *free-market argument*. The free-market argument proposes that, if executives take social and environmental considerations into account instead of just making as much profit as they can, they will interfere with the smooth operation of free markets. And, for Friedman, to do this is to interfere with a fundamental right of companies and their stakeholders to conduct voluntary exchanges of property.

Economic activity as voluntary exchange

Friedman's free-market argument touches on a theme that is central to his broader thinking about economic arrangements. This is that economic activity should be shaped by market transactions between buyers and sellers, who participate in those transactions of their own free will. For Friedman, when a customer buys something from a company, they are making a voluntary purchasing choice; they are free to buy or not to buy the product that is offered at the price at which it is offered. Companies should be similarly free to provide products and services as they choose. Buyer-seller transactions are and should be the outcome of freely made choices on behalf of both parties to exchange money for goods at a particular price, which reflects the demand and supply of those products and services.

Other stakeholder relationships might be viewed in the same light. Thus, employees have a choice whether or not to work for a company at the wage that is offered: they can take it or leave it. Conversely, companies should be free to hire or not to hire employees at what they consider to be an appropriate wage. Likewise, according to this analysis, suppliers are free to supply or not to supply a company at prices established by market mechanisms; the choice is theirs. Meanwhile, a company is, and, according to Friedman, should be free to buy or not to buy at that price. The relationship between a company and its shareholders can also be viewed as a voluntary exchange, in which shareholders are and should be free to buy and sell shares in companies as they choose.

As far as Friedman is concerned, then, corporate activity should be shaped by voluntary buying-and-selling choices made by corporations and their stakeholders. The right to make such choices, for Friedman, is of fundamental importance.

Pause for Reflection

In an open market, where there are no restrictions on economic activity, do you think all people are equally free to choose whether or not to enter into economic exchanges? Can you envisage circumstances within an open market that might restrict, for example, an individual's freedom to choose whether or not to work for a particular company at the going wage?

Interfering with voluntary economic exchanges

Now, consider what happens when a corporate executive makes business decisions based on environmental and social considerations. When they do this, they allow those environmental and social considerations to disrupt market mechanisms. They thus interfere with the right of corporations and their stakeholders to participate in voluntary economic exchanges. According to Friedman, any corporate executive who does such a thing is guilty of breaching what he considers to be a fundamental human right: the right to participate in voluntary, non-coerced exchanges of property. As Friedman puts it:

> The political principle that underlies the market mechanism is unanimity. In an ideal free market resting on private property, no individual can coerce any other, all cooperation is voluntary, all parties to such cooperation benefit or they need not participate. There are no values, no 'social' responsibilities in any sense other than the shared values and responsibilities of individuals. (Friedman, 1970)

The free-market argument and property rights

Friedman's free-market argument, like the agency argument discussed above, is a rights-based rationale. And like the agency argument, it appeals to the primacy of property rights.[2] According to Friedman's analysis, market transactions are essentially exchanges of property: companies exchange their property (in the form of goods and services) for the property of customers (their money). Meanwhile, suppliers offer to companies the things that they own in exchange for money that belongs to those companies. And shareholders exchange money that they own for a share in the ownership of the company in which they thus invest. Even employment relationships, according to this account, can be conceptualized as exchanges of property: on Friedman's Lockean analysis (see Chapter 1), employees give up a particularly important form of their property – their own labour – in exchange for money that belongs to their employer.

For executives to allow considerations of social and environmental responsibility to shape economic activity would be to interfere with the exercise of these vitally important property rights. For this reason, the very notion of corporate social responsibility is, for Friedman, a 'fundamentally subversive doctrine' (1970) which strikes at the heart of a free society. Friedman concludes that in a free society, 'there is one and only one social responsibility of business – to use its resources and engage in activities designed to increase its profits so long as it stays within the rules of the game, which is to say, engages in open and free competition without deception or fraud' (Friedman, 1970).

Video Activity 10.1

During the last decade, fixed-odds betting terminals (FOBTs) have become a common feature in UK betting shops. These gaming machines offer customers a different sort of gambling experience to the over-the-counter format with which betting shops are traditionally associated. Customers using FOBTs are able to wager

[2]Friedman is actually rather ambiguous on this point. Although he often talks of the importance of freedom and property rights, he also offers a utilitarian-style justification for free markets in his 1970 paper and elsewhere. That is, he suggests that it will be better for everybody in the long term if economic activity is shaped purely by market mechanisms. Here, though, I focus on Friedman's appeal to rights.

up to £100 every 20 seconds on games like blackjack and roulette, interacting only with a machine and having no contact with other humans.

Since their introduction in 1999, FOBTs have aroused a lot of concern. Critics suggest that the short, 20-second timescale of each bet offers a gambler little opportunity for reflection and encourages compulsive, repetitive betting. Since users are able to lose £300 in a minute, a gambler can rack up huge losses in a single betting session. Moreover, the absence of human interaction whilst betting means that nobody is in a position to encourage a gambler to take a break and consider the consequences of what they are doing. The recent proliferation of betting shops on most UK high streets makes access to FOBTs very convenient. This also makes it hard for habitual gamblers to avoid the temptation they present. In commenting on FOBTs, Aditya Chakrabortty has concluded that 'This is what predatory capitalism looks like: betting shops with machines designed to suck cash out of communities, run by FTSE firms' (Chakrabortty, 2014).

In response to criticisms such as these the Association of British Bookmakers has agreed a voluntary 'Code for Responsible Gambling and Player Protection', which contains 'a series of harm minimisation measures that go far beyond those that are legally required' (ABB, 2013). According to the code, these measures include the following:

> machine players will be able to set their own monetary and time limits. When they reach either of those limits, then game play will be suspended for thirty seconds, and a message will pop up on the screen asking them if they want to stop playing.
>
> During that thirty second break, responsible gambling messages will appear on screen and staff behind the counter will also be alerted to the fact a player has reached their chosen limit.
>
> On top of that, all customers will receive mandatory reminders on screen when they have been playing for 30 minutes or lost £250, giving the player the opportunity to decide whether they want to continue or not. Again, staff behind the counter will be alerted that someone has reached those mandatory limits. (ABB, 2013)

Watch the following video, entitled 'Betting Britain: Social responsibility takes back seat as gambling flourishes', which shows an RT news item about FOBTs.

www.youtube.com/watch?v=KNKzYIs28pI&list=PLvWoMVGdsAKawOFs58r9Xo6oD6eccdqd0

(Continued)

(Continued)

Questions

1 How might the development of FOBTs and their introduction into betting shops serve the interests of betting-shop companies' shareholders?
2 In what ways might this have a negative social impact?
3 The use of FOBTs might be described, in Friedman's terms, as voluntary economic exchanges involving betting-shop companies and their customers. How might the British Bookmakers Association's Code for Responsible Gambling and Player Protection affect the right of betting-shop companies and their customers to participate in these voluntary exchanges?
4 Can you think of any ways in which the voluntariness of customers' participation in those exchanges might be inhibited by the design of FOBTs?

Usurpation argument

A third argument that Friedman makes in his 1970 article has been called his *usurpation argument* (Chryssides and Kaler, 1993). It is also sometimes referred to as the *tax argument.* It proposes that, if executives devote corporate resources to social and environmental causes they are, in effect, levying a tax on the company's stakeholders. And in doing this they are usurping a right that belongs to government alone.

Defining usurpation

The word 'usurp' is generally used to refer to the act of taking up a position or a role that rightfully belongs to somebody else. For instance, if somebody were to mount a coup d'état and depose the President of the USA, stepping into the role of leader of the nation, it could be said that that person was 'usurping' the President, or that they were 'usurping' the President's role. Friedman's usurpation argument draws on this meaning of usurpation. It proposes that if corporate executives devote resources to anything other than maximizing profit they are usurping a role that rightfully belongs to somebody else.

Social and environmental spending constitutes a form of taxation

Friedman's argument goes like this. If executives focus their efforts on social or environmental causes, this costs money. For instance, suppose the executives of a large, building-aggregates company decide that the law regarding waste disposal at their cement quarries is too lax, and that they have a responsibility to install waste-disposal measures that go beyond legal environmental requirements. In other words, they believe that they have an ethical responsibility to do more than they are legally compelled to do to protect the environment. Friedman points out that this would have to be paid for somehow. The money might come from the company charging a little more for its products; it might mean paying its employees and suppliers a little less; or it might come from paying a smaller dividend to its shareholders. More likely the cost of the executives' environmental responsibility would be funded from a mixture of all these sources. Whichever is the case, somebody will have to pay. As Friedman describes it:

> In each of these cases, the corporate executive would be spending someone else's money for a general social interest. Insofar as his actions in accord with his 'social responsibility' reduce returns to stockholders, he is spending their money. Insofar as his actions raise the price to customers, he is spending the customers' money. Insofar as his actions lower the wages of some employees, he is spending their money. (Friedman, 1970)

Freidman compares spending other people's money in this way to taxation. He suggests, therefore, that devoting corporate resources to environmental or social causes is the same as imposing a tax on customers, employees, suppliers, shareholders or whoever ends up paying for that expenditure: an executive who does this 'is in effect imposing taxes, on the one hand, and deciding how the tax proceeds shall be spent, on the other' (Friedman, 1970).

Only government has the right to impose and spend taxes

Friedman goes on to point out that no business executive has the right to levy taxes. This is something that only government has a right to do:

> the imposition of taxes and the expenditure of tax proceeds are governmental functions. We have established elaborate constitutional, parliamentary and judicial provisions to control these functions, to assure that taxes are imposed so far as possible in accordance with the preferences and desires of the public. (Friedman, 1970)

For an executive to devote corporate resources to social or environmental causes, then, is to usurp the role of government; it is to do something which no executive has a right to do. Moreover, since governments in most Western nations (Friedman is speaking primarily of the USA in his 1970 paper) are elected on the basis of manifestos which outline their tax policies and their social and environmental policies, these matters are usually agreed democratically. For an executive to 'decide whom to tax by how much and for what purpose' (Friedman, 1970) would therefore not only usurp government; it would be an affront to the democratic process. As Friedman sees things, it would amount to corporate executives spending other people's money on their own pet projects without even consulting those people:

What it amounts to is an assertion that those who favor the taxes and expenditures in question have failed to persuade a majority of their fellow citizens to be of like mind and that they are seeking to attain by undemocratic procedures what they cannot attain by democratic procedures. (Friedman, 1970)

Pause for Reflection

Friedman's usurpation argument assumes that corporate spending on social and environmental causes is undemocratic because it involves executives spending money on matters that *they* consider to be important, which may not be considered important by other people. Drawing on the ideas concerning discourse ethics discussed in Chapter 7 of this book, can you think of ways in which decisions about corporate social and environmental spending might be taken in a more democratic manner than Friedman envisages?

Rights and the usurpation argument

Like his agency and free-market arguments, Friedman's usurpation argument is a rights-based rationale. In this case, it appeals to the right of government officials to levy taxes and decide how they are to be spent. By devoting corporate resources to anything other than making profit, executives would be usurping that right. But even worse, since citizens have a democratic right to choose governments based on, among other things, their policies on taxation and public spending, for corporate executives to get involved in such matters would be anti-democratic: it would amount to executives spending people's money on issues that they consider important rather than that money being spent on issues that the voting public see as important. For Friedman, it would thus breach a fundamental democratic right of citizens to decide such matters.

Theory in Practice

Making the world a better place while making money from selling healthcare products

GSK is one of the world's largest providers of pharmaceutical, vaccines and consumer-healthcare products. It has offices in 115 countries, operates major product-research centres in the UK, USA, Spain, Belgium and China, and runs a global manufacturing network of 87 sites (GSK, 2013a).

The 'responsibility' pages of GSK's website tell of the resources the company devotes to social causes (GSK, 2013b). This includes PULSE, a programme which gives employees the opportunity to spend up to six months working for healthcare and child-support organizations at home and abroad. Employees are thus able to use the skills and expertise developed with GSK to help poor communities around the world solve the healthcare challenges that they face. It also includes Orange Day, an initiative that gives GSK employees one paid day off each year to volunteer for their chosen local community project. As an example of how this works in practice, in 2011 thousands of GSK's USA staff spent a day on charitable projects, which included packing more than 120,000 meals for flood victims in the USA and for victims of extreme weather events in Haiti, Kenya and Nicaragua.

GSK's website also proclaims the company's commitment to look after 'Our planet' (GSK, 2013c). It reports that the company has developed an environmental sustainability strategy, which includes challenging targets to reduce carbon dioxide and other emissions that contribute to climate change, to cut its water consumption, to reduce the waste that it produces, and to enhance the efficiency of its recycling processes. GSK's description of its environmental sustainability strategy implies that the company has committed itself to going well beyond legal minimum requirements in environmental care and that it has committed the necessary resources to achieve this.

Questions

1 Presumably, GSK's senior executives have decided the company's policies regarding social and environmental sustainability. How might Milton Friedman interpret their action as usurpation of a right that properly belongs to government?
2 GSK's investor pages state that the company has 'focused its business around three strategic priorities which aim to increase growth, reduce risk and improve long-term financial performance' (GSK, 2013d). On the face of it, this seems to contradict the statements made elsewhere about fulfilling social and environmental responsibilities, since it implies that enhancing commercial performance is GSK's primary objective. How might these two apparently contradictory sets of commitments be reconciled?

Summarizing shareholder rationales

To sum up Friedman's position, corporate executives have one responsibility: that responsibility is to make as much profit as they can in order to maximize the value of the company they manage for the benefit of its shareholders. The rationales Friedman offers to support this position are notable for the emphasis that they place on rights, particularly on property rights. Friedman's perspective is consistent with an understanding of stakeholders, including shareholders, as autonomous individuals, or groups of autonomous individuals, each with specific rights which must be respected. It resonates with the idea of business activity as comprising a range of transactions between rights-bearing entities, each of whom should be able to extract what they wish from those transactions as long as this neither breaks the law nor infringes any rights that are more compelling than their own. And, given the importance that Friedman places on peoples' right to use their property as they choose, property rights must occupy an especially privileged position in these rights-governed transactions.

Normative stakeholder theory

Normative stakeholder theory contests the notion that shareholders must always come first. It proposes that business executives should take account of all of the stakeholders who are affected by corporate activity. It thus challenges Milton Friedman's view that the property rights of shareholders must be executives' most pressing ethical consideration (Donaldson and Preston, 1995). It also suggests that the notion of corporate social responsibility may not be as preposterous as Friedman (1970) supposes.

In order to explain the commitments entailed by normative stakeholder theory, it might help to distinguish it from two perspectives with which it may get confused. The first of these perspectives has been called 'instrumental stakeholder theory'; the second is sometimes referred to as 'enlightened shareholder theory'. An overview of these various perspectives and the relationships between them is offered in Figure 10.1 (p. 388).

Distinguishing normative stakeholder theory from instrumental stakeholder theory

The distinction between *instrumental stakeholder theory* and *normative stakeholder theory* has been made by Thomas Donaldson and Lee Preston (1995) in their influential paper entitled 'The stakeholder theory of the corporation: concepts, evidence and implications'. In this paper, Donaldson and Preston differentiate three versions of stakeholder theory, but only two versions – the instrumental and normative forms – are relevant here. Instrumental stakeholder theory, they suggest, 'establishes a framework for examining the connections, if any, between the practice of stakeholder management and the achievement of various corporate performance goals' (Donaldson and Preston, 1995: 67). They contrast this to normative stakeholder theory, according to which 'the interests of all stakeholders are of intrinsic value. That is, each group of stakeholders merits consideration for its own sake and not merely because of its ability to further the interests of some other group, such as the [shareholders]' (1995: 67).

Instrumental stakeholder theory: highlighting the instrumental importance of influential stakeholders

Instrumental stakeholder theory, as described by Donaldson and Preston, builds on the notions of *influential stakeholders* and *instrumental relationships*, which were introduced in Chapter 1 of this book. Influential stakeholders, you may remember, were defined as groups or individuals upon whom the success of a business depends. Those groups or individuals therefore have influence over its commercial performance. Another way of saying this is that influential stakeholders have an *instrumental relationship* with a company; that is, their support is *instrumental* to its success.

As pointed out in Chapter 1, groups such as customers, employees, suppliers and shareholders can be counted amongst a company's influential stakeholders, since without their support no company would be in business for long. In other words, customers, employees, suppliers and shareholders have an instrumental relationship with a company; their support is instrumental to its commercial success. However, in addition to stakeholders who have a *direct* influence relationship with a company, there may be others who are able to influence its success *indirectly*. For example, policies implemented by local and national government might impact on the business environment in ways that support or hinder the activities of particular corporations and specific industries, so government can be thought of as an indirect influential stakeholder. Newspapers, TV companies and high-profile bloggers are sometimes supportive or critical of corporations, and their stance may influence the attitudes of customers, employees and so on. Therefore, they might also be thought of as having an indirect, instrumental relationship with a company. Moreover, the activities of non-government organizations and pressure groups, such as Greenpeace, Amnesty International and Friends of the Earth, may also enhance or tarnish a company's reputation. This, in turn, might impact on its commercial performance. Indeed, such groups sometimes even take direct action against a corporation, which may interfere with its operations. Non-government organizations and pressure groups, then, might also be included under the heading of indirect influential stakeholders.

Instrumental stakeholder theory, as Donaldson and Preston define it, acknowledges the instrumental importance of direct and indirect influential stakeholders such as these and adds the observation that effective management of such stakeholders is an important ingredient to commercial success. As Donaldson and Preston put it, instrumental stakeholder theory identifies 'the connections, or lack of connections, between stakeholder management and the achievement of traditional corporate objectives (e.g., profitability, growth)' (1995: 71). In highlighting the importance of customers, employees, suppliers, the media, the government, non-government organizations and pressure groups to corporate success, instrumental stakeholder theory draws attention to the need for companies to keep these groups happy if they are to prosper.

Understood in this way, instrumental stakeholder theory is consistent with shareholder theory. Since the interests of shareholders are linked to corporate success, effective management of instrumental stakeholders is in the interests of shareholders. Consider this connection in relation to a company that runs a chain of large supermarkets. That company's influential stakeholders include the people who work in its stores, the customers who shop at them, the firms and individuals who supply the goods the company sells, and, of course, its shareholders. Influential stakeholders also include local authorities who might grant or refuse planning permission for new stores; journalists and bloggers who might say good or bad things about the supermarket company and thus influence public opinion; and pressure groups that might support or oppose the construction of a new supermarket in a particular town. Clearly, a supermarket company needs to get as many of these stakeholders as possible on its side if it is to be successful. Instrumental stakeholder theory draws attention to this need. If the supermarket company's executives succeed in securing the support of all those stakeholders, business is likely to prosper. And this will be good news for the company's shareholders.

Normative stakeholder theory: highlighting the ethical importance of all stakeholders

Normative stakeholder theory, on the other hand, rests on a different understanding of the importance of stakeholders. As Donaldson and Preston put it, normative theory 'is used to interpret the function of the corporation, including the identification of moral or philosophical guidelines for the operation and management of corporations' (1995: 71). As far as normative stakeholder theory is concerned, stakeholders are not just instrumentally important; they are normatively, or ethically, important. Whereas instrumental stakeholder theory would highlight the need for the executives of our imaginary supermarket chain to maintain good relationships with customers, employees, suppliers, shareholders, politicians, journalists and campaigners on the grounds that this is good for business, normative stakeholder theory would draw attention to ethical reasons why executives should take stakeholders into account.

It is important to note that *instrumental stakeholder theory* does not necessarily accord intrinsic ethical significance to influential stakeholders. It merely highlights their importance to the achievement of corporate success. According to instrumental stakeholder theory, any responsibility that executives have to take stakeholders into account derives purely from their instrumental importance. *Normative stakeholder theory*, on the other hand, attributes intrinsic ethical significance to stakeholders. It suggests that stakeholders matter in their own right regardless of their importance to corporate success. Whereas instrumental stakeholder theory only acknowledges stakeholders' usefulness, normative stakeholder theory accords them intrinsic ethical importance.

The significance of this distinction becomes apparent when we consider the practical implications of instrumental stakeholder theory and normative stakeholder theory respectively. As far as instrumental stakeholder theory is concerned, only commercially useful people matter. If somebody is not in a position to influence the success of a company, that company's executives have no reason to take that person into account. For example, instrumental stakeholder theory offers executives no reason to consider the interests of those communities who have no influence over corporate success but who are nevertheless affected by their decisions. Nor does it offer grounds to take into account employees who are no longer needed, suppliers who no longer offer the best deal, or customers who no longer present an attractive sales proposition. As far as instrumental stakeholder theory is concerned, these people cease to matter as soon as they no longer offer the most effective means of achieving corporate success. Normative stakeholder theory, on the other hand, suggests that such people should still matter to executives, even when they become superfluous to corporate requirements.

Theory in Practice

Do banks have a responsibility to provide all customers with free access to their funds?

Most people who use cashpoint machines in the UK are able to do so free of charge. That is, they do not have to pay a commission to the provider of the machine in order to access their funds. However, there are exceptions. Although banks provide free-access machines in most high streets, shopping centres and other public places, cash machines are also sometimes found on private premises – in shops, casinos, and so on – and some of the owners of these premises charge people a commission to use the machine. So, whether access is free or not depends largely on whether a bank has chosen to install a machine in a particular location, or whether users have to rely on cash machines provided by other operators.

In January 2014, a newspaper report (Ramesh, 2014) suggested that many people who live in less-affluent areas are more likely to have to pay to withdraw money from cash-dispenser machines than those who live in more-wealthy areas. The report referred to findings of a survey undertaken by the *Which?* organization (Which, 2013). For instance, the survey found that, in the relatively poor London region of Hackney Wick, all of the 10 cash machines within a half-mile radius charged users between £1.75 and £1.85 to make a withdrawal. Similarly,

(Continued)

(Continued)

in Tottenham 27 of the 35 cash machines found by *Which?* charged users a £1.50–£1.85 fee. Meanwhile, in the wealthy areas of Hampstead, Kensington and Chelsea, 52 of the 64 cash machines located by *Which?* could be used free of charge.

More generally, the newspaper report quoted figures provided by Link, the body responsible for running Britain's cash machines, which found that more than 300,000 of Britain's poorest people, who live in 269 low-income areas, have to travel at least 1 km to use a free-to-use cash machine.

The implication of these findings is that banks have chosen not to locate branches and cash machines in less-affluent areas because the value of custom in these areas does not justify it. People who live in such areas therefore have no choice but to pay to use machines run by other providers. On the other hand, banks are keen to look after customers who live in affluent areas, since those customers bring far more value to the bank. Wealthy customers therefore have access to conveniently located, free-to-use machines. Remarking on this state of affairs, the Labour MP Frank Field observed that 'Getting the poor to pay for the privilege of taking out their own money is a grotesque practice, which should end immediately' (cited in Ramesh, 2014).

Questions

1 Customers comprise an important group of *influential stakeholders*. Which customers do you think are better placed to contribute to a bank's commercial success; in other words, which customers are more influential: its wealthy customers or its poor customers?

2 *Instrumental stakeholder theory* proposes that bank executives should take the greatest care to manage relationships with those stakeholders who have the most influence over the commercial success of their bank. How would the practice of offering their wealthiest customers the most convenient and cheapest access to their funds, whilst denying this service to their less-affluent customers, stand up to the demands of instrumental stakeholder theory?

3 *Normative stakeholder theory* proposes that bank executives should treat their stakeholders as ethically significant in their own right, regardless of their influence over commercial performance. How would the practice of offering their wealthiest customers the most convenient and cheapest access to their funds, whilst denying this service to their less affluent customers, stand up to the demands of normative stakeholder theory?

Distinguishing normative stakeholder theory from enlightened shareholder theory

A second approach that sometimes gets confused with normative stakeholder theory has been referred to as *enlightened shareholder theory* (for example Pichet, 2011). Enlightened shareholder theory builds upon the idea of 'enlightened value maximization' (Jensen, 2002). This is the observation that if a corporation is to build shareholder value in the long term then it cannot just focus on short-term commercial performance; it must build the resources and relationships needed for sustained commercial success.

Enlightened shareholder theory: highlighting the potential commercial importance of all stakeholders

Enlightened shareholder theory is related to instrumental stakeholder theory in that it is also based on the observation that sound management of stakeholders is important to long-term corporate success. Consider again our imaginary supermarket group. Suppose its executives mistreat its suppliers in order to boost short-term profits. Perhaps they delay payment beyond reasonable limits, so that suppliers experience cash-flow difficulties; or maybe they use the company's purchasing power to force prices down to levels that are unsustainable for suppliers; or they might put pressure on suppliers to drop the price of goods already supplied. All these things will probably boost short-term profitability, but they are also likely to impair the company's relationship with those suppliers. As a consequence, those suppliers may be less inclined to do business with that particular supermarket company in the future, which will not be in its long-term commercial interests. And neither will it be in the long-term interests of its shareholders.

Short-term profiteering such as this might be described as a case of bad management of one particular group of influential stakeholders: by prioritizing short-term profit, executives may impair relationships with their suppliers. However, by maximizing short-term profit in this way, a company may also undermine relationships with other influential stakeholder groups. For instance, if our imaginary supermarket company gets a reputation for mistreating its suppliers, people may be less willing to shop in its stores, or prospective employees may decide to go and work elsewhere. Executives may even find that potential investors decide not to buy shares in their company because they do not approve of the way it treats its suppliers.

By mistreating one group of influential stakeholders, then, executives might impair their company's relationships with many other influential stakeholders, which will damage long-term commercial performance. And, clearly, this will not serve the interests of the company's shareholders. However, this may also happen if executives treat stakeholders who do not have an influence-based relationship with the company badly. For instance, suppose our imaginary supermarket sells products whose manufacture involves cruelty to animals. Those animals have no influence over the corporation, so they cannot be thought of as influential stakeholders. Nevertheless, selling such products may damage the company's reputation which may, in turn, lead to the loss of support of those influential stakeholders who disapprove of animal cruelty: some customers may take their custom elsewhere; some employees may choose to work elsewhere; and some shareholders may sell their shares if the supermarket group gets a reputation for indirectly supporting the mistreatment of animals.

It might therefore be argued that a company needs to treat *all* its stakeholders – influential and non-influential – well in order to achieve long-term commercial success. This is why enlightened shareholder theory is referred to as 'enlightened': it can be described as an *enlightened* approach to building shareholder value, which takes a long-term perspective, as opposed to a *non-enlightened* approach which only focuses on short-term profits. Enlightened shareholder theory therefore seems to go a stage further than instrumental stakeholder theory in calling upon executives to respect all stakeholders' interests and expectations. Whereas instrumental stakeholder theory just draws attention to the commercial importance of influential stakeholders, enlightened shareholder theory proposes that all stakeholders should be taken into account by executives because not doing so could impair their company's reputation, which, eventually will undermine profitability and share value.

Enlightened shareholder theory: the ethical importance of stakeholders derives from the ethical importance of shareholders

It might therefore seem that since long-term commercial success, which is in the interests of shareholders, demands that executives take *all* stakeholders into consideration, there is no conflict between enlightened shareholder theory and normative stakeholder theory. However, there is one very important difference between enlightened shareholder theory and normative stakeholder theory. This is that enlightened shareholder theory only accords intrinsic ethical significance to shareholders. The value of all other stakeholders, and the reason for treating them with respect, is derivative: these other stakeholders are only important as a means to the end of looking after shareholders. In the case of our imaginary supermarket company, enlightened shareholder theory suggests that looking after shareholders is the only thing that really matters. Being nice to suppliers and animals is only important as a means to that end. Suppliers and animals have no intrinsic normative significance; they do not matter to executives in their own right.

Normative stakeholder theory: stakeholders have intrinsic ethical importance

Normative stakeholder theory, on the other hand, suggests that all stakeholders should be treated as ethically significant *in their own right*. It does not consider suppliers and animals to be ethically important just because they help to build share value. It accords ethical relevance to them regardless of any relationship they might have with corporate performance. Unlike enlightened shareholder theory, normative stakeholder theory proposes that executives should take those who are affected by corporate activity into account even when doing so has no impact on profitability.

The importance of this difference in the attribution of ethical significance becomes clear if we envisage a situation in which the interests of a particular group of stakeholders are not consistent with commercial performance. Consider, again, the case of our imaginary supermarket chain and its policies concerning suppliers. Suppose there are many alternative suppliers of a particular product, so the supermarket company's executives need not worry too much about tarnishing relationships with one particular supplier. Or suppose that particular supplier is so dependent upon the supermarket's custom that she could not withdraw from the supply relationship even if she wanted to. And suppose, furthermore, that most of a supermarket company's influential stakeholders are unaware of how that company treats its suppliers and, anyway, they would not be too bothered even if they were to be made aware. In this case, according to enlightened shareholder theory, there is no reason for the executives of the supermarket company to bother about that particular supplier; she has no commercial importance so she has no ethical significance. If influential stakeholders do not know, or do not care about how a particular non-influential stakeholder is treated by a company, then its executives have no reason to care about that non-influential stakeholder.

According to normative stakeholder theory, on the other hand, suppliers and all other stakeholders are deserving of consideration no matter what their commercial importance to the corporation may be. Therefore, even an easily replaceable, heavily dependent supplier, about whom influential stakeholders neither know nor care, is deserving of executives' consideration.

Video Activity 10.2

Watch the following two videos. Both relate to events that took place during the 1990s involving the Shell oil company. Although these events took place nearly 20 years ago, they are landmark cases in the development of public and corporate attitudes to business ethics. Moreover, their repercussions continue to affect Shell and its stakeholders today.

www.youtube.com/watch?v=KToV-c8uvPc

www.youtube.com/watch?v=htF5XElMyGI

The first video is a Planetinternational film entitled 'Brent Spar Greenpeace vs. Shell'. It tells of Greenpeace's efforts to prevent Shell from dumping the Brent Spar

(Continued)

(Continued)

oil rig on the ocean bed after it had become obsolete. Greenpeace waged a high-profile campaign against the proposed sinking of the rig, which attracted a lot of media interest and political support. It also inspired a consumer boycott of Shell petrol stations. Shell's executives eventually decided not to sink the Brent Spar. Instead, they took the more costly action of dismantling the rig and recycling as much of its material as possible.

The second film, made by ShellGuilty, is called 'The Case Against Shell: "The Hanging of Ken Saro-Wiwa Showed the True Cost of Oil"'. It reports Shell's oil-drilling activities in the Ogoni region of the Niger Delta, local protest against Shell, and Nigerian government action to suppress that protest.

Questions

1 In the case of Brent Spar, can you identify one particular group of stakeholders, who had *direct influence* over the commercial success of Shell, whose response to the proposed sinking of the rig may have encouraged Shell's executives to change their plans? (A clue to the identity of this group can be found in the last words spoken on the video.)
2 Can you identify other groups of stakeholders, who had an *indirect influence* over Shell's commercial success and who, by drawing attention to the proposed dumping of the rig, encouraged the response from the stakeholders referred to in Question 1?
3 *Instrumental stakeholder theory* suggests that Shell's executives need to manage influential stakeholders effectively if their company is to prosper. How might the initial decision to dump Brent Spar be interpreted as poor management of influential stakeholders?
4 Do you think Shell's executives changed their minds about what to do with Brent Spar because they recognised that the natural environment, along with all those who are impacted by it, are intrinsically deserving of their consideration (as proposed by *normative stakeholder theory*)? Or were they just trying to manage their influential stakeholders more effectively than they had done initially (as proposed by *instrumental stakeholder theory*)?
5 The case of Brent Spar might be offered in support of *enlightened shareholder theory*. That is, it seems to demonstrate that looking after the environment and those who are affected by it is ultimately good for shareholders (on the basis that had Shell's executives gone ahead with the sinking of Brent Spar they would have lost the support of many customers, which would have been bad for business,

which would have been bad for shareholders). Therefore, there seems to be no conflict between looking after shareholders and looking after other stakeholders. However, the second video suggests that this may not always be the case. In this second set of events, profit maximization (and the interests of Shell's shareholders) seems to have conflicted with the interests of one particular group of stakeholders who are deeply affected by Shell's activities: namely, the Ogoni people. Why do you think, in this case, Shell's executives prioritized their responsibilities to maximize shareholder value over the interests of the Ogoni people?

Why it is important to distinguish normative stakeholder theory from instrumental stakeholder theory and enlightened shareholder theory

Despite the importance of the distinction between, on the one hand, normative stakeholder theory and, on the other hand, instrumental stakeholder theory and enlightened shareholder theory, this distinction is often overlooked by businesspeople and by some business ethicists. It is by no means unusual for practitioners and theorists to suggest that looking after shareholders and looking after other stakeholders amount to one and the same thing because, if executives did not treat all their stakeholders well, they would lose the support of those stakeholders and their reputation would be damaged, which would be bad for business. And this, it is argued, would be bad for shareholders. Therefore, it is often concluded, it is in the interests of shareholders that executives treat all other stakeholders well: looking after stakeholders is therefore good for shareholders, and looking after shareholders is good for stakeholders.

As the above discussion indicates, this may indeed be the case as far as some stakeholders are concerned. But it is not the case for all stakeholders. There are always likely to be stakeholders who are affected by corporate activity who have no influence over a business, so instrumental stakeholder theory offers executives no reason to take them into account. And there are always likely to be stakeholders who are affected by corporate activity about whom influential stakeholders neither know nor care, so enlightened shareholder theory offers no reason for executives to take them into account. Nevertheless, normative stakeholder theory proposes that such people ought to be taken into account by executives. To suggest that there is no conflict between shareholder theory and normative stakeholder theory, then, amounts to misplaced optimism. A corporate executive will inevitably encounter instances where the interests of shareholders conflict with the interests of certain other stakeholders. For this reason, normative stakeholder theory should not be brushed under the carpet as an irrelevancy. It offers an alternative to shareholder theory, and it often entails contrasting courses of action to those indicated by the application of shareholder theory.

Shareholder theory

Executives' main ethical responsibility is to shareholders

Normative stakeholder theory

Executives have an ethical responsibility to take into account all those stakeholders who are affected by corporate activity (all affected stakeholders).

Instrumental stakeholder theory

Executives must manage relationships with influential stakeholder if they are to ensure corporate success

Instrumental stakeholder theory **is consistent with** *shareholder theory* because:

- executives must take *influential stakeholders* into account if they are to ensure corporate success;
- corporate success is in the interests of *shareholders*;
- therefore taking *influential stakeholders* into account is in the interests of *shareholders*.

However, *instrumental stakeholder theory* **differs from** *normative stakeholder theory* in that:

- as far as *instrumental stakeholder theory* is concerned, if somebody who is affected by corporate activity has no influence over corporate success, executives have no reason to take that person into account;
- for *normative stakeholder theory*, on the other hand, all people who are affected by corporate activity should be taken into account regardless of the influence they may or may not have over corporate success.

Enlightened shareholder theory

Executives' main ethical responsibility is to shareholders, but they should take a long-term (enlightened) perspective on shareholders' interests

Enlightened shareholder theory **seems to be consistent** with *normative stakeholder theory* because:

- long-term corporate success is in the long-tern interests of *shareholders*;
- executives must take *influential stakeholders* into account if they are to ensure long-term corporate success;
- *influential stakeholders* care about the way companies treat their *affected stakeholders*;
- therefore, executives must also take *affected stakeholders* into account if they are to ensure corporate success in the long term;
- so, executives must take *affected stakeholders* into account if they are to serve the long-term interests of *shareholders*.

However, *enlightened shareholder theory* **differs from** *normative stakeholder theory* because:

- *influential stakeholders* may neither know nor care about how a company is treating some of its *affected stakeholders*, in which case *enlightened shareholder theory* offers no reason why executives should take those *affected stakeholders* into account;
- for *normative stakeholder theory*, on the other hand, executives should take all *affected stakeholders* into account regardless of whether *influential stakeholders* know or care about them.

Figure 10.1 Comparing shareholder and stakeholder theories

Some supporting rationales for normative stakeholder theory

Although it is tempting to draw on instrumental stakeholder theory or enlightened shareholder theory to suggest that the interests of shareholders and normative stakeholders are in harmony as long as we acknowledge the importance of influential-stakeholder management, or as long as we take a long-term, enlightened perspective on shareholder value, this temptation should be avoided. The interests of shareholders and certain normative stakeholders are often in conflict. Therefore, it will not do to dismiss the importance of normative stakeholder theory on the basis that it is not really opposed to shareholder theory. The question remains, then: how should executives respond when they encounter tensions between the interests of shareholders and those of other stakeholders? In particular, given the compelling rationales that are offered in favour of shareholder theory, and given the weight of expectation upon executives to put the interests of shareholders first, what justification might those executives have for acting in the interests of other stakeholders?

Here, I will outline three justifications that have been put forward in support of normative stakeholder theory: a *stakeholder-investments argument*; a *respect-for-persons argument*; and a *reciprocity argument*. After describing each, I will highlight some presuppositions upon which they are based concerning the ranking of ethical considerations and the relationship between business and society. I will also point out some ways in which these presuppositions differ from those which underpin Milton Friedman's justifications for shareholder theory.

Stakeholder-investments argument

The first of these rationales, the *stakeholder-investments argument*, proposes that if somebody makes an investment in a company they are entitled to have their interests taken into account by corporate decision makers. However, whereas shareholder theory focuses only on the investments made by shareholders, the stakeholder-investments argument also highlights significant investments that other stakeholders make in a company, some of which carry a high level of risk. Therefore, according to this argument, those stakeholders also have a right to consideration.

Shareholder investments

The practice of *investing* is very important to capitalist business models. Most businesses are only able to thrive if people invest in them. For example, the money that shareholders invest in a company enables that company to buy the things it needs to run its operations and to make a profit. Such investment also helps a company to grow. In return for their investment, shareholders become part-owners of a company. Usually, they do this in the hope that they will receive a return on that investment. This tends to happen through the award of dividend payments to shareholders or through an increase in the value of their shares, which enables them to sell those shares at a higher price than they paid for them.

Investing is, of course, a risky affair. Although investors hope for a return on their investment, this can never be guaranteed. The company that shareholders invest in may not perform as well as they hoped, in which case their investment will lose value. The company may even go bust, in which case shareholders will probably lose their investment altogether.

Shareholder theory places a great deal of importance on the investments made by shareholders. It proposes that by investing their property (their money) in a company, shareholders earn a right to be given priority by the company's executives. The risk that shareholders take by investing in a company makes this right even more compelling. If somebody is prepared to take a risk by investing in a business, it seems even more important that those who look after that investment should do so in the best interests of the investor. This idea is implicit in Milton Friedman's agency argument: shareholders take a risk by investing their property (their money) in a company; therefore their agents (the company's executives) have a responsibility to look after that investment to the best of their ability. As far as shareholder theory is concerned, this offers a good reason for executives to place shareholders' interests above all other considerations.

Other stakeholder investments

However, normative stakeholder theorists point out that shareholders are not the only people who make investments in a company (Boatright, 2002). The investments made by other stakeholders may not be as obvious as those made by shareholders, and they may not be so easy to quantify in financial terms. Nevertheless, those investments are often considerable and, as far as normative stakeholder theory is concerned, they also create rights on the part of the people who make them.

Consider, for example, some of the investments that a company's employees make in the business they work for. Some may work for a company for many years. They therefore invest a considerable part of their lives in helping it to prosper. Employees may also spend considerable time and effort developing specific skills that a company needs. And in doing all this, employees may forego opportunities to progress their careers elsewhere. Also, employees may have had to relocate to take up a job with a company, which involves all sorts of costs on their part. For a start, there are the financial costs of moving home. But there may also be social costs associated with taking up a new job. For instance, children's education may be interrupted as a consequence of a family relocating; a partner may have to interrupt their own career; old friends may be left behind and new friends may have to be made in the process of switching jobs. All of this represents a significant investment on the part of those employees; investments which enable a business to do well. Employees may therefore feel that, after all they have invested in a company, they have a right to consideration by its executives.

Customers also make important investments in a company just by purchasing its products. Those purchases are as important to commercial success as the financial investments made by shareholders. In buying a company's goods and services, customers may even become dependent on that company for continuity of supply or for the provision of ongoing, post-sale support. They invest in the expectation that this provision will be forthcoming. For instance, if I buy a new car I would expect the car manufacturer to carry on producing spares for my car over the life-cycle of the vehicle. By investing in that particular car, I become dependent on that provision. I would feel pretty aggrieved if I needed a new gear box in three years only to be told by my garage that the car maker had stopped supplying gear boxes for my model because its executives had decided to concentrate their resources on more profitable lines.

Investments made by suppliers also make an important contribution to a company's success. Suppliers might go to a lot of trouble to develop particular products in order to service the specific needs of the companies they supply. For instance, farmers often go to great lengths to develop particular strains of fruit, which conform to precise criteria concerning shape, size and colour, in order to meet the demands of supermarkets. In doing this, they forego opportunities to develop alternative strains, or to develop their land for other forms of agricultural production. If a supermarket drops a farmer with whom it had established a long-standing supply relationship, simply because its shareholders' interests are better served by sourcing its fruit in a cheaper market, that farmer is likely to suffer hardship as a result.

Investments made by stakeholders such as employees, customers and suppliers may therefore be as significant as those made by shareholders. In addition, those investments may carry as much risk, or perhaps even greater risk, as those made by shareholders (Blair, 1995; Boatright, 2002). This is because certain non-shareholder investments may not be as easy to withdraw from as those made by shareholders. If shareholders in a public company lose confidence in that company, there is usually a ready market on which they can dispose of their shares and thus redeem at least part of their investment; an alert investor can usually get out before things get too bad. Withdrawing from an investment is not always so easy for other stakeholders. It may not be so simple, for example, for an employee to switch jobs if she spots an impending change in her employer's HR policies, which may eventually lead to her redundancy. She is firmly locked into the investment she has made with that company; getting out is no simple matter.

Pause for Reflection

Think of a company in which you have recently invested as a customer, an employee, a supplier, or a shareholder. In what ways might the decisions made by the executives of that company impact on your interests? How easy would it be for you to redeem your investment if those executives made decisions that were against your interests? In other words, how easy would it be for you to get back what you have invested in the company if its executives did not do what you wanted them to do?

Now, to suggest that investments made by stakeholders such as employees, customers and suppliers entitle those stakeholders to be taken into account is not to say that the interests of any one of these groups should come first in executive decision making. It is merely to propose that they merit consideration. The investment made by a particular person does not necessarily entitle that person to special treatment; it just entitles them to be taken into account. But this is also the case for shareholders. Their investment entitles them to consideration, but it offers no grounds for their interests to be put above those of all others who make equally significant and equally risky investments in a business. Instead, they should be considered alongside those others. Executive responsibility is therefore conceived as a matter of balancing entitlements to consideration; of taking the interests of all stakeholders into account, rather than privileging those of shareholders.

Respect-for-persons argument

A second argument in support of normative stakeholder theory has been referred to as the *respect-for-persons* argument. It points out that shareholder theory entails that all other stakeholders should be treated purely as a means to the end of generating shareholder wealth, which is inconsistent with treating people with the respect that is due to them as rational beings.

Immanuel Kant: never treat people purely as a means to an end

The respect-for-persons argument draws on Immanuel Kant's *formula of the end in itself*, which was discussed in Chapter 3. The formula of the end in itself proposes that we have a duty to treat all other people as ends in themselves and never simply as a means to an end. In Kant's words, everybody has a duty to '*Act in such a way that you always treat humanity, whether in your own person or in the person of any other, never simply as a means, but always at the same time as an end*' (1948/1785: 91/66–7). Another way of putting this is that we should never use other people to bring about some objective that we desire.

Kant's formula of the end in itself is sometimes referred as the *principle of respect for persons* (Evan and Freeman, 1993), since it implies that we should always respect the dignity of human beings by treating them as having intrinsic worth rather than just having worth only because they help us to achieve something that we wish to achieve. Applied to business, the principle of respect for persons suggests that executives should respect the intrinsic worth of all people; they should not use some in order to serve the interests of others.

Shareholder theory involves using all other stakeholders to create shareholder wealth

William Evan and Edward Freeman (1993) point out that if business executives were to act in accordance with shareholder theory, the only people they would treat as an end would be their shareholders. Since shareholder theory proposes that shareholders take priority over all other stakeholders, it implies that every other stakeholder should be treated as a means to the end of building shareholder wealth. Customers, employees, suppliers, local communities and anybody else who is affected by business activity would not therefore be treated as an end in themselves; they would be treated purely as a means to the end of promoting the interests of shareholders. As Evan and Freeman point out, shareholders would thus be the only people whose human dignity would be respected. Executives' treatment of all other stakeholders would lack the respect for persons that philosophers such as Kant consider to be a fundamental criterion of ethical conduct.

For this reason, Evan and Freeman suggest that it is unethical to regard corporations as no more than vehicles for creating shareholder wealth. They should, instead, be treated as institutions in which the interests of all stakeholders can be accounted for. As they put it, 'The very purpose of the firm is, in our view, to serve as vehicle for coordinating stakeholder interests' (Evan and Freeman, 1993: 262).

All stakeholders should be represented in executive decision making

Furthermore, Evan and Freeman suggest that the best way of coordinating the interests of stakeholders is to allow all to be represented in corporate decision making: 'each of these stakeholder groups has a right not to be treated as a means to some end, and therefore must participate in determining the future direction of the firm in which they have a stake' (Evan and Freeman, 1993: 255). According to this proposal, instead of making unilateral decisions about what they believe to be best for shareholders, and using these judgements as a template for corporate action, corporate executives should put processes in place which allow all stakeholders to have a say in the direction of the company.

Pause for Reflection

William Evan and Edward Freeman (1993) propose that giving stakeholders the opportunity to determine the future direction of the firm in which they have a stake is the best way of respecting the human dignity of those stakeholders.

Suppose that you were an executive of a large corporation. Suppose also that you had read Evan and Freeman's work and that you agreed that you had a responsibility to respect the dignity of all your stakeholders by giving them the opportunity to determine the company's future direction. What practical measures could you put in place to put this commitment into practice?

Reciprocity argument

A third argument that has been put forward in support of normative stakeholder theory draws on the notion of *reciprocity*; that is, it draws on the idea that when we benefit from something that is given to us we have a responsibility to give something back in return. It proposes that, since companies receive a range of different forms of support from the society within which they operate, company executives have a responsibility to give something back to society.

Reciprocity and specific stakeholders

Reciprocity was offered as a rationale for stakeholder rights in Chapter 1. It is based on the idea that if a group of stakeholders gives something to a corporation, they are entitled to expect something back from that corporation. Reciprocity can be applied to stakeholders in different ways. Firstly, it can be applied to relationships between a company and specific stakeholder groups on the basis that if a particular stakeholder gives something to a business, then, in return, that stakeholder has a right to consideration. Chapter 1 discussed how this argument might be used as an ethical justification for the rights of a company's influential stakeholders. The principle of reciprocity suggests that since influential stakeholders such as customers, employees and suppliers contribute to the prosperity of a company, that company owes them something in return.

Of course, shareholders are also influential stakeholders. They make an important contribution to corporate prosperity so they also deserve something in return. However, normative stakeholder theorists suggest that this does not entitle them to special treatment. Instead, their reciprocity rights should be considered alongside those of all other stakeholders who have helped to get a company where it is.

Pause for Reflection

It could be argued that the support given by influential stakeholders to a corporation is adequately reciprocated by, for example, the wages that corporation pays its staff, the goods and services it provides for its customers, the money that it pays to its suppliers, and the dividends and uplift in value enjoyed by its shareholders. According to this view, the relationships between a corporation and its stakeholders should be understood in terms of explicit economic agreements. Stakeholder relationships, on this understanding, begin and end with the terms of those explicit economic agreements. Therefore, corporate executives' reciprocity-based obligations should be confined to honouring those terms.

Do you agree that this is the best way to think about human relationships? Do you believe that our rights and obligations are confined to the explicit economic agreements that we make, or do you think they go beyond this? Consider this question specifically in the context of the relationships between a corporation and its customers, its employees, its suppliers and its shareholders. As a customer, an employee, a supplier or a shareholder of a company can you think of any things that you would expect in return for your support that are not clearly defined in economic terms?

Reciprocity and society

There is also a further, less-specific way in which reciprocity might apply to relationships between companies and stakeholders. This does not concern specific relationships between business and particular groups of influential stakeholders. Rather, it concerns the broader relationship between business and society. It is based on the supposition that society provides a range of important services to business; services that are essential to business's existence. Therefore, business owes society a certain amount of consideration in return.

One example of the kind of support given by society to business is the transport and communication infrastructure upon which most companies depend. Roads, railways, canals, seaports, airports and telecommunication networks have been developed over many years at public expense. In other words, it is society that has provided those resources. Another example is the education provided to company employees. Most of the employees on whose skills companies depend acquire the early education upon which those skills are built in schools that are run at public expense. Moreover, most companies rely on public health services to keep their employees in a fit state to go to work. If employees fall ill, it is usually publicly funded medical services that cure them. And corporations would find it hard to run their businesses without the law and order provided by publicly funded police forces and judiciaries. Furthermore, the advanced technologies upon which the prosperity of many corporations is based are usually developed, at least in part, in universities and research institutes that are paid for by the state or by public funding bodies.

As well as these indirect forms of support, companies are often supported in more direct ways by the public purse. For instance, state-funded grants are often given to corporations to encourage investment in a particular region or to promote certain industry sectors. Government fiscal policy is often designed to stimulate consumer demand and to thus promote the prosperity of the corporations who supply that demand. Furthermore, specific companies and industry sectors are sometimes given tax concessions to encourage their development and to help them play a mutually supportive role in society.

Given the significance of this societal support for corporations, normative stakeholder theorists argue that society has a right to be taken into account by business executives. For a corporation to take all it needs from society without, in return, treating society with consideration would be to overlook that right to reciprocity. Therefore, all of the stakeholders who are embraced under the rubric of 'society', which includes a company's influential stakeholders but which also includes everybody who may be affected by corporate activity, have a right to consideration.

Theory in Practice

Offshoring: Good business sense or an abrogation of responsibility to stakeholders?

Chapter 3 of this book discussed the practice of offshoring, which has become common amongst Western corporations in recent decades. Offshoring usually involves companies that have built up their manufacturing, assembly and customer-service operations in their home country over many years, and which have developed a close relationship with their home localities, transferring those operations to the developing world. This permits them to achieve substantial cost savings, since land and labour costs are usually cheaper in these new locations. However, the loss of jobs in companies' home nation can have serious implications for the local economy.

Offshoring is particularly contentious when a company has traditionally been associated with a particular area. For instance, Levi Strauss, a renowned American brand, has long been associated with the culture and the economy of the southwest of the USA, where its iconic blue jeans were produced for most of the twentieth century (Levi Strauss, 2013). During this time, close interdependency developed between the prosperity of Levi Strauss and the prosperity of that region. For instance, in the town of El Paso in Texas, Levi Strauss had long been the largest employer, with nine manufacturing plants and over 3,000 employees (Mauleon and Ting, 2000). However, from 1995, Levi Strauss has been closing its factories in the USA, eventually transferring all the work to suppliers in the Caribbean, Latin America and Asia (*Baltimore Sun*, 2003). Since most of the closed factories were located in areas that suffer from high unemployment and depressed wages, the chances of Levi Strauss's former employees finding alternative work when business moved elsewhere were not good (Jones, 1999).

Questions

1 Who is likely to gain the most from the cost savings enabled by Levi Strauss's offshoring of production?
2 Which stakeholders are likely to lose the most?
3 How might the *respect-for-persons argument* discussed earlier be used to criticize the offshoring of Levi's manufacturing?
4 What insights might the *reciprocity argument* offer on the practice of offshoring?

Summarizing normative stakeholder rationales

I suggested earlier in this chapter that Milton Friedman's rationales can be characterized by their depiction of business as a set of transactional arrangements involving corporations and their stakeholders. According to this depiction, stakeholders are seen as separate individuals or groups of individuals, who stand apart from the corporation and from one another, conducting those transactions in a detached manner. According to Friedman's arguments, in order to consider the ethical responsibilities entailed by those transactions, executives should evaluate the rights of each distinct set of stakeholders. And, for Friedman, in that rights-based ethical evaluation, property rights should be accorded pre-eminence.

The normative stakeholder rationales discussed above point to a rather different understanding of business and of the relationship between corporations and stakeholders. Instead of casting corporations and their stakeholders as discrete, autonomous entities, who carry out economically based transactions at a distance, they place greater emphasis on the interconnections that exist between them. Moreover, instead of suggesting a rights-based rationale, in which property reigns supreme and in which ethical evaluation looks only to explicit, transactional agreements, normative stakeholder rationales highlight responsibilities that are associated with membership of an interdependent, mutually supportive community.

The term *corporate citizenship* is relevant to this way of thinking about business. Corporate citizenship frequently arises in academic discussions about business responsibilities and the term is often used by large corporations when speaking of their social and environmental policies. Despite its widespread use, though, it is not always clear precisely what is meant by corporate citizenship (Matten and Crane, 2005). One source which might offer some substance to this vague and ephemeral notion is the social-contract theory that was discussed in Chapter 4. Social-contract theory highlights tacit agreements that we enter into voluntarily by participating in certain relationships. As far as citizenship relationships are concerned, social-contract theory encourages us to think about tacit obligations we take on by enjoying the advantages associated with being a citizen. In particular, it suggests that, by benefiting from being part of society, we tacitly assume a responsibility to contribute to that society.

To apply this understanding of citizenship to a corporate context is partly to highlight specific, tacit obligations that corporations take on by enjoying the benefits of being part of society; it is to draw attention to specific resources, services and facilities provided to corporations by society, and to the reciprocity-based obligations that are tacitly assumed by corporations in taking advantage of them. However, the notion of corporate citizenship also encourages us to reflect more widely on business's place in society, and on the unavoidable interdependency that exists between society and business.

Rather than thinking of corporations as independent, self-sustaining entities that hover beyond the periphery of society, ducking into society to take what they need before promptly ducking back out again with their spoils, the notion of corporate citizenship encourages us to regard them as deeply embedded within society. To see business in this way is to see corporations as implicated in complex webs of interaction, which provide a context that is essential for their very being. According to this perspective, for corporations to take what they need from this supportive system before retreating to a separate space where they acknowledge only their debt to their shareholders would seem curious.

Conclusion

Shareholder theory provides a clear-cut, unambiguous template for executive responsibility. It calls upon executives to do what is best for business and to ignore any distractions that might deter them from that mission. The straightforward simplicity of shareholder theory ensures its practicality as a guide to executive decision making. In addition, the attention it places on the rights of individuals, and particularly their property rights, accords with contemporary ethical preoccupations: we like to think about ethics in terms of individual rights nowadays, and we are accustomed to according particular significance to property rights. Moreover, privileging the rights of shareholders resonates with the understandable desire of most business executives to do what is best for business. However, the simplicity, the intuitive appeal, and the practical allure of shareholder theory should not be allowed to mask its ethical shortcomings. Despite optimistic suggestions by business practitioners and business ethics academics that there is no conflict between looking after shareholders and looking after other stakeholders, absolute focus on the property rights of shareholders can only be sustained if the entitlement of other stakeholders to be taken into account is overlooked. Furthermore, to focus entirely on rights is to ignore broader ethical considerations that may also merit executives' attention.

Milton Friedman's rationales in support of shareholder theory encourage us to think of the business environment as an arena that is shaped by explicit, voluntary transactions between autonomous individuals and groups. The rights entailed by those transactions offer a helpful way of thinking about business ethics. However, to think of business ethics purely in these terms is to overlook the extent to which business is embedded within social contexts. It ignores the interdependencies that exist between corporations and their stakeholders, and it neglects any responsibilities entailed by those interdependencies. Therefore, although shareholder theory offers a simple, intuitively appealing, and practically relevant model for executive decision making, a comprehensive evaluation of executive responsibilities should embrace a broader understanding of corporate citizenship and the obligations that it entails.

Discussion questions

1. Think of an ethically contentious action carried out by a large corporation. When the executives of that corporation decided to take that action, which of their stakeholders' interests do you think they were prioritizing? Were they thinking only of shareholders, or did they take other stakeholders into account? What ethical rationales can you offer for and against their decision? Can you think of any considerations other than ethical ones that may have motivated those executives to make that decision?
2. Edward Freeman (1994) observes that shareholder theory tends to offer property rights as a unique 'normative core' for ethical evaluation of executive

(Continued)

(Continued)

responsibilities. In other words, it appeals to the property rights of shareholders as the only basis for ethical evaluation of executive responsibilities. Freeman suggests that we should consider other normative cores which might be more supportive of a normative stakeholder approach. In his paper, he draws specifically on a version of social-contract theory to do just this. He also suggests that feminine ethics and environmental ethics may offer alternative normative cores around which normative stakeholder justifications might be built. Can you identify ways in which the feminine ethics theories discussed in Chapter 8 of this book and the environmental theories discussed in Chapter 9 might be supportive of a normative stakeholder approach?

3. Chapter 5 on Virtue Theory discusses two contrasting ways of conceiving the purpose of business: those offered by Elaine Sternberg and Robert Solomon. How might these contrasting notions of purpose relate to the identification of executive responsibilities? In other words, what contrasting roles might executives play in achieving these contrasting conceptions of business purpose?

Further study

Milton Friedman's (1970) article 'The social responsibility of business is to increase its profits' contains the arguments in favour of shareholder theory discussed here, along with a few others.

Thomas Donaldson and Lee Preston's (1995) paper 'The stakeholder theory of the corporation: concepts, evidence and implications' is an influential discussion of various ways of thinking about stakeholders.

Will Hutton's (1997) edited book *Stakeholding and it Critics* offers a collection of short, readable articles associated with the shareholder theory–normative stakeholder theory debate.

The following video, entitled '"Stakeholders vs. Shareholders": Haas faculty debate "Whom exactly should business serve?"', shows a debate that took place at Haas School of Business at the University of California, Berkeley. The participants in this debate raise some of the points covered in the chapter along with a number of related arguments concerning executive responsibilities and business ethics in general: www.youtube.com/watch?v=yQ1x8jKLWDg.

Some Closing Thoughts 11

Chapter objectives

This chapter will:

- reflect on the perplexing nature of business ethics;
- suggest that, rather than inhibiting ethical evaluation, sensitivity to perplexity can actually enhance its quality;
- draw attention to the possibility of ethical ambivalence in relation to business practice;
- suggest that we may not have to put up with the ethical downsides of business activity in order to reap the ethical upsides;
- highlight the need for business to retain ethical legitimation;
- draw attention to some opportunities that the need for legitimation presents for ordinary people to influence the ethical performance of businesses;
- highlight some ways in which heightened public and corporate interest in business ethics might make it harder to evaluate the ethicality of business activity.

Introduction

At the start of this book I pointed out that the book aims to encourage you to think about what ethical business practice and unethical business practice consist of and to provide you with some conceptual frameworks that will help you do this. Each chapter has sought to offer some such conceptual frameworks; each has introduced some distinctive ways of thinking about ethics that might assist you in developing your ideas about the ethical ramifications of business.

So, now that you are approaching the end of the book, where has this exploration of business ethics got you? It is possible that you are now feeling a little *perplexed* because the book has offered a number of contrasting insights to business practice, some of which push your ethical judgement in one direction while others push it in other directions. As a consequence, you may feel even less certain about what is ethical and what is unethical now than you were before you opened the book. You may also be left with feelings of ethical *ambivalence* about the way that business is conducted in contemporary society. The book has probably drawn your attention to some ethically estimable aspects of contemporary business practice whilst also highlighting some of its ethically problematic features. As a result, you may not be sure quite how you feel about contemporary business practice: whether, in general, you approve of it or whether you disapprove of it. And lastly, the book may have left you with a feeling of *powerlessness*. Whatever conclusions you may have reached about what ethical and unethical business practice consists of, and whatever you may think about the ethical desirability or otherwise of contemporary business arrangements, you may be thinking: so what – what does this all have to do with me? What can I do to change anything?

This chapter will reassure you that these are not unusual responses. Most people feel similarly perplexed, ambivalent and powerless when they take a philosophically based approach to business ethics. However, I suggest that these reactions need not give you cause for despair. Rather, in this concluding chapter, I will suggest that perplexity about what is right and wrong need not preclude ethical conviction. Indeed, I will argue that a certain amount of ethical perplexity is a good thing because it can actually enhance the quality of our beliefs about business ethics. Secondly, I will suggest that ambivalence need not entail resignation: the fact that there are good things and bad things about contemporary business practice does not mean that we have to resign ourselves to those bad things in order to get the good things. Rather, it might encourage us to explore ways in which business arrangements can be transformed so as to encourage more of the good things that business has to offer whilst minimizing the bad things. Thirdly, I will try to convince you that you have a lot more influence over what business does than you may think.

However, I will also draw attention to the need to be on your guard when trying to evaluate corporate activity from an ethical perspective. Indeed, I will suggest that, as a consequence of growing interest in business ethics and corporate social responsibility, it may actually be getting harder, rather than easier, to work out precisely what corporations are up to.

Perplexity

Perplexity is an unavoidable feature of philosophically based ethical enquiry. Ethics is not like mathematics, physics and engineering. It does not lend itself to the delivery of precise conclusions. The Greek philosopher Aristotle captured this insight over 2,000 years ago when he observed that:

> Our discussion will be adequate if it has as much clearness as the subject-matter admits of, for precision is not to be sought for alike in all discussions, any more than in all the products of the crafts … it is the mark of an educated man to look for precision in each class of things just so far as the nature of the subject admits. (2009/circa 323BC: 4/1094b)

Aristotle had ethical enquiry in mind when he suggested that some kinds of subject-matter do not lend themselves to precision. And he proposed that a well-informed approach to the study of ethics will take this into account. Nevertheless, this lack of precision need not preclude ethical conviction: just because ethical evaluation cannot deliver incontestable conclusions about right and wrong does not mean that we cannot have firm opinions; nor does it mean that we cannot have good grounds for holding those opinions.

The precarious nature of ethical evaluation

The French philosopher Jean-Paul Sartre was well aware that the absence of certainty can leave us feeling rather anxious about ethics. Sometime after Aristotle's wise observation about the nature of ethical enquiry, Sartre (1973/1946) offered a vivid illustration of the anguish that ethical perplexity can evoke. However, he also suggested an appropriate response to such anguish. Sartre relates a conversation he had had with one of his students during the Second World War. At the time, France was occupied by Hitler's German forces. The student told Sartre that his father and mother were separated and that the father had further alienated his family by collaborating with the occupying German forces. Moreover, the student's brother had died in the German offensive of 1940. As a consequence, the student was living alone with his mother, who was distressed by the treason of her husband and by the loss of her elder son. Her one consolation was her only surviving son. However, although he knew how much his mother depended upon him, the student also felt a duty to leave home and undertake a perilous journey to the United Kingdom. There he would join the Free French Forces, which were being assembled with the intention of continuing the struggle against German occupation.

The student was in an ethical quandary. On the one hand, he felt a duty to atone for the collaboration of his father, to avenge the death of his brother, and to help to rid his country of the occupying German army. But, on the other hand, he was driven by his love for his mother and by a deep sense of responsibility to care for and comfort her. He knew that if he left, not only would she be deprived of his support; she would have to live with the additional burden of knowing that she may never see him again. He was racked with indecision. He approached Sartre, who was his philosophy teacher, to ask what he should do. Sartre's response was simple: 'You are free, therefore choose – that is to say, invent. No rule of general morality can show you what you ought to do: no signs are vouchsafed in this world' (Sartre, 1973/1946: 38).

The importance of ethical conviction

Sartre relates this story to draw attention to the unavoidably precarious nature of ethical evaluation; that there are no unquestionable formulas that we can apply to deliver irrefutable verdicts of right and wrong. Nevertheless, Sartre also used the story to illustrate the inescapability of our responsibility to make ethical judgements. Just because we are confronted with choices between apparently irreconcilable and incomparable alternatives does not mean that ethical evaluation is a meaningless undertaking. Rather, it means that each of us is our own ultimate arbiter of right and wrong. It is easy to imagine Sartre giving the same advice to a student who sought his guidance on an ethically charged business scenario, or to a businessperson confronted by a particularly vexing ethical dilemma. In each case he would point out that there are no rules or principles that can tell a person unequivocally what is the right thing to do; that person must make their own choice. Nevertheless they can and they should make that choice.

As far as Sartre was concerned, then, the best response to ethical perplexity is not prevarication but conviction. He suggested that we should not use the uncertainty of ethical evaluation as an excuse to avoid making judgements; rather we should grasp the creative possibilities that uncertainty offers. However, it is important to recognise that the absence of hard and fast rules for telling right from wrong does not mean that ethical evaluation is no more secure than the toss of a coin. In this respect, the words of Aristotle are again instructive: 'The man who has been educated in a subject is a good judge of that subject, and the man who has received an all-round education is a good judge in general' (Aristotle, 2009/circa 323BC: 4–5/1094b-1095a). The point that Aristotle is making here is that, although ethical judgement lacks the precision of scientific calculation, we can nevertheless distinguish a well-informed ethical choice from a poorly informed ethical choice. A well-informed choice is one that draws on comprehensive consideration of an issue; consideration which is undertaken by somebody who is well versed in the subject, and which embraces a range of perspectives. A less well-informed choice is one that is based upon a more limited purview.

This book has, I hope enhanced your ability to make well-informed evaluations of ethically charged business scenarios. By offering a range of perspectives from which those scenarios can be viewed, it has sought to help you to establish well-informed opinions, rather than poorly informed opinions, about ethical right and wrong in business.

The merit of perplexity: a corrective to ethical dogmatism

But not only is perplexity an unavoidable feature of ethical evaluation. I suggest that sensitivity to the uncertainty of ethical evaluation is also a good thing because it helps us to avoid ethical dogmatism. I understand ethical dogmatism as a tendency to assume that ethical principles or opinions are incontrovertibly true. Ethical dogmatism entails a disinclination to consider the possibility of alternatives. And since it is consideration of alternatives that broadens the basis upon which our ethical evaluations are formed, and which thus enhances their quality, ethical dogmatism is not likely to lead to well-informed ethical convictions. So while perplexity should not prevent us from forming ethical views, we should always be alert to the possibility that those views can be improved. And the best way to improve our ethical views is to engage with any new perspectives that might come our way.

The hazard of ethical dogmatism has particular resonance for the practical application of business ethics. Chapter 6 of this book discussed the insights that Friedrich Nietzsche offers to business ethics. In particular it highlighted the extent to which our ethical opinions might be influenced by interests and agendas that pervade the community of which we are part. We should therefore be alert to the possibility of such influences, and we should embrace opportunities to expose ourselves to alternatives. However, the circles in which we move may not always encourage this. We might spend most of our time associating with people who reinforce our ethical convictions rather than challenging them. As a consequence, our interest-driven perspectives are liable to become more, rather than less dogmatic. The singer-songwriter Tom Russell sums up what this might entail for businesspeople in his song, 'Who's gonna build your wall', from which the following lines are taken:

We've got fundamentalist Muslims
We've got fundamentalist Jews
We've got fundamentalist Christians
They'll blow the whole thing up for you

But as I travel around this big old world
There's one thing I fear most

It's a white man in a golf shirt

With a cell phone at his ear (Russell, 2007)

Russell's allusion to the 'white man in a golf shirt with a cell phone at his ear' offers a stereotypical depiction of the business executive of the Western world. His reference to fundamentalism, and his implicit comparison of the fundamentalism of the business executive to various types of religious fundamentalism, encourages us to reflect on the extent to which businesspeople, as a result of moving in professionally and socially exclusive circles, may miss out on exposure to ethical perspectives that challenge their own, and how they may thus run the risk of ethical dogmatism. Such considerations highlight the merits of businesspeople actively seeking out alternative points of view so as to avoid such dogmatism. If ethical perplexity helps businesspeople, as well as those of us who reflect on the ethics of business practice, to avoid the fundamentalism to which Russell alludes, then perhaps ethical perplexity is no bad thing.

Video Activity 11.1

The following video clip shows the Nobel Prize winning economist, Milton Friedman, lecturing to a group of students in 1977. Friedman was very influential in the formation of economic policy in the USA, the UK and parts of South America towards the end of the twentieth century. In the video, Friedman responds to a question from a student about the Ford Pinto, which was, at the time, the subject of ethical controversy (see Dowie, 1977 for more information).

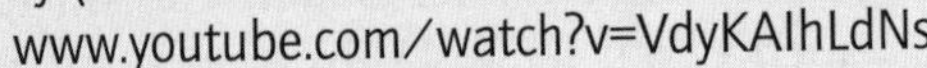

www.youtube.com/watch?v=VdyKAIhLdNs

Questions

1. To what extent do you think, in responding to the student's question, Milton Friedman demonstrates a willingness to engage with perspectives that challenge his own?
2. Would you say that Friedman shows *sensitivity to the perplexity of ethical evaluation* or is he more inclined to *ethical dogmatism*?

Ambivalence

A second possible reaction to reading a book of this nature is a feeling of ethical ambivalence about the business arrangements that prevail in contemporary society.

You may end up thinking that businesses do many things that are ethically praiseworthy but that they also do some things that are ethically questionable.

For instance, businesses provide affordable goods and services upon which most of us depend. Businesses also generate wealth for lots of people, either by creating jobs or by giving investors the opportunity to share in corporate success. And, of course, lots of corporations spend substantial sums supporting charitable projects. All of these things seem to point to the ethical desirability of business practice.

However, businesses also do many things that raise our ethical hackles. For example, in order to make their shareholders and some of their employees wealthy, some companies produce goods and services that are of dubious social benefit. Some create environmental problems in the process of giving their customers what they want. Some companies treat their workers in ways that leave a lot to be desired. Moreover, just as companies create vital jobs, so do they sometimes take those jobs away, thus depriving individuals, families and communities of the income upon which they have come to depend. Meanwhile, the management structures and decision-making procedures that prevail in firms rarely conform to the democratic principles that are acclaimed in most other walks of contemporary life. And the fruits of corporate activity are often distributed in what seems to be a highly inequitable manner.

So what are we to make of all this? Businesses seem to do lots of good things, but they also seem to do lots of bad things. To complicate matters still further, it is often the same companies doing the good things and the bad things. How, then, should we react? Should we assume that that is the way it has to be; that you cannot get the smooth without a bit of rough? Must we conclude that ethical purity is a utopian chimera that no business can ever achieve in practice, so we just have to put up with things as they are?

Some organization theorists have used the word *naturalization* to refer to the belief that things have to be the way they are. Mats Alvesson and Stanley Deetz define naturalization as follows:

> In naturalization a social formation is abstracted from the historical conflictual site of its origin and treated as a concrete, relatively fixed entity. As such [it] becomes the reality rather than life processes. Through obscuring the construction process, institutional arrangements are no longer seen as choices but as natural and self-evident. The illusion that organizations and their processes are 'natural' objects and functional responses to 'needs' protects them from examination as produced under specific historical conditions (which are potentially passing) and out of specific power relations. (Alvesson and Deetz, 2005/1996: 75)

The assumption that we must put up with the ethical burdens of business activity if we wish to derive the benefits that business offers can be seen as a form of naturalization. Such a view takes it for granted that business can only be organized in a particular way and that we must take it as it is, warts and all. It proposes that this is the way things have to be; that if we want the good things that business brings we have no choice but to accept the less desirable things. In other words, if we want high-quality, affordable goods and services, interesting jobs, prosperity and the charitable bounties that corporations bestow we must resign ourselves to the social disharmony, the environmental despoliation, the inequitable distribution of benefits and burdens, the anti-democratic management structures, and the marginalization of any considerations that do not add eventually to the bottom line.

Alvesson and Deetz suggest that such naturalization is a misguided perspective. They point out that to naturalize is to overlook the fact that the form taken by most businesses is only one possible form amongst many; it is a particular form that has been selected by those who are influential in creating and sustaining a particular type of corporate environment. Naturalization overlooks the possibility that things could be otherwise; that other forms could have been chosen. And in downplaying the possibility of other ways of doing business, it suppresses consideration of how those alternatives might come about. As Deetz puts it: 'Naturalization frequently stops discussion … at precisely the place it should be started' (Deetz, 1992: 190–91).

So while ambivalence is an understandable response to business-ethics study, it need not entail that we resign ourselves to the way things are. Rather, it can act as a spur to the exploration of alternative corporate forms which may enable us to reap the ethical fruits of business activity whilst avoiding the ethical decay that sometimes comes with it.

Theory in Practice

The Mondragon Corporation: another way of doing business

Mondragon is one of Spain's ten biggest corporations (Wolff, 2012). Based in the country's Basque region, Mondragon has over 100 subsidiaries with a combined annual turnover of 15bn (Tremlett, 2013). It employs over 83,000 people worldwide (Mondragon, 2013). However, Mondragon is very unlike the multi-national corporations we are more familiar with, having been described as offering 'a stunningly successful alternative to the capitalist organization of production' (Wolff, 2012).

The corporation that eventually became Mondragon was founded in 1956. Its founders sought to generate employment in a region that had been impoverished by years of war and neglect (Lafuente, 2012). They hoped to do this by creating a new kind of workplace; one which would be owned by its employees and which would be based around the principles of cooperation, participation, social responsibility and innovation that continue to imbue the business (Mondragon, 2013). The business that those founders initially set up was soon complemented by a number of other cooperative enterprises (Lafuente, 2012). These became affiliated under the Mondragon name and eventually grew into a highly diversified corporation, which today includes: banking and insurance groups; a supermarket chain and various other retailers; research and development firms; and manufacturing companies producing consumer goods, industrial components and construction materials. Mondragon even runs its own university, which currently has over 9,000 students (Lafuente, 2012; Mondragon, 2013).

All these enterprises are characterized by cooperative ownership structures and by democratic decision-making processes. Employees, who are referred to as 'members', collectively own the corporation, appoint Mondragon's directors, and retain the power to make decisions concerning the direction the business takes and the general rules that will govern it (Wolff, 2012). This has generated a higher level of employee engagement than is found in most workplaces. In random encounters with workers, University of Massachusetts economics professor, Richard Wolff, found 'a familiarity with and sense of responsibility for the enterprise as a whole that I associate only with top managers and directors in capitalist enterprises' (Wolff, 2012). Wolff also notes the relatively high profile taken by women in the corporation: 'Over 43% of MC members are women, whose equal powers with male members ... influence gender relations in society different from capitalist enterprises' (Wolff, 2012).

One of the rules decided by Mondragon's members sets limits to senior executives' pay. Unlike in conventional corporations, where bosses can earn hundreds of times the salary of their employees, Mondragon senior executives earn no more than 6.5 times the pay of their most junior workers (Wolff, 2012). An indication of the extent to which bosses eschew privilege is that José María Ormaetxea, one of the Mondragon corporation's co-founders, still drives a Ford Fiesta and lives in an ordinary flat in Mondragon town (Tremlett, 2013).

The Mondragon corporation also takes an unconventional approach to fluxes in the fortunes of its constituent businesses. Whereas most conglomerates ruthlessly cull subsidiaries which lag behind, along with the associated jobs, Mondragon supports poorly performing enterprises through cross-subsidies and loans. Mikel Zabala, human resources manager at the corporation's headquarters, explains that 'If someone has money left over, and another co-operative has run out, then they can lend them that money... Some of our most successful companies today are ones that needed help when things were going badly for them years ago. Now they, in turn, are helping others in need' (cited in Tremlett, 2013).

Mondragon adopts a similarly flexible, mutually supportive approach to fluctuations in staffing needs in its constituent enterprises (Wolff, 2012). If demand is

(Continued)

(Continued)

down in one business, leading to the need for a reduction in headcount, employees are transferred to vacant posts in other enterprises. Members have agreed on open and transparent rules, which govern these transfers and which award compensation for any costs associated with relocation. This provides a degree of financial security for employees, their families and their local communities that is rare in modern industry.

Richard Wolff observes that Mondragon also differs from conventional, shareholder-owned corporations in its long-term perspective towards research and development. Wolff reports that a portion of each enterprise's annual revenue goes into a central fund to pay for new product development. 'R&D within MC now employs 800 people with a budget over $75m. In 2010, 21.4% of sales of MC industries were new products and services that did not exist five years earlier' (Wolff, 2012).

The Mondragon corporation has grown dramatically since its early days and it continues to trade strongly. However, the economic difficulties that have followed the 2008 banking crash have caused major problems for Spanish businesses and Mondragon is no exception. With the Spanish economy shrinking at 1.9 per cent annually, sacrifices have been unavoidable. Instead of cutting back on jobs and making people redundant, though, Mondragon members have agreed to across-the-board wage reductions of around 5%, with managers taking the biggest cuts (Tremlett, 2013). In this way, Mondragon has mostly avoided adding to the 3.5 million people on Spain's dole queues (Tremlett, 2013).

Mondragon has its critics (see for example Kasmir, 1996). Indeed, even some of its own workers have reacted negatively to the recent wage cuts and have expressed their displeasure in some 'stormy' members' meetings, particularly in those enterprises that are feeling the squeeze most acutely (Tremlett, 2013).

But a particularly compelling recent criticism of Mondragon concerns the treatment of its overseas workers. Fierce competition from rival companies, which produce their goods using cheap labour in the developing world, has encouraged Mondragon to follow their lead. Mondragon now has 94 subsidiaries producing goods in countries ranging from Vietnam to Chile, Morocco and Russia (Tremlett, 2013). Workers at these plants are not treated as members of the cooperative, so are denied the ownership and participation rights that go with Mondragon membership (Tremlett, 2013). Moreover, it has been suggested that these non-member, overseas workers are often employed on part-time or temporary terms, so they are denied the job security enjoyed by Mondragon's members (Tremlett, 2013).

In defending Mondragon against such criticisms, Mikel Zabala acknowledges that non-members do not enjoy all the benefits of members but he argues that even non-member workers are treated better than workers in most companies: 'We do not really know how to behave like simple exploitative capitalists ... Even where we cannot fully behave as a co-operative, we at least try to implant the model of co-operative administration' (cited in Tremlett, 2013).

Questions

1 According to your ideas about ethical business practice, can you identify ways in which Mondragon is more ethical than traditional corporations?
2 Can you identify any ways in which Mondragon is less ethical than traditional corporations?
3 According to your understanding of ethical business, in what ways could Mondragon's ethicality be improved?
4 What factors might have caused Mondragon to act in a less ethical manner than its members would wish?

Powerlessness

So far in this concluding chapter I have suggested that perplexity about what is right and wrong in relation to business practice need not prevent us from forming firm opinions on the topic. Indeed, a certain amount of perplexity is a good thing if it encourages us to be receptive to the possibility that those opinions might be enhanced by engagement with other points of view. I have also suggested that ambivalence about the rights and wrongs of contemporary business need not entail that we must accept things as they are. Rather, it might encourage us to explore alternative ways of doing business, which deliver the ethical upsides whilst avoiding, or at least minimizing, the downsides. A further thought may occur to you as you come to the end of this book. You may be thinking that all this has very little to do with you because you can do nothing to influence corporate activity. It is one thing for presidents, prime ministers and corporate leaders to have opinions about business ethics, because they can put those opinions into practice. However, there is nothing that ordinary people like you and me can do to affect the way businesses and businesspeople carry on.

This would be an understandable reaction. The study of applied ethics can sometimes seem like a very hypothetical undertaking, particularly when applied to the activities of large, powerful organizations like business corporations. We are inclined to think that, even though we do not like what some of those corporations do, we can do nothing about it; they are just too big and too powerful to take any notice of us. However, I will offer some perspectives that suggest that we may not be quite as powerless as we seem. I will begin by introducing Jürgen Habermas's observation that economic systems need sociocultural legitimation if they are to prevail, which suggests that if we do not like what businesses are doing then, eventually, they will have to act differently. Then I will highlight some ways in which the capacity that we all have to influence the direction that business takes might be exercised; firstly, through the relationship we have with businesses as influential stakeholders; secondly, through the activities of new social movements.

The need for ethical legitimation

It is tempting to think that business leaders and politicians set society's economic direction and that the rest of us just get sucked along in the slipstream. However, a number of social theorists have suggested that things may not quite be so simple. For instance, by drawing attention to the inevitable interconnections between economic and political systems and the 'sociocultural realm', Jürgen Habermas (1975/1973, 1979/1976) highlights the need for business arrangements to retain public legitimacy if they are to continue. The *sociocultural realm*, for Habermas, is concerned with the norms, values and attitudes that prevail within society. It is the realm in which, amongst other things, our ethical expectations are expressed.

According to Habermas, if economic and political systems get out of synch with the sociocultural realm they will encounter crises in legitimation, which may undermine their ongoing viability. To borrow Habermas's terminology, the money-oriented and power-oriented 'steering media' of economics and politics need to be compatible with 'lifeworld' understandings that pervade the sociocultural realm. An important implication of this is that business processes cannot survive if they get out of touch with people's ethical expectations.

In considering some fundamental expectations that pervade the sociocultural realm, Habermas highlights the expectation that certain 'structural risks' (1979/1976) associated with developed capitalist economies will be controlled. Habermas draws attention, in particular, to three structural risks: the risk of economic instability; the risk that collective interests will be subordinated to the interests of specific groups; and the risk of gross inequality.

In highlighting these particular risks, Habermas draws attention to the need for business leaders and political leaders to ensure the following: firstly, that prevailing business arrangements permit people to lead their lives without fear of financial upheaval; secondly, that economic activity is arranged in such a way that it will meet collective needs, rather than just serving the needs of privileged elites; and thirdly, that patterns of social inequality do not get out of hand. If the economic and political system fails to meet these fundamental ethical expectations, Habermas suggests that a legitimation crisis will ensue. This means that the economic and political system will lose the public support that it must have if it is to survive.

Pause for Reflection

In speaking, over 30 years ago, of the ethical expectations of business that operate in the sociocultural realm, Habermas drew attention to the following three needs:

- the need for business structures to avoid catastrophic financial insecurity;
- the need for business activity to be oriented towards meeting collective needs;
- the need for the patterns of social inequality that arise from business activity to be kept within reasonable limits (Habermas, 1979/1976).

Habermas therefore focused primarily on economically oriented ethical expectations. Are there any other expectations that you would add to this list today, which you feel must be met if business arrangements are to remain in tune with prevailing ethical expectations?

Of course, the interconnections between economic and political systems, on the one hand, and, on the other hand, the sociocultural realm work in both directions. The ethical expectations that operate in the sociocultural realm set limits on the direction that economic and political structures can take but, at the same time, sociocultural expectations can be influenced by economic and political activity. In particular, all sorts of tactics might be used by those who hold political and economic power to try to shape sociocultural norms, values and attitudes and to shift ethical expectations in directions that they want them to take. The prevalence of political spin and the use of sophisticated corporate marketing activities are examples of such tactics. Nevertheless, Habermas's account suggests that such ruses will only take things so far. Eventually, the sociocultural realm will dig its heels in and refuse to go any further.

Video Activity 11.2

The following video, entitled 'Detox: A song about PeoplePower and Winning!' shows people taking a stand against the pollution of water systems by large clothing manufacturers.

(Continued)

(Continued)

http://www.greenpeace.org/international/en/multimedia/videos/Detox-A-song-about-PeoplePower-and-Winning-/

Questions

1 How might this video be interpreted as a manifestation of what Jürgen Habermas would call *legitimation crisis*? In other words, how might it demonstrate that *economic and political systems* have got out of tune with the ethical expectations that operate in the *sociocultural realm* and that the sociocultural realm is digging its heels in?
2 What actions might large corporations take to shape *sociocultural expectations* so as to avoid a *legitimation crisis* in relation to this issue?

Leveraging stakeholder influence

By alerting us to the potential of the sociocultural realm, and particularly ethical expectations, to put the brakes on economic systems, Habermas encourages reflection on ways in which this might happen. One way in which Habermas's ideas might be applied to contemporary business practice draws on the notion of stakeholding that was first introduced by Edward Freeman (1984) and developed by, amongst others, Thomas Donaldson and Lee Preston (1995). Chapter 1 of this book outlined the relevance of stakeholding to business ethics, distinguishing between different types of stakeholder relationship. The type of relationship that is particularly relevant in the present context is that which *influential stakeholders* have with corporations. You may remember that influential stakeholders were defined as people who are in a position to influence the success or failure of a corporation. They include its customers, its employees and its shareholders. Without the support of such stakeholders a company is deprived of a market for its products, a workforce to produce them, and the capital it needs to prosper and grow.

Most of us relate to business as influential stakeholders in at least one of these respects. We therefore have the capacity to make ethical statements via the purchasing decisions we make, the career paths we follow, or the companies in which we choose to invest. If we do not like the ethics of a particular company, we are at liberty to take our custom elsewhere. If we do not like the way that some businesses carry on, then we can simply cross them off our list of potential employers. And if we find ourselves with money to invest, there are many brokers offering portfolios which enable investors to choose the businesses they support according to ethical criteria.

Of course, exercising our ethical agency in this way may demand sacrifices on our part. For instance, if we do not like the way that our favourite smartphone manufacturer treats its workforce, we may need to choose a less-preferred brand; or we may even need to stop using smartphones altogether. If we choose not to work for a particular type of employer, we are likely to reduce our employment options, which, for all but the most sought-after employees, is a brave thing to do. And if we choose to invest only in companies that conform to particular ethical criteria, we may find there are not so many places to put our savings. However, as Jean-Paul Sartre (1973/1946) was at pains to remind his readers, these choices are ours to make. Moreover, only if we exercise such choices in ways that are consistent with our ethical convictions will companies be encouraged to fall into line with those convictions.

Video Activity 11.3

The following video is another by Greenpeace, entitled 'Alien Invasion'.

http://www.greenpeace.org/international/en/multimedia/videos/Alien-Invasion-/

In this video, the character played by Eddie Izzard suggests that the majority people who live on Earth will not prevent the environmental despoliation of their planet. He observes that they just do not care enough and, anyway, the 10 per cent who run the planet are just too powerful for the other 90 per cent to do anything. On the other hand, the character Zarg, played by Joe McFadden, suggests that the other 90 per cent *do* care about their planet and that they *can* prevent it from being destroyed.

Questions

1 How might Zarg's perspective be interpreted as faith in the power of *influential stakeholders* to make corporations act in a more ethically responsible fashion?
2 The video ends by suggesting several things that consumers might do to encourage corporations to act in a more environmentally sensitive manner. Can you identify five practical steps that you can take to discourage what you consider to be ethically problematic corporate activity and to encourage ethically acceptable businesses?
3 As well as highlighting the potential for consumers and other influential stakeholders to make their ethical views count, this video offers a satirical depiction of the governance of major corporations. Can you identify any ethically contentious features of the board of directors of the Tripartium Corporation, shown here, which may be found in contemporary corporations?

New social movements

To highlight the influence that stakeholding gives us over business is not to suggest that the purchasing, employment and investment decisions made by one person will alter the direction of corporate activity. A supermarket chain will not go out of business just because you or I choose to buy our vegetables from a small, independent greengrocer that treats its suppliers with greater consideration. Nevertheless, although the actions of one stakeholder standing alone may not force a company to change direction, there are very few stakeholders who actually stand alone. Rather, most of us continuously interact with other people, formally and informally, as members of social and professional groups. The conversations we have and the examples we set influence the ideas and the behaviour of others, just as those others influence us.

Habermas uses the term 'public sphere' to refer to the forums within which such interaction takes place. The public sphere was discussed in some detail in Chapter 7; it was described as a collection of physical, literary, media (press, radio and TV) and virtual spaces where people can access information, exchange ideas and debate matters of general interest. It is largely through participation in the public sphere that our ideas about the ethicality of corporate conduct get developed. And it is also in the public sphere that each of us is able to influence other people's ideas, thus amplifying the potential we have to influence business activity.

In this respect, Habermas (1981) drew attention to way that *new social movements* are providing platforms upon which people might come together to question dominant ways of doing things and to explore alternatives that are in keeping with shared ethical expectations. Nick Crossley has summarized Habermas's understanding of new social movements as follows:

> These ... groups do not defend traditions. They question them and, in doing so, both remoralize and repoliticize politics, simultaneously revitalizing the flagging public sphere. They generate a public debate about matters of public morality and social organization, contesting the norms by which we live our lives. And they are genuinely 'public', in that they stand outside of the stage show and bureaucracy of the political system. Furthermore, at the more private level they institute transformations of lifestyle and identity that serve to remoralize and reinvigorate 'everyday life', restoring the moral and symbolic texture that is undermined by colonization. (Crossley, 2003: 295–6)

For Habermas, then, new social movements play an important role in challenging the legitimacy of economic and political systems. They therefore help to keep those systems in tune with people's fundamental ethical expectations. Habermas's analysis relates specifically to the preoccupations of the latter half of the twentieth century, and the new social movements he speaks of reflect the preoccupations of that era. However, Nick Crossley suggests that a great deal of what Habermas had to say in the early 1980s is still relevant today. Crossley updates Habermas's ideas to embrace groups which express dissatisfaction with what they consider to be unethical corporate activity in the early twenty-first century. Depicted in this manner, these contemporary social movements play an important role in the formation of public opinion, in expressing deficits in the legitimation of prevailing business arrangements, and in keeping corporate activity in line with people's ethical expectations.

The implication of this is that our ethical convictions do matter. Perhaps no single person is able, alone, to change the direction of global corporate activity. Nevertheless, as members of collectives that communicate, debate, share information, critically evaluate and resist things we do not approve of, we all have the capacity to make a difference.

Theory in Practice

The banking crash: a trigger for legitimation crisis?

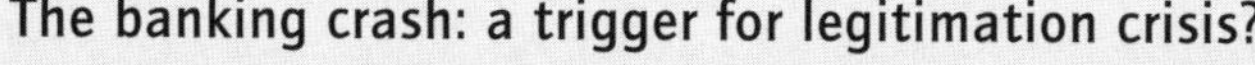

The crash

2007 saw the beginning of a banking crash, which, during the following two years, nearly brought the global financial system to its knees. In order to retain public faith in the banking industry, national governments and international financial institutions spent vast sums of public money buying out failing banks and providing financial support to prevent other banks from failing. The associated breakdown in confidence in the banking system led to a widespread reluctance to invest, which, in turn, slowed down economic activity in most parts of the world. The financial costs of bailing out the banks and the associated economic slowdown have caused great hardship, as fiscal austerity has led to cuts in spending on public services and as businesses have gone bust due to falling demand for their products and the inability to raise credit (see for example, *The Telegraph*, 2011; Kingsley, 2012a; BBC, 2013a for more detail).

The precise causes of the banking crash and the ensuing recession are matters about which there is some disagreement. The finger of blame has been pointed at a range of individuals, groups, policies and practices inside and outside the banking sector (see *The Economist*, 2013 for a concise overview; or Davies, 2010; Buckley, 2011; and Friedman, 2011 for comprehensive discussion), with some commentators (for example, Callinicos, 2010) proposing that the crash has exposed fundamental contradictions within the entire system of capital accumulation that pervades contemporary society.

Despite disagreements about the causes of the crash, though, several features of it are noteworthy. The first is that, during the period prior to the crash, the financial services industry became increasingly profitable whilst taking on increasingly risky investments. Although complex financing structures were devised to safeguard specific investments, this protection was dependent on the support of a

(Continued)

(Continued)

system which, in itself, ultimately proved unstable. A second feature is that participation in and support for this increasingly profitable and risky financial system brought considerable wealth to many people, including bank executives, traders, regulators, consultants and academic advisers. A third feature is that many nations are currently going through a period of extreme hardship as a consequence of the crash, with the poorest and most vulnerable members of society bearing the brunt of this hardship and with little relief in sight.

New social movements

In the last few years, governments and regulators have introduced some measures to control what goes on in the banking industry in the hope of avoiding a recurrence of the problems that led to the crash (see, for example, BBC, 2013b). However, there have also been other, less-formal responses. One has been the emergence of a number of movements calling not only for fundamental change in the banking industry but also for a reappraisal of the dominant capitalist model of economic organization.

Notable in this respect has been the Occupy movement, which sprung up in the aftermath of the crash. In 2011, during the early days of Occupy, a four-week period saw demonstrations and occupations, which were either directly or loosely affiliated to Occupy, taking place in over 900 cities around the world (Addley, 2011). Occupy has subsequently provided a focal point for protest against the banking system and associated austerity measures, whilst also providing a vehicle for general anti-corporate sentiment. The movement has been described by UN secretary general Ban Ki-moon as 'evidence of a growing wave of global anger at social and economic injustice' (cited in Addley, 2011), while the Occupy Together website states that Occupy 'takes to the streets to protest corporate greed, abuse of power, and growing economic disparity ... We simply want a system that operates in the interest of the people and to empower people to be a part of the process' (Occupy, 2013). The Occupy movement offers a departure from some other forms of recent, anti-corporate protest in that the demonstrations and occupations that have taken place in its name have been mostly peaceful.

As well as providing the opportunity for symbolic expressions of dissatisfaction with the economic status quo, Occupy seeks to provide opportunities for the exploration of alternatives. Occupy events are characterized by debate, organized along the lines of consensus-based decision making (Occupy, 2013), which not only provides a forum for considering alternative forms of organizing but which also embodies one such alternative. Notably, Occupy has no formal 'leaders', since its members challenge the need for and the desirability of the formal, hierarchical power structures that are usually associated with conventional visions of leadership. As the Occupy Together web site puts it:

> Anyone can be involved in the process and pick up the flag to address the problems they face in their community. We do not believe in placing the power of the movement in the hands of the few, but rather empowering everyone to be involved and share the responsibility together. (Occupy, 2013)

Stakeholder reaction

A further, more direct, consequence of the crash is that many bank customers have shown an interest in alternative forms of banking provision. In short, these people want to transfer their accounts to providers that offer what they consider to be more ethically sustainable forms of banking (Goff, 2011; BBC, 2012b; Channel 4, 2012). One UK consumer-support group, Move Your Money, has identified a number of specific customer concerns with mainstream banks. These include banks' contribution to the financial crisis; their involvement in dishonest trading practices; poor customer service; a 'toxic culture', which embraces 'crazy, casino gambling', 'macho risk taking', and an overwhelming focus on short-term profit; the concentration of business in a few, massive enterprises; excessive pay for senior executives and traders; unwillingness to lend money to small businesses; and a general lack of social or environmental responsibility (Move Your Money, 2013).

As a result of concerns such as these, a number of smaller banks, which have been less-overtly associated with such issues, have picked up new business. The UK's Channel 4 news reported in July 2012 that:

> Britain's public are voting with their feet ... According to Moneyfacts, enquiries about how to change current accounts are at the highest level since September 2010. The number of UK accounts opened on 2 July of this year was three times the usual rate. It is the ethical banking sector that appears to be benefiting ...Nationwide Building Society reported a 40 per cent increase in current account in one week, Triodos Bank had a 51 per cent increase in online savings account applications, and web traffic to Charity Bank has increased by 500 per cent in the last two weeks. (Channel 4, 2012)

(Continued)

(Continued)

A number of UK Student Unions are amongst the customers who have acted against mainstream banks by transferring their capital and their operating accounts to so-called ethical banks. Describing this trend amongst member organizations, Danielle Grufferty, a Vice-President at the National Union of Students, observes that:

> Students have a long history of using our power as consumers to put pressure on big companies and bring about an end to unethical practices. Young people are suffering because of an economic crisis that they did not create and moving our money is a simple way to demand better for banks in the future. (NUS, 2012)

Questions

1 How might the banking crash of 2008 and subsequent economic recession have evoked a *legitimation crisis* for the prevailing economic system? In other words, how has it demonstrated that economic arrangements have got out of synch with *sociocultural expectations*?
2 How might these events be seen as a consequence of inadequate management of *the structural risks* that Jürgen Habermas associates with developed, capitalist economies?
3 Can you identify any *new social movements* that have provided an outlet for sociocultural discontent?
4 How might *stakeholders* be influencing the future structure of banking?
5 Do you think the combined effects of *new social movements* and *stakeholder action* will result in significant, lasting changes to the banking industry?
6 What else might help to make such change a reality and thus bring banking back into line with *sociocultural expectations*?

The co-optation of business ethics

In order to decide which aspects of business practice we approve of or disapprove of, in order to decide whether prevailing forms of business activity merit ethical legitimation, and in order to decide which specific companies are deserving of our support, we may need to do some detective work. This is because, in business ethics as in any other walk of life, what you see is not always what you get. Some companies have been accused (for example, by Fleming and Jones, 2013) of taking a cynical approach to business ethics or, as it is often referred to, 'corporate social responsibility'. Such corporations are charged with taking business ethics/corporate social responsibility seriously only insofar as it helps them to massage their public image. For corporate executives to take such an approach is not to use business ethics/corporate social responsibility study as a way of identifying and preventing cases of unethical conduct. Rather, it is to use it as a basis for emphasizing the 'good' things their firms do whilst diverting attention from any ethically troubling aspects of their activities.

One concern with this approach is that it entails a co-optation of ethics. It takes the subject of business ethics away from its customary use and uses it for something different. In so doing, it deceives; it masquerades under false pretences. Specifically, it eschews the aim that books such as this one envisage for business ethics – which is to explore what ethical business practice looks like – and uses it, instead, as one more marketing tool to drive commercial performance. Rather than firms using business ethics enquiry to help them become more ethical, they just use it to inform their public relations activities. As a result, it becomes very difficult to work out just what corporations are really up to.

Video Activity 11.4

In this video, Anita Roddick, who founded The Body Shop and was a key player in efforts to inject social and environmental purposes into business activity, discusses corporate social responsibility.

www.youtube.com/watch?v=k44WifxDSX4

Questions

1 Roddick suggests in this video that large management consulting companies have 'hijacked' corporate social responsibility, turning it into a commodity that they can market in order to serve their own commercial ends and those of the corporations they advise. What sort of thing do you think Roddick has in mind here?

2 Roddick suggests that this hijacking of corporate social responsibility has taken it away from its true purpose. What is the difference between the social responsibility that Roddick envisages and the corporate social responsibility that, as she sees it, prevails in today's business world?

3 Roddick highlights an important limiting factor that, she suggests, will inhibit corporations from genuinely acting in a socially responsible fashion. What is this limiting factor?

The growing interest in business ethics or in corporate social responsibility may therefore serve to complicate the issue of legitimation by making it harder for people like you and me to decide which businesses are deserving of our ethical esteem and which ones are undeserving. Books such as this seek to highlight contradictions between certain forms of business practice and notions of ethicality. This agenda might help businesspeople reflect on the ethicality of their activities and shape those activities accordingly. It also seeks to assist observers who wish to evaluate businesspeople's success in doing this. There is a danger, however, that by highlighting contradictions between business practice and notions of ethicality, the subject of business ethics may just offer to those businesspeople who wish to mask those contradictions another tool to help them do so.

The fundamental purpose of business ethics, as I see it, is a *normative* one. Oskari Kuusela defines a normative approach to ethics as one which aims

> to determine the basis for answering questions about what is morally right or wrong, good or bad, what our obligations or rights are, how we should live, and so on. It seeks, in other words, to determine the ground or 'value basis' for our regarding certain things as having moral worth as opposed to others. Through such determinations, normative ethics then also aims to provide guidance for action and choice. (Kuusela, 2011: 73)

This normative agenda is contrasted to an *instrumental* one, which regards ethics as no more than an instrument that can be used to pursue a particular objective. In the case of business ethics, an instrumental approach uses it primarily as a means to drive the commercial performance of a particular firm. In order to derive the normative fruits of business ethics enquiry, then, it is wise to be wary of the possibility of its instrumental co-optation.

Theory in Practice

The tobacco industry: good guys or bad guys?

Some tobacco companies try hard to spread awareness of the ethically desirable things they do. A glance at the 'responsibility' and 'sustainability' pages of some leading tobacco corporations confirms how seriously they take ethics. For instance, Imperial Tobacco points out that 'Our goal is to make positive societal contributions' (IT, 2013), while British American Tobacco tells of its commitment 'to embed the principles of corporate responsibility around the Group' (BAT, 2013).

Part of the tobacco companies' ethical agenda involves generating prosperity for the many stakeholders who are associated with their businesses. As Imperial Tobacco tells us 'Governments, investors, employees and a wide range of other stakeholders benefit economically through the wealth created by our business' (IT, 2013). And in achieving this beneficent, wealth-creation agenda, tobacco companies say they are keen to maintain respectful and supportive relationships with their suppliers and with the communities within which those suppliers live. For instance, Philip Morris International refers to its 'responsibility to help support the communities where the tobacco we purchase is grown' (PMI, 2013). Similarly, Imperial Tobacco is sensitive to the need to build and maintain 'honest, co-operative trading relationships with our suppliers, treating them fairly and with respect'. Meanwhile, British American Tobacco proclaims its desire 'to provide a reliable source of income that can help support food security' (BAT, 2013).

The well-being of their employees is particularly high on tobacco corporations' list of priorities. At Philip Morris International, 'The health and safety of employees and contractors is a top priority' (PMI, 2013), while Imperial Tobacco says that it does what it can to ensure 'the continued development of our people enabling employees to fulfil their potential' (IT, 2013). British American Tobacco also emphasizes its commitment to encouraging employees to participate in decision making, since it believes that 'listening to their views [is] also fundamental' (BAT, 2013).

It seems that care for the natural environment is also very important to tobacco companies. For instance, Philip Morris International states that 'Tackling climate change is an important part of our sustainability strategy' (PMI, 2013) while British American Tobacco is 'working to actively address the impact of our business on the natural environment' (BAT, 2013). Imperial Tobacco also tells that 'We respect the natural resources we use, whether it's tobacco leaves, wood for paper and packaging or water to grow and then process our tobacco ... we focus on reducing our environmental impact (IT, 2013).

Tobacco companies' ethical purpose is also apparent in their enthusiasm for supporting charitable projects. For example, Philip Morris International's Charitable Giving Program focuses on a broad range of worthy causes, including the relief of hunger and extreme poverty, the provision of education opportunities, improving rural living conditions, discouraging domestic violence, and providing disaster relief. Similarly, Imperial Tobacco seeks 'to support social and environmental activities in geographical areas where we operate, responding to local and significant international needs' (IT, 2013).

In general, then, the major tobacco corporations tell us that they bring a great deal of good into the world by generating wealth, developing local communities, promoting the physical and psychological well-being of their employees, caring for the natural environment, and devoting a substantial proportion of their profits to

(Continued)

(Continued)

charitable projects. However, critics of the tobacco industry have suggested that tobacco companies may not always live up to these claims. For one thing, it has been suggested that tobacco companies are not quite as supportive of the welfare of the communities from which they buy their tobacco as they say they are. Some firms have been accused of using market power to drive down the prices paid to local farmers, which encourages the latter to depress wages and even to use cheap, child labour (Dugan, 2011). Indeed, in Malawi, where tobacco farming is an important part of the national economy, the country's anti-corruption bureau has accused tobacco companies of colluding to keep prices paid to farmers for the raw product low (Dugan, 2011).

Some of the strongest criticism of the tobacco corporations, however, relates to the marketing of a product which, it is claimed, killed 100 million people in the twentieth century and which, if current trends continue, will kill a billion people in the twenty-first century (Dugan, 2011). In particular, criticism has been levelled at tobacco-marketing activity in the developing world, especially that aimed at young people. As legislation and attitudes have turned against smoking in wealthy, developed nations, it has been suggested that tobacco companies are putting more emphasis on encouraging tobacco consumption in the developing world, where legal constraints on selling and advertising tobacco-related products are less restrictive (Dugan, 2011; Brodwin, 2013; Fernholz, 2013). Moreover, when governments try to introduce anti-tobacco legislation, corporations have been accused of using their financial muscle to block it. Emily Dugan observes that:

> When countries in these emerging markets try to clamp down on tobacco, the battle often ends up in the court room. In Uruguay, for example, the government had been leading the way under President Tabaré Ramón Vázquez Rosas, a former oncologist. In 2006 it became the first in the region to ban smoking in public places and now it wants 80 per cent of every pack of cigarettes to be taken up with health warnings. In response, Philip Morris has sued the government. It is thought that the company will demand at least $2bn in damages if Uruguay loses. (Dugan, 2011)

Laurent Huber, director of the Framework Convention Alliance on tobacco control, has pointed out that such legal actions can dissuade governments in less-affluent nations to act against tobacco: 'In countries like Uruguay, the tobacco industry uses its vast wealth to tie up public health measures in court battles. Win or lose, this has a chilling effect on other governments' (cited in Dugan, 2011).

A particularly contentious ethical issue concerns the marketing of tobacco products to children and young people. On the one hand, some tobacco companies deny that they encourage their customers to take up smoking, suggesting that they merely compete for market share of already-committed smokers, and that their marketing activities are aimed at adult smokers rather than children. And they put a lot of emphasis on the fact that those consumers *choose* to smoke. British American Tobacco, for instance, says that it merely seeks to grow its market share 'by encouraging existing adult smokers to choose our products over those of our competitors, not by trying to increase the number of people who smoke or how much they smoke' (BAT, 2013). Meanwhile, Imperial Tobacco says that 'We structure our responsible approach with our Values at the core of how we operate' (IT, 2013). This includes marketing and selling 'our products in a responsible way by focusing on adult consumers' (IT, 2013); that is, by focussing on those 'Millions of people around the world [who] choose to enjoy our tobacco products every day' (IT, 2013). Similarly, British American Tobacco's 'Focus on Harm Reduction' (BAT, 2013) aims at 'reducing ... risks and making available a range of less risky tobacco and nicotine-based alternatives' for the 'many adults [who] choose to smoke' (BAT, 2013).

However, a number of critics have suggested that tobacco companies may not actually live up to principles such as these. For instance, Pamela Ling and Stanton Glantz (2002) and Erin Brodwin (2013) have alluded to a sophisticated range of marketing tactics used by tobacco marketers to hook in young people and to retain their custom through various stages in the smoker's lifecycle, including measures aimed specifically at discouraging those who are trying to quit smoking from doing so. Moreover, it has been suggested that some tobacco companies specifically target young people by selling sweetly flavoured cigarettes (Carpenter et al., 2005; Manning et al., 2009; Gormley, 2013) and cigars (CfTFK, 2013), by using youth-oriented music in tobacco advertising (Hafez and Ling, 2006), by placing tobacco advertisements in magazines with high youth readership (Alpert et al., 2008), and by sponsoring club nights and parties with the aim of attracting new, young customers (Dugan, 2011; Lynch, 2013).

Questions

1. With reference to the ethics theories discussed in this book, can you list some ethically desirable features of the tobacco industry?
2. With reference to the theories discussed in this book, can you identify some ethically questionable features of the tobacco industry?

(Continued)

(Continued)

3 Which influential stakeholders do you think the content of the 'sustainability' and 'responsibility' pages of tobacco companies' websites is primarily aimed at?
4 Do you think people take what companies such as the major tobacco corporations say on their websites at face value, or are we becoming increasingly cynical when we read such material?

Conclusion

This book has offered a range of ethics theories as lenses through which business scenarios can be viewed in order to develop a comprehensive understanding of the ethical implications of those scenarios. This final chapter has anticipated some observations that such an undertaking might evoke. Namely, that different theories might offer contrasting perspectives, making it harder rather than easier to work out what right and wrong consists of; that, business-ethics enquiry might leave you feeling ambivalent about the ethicality of business; and that you might be wondering what this all has to do with you anyway, since there is little you can do to change anything.

While sympathizing with these reactions, this chapter has suggested that they need not give cause for despair. Indeed, perplexity might be turned to good use if it encourages us to engage with any new perspectives that come along and to consider how these might enhance the quality of our own ethical opinions. Meanwhile ambivalence, rather than giving cause for putting up with things as they are, might act as a spur to the exploration of business arrangements which enable more of the ethical and less of the unethical. And although it is tempting to think that we can do little to put our ethical convictions into practice, business's reliance on sociocultural legitimation may present opportunities for us to make our views count.

In general, this last chapter has highlighted the merits of developing as comprehensive an overview of the ethical implications of business practice as we can, of engaging critically with diverse perspectives, of being open to alternatives, and of having both the willingness and the confidence to stand up for our ethical convictions, even if this means challenging the status quo.

Discussion questions

1. Discuss the following statement: there is no point in using ethics theory to evaluate business practice because ethics theories often deliver conflicting perspectives. Therefore, you are better off just following your own ethical judgement and ignoring anyone who thinks differently.

2. The business world is increasingly dominated by large corporations, which operate transnationally, in which highly paid senior executives make the key decisions, and in which profit, growth and shareholder value are the key priorities. Is this the way things have to be, or could business arrangements be structured differently?
3. Local, national and international groups often emerge to pressurize large corporations to stop doing things which group members consider to be unethical. Do you think this is a legitimate form of protest? Are such groups fulfilling a useful social purpose or are they just coalitions of idealists, who are divorced from the practicalities of the real world, who try to use undemocratic means to pursue their utopian agendas, and who have little impact on what goes on?
4. Choose a well-known global corporation. Look at that corporation's website. What does it say about its ethical commitments? (You will probably find this under headings like 'responsibility' and 'sustainability'.) Does the corporation provide concrete instances of how it actually puts these commitments into practice? If you met the person who wrote those web pages, what questions might you want to ask them in order to form a comprehensive understanding of the ethicality of the corporation's activities? From what you can work out, do you think, overall, that this company does more good things than bad?

Further study

Simon Birch's (2012) article, 'How activism forced Nike to change its ethical game', discusses changes in the approach of one major global corporation to issues such as labour standards and environmental responsibility, suggesting that these changes have come about as a result of the combined influences of stakeholder action and new social movements.

Mark Achbar, Jennifer Abbott, and Joel Bakan's (2005) film *The Corporation* offers many interesting, critical insights on contemporary corporate activity and encourages exploration of alternative ways of doing business.

Martin Parker's (2002) book *Against Management* explores some concerns with conventional ways of managing organizations, highlighting the attractions of alternative, non-hierarchical forms of organization. Parker draws attention to a cultural shift in the way that we conceive management, and he encourages his readers to grasp the opportunities that this presents for the exploration of alternatives.

In *The End of Corporate Social Responsibility* (2013) Peter Fleming and Marc Jones argue that the current corporate preoccupation with corporate social responsibility (and, by implication, business ethics) is instrumentally, rather than normatively, motivated. They suggest that this instrumental co-optation of ethics may make corporations less ethical rather than more ethical.

E.F. Schumacher's *Small is Beautiful* (1993/1973) is a collection of essays that highlight some problems associated with the economic arrangements of the Western world. In particular, Schumacher suggests that the modern preoccupation with creating vast corporations, in which people perform highly specialized roles, creates all sorts of environmental, social and personal problems and may even undermine the economic efficiency it seeks to promote. Although *Small is Beautiful* was first published some 40 years ago, the ideas presented in it are highly relevant today.

Dan Hancox's *The Village Against the World* (2013) is a factual account of a small Spanish village, which has chosen to structure its economic, social and political affairs differently to the dominant Western model. This has had a major effect on the work and life experiences of the village's inhabitants. Hancox's book offers an interesting exploration of some ways in which an alternative approach to economic organization has been implemented as well as describing some challenges that such undertakings might encounter.

For Business Ethics by Jones, Parker, and ten Bos (2005) includes discussions about some of the ethics theories explored in this book, as well as some other theories, adding some interesting further perspectives to those offered here.

Ethics and Organizations (1998) is a collection of papers, edited by Martin Parker, which discusses ethically charged organizational issues, many of which relate especially to business. The book introduces some ethics theories, and some ethically oriented social theories, that are not discussed in this book, drawing out their implications for business ethics. It also includes some chapters that look at specific business disciplines, such as HRM, marketing and accounting, from an ethical perspective.

Business Ethics: Perspectives on the Practice of Theory, edited by Christopher Cowton and Roger Crisp (1998), contains many informative discussions about the study of business ethics and how it might be applied to practice.

References

You will notice that many of the references in this book show two dates; a later date followed by an earlier date. For example, you will find Immanuel Kant's *Critique of Practical Reason* referred to as Kant (2003/1787). In such cases, the first date refers to the particular edition of this text upon which I have drawn; the second date refers to the date on which the text was first published. I have included this second date to give readers some idea of when the ideas being discussed were initially formulated.

In some cases I have also added two separate page numbers when referencing direct quotations. For example, a quotation from Kant's work is referenced as (Kant, 2003/1787: 59/25). The first number refers to the page in the more recent edition from which the quote is taken; the second number relates to the original text. This second number may refer to a page, a paragraph, or a chapter depending on the format that is usually adopted for that particular original text. The inclusion of this second number will help readers who wish to access classic texts directly, since many printed editions and online copies of these works are available.

ABB (2013) 'ABB code for responsible gambling and player protection', Association of British Bookmakers website, 1 October. Available at: www.abb.uk.com/news/abb-code-for-responsible-gambling-and-player-protection/ (accessed January 2014).

Achbar, M., Abbott, J. and Bakan, J. (dirs.) (2005) *The Corporation*. Big Picture Media Corporation.

Acselrad, H. (2008) 'Grassroots reframing of environmental struggles in Brazil', in D. Carruthers (ed.), *Environmental Justice in Latin America: Problems, Promise, and Practice*. Cambridge, MA: MIT Press. pp. 75–97.

Acton, H.B. (1970) *Kant's Moral Philosophy*. Basingstoke: MacMillan.

Addley, E. (2011) 'Occupy movement: from local action to a global howl of protest', *The Guardian*, 18 October. Available at: www.theguardian.com/world/2011/oct/17/occupy-movement-global-protest (accessed November 2013).

Agger, B. (1987) 'The dialectic of deindustrialization: an essay on advanced capitalism', in J. Forester (ed.), *Critical Theory and Public Life*. Cambridge, MA: MIT Press. pp. 3–21.

Allen, I.E. and Todd, A.A. (2013) 'The fishing has been spoiled by the trawling', *Scarborough Maritime Heritage Centre*. Available at: www.scarboroughsmaritimeheritage.org.uk/atrawlingoverfishing.php (accessed August 2013).

Almond, B. (1993) 'Rights', in P. Singer (ed.), *A Companion to Ethics*. Oxford: Blackwell. pp. 259–69.

Alpert, H.R., Koh, H.K. and Connolly, G.N. (2008) 'After the master settlement agreement: targeting and exposure of youth to magazine tobacco advertising', *Health Affairs*, 27/6: 503–12.

Alvesson, M. and Deetz, S. (2005/1996) 'Critical theory and postmodernism', in C. Grey and H. Willmott (eds), *Critical Management Studies: A Reader*. Oxford: Oxford University Press. pp. 60–106.

Ames, K. and Wright, M. (2007) 'The wage and employment effects of leveraged buyouts in the UK', *International Journal of the Economics of Business*, 14/2: 179–95.

Amnesty International (2012a) 'Shell's wildly inaccurate reporting of Niger Delta oil spill exposed', 23 April. Available at: www.amnesty.org/en/news/shell-s-wildly-inaccurate-reporting-niger-delta-oil-spill-exposed-2012-04-23 (accessed November 2012).

Amnesty International (2012b) 'Report slams failure to prevent toxic waste dumping in West Africa', 25 September. Available at: www.amnesty.org/en/news/report-slams-failure-prevent-toxic-waste-dumping-west-africa-2012-09-25 (accessed February 2013).

Amnesty International and Greenpeace Netherlands (2012) *The Toxic Truth*. Available at: www.amnesty.org/en/library/asset/AFR31/002/2012/en/7336d72a-6b14-453a-bc1e-afd1e1117bde/afr310022012eng.pdf (accessed February 2013).

Aquinas, T. (2010/1264–73) 'Humans as moral ends', in D.R. Keller (ed.), *Environmental Ethics: The Big Questions*. Chichester: Wiley Blackwell. pp. 63–4.

Archer, D., Iritani, B., Kimes, D. and Barrios, M. (1983) 'Face-ism: five studies of sexual difference in facial prominence', *Journal of Personality and Social Psychology*, 45: 725–35.

Aristotle (2009/circa 323BC) *The Nicomachean Ethics*, D. Ross (transl.), L. Brown (ed.). Oxford: Oxford University Press.

Arnold, D. (2011) '*News of the World*: What was it like on the inside?', *BBC News Magazine*, 10 July. Available at: www.bbc.co.uk/news/magazine-14078182 (accessed April 2013).

Ashman, I. and Winstanley, D. (2006) 'Business ethics and existentialism', *Business Ethics: A European Review*, 15/3: 218–33.

Atlas Iron (2013) *Atlas Iron Limited Annual Report*, Atlas Iron corporate website. Available at: www.atlasiron.com.au/irm/content/annualreport2012/index.html# (accessed April 2013).

Austin, K. (2010) 'The "hamburger connection" as ecologically unequal exchange: a cross-national investigation of beef exports and deforestation in less developed countries', *Rural Sociology*, 75/2: 270–99.

Averis, M. (2011) 'Harlequins' Bloodgate physiotherapist has ban on practising overturned', *The Guardian*, 21 January. Available at: www.guardian.co.uk/sport/2011/jan/21/harlequins-bloodgate-physiotherapist-ban (accessed May 2013).

Bacon, N., Wright, M., Scholes, L. and Meuleman, M. (2010) 'Assessing the impact of private equity on industrial relations in Europe', *Human Relations*, 63/9: 1343–70.

Bailey, D. and de Ruyter, A. (2012) 'Re-examining the BMW-Rover affair: a case study of corporate, strategic and government failure?', Coventry University SURGE Working Paper Series, Number 1.

Baltimore Sun (2003) 'Levi's set to close last U.S. factory', 9 October. Available at: http://articles.baltimoresun.com/2003-10-19/news/0310190003_1_levi-strauss-blue-jeans-antonio (accessed August 2013).

Barrick (2013) 'Responsibility', Barrick Gold Corporation corporate website. Available at: www.barrick.com/responsibility/default.aspx (accessed December 2013).

Bartky, S.L. (1990) *Femininity and Domination: Studies in the Phenomenology of Oppression*. New York: Routledge.

BAT (2013) British American Tobacco corporate website. Available at: www.bat.com/group/sites/uk__3mnfen.nsf/vwPagesWebLive/DO52AD7G?opendocument&SKN=1 (accessed November 2013).

Baudrillard, J. (1997/1970) *The Consumer Society: Myths and Structures*. London: Sage.

Bauman, Z. (1993) *Postmodern Ethics*. Malden, MA: Blackwell.

BBC (2003) 'Bust company sacks workers by text', 30 May. Available at: http://news.bbc.co.uk/1/hi/business/2949578.stm (accessed April 2013).

BBC (2007) 'Pair jailed over royal phone taps', *BBC News*, 26 January. Available at: http://news.bbc.co.uk/1/hi/6301243.stm (accessed April 2013).

BBC (2008) *Tribe*. Available at: www.bbc.co.uk/tribe/topics/issues.shtml (accessed July 2012).

BBC (2009a) 'Richards resigns Harlequins post', *Sport: Rugby Union*, 8 August. Available at: http://news.bbc.co.uk/sport1/hi/rugby_union/my_club/harlequins/8191209.stm (accessed May 2013).

BBC (2009b) 'Richards banned for three years', *Sport: Rugby Union*, 17 August. Available at: http://news.bbc.co.uk/sport1/hi/rugby_union/my_club/harlequins/8191371.stm (accessed May 2013).

BBC (2009c) 'Trafigura knew of waste dangers', *Newsnight*, 16 September. Available at: http://news.bbc.co.uk/1/hi/programmes/newsnight/8259765.stm (accessed February 2013).

BBC (2010a) '"Bloodgate" saga will forever haunt Quins – Mark Evans', *Sport: Rugby Union*, 26 March. Available at: http://news.bbc.co.uk/sport1/hi/rugby_union/8588557.stm (accessed May 2013).

BBC (2010b) 'Timeline: BP oil spill', *BBC News: US and Canada*, 19 September. Available at: www.bbc.co.uk/news/world-us-canada-10656239 (accessed June 2014)

BBC (2012a) 'Billionaires behaving badly?', *Panorama*, 23 April. Available at: www.bbc.co.uk/iplayer/episode/b01gk8zc/Panorama_Billionaires_Behaving_Badly/ (accessed March 2113).

BBC (2012b) 'Rise in customers who use "ethical banks"' *BBC News*, 11 July. Available at: www.bbc.co.uk/news/business-18793181 (accessed November 2013).

BBC (2012c) 'News of the World phone-hacking scandal', *BBC News UK*, 4 August. Available at: www.bbc.co.uk/news/uk-11195407 (accessed April 2013).

BBC (2012d) 'UK Uncut protests over Starbucks "tax avoidance"', *News UK*, 8 December. Available at: www.bbc.co.uk/news/uk-20650945 (accessed April 2013).

BBC (2013a) 'Global recession timeline', *BBC News*. Available at: http://news.bbc.co.uk/1/hi/8242825.stm (accessed November 2013).

BBC (2013b) 'Banking reform: What has changed since the crisis?', *BBC Business News*, 4 February. Available at: www.bbc.co.uk/news/business-20811289 (accessed November 2013).

BBC (2013c) 'Ivory Coast Profile', *BBC News Africa*, 18 June. Available at: www.bbc.co.uk/news/world-africa-13287216 (accessed December 2013).

BBC (2013d) 'Bangladesh disaster: '"Little help" for Rana Plaza victims', BBC News Asia, 24 October. Available at: www.bbc.co.uk/news/world-asia-24649848 (accessed November 2013).

Beadle, R. and Moore, G. (2006) 'MacIntyre on virtue and organization', *Organization Studies*, 27/3: 323–40.

Becker, D. (1993) 'Kant's moral and political philosophy', in R.C. Solomon and K.M. Higgins (eds), *The Age of German Idealism*. Abingdon: Routledge. pp. 68–102.

Bennett, T. (2012) 'Why does Starbucks pay so little tax?' *Money Week*, 2 November. Available at: www.moneyweek.com/investment-advice/how-to-invest/video-tutorials/why-does-starbucks-pay-so-little-tax-61302 (accessed April 2013).

Bentham, J. (2000/1789) *An Introduction to the Principles of Morals and Legislation*, reproduced in T. Griffin (ed.), *Selected Writings on Utilitarianism*. Ware: Wordsworth.

Bernstein, R.J. (1983) *Beyond Objectivism and Relativism: Science, Hermeneutics and Praxis*. Philadelphia, PA: University of Pennsylvania Press.

Bernstein, R.J. (ed.) (1985) *Habermas and Modernity*. Cambridge: Polity.

Bertram, C. (2004) *Rousseau and the Social Contract*. Abingdon: Routledge.

BHP Billiton (2013) 'Sustainability', BHP Billiton corporate website. Available at: www.bhpbilliton.com/home/aboutus/sustainability/Pages/default.aspx (accessed December 2013).

Birch, S. (2012) 'How activism forced Nike to change its ethical game', *The Guardian*, 6 July. Available at: www.guardian.co.uk/environment/green-living-blog/2012/jul/06/activism-nike (accessed November 2013).

Blair, M.M. (1995) *Ownership and Control: Rethinking Corporate Governance for the Twenty-First Century*. Washington: Brookings Institution.

Boatright, J.R. (2002) 'Contractors as stakeholders: reconciling stakeholder theory with the nexus-of-contracts firm', *Journal of Banking and Finance*, 26/9: 1837–52.

Bonner, R. (1993) *At the Hand of Man: Peril and Hope for Africa's Wildlife*. New York: Alfred A. Knopf.

Bookchin, M. (2010/1993) 'What is social ecology?', in D.R. Keller (ed.), *Environmental Ethics: The Big Questions*. Chichester: Wiley Blackwell. pp. 268–75.

Borgerson, J.L. (2007) 'On the harmony of feminist ethics and business ethics', *Business and Society Review*, 112/4: 477–509.

Boucher, D. and Kelly, P. (eds) (1994) *The Social Contract from Hobbes to Rawls*. London: Routledge.

Bowie, N. (1999) *Business Ethics: A Kantian Perspective*. Malden, MA: Blackwell.

Bowie, N. (2002) 'A Kantian approach to business ethics', in R.E. Fredericks (ed.), *A Companion to Business Ethics*. Oxford: Blackwell. pp. 3–16.

Brady, C. (2005) 'English patient unsuitable case for treatment', *The Observer*, 10 April. Available at: www.guardian.co.uk/business/2005/apr/10/carindustry.politics1 (accessed January 2013).

Brady, C. and Lorenz, A. (2005) *End of the Road – The True Story of the Downfall of Rover.* Harlow: Pearson.

Brandt, R. (1971) 'Some merits of one form of rule utilitarianism', in T.K. Hearn Jnr (ed.), *Studies in Utilitarianism*. New York: Meredith. pp. 169–99.

Brandt, R. (1978/1963) 'Toward a credible form of utilitarianism', in M.D. Bayles (ed.), *Contemporary Utilitarianism*. Gloucester, MA: Peter Smith. pp. 143–86.

Brennan, A. (1995) 'Ethics, ecology and economics', *Biodiversity and Conservation*, 4: 798–811.

Bridge, G. (2004) 'Mapping the bonanza: geographies of mining investment in an era of neoliberal reform', *The Professional Geographer*, 56/3: 406–21.

Brodwin, E. (2013) 'Tobacco companies still target youth despite a global treaty', *Scientific American*, 21 October. Available at: www.scientificamerican.com/article.cfm?id=tobacco-companies-still-target-youth (accessed November 2013).

Brodzinski, S. (2003) 'Coca-Cola boycott launched after killings at Colombian plants', *The Guardian*, 24 July. Available at: www.theguardian.com/media/2003/jul/24/marketingandpr.colombia (accessed August 2013).

Buckley, A. (2011) *Financial Crisis: Causes, Context and Consequences*. Harlow: Pearson.

Bullard, R.D. (2010/1994) 'Environmental justice for all', in D.R. Keller (ed.), *Environmental Ethics: The Big Questions*. Chichester: Wiley Blackwell. pp. 491–501.

Bunker, S. (1985) *Underdeveloping the Amazon: Extraction, Unequal Exchange, and the Failure of the Modern State*. Urbana, IL: University of Illinois Press.

Burton, B.K. and Dunn, C.P. (1996) 'Feminist theory as a moral grounding for stakeholder theory', *Business Ethics Quarterly*, 6/2: 133–47.

Butler, J. (2004/1987) 'Variations on sex and gender: Beauvoir, Wittig, Foucault', in S. Salih (ed.), *The Judith Butler Reader*. Malden, MA: Blackwell. pp. 22–38.

Butler, S. and Hammadi, S. (2013) 'Rana Plaza factory disaster: victims still waiting for compensation', *The Guardian*, 23 October. Available at: www.theguardian.com/world/2013/oct/23/rana-plaza-factory-disaster-compensation-bangladesh (accessed November 2013).

Calhoun, C. (ed.) (1992) *Habermas and the Public Sphere*. Cambridge, MA: MIT Press.

Callicott, J.B. (2003) 'Wetland gloom and wetland glory', *Philosophy and Geography*, 6: 33–45.

Callinicos, A. (2010) *Bonfire of Illusions: The Twin Crises of the Liberal World*. Cambridge: Polity.

Campbell, T. (2006) *Rights: A Critical Introduction*. Abingdon: Routledge.

Card, C. (1991) 'The feistiness of feminism', in C. Card (ed.), *Feminist Ethics*. Lawrence, KS: University Press of Kansas. pp. 3–31.

Carpenter, C.M., Wayne, G.F., Pauly, J.L., Koh H.K. and Connolly, G.N. (2005) 'New cigarette brands with flavors that appeal to youth: tobacco marketing strategies', *Health Affairs*, 24/6: 1601–10.

Carrington, D. (2013) 'Political pressure is mounting on polluting water companies', *The Guardian*, 5 August. Available at: www.theguardian.com/environment/damian-carrington-blog/2013/aug/05/water-companies-pollution (accessed November 2013).

Carrington, D. and Barnes, S. (2013) 'Revealed: how UK water companies are polluting Britain's rivers and beaches', *The Observer*, 3 August. Available at: www.theguardian.com/environment/2013/aug/03/water-companies-polluting-rivers-beaches (accessed November 2013).

Center for Emerging Issues (2001) 'Nature travel and ecotourism: animal and human health concerns', October. Available at: www.aphis.usda.gov/animal_health/emergingissues/downloads/ecotourism.pdf (accessed March 2013).

Center for Responsible Travel (2013) 'Responsible travel: global trends & statistics'. Available at: www.responsibletravel.org/news/Fact_sheets/Fact_Sheet_-_Global_Ecotourism.pdf (accessed March 2013).

CfTFK (2013) 'Not your grandfather's cigar: a new generation of cheap and sweet cigars threatens a new generation of kids', Campaign for Tobacco-Free Kids website, 13 March. Available at: www.tobaccofreekids.org/what_we_do/industry_watch/cigar_report/?utm_source=home&utm_medium=carousel&utm_campaign=home (accessed November 2013).

Chakrabortty, A. (2014) 'Betting-shop machines sucking cash out of communities … this is what predatory capitalism looks like', *The Guardian*, 6 January. Available at: www.theguardian.com/commentisfree/2014/jan/06/betting-shop-machines-predatory-capitalism (accessed January 2014).

Chamberlain, G. (2011) 'Apple's Chinese workers treated "inhumanely, like machines"', *The Observer*, 30 April. Available at: www.guardian.co.uk/technology/2011/apr/30/apple-chinese-workers-treated-inhumanely (accessed July 2013).

Chandrasekhar, I., Wardrop, M. and Trotman, A. (2012) 'Phone hacking: timeline of the scandal', *The Telegraph*, 23 July. Available at: www.telegraph.co.uk/news/uknews/phone-hacking/8634176/Phone-hacking-timeline-of-a-scandal.html (accessed April 2013).

Channel 4 (2012) 'Banking: Five banks blazing the ethical trail', *4 News*. Available at: www.channel4.com/news/banking-five-banks-blazing-the-ethical-trail (accessed November 2013).

China Labor Watch (2014) 'Beyond Foxconn: deplorable working conditions characterize Apple's entire supply chain', China Labor Watch. Available at: www.chinalaborwatch.org/pro/proshow-176.html (accessed February 2014).

Chryssides, G.D. and Kaler, J.H. (1993) *An Introduction to Business Ethics*. London: International Thompson Business Press.

Chu, B. (2013) '"Wake up and smell the coffee": G8 must tackle tax evasion, says David Cameron', *The Independent*, 24 January. Available at: www.independent.co.uk/news/uk/politics/wake-up-and-smell-the-coffee-g8-must-tackle-tax-evasion-says-david-cameron-8464977.html (accessed April 2013).

Clapp, J. (1994) 'The toxic waste trade with less-industrialised countries: economic linkages and political alliances', *Third World Quarterly*, 15/3: 505–18.

Coca-Cola (2013a) 'FAQs: Advertising', Coca-Cola corporate website. Available at: www.coca-colacompany.com/contact-us/faqs (accessed October 2013).

Coca-Cola (2013b) 'Global mutual respect policy', Coca-Cola corporate website. Available at: http://assets.coca-colacompany.com/cd/8f/106258bd4dbb89663257047f50f1/global-mutual-respect-policy-english-pdf.pdf (accessed August 2013).

Coca-Cola (2013c) 'Human & workplace rights', Coca-Cola corporate website. Available at: www.coca-colacompany.com/our-company/human-workplace-rights (accessed August 2013).

Coca-Cola (2013d) 'The Coca-Cola Foundation', Coca-Cola corporate website. Available at: www.coca-colacompany.com/our-company/the-coca-cola-foundation (accessed October 2013).

Coca-Cola (2013e) 'Who we are', Coca-Cola corporate website. Available at: www.coca-colacompany.com/careers/who-we-are-infographic (accessed October 2013).

Coca-Cola (2013f) 'Workplace rights policy', Coca-Cola corporate website. Available at: http://assets.coca-colacompany.com/65/e0/36fa0f6e4aa9bae055a644ad15d6/workplace_rights_policy.pdf (accessed August 2013).

Commons Select Committee (2011) 'Uncorrected transcript of oral evidence given at the House of Commons Culture, Media and Sport committee's inquiry into phone hacking by James Murdoch, Rupert Murdoch and Rebekah Brooks', 19 July. Available at: http://www.publications.parliament.uk/pa/cm201012/cmselect/cmcumeds/uc903-ii/uc90301.htm (accessed July 2014). NB: since neither witnesses nor Members have had the opportunity to correct the record, the transcript is not yet an approved formal record of these proceedings and sections quoted from it should be read on that understanding.

Conway, N. and Briner, R.B. (2005) *Understanding Psychological Contracts at Work: A Critical Evaluation of Theory and Research*. Oxford: Oxford University Press.

Co-operative News (2011) 'UK's biggest workers' co-op celebrates win'. Available at: http://www.thenews.coop/36885/news/consumer/uk%E2%80%99s-biggest-workers%E2%80%99-co-op-celebrates-win-co-operative-news/#.U77RifldWCs (accessed July 2014).

Cowton, C. and Crisp, R. (eds) (1998) *Business Ethics: Perspectives on the Practice of Theory*. Oxford: Oxford University Press.

Crane, A. and Matten, D. (2010) *Business Ethics* (3rd edn). Oxford: Oxford University Press.

Crary, J. (2013) *24/7: Late Capitalism and the Ends of Sleep*. London: Verso.

Crossley, N. (2003) 'Even newer social movements? Anti-corporate protests, capitalist crises and the remoralization of society', *Organization*, 10/2: 287–305.

Danto, A.C. (1994/1986) 'Some remarks on *The Genealogy of Morals*', in R. Schacht (ed.), *Nietzsche, Genealogy, Morality*. Berkeley, CA: University of California Press. pp. 35–48.

Darwall, S. (ed.) (2003) *Virtue Ethics*. Malden, MA: Blackwell.

Davies, H. (2010) *The Financial Crisis: Who is to Blame?* Cambridge: Polity.

Davies, N. (2009) 'Murdoch papers paid £1m to gag phone-hacking victims', *The Guardian*, 8 July. Available at: www.guardian.co.uk/media/2009/jul/08/murdoch-papers-phone-hacking (accessed April 2013).

Davies, N. and Hill, A. (2011) 'Missing Milly Dowler's voicemail was hacked by News of the World', *The Guardian*, 5 July. Available at: www.guardian.co.uk/uk/2011/jul/04/milly-dowler-voicemail-hacked-news-of-world (accessed April 2013).

Davis, M. (2009) *Comrade or Brother: A History of the British Labour Movement* (2nd edn). London: Pluto.

De George, R.T. (1993/1978) 'Moral issues in business', in G. Cryssides and J. Kaler (eds), *An Introduction to Business Ethics*. London: Thomson. pp. 37–49.

Deetz, S.A. (1992) *Democracy in an Age of Corporate Colonization: Developments in Communication and the Politics of Everyday Life*. Albany, NY: State University of New York.

Dihigg, C. and Barboza, D. (2012) 'In China, human costs are built into an iPad', *New York Times*, 25 January. Available at www.nytimes.com/2012/01/26/business/ieconomy-apples-ipad-and-the-human-costs-for-workers-in-china.html?pagewanted=all&_r=0 (accessed July 2013).

Donaldson, T. and Preston, L. (1995) 'The stakeholder theory of the corporation: concepts, evidence and implications', *Academy of Management Review*, 20–1: 65–91.

Doward, J. (2002) 'Lord of the lap dance', *The Observer*, 3 February. Available at: www.guardian.co.uk/business/2002/feb/03/theobserver.observerbusiness11?INTCMP=SRCH (accessed November 2012).

Dowie, N. (1977) 'Pinto Madness', *Mother Jones*, September/October. Available at: www.motherjones.com/politics/1977/09/pinto-madness (accessed November 2013).

Dugan, E. (2011) 'The unstoppable march of the tobacco giants', *The Independent on Sunday*, 29 May. Available at: www.independent.co.uk/life-style/health-and-families/health-news/the-unstoppable-march-of-the-tobacco-giants-2290583.html (accessed November 2013).

Economist, The (2012) 'Wake up and smell the coffee', *The Economist*, 15 December. Available at: www.economist.com/news/business/21568432-starbuckss-tax-troubles-are-sign-things-come-multinationals-wake-up-and-smell (accessed April 2013).

Economist, The (2013) 'The origins of the financial crisis', *The Economist*, 7 September. Available at: http://www.economist.com/news/schoolsbrief/21584534-effects-financial-crisis-are-still-being-felt-five-years-article (accessed November 2013).

Evan, W.M. and Freeman, R.E. (1993) 'A stakeholder theory of the modern corporation: Kantian capitalism', in G.D. Chryssides and J.H. Kaler, *An Introduction to Business Ethics*. London: International Thompson Business Press. pp 254–66.

Fast Food Forward (2013) *We can't survive on $7.25!* Available at: www.fastfoodforward.org/en/ (accessed August 2013).

Fernholz, T. (2013) 'How cigarette companies use free trade deals to sell more cigarettes to women and kids', *Quartz*, 10 September. Available at: http://qz.com/122436/how-cigarette-companies-use-free-trade-deals-to-sell-more-cigarettes-to-women-and-kids/ (accessed November 2013).

Finch, J. and Bowers, S. (2009) 'Executive pay keeps rising', *The Guardian*, 14 September. Available at: www.guardian.co.uk/business/2009/sep/14/executive-pay-keeps-rising (accessed April 2013).

Fleming, P. and Jones, M. (2013) *The End of Corporate Social Responsibility: Crisis and Critique*. London: Sage.

Francis, H. and Smith, D. (1980) *The Fed: A History of the South Wales Miners in the Twentieth Century*. London: Lawrence and Wishart.

Fraser, N. (1992) 'Rethinking the public sphere', in C. Calhoun (ed.), *Habermas and the Public Sphere*. Cambridge, MA: MIT Press. pp. 109–42.

Freeman, M. (2002) *Human Rights: An Interdisciplinary Approach*. Cambridge: Polity.

Freeman, R.E. (1984) *Strategic Management: A Stakeholder Approach*. Boston: Pitman.

Freeman, R.E. (1994) 'The politics of stakeholder theory: some future directions', *Business Ethics Quarterly*, 4/4: 409–21.

Friedman, J. (ed.) (2011) *What Caused the Financial Crisis*. Philadelphia, PA: University of Pennsylvania Press.

Friedman, M. (1970) 'The social responsibility of business is to increase its profits', *New York Times Magazine*, 13 September. Available at: www.colorado.edu/studentgroups/libertarians/issues/friedman-soc-resp-business.html (accessed July 2013).

Friedman, T.L. (2005) *The World is Flat: A Brief History of the Twenty-First Century*. New York: Farrar, Straus and Giroux.

Fryer, M. (2011) *Ethics and Organizational Leadership: Developing a Normative Model*. Oxford: Oxford University Press.

Fryer, M. (2012) 'Facilitative leadership: drawing on Jürgen Habermas' model of ideal speech to propose a less impositional way to lead', *Organization*, 19/1: 25–43.

Furnham, A. and Mak, T. (1999) 'Sex-role stereotyping in television commercials: a review and comparison of fourteen studies done in five continents over 25 years', *Sex Roles*, 41/5&6: 412–37.

Gabbatt, A. (2013) 'US fast food workers walk out in organised strike against low wages', *The Guardian*, 29 July. Available at: www.theguardian.com/world/2013/jul/29/fast-food-workers-strike-wages?INTCMP=SRCH (accessed August 2013).

Galbraith, J.K. (1999/1958) *The Affluent Society*. St Ives: Penguin.

Gardiner, P. (1993) 'Kant: *Critique of Judgement*', in R.C. Solomon and K.M. Higgins (eds), *The Age of German Idealism*. Abingdon: Routledge. pp. 103–37.

Garside, J. (2012) 'Executive pay soars as bosses set each others' awards', *The Guardian*, 2 April. Available at: www.guardian.co.uk/business/2012/apr/02/executive-pay-ftse-firms (accessed April 2013).

Garvin, T., McGee, T.K., Smoyer-Tomic, K.E. and Ato Aubyn, E. (2009) 'Community-company relations in gold mining in Ghana', *Journal of Environmental Management*, 90: 571–86.

Gilbert, J. (2005) 'Cultural rights' in R.K.M. Smith and C. van der Anker (eds), *The Essentials of Human Rights*. London: Hodder Arnold. pp. 76–9.

Gilligan, C. (1987) 'Moral orientation and moral development', in E.F. Kittay and D.T. Meyers (eds), *Women and Moral Theory*. Savage, MD: Rowman and Littlefield. pp. 19–33.

Gilligan, C. (1993/1982) *In a Different Voice: Psychological Theory and Women's Development*. Cambridge: Cambridge University Press.

Gilligan, C. (1995) 'Hearing the difference: theorizing connection', *Hypatia*, 10/2: 120–7.

Glencore Xstrata (2013) 'Sustainability: our approach', Glencore Xstrata corporate website. Available at: www.glencorexstrata.com/sustainability/our-approach/ (accessed August 2013).

Global Exchange (2011) 'Sweatfree', Global Exchange website. Available at: www.globalexchange.org/fairtrade/campaigns/sweatfree (accessed September 2012).

Goergen, M. (2012) *International Corporate Governance*. Harlow: Pearson.

Goff, S. (2011) 'Ethical banking: Strong principles foster growth', *Financial Times*, 15 June. Available at: www.ft.com/cms/s/0/93502918-9716-11e0-9c9d-00144feab49a.html#axzz2jmyraJ9F (accessed November 2013).

Goffman, E. (1979/1974) *Gender Advertisements*. London: Macmillan.

Goldcorp (2013) 'Responsible mining', Goldcorp Inc. corporate website. Available at: www.goldcorp.com/English/Responsible-Mining/default.aspx (accessed December 2013).

Goldstein, K. (2000/1939) *The Organism: A Holistic Approach to Biology Derived from Pathological Data in Man*. Cambridge, MA: MIT.

Goodin, R. (1993) 'Utility and the Good', in P. Singer (ed.), *A Companion to Ethics*. Oxford: Blackwell. pp. 241–48.

Goodley, G. and Wearden, S. (2010) 'FTSE 100 bosses criticised as boardroom pay leaps by 55%', *The Guardian*, 29 October. Available at: www.guardian.co.uk/business/2010/oct/29/ftse-boardroom-pay-soars (accessed April 2013).

Google (2013) 'Ten things we know to be true', Google corporate website. Available at: www.google.com/about/company/philosophy/ (accessed September 2013).

Gordon, L. (1997) *Her Majesty's Other Children: Sketches of Racism from a Neocolonial Age*. Lanham, MD: Rowman and Littlefield.

Gormley, M. (2013) 'Flavored tobacco ban in NY convenience stores? Cancer society says products aimed at kids', *Huffington Post*, 31 May. Available at: www.huffingtonpost.com/2013/06/01/flavored-tobacco-ban-in-ny-convenience-stores-cancer-society-says-products-aimed-at-kids_n_3371834.html (accessed November 2013).

Gray, L. (2013) 'Thousands of wind turbines to go up as subsidies cut', *The Telegraph*, 8 February. Available at: www.telegraph.co.uk/earth/energy/windpower/9858849/Thousands-of-wind-turbines-to-go-up-as-subsidies-cut.html (accessed March 2013).

Greenpeace (2009) 'Krill: the food that keeps Antarctica alive is under threat'. Available at: http://www.greenpeace.org/seasia/ph/What-we-do/oceans/polar-seas/antarctic/krill-antarctica-foodchain-under-threat/ (accessed March 2013).

Greenpeace (2014) 'Whaling'. Available at: http://www.greenpeace.org/international/en/campaigns/oceans/fit-for-the-future/whaling/ (accessed July 2014).

Greenwood, D.J. (1989) 'Culture by the pound: an anthropological perspective on tourism as cultural commoditization', in V.L. Smith (ed.), *Hosts and Guests. The Anthropology of Tourism*. Philadelphia, PA: University of Pennsylvania Press. pp. 171–85.

Groom, B. (2011) 'Executive pay: The trickle-up effect', *Financial Times*, 27 July. Available at: www.ft.com/cms/s/0/0a752f2e-b883-11e0-8206-00144feabdc0.html#axzz1Udci9Vlq (accessed April 2013).

Groom, B. (2013) 'Top pay rises despite struggling economy', *Financial Times*, 10 April. Available at: www.ft.com/cms/s/0/5caa3636-a13e-11e2-990c-00144feabdc0.html#axzz2QAU8U4xZ (accessed April 2013).

GSK (2013a) 'What we do', GSK corporate website. Available at: www.gsk.com/about-us/what-we-do.html (accessed December 2013).

GSK (2013b) 'Our people', GSK corporate website. Available at: www.gsk.com/responsibility/our-people.html (accessed December 2013).

GSK (2013c) 'Our planet', GSK corporate website. Available at: www.gsk.com/responsibility/our-planet.html (accessed December 2013).

GSK (2013d) 'Investing in GSK', GSK corporate website. Available at: www.gsk.com/investors/investing-in-gsk.html (accessed December 2013).

Guardian, The (2010) 'Bloodgate doctor Wendy Chapman given warning by disciplinary panel', *The Guardian*, 1 September. Available at: www.guardian.co.uk/sport/2010/sep/01/bloodgate-wendy-chapman-gmc-warning (accessed May 2013).

Guest, D.E. and Conway, N. (2002) *Pressure at Work and the Psychological Contract*. London: CIPD.

Guha, R. (1997/1989) 'Radical American environmentalism and wilderness preservation: a third world critique', in R. Guha and J. Martinez-Alier, *Varieties of Environmentalism: Essays North and South*. London: Earthscan. pp. 92–108.

Guha, R. and Martinez-Alier, J. (1997) *Varieties of Environmentalism: Essays North and South*. London: Earthscan.

Habermas, J. (1974/1964) 'The public sphere: an encyclopaedia article', S. Lennox and F. Lennox (transls), *New German Critique*, 3: 49–55.

Habermas, J. (1975/1973) *Legitimation Crisis,* T. McCarthy (transl.). Boston, MA: Beacon Press.

Habermas, J. (1979/1976) *Communication and the Evolution of Society*, T. McCarthy (transl.). London: Heinemann.

Habermas, J. (1981) 'New Social Movements', *Telos*, 49: 33–37.

Habermas, J. (1984/1981) *The Theory of Communicative Action, Volume One: Reason and the Rationalisation of Society*, T. McCarthy (transl.). Boston, MA: Beacon Press.

Habermas, J. (1987/1981) *The Theory of Communicative Action, Volume Two: Lifeworld and System: A Critique of Functionalist Reason*, T. McCarthy (transl.). Boston, MA: Beacon Press.

Habermas, J. (1990/1983) *Moral Consciousness and Communicative Action*, C. Lenhardt and S.W. Nicholson (transls). Cambridge, MA: MIT Press.

Habermas, J. (1994/1991) *Justification and Application: Remarks on Discourse Ethics*. C.P. Cronin (transl.). Cambridge, MA: MIT Press.

Hafez, N. and Ling, P.M. (2006) 'Finding the Kool Mixx: how Brown & Williamson used music marketing to sell cigarettes', *Tobacco Control*, 15: 359–66.

Halliday, J. (2012) 'Surfthechannel owner sentenced to four years over piracy', *The Guardian*, 14 August. Available at: www.guardian.co.uk/technology/2012/aug/14/anton-vickerman-surfthe channel-sentenced (accessed August 2012).

Hamilton, C. (2003) *Growth Fetish*. Crows Nest, NSW: Allen and Unwin.

Hancox, D. (2013) *The Village Against the World*. London: Verso.

Harkaway, N. (2012) *The Blind Giant: How to Survive in the Digital Age*. London: John Murray.

Hegel, G.W.F. (1969/1831) *Hegel's Science of Logic*, A.V. Miller (transl.). Amhurst, NY: Prometheus Books.

Hegel, G.W.F. (1975/1830) *Hegel's Logic: Being Part One of The Encyclopaedia of Philosophical Sciences*, W. Wallace (transl.). Oxford: Oxford University Press.

Hegel, G.W.F. (1977/1807) *Hegel's Phenomenology of Spirit*, A.V. Miller (transl.). Oxford: Oxford University Press.

Hegelsen, S. (1990) *The Female Advantage: Women's Ways of Leadership*. New York: Doubleday.

Helmore, E. (2013) 'US fast-food workers in vanguard of growing protests at "starvation wages"', *The Observer*, 10 August. Available at: www.theguardian.com/world/2013/aug/10/us-fast-food-protests-wages (accessed August 2013).

Hepburn, R. (1966) 'Contemporary aesthetics and the neglect of natural beauty', in B. Williams and A. Montefiore (eds), *British Analytic Philosophy*. London: Routledge. pp. 285–310.

Herbert, G.B. (2002) *A Philosophical History of Rights*. New Brunswick, NJ: Transaction.

Hoagland, S.L. (1991) 'Some thoughts about "caring"', in C. Card (ed.), *Feminist Ethics*. Lawrence, KS: University Press of Kansas. pp. 246–63.

Hobbes, T. (1994/1651) *Leviathan*, E. Curley (ed.). Indianapolis, IN: Hackett.

Hobsbawm, E. (1997/1975) *The Age of Capital: 1848–1875*. London: Abacus.

Hobsbawm, E. (2003/1962) *The Age of Revolution: 1789–1848*. London: Abacus.

Honig, B. (1996) 'Difference, dilemmas and the politics of home', in S. Benhabib (ed.), *Democracy and Difference: Contesting the Boundaries of the Political*. Princeton, NJ: Princeton University Press. pp. 257–77.

Hughes, G.H. (2001) *Aristotle on Ethics*. London: Routledge.

Hughes, M., Gardham, D., Bingham, J. and Bloxham, A. (2011) 'Phone hacking: families of war dead 'targeted' by News of the World', *The Telegraph*, 7 July. Available at: www.telegraph.co.uk/news/uknews/phone-hacking/8621797/Phone-hacking-families-of-war-dead-targeted-by-News-of-the-World.html (accessed April 2013).

Hutton, W. (ed.) (1997) *Stakeholding and its Critics*. London: IEA.

ICBL (2013) 'Arguments for a ban', *International Campaign to Ban Landmines*. Available at: http://www.icbl.org/en-gb/problem/arguments-for-the-ban.aspx (accessed April 2013).

Industriall (2013) 'Bangladesh safety accord welcomes 100 brand milestone', Industriall Global Union website. Available at: www.industriall-union.org/bangladesh-safety-accord-welcomes-100-brand-milestone (accessed November 2013).

International Ecotourism Society (2000) 'Ecotourism statistical fact sheet'. Available at: www.active-tourism.com/factsEcotourism1.pdf (accessed March 2013).

Irigaray, L. (2004/1984) *An Ethics of Sexual Difference*, C. Burke and G.C. Gill (transls). London: Continuum.

Irwin, T. (1999) *Aristotle: Nicomachean Ethics*. Indianapolis, IN: Hackett.

IT (2013) Imperial Tobacco corporate website. Available at: www.imperial-tobacco.com/index.asp?page=5 (accessed November 2013).

ITUC (2007) *Where the House Always Wins: Private Equity, Hedge Funds and the New Casino Capitalism*. International Trade Union Confederation Report. Available at: www.ituc-csi.org/IMG/pdf/ITUC_casino.EN.pdf (accessed June 2012).

Iyer, P. (2000/1988) 'Bali: on Prospero's Isle', in F.J. Lechner and J. Bili (eds), *The Globalization Reader*. Malden, MA: Blackwell. pp. 111–14.

Jackson, K.T. (2005) 'Towards authenticity: a Sartrean perspective on business ethics', *Journal of Business Ethics*, 58: 307–25.

Jaggar, A.M. (1991) 'Feminist ethics: projects, problems, prospects', in C. Card (ed.), *Feminist Ethics*. Lawrence, KS: University Press of Kansas. pp. 78–104.

Jelic, R. and Wright, M. (2011) 'Exits, performance, and late stage private equity: the case of UK management buy-outs', *European Financial Management*, 17/3: 560–93.

Jensen, M.C. (2002) 'Value maximization, stakeholder theory, and the corporate objective function', *Business Ethics Quarterly*, 12/2: 235–56.

Johnson, P. (1976) 'Women and power: towards a theory of effectiveness', *Journal of Social Issues*, 32/3: 99–110.

Johnson, P. (2006) 'Whence democracy? A review and critique of the conceptual dimensions and implications of the business case for organizational democracy', *Organization*, 13/2: 245–74.

Jones, C., Parker, M. and ten Bos, R. (2005) *For Business Ethics*. London: Routledge.

Jones, S. (1999) 'Jeans maker Levi Strauss to cut 5,900 jobs in the US and Canada', World Socialist Website, 26 February. Available at: www.wsws.org/en/articles/1999/02/levi-f26.html (accessed August 2013).

Jones, T.M. and Hunt, R.O. (1991) 'The ethics of leveraged management buyouts revisited', *Journal of Business Ethics*, 10: 833–40.

Jorgenson, A. (2003) 'Consumption and environmental degradation: a cross-national study of the ecological footprint', *Social Problems*, 48: 122–45.

Jorgenson, A. (2006) 'Unequal ecological exchange and environmental degradation: a theoretical proposition and cross-national study of deforestation, 1990–2000', *Rural Sociology*, 71/4: 685–712.

Jorgenson, A., Austin, K. and Dick, C. (2009) 'Ecologically unequal exchange and the resource consumption/degradation paradox: a panel study of less-developed countries, 1970–2000', *International Journal of Comparative Sociology*, 50/3–4: 263–84.

Jowit, J. (2008) 'Krill fishing threatens the Antarctic', *The Guardian*, 23 March. Available at: www.guardian.co.uk/environment/2008/mar/23/fishing.food (accessed March 2013).

Kaimowitz, D., Mertens, B., Wunder, S. and Pacheco, P. (2013) 'Hamburger connection fuels Amazon destruction: cattle ranching and deforestation in Brazil's Amazon', *Center For International Forestry Research*. Available at: www.cifor.org/publications/pdf_files/media/Amazon.pdf (accessed March 2013).

Kalleberg, A.L. (2011) *Good Jobs, Bad Jobs*. New York: Russell Sage Foundation.

Kant, I. (1948/1785) 'Groundwork to the metaphysic of morals', H. J. Paton (trans. and ed.), *The Moral Law: Kant's Groundwork to the Metaphysic of Morals*. London: Hutchinson. pp. 51–123.

Kant, I. (1997/1788) *Critique of Practical Reason*, M. Gregor (trans. and ed.). Cambridge: Cambridge University Press.

Kant, I. (2003/1787) *Critique of Pure Reason*, N. Kemp Smith (trans.). Basingstoke: Palgrave Macmillan.

Kasmir, S. (1996) *The Myth of Mondragón: Cooperatives, Politics, and Working-class Life in a Basque Town*. Albany, NY: State University of New York Press.

Kaufmann, W. (ed.) (1956) *Existentialism from Dostoevsky to Sartre*. New York: Meridian.

Kavka, G.S. (1999/1983) 'Hobbes war of all against all', in C.W. Morris (ed.), *Critical Essays on Hobbes, Locke, and Rousseau*. Lanham, MD: Rowman and Littlefield. pp. 1–22.

Keller, D.R. (2010) (ed.) *Environmental Ethics: The Big Questions*. Chichester: Wiley Blackwell.

Kierkegaard, S. (1997/1843) 'Either/or, a fragment of life', in H.V. Hong and E.H. Hong (eds), *The Essential Kierkegaard*. Princeton, NJ: Princeton University Press. pp. 37–83.

Kingsley, P. (2012a) 'Financial crisis: timeline', *The Guardian*, 7 August. Available at: www.theguardian.com/business/2012/aug/07/credit-crunch-boom-bust-timeline (accessed November 2013).

Kingsley, P. (2012b) 'A business with no bosses', *The Guardian*, 8 October. Available at: www.theguardian.com/society/2012/oct/08/business-with-no-bosses (accessed September 2013).

Klein, N. (2001) *No Logo*. London: Harper Collins.

Knudsen, H., Busck, O. and Lind, J. (2011) 'Work environment quality: the role of workplace participation and democracy', *Work Employment & Society*, 25/3: 379–96.

Kokou, E. (2006) 'Third World used as a dumping ground for toxic waste', *Socialist Worker*, 14 October. Available at: www.socialistworker.co.uk/art.php?id=9903 (accessed February 2013).

Kraut, R. (2010) 'Aristotle's ethics', *Stanford Encyclopaedia of Philosophy*. Available at: http://plato.stanford.edu/entries/aristotle-ethics/ (accessed May 2013).

Kuusela, O. (2011) *Key Terms in Ethics*. London: Continuum.

Lafuente, J.L. (2012) 'The MONDRAGON cooperative experience: humanity at work', *Management Innovation eXchange*, 11 May. Available at: www.managementexchange.com/story/mondragon-cooperative-experience-humanity-work (accessed November 2013).

Langiulli, N. (1971) *The Existentialist Tradition*. New Jersey: Humanities Press.

Leigh, D. (2009) 'How UK oil company Trafigura tried to cover up African pollution disaster', *The Guardian*, 16 September. Available at: www.theguardian.com/world/2009/sep/16/trafigura-african-pollution-disaster (accessed December 2013).

Leigh, D. and Evans, R. (2003) 'BAE accused of arms deal slush fund', *The Guardian*, 11 September. Available at: www.guardian.co.uk/world/2003/sep/11/bae.freedomofinformation (accessed July 2013).

Leigh, D. and Evans, R. (2011a) 'The Iranian deals', *Guardian*. Available at: www.guardian.co.uk/baefiles/page/0,,2095222,00.html (accessed July 2013).

Leigh, D. and Evans, R. (2011b) 'Secrets of al-Yamamah', *Guardian*. Available at: www.guardian.co.uk/baefiles/page/0,,2095831,00.html (accessed July 2013).

Leigh, D. and Evans, R. (2011c) 'BAE's secret money machine', *Guardian*. Available at: www.guardian.co.uk/baefiles/page/0,,2095840,00.html (accessed July 2013).

Leigh, D. and Evans, R. (2011d) 'Nobbling the police', *Guardian*. Available at: www.guardian.co.uk/baefiles/page/0,,2098531,00.html (accessed July 2013).

Leigh, D. and Evans, R. (2011e) 'Healey's machine', *Guardian*. Available at: www.guardian.co.uk/baefiles/page/0,,2093320,00.html (accessed July 2013).

Leigh, D. and Evans, R. (2011f) 'The unlovable Saudis', *Guardian*. Available at: www.guardian.co.uk/baefiles/page/0,,2095803,00.html (accessed July 2013).

Leigh, D. and Evans, R. (2011g) 'The Ray Brown years', *Guardian*. Available at: www.guardian.co.uk/baefiles/page/0,,2095209,00.html (accessed July 2013).

Leiter, B. (2002) *Nietzsche on Morality*. London: Routledge.

Leopold, A. (2003/1949) 'The land ethic', in A. Light and H. Rolston (eds), *Environmental Ethics: An Anthology*. Malden, MA: Blackwell. pp. 38–46.

Levi Strauss (2013) 'Levi Strauss & Co: timeline', Levi Strauss corporate website. Available at: http://www.levistrauss.com/our-story/heritage-timeline/heritage-timeline-2/ (accessed July 2014).

Levinas, E. (1969/1961) *Totality and Infinity: An Essay on Exteriority*. Pittsburgh, PA: Duquesne University Press.

Libcom (2013) 'The house of cards – the Savar building collapse', libcom.org website. Available at: http://libcom.org/news/house-cards-savar-building-collapse-26042013 (accessed November 2013).

Ling, P.M. and Glantz, S.A. (2002) 'Why and how the tobacco industry sells cigarettes to young adults: evidence from industry documents', *American Journal of Public Health*, 92/6: 908–16.

Lloyd, C., Mason, G. and Mayhew, K. (eds) (2008) *Low Wage Work in the United Kingdom*. New York: Russell Sage Foundation.

Locke, J. (1988/1690) *Two Treatises of Government*, P. Laslett (ed.). Cambridge: Cambridge University Press.

Luke, T.W. and White, S.K. (1987) 'Critical theory, the information revolution, and an ecological path to modernity', in J. Forester (ed.), *Critical Theory and Public Life*. Cambridge, MA: MIT Press. pp. 22–53.

Lynch, L. (2013) 'Buying Eastern Europe: the tobacco industry takeover', *Balkanist*, 14 September. Available at: http://balkanist.net/buying-eastern-europe-tobacco-industry-takeover/ (accessed November 2013).

Macalister, T. (2013a) 'Government invests £50m in windfarms', *The Guardian*, 6 February. Available at: www.guardian.co.uk/business/2013/feb/06/government-invests-50million-pounds-windfarms (accessed March 2013).

Macalister, T. (2013b) 'Big six energy firms accused of "cold-blooded profiteering"', *The Guardian*, 12 April. Available at: www.theguardian.com/business/2013/apr/12/big-six-energy-firms-accused-profiteering (accessed August 2013).

MacIntyre, A. (1985/1981) *After Virtue*. London: Duckworth

MacIntyre, A. (1994) 'A partial response to my critics', in J. Horton and S. Mendus (eds), *After MacIntyre: Critical Perspectives on the Work of Alasdair MacIntyre*. Cambridge: Polity. pp. 283–304.

MacLeod, S. (2005) 'Business and human rights', in R.K.M. Smith and C. van der Anker (eds), *The Essentials of Human Rights*. London: Hodder Arnold. pp. 27–31.

Mahoney, J. (2007) *The Challenge of Human Rights*. Malden, MA: Blackwell.

Mallin, C.A. (2007) *Corporate Governance*. Oxford: Oxford University Press.

Manning, K.C., Kelly, K.J. and Comello, M.L. (2009) 'Flavoured cigarettes, sensation seeking and adolescents' perceptions of cigarette brands', *Tobacco Control*, 18: 6459–65.

Mansbridge, J. (1996) 'Using power/fighting power: the polity', in S. Benhabib (ed.), *Democracy and Difference: Contesting the Boundaries of the Political*. Princeton, NJ: Princeton University Press. pp. 46–66.

Marcuse, H. (2002/1964) *One Dimensional Man: Studies in the Ideology of Advanced Industrial Society*. London: Routledge.

Marine Stewardship Council (2013) 'Vision and mission'. Available at: www.msc.org/about-us/vision-mission (accessed March 2013).

Marshall, J. (1995) *Women Managers Moving On: Exploring Career and Life Choices*. London: Routledge.

Martinez-Alier, J. (2001) 'Mining conflicts, environmental justice, and valuation', *Journal of Hazardous Materials*, 86: 153–170.

Marx, K. (2000/1843) 'On the Jewish question', in D. McLellan (ed.), *Karl Marx Selected Writings* (2nd edn). Oxford: Oxford University Press. pp. 46–70.

Marx, K. (2000/1849) 'Wage labour and capital', in D. McLellan (ed.), *Karl Marx Selected Writings* (2nd edn). Oxford: Oxford University Press. pp. 273–94.

Marx, K. (2000/1867) *Capital*, in D. McLellan (ed.), *Karl Marx Selected Writings* (2nd edn). Oxford: Oxford University Press. pp. 452–546.

Marx, K. and Engels, F. (2000/1848) *The Communist Manifesto*, in D. McLellan (ed.), *Karl Marx Selected Writings* (2nd edn). Oxford: Oxford University Press. pp. 245–72.

Maslow, A.H. (1943) 'A theory of human motivation', *Psychological Review*, 50: 370–96.

Matten, D. and Crane, A. (2005) 'Corporate citizenship: toward and extended theoretical conceptualization', *Academy of Management Review*, 30/1: 166–79.

Mauleon, V. and Ting, C. (2000) 'El Paso: Texas colonias', *At the Breaking Point: US-Mexico Border*, UC-Berkeley Graduate School of Journalism Report on the Effects of the NAFTA. Available at: http://journalism.berkeley.edu/projects/border/elpasocolonias.html (accessed August 2013).

McKibbin, B. (2010/1998) 'A special moment in history', in D.R. Keller (ed.), *Environmental Ethics: The Big Questions*. Chichester: Wiley Blackwell. pp. 469–75.

Mendick, R. (2013) 'Foreign firms' £100bn wind farm subsidies', *The Telegraph*, 3 February. Available at: www.telegraph.co.uk/earth/energy/windpower/9844140/Foreign-firms-100bn-wind-farm-subsidies.html (accessed March 2013).

Miceli, M.P., Near, J.P. and Dworkin, T.M. (2008) *Whistle-blowing in Organizations*. New York: Routledge.

Mid Wales Wind Farm Planning (2013) Available at: www.midwaleswind.co.uk/ (accessed March 2013).

Mill, J.S. (1962/1861) *Utilitarianism*, reproduced in M. Warnock (ed.), *Utilitarianism*. London: Collins Fontana.

Mill, J.S. (2010/1874) 'The amoral status of nature', in D.R. Keller (ed.), *Environmental Ethics: The Big Questions*. Chichester: Wiley Blackwell. pp. 73–77.

Miller, D. (1994) 'Ontology and style', in J. Friedman (ed.), *Consumption and Identity*. Amsterdam: Harwood. pp. 71–96.

Milmo, C. (2009) 'Dumped in Africa: Britain's toxic waste', *The Independent*, 18 February. Available at: www.independent.co.uk/news/world/africa/dumped-in-africa-britain8217s-toxic-waste-1624869.html (accessed July 2014).

Monbiot, G. (2001) *Captive State: The Corporate Takeover of Britain*. London: Pan.

Mondragon (2013) Mondragon Corporation corporate website. Available at: http://www.mondragon-corporation.com/eng/ (accessed July 2014).

Moody-Adams, M. (1991) 'Gender and the complexity of moral voices', in C. Card (ed.), *Feminist Ethics*. Lawrence, KS: University Press of Kansas. pp. 195–212.

Moore, G. (2002) 'On the implications of the practice-institution distinction: Macintyre and the application of modern virtue ethics to business', *Business Ethics Quarterly*, 12/1: 19–32.

Moore, G. (2005) 'Humanizing business: a modern virtue ethics approach', *Business Ethics Quarterly*, 15/2: 237–55.

Moore, G. (2008) 'Re-imagining the morality of management: a modern virtue ethics approach', *Business Ethics Quarterly*, 18/4: 483–511.

Moore, G. (2012) 'Virtue in business: alliance boots and an empirical exploration of Macintyre's conceptual framework', *Organization Studies*, 33/3: 363–87.

Moore, G. and Beadle, R. (2006) 'In search of organizational virtue in business: agents, goods, practices, institutions and environments', *Organization Studies*, 27/3: 369–89.

Moore, G.E. (1993/1903) *Principia Ethica*. Cambridge: Cambridge University Press.

Moore, G.E. (2005/1912) *Ethics*. Oxford: Oxford University Press.

Moore, M. (dir.) (1998) *The Big One*. Miramax Films.

Morgan, G. (1998) *Images of Organization* (The Executive Edition). Thousand Oaks: Sage.

MORI (2001) *The Springboard MBI Report 2001: A Survey into the Reality of Management Buy-ins from the Candidates' Perspective*. Springboard plc.

Morozov, E. (2011) *The Net Delusion: How Not to Liberate the World*. London: Penguin.

Morris, C.W. (1999) (ed.) *Critical Essays on Hobbes, Locke, and Rousseau*. Lanham, MD: Rowman and Littlefield.

Move Your Money (2013) Available at: http://moveyourmoney.org.uk/ (accessed November 2013).

Muir, J. (2010/1901) 'The wild parks and forest reservations of the West and Hetch Hetchy Valley', in D.R. Keller (ed.), *Environmental Ethics: The Big Questions*. Chichester: Wiley Blackwell. pp. 96–7.

Murphy, R. (2012) 'Amazon, Google and Starbucks are struggling to defend their tax avoidance' *The Guardian*, 13 November. Available at: www.guardian.co.uk/commentisfree/2012/nov/13/amazon-google-starbucks-tax-avoidance (accessed April 2013).

Myers, N. (1981) 'The hamburger connection: how Central America's forests become north America's hamburgers', *Ambio*, 10/1: 3–8.

Naagbanton, P. (2011) 'Shell has admitted liability but has a long way to go to make amends', *The Guardian*, 4 August. Available at: www.guardian.co.uk/commentisfree/2011/aug/04/shell-nigeria-oil-spills (accessed April, 2013).

Næss, A. (1973) 'The shallow and the deep, long-range ecology movement. A summary', *Inquiry*, 16/1: 95–100.

Næss, A. (2010/2008) 'The shallow and the deep ecology movement', in D.R. Keller (ed.), *Environmental Ethics: The Big Questions*. Chichester: Wiley Blackwell. pp. 230–35.

Near, J.P. and Miceli, M.P. (1985) 'Organizational dissidence: the case of whistle-blowing', *Journal of Business Ethics*, 4/1: 1–16.

Newmont (2013) 'Sustainability', Newmont Mining Corporation corporate website. Available at: http://newmont.com/sustainability (accessed December 2013).

Nietzsche, F. (2003/1887) *The Genealogy of Morals*. New York: Dover.

Nietzsche, F. (2006/1886) 'Beyond good and evil: prelude to a philosophy of the future', in K. A. Pearson and D. Large (eds), *The Nietzsche Reader*. Malden, MA: Blackwell. pp. 311–61.

Nietzsche, F. (2006/1887) 'The gay science', in K. A. Pearson and D. Large (eds), *The Nietzsche Reader*. Malden, MA: Blackwell. pp. 362–83.

Noddings, N. (2003) *Caring: A Feminine Approach to Ethics and Moral Education* (2nd edn). Berkeley, CA: University of California Press.

NUS (2012) 'Students' unions join NUS and Move Your Money ethical banking campaign', NUS website. Available at: www.nus.org.uk/en/news/students-unions-join-nus-and-move-your-money-ethical-banking-campaign/ (accessed November 2013).

Object (2012a) 'Stripping the illusion: lap-dancing – frequently asked questions'. Available at: www.object.org.uk/faqs (accessed November 2012).

Object (2012b) 'Stripping the illusion: frequently asked questions about lap-dancing'. Available at: www.object.org.uk/files/lap%20dancing%20FAQ%202010.pdf (accessed November 2011).

Occupy (2013) #occupytogether web site. Available at: www.occupytogether.org/aboutoccupy/ (accessed November 2013).

O'Connell, D. (2009) 'How the Phoenix gang plundered MG Rover', *The Sunday Times*, 13 September: 10–11.

O'Neill, O. (1993) 'Kantian ethics', in P. Singer (ed.), *A Companion to Ethics*. Oxford: Blackwell. pp. 175–85.

Owen, G. (1999) *From Empire to Europe: The Decline and Revival of British Industry Since the Second World War*. London: Harper Collins.

Pariser, E. (2011) *The Filter Bubble*. New York: Penguin.

Parker, M. (2002) *Against Management*. Cambridge: Polity.

Parker, M. (ed.) (1998) *Ethics and Organizations*. London: Sage.

Paton, H.J. (1948) *The Moral Law: Kant's Groundwork to the Metaphysic of Morals*. London: Hutchinson.

Perlis, M.F. and Chais, W.E. (2010) 'Will whistle-blowing be millions well spent?', *Forbes*, 15 September. Available at: www.forbes.com/2010/09/15/whistle-blowers-sec-opinions-columnists-perlis-chais.html (accessed July 2013).

Pichet, E. (2011) 'Enlightened shareholder theory: whose interests should be served by the supporters of corporate governance?', *Corporate Ownership & Control*, 8/2–3: 353–62.

PMI (2013) Philip Morris International corporate website. Available at: www.pmi.com/eng/sustainability/pages/sustainability.aspx (accessed November 2013).

Politics Home (2011) 'Statement from James Murdoch on the closure of the News of the World', 7 July. Available at: www.politicshome.com/uk/article/31458/ (accessed April 2011).

Project Tiger (2013) 'Introduction', *Project Tiger India*. Available at: http://projecttiger.nic.in/ (accessed March 2013).

PSE (2007) *Hedge Funds and Private Equity: A Critical Analysis*, Socialist Group in the European Parliament. Available at: www.socialistsanddemocrats.eu/sites/default/files/2239_EN_publication_hedge_funds_1.pdf (accessed July 2014).

Ramesh, R. (2014) '300,000 poor people live more than 1km from free cash machine', *The Guardian*, 1 January. Available at: www.theguardian.com/society/2014/jan/01/poor-people-free-cash-machines (accessed January 2014).

Rawls, J. (1999/1971) *A Theory of Justice*. Oxford: Oxford University Press.

Read, J. (2012) 'Ford deals blow to UK economy', *Financial Times*, 25 October. Available at: www.ft.com/cms/s/0/0b4e1da4-1ea1-11e2-bebc-00144feabdc0.html (accessed November 2012).

Rees, P. (2009a) 'Tom Williams admits he asked for doctor to cut his lip to corroborate blood injury claims', *The Guardian*, 26 August. Available at: www.guardian.co.uk/sport/2009/aug/26/doctor-blood-harlequins (accessed May 2013).

Rees, P. (2009b) 'Harlequins' Charles Jillings resigns, bagging Dean Richards into the bargain', *The Guardian*, 28 August. Available at: www.guardian.co.uk/sport/2009/aug/28/charles-jillings-harlequins-resign-bloodgate (accessed May 2013).

Rees, P. (2010) 'Former Harlequins physio Steph Brennan struck off over Bloodgate', *The Guardian*, 14 September. Available at: www.guardian.co.uk/sport/2010/sep/14/steph-brennan-harlequins-bloodgate (accessed May 2013).

Regan, T. (1983) *The Case for Animal Rights*. Berkeley, CA: University of California Press.

Rice, J. (2007) 'Ecological unequal exchange: consumption, equity, and unsustainable structural relationships within the global economy', *International Journal of Comparative Sociology*, 48: 43–72.

Riley, P. (1999/1970) 'A possible explanation of Rousseau's general will', in C.W. Morris (ed.), *Critical Essays on Hobbes, Locke, and Rousseau*. Lanham, MD: Rowman and Littlefield. pp. 167–90.

Rio Tinto (2013) 'Communities', Rio Tinto corporate website. Available at: www.riotinto.com/ourcommitment/communities-4796.aspx (accessed December 2013).

Rolston, H. (2000) 'Aesthetics in the swamps', *Perspectives in Biology and Medicine*, 43/4: 584–97.

Rosener, J.B. (1990) 'Ways women lead', *Harvard Business Review*, November-December: 119–25.

Rousseau, J-J. (1993/1751) 'A discourse on political economy', in G.D.H. Cole (transl.), *The Social Contract and The Discourses*. New York: Everyman. pp. 127–68.

Rousseau, J-J. (1993/1755) 'A discourse on the origin of equality', in G.D.H. Cole (transl.), *The Social Contract and The Discourses*. New York: Everyman. pp. 31–125.

Rousseau, J-J. (1993/1762) 'The social contract' in G.D.H. Cole (transl.), *The Social Contract and The Discourses*. New York: Everyman. pp. 179–304.

Rushe, D. (2013a) 'Dow closes at record high as markets shrug off slow US growth', *The Guardian*, 15 March. Available at: www.theguardian.com/business/2013/mar/05/dow-jones-record-high-budget (accessed August 2013).

Rushe, D. (2013b) 'Dow Jones sets new high in closing above 15,000', *The Guardian*, 7 May. Available at: www.theguardian.com/business/2013/may/07/dow-jones-new-high-15000 (accessed August 2013).

Russell, T. (2007) 'Who's gonna build your wall', on Assorted Artists, *Wounded Heart of America*. Highstone Records.

Ryder, R.D. (2011) *Speciesism, Painism and Happiness: A Morality for the 21st Century*. Exeter: Societas.

Saad-Filho, A. and Johnston, D. (eds) (2005) *Neoliberalism: A Critical Reader*. London: Pluto Press.

Saito, Y. (1998) 'The aesthetics of unscenic nature', *Journal of Aesthetics and Art Criticism*, 56/2: 101–11.

Sanders, L. (1997) 'Against deliberation', *Political Theory*, 25: 347–76.

Sandler, R. (2010/2005) 'Environmental virtue ethics', in D.R. Keller (ed.), *Environmental Ethics: The Big Questions*. Chichester: Wiley Blackwell. pp. 252–6.

Sartre, J-P. (1973/1946) *Existentialism and Humanism*, P. Mairet (transl.). London: Methuen.

Sartre, J-P. (2003/1943) *Being and Nothingness*, H.E. Barnes (transl.). Oxford: Routledge.

Saul, H. (2013) 'Primark offers compensation to Bangladesh Rana Plaza collapse victims', *The Independent*, 24 October. Available at: www.independent.co.uk/news/world/asia/primark-offers-compensation-to-bangladesh-rana-plaza-collapse-victims-8901572.html (accessed July 2014).

Schaper, E. (1992) 'Taste, sublimity and genius: the aesthetics of nature and art', in P. Guyer (ed.), *The Cambridge Companion to Kant*. Cambridge: Cambridge University Press. pp. 367–93.

Schneewind, J.B. (1992) 'Autonomy, obligation and virtue: An overview of Kant's moral philosophy' in P. Guyer (ed.), *The Cambridge Companion to Kant*. Cambridge: Cambridge University Press. pp 309–41.

Schroeder, J.E. and Borgerson, J.L. (2005) 'An ethics of representation for international marketing communication', *International Marketing Review*, 22/5: 578–600.

Schumacher, E.F. (1993/1973) *Small is Beautiful: A Study of Economics as if People Mattered*. London: Vintage.

Shandra, J.M., Leckband, C., McKinney, L.A. and London, B. (2009) 'Ecologically unequal exchange, world polity, and biodiversity loss', *International Journal of Comparative Sociology*, 50/3–4: 285–310.

Shell (2012) Shell Global corporate website. Available at: www.shell.com/ (accessed November 2012).

Singer, P. (1995) *Animal Liberation* (2nd edn). London: Pimlico.

Sison, A.J.G. (2003) *The Moral Capital of Leaders: Why Virtue Matters*. Cheltenham: Edward Elgar.

Smart, J.J.C. and Williams, B. (1973) *Utilitarianism: For and Against*. Cambridge: Cambridge University Press.

Smith-Spark, L. (2006) 'Turkey dam project back to haunt Kurds', BBC. Available at: http://news.bbc.co.uk/1/hi/world/europe/5243588.stm (accessed July 2012).

Solomon, R.C. (1991) 'Business ethics', in P. Singer (ed.), *A Companion to Ethics*. Oxford: Blackwell. pp. 354–65.

Solomon, R.C. (1992) *Ethics and Excellence: Cooperation and Integrity in Business*. Oxford: Oxford University Press.

Sternberg, E. (2000) *Just Business: Business Ethics in Action* (2nd edn). Oxford: Oxford University Press.

Stornoway Wind Farm (2013) Available at: www.stornowaywind.com/ (accessed March 2013).

Street-Porter, J. (2012) 'Google, Amazon, Vodafone and Starbucks might not be breaking laws. But they deserve to be punished', *The Independent*, 9 December. Available at: www.independent.co.uk/voices/comment/google-amazon-vodafone-and-starbucks-might-not-be-breaking-laws-but-they-deserve-to-be-punished-8395842.html (accessed July 2014).

Suma (2013) 'Cooperation', Suma corporate website. Available at: www.suma.coop/about/cooperation/ (accessed September 2013).

Sun, The (2011) 'News of the World closing down', 11 July. Available at: www.thesun.co.uk/sol/homepage/news/3683538/News-of-the-World-closing-down.html (accessed April 2013).

Sweeney, J. (2012) 'Mining giant Glencore accused in child labour and acid dumping row', *The Observer*, 14 April. Available at: www.theguardian.com/business/2012/apr/14/glencore-child-labour-acid-dumping-row (accessed August 2013).

Sylvan (Routley), R. (2003/1973) 'Is there a need for a new, and environmental, ethic?', in A. Light and H. Rolston (eds), *Environmental Ethics: An Anthology*. Malden, MA: Blackwell. pp. 46–52.

Taylor, C.C.W. (2005) 'Eudaimonia', in T. Honderich (ed.), *The Oxford Companion to Philosophy*. Oxford: Oxford University Press. p. 271.

Telegraph, The (2009) 'Dean Richards ban: ERC decisions in full', *The Telegraph*, 18 August. Available at www.telegraph.co.uk/sport/rugbyunion/club/6048208/Dean-Richards-ban-ERC-decisions-in-full.html (accessed July 2014).

Telegraph, The (2011) 'Timeline of world financial crisis', *The Telegraph*, 23 June. Available at: www.telegraph.co.uk/finance/financialcrisis/8592990/Timeline-of-world-financial-crisis.html (accessed November 2013).

Telegraph, The (2012) 'Spearmint Rhino boss urges students to strip to pay for degrees'. *The Telegraph*, 4 October 2011. Available at: www.telegraph.co.uk/education/education-news/8806091/Spearmint-Rhino-boss-urges-students-to-strip-to-pay-for-degrees.html (accessed November 2012).

Telegraph, The (2013) 'Bangladesh panel blames building owner for disaster', *The Telegraph*, 22 May. Available at: www.telegraph.co.uk/news/worldnews/asia/bangladesh/10073797/Bangladesh-panel-blames-building-owner-for-disaster.html (accessed November 2013).

ten Bos, R. (1997) 'Essai: business ethics and Bauman ethics', *Organization Studies*, 18/6: 997–1014.

Theprisma (2012) 'Gold for Suárez … miners and tradition', *Theprisma*, 22 April. Available at: www.theprisma.co.uk/2012/04/22/gold-for-suarez%E2%80%A6miners-and-tradition/ (accessed December 2013).

Therborn, G. (2011) *The World: A Beginners Guide*. Cambridge: Polity.

Thoreau, H.D. (2010/1883) 'Walking', in D.R. Keller (ed.), *Environmental Ethics: The Big Questions*. Chichester: Wiley Blackwell. pp. 93–5.

Tong, R. (1997/1989) *Feminist Thought: A Comprehensive Introduction*. Abingdon: Routledge.

Trafigura (2014a) 'Trading', Trafigura corporate website. Available at: www.trafigura.com/trading/ (accessed March 2014).

Trafigura (2014b) 'Our global locations', Trafigura corporate website. Available at: www.trafigura.com/about-us/the-group/ (accessed March 2014).

Trafigura (2014c) 'Responsibility', Trafigura corporate website. Available at: www.trafigura.com/about-us/responsibility/ (accessed March 2014).

Tremlett, G. (2013) 'Mondragon: Spain's giant co-operative where times are hard but few go bust', *The Guardian*, 7 March. Available at: www.theguardian.com/world/2013/mar/07/mondragon-spains-giant-cooperative (accessed November 2013).

Trevino, L.K. and Nelson, K.A. (2004) *Managing Business Ethics: Straight Talk About How To Do It Right* (3rd edn). Hoboken, NJ: Wiley.

UNEP (2013) 'Negative socio-cultural impacts from tourism' *United Nations Environmental Programme*. Available at: www.unep.org/resourceefficiency/Business/SectoralActivities/Tourism/FactsandFiguresaboutTourism/ImpactsofTourism/Socio-CulturalImpacts/NegativeSocio-CulturalImpactsFromTourism/tabid/78781/Default.aspx (accessed August 2013).

Unger, R.M. (2009/2005) *The Left Alternative*. London: Verso.

United Nations (2013a) 'Global issues: demining', United Nations. Available at: www.un.org/en/globalissues/demining/ (accessed April 2013).

United Nations (2013b) *Universal Declaration of Human Rights*, United Nations. Available at: www.un.org/en/documents/udhr/ (accessed August 2013).

United Nations Global Compact (2006) 'Case story: Marine Stewardship Council'. Available at: www.unglobalcompact.org/case_story/198 (accessed March 2013).

Urkidi, L. (2010) 'A glocal environmental movement against gold mining: Pascua–Lama in Chile', *Ecological Economics*, 70: 219–27.

Urkidi, L. and Walter, M. (2011) 'Dimensions of environmental justice in anti-gold mining movements in Latin America', *Geoforum*, 42: 683–95.

Urmson, J.O. (1978/1953) 'The interpretation of the moral philosophy of J.S. Mill', in M.D. Bayles (ed.), *Contemporary Utilitarianism*. Gloucester, MA: Peter Smith. pp. 13–24.

Urmson, J.O. (1980/1973) 'Aristotle's doctrine of the mean', in A.O. Rorty (ed.), *Essays on Aristotle's Ethics*. Berkeley, CA: University of California Press. pp. 157–70.

Vidal, J. (2010) 'Nigeria's agony dwarfs the Gulf oil spill. The US and Europe ignore it', *The Observer*, 30 May. Available at: www.guardian.co.uk/world/2010/may/30/oil-spills-nigeria-niger-delta-shell (accessed April 2013).

Vidal, J. (2011a) 'Shell accepts liability for two oil spills in Nigeria', *The Guardian*, 3 August. Available at: www.guardian.co.uk/environment/2011/aug/03/shell-liability-oil-spills-nigeria (accessed April 2013).

Vidal, J. (2011b) 'Shell oil spills in the Niger delta: "Nowhere and no one has escaped"', *The Guardian*, 3 August. Available at: www.guardian.co.uk/environment/2011/aug/03/shell-oil-spills-niger-delta-bodo (accessed April 2013).

Wachman, R. (2011a) 'Sex in the city: Spearmint Rhino pulls bankers bearing bonuses', *The Guardian*, 20 February. Available at: www.guardian.co.uk/business/2011/feb/20/banking-executive-pay-bonuses (accessed November 2012).

Wachman, R. (2011b) 'Glencore valued at £38bn as it reveals its flotation price', *The Guardian*, 18 May. Available at: www.theguardian.com/business/2011/may/18/glencore-ipo-price-london-flotation (accessed August 2013).

Waldron, J. (1994) 'John Locke: social contract versus political anthropology', in D. Boucher and P. Kelly, (eds) *The Social Contract from Hobbes to Rawls*. London: Routledge. pp. 51–72.

War on Want (2006) 'Coca-Cola: The Alternative Report'. Available at: www.waronwant.org/attachments/Coca-Cola%20-%20The%20Alternative%20Report.pdf (accessed August 2013).

War on Want (2013) 'Bangladesh building collapse – Rana Plaza', War on Want briefing document, 1 October. Available at: www.waronwant.org/attachments/Bangladesh%20building%20collapse%20briefing.pdf (accessed November 2013).

Warburton, N. (2001) *Philosophy: The Classics* (2nd edn). London: Routledge.

Warren, K. (1994) (ed.) *Ecological Feminism*. London: Routledge.

Warren, K. (2010/1990) 'The power and promise of ecological feminism', in D.R. Keller (ed.), *Environmental Ethics: The Big Questions*. Chichester: Wiley Blackwell. pp. 281–91.

Wenz, P.S. (2010/1995) 'Just garbage', in D.R. Keller (ed.), *Environmental Ethics: The Big Questions*. Chichester: Wiley Blackwell. pp. 501–08.

Which (2013) 'Shocking cash machine charges', *Which?* 25 January. Available at: www.which.co.uk/news/2013/01/shocking-cash-machine-charges-308696/ (accessed January 2014).

White, R. (1994/1988) 'The return of the master: an interpretation of Nietzsche's *Genealogy of Morals*', in R. Schacht (ed.), *Nietzsche, Genealogy, Morality*. Berkeley, CA: University of California Press. pp. 63–75.

Wicks, A.C., Gilbert, D.R. and Freeman, R.E. (1994) 'A feminist reinterpretation of the stakeholder concept', *Business Ethics Quarterly*, 4/4: 475–97.

Williams, L.L. (2001) *Nietzsche's Mirror: The World as Will to Power*. Lanham, MD: Rowman and Littlefield.

Wolff, J. (2002) *Why Read Marx Today*. Oxford: Oxford University Press.

Wolff, R. (2012) 'Yes, there is an alternative to capitalism: Mondragon shows the way', *The Guardian*, 24 June. Available at: www.theguardian.com/commentisfree/2012/jun/24/alternative-capitalism-mondragon (accessed November 2013).

Wood, A.W. (2000) 'Kant's practical philosophy', in K. Ameriks (ed.), *The Cambridge Companion to German Idealism*. Cambridge: Cambridge University Press. pp. 57–75.

Wood, G. and Wright, M. (2010) 'Private equity and human resource management: An emerging agenda', *Human Relations*, 63/9: 1279–96.

Woodman, C. (2012) *Unfair Trade*. London: Random House.

Wright, M., Bacon, N. and Amess, K. (2009) 'The impact of private equity and buyouts on employment, remuneration and other HRM practices', *Journal of Industrial Relations*, 51: 501–15.

Wright, M., Thompson, S. and Burrows, A. (2005) 'Corporate governance: the role of venture capitalists and buy-outs', in K. Keasey, S. Thompson and A. Burrows (eds), *Accountability, Enterprise and International Comparisons*. Chichester: Wiley. pp 207–33.

Wright, W.A. (1993) 'Treating animals as ends', *The Journal of Value Inquiry*, 27/3–4: 353–66.

Young, I.M. (1996) 'Communication and the other: beyond deliberative democracy', in S. Benhabib (ed.) *Democracy and Difference: Contesting the Boundaries of the Political*. Princeton, NJ: Princeton University Press. pp. 120–36.

Zebich-Knos, M. (2008) 'Ecotourism, park systems, and environmental justice in Latin America', in D.C. Carruthers (ed.), *Environmental Justice in Latin America*. Cambridge, MA: MIT Press. pp. 185–211.

Zuboff, S. (1988) *In the Age of the Smart Machine: the Future of Work and Power*. New York: Basic Books.

Index

Accident Group, 134
accountability, 241
Ackroyd, N., 192
acquisition of knowledge, 63
act utilitarianism, 72–75
Acxiom, 281
aesthetic anthropocentrism, 330–331, **340**, 341
affected stakeholders
  definition of, 32, *33*, 79, *80*
  normative and instrumental importance of, 37–41
  right to consideration and, 34–35, 36
Africa
  mining industry in, 348–351
  wilderness and wildlife tourism in, 343, 344–345
After Virtue (MacIntyre), 193
Alvesson, M., 407–408
ambivalence, 402, 406–411
American News Project, 160
Amnesty International, 349–351
amour-propre, 143–144, 147, 148
Amulet Group, 134
animals, 337. *See also* environmental ethics; wilderness and wildlife preservation and tourism
anthropocentrism
  aesthetic anthropocentrism, 330–331, **340**, 341
  atomistic presupposition of, 337–338, **340**
  definition of, 326
  emotional anthropocentrism, 331–333, **340**, 341
  enlightened anthropocentrism, 329–330, **340**
  resource anthropocentrism, 327–329, 337, **340**
  wind farms and, 334
anti-personnel landmines, 82–83
appreciation of beauty, 63
The Apprentice (television programme), 180–182
Aquinas, T., 327–328, 336
Archer, D., 319
Aristotle
  on ethics, 12, 403, 404
  on virtue, 171–172, 173–180, 182–184, 192–194
arms trade, 242–245
Arnold, D., 153
Ashman, I., 242
Association of British Bookmakers, 373
Atlas Iron Limited, 74–75
atomism, 293–294, 337–338, **340**
Austin, K., 360
Australianetworknews, 40–41
authenticity, 238–239, 241–245

bad faith, 236–237, 240–242
BAE Systems, 242–245
Bailey, D., 309
Balfour Beatty, 28–29
Bandar, 244–245
banks, 381–382, 417–420
Barboza. D., 219
Barclays Bank, 237–238
Bauman, Z., 357, 358
Beadle, R., 181, 207–208
beauty, 63, 331
Becker, D., 95
Bell, T. W., 45
Ben and Jerry's Ice Cream, 295–296
Bennett, T., 138
Bentham, J., 56, 61–62
Bernstein, R.J., 250
Beyond good and evil (Nietzsche), 224
The Big One (documentary film), 182
biocentrism, 326–327, 335–340, **340**, 341
biotic pyramid, 338–340
Blair, T., 243
Bloodgate, 204–207
BMW, 307–311
The Body Shop, 421
Boiler Room (film), 143–144
Bonner, R., 343

Bookchin, M., 355, 356
Borgerson, J.L., 319–321
BP, 258–261
Brandt, R., 71, 73–74
Brennan, A., 335–337
Brennan, B., 224–225
bribery, 242–245
British American Tobacco (BAT), 422–426
Brodwin, E., 425
Brooks, R., 151
Burton, B.K., 295
business
  definition of, 3–4
  purpose of, 185–188
business ethics
  anthropocentrism and, **340**
  authenticity and, 238–239, 241–245
  bad faith and, 237
  biocentrism and, **340**
  co-optation of, 420–426
  dilemmas in, 7–9
  discourse ethics and, 252–254, 258–261
  environmental sustainability and, 359–360
  ethical relativism and, 230–232, *234*, 240–245
  existentialism and, 240–245
  feminine ethics and, 305–311, **306**
  Kant and, 115–123
  Nietzsche and, 230–232
  scope of, 6–7
  social contract theory and, 135–155, *140*
  study of, 9–11
  subject matter of, 5–6
  theory of justice and, 159–160, 163–165
  utilitarianism and, 57–60, 77–85
  virtue theory and, 185–192, 207–208
business executives, 363–365. *See also* shareholder theory
Butler, J., 314–316

Cameron, D., 138–139
Campbell, T., 19–20, 24
Captive State (Monbiot), 106, 107–109
Card, C., 302
care-ethics theory. *See* feminine ethics
Caring (Noddings), 296
categorical imperative
  business ethics and, 118–123
  end in itself and, 104–109, 392–393
  vs hypothetical imperatives, 99–100
  perfect duties and, 112–114, 118
  universal acceptability and, 109–112
  universal law and, 100–104

Cavite EPZ, 117
Chakrabortty, A., 373
China Labor Watch (pressure group), 219
Chumbawamba, 332–333
CNBC, 65–66, 75–76
Coca-Cola, 10–11, 23–24
communicative action, 266–267
community
  discourse ethics and, 259–261
  virtue theory and, 176–177, 188–189, 196
Compagnie Tommy, 350–351
compassion, 144–145, 146–147, 148
consequentialism, 54–55. *See also* utilitarianism
consumer marketing, 316–321
consumer society, 352–354
contracts of employment, 133–134
copyright infringement, 102–104
corporate citizenship, 398
Corporate Europe Observatory, 20–21
Corporate Finance Television, 192
corporate lobbying, 20–21
corporate social responsibility, 366, 420–421
The Corporation (film), 45, 183, 326
corporations
  biocentrism and, 335
  colonization of public sphere by, 277, 278–285
  environmental impact and, 325
  political rights and, 19–20
  public sphere and, 277
  responsibilities and, 29–30
  social rights and, 22
  taxation and, 137–139
corruption, 242–245
courage, 197
Crane, A., 111
Crary, J., 278
Critique of Pure Reason (Kant), 89
Crossley, N., 416
The Cruel Sea (film), 56–57
cultural rights, 24–26, 28–29

de Ruyter, A., 309
deep ecology, 352
Deepwater Horizon, 258–261
Deetz, S., 407–408
democracy, 252–254
denial of proximity, 357
dependent stakeholders, 79–83, *80*
DesJardins, J., 354
dialectical opposition, 255–258
difference, 355–356
difference principle, 161–168

Dihigg, C., 219
direct utilitarianism. *See* act utilitarianism
discourse, 250
discourse ethics
  business ethics and, 252–254, 258–261
  features of, 251–258
  introduction to, 249–251, *262*
  public sphere and, 275–285
  See also workplace democracy
discrimination, 164
discursive democracy, 252–254
distributive justice, 156
Dolce & Gabbana, 318
Donaldson, T., 36, 378–380, 414
Dowler, M., 150–151
Dugan, E., 424
Dunn, C.P., 295
duty, 2, 92

ecological feminism, 355
emotion, 214, 216–217
emotional anthropocentrism, 331–333, **340**, 341
employment practices, 219–221
employment relations. *See* workplace democracy
end in itself, 104–109, 119–120, 392–393
energy companies, 368–369
enlightened anthropocentrism, 329–330, **340**, 341
enlightened shareholder theory, 383–389, *388*
Environmental Audit Committee (EAC), 111–112
environmental ethics
  anthropocentrism and, 326–334, 337–338, 341
  biocentrism and, 326–327, 335–340, 341
  environmental justice and, 345–351
  environmental sustainability and, 352–360
  introduction to, 324–326
  wilderness and wildlife preservation and, 341–345
environmental justice, 165, 345–351
environmental sustainability, 352–360
epistemic closure, 321
equal liberty, 161
equality, 156, 158–160
essentialism, 312–314
ethic of care, 289–293, **292**, **306**, 307–311
ethical absolutism
  vs. discourse ethics, 249–250
  vs. ethical relativism, 214–218, *216*, 219–221
  Nietzsche on, 222–229
Ethical Addictions, 106–107
ethical care, 297
ethical consensus, 254–255, 257–258, 260
ethical conviction, 235–236, 404–405
ethical dogmatism, 405–406
ethical evaluation, 403–404
ethical ideal, 296–298
ethical legitimation, 412–414
ethical relativism
  business ethics and, 230–232, *234*, 240–245
  vs. discourse ethics, 250
  existentialism and, 232–245
  features of, 214–221, *216*
  introduction to, 212–213
  Nietzsche and, 213, 221–232
ethical universalism. *See* ethical absolutism
ethics, definition of, 2
eudemonia, 173n1
European Union Expert Groups, 20–21
Evan, W.M., 393–394
Evans, R., 242–244
excellence, 192–197, 199–200
existentialism
  business ethics and, 240–245
  overview, 213, 232–240
Export Processing Zones (EPZs), 116
external goods, 193, 195–196, 198–204
extreme utilitarianism. *See* act utilitarianism

face-ism, 319
facticity, 236
fair equality of opportunity, 164
fairness, 2, 185
Fairtrade, 106
Fast Food Forward, 50
feminine ethics
  business ethics and, 305–311, **306**
  criticism of, 301–305
  gender stereotyping and, 316–321
  Gilligan on, 289–293, **292**, 296, 305–306, 313
  introduction to, 287–289
  nature of gender and, 312–316
  Noddings on, 296–301, 304, 305–306
  stakeholders and, 293–296, 298–301
feminine touch, 317
Ferguson, N., 300–301
The Filter Bubble (Pariser), 280–284
fisheries industry, 330, 338–340
fixed-odds betting terminals (FOBTs), 372–374
Flint, C., 369
Ford Motor Company, 59–60
Fortune (magazine), 65–66
Foxconn Technology, 219–221
free will, 94–95, 96

freedom
existentialism and, 234–235, 240
Kant on, 93–95
objective-good utilitarianism and, 63
social contract theory and, 130–131
theory of justice and, 156–157
freeloading, 103–104
Freeman, E., 32–35, 79, 293–295, 414
Freeman, R.E., 187–188, 393–394
Friedman, M.
agency argument and, 366–370, 377–378
free-market argument and, 370–374, 377–378
perplexity and, 406
shareholder theory and, 83, 364–365, 397
usurpation argument and, 374–378
Fuel Poverty Action (pressure group), 369
Fuld, R., 160
function ranking, 317
Furnham, A., 318–319

Garvin, T., 348
gender
essentialism and, 312–314
social constructionism and, 312–313, 314–316
See also feminine ethics
gender displays, 316–318
gender stereotypes, 303, 316–321
Genealogy of Morals (Nietzsche), 224, 233
Gilbert, D., 293–295
Gilligan, C., 289–293, **292**, 296, 305–306, 313
Gilmour, I., 244
Glantz, S.A., 425
Glasenberg, I., 37–38
Glencore, 37–38
Glengarry Glen Ross (film), 231
global warming, 339, 345–346
Goergen, M., 365–366
Goffman, E., 316–318
good, 56, 60–70
Goodin, R., 62
Goodman, C., 149
Google, 284–285
Gray, J., 67–68, 69
Greenpeace, 338–340, 349–351, 385–386, 415
Groom, B., 166–167
Groundwork of the Metaphysic of Morals (Kant), 90, 100
Grufferty, D., 420
GSK, 376–377
The Guardian (newspaper), 149, 242, 368–369
Guha, R., 342–343

Habermas, J.
on communicative action, 266–267
on discourse ethics, 251, 263
on public sphere, 276, 278–279, 284, 416
on shared understanding, 267–270
on sociocultural realm, 412–413
on validity claims, 268, 270–273
Haley, J.M., 304–305
'Half the Man' (song), 174–175
Halliday, J., 102–103
hamburger connection, 359–360
Harkaway, N., 278
Harlequins (rugby club), 205–207
Healey, D., 244
hedonistic utilitarianism, 61–62, 67–69, 70
Hegel, G.W.F., 257n4
Hegelsen, S., 314
highly leveraged deals, 191
Hitler, A., 230
Hoagland, S.L., 304
Hobbes, T.
on community, 176n2
on human nature, 146
social contract theory and, 127, 128, 136–137, 141–142, 143
on state of nature, 136–137, 141–142, 143
honesty, 185, 197
Huber, L., 424
Hughes, G.H., 173n1, 184
Hughes, S., 112
human chauvinism, 336
human dignity, 63
human flourishing, 172–177
hypothetical imperatives, 99–100

ideal utilitarianism. *See* objective-good utilitarianism
Ilisu Dam (Turkey), 28–29
imperfect duties, 112–114, 118
Imperial Tobacco (IT), 422–426
In a Different Voice (Gilligan), 289
India, 342–343
indirect utilitarianism. *See* rule utilitarianism
influential stakeholders
definition of, 32, *33*, 79, *80*
instrumental stakeholder theory and, 379
normative and instrumental importance of, 36–41
powerlessness and, 414–415
reciprocity rights and, 33–34, 36, 39
information and communication technology (ICT), 264–265, 277–279

institutional investors, 365
instrumental relationships, 36–37, 379
instrumental stakeholder theory, 378–382, 387–389, *388*
intellectual property rights, 41
intentions, 90, 95–96, 273
internal goods, 193, 194–195, 198–201
International Campaign to Ban Landmines, 82
International Monetary Fund, 346–347
internet, 277–285
Irigaray, L., 313–314, 315–316
Ivory Coast, 349–351

Jackson, K.T., 242
Jaggar, A.M., 289, 302–303, 306
Jillings, C., 206
Johnson, P., 314
Jurassic Park (film), 217–218
Just Business (Sternberg), 185
justice, 197. *See also* theory of justice
justice perspective, 289–293, **292**, **306**, 307–311

Kant, I.
  animals and, 337
  business ethics and, 115–123
  on categorical imperative, 99–115, 118–123
  normative stakeholder theory and, 392–393
  overview of moral philosophy by, 89–98, *115*
  on reason, 88–89, 91–93, 95, 96, 100, 101, 216
  on the sublime, 331
Keeper, D., 106–107
Keller, D.R., 165
Kierkegaard, S., 235
Kinder Scout Mass Trespass (1932), 332–333
Klein, N., 117
Knight, P., 182
knowledge, 63
Kohlberg, L., 289
Kraut, R., 173n1
Kuusela, O., 422

labor unions, 22–24
labour standards, 115–123
Lagarde, C., 300–301
last-person argument, 335, **340**
Latin America, 343–344
Learn Liberty, 45
Lehman Brothers, 160
Leigh, D., 242–244
Leopold, A., 338
Levi Strauss, 397
liberal democracy, 252n2
LIBOR, 237–238
Ling, P.M., 425
living wage, 49–50
Locke, J.
  on nature, 328
  on property rights, 42–46, 47, 129
  social contract theory and, 127, 129, 132
logic of domination, 354–357

MacIntyre, A., 173–174, 192–204, *202*
Mackey, J., 187–188
Mak, T., 318–319
management buyouts (MBOs), 189–192
Margin Call (film), 239–240
Marine Stewardship Council (MSC), 330
Martinez-Alier, J., 342, 348
Marx, K., 42, 46–50
maternalistic authoritarianism, 303–304
Matten, D., 111
McCann, M., 150–151
McKibbin, B., 353
Meredith, I., 106–107
Michelak, R., 295–296
Mill, J.S.
  on nature, 328, 332
  utilitarianism and, 64–66, 69–70
mining industry, 25–26, 37–38, 346–348
Monbiot, G., 106, 107–109
Mondragon Corporation, 408–411
Moody-Adams, M., 302, 303
Moore, G., 181, 207–208
Moore, G.E., 63
Moore, M., 182
moral community, 335–337, **340**
Moral Consciousness and Communicative Action (Habermas), 267
morality
  definition of, 2–3
  Nietzsche on, 221–229
  Rousseau on, 145–146, 147, 148
Morgan, G., 356
Morozov, E., 280
Morris, H., 25–26
Move Your Money (consumer-support group), 419
movie piracy, 102–103
Muir, J., 332–333
Mulally, A., 59–60
Mulcaire, G., 149
Murdoch, J., 151–152, 155
Murdoch, R., 151, 153–155
music piracy, 104
Myers, N., 359–360

Naagbanton, P., 85
Næss, A., 352, 356, 358
natural care, 297
natural environment, 35. *See also* environmental ethics
naturalization, 407–408
negative responsibilities, 30–31
Nelson, K., 111
New York Times test, 111, 112
News of the World (newspaper), 149–155
Nicomachean Ethics (Aristotle), 171–172
Nietzsche, F.
  business ethics and, 230–232
  ethical relativism and, 213, 221–229
  nihilism and, 233
nihilism, 233
Noddings, N., 296–301, 304, 305–306
non-consequentialist ethical approaches, 55
non-dependent stakeholders, 82–85
normative stakeholder theory
  vs. enlightened shareholder theory, 383–389, *388*
  vs. instrumental stakeholder theory, 378–382, 387–389, *388*
  introduction to, 364
  reciprocity argument, 394–398
  respect-for-persons argument and, 392–394, 397–398
  stakeholder-investments argument and, 389–392, 397–398

Obama, B., 50
Object (pressure group), 68–69
objective-good utilitarianism, 62–64, 69, 70
objectivism, 215
obligations, 2
The Observer (newspaper), 111
Occupy (movement), 418–419
offshore production
  labour standards in, 115–123
  overview, 116–117
  stakeholders' rights and, 40–41
offshoring, 396–397
opposition, 255–258
original position, 156–163

Paisder, P., 129
Pariser, E., 280–284
paternalistic authoritarianism, 303–304
Paton, H.J., 100
perfect duties, 112–114, 118
perplexity, 402, 403–406
personal data, 280–281
personal freedom, 63
Philip Morris International, 423
Phoenix consortium, 308–311
piracy, 102–104
Planetinternational, 385–386
political rights, 19–21, 22–23
pornography industry, 61
positive responsibilities, 30–31
powerlessness, 402, 411–420
practices, 192–197
Preston, L., 36, 378–380, 414
Primark, 122
principle of corporate maximization, 77–85
principle of respect for persons, 393. *See also* end in itself
private equity (PE) firms, 190–192
profit, 47–48
Project Tiger (India), 342
property rights
  overview, 41–50
  shareholder theory and, 369–370, 372
  social contract theory and, 129
proximity, 299–300, 357–358
psychological contract, 133–134
public sphere
  corporations and corporate colonization of, 277, 278–285
  ICT and, 277–278
  importance of, 275–276
  powerlessness and, 416
Pumba Private Game Reserve (South Africa), 344–345
purpose, 183–192

Radical American Environmentalism, 344
Rana Plaza, 121–123
rationality, 156, 157–158
rationalization programmes, 57–60
Rawls, J.. *See* theory of justice
Reagan, J., 114
reason
  Aquinas on, 327–328
  ethical relativism and, 216–217
  Kant on, 88–89, 91–93, 95, 96, 100, 101, 216
reciprocity rights, 33–34, 36, 39, 394–397
redundancy programmes, 9
Regan, T., 337
resource anthropocentrism, 327–329, 337, **340**
responsibility, 2, 29–31
Richards, D., 206

rights
  animals and, 337
  characteristics of, 27–31
  definitions of, 2, 17–18
  shareholder theory and, 376
  stakeholders and, 31–41, *33*
  See also property rights
rights theory
  characteristics of rights and, 27–31
  cultural rights and, 24–26, 28–29
  introduction to, 18–19
  political rights and, 19–21, 22–23
  social rights and, 21–24
  Universal Declaration of Human Rights and, 23, 26–27, 31, 49
Riley, P., 131
ritualization of subordination, 317
Robertson, S., 369
Roddick, A., 421
Romney, M., 75–76
Rosener, J.B., 314
Rousseau, J-J.
  on *amour-propre*, 143–144, 147, 148
  on compassion, 144–145, 146–147, 148
  compassion on, 144–145
  on morality, 145–146, 147, 148
  social contract theory and, 127, 128, 129, 142–146
  on state of nature, 142
Rover, 307–311
Royal Horticultural Society, 196–197
rugby, 205–207
rule utilitarianism
  vs act utilitarianism, 72–76
  management and, 77–85
Russell, T., 405–406
Ryder, R.D., 336

Safeway, 107–109
Sandler, R., 337
Sartre, J.-P.
  on authenticity, 238–239, 241
  on bad faith, 236, 240
  on choice, 415
  on ethical evaluation, 403–404
  existentialism and, 213, 233
  on freedom, 235, 240
Save the Whale (campaign), 338–340
Schneewind, J.B., 123–124
Schroeder, J.E., 319–321
self-actualization, 63
self-ownership, 43–44
senior-executive pay, 166–168
sentiment, 92–93, 95, 100, 112–114
shallow ecology, 352
shared understanding, 267–270
shareholder theory
  agency argument and, 366–370, 377–378
  free-market argument and, 370–374, 377–378
  introduction to, 364–365
  vs. normative stakeholder theory, 397
  primacy of shareholders and, 365–366
  usurpation argument and, 374–378
Shell (oil company), 84–85, 385–386
ShellGuilty, 386
Sinaltrainal (Colombian food and drink union), 23–24
Singer, P., 337
SkillBoostersTV, 164
The Smartest Guys in the Room (film), 146
social constructionism, 312–313, 314–316
social contract theory
  business ethics and, 135–155, *140*
  introduction to, 126–127
  origins of, 127–131
  social contract as hypothetical construction in, 135, 136, 138–139, 157
  tacit agreements and, 132–134, 136, 138–139
  voluntarism and, 131–132, 136, 138–139, 157
  See also theory of justice
social movements, 415–420
social-networking sites, 282–283
social rights, 21–24
sociocultural realm, 412–413
Solomon, R., 181, 185–186, 187, 188–189, 356
Spearmint Rhino, 66–70
Specht, J., 67
speciesism, 336
sports corporations, 204–207
stakeholders
  definition of, 31
  discourse ethics and, 259–261
  feminine ethics and, 293–296, 298–301
  normative and instrumental importance of, 36–41
  rights and, 31–41, *33*
  rule utilitarianism and, 79–80, *80*
  See also affected stakeholders; influential stakeholders
Starbucks, 138–139
state of nature, 128, 136–137, 141–146
Sternberg, E., 185, 186–187, 188–189
stockholders, 365. *See also* shareholder theory
strategic action, 266–267

subjectivism, 215
the sublime, 331
Sugar, A., 180–182
Suma, 274–275
surfthechannel.com (website), 102
surplus value, 47–48
Sweeney, J., 38
Sylvan, R., 335, 336

tacit agreements, 132–134, 136, 138–139
Tarling, G., 339
taxation
  shareholder theory and, 374–378
  social contract theory and, 137–139
The Telegraph (newspaper), 150
theory of justice
  business ethics and, 159–160, 163–165
  difference principle and, 161–168
  distributive justice and, 156
  equal liberty and, 161
  equality and, 156, 158–160
  freedom and, 156–157
  original position and, 156–163
  overview, 155–156, *157*
  rationality and, 156, 157–158
  veil of ignorance and, 156, 158–160
Theprisma, 25–26
Thomson Holidays, 319
Thoreau, H.D., 332–333
Thurlbeck, N., 154
tobacco industry, 422–426
tourism industry
  cultural rights and, 25
  tour operation and, 198–199, 204
  wilderness and wildlife tourism, 333, 342–345
trade unions, 22–24
Trafigura, 348–351
Trevino, L., 111
Troy (film), 223–224
Trump, D., 180–182
Two Treatises of Government (Locke), 42

UBS (Swiss bank), 28–29
unethical business conduct
  culture-focused approach on, 148, 149–155
  overview, *140*
  person-focused approach on, 147–148, 149–155
Unfair Trade (Woodman), 106–107
Unilever, 330
United Nations, 82, 85. See also *Universal Declaration of Human Rights*
universal acceptability, 109–112, 120–121
Universal Declaration of Human Rights, 23, 26–27, 31, 49
universal law, 100–104, 118–119
Urkidi, L., 347–348
utilitarianism
  animals and, 337
  Bentham and, 56, 61–62
  business and, 57–60
  business ethics and, 77–85
  challenges to, 70–72
  good and, 56, 60–70
  hedonistic utilitarianism, 61–62, 67–69, 70
  introduction to, 55–57
  management and, 77–85
  Mill and, 64–66, 69–70
  objective-good utilitarianism, 62–64, 69, 70
  overview, *76*
  rule utilitarianism, 72–76
utilities, 56

validity claims, 267, 268, 270–273
veil of ignorance, 156, 158–160
Vickerman, A., 102–103
Vidal, J., 85
virtue, definition of, 2
virtue theory
  business ethics and, 185–192, 207–208
  excellence in practices and, 192–204, *202*
  human flourishing and, 172–177
  introduction to, 171–172
  natural environment and, 337
  purpose and, 183–192
  virtuous mean and, 178–183
virtuous mean, 178–183
Volkswagen, 319
voluntarism, 131–132, 136, 138–139, 157

Waldron, J., 135
Walley, J., 111–112
Walter, M., 347–348
War on Want, 11, 121–123
water companies, 111–112
Watson, T., 154
Waxman, H., 160
Which? (organization), 381–382
White, R., 233
Wicks, A.C., 293–295, 299
wilderness, 332–333
wilderness and wildlife preservation and tourism, 333, 341–345
will to power, 224–226

Williams, L., 227
wind farms, 334
Winstanley, D., 242
Wolff, R., 263, 408–411
women, 300–301. *See also* feminine ethics; gender
Woodman, C., 106–107
Woods, T., 196–197
workplace democracy
  feasibility and benefits of, 261–263, *262*
  involvement of employees in, 263–266
  motivation and, 266–267
  shared understanding and, 267–270
  Suma and, 274–275
  validity claims and, 267, 270–273
workplace discrimination, 164
World Bank, 346–347
World Wildlife Fund (WWF), 330
Wright, W.A., 337

'You Can (Mass Trespass, 1932)' (song), 332–333

Zabala, M., 409–411
Zara, 122
Zebich-Knos, M., 343–344